P9-CQH-310

Dedicated to Warren Fraleigh, in gratitude for his monumental contribution to the founding and development of the philosophy of sport.

CONTENTS

Contributors   x

A historical introduction to the philosophy of sport   1
Mike McNamee and William J. Morgan

SECTION I
Philosophical approaches to the conceptualization of sport   **9**

1 Formalism and sport   11
   Scott Kretchmar

2 Internalism and sport   22
   Robert L. Simon

3 Conventionalism and sport   35
   William J. Morgan

4 An institutional theory of sport   53
   Graham McFee

SECTION II
Philosophical theories and sport   **67**

5 Aesthetics of sport   69
   Andrew Edgar

6 Bioethics and sport   81
   Silvia Camporesi

7 Eastern philosophy   98
   Jesús Ilundáin-Agurruza and Takayuki Hata

8 Epistemology and sport   115
   Steffen Borge

9 Ethics and sport   131
   Mike McNamee

10 Existential philosophy and sport   142
    Kenneth Aggerholm

11 Feminism in the philosophy of sport   161
    Leslie A. Howe

12 Phenomenology and sport   178
    Irena Martínková

13 Philosophy of mind and sport   192
    Paul Davis

14 Pragmatism and the philosophy of sport   207
    John Kaag

15 The radical critique of sport   218
    Lev Kreft

16 Religion, theology and sport   238
    Gregg Twietmeyer

17 Sport as a legal system   255
    John S. Russell

18 Metaphysics and sport   274
    Stephen Mumford

SECTION III
Key issues and themes in the philosophy of sport   285

19 Competition   287
    Paul Gaffney

20 Disability and Paralympic sport   300
    Steve Edwards and Mike McNamee

21 Doping and anti-doping: an inquiry into the meaning of sport   315
    Thomas H. Murray

22 Fair play   333
    Sigmund Loland

23 Genetics, science fiction and the ethics of athletic enhancement 351
    W. Miller Brown

24 Olympism – a philosophy of sport?   368
    Heather L. Reid

25 Philosophical approaches to coaching   383
    Jeffrey P. Fry

26 Spectatorship – watching and following sport   401
    Carwyn Jones

27   Sport, commerce and the market   411
    Adrian Walsh

28 Technology and sport   426
    Rasmus Bysted Møller and Verner Møller

    Index   439

CONTRIBUTORS

Kenneth Aggerholm
Department of Sports Science and Clinical Biomechanics, University of Southern Denmark, Denmark.

Steffen Borge
UiT The Arctic University of Norway, Norway.

W. Miller Brown
Professor of Philosophy, Trinity College, USA.

Silvia Camporesi
Lecturer in Bioethics and Society, Department of Social Science, Health and Medicine, King's College London, UK.

Paul Davis
Senior Lecturer in the Sociology of Sport and Exercise, Faculty of Applied Sciences, University of Sunderland, UK.

Andrew Edgar
Reader in Philosophy, School of English Communications and Philosophy, Cardiff University, UK.

Steven D. Edwards, Professor of Philosophy of Health Care, College of Health and Human Sciences, Swansea University, UK.

Jeffrey P. Fry
Associate Professor, Department of Philosophy and Religious Studies, Ball State University, USA.

Paul Gaffney
Associate Professor of Philosophy, St. John's University, USA.

Takayuki Hata
Professor of Sport Philosophy and Physical Education, Graduate School of Education, Okayama University, Japan.

Leslie A. Howe
Professor of Philosophy, Philosophy Department, University of Saskatchewan, Canada.

Jesús Ilundáin-Agurruza
Associate Professor, Department of Philosophy, Linfield College, USA.

Carwyn Jones
Reader in Sports Ethics, Cardiff School of Sport, Cardiff Metropolitan University, UK.

John Kaag
Associate Professor of Philosophy, University of Massachusetts Lowell, USA.

Lev Kreft
Professor of Philosophy, Department of Philosophy, University of Ljubljana, Slovenia.

R. Scott Kretchmar
Professor of Exercise and Sport Science, Department of Kinesiology, Penn State University, USA.

Sigmund Loland
Professor of Philosophy of Sport, Norwegian University of Sport Sciences, Olso, Norway.

Irena Martínková
Assistant Professor of Philosophy and Ethics of Sport, Faculty of Physical Education and Sport, Charles University in Prague, Czech Republic.

Graham McFee
Emeritus Professor of Philosophy, University of Brighton, UK, and Professor, Department of Philosophy, California State University Fullerton, USA.

Mike McNamee
Professor of Applied Ethics, College of Engineering, Swansea University, UK, and Visiting Professor, College of Sport, Hunan Normal University, China.

Rasmus Bysted Møller
Department of Public Health, Section for Sport, Aarhus University, Denmark.

Verner Moller
Professor of Sport Studies, Aarhus University, Denmark.

William J. Morgan
Professor, Division of Occupational Science and School of Communication, University of Southern California, USA.

Stephen Mumford
Professor of Metaphysics, Department of Philosophy, University of Nottingham, UK, and Professor II, Norwegian University of Life Science (NMBU), Norway.

Thomas H. Murray
President Emeritus, The Hastings Center, USA; Chen Su Lan Centennial Professor, Centre for Biomedical Ethics, National University of Singapore.

Heather L. Reid
Professor of Philosophy, Morningside College, USA.

John S. Russell
Instructor, Philosophy Department, Langara College, Canada.

Robert L. Simon
Bartlett Professor of Philosophy, Hamilton College, USA.

Gregg Twietmeyer
Associate Professor, School of Kinesiology, Marshall University, USA.

Adrian Walsh
Associate Professor in Philosophy, School of Humanities, University of New England, Australia.

A HISTORICAL INTRODUCTION TO THE PHILOSOPHY OF SPORT

Mike McNamee and William J. Morgan

We are delighted to have co-edited this *Handbook of the Philosophy of Sport*, the publication of which coincides with a half-century or so of philosophical scholarship devoted to sport. We have enlisted an international team of leading scholars to address the main philosophical issues and concerns of the subject. We have tried to be as comprehensive as possible in our coverage of the relevant topics. Each chapter features an original contribution that summarizes and critically analyzes the best philosophical work to date relevant to the topic. Our intent throughout was to produce a major reference work for scholars interested in the philosophy of sport. We also sought to highlight the important normative and practical connections of these topics to issues that presently beset the world of sport, to assist serious observers and students of sport interested in the often outsized role it plays in their lives both on and off the field. By presenting a comprehensive picture of the intellectual development of sport philosophy to the present, we further intended the *Handbook* to serve as a guide for possible future theoretical advances in each of these topical areas. These are, admittedly, ambitious goals and, as such, hard to fulfil. So there will be inevitable gaps in our coverage and, no doubt, areas where readers will have wished for a different treatment of some of the topics discussed. Nevertheless, we believe that we have achieved our main goals, and that this compendium of work will prove useful to scholars, students, and interested parties alike, no matter their particular philosophical tastes or interests.

In the remaining part of this introductory essay, we take a look back at the major events that led to the development of the philosophy of sport as an intellectual field of study from its inception in North America to its present international standing across Europe and the rest of the world.

A brief history of the philosophy of sport in North America

The philosophy of sport, like its close academic cousins the history and sociology of sport, is a recent addition to the academic world. It established itself first in North America, but spread soon after to Europe and much of the rest of the world. It was in the middle to late 1960s that it experienced its first growing pains in the United States, fuelled by a booming economy that greatly expanded both the size and number of colleges and universities, and more importantly – for our purposes – the scope of their curricula. Perhaps even more important in this regard was the overheated, anti-authoritarian social and political climate of the 1960s, which prompted a large number of Americans, especially those under the age of 30, to challenge the old orthodoxies and traditions both in and outside the academy. If ever there was a time ripe for great political and intellectual change, this was it. It played a significant part in the development of new academic disciplines like sport studies and its various cognates, and new subdisciplines like the philosophy of sport, which began to regularly show up in college and university curricula across the country and in Canada.

The birth of the philosophy of sport was not an "immaculate" theoretical conception; a new subject that sprung up suddenly and seemingly out of nowhere. It developed out of, and in many respects was a critical response to, what used to be called the philosophy of physical education, which considered itself a subdiscipline of the philosophy of education rather than of philosophy in general. The main aim of the philosophy of physical education in the UK and USA was to bolster the educational credentials of physical activity in all its various forms, ranging from rudimentary human movement and spontaneous play to highly organized games and sports. This task was often carried out with a sense of urgency by philosophers of physical education because many leading educational theorists of the time (pre-1960s) were persuaded that physical education was not an appropriate educational subject because it lacked the requisite intellectual and cognitive content. Put bluntly, the prevailing view was that physical education was an affair of the body rather than of the mind, and thus should be denied educational franchise. It is little wonder, therefore, that philosophers of physical education did everything they could to undermine the crude mind–body dualism that informed such jaundiced views of their subject.

By the mid to late 1960s in the USA, however, the philosophy of sport had eclipsed the philosophy of physical education, and had supplanted it as a central academic subject and focus of scholarly inquiry. This important intellectual shift was owed in part to the explosion of interest in sport itself in the middle of this decade in both the USA and the larger world – a trend that shows no sign of abating even today, let alone of being reversed. Moreover, this upsurge of philosophical interest in sport was also due to two other important developments in the USA. The first had to do with the publication of three path-breaking books that helped put the study of sport on the philosophical map. The second had to do with the establishment of a liberal arts model of physical education in a small, relatively obscure northeastern university, which remarkably showcased the philosophy of sport as its core curricular offering, and which set in motion a dialogue about the philosophical significance of sport that eventually spilled over into the larger scholarly community.

With regard to the first development, two of the landmark philosophy of sport texts were authored by physical education professors from the University of Southern California: Howard Slusher's *Man, Sport, and Existence* (1967), and Eleanor Metheny's *Movement and Meaning* (1968). Slusher's book was an existential take on the significance and meaning of athletic engagement. Metheny's pioneering work was a more ambitious and original contribution, which featured a full-blown philosophical theory of human movement and sport. The back-to-back publication of these scholarly treatises helped propel this new philosophical study of sport forward, and played a central role in bringing to an end the dominance that the philosophy of physical education previously enjoyed in higher educational and scholarly circles.

Notwithstanding these seminal texts, it was the publication of the third book of this period, Paul Weiss's *Sport: A philosophic inquiry* (1969), which made the greatest contribution to the legitimation of sport philosophy, especially in the philosophy community, where it had started to gain some attention, not all of which was positive. The distinguished English analytical philosopher, Lord Anthony Quinton (1969) wrote a very critical review essay "Locker Room

Metaphysics" in the *New York Review of Books*. He was particularly dismissive of Slusher's book, although this appears in part because of his antagonistic posture towards continental philosophy (McNamee, 2012).

The reason why Weiss's book created such a fuss in philosophical circles was not so much owing to the intellectual merits of the book itself, but rather to Weiss's commanding stature in philosophy and the larger intellectual world. Weiss was widely esteemed as one of America's premier philosophers, and one of its most celebrated spokespersons outside of the academic philosophical community. It was hardly lost on humanists in academe at the time that if a world-famous philosopher like Weiss had thought sport worthy of a book-length study, perhaps they should take a more serious look at this topic themselves.

To be sure, Weiss was not the only major philosopher to ever write about sport. On the contrary, such philosophical giants as Plato and Aristotle wrote approvingly and even at times enthusiastically, of play, athletics and gymnastics, as did such philosophical luminaries as Friedrich Nietzsche, Martin Heidegger, and Jean-Paul Sartre, whose respective conceptions of play figured not insignificantly in their own world views. The famous twentieth-century Austrian analytical philosopher Ludwig Wittgenstein should also be included in this august group, because he used the notion of a game, specifically a language game, to explicate some of his most original philosophical views (see Midgley, 1974). Though none of these philosophers ever produced a systematic work of the kind that Weiss did, nor even a systematic essay devoted to sport (with the possible exception of Sartre's treatment of play and skiing in the last sections of his tome *Being and Nothingness*), which meant the interested reader had to comb carefully through their writings to find scattered references to play and sport, what they did write about sport was not insignificant. Despite this fact, most contemporary philosophers simply ignored sport, presupposing or assuming that it was too trivial a human affair to merit serious philosophical attention and analysis. It took someone with the intellectual stature of Paul Weiss, therefore, to jolt the philosophy community out of its complacency and give sport the philosophical kudos it needed if it were ever to rival the stature of other philosophical subdisciplines such as the philosophy of science, religion, history, law, and politics.

The second part of the story of the philosophy of sport's rise to academic respectability, as noted, had specifically to do with its institutionalization in the academy. By the end of the 1960s and beginning of the 1970s, departments of physical education in colleges and universities in the USA and Canada had begun to give serious attention to the study of sport, and as a result initiated wholesale changes in their curricula to accommodate this new interest. Most noteworthy in this regard was the State University of New York at Brockport, where the charge to change the disciplinary focus of the physical education department came from the President, Albert Brown.[1] Brown proposed that a new physical education "major" (i.e. undergraduate or Bachelor degree program) be developed at Brockport with one novel and important twist: that it be based on a liberal arts model rather than the more prevalent and traditional educational and professional model. He subsequently hired Warren Fraleigh in 1970 from San Jose State University to be Dean of the College of Physical Education and Recreation, and to carry out his programme to transform the physical education curriculum. The following year was a remarkable one for the nascent discipline. Fraleigh hired six specialists in the philosophy of sport, and, in addition, scholars in related fields like sport sociology, and installed the philosophy of sport as one of the core subjects of the new curriculum. The clustering together of such like-minded and academically trained sport philosophers was an innovation – unlikely to be repeated in scale and significance – that, unsurprisingly, created quite a stir in both Fraleigh's own institution and in physical education departments across the USA and Canada.

Brockport was already the home of the Center for Philosophic Exchange, directed by Howard Kiefer. Its main aim was to encourage philosophical inquiry into pressing social and public issues and to disseminate the results of that inquiry to the greater academic and public community. To meets its charge, the Center annually hosted two renowned philosophers to speak to some important and timely issue. These sessions were conducted according to a question-and-answer format. They were videotaped and loaned out at no cost to interested educational institutions and public organizations. In addition, the two invited philosophers also presented formal papers to a public audience, which were subsequently published in the journal, *Philosophical Exchange*. In 1971, Fraleigh contacted Kiefer to see if the Center would be interested in bringing Paul Weiss to campus to give a paper on sport along with Richard Schacht, then an up-and-coming philosopher from the University of Illinois, to give a critical response to Weiss's paper. Fraleigh's plan was to have the Weiss–Schacht exchange front a larger symposium that his department would sponsor devoted to the philosophy of sport. Kiefer gave his support, and, in 1972, Brockport hosted the first ever philosophy conference dedicated to the philosophical study of sport in North America, and, to the best of our knowledge, likely the first sport philosophy conference of its kind ever held.

The conference was a resounding success, as attested by the large number of philosophers, philosophically trained sport studies scholars, and public parties who both presented papers and attended its several sessions.[2] It also proved to be an intellectual success in terms of the lively discussions it sparked among conferees. Of special importance in this regard was the discussion it led to between Fraleigh and Weiss, among others, about forming a philosophical society of sport and starting a philosophy journal devoted to sport. In 1971–72, a steering committee was formed for these very purposes that included, besides Weiss and Fraleigh, Richard Zaner, a philosopher, and Ellen Gerber, a sport philosopher.[3] At the 1972 Eastern Division Meeting of the American Philosophical Association, held in Boston, Massachusetts, the Philosophic Society for the Study of Sport (PSSS) was formally established. The following year, plans were drawn up to launch a new journal to be called the *Journal of the Philosophy of Sport*, and Robert Osterhoudt, a former sport philosophy professor at Brockport who had just relocated to the University of Minnesota, was appointed its first editor. The first volume of the *Journal* was published in 1974. In 1999, PSSS formally changed its name to the International Association of the Philosophy of Sport (IAPS) to reflect its growing international membership. Today, IAPS is a strong and vibrant scholarly association that holds its annual conferences all over the world, and its signature publication, the *Journal of the Philosophy of Sport*, remains one of the premier journals in the field.

A brief history of the philosophy of sport in the rest of the world

Having concentrated thus far on the American context for the development and institutionalization of the discipline, it is worth noting that the global development of the philosophy of sport proceeded apace, although somewhat unevenly. In the 1970s, for instance, only Germany (German Society of Sports Science, which contained a philosophy of sport section) had some kind of national organization devoted to the discipline. Important early work had been undertaken by Hans Lenk, himself a well-known philosophical figure in Germany, in the philosophy of sport. His text, *Social Philosophy of Athletics*, was published in Germany in 1975 and appeared in the English language in 1976. Similarly, in Japan, the Japan Society for the Study of Sport had formed national associations of sport philosophy. The Japan Association subsequently began publishing the *Journal of the Philosophy of Sport and Physical Education*.

The development of sport philosophy in Japan (Hata and Sekine, 2010) and Britain followed a similar trajectory as it had in the USA with regard to its initial ties to the philosophy of education. Indeed, much of the early philosophical scholarship on sport could be found in journals of the philosophy of education, where philosophers of physical education had found an academic niche. This continued into the 1980s, although in the UK and British Commonwealth countries (notably Australia and Canada), there was something of an interlude as no-vocational degree courses sprang up in human movement studies. Although a short-lived phenomenon, by the end of the 1990s, most of such courses were replaced by degree programs in sports studies or sports science. This period did produce one classic text: *Philosophy and Human Movement* by the British philosopher David Best. Although not focusing on sports exclusively (it notably included dance), it was deeply critical of early phenomenological work (such as Metheny's), and initiated a debate regarding sports status as art that ran for decades.

Despite this activity, it was not until early in the next century, 2002 to be precise, that another national association of sport philosophy was established. This was the British Philosophy of Sport Association (BPSA), which was started at a conference organized by Mike McNamee at the University of Gloucestershire. This organization also started publishing a new journal called *Sport, Ethics and Philosophy*, which in short order became a major international journal publishing philosophical work on sport. In 2003, the BPSA held its first annual meeting and has met annually thereafter. It has drawn presenters from around the world and has created a working group that initiated the European Association for the Philosophy of Sport (EAPS), which coexisted with the BPSA and developed formal links with its official journal (*Sport, Ethics and Philosophy*) and associated conferences.

Under the leadership of Lev Kreft in Slovenia, the EAPS helped support a number of initiatives that led to the developments of national associations in Slovenia (2010); the Czech Republic (2011), which had strong relations with Polish (Kosiewicz, 2012), and Hungarian scholars, although they have not yet developed into national organizations. Similarly, in the Netherlands, there has long been an interest in scholarship in the field without a leading institution (Hilvoorde *et al.* 2010). The Scandinavian and Germanic regions have a long tradition of sustained philosophical interest in sports (Brevik, 2010; Pawlenka, 2010), although neither has a developed an independent national association. By contrast, in China, relatively little philosophical reflection on sport has been promoted, although there is current interest in the subject that is beginning to bear fruit (Hsu, 2010).

A final development is worthy of note, in this respect. It concerns the recent development of Asociación Latina de Filosofía del Deporte (ALFiD; Latin Association for Philosophy of Sport), which does not follow the national institution development of the subject but rather integrates the discipline in Latin languages – French, Italian, Portuguese, and Spanish (Torres and Campos, 2012). The history of philosophy of sport in these countries is long though sporadic. In Spain, José Ortega y Gasset published some articles about the relevance of sport in the society at the beginning of twentieth century. But perhaps the author that made a deeper contribution to the philosophy of sport in Spain during the 1960s and 1970s was José María Cagigal. Although his main concern was the social meaning of the sport, some of his writings contained original philosophical insights. The culmination of work in the Spanish language, in particular, occurred in 2013 with a new journal, published in both Spanish and English, *Fair Play: Journal of Sport: Philosophy, Ethics and Law*, and a newly formed Spanish Association for the Philosophy of Sport.

Interestingly, in both these countries, the philosophical background, drawing extensively on the phenomenological tradition, developed its own nomenclature. The terms, favored here include "physical culture" and "movement culture" over sport as the object of their philosophical interest, and, in the Czech Republic, at least, the phrase "philosophical kinanthropology"

(Jirasek, 2003; Jirasek and Hopsicker, 2010) identified the field that is internationally known as the philosophy of sport.

Philosophical traditions and the philosophy of sport

The linguistic economies generated by these heterogeneous organizations and fields of scholarship in the philosophy of sport – loosely understood – indicate more than mere linguistic differences. For instance, what is commonly called "sport" in the West draws upon a rich history of Greek and Roman athletics (Reid, 2010) that extends all the way to the modern incarnation of educational sports in Victorian Britain and finally to the rebirth of the Olympic Games by Baron Pierre de Coubertin and others (Reid and Austin, 2012; McNamee and Parry, 2012). While across Europe the paradigmatic sports recognized as Olympic sports were practiced and promoted, so too were alternative movement cultures including fitness- and health-related activities groups, and sport-for-all organisations, which bore only a family resemblance to the rule-governed and competitive activities we typically think of and classify as "sports" in the West. Notably, in France, work in the philosophy of the body and in social theory of sport have gone hand in hand with reflections on movement forms that would not fall under a narrower conception of "sport" such as articulated by the founding scholars of the field.

There is, however, even a deeper and more philosophically interesting difference between published philosophical work on sport in North America, particularly the *Journal of the Philosophy of Sport*, and Britain and larger Europe. That difference has to do with the dominance of analytical philosophical approaches to sport in the USA and Canada. This is not to deny that Continental philosophy has not developed a sport philosophical literature. Indeed the labels themselves, as Bernard Williams (1995) once noted, are somewhat misleading – and both, being traditions of Western philosophy, take no significant account of Eastern philosophy, which is a major source of published work in the philosophical literature on sport in Japan.

Given that philosophical research is always and everywhere internally related to the expression of ideas particular to different cultures, the idiom of that expression shapes somewhat the boundaries of what can be said. In contrast to the biomedical sciences of sport, which make ready use of a technical language (the scientific method) spoken and understood the world over, philosophers working in the Continental tradition speak a much more specialized language understood only by specialists in fields such as existentialism, hermeneutics, ontology and phenomenology (see Martinkova and Parry, 2012).

Although the label "Continental" itself reflects geocultural considerations (the work emanated from communities of scholars in France (Andrieu, 2014), Germany, and more broadly in Continental Europe), one finds philosophers of sport across the globe drawing upon those traditions. Similarly, analytical philosophy, though the dominant tradition in the Anglo-American tradition of Western philosophy, is misleading in the sense that some of its founding fathers were indeed from Continental Europe. The drawing of distinctions to represent our experience of the world, however, is common to all schools or traditions of philosophical and sport philosophical endeavour.

Conclusion

In this volume we hope to have given full voice to individual scholars and traditions that represent the best of such work independent of its self-identification. Although omissions and errors will always remain in compendium works, we hope that this volume will give newcomers to the field a sense of the import and vitality of the field. Equally, we hope that those who have ploughed their own furrows in the field of philosophy of sport, however long or deep, will find here continuing nourishment for their critical reflections. What is clear is that owing to both the high quality of its scholarship and the internationalization of the field, the philosophy of sport can be said without exaggeration to be flourishing.[4]

Notes

1 The background material for the historic role that Brockport played in the institutionalization of sport philosophy as an academic subject comes from an oral history that Bill Morgan conducted with one of its central figures, Warren Fraleigh. A version of that history appeared in Fraleigh (1983).
2 Bill Morgan personally attests to its success, having presented a paper and attended many of the sessions, including the Weiss–Schacht exchange, as a newly graduated 21-year-old.
3 We have not made comment on English-language nomenclature and have taken as synonymous the phrases philosophy of sport and sport philosophy, and also sport philosopher and philosopher of sport. In each case, the former tends to be more widely used than the latter in North America.
4 Thanks to Bernard Andrieu, Warren Fraleigh, Lev Kreft, Irena Martinkova, Cesar Torres, Jose Luis Triviño, for their assistance with particular developments of the subject in their respective regions.

References

Andrieu, B. (2014). "The Birth of the Philosophy of Sport in France 1950–1980. Part 1: from Ulmann to Rauch through Vigarello," *Sport, Ethics and Philosophy*, 8(1), 32–43.

Best, D. (1978). *Philosophy and Human Movement*, London: Lepus.

Breivik, G. (2010). "Philosophy of Sport in the Nordic Countries," *Journal of the Philosophy of Sport*, 37(2), 194–214.

Fraleigh, W. P. (1983). "The Philosophic Society for the Study of Sport," *Journal of the Philosophy of Sport*, X, 3–7.

Hata, T. and Sekine, M. (2010). "Philosophy of Sport and Physical Education in Japan: Its History, Characteristics and Prospects," *Journal of the Philosophy of Sport*, 37(2), 215–224.

Hsu, L. H. (2010). "An Overview of Sport Philosophy in Chinese-Speaking Regions (Taiwan and Mainland China)," *Journal of the Philosophy of Sport*, 37(2), 237–252.

Jirasek, I. (2003). "Philosophy of Sport, or Philosophy of Physical Culture? An experience from the Czech Republic: philosophical kinanthropology," *Sport, Education and Society*, 8(1), 105–117.

Jirasek, I. and Hopsicker, P. M. (2010). "Philosophical Kinanthropology (Philosophy of Physical Culture, Philosophy of Sport) in Slavonic Countries: The Culture, the Writers, and the Current Directions," *Journal of the Philosophy of Sport*, 37(2), 253–70.

Kosiewicz, J. (2012). "Philosophy of Sport in Poland: Observations," *Physical Culture and Sport. Studies and Research*, 54(1), 86–102.

Lenk, H. (1979). *Social Philosophy and Athletics*, Champaign, IL: Stipes.

McNamee, M. J. (2012). "Locker Room Metaphysics (Revisited)," *Sport, Ethics and Philosophy*, 6(4), 407–9.

McNamee, M. J. and Parry, S. J. (eds) (2013). *Olympic Ethics and Philosophy*. Abingdon: Routledge.

Martinkova, I. and Parry, S. J. (2012). *Phenomenological Approaches to Sport*. Abingdon: Routledge.

Metheny, E. (1968). *Movement and Meaning*, New York: McGraw-Hill.

Midgley, M. (1974). "The Game Game", *Philosophy*, 49(189), 231–253.

Pawlenka, C. (2010). "Philosophy of Sport in Germany: An Overview of its History and Academic Research," *Journal of the Philosophy of Sport*, 37(2), 271–291.

Quinton, A. (1969) "Locker Room Metaphysics," *New York Review of Books*, August 21, 21–3.

Reid, H. L. (2010). Athletics and philosophy in Ancient Greece and Rome: Contests of virtue, *Sport, Ethics and Philosophy*, 4(2), 109–234.

Reid, H. L., and Austin, M. W. (eds) (2012). *The Olympics and Philosophy*. Lexington, KY: University Press of Kentucky.

Sartre, J. P. (1956). *Being and Nothingness*, New York : Philosophical Library.

Slusher, H. (1967). *Man, Sport and Existence: A critical analysis*. Philadelphia: Lea and Febiger.

Torres, C. R. and Campos, D. G. (2010). "Philosophy of Sport in Latin America," *Journal of the Philosophy of Sport*, 37(2), 292–309.

van Hilvoorde, I., Vorstenbosch, J. and Devisch, I. (2010). "Philosophy of Sport in Belgium and the Netherlands: History and characteristics," *Journal of the Philosophy of Sport*, 37(2), 225–236.

Weiss, P. (1969). *Sport: A philosophic inquiry*. Carbondale, IL: Southern Illinois University Press.

Williams, B. (1995). *Making Sense of Humanity: And other philosophical papers 1982–1993*, Cambridge: Cambridge University Press.

Wittgenstein, L. (1958). *Philosophical Investigations*, translated [from the German] by G. E. M. Anscombe. Oxford: Blackwell.

SECTION I

Philosophical approaches to the conceptualization of sport

1

FORMALISM AND SPORT

Scott Kretchmar

In certain philosophic circles, formalism has something of a bad name.[1] It has been described as narrow, insufficient, inflexible, and counter-intuitive. It is said to be a philosophic position that has implausible implications and one that serves as a home for hidden essentialisms. It is also thought to lack critical resources for adjudicating issues not clearly covered by the rules on which it relies and, partly because of this, has little if any normative potency. Some have argued that a formalist account of sport underplays its aesthetic components by portraying it more as craft than art, as having a grammar and syntax but no semantics. Even for those who argue that formalist perspectives shed some light on games and game playing, such assets are thought to pale in comparison to those found in rival positions – most notably conventionalism or critical ethnocentrism and broad internalism or, as it is also sometimes called, interpretivism.[2]

In this essay, I attempt to argue that formalism does not deserve this fate, or at least not all of it. I discuss the basic tenets of formalism and the logic on which it is grounded, review its putative weaknesses, and finally present arguments that would support my thesis about its often under-appreciated assets. This final section includes what I regard to be a noncontroversial reinterpretation of formalism, one that reduces some of its rigidity but still remains true to its central principles.

A definition of formalism

Formalism is a position attributed to Suits (2005) and others who argued that games are a product of their constitutive rules. That is, these rules jointly create and define the game – its purpose, the means allowed for achieving the purpose, penalties for rule violations, methods for scoring, indications of how the game begins and ends, and methods by which game tests (particularly in parallel or sequential sports) are shared in competitive formats. Constitutive rules, in short, do a lot of work.[3] The work they accomplish, moreover, is regarded by many formalists as sufficient. Nothing is needed that would fall outside the lines drawn by a game's rules. While constitutive rules can be tightened, loosened, or otherwise modified, a game at any point in time is nothing more or less than what its constitutive rules say it is.

This close relationship between the game and its rules has important consequences, including those detailed in the so-called "logical incompatibility thesis." Here is how Morgan described its implications related to cheating:

> The logical incompatibility thesis holds that one cannot win, let alone compete, in a game if one resorts to cheating. This is so, it argues, because in an important sense the rules of a game are inseparable from its goal. That is, the goal of golf is not simply to put the ball into the hole, but to do so in a quite specified way – by using the fewest number of strokes possible. Hence, if one cannot really win a game unless one plays it, and if one cannot really play a game unless one obeys its rules, then it follows that winning and cheating are logically incompatible.
>
> *(Morgan 1988: 50)*

These principles then constitute the bare bones of formalism, the position that I analyze in this essay and, in at least modest ways, defend. This defense rests in part on an appreciation of formalism's roots, a topic to which we must now turn.

The foundations of formalism

Formalism rests on a fundamental distinction that goes back to Kant and beyond, one that runs between what is given and constructed, the natural and unnatural, brute reality and its conventional counterpart (Searle 1969). Things that are part of the natural world are encountered, known, and dealt with directly in the normal course of living and learning. We come to know these givens of life by bumping up against them (or their bumping up against us) and then learning to negotiate the conditions they impose. We do this through observation, trial and error, listening to our parents, becoming apprentices, learning rules of thumb, reflecting, benefiting from formal education, and so on.

If we encounter a heavy object and need to lift it out of the way, for instance, we are constrained and enabled – whether tacitly or explicitly – by certain rules of biomechanics, physics, metabolism, and the like. We may watch someone carry out this task and mimic his or her behavior. One way or another, however, we learn what works and what does not when trying to remove large rocks from one's path.

Brute reality also includes the normative world. If we want to understand differences between good living and its counterpart, we once again learn this through a variety of means – perhaps by observing the choices of a wise parent, reading good literature, or reflecting carefully on our own life experiences. We are likely to surmise that a life filled with love, friendship, and meaning, for example, is superior to one composed primarily of distrust, alienation, and boredom. Similarly, we learn, through reflection and a variety of other means, about the rights of our neighbors and the kinds of obligations we may have toward them.

While discoveries in the normative domain may be held in more tentative ways than some that come from measuring and observing the physical world, and while cultural norms and historical traditions often cast a different light on these basic human activities, nothing here is constructed through stipulation. We do not establish principles of good living or rules of ethics through conventional agreements, by stipulating that "this counts as good" and "that counts as bad". Whether through what Habermas (1994) has called "practical reason" or some other method of discourse and reflection, we attempt to see why some thing or some behavior *deserves* to be identified as good or bad.

Institutions, by way of contrast, are second-order, conjured-up, or constructed realities. They are produced out of the dust, as it were, when people agree on stipulated relationships. Both elements are needed – the stipulations and the agreements. Without the stipulations, there would be no second-order reality, no institution. Without the agreements, the institutions could not do their work.

This can be seen by noticing how language functions. When we stipulate that marks on piece of paper that spell "d-o-g-s" mean four-legged, furry, domesticated pets, we have begun to create a language institution. But without agreement from others on this arrangement, the language cannot do its work related to successful communication.

Two different kinds of rules, according to Searle (1969), are associated with natural and conventional behavior, respectively. Encounters with brute reality (like the need to lift a heavy rock out of one's way or desires to understand the good life and ethical responsibilities) can be codified in what Searle called "regulative rules." Such rules do not add anything new to the behavior or its meaning. They merely describe what many have already experienced and come to know.

Searle used the example of fishing to make this point. We could describe an act of successful fishing in the following way. "The young boy used barbed steel hooks to catch fish this afternoon." The corresponding regulative rule might be this: "If one wants to catch fish, it is better to use steel hooks than hooks made out of butter." This regulative rule adds nothing new to our common understanding of the properties of steel and butter or how fish are effectively caught. Here is how Searle put it:

> In the case of fishing the ends–means relations … are matters of natural physical facts; such facts for example, as … hooks made of steel hold fish, hooks made of butter do not. [The] conditions [under which] one catches a fish is not a matter of convention or anything like a convention.
>
> *(Searle 1969: 37)*

Regulative rules are primary and cover the larger portion of what might be called day-to-day living. They provide the foundation for both human and nonhuman animal behavior. They include the laws of physics, the characteristics of chemicals, the principles of biology and nutrition, guidelines for safety, and many interpersonal norms of decent behavior, including common rules of etiquette. They may be hard-wired, learned, or a little bit of both. These laws, principles, guidelines, rules of thumb, and norms exist, have their effect, and thus, influence our behavior, whether we articulate and reflect on them or not. In point of fact, we internalize most of these regulations in the normal course of growing up, learning how things work, and developing useful skills and habits. Some are even embedded in our emotional reactions to various life events (Damasio 1999, 2003).[4]

Because we come to embody most of these rules, we no longer find it necessary to consult them. But, once again, if for whatever reason it became helpful to articulate regulative rules, they merely describe brute reality and our behavior as part of it. Nothing new is constructed. No new behaviors like speaking English, hitting homeruns, spending dollars, or voting for presidents are created.

These latter kinds of actions require conventional agreements, and such agreements require constitutive rules. Conventions and the institutions they create literally come into existence on the backs of their own rules. Where no constitutive rules exist, in other words, no conventions (and thus too, no institutions) will be found. None of our common institutions – not the English language, baseball, money, or democratically elected heads of state – existed until constitutive rules fleshed out the conventions that brought them to life and allowed them serve the functions they were created to serve.

Human needs predate convention-grounded institutions and serve as their sufficient cause. Thus, prior to the development of conventions, such needs had to be met with greater or lesser success by other means. Functions related to successful communication, for instance, were and are carried out with varying degrees of efficacy in the absence of any conventions. Animals, for example, communicate in fairly sophisticated ways by employing what Tomasello (2008) has called a proto-language via a variety of gestures, body postures, and sounds. Natural communication, in other words, preceded more powerful and complex forms of conventional communication such as English, Russian, and Chinese, or computer languages like XML, HTML and XSLT.

According to Searle, most constitutive stipulations can be converted into the following formula: "X counts as Y in context C." As noted, the word "dog" (X) counts as a certain furry, four-legged animal (Y) in the context of the English language (C). By agreeing to a number of such stipulations, we end up sharing vocabularies, grammatical constructions, and rules of syntax that allow us to say more than we could say by using regulative rules and their pre-conventional methods of communication – once again, methods such as grunting, pointing, or drawing pictures.

Human needs also generated convention-based institutions called sport – perhaps needs related to improved forms of play, better pastimes. Thus, sport stands in the same relationship to its constitutive rules as language. A ball that passes over the net, hits the table, and is not returned (X) counts as one point (Y) in the context of table tennis (C). By agreeing to a number of such stipulations, we benefit from a challenging game that provides a richer pastime than we would have if we used regulative rules and their pre-conventional methods of promoting intrinsically satisfying experiences through, for instance, simple physical play.[5] Thus, just as language conventions permit superior communication in comparison to proto-language, so too do games produce superior problem-based pastimes in comparison to the occasionally enjoyable and less reliable challenges found in work or some natural forms of play.

This reasoning provides the central warrant for formalism – both its logic and its utility. Table tennis and other game institutions are simply the sum of their constitutive parts, and those parts are joined to effect certain ends, to meet certain human needs and interests. In games, arguably, those needs and interests are related to confronting and solving valid problems. These ends can be achieved and these functions served only if the institutions are built well.

Consequently, building game tests is not a random process. Conventional agreements codified in constitutive rules are not arbitrary arrangements. Constitutive game rules perform a number of functions and they have to perform them effectively. Some of these functions are more foundational, others more culturally relative. But all of them have plausible roles to play in producing high quality games. I listed some of these at the start of the chapter and provide clarifications of these functions below:[6]

- The modulation of means and ends to create a good problem, one that is neither too hard nor too easy, is durable and does not lose its charm after being played only a few times, one that is flexible enough to be played by people of different ages and skill levels, one that has good symbolic potential or otherwise fits the culture in which it is to be played.
- The restoration of games that have gone awry, indications of what counts as a violation, which violations deserve penalties, how to make sure penalties effectively compensate for unearned or illegal advantages gained, how to mimic or otherwise respect the constitutive skills of the game in the restoration process, how to promote restorative efficiencies so that players do not spend more time restoring the game (e.g., taking foul shots in basketball) and less time playing it (e.g., experiencing the full five on five challenge of the game).
- The establishment of effective methods for scoring, for accurately and fairly marking achievements in the face of the game test and noting relative or comparative levels of

achievement in contests; the determination of how subjectively scored games (e.g., diving, figure skating) can achieve acceptable levels of reliability and validity.

- The determination of how games start, continue, and stop, what counts as too long or short a game, how to guarantee skill-based action in time-regulated games where stalling can undermine the integrity of the contest, how to assure that methods for starting and stopping games do not provide unfair advantages to any of the competitive parties.
- The adjudication of how games will be shared in competitive situations,[7] the order of performance in serial competitions (e.g., downhill skiing where fairness is affected by racing order), indications of how parallel contests are to be conducted (e.g., in races around a track, staggered starts designed to promote fairness, rules about sharing space, when and how a runner can cut in), and the allowances and limitations for interactive contests (e.g., in basketball who gets the ball first, how offensive and defensive opportunities are regulated).

Constitutive rules are the tools used by mortal gamewrights[8] to carry out these various functions. I mention that gamewrights are mortal to underline the sheer difficulty of meeting the aforementioned requirements effectively, let alone, perfectly or ideally. All games have flaws – chess, Sudoku puzzles, baseball, even soccer – the so-called "beautiful game" (see, e.g., Kretchmar 2005b). Rule makers sit down at the end of every season (sometimes even in the middle of a season) and revisit their game's constitutive rules. They tinker; they amend; occasionally they make dramatic changes. Sometimes they agree that the game needs to be subdivided – racquetball separating from paddleball, motorcycling emerging from cycling, and possibly "drug-free games" complementing "enhanced" versions of the same basic activity (Gleaves 2011).

The admission that game rules are flawed, vague, and variable, raises important questions about the sufficiency of formalism. Games, it would appear, need something that goes beyond the rules, both to enhance or assure game quality and to provide guidance for reformation or other adjustments. This leads us to the criticisms that have been leveled at formalism and common preferences expressed for alternate theories – either broad internalism/interpretivism or some brand of conventionalism.

A critique of formalism

A basic criticism leveled at formalism is epistemological in nature and it is a strong one. Rules are commonly open to interpretation, and rules cannot interpret themselves. That is, the people who play the games must decide, for instance, what "non-contact" means and whether or not a prohibition against fouling really applies at the end of a game when the other team is stalling and no other game-related methods exist for advancing one's competitive commitments. These decisions and interpretations become part of the ethos of the game, a more-or-less common understanding of how the game is interpreted, how the rules are to be applied, even when rules can and should be ignored (D'Agostino 1995).

Broad internalists have made much of this concern and for good reason. They have rightly observed that game rulebooks are never complete. This insufficiency can be traced to specific causes including: a) actions that were never imagined by rule makers (e.g. Wilt Chamberlain once dunked foul shots legally when he realized he could run from midcourt, leave the ground at the foul line, and slam the ball through the basket before touching the floor); b) actions that are variably significant depending on context (e.g. in basketball, a push near the basket may confer a clear illegal advantage or, in other cases or locations on the court, have no appreciable

effect on the game at all); c) actions that may be intentional or accidental and where this difference is important to the integrity of the game (e.g. a baseball pitcher who has a history of control
problems hits a batter with a fast ball – third parties, like umpires, cannot always tell for sure if
the pitch was thrown intentionally); d) actions for which there are no rules and for which rules
would not even be helpful (e.g. the common maxim "you should play hard" cannot be usefully
stipulated in rulebooks; Reddiford 1985). For these reasons and others, it seems clear that the
formalist account is insufficient: games *are* more than their constitutive rules say they are.

Other criticisms are related to logical conundrums created by formalism and the logical
incompatibility thesis. For instance, if a game is literally the sum total of its many constitutive
rules, and if one is no longer playing that game when any one of these rules is broken, and if
it is certain or likely that at least one rule will be broken during the course of any game, then
it follows that players will certainly or likely never complete a game. To say the least, this is an
odd conclusion. It is odd because most games, even those that include multiple rule violations,
almost always appear to be successfully completed.

Similarly, it has been argued that formalism cannot account for game penalties (D'Agostino
1995). The argument might go as follows: If penalties in baseball, for instance, are designed to
levy fines on players who violate rules of the game; and if those who violate baseball rules are
by definition no longer in the game, it follows (oddly) that baseball penalties are levied on those
who are no longer playing baseball. A consequence of this line of reasoning is the effacement
of the well-known distinction between playing fairly and unfairly.

A third criticism of formalism is related to its putative rigidity (D'Agostino 1995). In its
worst form, this can appear as a kind of Platonism. What seems to be a pragmatically
constructed and revision-prone activity known as baseball becomes Baseball, an ideal game.
This promotes a rigid and most likely traditionalist reading of game rules. It would have baseball gamewrights at the table arguing for honoring and preserving a certain essence of the
game. Conventionalists and broad internalists alike rightly criticize both the ambitious epistemology behind such a position and the metaphysical inflexibility it produces.

A formalist, however, does not have to be a Platonist. One can argue that a game at any one
point in time is nothing more than its rules, but also agree that those rules are imperfect and
open to revision. But this raises another question. On what grounds, if any, can and should a
game be changed? This leads to a final important criticism of formalism – namely, that it lacks
critical resources for making just these kinds of decisions (Simon 2000).

This very question bothered Ronald Dworkin (1986), a philosopher of law. In the domain
of jurisprudence, he argued that legal precedent rather than inherited game rules presents reformation and adjudication problems. How much weight should precedent carry? How should it
be interpreted? On what grounds can precedent be redefined or even ignored? In effect,
Dworkin asked the same question that thoughtful gamewrights ask. How can we duly respect
antecedent rules while not being bound blindly or inexorably to them?

Dworkin suggested that thoughtful individuals can come to understand what the law is
about and that principles emerging from such reflection can provide guidance for both the
interpretation of precedent and warranted deviations from it. This led to his conclusion that
precedent, even good precedent, is not sufficient and Russell's (1999) similar claim that "rules
are not all an umpire has to work with."

The bottom line, from this particular critical perspective, is that formalists lack a rational
foundation for determining the merits of the current version of any game or reasons for reformation where it is needed (Simon 2000). Something in addition to the constitutive rules of
games is needed to account for the games themselves, permit effective or fruitful game playing, and guide any efforts related to game modifications. This something else is either the

principles of the broad internalists (and the realist commitments that go with them) or well-conceived "deep conventions" (and the anti-realist commitments that go with them) (Morgan 2012). But this is another story. For purposes here, formalism is seen as flawed on either account. Formalist interpretations need to be fortified either by rational insight and a consensus regarding what sport is about (broad internalism) or by thoughtful discourse on variable social practices and traditions and an agreement that epistemological certainty will never be achieved (conventionalism or critical ethnocentrism).

A defense and revision of formalism

After reading these criticisms, it may sound odd to claim that most everyone agrees that formalism is, partially, true. But this, in fact, is the case. Nearly everyone agrees with Searle and Suits that games are institutions and that institutions are products of their constitutive rules. Even more importantly, there is general agreement with the tenets of the incompatibility thesis. At some point – albeit perhaps a difficult-to-define-point – a failure to follow game rules is a failure to play the game. Many also agree that the most direct and efficacious route to game reformation is taken when individuals consent to formal rule changes, and not rely on vague game principles or a commonly held ethos. Clearly articulated game rules would seem to be the best means we have for knowing how to play a game and for assuring a level playing field (Fraleigh 2003).

Without courting essentialism or Platonic idealism, one can make an even stronger argument. Some longstanding games and their constitutive rules are not only efficacious. They also deserve a degree of respect. Dworkin (1986) made just this kind of argument in trying to balance legal needs for predictability, on the one hand, with flexibility, on the other. Predictability comes when "people accept that they are governed not only by explicit rules laid down in past political decisions but by whatever other standards flow from the principles these decisions assume" (1986: 188). By analogy, we can say that athletes and spectators should respect morally defensible games that have withstood the test of time, honor their constitutive rules and the principles that went into their development, and counsel caution when anyone would tinker with their defining characteristics. If these games are to change, they should be modified with care.

While Dworkin is considered a liberal philosopher, there is a high degree of conservatism in his work as well. Some of this conservatism comes to the fore when he acknowledges the wisdom that can be embedded in the law or, for our purposes here, in any game's constitutive rules. But he gives an even stronger endorsement of formalism when he argues that the best defense for the legitimacy of rules rests "not in the hard terrain of contracts or duties of justice or obligations of fair play that might hold among strangers … but in the more fertile ground of fraternity, community, and their attendant obligations" (1986: 206). The warrant for honoring game rules, according to Dworkin, would stem from "obligations in virtue of collective community decisions" (p. 206) as represented in a game's constitutive rules. The doorway for change and flexibility is kept open by Dworkin with his reliance on "the principles these decisions assume," but the crack is not very wide. So, while neither legal precedent nor constituted game traditions deserve anything like blind allegiance, they arguably deserve a healthy degree of respect.[9]

A final argument in support of formalism is an important one. It speaks to claims that formalism is counter-intuitive, that it presents logical conundrums. Many of these criticisms are related to the logical incompatibility thesis and its consequences. Ironically, these criticisms carry force only if one ignores the full analysis provided by the often-cited progenitor of formalism – John Searle.

My claim here is that formalism becomes illogical when interpreted in a wooden, analytic way. D'Agostino (2005), for instance, stipulated that playing a game required adherence to *all* its constitutive rules, and that game playing or defection was an *all or nothing phenomenon*. That is, one is either playing in accordance with all game rules (or not) and, consequently, one is either in the game (or not). Neither one of these stipulations is required by formalism, neither one is supported by Searle, and neither one makes much sense.

Searle (1969) argued that not all constitutive rules of language are created equal. Some are more important than others. Consequently, the violation of some rules does more damage to communication acts and purposes than does the violation of others. In speaking of chess and American football Searle wrote, "There will always be degrees of centrality in any system of constitutive rules." It would not be true, therefore, that "a slight change in a fringe rule makes it a different game" (p. 34). Similarly, the violation of a fringe rule of, say, football would not mean that one was no longer playing football.

It makes much more sense to portray formalism in terms of constitutive rules that perform greater and lesser roles in making any game what it is. Earlier, I detailed the many functions of constitutive rules. Those regulations related to creating a game problem that is neither too diffi-cult nor too easy, that specify the use of certain physical skills, certain strategic decisions, and certain interactions among teammates would typically lie closer to the heart of the game. A violation of those rules might well damage the game beyond repair, make a mockery of it, or otherwise ruin the contest. On the other hand, wearing a jersey with an illegally small number on it, standing an inch outside the batter's box in baseball, or creating incidental contact that confers no significant advantage in basketball, are relatively trivial violations of constitutive rules. A failure to heed their requirements does little or no damage to the game itself.

Searle argued that language institutions are built to perform a function. So, too, it is with games. When language conventions fail because someone fails to follow the rules of vocabu-lary, syntax, grammar, and semantics we suffer the results – probably some form of non- or miscommunication. In language, there are no formal penalties for rule violations. We simply do not get the message, or have to put up with unnecessary ambiguities when we need clarity.

In sport, the failure to follow rules has analogous effects. The game might be ruined or damaged. However, gamewrights invoke penalties that would restore games to something of their pre-violation status. But again, not all violations threaten games to the same degree.

In light of these reflections, we might picture four levels of violations of constitutive rules and the typical responses for each one. Level I involves a violation of a central rule or attitude required for game play.[10] It is met with disqualification or other brands of strong punishment such as a red card in soccer or some other form of warning. Such violations are, in effect, fail-ures to play the game or play it in accord with common tenets of fair play or moral decency.

A level-II violation does not merit disqualification. Nevertheless, it is serious because it immediately confers significant unearned advantage. It is met with compensations designed to erase the advantage and also with threats of eventual disqualification for continued or excessive violations – as is the case in basketball, where a person can foul out of the game.

Level-III violations confer insignificant advantages. Thus, compensatory penalties are typi-cally not needed or, when used, their effect is minimal. Many such violations at this level are unintended, as when a pass in soccer misses a teammate and the ball goes out of bounds. Possession, in such cases, is simply awarded to the other team. Such minimal indiscretions blend at some point into what I am calling level-IV violations of constitutive rules. These are of such little consequence that they normally invoke no penalties whatsoever. Even where penalties could be levied, officials often "overlook" such violations for purposes of preserving the flow of the game.

This stratified, functional approach to formalism allows us to avoid some of the odd conclusions required by an analytic, dichotomous account. People who violate rules are still in those games and can still win them. The violation of a single, trivial constitutive rule does not effectively change the game. Penalties make sense because violations (at least at levels II, III, and IV) do not nullify games or necessarily render game outcomes invalid. They merely harm them, make them less likely to function well and may render game outcomes less reliable. Thus, the distinction between playing unfairly and fairly is preserved.

When all is said and done, and if my arguments carry any weight, the common ethical recommendation to "follow game rules" is not bad advice. While I have not argued that a formalist account of games is sufficient, it is nonetheless powerful. I say it is powerful because many games and their variations have been with humankind for centuries. Their enduring popularity speaks to the fact that their constitutive rules are doing their jobs well.

It is also powerful because many current game rules, I think, combine elements of the two other adjudicatory options. Many of our popular games do, in fact, reveal principles related to good physical tests, good ways of measuring success or progress, good ways to share tests and compete, and so on. This would suggest that broad internalism can be useful.

But the variety of games available and the variable ethos that surrounds them also speaks to the importance of pluralism and thus, too, conventionalist interpretations of sport. Such values as excellence, drama, knowledge, excitement, improvement, opportunity or having a chance, among other goods that arguably have intrinsic connections to gratuitous physical testing and contesting are alternately featured, or given lesser roles, from one time or one culture to another (Kretchmar 2014).

I would add a third adjudicatory factor and one that is often overlooked – namely biology and our evolutionary history. Games are made by us and for us. They have to fit our nature – our capacities, our tendencies, our genetic leanings. This is obviously true at the physical level, but it is less obviously the case at the human level. Yet we hominins have been built to play, seek meaning, solve problems and so much more. Gamewrighting, whether explicitly or tacitly, must take these givens of human nature into account if it is to be successful.

Thus, effective constitutive rules and the strength of formalism may rest on the deft deployment of principled thinking, an appreciation for cultural pluralism, and a sensitivity to what we humans are. But these speculations reach far beyond the central purposes of this chapter. As this debate over interpretive foundations continues, we might be well advised to take game rules seriously and treat them with a degree of respect. As Dworkin argued, precedent provides the necessary cultural stability and predictability that would counterbalance any drive for excessive change and the uncertainty that comes with it.

Notes

1 Criticism of formalism has been around for years. D'Agostino (1988/1995) was one of the first to attack formalist interpretations of sport, but many others followed. Among the most notable are Dworkin (1986), Morgan (1987, 2004, 2012), Russell (1999, 2004, 2007, 2011), Simon (2007) and Edgar (2013).
2 A recent example is found in Morgan (2012), he identified formalism as the least useful of the three major options for interpreting sport, the other two being broad internalism and his preferred interpretative framework, deep conventionalism.
3 My understanding of the work accomplished by constitutive rules is taken from Searle. That is, the constitutive rules of language (or games) are all stipulations that, in any way, contribute to the creation of the entire language (or game) institution and its ability to perform its functions. Clearly, some constitutive rules meet this requirement more fully than others. In this sense, as argued later in the chapter, not all constitutive rules are created equal. For a more complete discussion of this, see Kretchmar (2001).

4   The work of Bernard Suits (1978/2005) is often regarded to be a prime example of formalist think-
    ing. Interestingly, he never (to this author's knowledge) mentioned regulative rules. This may be due
    to the fact that he was interested in defining a convention, not its preconditions. Nevertheless, he at
    least tacitly acknowledged this distinction be noting that there are two ways by which hurdles make
    tasks more difficult. Game hurdles are placed in one's way solely for the sake of the challenges they
    make possible. This, as noted, is a consequence of what Suits called the lusory attitude. But natural
    hurdles (he used an example from ethics) are accepted for non-lusory reasons. In Searle's conceptual
    scheme, such natural hurdles are comprehended vis à vis regulative rules. Thus, Suits made use of the
    distinction even if he did not formally acknowledge or emphasize it.

5   Some would argue that I am begging a question here by identifying sport as a pastime. To an extent,
    this is true. But my argument here is that this is arguably no more indefensible than identifying the
    foundational function of language as one of communication or the function of money as facilitating
    trade or the exchange of goods and services. Also, the identification of games as pastimes does not
    preclude their use for other purposes such as the pursuit of excellence or making a living. Similarly,
    language can be used for a variety of purposes—for instance, to intimidate, intentionally deceive, solid-
    ify one's power, and so on.

6   See Kretchmar (2005a, 2005b) and Torres (2000) for further analyses of game rules and their func-
    tions.

7   According to most analyses, games are tests. Thus, contesting and competition are not assumed when
    one speaks of game tests. Many of our sporting games (e.g., bowling, golf, running and swimming for
    time) can be done alone and non-competitively, in non-competitive groups, or alternately in compet-
    itive settings were two or more opponents (or teams of opponents) are present.

8   I am not claiming that games are all invented by individuals. The process of gamewrighting is
    undoubtedly messy, one that often involves antecedent activities of uncertain origin that are then
    modified and re-modified by individuals or groups.

9   The qualifier here is important. Some brutal or wicked games, for instance, deserve little or no respect.
    Dworkin was sensitive to criticisms related to corrupt legal precedent, like those established during
    the Nazi regime. Likewise, the argument for respect here speaks to a critical and qualified respect.

10 Interestingly, it is not just a violation of constitutive rules that generate disqualification. We saw that
    in the recent summer games when Korea was disqualified for a failure to try to win – something, as
    Reddiford (1985) argued, that cannot be helpfully stipulated in the rules. Suits' categories of "triflers"
    and "spoilsports" also identify game playing failures for which there may be no constitutive rules. Of
    course, egregious cheats who do, in fact, violate constitutive rules, count among the others who may
    be thrown out of games.

References

D'Agostino, F. (1995). "The ethos of games," in *Philosophic Inquiry in Sport*, 2nd ed., edited by W. Morgan.
    Champaign, IL: Human Kinetics, pp. 42–49.

Damasio, A. (1999). *The Feeling of What Happens: Body and Emotion in the Making of Consciousness*. New
    York: Harcourt.

Damasio, A. (2003). *Looking for Spinoza: Joy, Sorrow, and the Feeling Brain*. New York: Harcourt.

Dworkin, R. (1986). *Law's Empire*. Cambridge, MA: Harvard University Press.

Edgar, A. (2013). "A hermeneutics of sport," *Sport, Ethics and Philosophy* 7: 140–67.

Fraleigh, W. (2003). "Intentional rule violations – one more time," *Journal of the Philosophy of Sport 30*, 166–76.

Gleaves, J. (2011). *From Science to Sport: A cross-disciplinary examination of the justification for doping bans*.
    Unpublished doctoral dissertation, Pennsylvania State University.

Habermas, J. (1994). *Justification and Application: Remarks on discourse ethics*. Cambridge, MA: MIT Press.

Kretchmar, S. (2001). "A functionalist analysis of game acts: Revisiting Searle," *Journal of the Philosophy of
    Sport XXVIII*: 160–72.

Kretchmar, S. (2005a). *Practical Philosophy of Sport and Physical Activity*, 2nd ed. Champaign, IL: Human
    Kinetics.

Kretchmar, S. (2005b). "Game flaws," *Journal of the Philosophy of Sport XXXII*: 36–48.

Kretchmar, S. (2014). "Pluralistic internalism," *Journal of the Philosophy of Sport* published online April 16,
    2014. DOI:10.1080/00948705.2014.911101.

Loland, S. (1998). "Fair play: Historical anachronism or topical ideal?" in *Ethics and Sport*, edited by M.
    McNamee and S. J. Parry. London: E & FM Spon, 79–103.

Morgan, W. (1987). "The logical incompatibility thesis and rules: A reconsideration of formalism as an account of games," *Journal of the Philosophy of Sport XIV*, 1–20.

Morgan, W. (1988). "The logical incompatibility thesis and rules: A reconsideration of formalism as an account of games," in *Philosophic Inquiry in Sport,* (2nd ed.), edited by W. Morgan. Champaign, IL: Human Kinetics, 50–63.

Morgan, W. (2004). "Moral antirealism, internalism, and sport," *Journal of the Philosophy of Sport 31*, 161–83.

Morgan, W. (2012). "Broad internalism, deep conventions, moral entrepreneurs, and sport," *Journal of the Philosophy of Sport 39*: 65–100.

Reddiford, G. (1985). "Constitutions, institutions, and games," *Journal of the Philosophy of Sport XII*, 41–51.

Russell, J. S. (1999). "Are rules all an umpire has to work with," *Journal of the Philosophy of Sport, XXVI*: 27–49.

Russell, J. S. (2004). "Moral realism in sport," *Journal of the Philosophy of Sport 31*: 142–60.

Russell, J. S. (2007). "Internalism and internal values in sport," in *Ethics in Sport*, (2nd ed.), edited by W. Morgan. Champaign, IL: Human Kinetics, 35–50.

Russell, J. S. (2011). "Limitations of the sport-law comparison," *Journal of the Philosophy of Sport 38*: 254–72.

Searle, J. (1969). *Speech Acts: An essay in the philosophy of language*. Cambridge: Cambridge University.

Simon, R. (2000). "Internalism and internal values in sport," *Journal of the Philosophy of Sport XXVII*, 1–16.

Suits, B. (2005). *The Grasshopper: Games, life and utopia*. Introduction by T. Hurka. Plymouth: Broadview.

Tomasello, M. (2008). *Origins of Human Communication*. Cambridge, MA: MIT Press.

Torres, C. (2000). "What counts as part of a game: A look at skills," *Journal of the Philosophy of Sport 27*, 81–92.

2

INTERNALISM AND SPORT

Robert L. Simon

Internalism is a theoretical approach to understanding and assessing sport that provides a framework for examining questions such as the following: Is athletic competition morally defensible or does it by its very nature overemphasize winning and denigrate those who don't win as losers? How should we understand sportsmanship and what does it require? What is fair play? How should coaches distribute playing time among their team members? More broadly, what if anything accounts for the interest and passion shown by participants in and spectators of sport around the world? Do the features that account for fascination with sport morally legitimize it or is sport, especially elite competitive athletics, a practice that perniciously distracts us from the issues of the day and instills an unethical win-at-all cost attitude that carries over in all aspects of our culture?

Theorists of sport have developed philosophical frameworks to provide intellectually defensible responses to these and many other conceptual, explanatory, and ethical questions about sport. These frameworks for inquiry may be called theories of sport.[1] These theories can be assessed by how well they meet at least the following criteria: Do they provide a characterization of sport that distinguishes it from other practices, do they offer an explanation or account of what so many people find attractive or fascinating about sport, and do they provide resources for the moral and aesthetic evaluation of sporting practices? Internalism, the subject of this chapter, is one approach or strategy for developing a theory of sport.

The internalism–externalism distinction

In understanding a social practice, we might on one hand try to place it in a social context, for example by examining the function or role it plays in a broader social setting. Thus, we might explain what goes on in college classrooms, such as discussion, writing papers, and taking examinations, in terms of the role grading plays in sorting students so they can be assessed for employment or admission to selective graduate programs. On the other hand, we can look at values that might be embedded in the practice itself. For example, an internal assessment of the ethics of discussion within college classrooms might find not only that students are to be treated with the respect due them as persons (the broad Kantian ethical principle of not treating others as mere means) but also that the manner in which they are respected requires that all parties encourage open discussion, that the professor normally has the right to select texts and direct participation in the classroom, and that following the argument where it leads may sometimes make some students uncomfortable, as when they are confronted with philosophical arguments that conflict with their previously unexamined religious beliefs. These latter considerations, while they need not conflict with broad ethical principles, such as the abstract Kantian formula, are presupposed by a paradigm or interpretation of the internal values that normally should govern college classrooms.

With this distinction in mind, is the best way to understand and assess sport and sporting practice to place it in a broader social context or to attend to its internal features? The first approach, often called "externalism," is the view that sport is best understood and assessed in terms of the social role it plays, the social function it serves, or its place in a broad sociocultural context. Perhaps the best example of an externalist approach is functionalism; the idea that sport is best looked at *as* fulfilling some social need or goal. For example, sport may be identified and assessed according to whether it produces social cohesion among some group, such as fans, residents of an area, or even at a national or global level.

"Internalism" can be defined minimally as asserting that some internal features of sport are necessary to understanding and evaluating it or more strongly as maintaining that it is the internal features of sport alone that are fundamental for conceptual, explanatory, and justificatory purposes. On this account, minimalist versions of internalism may be compatible with some weak or modest forms of externalism since all it asserts is that any satisfactory theory will have to consider some internal features of sport. Stronger forms of internalism, however, may be less easy or impossible to reconcile with externalist approaches.

Moreover, the externalism–internalism distinction itself may be problematic, not only because some combinations of each approach may be compatible but also because of lack of clarity about what constitutes an "internal" feature of sport and what is "external." For example, is the pursuit of new records in swimming and track and field inherent to the presumably internal ideal of athletic competition as the pursuit of excellence, or is identifying breaking records as opposed to say simply doing one's best, a goal fostered by some social and historical contexts but not others?

Nevertheless, even if the internal–external distinction is not always sharp, it may nevertheless be useful. It not only suggests differing strategies for theorizing about sport and athletic competition but also, at least where strong internalism is concerned, a way of taking sport seriously as an important practice in its own right, independent of its social roles.

Functionalism, which, as we noted above, is a form of externalism, seems particularly deficient on this point. Even if sport does serve the social goals of promoting social unity, promoting health by combating obesity, or discharging aggression harmlessly, or some other social function, this approach tells us nothing about why sport in particular serves this goal rather than some other practice. Still less does it tell us whether fulfilling the function is morally valuable (or even morally required), let alone whether sport is the morally best way (or even a morally defensible way) of doing it. Finally, it also provides little if any basis for resolving ethical issues that may arise within athletic competition, such as how much importance to assign to winning, whether doping should be permitted or prohibited, what counts as fair play, and many others.[2]

Internalists, then, believe that attending to what William J. Morgan has called "the gratuitous logic of sport," its internal characteristics, values, and principles, not only sheds the most light on sport but best provides the resources for assessing it morally as well (Morgan, 1994, especially Chapter 5).

Internalism: formalist approaches

An important form of internalism suggests that sports are best understood in terms of their formal structures, which consist primarily of the constitutive rules of various sports. Much as a developed legal system can be viewed as a system of different kinds of rules, sports also can be understood along such lines. For example, baseball, soccer and basketball can be distinguished from one another because the rules of each are so different.

But not all rules are of the same logical type. Thus, in law, we can distinguish what H. L. A. Hart called primary rules, such as the legal rules for making wills, or buying a house, or designating certain acts as crimes from secondary rules, such as rules for identifying and changing the primary ones. Different kinds of rules can be found in sports as well (Hart, 1997).

In his fascinating analysis of the nature of games, *The Grasshopper: Games, Life and Utopia,* Bernard Suits (2005) emphasized the importance of constitutive rules. Constitutive rules are those that define what counts as permissible moves within a game and what counts as winning. Thus, in American football, they transform pursuit of an easily obtainable pre-lusory goal, such as carrying a ball of a certain shape over a line drawn in the ground, to a lusory goal of scoring more touchdowns than the opposition. The lusory goal can be achieved only within the framework of existing rules; in this view, (American) football would not exist without the constitutive rules that define it. These rules create the conditions under which achieving an otherwise unchallenging state of affairs – carrying the ball over the line – becomes a challenge that can test our mettle. Indeed, Suits' informal definition of games is that they are "voluntary attempts to overcome unnecessary obstacles" (Suits, 2005: 55).

Formalism is a theory of sport (or, better, a family of related theories) that draws on Suits' analysis. As I consider it here, however, its main point is that, just as the legal system, as suggested by Hart, may be seen to be characterized by its formal structure of rules, so too sports may be characterized and distinguished from one another by their formal structures of constitutive rules as well. Of course, sports also contain others sorts of rules, such as regulative rules which may recommend good strategies for winning, but it is the constitutive rules that define the sport.

Formalism is an internalist theory because it identifies sport by the internal features of its formal structure rather than by any social or psychological function it serves. Formalism also at least suggests a normative framework for ethical assessment in sport; namely, respect for the rules and fair play understood as the prohibition of cheating.

Formalism does shed important light on the nature of sports, and games generally, through its emphasis on constitutive rules. Fans of the comic strip *Calvin and Hobbes*[3] will remember the fictional game called "Calvinball" in which the players make up the rules as they go along. Of course, "Calvinball" is not a game, since anything can count as a move within the activity as players make up new and more complicated "rules" as the game goes along.

> Player A: You lose because your car has more than 15,000 miles on its mileage meter.
> Player B: But that rule doesn't apply in this universe, only elsewhere in the multiverse.
> Player A: Except that clause is negated when stated in North America.

Formalists, as "Calvinball" illustrates, are quite right to assert that without the formal structure of constitutive rules, we would not have sports in the first place.

I have argued elsewhere, however, that formalism is deficient on at least two fundamental grounds. Most important, the resources it provides for the moral assessment of behavior in sport seem far too limited (Simon, 2010: 3–8). Although respect for the rules and the prohibition of cheating are important moral guidelines, many significant moral issues that arise in sporting contexts require a broader moral perspective than that provided by the model of rules. For example, consider such issues as whether a proposed rule change is an improvement to the game, how playing time should be distributed among players on a team, whether opponents always have an obligation to play their best against opponents, whether the winning team should seek to correct a crucial but egregiously bad call by an official in its favor and whether trash talking is an acceptable practice at different levels of athletic competition. Dealing with these and many other complex issues that arise in sport requires richer resources for moral inquiry than provided by narrow forms of formalism.

A second line of criticism has been advanced by theorists who are often called conventionalists. They argue that, in addition to rules, sports involve the application of social conventions (which may differ among different social, historical or cultural contexts). Since all actual games involve some form of rule breaking – a soccer game does not cease to be a soccer game if a player, without being detected by officials intentionally uses her hands to guide the ball in violation of the rules – we also need to understand the social conventions or "ethos of the game" to understand sport (D'Agostino, 1981).

Is conventionalism an internalist or externalist theory? I suggest that it depends: if sports in a particular socio-historical context turns out simply to mirror values imported from elsewhere, then conventionalism in that context is externalist. On the other hand, if the conventions arise from within the sporting community (itself a notion without clear boundaries) and reflect internal features of sport, it may be internalist. For example, if the broader society practices strict racial segregation but the sporting community allows participation and evaluates players solely on their merits, its conventions may be internalist, especially if it views sport as essentially a meritocratic enterprise where players should be judged on their athletic skills alone.

Be that as it may, conventionalism of the kind I have described so far is open to the same objection made against narrow versions of formalism; namely, it lacks adequate resources for the moral evaluation of sport. Surely conventions are not morally acceptable just because they are followed or exist in a given context. Thus, if diving became the norm in soccer, that would not necessarily make the game of soccer better, let alone make the practice of diving morally acceptable.[4] In other words, unless modified, conventionalism lacks the resources for the critical evaluation of sport; it runs the risk of confusing what is (what conventions are followed at any given time) with what ought to be.

Later in the chapter, we examine a more sophisticated form of conventionalism that claims to overcome this difficulty. But first, we need to explore an internalist theory that arguably overcomes the weaknesses of narrow forms of formalism.

Broad internalism: an interpretive account

In his now-classic contribution to jurisprudence, *The Concept of Law*, Hart (1997) offered a characterization of law that can be thought of as a relatively complex version of formalism. In his view, sophisticated systems of law can best be thought of as the union of primary and secondary rules. Primary rules include the prohibitions of criminal law but, as Hart pointed out, also include enabling rules, such as rules for how to enter into a contract, make a will, or marry. Secondary rules (which may be thought of as meta-rules), include rules for changing the primary rules, rules for adjudicating disputes about their meaning, scope and application, and a rule of recognition (perhaps the United States Constitution is such a rule) for identifying the other rules of the system.

This influential approach to the characterization of law was challenged by Ronald Dworkin (1977) who pointed out that, in complex cases, which he called "hard cases," judges not only do rely on more than the rules but also should do so as well. Dworkin was not suggesting that judges be permitted to simply apply their own moral or political views to the law, as the following example of his illustrates. In an early New York State case, *Riggs v. Palmer*, a grandfather makes a legitimate will leaving his estate to the grandson. Apparently lacking patience, the grandson hurries things along and murders his grandfather. The issue at stake is whether the grandson, although charged for murder, nevertheless should get his inheritance. In considering the case, the New York court looked at a variety of factors. For one thing, under the law, the will was valid (i.e. it was properly drawn), was signed by the required number of witnesses, and so forth. Yet the majority of the court overturned the will, citing the legal principle, sometimes applied in other areas of criminal law, that a wrongdoer should not profit from his own wrongdoing. Dworkin argues then that the law consists of *principles* as well as *rules* (I discuss this distinction more fully below). Legal principles on Dworkin's account are not the personal moral values of the judge but are presupposed by or embedded in the best overall interpretation of the areas of law relevant to the case at hand.

In an influential paper that explicitly acknowledges Dworkin's influence, J. S. Russell (1999) cites several example from the history of baseball that raise questions about formalism, or the model of rules, that are similar to those raised by *Riggs v. Palmer*. One case involves an 1897 Major League baseball game between Louisville and Brooklyn. A Louisville player, Reddy Mack, crossed home plate to score and then apparently reasoned that the rule restricting interference with fielder as worded at the time implied that he was no longer a base-runner since he already had scored. Mack then held the opposing catcher down while his own teammate also scored. Should this act have been allowed, assuming (as was the case) it was not explicitly prohibited under the rules?

Russell (1999) argues that the umpire of the game, Wesley Curry, was correct in calling the runner out for interference. If Mack's play had been allowed to stand, Russell points out, the game of baseball would have been radically changed. Wrestling fielders to the ground would become a skill valued in the sport. The beauty of great plays by fielders might be negated. Conversations such as the following would become intelligible and pertinent.

> A: Jones is a better hitter and fielder than Smith so he clearly is the better player.
> B: Ah, but Smith is much better at knocking catchers and other fielders down after he has crossed home plate.

Russell suggests that Curry's decision to call interference was justified, not by an explicit rule, but by a governing principle. The principle, which Russell calls the internal principle of sport, states that "rules should be interpreted in such a manner that the excellences embodied in achieving the lusory goal of the game are not undermined but are maintained and fostered" (Russell, 1999: 15). Since allowing Reddy Mack's tactic would undermine the lusory goal of determining which team is best at exhibiting the fundamental skills of baseball, such as hitting, fielding, throwing and base-running, Curry was justified in disallowing it.

What distinguishes Dworkinian principles from rules? On Dworkin's account, rules such as the "three strikes and you are out" in baseball are applied in an "all or nothing" manner while principles can conflict and often must be weighed against one another as well as against other relevant factors, as in *Riggs v. Palmer* (Dworkin, 1977: 101–5). More important, principles must be supported by their role in a coherent theory of the sport (or the law) that best applies to the case in hand and views the sport (area of law) in its best light (Dworkin, 1977; Russell, 1999:14; Simon, 2013: 52–4).

That is, according to broad internalism, we can support many ethical judgments in sport by appealing to an overall theory or account that satisfies the criteria of "fit" and "normativity". The theory satisfies the criterion of fit if it explains the salient features of a sport (or possibly competition in sports more generally); for example, by explaining which skills are fundamental to the sport, offering a coherent account of the challenge the sport is best construed as testing, or in other words, explaining the point of the constitutive rules of the sport. Although the exact meaning of "fit" in this context is debatable, fitting together the various elements of the practice being interpreted into a coherent and mutually reinforcing whole seems central. The second criterion of normativity is satisfied when the theory presents the sport (or athletic competition more generally) in its morally, and, as Cesar Torres (2012: 299 320) has reminded us, in its aesthetically best light.

Two examples may illustrate the application of this interpretative approach to understanding and evaluating sports.[5] One is Cesar Torres's distinction between the primary and restorative skills of a sport. The former are the fundamental skills the sport is best understood as testing while the latter skills are employed when the rules are violated and the game needs to be restored to its proper track, for example by compensating the offended competitor or team. Shooting from the field during the course of play is a primary skill of basketball while foul shooting is a restorative one.

This distinction seems to fit not only our intuitions about basketball but also the priority we give when evaluating players to such skills as dribbling, passing, and shooting from the field as opposed to foul shooting.[6] As a result, the priority given to primary skills implies that excessive fouling (such as strategically fouling to stop the clock) not only harms the game aesthetically by interrupting its flow but also makes the game worse by elevating a mere restorative skill to overriding importance down the stretch of a close or hotly contested game. While the latter implication surely is controversial, it does illustrate how an interpretation of a sport can have implications for practice.

A number of proponents of broad internalism have defended a specific interpretation, applying broadly to athletic competition across sports, that such competition should be understood as what I have called a mutual quest for excellence (Simon, 2010: 24–8; see also Boxill, 2003: 1–12). While critics of athletic competition have accused competitive sport of promoting selfishness (or a kind of team oriented nationalism – "My team right or wrong!"), a disregard for the humanity of opponents, and a tremendous overemphasis on winning as the sole criterion of success, I maintain that the model of sport as a mutual quest for excellence (sometimes called mutualism) offers a important response to such a critique.

According to the mutualist model, athletic contests are seen in their best ethical (and perhaps aesthetic) light when conceived of as the result of a voluntary (if sometimes unspoken) agreement by the competitors to test one another in the contest. Opponents of this model are not enemies or obstacles but facilitators engaged in a mutually beneficial activity, the test or contest, through which they challenge one another while striving for excellence. This activity is viewed both as valuable in itself – the testing of oneself through meeting challenges in sport can be viewed as a good for human beings, or a significant component of human flourishing, since it requires us to employ our higher-order physical and mental capacities. I also argue that athletic competition is educational, since we learn about ourselves and others through striving for achievement and competitive success (Simon, 2008).

The mutualist model arguably meets the test-of-fit criterion since it explains key features of athletic competition, such as why the rules (as Suits pointed out) create obstacles to what otherwise might be done quite easily and why sports fascinate so many, participants and spectators alike.[7] It also meets the criterion of "normativity" since the mutual quest for excellence normally is voluntary or uncoerced, does not require reducing opponents to mere objects or enemies but regards them as partners in a partially cooperative endeavor, and does not overemphasize winning. Winning, on my own view, is normally a sign of athletic success but not always. For example, is an athletically superior team that barely wins in spite of sloppy play over a vastly inferior opponent really successful?[8]

The argument in this section maintains that first, the broad internalist approach provides the kind of reasoning that should be used to develop an explanatory and justificatory model of competition in sports and, second, that mutualism (the mutual quest for excellence) is the model best supported by the broad internalist approach. Of course, whether this overall internalist approach is successful is debatable. While that issue is rightly subject to future inquiry and discussion, we can consider two important criticisms of it in the final sections of this paper.

First criticism: The relativity of ideals

Suppose we accept a broad internalist approach to understanding and assessing normative issues that arise in sport. Does a broad internalist approach lead to one account of sport that is most defensible, several that are about equally defensible, or does it lead to a kind of relativism of sport in which a multitude of theories of sport compete for our allegiance with none being more justifiable than any other? Let us call the first outcome "monism," the second "pluralism," and the last relativism. To put the question another way, is the ideal of the mutual quest for excellence (mutualism) a favored account or must it contend with rivals that would be equally reasonable to adopt?

John Rawls, in *A Theory of Justice* (1971: 50), raises a similar question concerning reflective equilibrium (an ideal balance in which our principles and our considered reaction to cases are in harmony) when he asks "does a reflective equilibrium (in the sense of a philosophical ideal) exist? If so, is it unique? Even if it is unique, can it be reached?"

Rawls was undoubtedly correct in indicating that such fundamental issues will continue to be the subject of further inquiry for the foreseeable future. In the passage quoted above, he also expresses doubt about whether we can answer such questions definitively at present. However, while debates about the justifiability of the mutualist approach and whether it is the most defensible interpretation of competitive sports surely will continue, several considerations suggest that currently it is the most warranted approach to the philosophical understanding and evaluation of sport.

First, it is plausible to conclude, along lines argued recently by Ronald Dworkin (2011: 23–98), that relativism is not in any privileged position. That is, the claim that no philosophical theory of sport is more defensible than any other is itself a first order assertion to the effect that the available evidence for all approaches is equal in force, either equally, strong, weak or even entirely absent. But that itself is a claim that requires justification that may be quite difficult for the relativist to provide. At the very least, such a claim is far from self-evident.

On the contrary, if we are to take a broad internalist approach, some version of mutualism has a claim to be the best existing internalist account and so needs to be taken seriously. First of all, it fits with central features of sport, explaining the value of artificial challenges created by the constitutive rules. These create challenges that we may value both for their own sakes, as meeting such challenges can be seen as an intrinsically valuable activity grounded in an ideal of human flourishing, and which, when carried out properly, may help participants and spectators to develop important character traits and learn about themselves and others. Because participation normally is voluntary, and because contests are unscripted narratives, sports provide a perhaps not unique but very public "moral laboratory" in which the nature and role of concepts such as fairness, sportspersonship, and respect for persons can be illustrated, expressed and debated. Finally, the drama of trying to overcome what Suits (2005) called "unnecessary obstacles" may also explain the attractiveness of athletic competition not only to participants but to spectators as well.

Similarly, a broad internalist approach, with its emphasis on principles as well as rules, provides resources for moral analysis of such hard cases as Reddy Mack's use of the fielder-interference rule of his time. While broad internalist approaches are open to the charge that they allow sports philosophers to spin abstract theories at will without evidence that the theories are actually well grounded, this itself is a claim about the nature of justification in philosophy of sport that also faces critical scrutiny that broad internalists claim has decisive force. That is, as we have seem, broad internalists claim to have improved upon both narrow versions of formalism and conventionalism, and have supported the ideal of the mutual quest for excellence by defending it as the model of competitive sport that both fits the main features of the practice and presents it in its best light.

Morgan's deep conventionalism: A critical contextualism

In a series of articles, William J. Morgan (2012, 2013) has argued for three theses. First, he maintains that many broad internalists such as myself have construed conventionalism too narrowly (or unsympathetically). Second, he argues that conventionalism properly construed can have critical force against prevailing conventional accounts of sport. Third, his "deep conventionalism" implies that different theories may be the best interpretation of sport in different social and historical contexts and so the search for a universal theory that is justifiable to all reasonable people is fruitless.

Our earlier discussion suggested that conventionalism lacked the resources to allow for a moral critique of sport. Conventions might be morally acceptable but they need not be. In addition, externalist versions of conventionalism, which suggest the conventional ethos of the game merely mirrors broader social conventions dominant in the culture generally, seemed to give the broader culture a free moral pass by exempting it from critical scrutiny. On the contrary, if moral critique is possible at all, existing conventions should not be simply accepted as given to us but should be subject to searching moral examination.

Morgan, however, maintains that this objection to conventionalism fails to distinguish between surface (or coordinating) conventions and what he calls deep conventions (Morgan, 2012: 70–9). The former might include some commonly accepted prescriptions as "Losing teams in basketball games may intentionally foul opponents so as to stop the clock and force the opponents to make free throws to hold their lead." As a number of writers have argued, this surface convention is not shown to be acceptable or justifiable just because it is accepted.

Perhaps Morgan's key contribution to an internalist defense of conventionalism is his argument that, in addition to surface conventions, such as the convention of basketball specified above, there also are deep conventions that do have critical force. These conventions express the underlying theory of sport that critical reflection finds to make the best sense of existing social practices.

According to Morgan, however, these social practices differ according to the historical social context in which they are embedded. Thus, strategic fouling in basketball *may* be morally acceptable in a deep reconstruction of the semi-professional ethic dominating much of contemporary American sport, but may be considered totally unethical in sporting contexts dominated by the ethic of gentlemanly generosity towards opponents prevalent in upper-class nineteenth- and early twentieth-century England (Morgan, 2013: 66–73).

Note that Morgan's approach is quite compatible with, and may even presuppose, broad internalism, in that it requires us to find the best overall interpretation of sporting practices within given sociocultural contexts. The dispute between Morgan and such writers as Russell, Nicholas Dixon and myself, if this account of Morgan's view is accurate, is not between internalism and externalism, or between broad internalism and non-interpretive approaches, but is over whether interpretations can justifiably be claimed to transcend particular contexts and at least make a claim to universal assent. Indeed, in Morgan's view, different deep conventional paradigms of sport are incommensurable and so reasoned dialogue between their supporters is bound to fail (Morgan, 2013: 70–1).

Morgan's deep conventionalism is an important variant of broad internalism and as such will continue to be the subject of further inquiry and discussion. I have suggested several criticisms of it elsewhere but after briefly summarizing two of them, I pursue the second in greater depth in what follows.[9]

First, Morgan's deep conventions seem to have many of the characteristics of the principles appealed to by broad internalism as discussed so far. They are not rules, often need to be weighed against one another when they conflict, and are derived from a broad interpretation of the practice under consideration. Second, principles are not ahistorical in origin or transcendent in any pejorative sense, but always are defended within a given historical context and so are always open to further refinement or even refutation (fallibilism).

What I want to question here, however, is the incommensurability thesis and the subsequent charge of transcendentalism that Morgan makes against his philosophical opponents. Morgan acknowledges "that the argumentative process of giving and asking for reasons presupposes that everyone so engaged is on the same page as to what qualifies as a reason" but cautions that "aiming for such universality in our rational judgments about sports, or anything else for that matter, is wishful thinking at best" (Morgan, 2013: 70).

As noted above, however, there is no reason to regard such skepticism about even the possibility of achieving universality as the default position. Whether or not it turns out to be acceptable depends on whether the arguments for it are stronger than those for other views.

Morgan, however, has provided an argument for his view that certainly deserves our consideration. I believe it goes something like this: different culturally embedded paradigms of sport embody different accounts of what counts as a reason. But since critical inquiry or discussion involves a common set of standards, norms or reasons to even get off the ground (see the quotation from Morgan above), critical inquiry or discussion designed to reconcile competing paradigms can never even get started. The common framework presupposed by inquiry is absent. How might the proponents of universalistic versions of broad internalism respond?

First, following a line of argument famously advanced by Donald Davidson, they can maintain that there can be no conception of sport radically different from our own since, if the difference was sufficiently radical, it would not be a conception of sport to begin with (Davidson, 1974).

Be that as it may, this point alone is insufficient to establish the possibility of universalism since it may be that while different paradigms have common elements or share family resemblances, different values may be weighted differently in different cultural and historical contexts. Consider the following quotation, cited by Morgan, from the novel *Chariots of Fire* (Weatherby, 1982), where the runner Harold Abrahams responds to the Cambridge dons who criticize him for his professional, and thus ungentlemanly, attitude that involved hiring a coach, that violated the dominant amateur paradigm of sportsmanship.

> You know, gentleman, you yearn for victory just as I do. But achieved with the appar-
> ent ease of gods. Yours are the archaic values of the prep school playground … I
> believe in the relentless pursuit of excellence – and I'll carry the future with me."
> *(Weatherby, 1982: 91–2, quoted by Morgan, 2013: 263)*

On what I take to be Morgan's view, the dons and Abrahams, while their conceptions of sport are intelligible to one another, weigh values differently, with Abrahams giving much more weight to excellence and victory than do his critics. But this hardly shows that the argument cannot be resolved or even that there is no best resolution capable of attracting the allegiance of all reasonable discussants. Thus, parties to both sides of the debate, if they are broad internalists, need to offer an interpretation of sport that does justice to its main features and presents them in what is arguably their normatively best light.

Morgan might object that there is no common conception of sport shared by both sides. That point is doubtful, since both sides view sport as a rule governed activity creating obstacles that exist to challenge the competitors and both sides presumably view the attempt to meet those challenges as valuable.[10] But even if Morgan's point is correct and there is no identical conception of sport shared by all, the Davidsonian argument implies there will be at least some commonalities that will enable proponents to at least understand each other's perspective. After all, it cannot be the case that the "gentlemanly amateur' view defended by the dons is unintel-ligible to us, since it is characterized all too well in *Chariots of Fire*, and gives the work its bite, as well as by Morgan himself. Given that, it is plausible to think that the different parties will at least appreciate or understand the points made by the other side. That suggests that given a common framework for discussion, the emergence of a hybrid view more acceptable to all parties than their starting point surely cannot be ruled out.

In fact, the ethics of elite golf competitions can be reconstructed as just such a hybrid. Competition at the better amateur and professional levels in golf certainly involves such "professional" aspects as coaching, hard training, a quest for excellence, and an intense desire to win. At the same time, golf etiquette (expressed in the formal rule book) requires courtesy towards opponents and respect for the excellences they exhibit. Indeed, generosity towards opponents is part of golfing lore. For example, in one of the most famous acts of sportsman-ship in modern sport, Jack Nicklaus, in the hotly contested 1969 Ryder Cup, conceded a very short but tricky putt to Tony Jacklin on the last hole of the last day, allowing the British team to tie the Americans. If Jacklin, one of the greatest golfers of his time, had missed, it not only would have forever tarnished his stature as a player but might have negatively affected his play from then on.[11] While such examples are perhaps rare, when compared with the world depicted in *Chariots of Fire*, they occur at various levels of sport, and not just in golf, and at least suggest that sport cannot neatly be divided into isolated paradigms immune from examination from any external viewpoints.

A number of philosophers of sport have also suggested approaches to competition which might represent a hybrid blend of tempered competitiveness that reasonable advocates who start from differing paradigms might well agree on. To take two recent examples. John Russell has argued that coaches, at least at certain levels of sport and in some contexts, have a duty to correct the competitive injustice of bad calls by officials that provide their own teams with unfair benefits (Russell, 2013: 103–19). His argument appeals to values that have a rational pull not only on those closer to the nineteenth-century gentlemanly model discussed by Morgan but also on contemporary athletes, coaches, and spectators, who believe that outcomes should reflect the skills of their contestants and their abilities to meet the challenges of the sport (Russell, 2013). On the other hand, Scott Kretchmar has reminded us that winning involves special skills, "knowing how to win," and that mutualists who regard winning as only one criterion of athletic success among many may give it much too short shrift (Kretchmar, 2012). Indeed, as Russell concedes, athletic contests at higher levels may, in addition to being a mutual quest for excellence, also reflect controlled ritualized rivalry as well.

Whether these values can be brought into a harmonized theoretical framework, a kind of Rawlsian reflective equilibrium, of course, remains debatable. Deep conventionalists may respond that debates take place within a specific sociohistorical context and community (twentieth- and twenty-first century Anglo-American philosophy) with its own criteria of what counts as reasonable. However, my examples above at least suggest that skepticism about achieving a reasonable universal consensus is itself open to very serious challenges. Even more, the examples suggest that current debates in the philosophy of sport do not represent a professional paradigm incommensurate with earlier ideals of sport but, at their very best, contain hybrid elements that make dialogue among proponents of different viewpoints not only possible but fruitful as well.

Conclusion

Be that as it may, internalism remains a fruitful approach to the understanding and assessment of practices in sport, including athletic competition at various levels of skill. After all, as noted above, deep conventionalism is a form of internalism. Both deep conventionalists and broad internalists such as Nicholas Dixon, John Russell, and me, who are sympathetic to universalism and moral realism, take what Morgan has called "the gratuitous logic" of sport seriously and regard the internal features of sport as both morally and explanatory salient. Thus, while broad internalism (interpretivism) will continue to be discussed and refined in the theoretical literature, it provides an approach to the understanding and evaluation of sport that is not only theoretically plausible but also, through its account of mutualism, has great potential to significantly affect practice as well.

Notes

1 I discuss the role of theories of sport more fully in "Theories of Sport" in Cesar Torres (ed.) *A Companion to the Philosophy of Sport*, (Bloomsbury Press, 2014).

2 Functionalists presumably would respond by saying such disputes should be resolved instrumentally by selecting the response that best achieves the function of sport, e.g. promoting social cohesion. But this begs two crucial questions: whether the alleged function itself is morally acceptable and whether other values besides or instead of instrumental ones need to be considered.

3 *Calvin and Hobbes*, by Bill Watterson, was published between 1985 and 1995. See www.gocomics.com/calvinandhobbes (accessed 4 October 2014).

4 Diving is the practice in soccer of faking an injury to stop play, with the intent of depriving the opponent of a tactical advantage gained through skillful play.

5 Broad internalism often is appropriately called interpretivism since, like Dworkin's approach to law, it requires us to try to formulate and defend an interpretation – say an interpretation of the fielder-interference rule in Russell's example.

6 However, the distinction does face a number of criticisms. For example, killing a penalty in ice hockey might be a restorative skill but is a highly complex activity that is fundamental to the game. Also, as Mike McNamee has pointed out to me, primary skills seem identified by their importance in the sport at issue, while restorative skills are identified by their function, which suggests different kinds of distinctions are being blurred together.

7 Presumably, the participants relish the process of learning to or trying to meet challenges, and spectators appreciate not only the skills and virtues exhibited in such a pursuit, but also the drama or twists and turns of the story of each contest, even each season or longer, as the sporting narrative develops over time.

8 See Dixon (1999) for an analysis of the factors that can diminish the importance of winning as a criterion of athletic superiority. For arguments that assign more significance to winning than many mutualists would allow, see Kretchmar (2003, 2012).

9 The first objection is also discussed in my paper (Simon, 2014). I first developed these criticisms of Morgan's position in an early pre-publication review of one of his papers for the *Journal of the Philosophy of Sport* but also am greatly indebted to discussion and correspondence with John Russell, who kindly allowed me to see his unpublished paper ("Does Metaethics Make a Difference in Philosophy of Sport," presented at the International Association for the Philosophy of Sport Conference on September 6, 2013, at California State University) well before the preparation of this chapter. Of course, I am fully responsible for any deficiencies in my analysis.

10 I owe this point to a suggestion from Mike McNamee.

11 Was Nicklaus applying an external value here; namely, that no one should be put under that sort of extreme pressure in a sporting contest? Perhaps; although golfers play under extreme pressure in elite tournaments all the time. More plausibly, Nicklaus was applying a principle internal to the ethics of golf, according to which one should win by hitting golf shots of quality and not because of a an opponent's miss of a very easy shot owing to the pressure of the situation. Indeed, both accounts might apply since, as noted earlier, the internal–external distinction is not a sharp one and borderline cases surely can arise.

References and bibliography

Boxill, Jan (2003) "The Moral Significance of Sport," in Jan Boxill (ed.), *Sports Ethics: An Anthology*. Malden, MA: Blackwell, 1–12.

D'Agostino, Fred (1981) "The Ethos of Games," *Journal of the Philosophy of Sport*, 8: 7–18.

Davidson, Donald (1974) "On the Very Idea of a Conceptual Scheme," *Proceedings and Addresses of the American Philosophical Association*, 47: 5–20.

Dixon, Nicholas (1999) "On Winning and Athletic Superiority," *Journal of the Philosophy of Sport*, 26: 10–26.

Dixon, Nicholas (2012) "Canadian Figure Skaters, French Judges and Realism in Sport," *Journal of the Philosophy of Sport*, 39: 103–16.

Dworkin, Ronald (1977) "Hard Cases" in *Taking Rights Seriously*. Cambridge, MA: Harvard University Press, 81–130.

Dworkin, Ronald (2011) *Justice for Hedgehogs*. Cambridge, MA: Harvard University Press.

Hart, H. L. A. (1997) *The Concept of Law*. New York: Oxford University Press (first published in 1961).

Kretchmar, Scott (2003) "In Defense of Winning," in Jan Boxill (ed.), *Sports Ethics: An Anthology* Malden, MA: Blackwell, 130–5.

Kretchmar, Scott (2012) "Competition, Redemption, and Hope," *Journal of the Philosophy of Sport*, 39: 101–16.

Morgan, William J. (1994) *Leftist Theories of Sport: A Critique and Reconstruction*. Urbana: University of Illinois Press.

Morgan, William J. (2012) "Broad Internalism, Deep Conventions, Moral Entrepreneurs," *Journal of the Philosophy of Sport*, 39: 65–100.

Morgan, William J. (2013) "Interpretivism, Conventionalism and the Ethical Coach" in Robert L. Simon (ed.), *The Ethics of Coaching Sports: Moral, Social, and Legal Issues*. Boulder, CO: Westview Press, 61–77.

Rawls John. (1971) *A Theory of Justice*. Cambridge: Harvard University Press.

Russell, J. S. (1999) "Are Rules All an Umpire Has to Work With," *Journal of the Philosophy of Sport*, 26: 27–49.

Russell, J. S. (2013) "Coaching and Undeserved Competitive Success," in Robert L. Simon, *The Ethics of Coaching Sports: Moral, Social and Legal Issues*. Boulder: Westview Press, 103–20.

Simon, Robert L. (2000) "Internalism and Internal Values in Sport," *Journal of the Philosophy of Sport*, 27: 1–16.

Simon, Robert L. (2008) "Does Athletics Undermine Academics? Examining Some Issues," *Journal of Intercollegiate Sport* 1: 40–58.

Simon, Robert L. (2010) *Fair Play*. Boulder, CO: Westview Press.

Simon, Robert L. (2013) "The Ethical Coach: An Interpretive Account of the Ethics of Coaching" in Robert L. Simon (ed.), *The Ethics of Coaching Sports: Moral, Social and Legal Issues*. Boulder, CO: Westview Press, 41–59.

Simon, Robert L. (2014) "Theories of Sport," in Cesar Torres (ed.), *The Bloomsbury Companion to the Philosophy of Sport*. London: Bloomsbury, 83–97.

Suits, Bernard (2005) *The Grasshopper: Games, Life and Utopia*, 2nd ed. Peterborough, ON: Broadview (first published in 1978).

Torres, Cesar R. (2012) "Furthering Interpretivism's Integrity: Bringing Together Ethics and Aesthetics," *Journal of the Philosophy of Sport*, 39: 299–319.

Weatherby, W. J. (1982) *Chariots of Fire*. New York: Dell.

3

CONVENTIONALISM AND SPORT

William J. Morgan

Introduction

The normative theory of conventionalism can claim very few adherents in sport philosophy circles. Its failure to garner any significant support in this regard cannot be attributed solely to benign neglect. For what little attention it has received in the literature has been mostly of the critical, dismissive, variety. It will come as no surprise, therefore, that my survey of this literature is notable, save for a few exceptions, only for the negative, unflattering picture it paints of conventionalism as a theory of sport. But it may well be surprising, given what I have just said, that the second section of my essay is devoted to a robust defense of conventionalism against its many critics, which in part draws from the work of those select few in the sport philosophy community who think there is more to this theory than initially meets the eye. That defense is long overdue, since I think its critics have not only failed to see what conventionalism has to contribute to normative discussions of sport, but have also badly mischaracterized as well what such a theory, rightly understood, looks like and stands for. These two apparent errors are, of course, related, since it is in part because critics of conventionalism mistake what conventionalism comes to as a normative theory that they have seen fit to reject it, root and branch, as a substantive approach to the critical study of sport. To be sure, my effort to restore conventionalism's good name depends on taking seriously the main criticisms that have been levelled against it, which, in turn, depends on giving those criticisms that comprise almost the whole of the extant literature a fair and comprehensive hearing.

Criticisms of sport conventionalism

The major criticism made against a conventionalist theory of sport claims that the norms in which it trades are too close to the athletic action they are supposed to guide, oversee, and evaluate, to do the kind of critical work any normative theory worthy of the name is supposed to do. That is, critics insist that conventional norms are too caught up in the status quo conception and regard for contemporary sport, too connected to how sport is presently thought about and practiced, to be able to justify whatever normative judgments are made in their name, let alone to criticize the status quo in which they are firmly entrenched. What such norms possess in descriptive force, in describing what actually goes on in sport today, they lack in prescriptive force, in prescribing what ought to go on in sport. And there is not any way to correct for this normative deficiency, critics further claim, because it is in virtue of what conventional norms are that they prove to be prescriptively impotent.

According to this criticism then, the main weakness of conventionalism is that its trademark norms have nothing more going for them than the fact that they are widely accepted. Since conventions on this view just are wide-ranging social agreements, and since the norms that issue from those agreements tell us only whether they meet with the approval of the relevant athletic practice community or society, they are immune to criticism. This means that criticizing these conventional norms is not only forbidden, but always mistaken, because they alone determine what is and is not normatively correct conduct (Dixon, 2003). This also means that because conventions always bottom out in some sort of agreement rather than, say, a rational argument or conviction, rational reflection and argument play no role in their normative calculus. Rather, then, to paraphrase Simon (2007: 48), on agreeing to normative principles because of the intellectual considerations in their favor, conventionalists would have us agree to normative principles because of the mere fact of their having been agreed upon. Surely, the critics insist, this gets things, normatively speaking, exactly and disastrously backwards, since it substitutes mere acceptance for rational concurrence.

If we are to reverse this fatal flaw in conventionalism and thus disabuse its adherents of the bad idea that normative theory can get along quite nicely by appropriating its standards from whatever the prevailing social morality happens to be, then we have basically two paths open to us to put sport on a firmer moral footing: either to invent a new and improved morality, or to discover a better one. Critics of conventionalism like Simon and Dixon favor the first, inventive approach, and adopt what the former calls a discourse approach, or what I call a "realism of reasons." The basic idea behind this approach is the simple one that "ethical justification is a common public practice carried out and through the give and take of reasons" (Simon, 2004: 127). What gives this exchange of reasons its normative force is that the standards by which it is conducted and its argumentative success assessed possess a "rational basis independent of cultural, linguistic, or pragmatic considerations" (Simon, 2004: 124). This means that in our deliberations over what normative principles should guide and govern sport we can entertain the diverse viewpoints of all parties to the discourse no matter their historical or social allegiances or circumstances so long as we consider them strictly on the basis of their intellectual merit. It is, therefore, because the reasons traded back and forth in normative discourse can be evaluated according to the intellectual contribution they make to the dialogue, we can be confident that whatever arguments survive such critical give-and-take and are put to use to construct a new moral theory of sport are rationally justified, and thus warrant our critical assent (Simon, 2004: 135). This explains why Simon contends that Russell's argument (Simon, 2014: 27) that "coaches … have a duty to correct the competitive injustice of bad calls by officials that provide their own teams with unfair benefits" would be as rationally compelling to an adherent of a nineteenth-century gentleman-amateur take on sport as it would be to a present-day enthusiast of contemporary elite sport.

Critics of conventionalism like Russell favor the second, discovery approach, and claim that on the basis of "certain perfectionist and voluntaristic arguments about the nature of sport," we can "track the truth and identify real facts" that underpin competitive sport (Russell, 2012: 9). It is from these fundamental non-moral facts about the purpose and point of sport, Russell argues, that we can confidently divine rationally justified normative principles for governing sport. Two such non-moral facts figure prominently in his normative account of sport, both of which he gleans from Suits's widely regarded conceptual analysis of sport (Suits, 2007). The first is that sport has a "clear underlying purpose, which is to provide "contexts for the exercise and display of skills in overcoming [rule-created] artificial obstacles," and the second is that the attempt to overcome these contrived challenges must be voluntarily pursued if that attempt is to be properly regarded as a sportive one (Russell, 2011: 257, 264). As Russell sees it then, it is because his normative theory corresponds to the facts of the matter that underlie sport, no matter, again, when, where, and by whom it is practiced, that we can be confident the principles he derives from these facts capture important moral truths about sport. That is why he thinks he is on firm ground in claiming that – in a reference to the famous George Brett pine-tar baseball bat controversy, in which he was first called out by umpires after hitting a home run for having pine tar (a sticky substance applied to the lower end of the bat for gripping purposes) too high on his bat (a technical violation), only to be later reversed on further review by the president of the American League and awarded a home run – "it really is a fact that baseball is a better game if home runs are not disallowed because pine tar is found high up on a bat … because there is no advantage to that … [and it] is in fact irrelevant to the game" (Russell, 2011: 267).

Social conventions and sport conventions

As I have claimed that many of the criticisms of conventionalism in the philosophy of sport literature misfire because they are based on mistaken conceptions of what a convention is, I first need to address the question what counts as a correct conception of a convention before I explicitly consider these criticisms. Of course, if I am right that the major critics of a conventionalist normative theory of sport go wrong in part because they rely on errant accounts of what a conventional norm is, then in trying to correct for these errors I have already begun to take up these criticisms, or at very least set the stage for doing so.

The first thing that probably should be said about conventions is how ubiquitous they are in our lives. Just about everything we do in our lives, from the most mundane to the most sublime, depends on various kinds of conventions. Indeed, conventions of language, etiquette, and courtesy are inescapable features of our lives; we could scarcely get by or interact with others without them (Marmor, 2009: 55). Even the conventions of social practices such as sport, art, music and the like, that affect us only if we voluntarily decide to pursue them, can scarcely be ignored once engaged.

The second thing that should be said about conventions follows from the first. For, if conventions figure in so much of what we do, it stands to reason that they take different forms and play different roles depending on what kind of activity or social practice we are participating in. The multiform character of conventions has not been fully appreciated in the philosophy literature owing, curiously enough, to David Lewis's path-breaking and widely regarded book, *Convention* (2002). This is because Lewis featured one kind of convention in his book: What he called "coordinating" conventions. The main function of conventions of this kind, naturally enough, is to solve large-scale, recurrent coordination problems. What he meant by such a coordination problem can easily be seen by borrowing one of his own examples: On which side of the road people should drive? This is a large-scale problem, obviously, because if drivers simply follow their own individual predilections or decide among some subset of their driving peers to drive on one side of the road as opposed to the other, the roads will not be safe to negotiate for anyone. It is a recurrent problem, of course, because every time people choose to drive they will face the same problem. What Lewis wanted us to notice about the role that conventions play when confronted with such a problem is, first, just what side of the road people end up driving on is utterly arbitrary (for it cannot be said that driving on the left side is a better alternative than driving on the right side, or vice versa), and, second, that the way to solve it requires synchronizing our actions with one another. But Lewis was also at pains to show that because of the sheer scale of the problem – the sizable numbers of the drivers involved – it could not be resolved by some sort of grand agreement. This is why he turned to game theory, specifically to cooperation rather than conflict games, to explain how conventions arrive on the social scene, and argued that they emerge when, to stick to the present example, the coordination of the drivers' actions are accomplished when all the relevant parties act out of "a general sense of common interest." Rather than each driver acting on their own strongest preferences, all are concerned to act only on what they expect everyone else's preferences to be (Lewis, 2002: 4). When enough drivers act in this requisite cooperative manner, and as a result end up driving on one side of the road rather than the other, driving on that side of the road becomes a convention, and remains one so long as drivers continue to comply with it.

What is so important about such coordinating conventions, as Lewis (2002) noted, is that so much of the lives we share with others involve precisely such large-scale recurrent problems, in which we have to figure out how to harmonize our actions with a lot of other people without the benefit of some sort of plebiscite. But Lewis had much bigger theoretical fish to fry in his analysis of conventions of this kind, for one reason he trained his philosophic sights on them was to dispute Quine's weighty claim that language cannot be conventional because conventions are agreements, and surely no one ever agreed with one another to follow "stipulated rules in our use of language". And even if we suppose our ancestors did, and we have since forgotten, language cannot be conventional since at least some of our predecessors "would have needed to provide the rudimentary language in which the first agreement was made" (Lewis, 2002: 2). However, Lewis countered, if we disabuse ourselves of the mistaken idea that conventions, at least of this broad scope, are mere agreements, then we will be able to see that some not insignificant features of our language are indeed conventional.[1]

So Lewis's classic book sheds much needed light on the nature and point of conventions. At least one of those lessons, that conventions are not, in a great many cases, agreements, is of special and obvious interest to my present analysis of sport conventions. That is because, to reiterate, I have claimed that many of the critics of a conventionalist theory of sport are of the view that conventions are essentially social agreements.[2] However, because Lewis's book was such a philosophical *tour de force*, it became a virtual article of faith in philosophical circles that conventions, at least the most theoretically and practically interesting ones, were mostly, if not wholly, of the coordinating variety. That was unfortunate because, as I have intimated, conventions play a much wider role in the life we share with others, and in one sense that I now wish to discuss, arguably a more important role.

The more important function that conventions perform in this respect is especially significant and relevant to social practices like sport because it is a distinctively normative rather than a mere coordinating function. It is distinctively normative because conventions also are centrally involved, together with the rules, in determining what is the point and purpose of sport, and, therefore, what specific mix of skills, values, and excellences are integral to its pursuit, not to mention what normative vocabulary and standards of reflective appraisal are best suited to evaluate the actions that take place there. Marmor (2009) was arguably the first philosopher to draw our attention to, and highlight the significance of, conventions of this normative stripe, and called them "deep" conventions, to distinguish them from coordinating conventions. We can readily see the importance of his distinction for sport by noting, as he did, the different response called for when asked why we follow a coordinating convention as opposed to why we follow a deep convention. For if we are asked why Americans *inter alia* drive on the right side of the road it makes perfectly good sense to reply "to coordinate our actions with other drivers," whereas if we are asked why, say, we play soccer, it makes no sense at all to reply "to coordinate our actions with other players" (Marmor, 2009: 23). That is because, prior to the invention of soccer, there was no coordination problem that needed solving. On the contrary, coordination of this sort comes on the scene in a game like soccer only after its deep conventions and its founding rules have completed their normative work. Deep conventions, then, are deep precisely because they are major forces in shaping and molding sport into the various historical and social perfectionist forms it has taken, and will take, and thus major players in our assessment of the importance and value they hold in our lives.

But how is it that the deep conventions of sport are able to exercise such a formative influence over its basic aim and character? The answer requires that I say something more about what they are, and what they add to the constitutive rules of sport.

With regard to the first point, deep conventions are best understood as normative responses to our "deep psychological and social" needs for playing sports in the first place, for taking on its contrived perfectionist challenges. The fact that we play sports at all, that they are such a vital part of our cultural life, is, therefore, "not a coincidence of history" (Marmor, 2009: 73). So while "we" can easily imagine a culture that plays different games than our own culture, we can hardly imagine a culture that does not play games at all, because such a culture would be so radically different from our own as to defy any explanation intelligible to us. However, the fact that sport figures so prominently in our own culture, not to mention cultures like ours, does not mean that it is an *a priori* fixture of our culture, that it somehow operates in a social and historical vacuum, and, therefore, is immune to the contingencies of time and place. On the contrary, because our normative responses to the deep psychological and social needs we have to play sport change as often as we and our social lives change, which is to say constantly, so do our deep sport conventions. That is why, as we shall shortly see, the kind of gentleman-amateur sport played in the latter part of the nineteenth and the early part of the twentieth century is quite different from the highly professionalized and specialized way in which we now play sport. So while it is no historical accident that sport has always been a part of our cultural life, it is very much an historical and contingent fact that sport has assumed the different forms it has to this point, and, no doubt, will likely assume yet different, perhaps even radically different, forms in the future.

With regard to the second point, the fact that the constitutive rules of sport cannot fix the aim and value of sport all by themselves, but require the normative support of deep conventions to do it, shows that, for all their obvious importance, they are neither self-interpreting nor exhaustive. That means that whenever significant normative conflicts arise in sport, we often must do more than consult the rules to resolve them. If rules were all we had to go on in such cases, then we would indeed be at a loss as to how to set our athletic normative compasses in such confounding circumstances. But no one thinks, save perhaps a strict formalist, that there is not more to sport than its rules, that sport does not also embody, as Marmor puts it, "certain conceptions of winning and losing, values related to what counts as a good game and a bad one or an elegant and a sloppy one" (2006: 352).[3] These conceptions, as I have argued, are what deep conventions bring to the normative table, and they are made up of the background understandings, reasons, and values we carry around with us as a result of our particular social enculturation into sport, of our internalization of historically grounded and bounded athletic moral ideals we share with our cultural peers. It is of capital importance, therefore, at least so far as their conventional pedigree is concerned, that these background normative understandings, meanings, values, and reasons are shared. For what they convey and give voice to are not only how the individual members of a culture conceive the point of athletic enterprise, but how the larger culture and society itself conceives the point of athletic enterprise. In other words, because these background understandings of sport are common ones, they are not the sort of things that, as Taylor (1975: 382) avers, "could be in the minds of certain individuals only", but rather are part of what Dworkin (1986: 63) referred to as our "form of [collective] mental life or group consciousness", or what Hegel called our "objective spirit" (a normative shareable state of mind or common like-mindedness).[4] Further, that the deep conventions of sport implicate our collective, cultural understandings of, and reasons for engaging in sport accounts not only for why they are subject to the interpretation and reinterpretation that are a constant feature of our larger cultural life, but explains as well why the normative story we tell about sport takes the historical twists and turns that it does, and why it defies any abstract, final encapsulation or summing up of its main *telos*.

But how can we be so sure, it might be reasonably asked, that these normative responses to our deep cultural needs and aspirations to play sport are, in fact, conventional norms as opposed to some other kind of norm? The answer is because they meet the three main criteria that most theorists, to include both Lewis and Marmor, regard as distinguishing features of conventions. These features include:

- some community or comparable social unit (C) that typically follows norms (N) in certain social practices (S);
- there is a reason or reasons R) for members of C to follow N in S; and
- there is at least one other alternative norm (N¹) that if members of C had actually followed in S, then R would have been a sufficient reason for members of C to follow N¹ instead of N in S.[5]

I will briefly explain each one of these three features in terms of my previously cited contrast between the gentleman-amateur and contemporary professional conceptions of sport.

To begin, then, with the first feature of conventions that some community or other, in my example the largely English community of amateur sport and for a time its chief rival and eventual historical successor, the largely American community of professional sport, generally follows norms regarding how its members should pursue the perfectionist point and purpose of sport.[6] The first question we need to ask here is whether these two supposed athletic cultures are, in fact, *bona fide* cultures or communities. After all, size matters in this regard, and it is not possible to set some determinate number as to how many members a particular culture or community must have to qualify as such (Marmor, 2009: 4). However, we need not quibble over whether these two athletic groups are real communities, if only because both have enough members to rule out the possibility that the norms they follow could have been the product of an actual agreement among them. This fact should give us confidence that the norms these two athletic communities follow are conventional ones, since, *pace* Lewis, conventions typically arise as an alternative to such agreements.

The next question we need to ask is, of course, what norms governed their athletic conduct. In the case of the gentleman-amateur community, the norms its members thought were integral to honoring the purpose of sport were derived from the view that sport is best understood as an intrinsic perfectionist enterprise which should be pursued for the love of the game itself and not for any instrumental benefits that might be obtained by engaging in it. This normative take on sport obviously put it at odds with the professional conception of sport that was to soon replace it, since it rejected any attempt to turn sport into a paid career or occupation.[7] What is more, the amateur conception that sport is an avocation rather than a vocation not only normatively militated against trying too hard to win, but also against adopting rationalized training methods based on the latest scientific advances, against employing professional coaches to aid one's athletic efforts, against "seeking a single-minded, focused [athletic] brilliance" at the expense of all-around athletic excellence (LaVaque-Manty, 2009: 99), and against the use of strategic tactics to achieve athletic success (to include both strategies in team sports in which members set the pace for teammates in a footrace or members of a cycling team attempt to box-in opponents to aid their side, and strategic efforts to manipulate the rules to one's advantage).[8]

The norms of professional sport, by contrast, turned those of the amateur conception on its head, which accounts for the unalloyed seriousness in which its enthusiasts pursued sport, and treated winning as its unambiguous aim. That gave a normative pass, then, to the idea that sport is a serious occupation rather than an non-serious pastime, and, as a consequence, to athletes trying to become the most accomplished competitors they could be, that is, well-trained, well-coached, strategically savvy (in both game tactics and rule-bending), extremely efficient, and highly specialized performers. In relatively short order, therefore, the wholehearted commitment to athletic success went from a much despised vice and normatively execrable way to engage in sport to a virtuous and normatively exemplary way to engage in sport.[9]

The second feature of conventional norms is that they not only generate norms to govern our conduct in sport but also concurrent reasons for complying with their directives. They are able to do the latter by virtue of the role they play, together with the rules, in establishing the point of athletic enterprise. For, by shaping our varying conceptions of what sports are all about, of what constitutes genuine athletic excellence, they allow us to distinguish between better and worse ways of achieving athletic success, and, therefore, between normatively good and bad reasons for pursuing athletic excellence. However, the kind of reason-giving that deep conventions make available to us is fundamentally unlike the kind of reasoning provided by coordinating conventions. Since in the latter, coordinating, case, our reasons for having and complying with a convention like driving on the right side of the road are identifiable independently of the conventions themselves. That is because the problem they were created to solve predates them (Marmor, 1996: 366). However, in the former, deep-conventional case, our reasons for having and complying with the relevant gentleman-amateur or professional conventions of sport are dependent on these very conventions themselves. That is because, without them, there would have been no such conceptions of sport in the first place. To put the same point differently, the reasons for having coordinating conventions is that they answer to a practice-independent, external purpose (in the present example, to make driving on the roads safe and efficient for all would-be drivers), but the reasons for having deep conventions is that they answer to a practice-dependent, internal purpose (to establish normatively credible reasons for seeking athletic excellence).

What is especially important to notice about the deep-conventional reasons authorized by the respective amateur and professional athletic communities is the very different assignments of athletic purpose and athletic excellence they make. For what the gentleman-amateur community regards as a good reason for pursuing sport (only in moderation), its successor professional community not only regards as a bad reason for pursuing sport but as no reason at all, since it fundamentally misconstrues what sport is all about and what constitutes genuine athletic excellence; and what, correspondingly, the professional community regards as a good reason for pursuing sport (only in a serious, wholehearted manner), its predecessor gentleman-amateur community not only regarded as a bad reason for pursuing sport but as no reason at all, since it, too, gets the point of sport altogether wrong, as well as that of true athletic accomplishment. This means what counts as a normatively intelligible and justifiable reason for engaging in sport is relative to the athletic practice community one belongs to, and, further, that giving and asking for reasons in sport, the dialogical process by which we reflectively justify our normative judgments of athletic success and failure, is a thoroughgoing interpretive matter, since it depends ultimately on the collective viewpoint of the relevant practice community. Thus, if we see the point of athletic enterprise through the eyes of the gentleman-amateur community, we will conceive the purpose of sport at its best as a pleasurable pastime. But if we see the point of competitive sport through the eyes of the professional community, we will conceive the purpose of sport at its best as a serious, full-time, intensely competitive, event. In short, everything depends in this conventional sense on how the relevant practice community interprets what is at stake in sport. This means that reason-giving and norm setting are not objective, agent (community)-independent matters, but entirely intersubjective, agent (community)-dependent matters.

The third, and last, distinctive feature of conventional norms concerns their arbitrary character. This feature requires careful elaboration because to say conventions are arbitrary can mean different things, only one of which captures the singular sense in which conventions can rightly be said to be arbitrary.

To say that conventions are arbitrary might mean that they became part of the social fabric for no apparent reason. This suggests that conventions are merely a natural byproduct of living with others, that they turn up without our conjuring them up simply as a consequence of our interactions with our peers. But that cannot be said of conventional norms because, as noted, they were created for quite specific reasons: either to coordinate our actions or to normatively orient, guide, and assess our actions.

To claim that conventions are arbitrary might also mean that, for example, whether we drive on the right or the left side of the road is inconsequential, so long as we coalesce around one of these alternatives, or that whether we treat sport as a leisurely pastime or as a serious competitive quest is equally inconsequential so long as, once again, we coalesce around one of these alternatives. In other words, either alternative followed in these examples will do the job of providing us the normative direction we need if we rally around it, and which one it turns out to be is immaterial. This sense of the arbitrary does seem to capture many coordinating conventions like those of driving because their sole satisfaction condition has to do with their efficacy in solving the problem for which they were created. In other words, it really does not matter what side of the road we drive on so long as the side we choose to do so chimes with what our peers opt to do. However, the deep conventions of sport and kindred practices are another matter. That is because the central satisfaction condition of deep conventions is their being true to the deep normative responses that give rise to perfectionist practices like sport. In these cases then, it does matter, really matter, what deep conventions an athletic practice community settles on, since these conventions, as noted, largely determine what that community takes to be the point and value of competitive sport.

In what sense, then, can it be said that the deep conventions of sport are arbitrary? The answer is in two related senses. The first is that the deep conventions followed by an athletic practice community have plausible alternatives that could have been followed instead without a "significant loss of purpose" (Marmor, 2009: 9). Thus, the amateur devotees of sport could have demonstrated the nobility of their enterprise by insisting that in their participation in the revived Modern Olympic Games both they and their opponents wear a common uniform to discourage any hostility that might arise between them as a result of nationalistic fervor instead of, say, clinging, as they did, to the ideal of balance and proportion to discourage ungentlemanly conduct. Similarly, the professional devotees of sport could have demonstrated the seriousness of their enterprise by refusing to adopt technical advances in equipment, as opposed, say, to training techniques, that might be thought to detract from distinctively human improvements in athletic performance. So long as these alternative norms that forbid nationalistic displays or mere technological improvements in athletic paraphernalia do not appreciably change the different athletic purposes they serve, then, Marmor (2009) assures us, they count as conventional norms.

The second sense in which the deep conventions of sport are arbitrary is that part of the "initial" reason people follow them is that their relevant peers follow them as well (Marmor 2009: 8). This means that the normative grip that such conventions have on people is owed in part to the fact that the members of the relevant athletic practice community actually follow them instead of their conceivable alternatives, that they are, in other words, "compliance-dependent." Such compliance, however, should not be confused with a *modus vivendi*; that is, with a mere compromise worked out by its members to serve their private interests. Rather, it points to the previously noted normative like-mindedness that is a characteristic feature of the reasoning of communities, in which, as Postema (2008: 42) nicely puts it, "the participation of others in the practice, indeed their characteristic reasoning about their participation and that of others, plays an important role in their own reasoning about how to act within the practice". So long as these common reasons and values to act in concert with others are stronger than the private preferences individuals might have for following one of the alternative conventions, we can be confident, first, that they are indeed conventional norms, and second that they exert real normative force, that people will feel bound by and, therefore, comply with them.

But if the conventional norms of sport are arbitrary in this double respect that they have conceivable alternatives and are compliance-dependent, then, a critic might plausibly rejoin, how can they be deep? For, contrary to my claim above, deep conventions seem to have nothing more going for them than the coordinating conventions of driving, since whether athletic practice communities follow amateur or professional conventions seems as immaterial as whether people drive on the right or left side of the road. This is an important objection, but, I hasten to add, Marmor (2009: 74) has a powerful reply to it. That reply is that the deep social features of our culture to which the respective conventions of amateur and professional sport are normative responses are "radically underdetermined" by these cultural features. For the deep cultural needs, reasons, and values that these deep conventions of sport embody and express, and that account for there being such forms of sport to begin with, might well have been fulfilled by any number of alternative deep conventions for playing sports without, again, any appreciable loss of their normative point or salience. However, that the deep conventions of sport have plausible alternatives that might have been followed instead does not in the least diminish how deeply ingrained they are in our sporting lives. For another important part of their normative hold on us is the significant normative contribution they make to our athletic lives once we commit to them in establishing, as noted, what is the aim and value of the contrived challenges they invite us to take on. And it is their deep connection to sport that explains why they have such significant normative pull and staying power, why their conventional character makes them less rather than more amenable to change and modification than even their formal rules. For we often tweak the rules of sports for a variety of instrumental purposes (for example, to make them more interesting or entertaining or profitable), but we much less often tinker with the deep conventions of sport because as the deep normative responses they are they have a lot to do with what we find at various times intrinsically valuable about athletic contests.

Conventionalism defended

My account of the distinguishing features of sport conventions, I want to claim, goes a long way in showing how the critics' main objection to their normative promise – that conventions are prescriptively ineffectual because they are nothing more than broad social agreements – can be defeated. There are at least two other accounts in the sport philosophy literature from which I can draw to help make my case for such a defensible conventional normative theory of sport. They include Bogdan Ciomaga's (2012) important essay, which persuasively argued that the critics' takedown of conventionalism was based on a mistaken conception of conventions, and William J. Morgan's (2012) essay, which argued that a conventional theory of sport is an improvement upon other normative theories prominent in the literature (formalism and broad internalism) because it corrects for what he regards to be their overly abstract account of the purpose of competitive sport.

The criticism that conventionalism is normatively suspect because it is critically suspect, because, that is, its norms are mere social agreements, is clearly mistaken. For most conventions, as Lewis (2002) insisted, and as we have seen in the previous section, arise as an alternative to social agreements, when such social agreements are not possible. Indeed, this is Lewis's answer to the pithy question Quine (2002: xi) asks in his Foreword to *Convention*: "What is convention when there can be no thought of convening?". However, even those conventions that are owed to actual convening are not merely social agreements. Rather, they, too, are rooted in the background understandings that deep conventions are normative responses to, and thus are an important source of the reasons we have for playing sports at particular times and places.

I doubt, however, that the critics of conventionalism would be more favorably disposed to it even if they could be persuaded that they had erred in writing off conventions as simple social agreements. That is because their fundamental problem with normative theories of sport of this kind is that their conventional starting points lack rational credibility because they have not themselves been reflectively vetted. So, even if I have succeeded in closing off the critics' favored way of making this point against conventionalism, by showing it cannot be so easily dismissed since its trademark norms are not, in fact, mere social agreements, they can simply shift their critical focus and attack the undisputed fact that conventions are grounded in historically contingent background understandings and not intellectually rigorous arguments to make essentially the same critical point. That would make the question whether conventions are social agreements or not, they would likely claim, entirely beside the point. Rather, what is at issue is the intellectual force of the normative principles we use to evaluate our actions in sport. And it is precisely because conventions lack such argumentative backing that critics would, no doubt, continue to regard them as normatively suspect.

But if we take the critics' objection to conventionalism to heart here, then we can see why it is self-undermining because it leads us into a conceptual and normative cul-de-sac. For the only apparent way of ensuring that our starting points are intellectually credible ones is if they enjoy argumentative backing and not simply, as we have seen in the case of conventions, the social backing of particular athletic practice communities. However, this presumes that when faced with conflicting and competing historical conceptions of sport we can go transcendent and search for some Archimedean point, some meta-normative, completely neutral and impartial standpoint from which to evaluate the normative viability of particular conceptions of athletic endeavor. But surely the search for such a perspective-independent vantage point, in which we try to approximate something like Nagel's famous view from nowhere and assess sport and the like by tapping into standards that are not peculiarly those of any actual athletic practice community, is a well-worn philosophical fiction that has outlived any normative utility it might once have had. For the price paid for trying to take normative inquiry to such great abstract heights is the too-heavy one of irrelevance to practice. That is because the level of reflective generality entailed by such a transcendent move would leave us with a conception of athletic purpose and excellence so conceptually barren and normatively threadbare –

something on the order of sport is about the pursuit of physical (bodily) perfection, that no actual historical conception of sport would have any trouble justifying its athletic bona fides. All of which means that normative inquiry conducted from such a lofty philosophical stand-point is singularly unsuited to serve as an arbiter of the kinds of actual normative conflict I have featured with regard to the rival amateur and professional renderings of sport, and, it goes without saying, of any other such conflict that might breakout between future athletic practice communities.

Suppose, however, there was a way to intellectually burnish our normative principles of sport without going transcendent, without abstracting from our on-the-ground social and historical conceptions of athletic enterprise. Robert Simon has recently proposed an alternative normative approach to sport, one that he claims avoids "the excessive abstraction of our actual situation, on the one hand, and too uncritical immersion in it, on the other" (Simon 2004: 126). Simon thinks we can avoid such excesses if we adopt a discourse version of normative theory, one that gives all the parties to rational dialogue a chance to say their piece and to receive a respectful hearing regarding the critical merits of their contributions. This can only happen, he thinks, if we take at least two crucial steps. The first is to disabuse ourselves of the bad idea that different conceptions of sport can be neatly "divided into isolated paradigms" (Simon 2014: 27), into pure types immune to external, outside scrutiny. The second is to further disabuse ourselves of the equally bad idea that "the second-order standpoint[s] of ... communit[ies]," in other words their internal standards of normative appraisal, should be treated as "sacrosanct" (Simon 2004: 128). That Simon has conventionalism in mind here is too obvious to miss, nor is there any doubt that he is persuaded conventionalism can be dealt a serious blow by following these steps without undermining itself in the process, as I claimed with regard to the former transcendent approach. For, if we can open normative dialogue in this way across different athletic practice communities and their respective conceptions of sport, Simon opines, we can begin to see the important commonalities in our respective notions of sport that unite us rather than the perhaps more obvious differences that divide us, and take critical advantage of this apparent overlap in our normative vocabularies. Simon thus envisages "a potential universal community of discoursers," in which a plurality of viewpoints on what is the central point of sport can be entertained and subjected to careful scrutiny from all quarters (Simon, 2004: 135). Whatever conception of sport is able to survive such a diverse, in-depth, and sustained rational give and take, he argues, is the one we can be sufficiently confident is the most intellectually meritorious one, the one most deserving of our rational assent.

This is, to say the least, a very attractive take on normative inquiry into sport. That is why I am happy to meet him half way, and in fact have already done so since I, too, have claimed that our historical conceptions of sport are mostly, if not entirely, hybrids and not ideal types or pure specimens.[10] But I cannot go the rest of the way with him because his second recommendation that we subject conflicting conceptions of sport like the present one between the gentleman-amateur and professional notions to external scrutiny is problematic if pushed too far. Let me explain.

As I have tried to show, both the gentleman-amateur and professional conceptions of sport are hybrid constructions. In the case of the former, the idea that sport is best conceived as a noble pastime rather than an all-out struggle to demonstrate athletic superiority is partly derived from a medieval conception of social hierarchy and partly from the Renaissance ideal of the courtier who was adept at many things "but supreme (by dint of hard practice) at none of them" (Guttmann, 1978: 31–2). Similarly, the professional conception, to reiterate, retained the amateur-based wariness of playing sports primarily for financial remuneration. So Simon is entirely right that our different historical understandings of the purpose of athletic endeavor are not ideal types, but amalgams of various athletic features, some of which at least have been purloined from their predecessors. The critical point not to be lost sight of here, however, is that we cannot infer from the fact that our varying conceptions of sport are mixed constructions that they are *ipso facto* rationally commensurable: that they do not and cannot conflict. On the contrary, what I argued with the amateur and professional athletic communities specifically in mind is that their decidedly mixed conceptions of athletic purpose and excellence in no way smoothed the way for their rational reconciliation and made it somehow possible to bridge the significant differences between them. So whether our particular historical conceptions of sport can be made to cohere rationally with one another seems to have nothing important to do, as Simon seems to think, with their ideal or non-ideal pedigree.

Nevertheless, it would be hard to deny Simon's further point that the job of rationally reconciling our different accounts of athletic endeavor requires as well that we subject these thoroughly "mongrelized" accounts to external scrutiny. This is easier said than done, however, since opening up these accounts to outside inspection requires, as Simon duly noted, we stop privileging the internal standards of reflective appraisal that lie behind them and by which we justify them to the members of our particular practice communities. I think, however, that Simon is skating on thin ice in this regard, because there are definite limits on how far we can push normative inquiry in this external direction.

Where, then, do we draw the line in this regard? One place there is no need to draw it is when we ask ourselves whether rival accounts of sport are indeed accounts of sport rather than of simulacra of sport. For there is surely enough overlap in the respective normative vocabularies of these two athletic practice communities for the enthusiasts of each to recognize that the other has an intelligible conception of sport, that what each are doing is sport and not something else. Here the differences in the two accounts are no obstacle to apprising the athletic bona fides of each from an outside perspective. Neither camp, therefore, will have any reason to doubt that the others' practices are indeed forms of sport. So far, then, so good. But it is worth noting that, if there is no obstacle to determining whether our rivals have intelligible conceptions of sport, if Simon is right about this, then it follows that he is also right that there is no obstacle to appropriating from other conceptions of sport one or more of their features to include in our own athletic practices, provided, of course, these additional features can be made to cohere with the other core features of our practices.[11] To be sure, incorporating all of the features of these other conceptions is not a possibility, since if the amateur and professional accounts do conflict, as I have claimed, then they could not be all made to cohere with one another. That does not mean, however, that members of these practice communities cannot selectively borrow from one another.

But what they cannot do, and where a line, therefore, needs to be drawn, is to rationally engage one another in an open-ended dialogue to determine by sheer dint of argument which conception of sport is the normatively superior. It was the very possibility of setting the stage for such an argumentative encounter, of course, that is the reason why Simon steered normative inquiry in this dialogical direction. For, if conceptions of sport, even as different as amateur and professional, can successfully be subjected to outside scrutiny in this dialogical fashion, Simon thought, then we will be able argue our way out of conflicts like these. The problem, however, is that while there is enough overlap in the amateur and professional conceptions for each to understand and borrow from the other, there is not enough overlap to sustain a fruitful rational exchange between them. So I do not see how Simon can make good on his admittedly attractive claim that rational dialogue can get us to the normative promised land, since, if we assume, as Simon rightly does, that the transcendent option is not an option at all, then any analysis of the normative merits of our actual conceptions of sport must, per necessity, take its rational cue from one or the other of these conceptions. But if these conceptions really do conflict with one another, then whatever conception we start our inquiry with will determine the outcome before the argument can even get off the ground; will, that is, beg the question at issue of which conception of sport is the most rationally superior.

We can see why such a dialogical normative enterprise is fated to fail by rehearsing how an argument of this sort would have to go, and actually did go in my example of the encounter between the amateur and professional communities, and why it cannot but lead to an argumentative impasse. Since we only can get such an argument going if, to reiterate, we start with one or the other of the socially and historically embedded accounts in question, let us begin with the professional position because it at least has the advantage of being closer to our own contemporary understanding of what counts as a genuine athletic challenge – of course, it does not matter which account we start with because it will end, or so I claim, in the same rationally disappointing way. It will be remembered that, in the professional rendering, both the use of strategies like boxing in one's opponents in a footrace, and strategically manipulating the rules to one's advantage were coveted features of athletic competitions, and comprised a vital part of the mix of skills that its adherents considered essential to athletic perfection. Members of the professional community were able to make a persuasive, rational case to their peers for why strategy should hold such a valued place in their account of competitive sport in the same standard inferential way in which all such cases are made, namely, by showing that they were justified in drawing such a normative conclusion because it logically followed from the premises with which they began their argument. The rub, however, is that these same arguments had no persuasive impact, nor could they have had such an impact, on the members of the rival amateur community, since by their very different lights these strategy-friendly arguments were no arguments at all, let alone compelling arguments that might cause them to change their mind. It is not that the rational give and take between them failed because one or both sides were being unreasonable, were deliberately trying to sabotage any rational interchange between them, but because they could not see rationally eye to eye on what, if any, place strategy should have in sport given their very different construals of its main purpose. All of which suggests that, *contra* Simon, the giving of and asking for reasons, argumentative discourse, is an inside game, one that can accomplish the normative work that Simon asks it to do, only if everyone is playing the same argumentative game, and thus playing by the same discursive rules. Put otherwise, there is no such thing as an intrinsically good reason or argument that can persuade any audience it is put to, but only a contextually good reason or argument that can persuade certain like-minded audiences but not others. So when extramural normative disputes break out, like the one waged between the amateur and professional athletic communities, all rational bets are off because we can no longer safely assume that everyone is making the same moves in the same language game.

The inability of the professional camp to persuade the amateur camp that strategy is integral to athletic contests, and the latter to persuade the former that it should be kept out of such contests, is seldom viewed by the disputants as the rational stalemate that, I would argue, it is. The conflict currently under discussion is no exception, since each side continued to think it was right, that reason was on its side, and that the dispute could be easily resolved if only the other side would acknowledge that its own arguments were too weak and feeble to makes its case successfully. But without any arguments that the other side would and did find convincing to back up their criticisms, such back-and-forth accusations amounted to nothing more than mere name-calling. Of course, that is not how the disputants saw it, because each side persisted in claiming it had, in fact, won the argument. But that very persistence suggests a further weakness in the positions of both, in which the inability of either camp to win the argument over strategy by the lights of the other puts in question whether either side has won the argument even by its own lights. After all, the idea behind Simon's discourse approach is that by inviting all of the disputants to make their case in an open argumentative setting we can arrive at a rational resolution of the conflict based on which view is best able to defend the criticisms made against it. Surely if the proponents of the professional conception of sport are unable to persuade proponents of the amateur conception that they have successfully defended their argument in favor of strategy as a legitimate athletic skill, then this also casts doubt as to whether its own positive view on this matter is indeed the objectively correct one. Simply by being right about the role of athletic strategy, or any thing else for that matter, by one's own lights alone hardly justifies that its anti-strategy alternative is not. That means any effort to determine who is right in such cases, who wins the argument, cannot be achieved by one side or the other pointing out that its view is correct by itself, according to its own terms.[12]

The moral of this story is not that there is no way forward when we come up against normative conflicts of this kind, but no *rational* way forward where what we mean by 'rational' is something that is neutral between normative conceptions of sport (the transcendent perspective) or non-circular justification (the discourse perspective). That means that the impasse reached by the professional and amateur communities on what is the purpose of sport and what skills are central to athletic excellence is indeed a genuine rational stalemate for which there is no rational resolution of the sort Simon envisaged. Rather, what such a stalemate signals is that both sides have depleted their argumentative resources, have run out of justifications, and when we reach this juncture, as Wittgenstein (1958, section 217) observed, we "have reached bedrock, and [our] spade is turned". So when we hit bedrock, insisting that the argument continue until one side comes to its rational senses is pointless. It misses the point.

But what about Simon's previously noted claim that the argument that coaches have a duty to correct the injustice of officials' bad calls would have succeeded in persuading adherents of both amateur and professional sport, not to mention those of contemporary elite sport, that coaches do indeed have such a duty (Simon 2014: 27). My first response is that I have not claimed that different athletic practice communities would never be able to agree on anything argued by their rivals, but only those core issues that speak to the core differences in their respective conceptions of sport.[13] My second response is that this issue does, in fact, touch on one such divisive core issue, which is why I think Simon is just wrong that both the amateur and professional communities would find this argument compelling. That is because amateurs of that era were convinced that only players should be entrusted to call penalties, which would include correcting whatever mistakes they make in this capacity, because no self-respecting gentleman would ever deign to intentionally contravene the rules. Assigning such a gentlemanly duty to ruling officials, and then to coaches when the officials make bad calls, would not only be seen in their eyes as an attack on their integrity, as, in effect, a denial that they are the gentleman they so assiduously claim to be, but as a complete sell-out of what they value most about sport.

I am also not convinced that Russell's earlier cited resolution of the George Brett pine-tar controversy would win the day, no matter the athletic audience it was presented to. Russell thought otherwise because he maintained there is a fact of the matter about baseball in this case that, when appealed to, should settle the controversy once and for all. The relevant objective fact he has in mind is that in baseball home runs should never be disallowed because of minor technical infractions like applying pine tar too high on bats when such violations have, and had, no effect on the athletic feat in question. I readily concede that what we are dealing with in this case is an important normative fact, but I would argue it is a conventional fact not, as Russell would have it, a hard, non-contextual realist fact. This leaves very much open, however, the possibility as we change our minds about what sport is all about and what skills are integral to athletic success, as we inevitably will if past history is any indication, that we might change our mind about this "fact" as well. And one such change relevant to the pine-tar case that we are already beginning to see, and that might well change our view on this matter, is the increasing importance assigned to managerial ingenuity as a relevant factor in determining athletic success. This bears on the present incident with regard to one important and unremarked feature, which is that it was the opposing Yankee's manager, Billy Martin, who brought Brett's bat to the attention of the umpire, yet he had noticed the illegality of the bat much earlier in the same season. Nevertheless, he decided to wait for the most strategically opportune time to make it public. Brett's home run later in the season and late in a game that gave his team a one run lead over the Yankees provided Martin with the most advantageous moment. What I am suggesting, therefore, is that, in sports like baseball, some future audience might well come to see Martin's timely intervention as a stroke of strategic managerial brilliance that ought to be recognized as an important athletic skill, perhaps even on par with that of hitting home runs, and that if that were to come to pass Martin's ingenuity would be rewarded by being reaffirmed rather than overturned by the relevant baseball administrators.[14]

I have been arguing that there is no rational way forward when confronted with normative conflicts as deep as the present one because there is no rational inferential path that leads from amateur to professional sport. This is because, to reiterate, the very different, conventionally laden starting points at issue here preempt any such inferential moves. Yet it is clear, as I earlier hinted, that we are able somehow to find our way past such disputes, since the amateur versus professional conflict is but one of many such conflicts that have occurred in the history of sport. Kuhn is the theorist to which many philosophers turn when trying to figure out how to get out of such conceptual and normative jams, and for good reason, because his advice when this happens in scientific circles, namely, to rely on one's creative imagination rather than one's present arsenal of arguments, is eminently generalizable to sport and most other social practices. For Kuhn (1970) showed that when what he calls "normal" science has run its course, has led to an explanatory and justificatory dead end, the leading lights of the scientific community were able to forge ahead by thinking outside the box, that is, by imaginatively conjuring up a new paradigm rather than repeating the same tiresome arguments of the old one. To pull off such a revolutionary, unconventional feat requires a new kind of dialectical move, one in which the aim, as Rorty (1989: 78) puts it, is to "play off vocabularies against one another, rather than … to infer propositions from one another," and, therefore, to substitute "redescription for inference". This is how visionaries in the athletic world were able to jumpstart their own gestalt switches that produced such innovations as women's sports and the Paralympic Games. For it was by redescribing the aim of sport, what skills, virtues, and features qualify as athletic excellence, and, not least of all, what kinds of bodies are properly regarded as athletic bodies, that they created a new practical and logical space in which such newfangled sports and new athletic bodies were able to find a genuine home for the first time. So what Einstein did for Newtonian science, Hegel for Platonist and Kantian philosophy, Rousseau for Hobbesian-styled politics, athletic feminists and advocates for the disabled did for amateur and professional sports. And because these normative entrepreneurs of gendered and disabled sports, like those of the "new" science, philosophy, and politics, could not make their case, initially at any rate, in the rationally justificatory fashion of their contemporaries, since the argumentative games their peers played were not only of no use to them but got in the way of their entrepreneurial efforts to change the topic rather than continue the old arguments, they had to draw attention to their novel views by making what at the time were unwarranted assertions and counter-intuitive claims in the hope their peers might out of curiosity take notice. In short, they had to de-conventionalize sport by redescribing it to make normative room for these new games and new athletes. At the same time, their only chance of success, of instigating "real" change, was to cause enough of their peers eventually to drop their favored conceptions of sport and adopt the new ones, which required that these new conceptions be, as it were, re-conventionalized, that is, become as conventional, as intuitive, and as amenable to rational argument, once firmly ensconced in new language games, as their predecessors.

Conclusion

In closing, I want to underscore that my claim that rational dialogue, the giving and asking for reasons, can do the normative work for which we depend on it in sport and other social practices only if everyone is playing by the same conventional rules of argument is no cause to despair. For the fact that rational argument is itself a conventional social practice does not wed us to the status quo, to what power speaks to truth rather than the other way around, nor does it commit us to the silly idea that we cannot be wrong about our own conventional views of sport and the like. What it does mean is that the more radical and immodest claim that an entire community or culture could be wrong about the point of athletic competition and how it should be normatively conducted is false. For, if that were true, it would mean that we could somehow plausibly distinguish between what such a community thinks is the purpose of sport and what it *really* is. But I don't think any such distinction can be plausibly made since, after all, what is the aim of sport and what standards we should use to evaluate actions within its precincts are not things we discover but rather things that we create. And because we, the relevant practice communities, are the ones who created them, it seems strange, to say the least, that we could be wholly wrong about what we have created. However, and this is the crucial point, it is completely plausible, and has certainly happened enough, that we get our normative assessments of sport wrong because we have drawn the wrong inferences from the premises formulated in our conventional normative vocabulary. So when we argue back and forth with our peers about sport with the aid of that vocabulary, we might well come to see that the premises of our arguments commits us to conclusions that we have not previously drawn; in other words, that we have erred in our inferential judgments and need to correct them by accepting these new conclusions and discarding the old ones. When argument leads to a result like this one, we will have achieved, in Simon's (2004: 127) words, "a more coherent understanding of the deeper cultural values" at stake in such arguments.[15] And that achievement, as I see it, is achievement enough to certify the critical credentials of a conventionalist normative theory of sport.

Notes

1 It also should be noted that the common reasoning conventions embody in such cases does not require "the interposition of a promise; since the actions of each of us have a reference to those of the other, and are performed upon the supposition that something is to be performed on the other part."

2 That is not to say, nor did Lewis say, that conventions are never mere social agreements, only that most of the more important conventions that concern our larger social lives are not simple social agreements.

3 The real dispute among sport philosophers is what are we to make of these normative complements to the rules; that is, of whether they are abstract, ahistorical and asocial principles, or, as I argue, historically and socially freighted deep conventions.

4 This notion that reasons are shared, that they say something about who "we" are in a first-person plural sense above and beyond what "I"' privately may or may not regard as a reason in a first-person singular sense, has often been criticized and even ridiculed in certain philosophical circles as some sort of

mysterious metaphysical claim for, as it were, a super, supra subject that governs how each of us reason and act from on high. But neither Dworkin's notion of "group consciousness nor Hegel's notion of "objective spirit" enjoins any such strange metaphysical collective subject, but rather only that, as Landen (2005: 353) nicely puts it, any account of practical reason that "start[s] from basic building blocks that can [only] be found within individuals," that is, individual mental features such as desires, preferences, or interests, "and works outward," is starting from the wrong place.

5 I am simply paraphrasing here, using slightly different nomenclature, Marmor's (2009: 2) rendering of a convention.

6 For a well-documented account of the rivalry between these two athletic practice communities, especially as it played out in the Olympic Games in the period between 1906 and 1924, see Dyreson (1998).

7 It should be noted that, by the turn of the twentieth century, this amateur-inspired ethical stricture against playing sport for money no longer contained the social class animus that its earlier version did, because the sharp edges of the traditional class distinctions between gentleman and working-class folk had been blunted by the burgeoning democratization of English society, as evidenced by its relatively new and growing middle class. What we have here and in the professional conception to come, then, are hybrid forms of sport and not ideal types.

8 Critics of the time derided tactics like pace setting and boxing-in opponents in team sports as contemptible forms of "collusion" (Collier, 1898: 382–8), and they denounced strategic bending of the rules as decidedly ungentlemanly, since no gentleman rightly so called would stoop so low as to resort to such rule tampering (LaVaque-Manty, 2009: 99).

9 As noted in footnote 7 above, what amounts to first iteration of modern professional sport is a hybrid form of sport rather that ideal type. For, like its amateur predecessor, the emergent professional view of sport was similarly wary of the monetary motive in sport. Both camps, as Rader (2004: 131) noted, were persuaded there were "higher purposes than merely making or spending money" both in and outside sport.

10 I do concede and regret, however, that in an earlier essay (Morgan, 2012), I did not make it sufficiently clear that both the amateur and professional conceptions of sport were hybrids and not ideal types.

11 This would, of course, explain how we end up with the hybrid conceptions of sport that we do have.

12 I have benefited greatly from Boghossian's (2007: 78–9) illuminating discussion of this issue. His citation of Fumerton's following point is instructive in this regard, "there is no philosophically interesting notion of justification … that would allow us to use a kind of reasoning to justify the legitimacy of using that reason" (p. 79).

13 Since the issue in question here, as I point out in the next sentence, does touch on such a core matter, I make this first point only to clarify my position.

14 Russell (1999: 37) astutely anticipates my claim here that Martin's strategic maneuver in this example might itself be construed as a relevant athletic skill, and, therefore, a legitimate form of athletic excellence. But he rejects the normative legitimacy of such a managerial tactic because, at present, we try to eliminate rather than incorporate such strategic interventions in our athletic contests. He is certainly right that our current athletic conventions speak against such a move. But my argument is that just as the professional athletic community waived aside the amateur athletic community's misgivings regarding the use of strategy in sport, a future athletic community might similarly waive aside our present misgivings regarding managerial interventions of the sort Martin attempted here.

15 Of course, Simon eventually rejected this gloss on argument in favor of his discourse realist alternative.

References

Boghossian, P. 2007. *Fear of knowledge*. New York: Oxford University Press.

Ciomaga, B. 2012. Conventionalism revisited. *Sport, Ethics and Philosophy* 6(4): 410–22.

Collier, P. 1898. Sport's place in the nation's well-being. *Outing* 32: 382–8.

Dixon, N. 2003. Canadian figure skaters, French judges, and realism in sport. *Journal of the Philosophy of Sport* 30: 103–16.

Dworkin, R. 1986. *Law's Empire*. Cambridge, MA: Harvard University Press.

Dyreson, M. 1998. *Making the American team: Sport, culture, and the olympic experience*. Urbana, IL: University of Illinois Press.

Guttmann, A. 1978. *From ritual to record: The nature of modern sports*. New York: Columbia University Press.

Kuhn, T. 1970. *The Structure of Scientific Revolutions*. Chicago, IL: University of Chicago Press.

Landen, A. S. 2005. Evaluating social reasons: Hobbes vs. Hegel. *Journal of Philosophy* 102: 327–56.

LaVaque-Manty, M. 2009. *The playing fields of Eton: Equality and excellence in modern meritocracy*. Ann Arbor, MI: University of Michigan Press.

Lewis, D. 2002. *Convention: A philosophical study*. Oxford: Blackwell.

Marmor, A. 2006. How law is like chess. *Legal theory* 12: 343–56.

Marmor, A. 2009. *Social conventions: From language to law*. Princeton, NJ: Princeton University Press.

Morgan, W. J. 2012. Broad internalism, deep conventions, moral entrepreneurs, and sport. *Journal of the Philosophy of Sport* 39(1): 65–100.

Postema, 2008 G. Salience reasoning. *Topoi* 27: 41–55.

Quine, W. V. 2002. Foreword. In *Convention: A philosophical study*, xi–xii. D. Lewis. Oxford: Blackwell.

Rader, B. 2004. *American sports: From the age of folk games to the age of televised sports*. Upper Saddle River, NJ: Prentice Hall.

Rorty, R. 1989. *Contingency, irony, and solidarity*. New York: Cambridge University Press.

Russell, J. 1999. Are rules all an umpire has to work with? *Journal of the Philosophy of Sport*, XXVI: 27-49.

Russell, J. 2012. Does metaethics make a difference in philosophy of sport? Paper presented at the 2012 Pacific Division Group, American Philosophical Association, April 4.

Russell, J. 2011. Limitations of the sport-law comparison. *Journal of the Philosophy of Sport* 38(2): 254–72.

Simon, R. 2004. From ethnocentrism to realism: Can discourse ethics bridge the gap. *Journal of the Philosophy of Sport* 31: 122–41.

Simon, R. 2007. Internalism and internal values in sport. In *Ethics in sport*, 2nd ed., ed. W. J. Morgan, 35–50. Chapmaign, Urbana, IL: Human Kinetics.

Simon, R. 2014. Internalism and Sport. In *Handbook of the philosophy of sport*, eds. M. McNamee and W. J. Morgan. New York: Routledge.

Suits, B. 2007. The elements of sport. In *Ethics in Sport*, 2nd ed., edited by W. J. Morgan, 9–19. Champaign, IL: Human Kinetics.

Taylor, C. 1975. *Hegel*. Cambridge: Cambridge University Press.

Wittgentsein, L. 1958. *Philosophical Investigations*. Oxford: Blackwell.

4

AN INSTITUTIONAL THEORY OF SPORT

Graham McFee

What content is possible for a truly philosophical account of, say, sport? In particular, how can its *conceptual* character (as philosophy) accommodate the need to recognize the *features* of particular sports as they occur through the contingencies of actual sporting events? Attempts to conceptualize narrowly the intrinsic features of a particular sport typically come to grief on the assumed need to cover *all* cases – for instance, applying to all the varied occasions on which that sport is played.

An institutional theory of sport belongs to such a broadly analytical philosophical approach to sport but represents a move towards greater sensitivity to context than was possible on traditional assumptions of the exceptionlessness of conceptual connections. Here, a parallel with concerns in philosophical aesthetics allows the elaboration of the features of institutional accounts, while emphasizing the variety of what must be accommodated to cover *sport*, given the different contexts of sporting performance. For the *real* sport cannot be accessible only through elite performance. Instead of such an idealization, an account of sport must acknowledge a place for (for example) the learning of the sport, and for its performance at all levels. Doing so requires the inclusion – on *some* occasions – of what might otherwise be dismissed as irrelevant or contingent features of sporting events, as well as some rethinking of the picture of rule-following adopted. Elaborating these points here elucidates the constraints an institutional account can offer; and, in particular, its explanation of the normative dimension of the rules of sport.

Background to institutional accounts in philosophy

To understand how the failures of a traditional conception of the philosophy of sport might lead to the development of an institutional account, it is helpful to begin with parallel questions in philosophical aesthetics since talk of an *institutional theory of sport* clearly owes something to the idea of an institutional theory of art.[1] There, the systematic failure of invitations to define 'art' (and its sub-categories) led to the suspicion that the project itself was misconceived, not least because counter-examples to the putative definitions of art were to be typically found in relatively ordinary or humdrum examples of artworks. Further, some writers (see McFee, 2004a: 23–31) suggested that the problem resided with the expectation of definition, or the conception of philosophy that placed such an expectation at its methodological heart. In this way, the general usefulness of such definitions (viewed strictly in terms of the provision of conditions that were individually necessary and jointly sufficient) was called into question. One response, elaborated by George Dickie (1974), attempted to define 'art' by appeal to what he called 'unobvious' or 'unexhibited' features of artworks: for instance, their relations to institutions associated with art such as art criticism, the curating of art galleries, the publishing of artworks (such as some poems or novels), the restoration of artworks – Dickie followed Danto in calling this 'the artworld', while conceding that there is not just one: and this view as a whole attempted to derive a definition that was purely descriptive of art, rather than evaluative.

Thus Dickie (1974: 34) produced his notorious institutional definition of art, which claimed that:

> A work of art in the classificatory sense is (1) an artifact (2) a set of the aspects of which has had conferred upon it the status of candidate for appreciation by some person or persons acting on behalf of a certain social institution (the artworld).

When this putative definition to succumbed to counter-examples (and other difficulties; see McFee, 2011a: 150–6), Dickie (1984) modified it in an attempt to generate conditions individually necessary and jointly sufficient, but now he conceded that this later account was circular, while insisting that this was just an accurate reflection of art's institutional nature, since it involves a social setting to include the changing practices and conventions of art, the heritage of artworks, the writings of critics, and such like.[2]

An alternative response to the failure of such attempts at definition was to reject *that* project, and its centrality to one's view of philosophy, yet to grant some of its explanatory power (vis-à-vis the treatment of artworks, art forms and art movements) in recognizing them as institutional. In particular, one effect was to bring within the compass of a concern with art a larger circle of cases and situations – roughly, the sorts of things to which Dickie had referred: that is, attention was directed not just to the artwork itself but also to the place of discussions of art making, of art restoring, the training of performers (for performing arts), practices of curating for art galleries, and publishing for works of literature. On such an account, these were not to be dismissed as mere ephemera, or social concomitants of art: instead, their constitutive role in the possibility of art was acknowledged. So these, as parts of the artworld, were recognized to have a potential place in the fuller story of acknowledging the historical and social settings of art-practices.

Turning to sport

Our thinking about an institutional account of sport can begin from there, both because the same sorts of disputes (about definition, and such like) that beset philosophical aesthetics have recurred in the philosophy of sport (McFee, 2004a: 15–16) and because the expectations for any institutional account for sport should have learnt from Dickie's mistakes. Further, the deficiencies of the previous strategies were the same, or similar, in both cases. Nevertheless, in this vein, two key differences between the situations for art and for sport must be stressed at the beginning. The first distinguishes strong institutional accounts, like that appropriate to *art*, from the case for sport (where only a weaker institutionalism is appropriate); the second identifies a mistaken understanding of the project of any institutional theory: since Dickie's institutional theory (for art) hunted for a definition, that might seem to carry over, but it does not – our institutional account of sport will not be concerned with definition. It is no part of such an account to attempt a definition of *sport*, or related concepts, nor will it assume that one would be desirable.

An institutional theory of art might be loosely characterised as one where such-and-such *is* art if the 'right people' say it is (but see McFee, 2011a: 148–50). This will roughly characterise any institutional theory (*mutatis mutandis*). Now, the term 'institutional' is regularly deployed within analytic philosophy in a second sense, one deriving from moral philosophy, where both Elizabeth Anscombe (1981: 24) and John Searle (1969: 50–2) have urged that, say, *promising* is an institutional concept, as a way to draw attention to its rule-governed character. For such weakly institutional notions, such as *language*, any 'Tom, Dick or Harriet' can pronounce on the grammaticality of utterances, at least insofar as he/she is a *native speaker* of the language. Roughly, the same is true of the identification of promises. And this is to be expected for an account of sport, since the term 'sport' here just has an ordinary, non-technical meaning: there are no genuine experts in its application. But that is not the sense of the term 'institutional' deployed for *art*. Rather, institutional theorists of art typically employ the term to emphasize a key feature of the institution: or, perhaps better, a key function it performs, namely the functioning of a so-called *authoritative body* (McFee, 2011a: 147–8; Baker and Hacker, 1984: 272–3). So, for strongly institutional concepts like 'art', the focus on the claim of institutionalism is more specific: not everyone has a 'say' in the art status of particular objects (or the artistic credentials of particular putative artists). Instead, in institutional theories of this strong sort, appeal must be made to the *authoritative body*: to what (for art) I call 'the Republic of Art' (following Diffey, 1991: 45–8). But this is not true of sport. So adopting an institutional account of sport would not just involve stressing the place of rule-regulating bodies for most sports. Rather, as with language, the institutional character of sport would be reflected in its rule-related character, but without this additional implication of an *authoritative body* for sport (as such). For what *counts* as sport varies from sport to sport – for instance, in the different degrees to which written rules specify acceptable and unacceptable behaviours, or the equipment that must, may or must not be employed; and the character of particular sports is typically partly in the hands of its players, as later examples illustrate.

Here, Mike McNamee[3] supplied a helpful example. As he reports it, ultimate Frisbee players had hitherto been self-regulating. Now a big dispute has broken out over whether an independent referee, or adjudicator, must be used to rule on disputed calls. With such a referee in place, is this still the same sport, ultimate Frisbee? Or are there two such sports now: (a) refereed ultimate Frisbee; and (b) non-refereed ultimate Frisbee? Or, as Mike put it, 'more rhetorically, which is the *real* ultimate Frisbee?' Such a debate is grist for our institutional mill (and see later): on the option urged here, defending a weaker version of institutionalism, that debate may be resolved (in principle) in any specific case where it *counts* for us – but not by appeal to experts (an authoritative body). For a motivation is needed for disputing any particular answer here, given the facts as we have agreed them. That is, why should one *then* insist that there were two similar sports, rather than one sport in two versions? Or vice versa? (Comparisons with rugby football suggest that either resolution is possible, giving no reason to prefer this or that.) Moreover, it does not follow that because the dispute is over the *regulation* of the sport, one can just appeal to the governing body (if any) for a resolution.

In this sense, then, *sport* – while only weakly institutional when compared with *art* – is more strongly institutional than, say, language because reference to the institutions of sport (or sporting practices)[4] retains more direct substance: the world of sport is replete with *real* institutions (with governing bodies and rules committees, with events organizers and those composing narrations of sporting events; for instance, for newspapers or magazines). Seeing that any adequate account of sport must sometimes require reference to these, or to other backgrounds in history and social practice, is a way to move away from focus on the sorts of (allegedly inherent) features of sports and sporting events to which putative definitions of sport usually refer.

Of course, this is just one way to expand the candidate features that might sometimes find a place in the narrative characterizing this or that sport on some particular occasion. To the degree that this is the right attitude, an institutional account of sport will enlarge the range of factors to which reference might realistically be made in discussing the 'nature' of sport.

Equally, not just *anything* could count here, even if it occurred during the passage of a sporting event. For instance, there would never be a place, as part of the sport *itself*, for the antics of English cricketer Derek Randall (1984: 30): '[experimenting] with a few somersaults, or throwing my sunhat in the air and catching it on my head.' But this occurred especially during important matches in India in 1976, where rates of play: 'were so painfully slow that they allowed ample opportunity to perform a cartwheel, do a somersault, play tricks with my sunhat, wink at a pretty girl' (Randall, 1992: 98).

Hence, as Randall implicitly concedes, these were things he did *outside* of the game itself. Of course, granting the formal irrelevance of such antics to the game itself does not deny the enjoyment they can give to spectators – a reason these were actually encouraged by Randall's captain in India, Tony Greig (Randall, 1984: 30). Yet they *are* irrelevant. But that again is an institutional fact, not one drawn directly from the rules.

It might seem that some special character attached to the concept *game* (and perhaps the concept *sport*) in this respect. Thus, Wittgenstein's discussion of the concept *game* (see Wittgenstein, 2001, sections 66–7), as well as his introduction into philosophy of the concept *language game* (Wittgenstein, 2001, section 7) might lead some people to think that somehow (and especially via the concept *language game*), Wittgenstein saw some *special* place for games (and hence perhaps of sport). Moreover, that this sort of thing should be avowed by a self-avowed Wittgensteinian (like me).

Of course, Wittgenstein did write about language games, by which he meant – roughly – simple, or simplified, linguistic forms, to include words, sentences and a context for their employment; but also diagrams and gestures as appropriate. These language games are created or described for use as '*objects of comparison*' (Wittgenstein, 2001, section 130 [original emphasis]) for philosophically puzzling concepts or contexts, often to exemplify misconceptions. Since such *objects of comparison* are designed so that their characteristics (their point and purpose) will be evident on inspection, the language games should be seen as complete (Wittgenstein, 2001, sections 2, 18), rather than as fragments of ordinary language. Further, the concept *game* was indeed used as an object of comparison (as above, see Wittgenstein, 2001, sections 66–7). Yet Wittgenstein was also clear that there was nothing special about games here. Like many other concepts, *game* can have philosophical implications or raise philosophical issues (in its contexts). But that is all. As he put it, 'the word "game" is not a metalogical word' (Wittgenstein and Waismann, 2003: 223); that *game* is not a metalogical concept. His idea is that the points that can be made in respect of the term 'game' could be made in respect of many other general terms. In particular, if our concern were with rule-governedness, we could 'make everything clear by means of chess' (Wittgenstein and Waismann, 2003: 223).

So the first feature differentiating an institutional theory, or account, of *sport* from an institutional account of art is that sport is only institutional in the weaker sense that follows from its rule-following character – in this, it resembles, say, language.[5] Yet it is *institutional* in that rule-following here is not reducible to a set of simply rules, easily and uncontentiously applied without regard for context. (For general points about rule-following, see McFee, 2004a: 44-49.)

As mentioned above, the second differentiating feature reflects the fact that, for art, institutional theories have typically been associated with the attempt to provide a *definition* of art; and especially, as above, with George Dickie's attempts at such a definition (see Dickie, 1974: 34; Dickie, 1984: 7; compare McFee, 2001a: 152). But this feature, this emphasis on definition and conceptual 'definiteness', has no special place in institutional accounts of art; and neither, of course, need it feature in an institutional account of sport, although (as we shall see) a contrast with definition clarifies our interest in institutional accounts.

One feature of institutional accounts – well-exemplified in respect of art – grants to the discussion a wider compass than is usual in, say, the search for a definition. Thus, the institutional account of art recognises the place of training in art making and art appreciating; the role of restoring art; and, for performing arts, the training of performers – in addition to the place of making and appreciating artworks. These others are not dismissed as just (say) aspects of the sociology of art. All of them bear on genuinely understanding what art really is: but they would not typically feature in standard attempts to define art.

Of course, this is part of the point here, as it might be applied to sport. For I will urge (and exemplify) that the net effect of an institutional account of *sport* is to introduce a radical contextualism; and, in particular, one that explains why the search for definitions (or something similar) is misplaced: what is sought is not, in fact, a property of words or expressions (see Travis, 2008: esp. 159–60).

Real sport?

When thinking of attempts to define 'sport' (and 'game'), many of us rightly turn our attention first to the works of Bernard Suits (1978; 1995a; 1995b: compare McFee, 2004a: 17–31). Here, it is interesting that one attempt to augment Suits' work, from within his formalist tradition, came from Klaus Meier's view that there were more rules to sport than Suits had initially granted, to include those that specify and regulate 'eligibility, admission, training and other pre-contest requirements' (Meier, 1985: 700). With different starting assumptions (in particular, the rejection of the hunt for a definition), the recognition of such 'auxiliary rules' (Meier, 1985: 70) might have been the beginning of a kind of institutionalism about sport. Equally, one might find such institutionalism prefigured in recognising sport as a *practice* – had that term not been appropriated by followers of MacIntyre[6] (for discussion, see McFee, 2004b).

But the central point of any institutional account must be to grant the importance for understanding whatever it is (*sport*, in our case) of activities seemingly surrounding *real* sport or 'central cases' of sport. For the institution extends beyond, say, just the playing field – and its extent and contours must themselves be addressed institutionally. In doing so, the institutional account makes any claims here strictly contextual (or occasion-sensitive; Travis, 2008). Hence, the claims made are no longer treated as just strings of words, as though repeating the words *automatically* repeated those claims.

Here, to elaborate the point about institutions, I shall stress one particular kind of example: that most sports are played at a number of different levels – from professional or elite to inter-family; and from the *serious* (for money or fame) to the purely recreational – say, dealing with children. Further, aspects of the sport practice tend to differ at these different levels: different activities are done (or not done) in playing the sport. Different equipment may be used, or not used, at least standardly. Sometimes such differences are reflected in the rules used (they might be modified by the league, or by local circumstances, as in an example below); sometimes in other practices or expectations. There may still be the thought that, somewhere in this medley, there is the *real* sport. But on which of these occasions is the *real* sport visible?

This question is crucial since traditional attempts to define 'sport' often founder at precisely these points, because the force of the project of definition will be undermined precisely where there are exceptions of this sort to its central claims or conditions, as then one no longer has 'a concise yet comprehensive characterisation' (McFee, 2004a: 21–2): genuine definitions must have an 'exact fit' on the concept defined – what is claimed as an X must be one; what is thereby denied X status must *not* be. That is, the definitions must apply exceptionlessly, or they are not *genuine* definitions (McFee, 2004a: 21–2). And such activities, reflecting the different levels of sports-playing, offer obvious counter-examples to the claim to exceptionlessness that the definition offers, the claim that this sport *really* involves doing (or not doing) such-and-such. Hence a kind of Platonising *idealisation* (terms from D'Agostino, 1995: 44) is common to many attempts to clarify the nature of sports: that is, it is assumed that there is a *full* or *complete* version of the playing of the sport (usually thought to take place at the elite level, with all the 'bells and whistles' of uniforms, umpires or referees, and an audience). As we will see below, this assumption of *completeness* is one false step here.

Of course, for the argument, it does not matter which level is identified as the *real* sport, for – whatever is selected – one must then decide on the sport status of the others. But if one takes (say) the sport as played at the elite level as one's model for *really* playing the sport or game (say, soccer or chess), its playing at these other levels seems to generate obvious counter-cases. After all, the playing of that very sport or game (at another level) *has features* not in one's real sport or game, or lacks such features. But this is just what the 'definers' had hoped to preclude by stressing the *real* sport. Above, it was urged that the character of particular sports is typically partly in the hands of its players, since who counts as the typical players, or as players of the *real* sport, will be contested in the discussion of such cases. And, if the sport is typically played in particular situation in *this* way, with *these* rules and *that* equipment, then – in that situation at least – these typically identify genuine sporting situations: genuine instantiations of that sport. For instance, soccer (football) played in the park may well lack eleven players on each side; or, in some cases (say, with groups of young children), may flourish with more than eleven! But, if this is still the playing of soccer, how many players are there in a *real* soccer team, the one to which our putative definition refers? There can be no answer to fit all cases, unless one denies the obvious, by denying that one or more of these levels is *really* sports-playing. In elaboration, I will mention two examples, to which I will return.

First, I play soccer with a bunch of friends in the local park: the goal posts are marked by coats; we do not usually manage eleven players on each side; there are no uniforms, no referees, and no audience; and (importantly) the 'hand-ball' rule permits a player to use his hand without penalty to stop the ball just in case it would otherwise have run to the other side of the park – there is no 'natural' boundary to the left. Of course, the 'hand-ball' rule has not disappeared: various kinds of 'hand-using' behaviour (up-to-and-including the 'goal' scored by the deliberate hand-ball, of the kind exemplified in elite sport with Maradona's 'hand of God' effort) would still be penalized. But that rule amounts to something different in our context than in, say, elite soccer – without our game ceasing to be soccer. So the key point is that we are clearly playing *football* (as we in the UK would all call it: in the USA, more properly called 'soccer'), despite our not using all the rules that characterise elite soccer; say, as played in the English Premier League. Certainly, we are not playing *another* sport (it is not rugby nor bridge); and we would see no point in doing so – we are football fans, after the model of Nick Hornby's *Fever Pitch* (1992). Someone who insists we are playing a defective version of the game, relative to (say) Premiership football, should be asked 'why?' – why is *that* the way to characterise the relationship among these different-ish activities? For our point is that these are not *different* games at all: rather both are soccer – a fact permitted by the institution of soccer, which includes this variety.

Similarly, I play chess with my grandson. I give him a queen advantage; and, on the relevant occasion, he wins. On the next Sunday, I play in a simultaneous tournament against the best player in the world (still Garry Kasparov, to my way of thinking): he gives me a queen advantage and, *per impossibile*, I win! What should we make of the similarities and differences between our situations? Who has won *at chess*? And what other games were involved? In summary, once we acknowledge the facts as I have presented them, the institutional character of sport permits us to discuss them just as we have: each counts, in context, as football or as chess (respectively), without postulating or presupposing some hidden essence, as a brief elaboration of the cases shows.

Two important principles drive our discussion of these cases, reflecting (in the first instance) our institutionalism about sport. The first is from Wittgenstein (2001, section 79): 'Say what you choose, so long as it does not prevent you from seeing the facts. (And when you see them there is a great deal you will not say.).' Our concern is not with particular words as such, nor with which word to use. Instead, it reflects what one wants to say, in that context – and nuances of context can radically alter this.

Similarly, the second principle reflects the fact that the truth of what one says reflects the context of utterance. As Austin remarked:

> It seems fairly generally realized nowadays that, if you take a bunch of sentence (or propositions …) impeccably formulated in some language or other, there can be no question of sorting them into those that are true and those that are false; for … the question of truth and falsity does not turn only on what a sentence *is*, nor yet what it *means*, but on, speaking very broadly, the circumstances in which it is uttered. Sentences are not *as such* either true or false.
>
> *(Austin, 1962: 110–11)*

So investigating what sport is will be connected at best loosely to the word 'sport', detached from contexts of utterance. Then that thought might be continued, as Austin (1979: 130) remarked on another occasion, that:

> statements [n.b. *not* sentences] fit the facts always more or less loosely, in different ways on different occasions for different intents and purposes. What may score full marks in a general knowledge test may in other circumstances get a gamma.
>
> *(Austin, 1979: 130; my insert)*

Hence, there are no absolute standards of what was said or meant, but only the current, contextual ones.

So, in the second case above, the chess case, did my grandson beat me at chess? Obviously, it will be important to him that the answer is 'Yes' – he beat Grandpa at chess for, say, the first time! But that does not give us a basis to generalise: I did *not* beat Garry Kasparov at chess (or, by my assumptions, I could claim to be the best player in the world) – at the least, I did not beat Garry at chess *without qualification* ('with a queen start, in a simultaneous display'). The context makes the same form of words, about winning at chess, ask a different question. And that is the key moral for an institutional account of sport as I understand it: that it will reflect the context (in its diversity), rather than trying to assign a single meaning, or a set of truth conditions, to particular forms of words.

So, turning to the first example, were we really playing soccer (football) in the park? Well, we have agreed that we were not playing rugby or tiddlywinks or cricket. We saw the activity as soccer, although 'modified' to our context; so that, in our context, that was just (one of the things) football was! In that context, doing something that (in the English Premier League) would count as *hand-ball* is *not* hand-ball. Moreover, one might with justice take the 'hand-ball' rule as 'definitive' of soccer. But that just shows us that, in the kinds of contexts the institution of sports playing can provide, such a fact takes us only so far. In particular, it does not resolve the question about what sport we are playing or what its rules are, although it does indicate that such questions cannot be treated as a matter about *words* only! And this is just where it can be helpful to take sport as *institutional* in the sense developed here.

One approach in the literature, following Morgan (1995: 53–4), is to distinguish different versions of a particular sport; in particular, contrasting *defective* instances with cases of play a *different* (if similar) game. But why should *this* one be regarded as somehow *defective*? (It works perfectly well in practice to play in this way, let us assume, with no more disputes about hand-ball or off-side than in the Premiership.) What is the paradigm to which our new case is supposed to be defective? And why should it be thought of as paradigmatic? The institution of soccer seems flexible enough to accommodate the playing of soccer in ways that, in a very different context, one might regard as defective; say, by stressing the contrasts between its particular version of the hand-ball rule and that played in (say) elite soccer or preserved in rulebooks. But we all know this. It does not compel us in any particular direction when asked previously what we were doing: once we agree on the facts, we can look to what we can best say *then* – in line with Wittgenstein's remarks in PI, section 79 (Wittgenstein, 2001), it may not be that one can, any longer, just say *anything*. But that would reflect the constraints this context sets on understanding this sport; and understanding this activity as *that* sport. So it would draw on the institution here, loosely conceived. Hence, it would be precisely the subject matter for an institutional account of sport.

Institutional constraints

Here, notice that an institutional account is not a licence to say just anything. Consider first an example from Mike McNamee concerning bog-snorkelling. As he quotes from the advertisement:

> Competitors have to complete two lengths of a 60-yard [50 metres] trench cut through the peat bog in the quickest time possible, wearing snorkels and flippers (wet suits optional but advisable) but without using any conventional swimming strokes.
>
> *(Mike McNamee 2008: 9–10)*

Asked about the sport status of this activity, we know that the desired answer cannot be an uncontentious 'yes' answer, as though bog-snorkelling were as clearly a sport as rugby, soccer, cricket and basketball. But, equally, there cannot be an uncontentiously 'no' answer – partly because that makes advocates of the 'yes' answer look uninformed in ways we have no reason to suggest; and partly because the activity shares features with other sports which seem relevant to the sport status of those activities. Here, one might look across to Suits' definition: bog-snorkelling does involve a physical skill, and it certainly has a following of some width; further, it seems to have continued past the phase of being a 'fad'. But both these last points can be contested: perhaps the activity's following is insufficiently wide; or perhaps it remains a fad – this is what those who deny it sport status must urge. So we have a debate here, which is just as we wanted – the sport status of bog-snorkelling is presently a matter for debate only; there is no clear answer. This is a genuine borderline case.

One might think, as perhaps Frege did, that a concept was sound only if it resembles a field in being bounded on all sides:

> To a concept without a sharp boundary there would correspond an area that had not
> a sharp boundary-line all around, but in places just vaguely faded away into the back-
> ground. This would not really be an area at all; and likewise a concept that is not
> sharply defined is wrongly termed a concept ... The law of excluded middle is really
> just another form of the requirement that the concept should have a sharp boundary.
>
> *(Frege, 1960: 159; see Wittgenstein, 2001: section 71)*

Then one must deny that this conception of the soundness of concepts applied to those above, whose application is not determinate in all cases – and this move might be offered even if we accepted the occasion sensitivity our contextualism ensured, for we might feel that, in *that* case, there was at least a clear answer once the context was properly identified, although the *general* requirement could not be sustained.

Sometimes, then, the institutional account of sport yields clear answers, so that one can genuinely 'get it wrong' in thinking of sport a certain way, or of a certain activity as sport – either uncontentiously or as a borderline example. Thus, we can imagine a time in the not-too-distant future where boxing was no longer regarded as a sport, for the sorts of obvious reasons that guarantee that *pankration* (the lethal Ancient Greek martial art) is *not* a sport, despite its place in the Ancient Olympics. The change I am speculating in respect of boxing would be a change in the institutional structure of boxing: perhaps it could not come about while there were large numbers of parents willing to send their children to participate in training in boxing. What is needed, then, might be called 'a cultural change' – a change to the culture surround-ing boxing – or 'an institutional change' but, if it occurred, the change to boxing would come about by changes not reflected in, say, the definition of 'boxing'. Or so one might think.

Moreover, this institutional perspective recognises innovations in sport, in ways that seem appropriate. Contrast the introduction of the Fosbury flop into high-jumping (where it is now ubiquitous) with the innovations suggested by the case of Oscar Pistorius. Because sport is (weakly) institutional, there was really no difficulty at the conceptual level in generating informed discussion of either case. For the concepts at issue were not bounded in the ways that Frege had supposed. Clearly, Fosbury's technique conferred an advantage on its user (he won gold at the 1968 Olympic Games). But this was a skill, of a sort – others could, and did, learn it – there was no serious issue as to whether or not it was fair, although it certainly revolu-tionised high-jumping. And we can imagine objectors claiming that it was not *real* high-jumping. But they were wrong; and history has made that point plainly. The case of the springs, or 'blades', that Pistorius used is different. Not everyone needs these 'blades' – only a double-amputee like Pistorius. But, if he had won Olympic gold in 2012 using them, one might have feared a rush to unnecessary amputations. Still, considerations of fairness rightly permitted Pistorius to run – there is no automatic corollary in future cases: they can be treated 'case-by-case' and regulated by obviously sport-relevant considerations, such as fairness.

A related example (discussed before: McFee, 2004a: 106–7) is the claim by Ronald Dworkin (1978: 24) for the arbitrary character of the rule in baseball 'that if a batter has had three strikes, he is out'. And of course Dworkin would be right were the choice, say, between three strikes and four: the selection of three would indeed be arbitrary! But the rule could not be 'one strike and he is out': that would not give the batter a reasonable chance to display his skill. And it could not be, say, '300 strikes and he is out' as that would make competition in the sport long and boring for the audience. So there are sport-relevant considerations at work here: the rule as we have it is not entirely arbitrary, after all, given the institutional character of sport.

The normativity of institutions

However, the expression 'institutional account of sport' might suggest a seemingly quite different structure: one aimed at explaining why sporting rules have the force they do. Now there is a sense in which the right reply, asked about the institutional account of sport, is to say that it stresses rule-following as institutional. That is what we are reiterating now. (Of course, an *authoritative body* would offer one way to elaborate that point, were *sport* institutional in the stronger sense.) So that only takes us so far.

To move forward, we should consider (again: McFee, 2004b) a distinction Morgan (1994: 226; 1995: 60) draws between two conceptions of *ethos*. The first, found in D'Agostino, is *descriptive* in reflecting the fact that:

> players and officials have … conspired to ignore certain of the rules of basketball …
> in order to promote certain interests … e.g. to make the game more exciting than it
> would be if the rules were more strictly enforced.
>
> *(D'Agostino, 1995: 47)*

Such behaviour reflects the 'social standards we presently use to judge and watch the games we judge and watch' (Morgan, 1994: 56): they amount to the rules we *actually* play by; and, to sort out what they are, 'we must make this determination *empirically*' (D'Agostino, 1995: 47). Thus, we might study how the LA Lakers basketball team 'interprets' the rules, through its play: which behaviours are regarded as acceptable despite being in conflict with a formal rule (say, against contact); and how penalties play into that situation. But this describes simply how 'we' do in fact act: such a *descriptive* conception offers no real basis for our behaving that way. What *usually* happens (say, the answer *usually* arrived at in a mathematical calculation) is formally irrelevant to the normative question of what *should* happen! Thus, I will concede for the sake of argument that – since most long division is performed by children in learning the skill – most of it arrives at the wrong answer. As Morgan (1994: 56) notes, this descriptive view of the *ethos* of a game 'confuses games with their social setting' and so offers no reason why one should behave in that way, beyond the fact that others do. D'Agostino (1995: 47) had written here of 'the interests of institutionalized forces'; but a descriptive account of *ethos* will not count as 'institutional' in the sense developed here.

By contrast, a *normative* conception of *ethos* will explain why one ought to, say, follow these rules in such-and-such a way. Such an *ethos* 'supplies a reason to take seriously and pursue diligently the standards of excellence that infuse the aim of the game, a reason to try to win in whatever way the game demands' (Morgan, 1994: 225). But how?

One account of rule-following in general (drawing on the work of Kripke, 1982) has attempted to justify the following of a particular rule by a specific person on a particular occasion in terms of the background provided by a rule-following community (to which the person belongs). But that in turn seems to suggest an extant community, whose practices could them be studied – which seems to return us to the *empirical* investigation suitable for *descriptive* conception of *ethos*.

Rather, the point here is just to identify the human power or capacity to recognise *normativity*: we are first trained into it; and later come to apply it in other cases. Wittgenstein (2001, sections 85, 87) exemplifies these two phases by discussing signposts: I learn how to follow them; and later I learn that they can be instantiated in various different forms, and not just by a wooden finger atop a post. But, given the signpost, what one ought to do to follow the path is not arbitrary. Still, nothing compels the behaviour, except the signpost – perhaps in combination with the *desire* to be following that path! It seemed as though there must be some other source of the normativity. But, as Wittgenstein (1969, secion 471) might put it, that thought is an example of *trying to go further back* than the beginning. There is actually no answer, but no genuine perplexity remains.

One might imagine that this discussion would prompt an attempt to formalise our account of rule-following; but earlier comments should be invoked to speak against that idea. As a first approximation, Wittgenstein (2001, section 354) recognized that, as he put, '[t]he fluctuation … between criteria and symptoms makes it look as though there were nothing at all but symptoms'. That is to say, what is on some occasions merely evidence for some claim (and hence potentially true *or* false) might, on other occasions, be used to in *explanation* of that claim. Then it would lack this bi-polarity. Thus, when a metal bar in Paris was used as an exemplar for one *metre*, it made no sense to ask whether that bar was a metre long: 'one can say neither that it is one metre long, nor that it is not one metre long' (Wittgenstein, 2001, section 50[b]). Given its role as an exemplar, it was a kind of 'definition', explaining what was meant by 'one metre': as a result, it would be misleading to assert that it *was* a metre long; and hence misleading to deny it. Here, the bar stood as a criterion of metre-hood! But, when no longer viewed as a exemplar, the bar's length could be questioned – had it perhaps expanded in the heat? Now its characteristics are merely symptomatic. So that, in different contexts, the very same form of words ('That bar is a metre long!') can be used to elaborate what Wittgenstein was calling criteria *or* symptoms. And criteria, as logical operators, are akin to rules – as symptoms are akin to the kinds of generalisations a descriptive account of *ethos* might suggest! So it is unlikely that any neat verbal differentia will be found, since in context one can 'fluctuate' into the other. As a result, what seem to be just rules deployed in *this* particular game might be or become treated as fundamental to the sport it was. Or vice versa. Thus, for example, the hand–ball rule in soccer can *seem* constitutive of the sport, but then (as we have seen above) not be deployed exceptionlessly. And that, in turn, will reinforce our rejection of the hunt for a definition of sport and cognate concepts, since definitions must be exceptionless.

So this discussion of the institutional character of rule-following connects our recent discussion to the initial one. For, although sport is institutional only in the weaker of the two senses sketched initially (it is not institutional in the sense in which *art* is institutional, that requiring an authoritative body), nevertheless, sport is perhaps more strongly institutional that some other candidate practices just because it has codified rules and, correspondingly, governing bodies explicitly regulating such activities. In this way, some of the institutions of sport are concrete. Moreover, they function just as we have described. Thus, suppose the question of the sport status of kabbadi were raised: how might one begin to answer it? Obviously this is not a question with any simple answer. But it is one that must be faced, and resolved, by the International Olympic Committee (IOC). Then, it is relevant here that the IOC takes the view that kabbadi lacks a sufficiently wide following to be an Olympic sport: that is, 'wide following' is read *other than* simply in terms of numbers. The sheer number of kabbadi's followers alone cannot guarantee a wide following (for instance, because they are all in the Indian subcontinent or its diaspora: so a kind of geographical width is required). Then one might ask whether all sports are Olympic sports: obviously, they are not: women's hammer is not in the Olympics; but, if men's hammer is a sport (as it obviously is), the same seems to follow for women's hammer. Still, is that case germane? Is women's hammer excluded from the Olympics for reasons that differentiate it from kabbadi?

My point here is simply to relate the theoretical institutional structure to the concrete one, with the second partly exemplifying the first. For then we see how the practical discussion (say, about kabbadi) might be thought an abstract discussion (also); one of the nature of sport. It helps if we have given up the idea that sport has an essence; if we are no longer expecting a single unifying account of sport (given in a few lines). And part of the strategy to point us in that direction will be recognising (as above) the various levels at which sport is played. Then we can see that what might be an example of soccer or chess *for these purposes* or *on this occasion* need not be so universally or exceptionlessly; but without either *soccer* or *chess* becoming something vague.

The suggestion of vagueness arises only when we think of our game or sport as necessarily complete: as comprising, say, a finite totality of rules. Here, Wittgenstein asks:

> What is to be understood by 'all the rules of tennis'? All the rules in a particular book, or all that are in a player's head, or all those that have ever been uttered, or even: all that can be listed?
>
> *(Wittgenstein, 2005: 200e)*

The point here is that no complete enumeration is possible, if one grants that these rules apply in those circumstances but that others might apply in different circumstances (as above). Further, it will not help to add 'and so on' – we have no way to expanding the list to cover all relevant examples (real and imaginary). As Wittgenstein (2003: 325) remarked, '[i]f one wished to give an enumeration ... then the question would arise: Is that *all*?'. Such a question admits of no helpful answer: at present, we might grant that our list (say, of rules) is incomplete but we have no conception either of how to complete it nor (having done so) how to demonstrate that it is complete.

In this way, the attempt to discuss sport by focusing solely on its rules is seen to be misguided: while recognising the importance of the rules in distinguishing this sport from that one, we grant that there is a limit here; and, again, one our institutionalism can address.

Conclusion

The institutional account of sport may not seem to offer much: there will be no neat definition of the kind the idealization of sport might suggest; and, while many factors will have a bearing on the identification of particular sports, none will do so exceptionlessly. Even those most regularly mentioned as perhaps always having *some* bearing, such as the rules of a particular sport, will typically apply in different ways in different contexts or faced with different difficulties. For this reason, although there are definitely regulative and constitutive *uses* of the rules of particular sports, we cannot expect particular rules to be exceptionlessly constitutive or regulative (McFee, 2004a: 43–4). The elegance of a definition, or the hope of exploring sport exclusively in terms of its rule-following character (say), has disappeared. But these facts, while describing the institutional account, conceal its power. The apparent lack of elegance is the price to be paid for a realistic picture of sport (rather than an idealized one), one engaged with the (sublunary) world of sport and, hence, that can reflect both the different contexts within which a particular sport is played (as in our soccer example, above) or the different interests we might have in discussing sport – as fan, teacher, anxious parent, philosopher, and a lot more. In this way, institutionalism licenses the detailed consideration of a particular sport: sports practices can be addressed as they are encountered by the variety of those engaged with sport. And all have a potential role here.

For one insight of institutionalism is the variety of what has a direct bearing on the nature of a particular sport (especially when compared with those who imagine a short list of intrinsic properties of sport): that is not to be reduced to, for instance, the sport's rules only; nor exemplified only at some elite level. Indeed, the features of elite sport are obviously not all *essential* for occurrences of that sport (that sport is instantiated without them) but that does not mean that, when present, they are not crucial, in that context, as a topic for informed discussion and (ideally) resolution in *this* case. Moreover, as we saw above, the lack of a (general) definiteness still permits normativity: this is not a case where 'anything goes'. Institutional regulation remains regulation.

Notes

1   In reality, the history of my interest in this idea reflects an invitation to fill in as speaker to sports students, using the only materials I had with me, on the institutional theory of art. The occasion forced me to consider the similarities and differences here, from my understanding of institutional accounts of art. This idea has also been explored independently in Mumford (2012, esp. 31–40), especially in relation to the watching of sport. Some paragraphs here draw directly, or fairly directly, on my article, "Making Sense of The Philosophy of Sport (McFee, 2013a), as reflecting the best way I found to express some points.
2   For more on definitions of art, see Davies (2013).
3   Thanks to Mike for both the information and for permission to use it.
4   This idea of a *practice* is introduced by John Rawls (1967: 144 note):

> I use the word 'practice' throughout as a sort of technical term meaning any form of activity specified by a system of rules which defines offices, roles, moves, penalties, defences, and so on, and which gives the activity its structure. As examples one may think of games and rituals, trials and parliaments.

As Rawls (1967: 164 note) continues:

> [t]hat there is a practice entails that there are instances of people having been engaged and now being engaged in it (with suitable qualifications).
>   In addition, "[t]he practice view leads to an entirely different conception of the authority which each person has to decide on the propriety of following a rule in particular cases" (Rawls, 1967. 164). Further, that "[o]nly by reference to the practice can one say what one is doing"; moreover, "[t]o explain or to defence one's own action, as a particular action, one fits it into a practice which defines it" (Rawls, 1967: 165 [both passages]. And Rawls elaborates this view with reference to sporting examples.

Alasdair MacIntyre (1985: 187–91) expands a related conception, on which:

> A practice involves standards of excellence and obedience to rules as well as achievement of goods. To enter a practice is to accept those standards and the inadequacy of my own performance as judged by them. ... to submit my own attitudes, choices, preferences and tastes to the standards which currently partially define the practice (MacIntyre 1985: 190).

This is then discussed (in relation to sport and citing MacIntyre) by both McNamee (2008: 43–68) and Morgan (1994: 131–7): in particular, appealing to "the distinctive rationality and the array of goods and virtues that define sporting practices" (Morgan 1994: 226). For some discussion of the importance thereby assigned to practices, see McFee (2004b).
5   Addressing the *application* of these rules in sporting contexts, and especially their application in contested cases, is an important task here for elaborating institutionalism: see McFee, 2011b; 2013b.
6   Clear examples, in addition to those of Morgan (1994) and McNamee (2003) above, and those they cite, would be Brown (1990), Kretchmar (2003) and Butcher and Schneider (2003), although some simply assume MacIntyre's position.

References

Anscombe, G. E. M. (1981) 'On brute facts' in G. E. M. Anscombe, *Metaphysics and the Philosophy of Mind.* Collected Papers Volume III. Oxford: Blackwell, 22–5.
Austin, J. L. (1962) *Sense and Sensibilia*, Oxford: Oxford University Press.

—— (1979) *Philosophical Papers* (3rd ed.). Oxford: Oxford University Press.

Baker, G. P. and Hacker, P. M. S. (1984) *Language, Sense and Nonsense*, Oxford: Blackwell.

Brown, W. M. (1990) 'Practices and prudence', *Journal of Philosophy of Sport*, 17(1): 71–84.

Butcher, R. and Schneider, A. (2003) 'Fair play as respect for the game', in J. Boxill (ed.) *Sports Ethics: An Anthology*. Oxford: Blackwell, 153–71.

D'Agostino, F. (1995) 'The ethos of games', in W. J. Morgan and K. V. Meier (eds) *Philosophic Inquiry in Sport* (2nd ed.). Champaign, IL: Human Kinetics: 42–9.

Davies, S. (2013) 'Definitions of Art' in Berys Gaut and Dominic Lopes (eds), *The Routledge Companion to Aesthetics* (3rd ed.). Abingdon: Routledge, 213–23.

Dickie, G. (1974) *Art and The Aesthetic: An institutional analysis*. Ithaca, NY: Cornell University Press.

—— (1984) *The Art Circle*. New York: Haven.

Diffey, T. J. (1991) *The Republic of Art*. New York: Peter Lang.

Dworkin, R. (1978) *Taking Rights Seriously*. Cambridge, MA: Harvard University Press.

Frege, G. (1960) *Philosophical Writings of Gottlob Frege* [translated P. Geach and M. Black] (2nd ed.). Oxford: Blackwell.

Hornby, N. (1992) *Fever Pitch*. London: Penguin.

Kretchmar, S. (2003) 'In defence of winning', in J. Boxill (ed.) *Sports Ethics: An Anthology*. Oxford: Blackwell, 130–5.

Kripke, S. (1982) *Wittgenstein on Rules and Private Languages*, Oxford: Blackwell.

McFee, G. (2004a) *Sport, Rules and Values*. London: Routledge.

—— (2004b) 'Normativity, justification and (MacIntyrean) practices: Some thoughts on methodology for the philosophy of sport', *Journal of Philosophy of Sport*, 31(1): 15–33.

—— (2011a) *Artistic Judgement*. Dordrecht: Springer Verlag.

—— (2011b) 'Fairness, epistemology and rules: A prolegomenon to a philosophy of officiating', *Journal of Philosophy of Sport*, 38(3): 229–53.

—— (2013a) 'Making sense of the philosophy of sport', *Sport, Ethics and Philosophy*, 7(4): 412–29.

—— (2013b) 'Officiating in aesthetic sports', *Journal of Philosophy of Sport*, 40(1): 1–18.

MacIntyre, A. (1985) *After Virtue* (second edition). London: Duckworth, 1985.

McNamee, M. J. (2008) *Sports, Virtues and Vices: Morality Plays*. London: Routledge.

Meier, K. (1995) 'Triad trickery: playing with games and sports', in W. J. Morgan and K. V. Meier (eds.) *Philosophic Inquiry in Sport* (second edition), Champaign, IL: Human Kinetics: 23-35.

Morgan, W. J. (1994) *Leftist Theories of Sport: A Critique and Reconstruction*, Chicago, IL: University of Illinois Press.

—— (1995) 'The logical incompatibility thesis and rules: a reconsideration of formalism as an account of games', in W. J. Morgan and K. V. Meier (eds.) *Philosophic Inquiry in Sport* (second edition), Champaign, IL: Human Kinetics: 50-63.

Mumford, S. (2012) *Watching Sport: Aesthetics, ethics and emotion*. Abingdon: Routledge.

Randall, D. (1984) *The Sun Has Got His Hat On*. London: Willow Books.

—— (1992) *Rags: The Autobiography of Derek Randall*. Nottingham: Sport-in-Print.

Rawls, J. (1967) "Two concepts of rules", reprinted in Philippa Foot (ed.) *Theories of Ethics*. Oxford: Oxford University Press, 144–70.

Searle, J. (1969) *Speech Arts*. Cambridge: Cambridge University Press.

Suits, B. (1978) *The Grasshopper: Games, Life and Utopia*, Edinburgh: Scottish Academy.

—— (1995a) 'The elements of sport', in W. J. Morgan and K. V. Meier (eds.) *Philosophic Inquiry in Sport* (2nd ed.). Champaign, IL: Human Kinetics, 8–15.

—— (1995b) 'Tricky triad: Games, play and sport', in W. J. Morgan and K. V. Meier (eds.) *Philosophic Inquiry in Sport* (second edition), Champaign, IL: Human Kinetics: 16-22.

Travis, C. (2008) *Occasion-Sensitivity: Selected Essays*. Oxford: Clarendon.

Wittgenstein, L. (2001). *Philosophical Investigations* (3rd ed.), trans. G. E. M. Anscombe. Oxford: Blackwell.

—— (1969) *On Certainty*, (trans. D. Paul and G. E. M. Anscombe) Oxford: Blackwell.

—— (2005) *The Big Typescript: Ts 213*. (trans. C. G. Luckhardt and M. A. E. Aue) Oxford: Blackwell.

Wittgenstein, L. and Waismann, F. (2003) *The Voices of Wittgenstein*, ed. Gordon Baker. London: Routledge.

SECTION II

Philosophical theories and sport

5

AESTHETICS OF SPORT

Andrew Edgar

Introduction

Aesthetics, as a philosophical discipline, covers two related but distinct issues: beauty and art. Thus, on the one hand, aesthetics is concerned with the nature of beauty and other aesthetic qualities, and the perception of such qualities through the faculty of taste, wherever they may be found. On the other hand, aesthetics is concerned with the nature of art and our appreciation and interpretation of art works, regardless of whether beauty is a core quality of that work. This dichotomy leads to two areas of study for the aesthetics of sport: an evaluative inquiry into the nature and relevance of aesthetic qualities (beauty, grace, drama, and so on) to the experience of playing and watching sport, and an ontological inquiry into the nature of sport and its relationship to art. At its extreme, the latter argues that sport is one of the arts, and so to be judged and assessed as such.

Aesthetics was a core concern of the philosophy of sport throughout the 1970s and 1980s. The first issue of the *Journal of the Philosophy of Sport*, for example, carried four papers on aesthetics (Kuntz 1974, Geakin and Maasterson 1974, Thomas 1974, Ziff 1974). Edited collections of philosophical papers on sport typically carried a section on aesthetics (see, for example, Gerber and Morgan 1979; Morgan and Meier 1988), as did monographs (Hyland 1990); edited collections devoted to the aesthetics of sport were published (see Whiting and Masterson 1974) and Lowe (1977) published a monograph, the culmination of work that began with his doctoral studies. While the aesthetics of sport was somewhat eclipsed by ethics in the following two decades, a number of recent publications – including special issues of both the *Journal of the Philosophy of Sport* (Lacerda 2012) and *Sports Ethics and Philosophy* (Mumford 2011; Edgar 2013) – signal a revival.

This chapter rehearses the core debates that have developed within the philosophy of sport over, firstly, the aesthetic evaluation of sport and, secondly, the possible identity of sport and art, before commenting on recent developments within the aesthetics of sport.

Sport and aesthetic quality

Evaluative and ontological questions have been debated side by side throughout the history of the aesthetics of sport and it is therefore little more than a matter of convenience to begin this exposition with the evaluative issues of aesthetic qualities such as beauty. C. L. R. James's 1963 essay, 'What is Art?' (a chapter from his paean to cricket, *Beyond a Boundary*, 1983: 195–211) is a case in point. James wants to establish an identity between sport and art and does so on the ground that both have qualities that yield what he calls 'aesthetic pleasure'. In the philosophical literature, aesthetic pleasure is typically understood as the response to the experience of beauty. An object is beautiful precisely in that one experiences aesthetic pleasure upon beholding it. For James, sport and art are alike created and performed to yield the experience of aesthetic pleasure and thus to be beautiful.

James illustrates this through cricket. The rules of cricket, like the rules of any sport, shape the possibility of the players' physical movements, albeit, for James, cricket realises this with unique subtlety. The movements of the bowler, constrained by the prohibition on straightening their arm during delivery, and of the batter, who while free to choose a range of shots is yet typically disciplined by the paradigmatic side-on stance of the coaching manual, are conventional. That is to say that, in comparison with the freedom of our mundane movements, they are constrained and shaped by conventions adopted simply for the purpose of playing cricket. So, just as a work of art, a sculpture say, refines the appearance of the mundane human body, posing it and shaping it so that it is beautiful, so too the rules of cricket, and sport in general, pose and shape the athlete's body. By highlighting only certain bodily gestures and behaviours, as well as through its repetitive structure of balls and overs, and in the core confrontation between batter and bowler, cricket, James argues, encourages a life-enhancing and pleasurable aesthetic contemplation closely akin to our experience of great art.

Despite its early date, James's argument is a subtle and sophisticated contribution to the aesthetics of sport. As such, it may be taken to highlight a number of the more fundamental issues within the discipline. Firstly, the essay implicitly raises a question as to exactly what the relevant aesthetic qualities of a sport might be. 'Beauty' may seem a self-evident aesthetic quality, yet James in fact only passingly refers to 'beauty', preferring the more sophisticated and rather technical terms, 'significant form', 'tactile values' and 'movement' borrowed from the art critic, Bernard Berenson. James's argument indeed works, in part, because Berenson understands art works as stirring the imagination of the viewer, so that one may feel the bulk of the objects represented in the art work, 'heft their weight, realize their potential resistance'. The art work encourages 'us, always imaginatively, to come into close touch with, to grasp, to embrace, or to walk around' the objects represented (Berenson 1950: 60). There is an embodiment to Berenson's engagement with art that readily lends itself, in James's hands, to articulating the spectator's involvement with the physical struggle and discipline of the athlete.

Others offer a more straightforward list for the appropriate aesthetic qualities of sport, such as Elliott's (1974: 112) 'swiftness, grace, fluency, rhythm and perceived vitality' or Aspin's (1974, 126) grace and elegance. It may be suggested here that the focus lies very much on the movement of the athletes and the formal patterns that they epitomise. While Hohler (1974: 55) similarly focuses on movement, his appeal to the integration of conflicting components broadens the scope of the aesthetic quality of the sport to the game as a whole. Kupfer (1995: 392–6) suggests a hierarchy from simple 'linear' games, such as the 100 metres or javelin, in which quantitative distances or times alone matter, through 'qualitative' sports, such as gymnastics, that are judged in terms of discipline and elegance of bodily movements, through to sports that entail direct competition between individuals or teams, such as tennis or soccer. These are 'dramatic' sports (Kupfer 1995: 396). The aesthetic possibilities become more subtle and complex as one moves up the hierarchy, and indeed the aesthetic qualities themselves, on this account, vary from sport to sport. The aesthetics of sport is then not merely a matter of the gracefulness of individual movements but of the dramatic development of the competition as a whole.

Kupfer (1979: 359) characterises the well-played and thus aesthetically pleasing game as a 'see-saw scoring, the delicate balance between offences and defences, the entire rhythm of the game … fulfilled in the ending which is, in addition to a terminus, a climax'. In effect, Kupfer's drama and James's significantly formed cricketer are alike picking up on a core theme that runs through much of the literature in philosophical aesthetics. This is the argument that beauty lies in the bringing together of disparate elements into a harmonious whole. It may be noted that such an approach presupposes that the aesthetic judgement of sport is, in fact, exclusively to do with the harmonious. There is, for Kupfer, something aesthetically troubling about a game that is won by the team that played less well and so deserved to lose, or perhaps even a win ground out against a more talented opponent.

Edgar (2013: 100–20) has argued that the exclusive focus on the harmonious and beautiful leads to a very narrow and rather conservative approach to the aesthetics of sport. It neglects the fact that much sport is ugly and not merely in the distorted physical gestures of athletes but, more importantly, in the ever-present threat of defeat and failure. Not everyone can be a winner, and there is a danger that an aesthetics akin to Kupfer's will see sport only from the perspective of the (deserved) winner. Edgar therefore argues for the aesthetics of sport to embrace something akin to modernism in the arts and thus to recognise that the aesthetic worth of much sport, like much modern art, lies in its defiance of simple harmony. A sporting aesthetic would then focus upon disruptive or, to use Nietzsche's term Dionysian, elements – such as the bitterness of defeat, the undeserved victory and an awareness of the everyday pain and suffering that underpins sporting achievement – that spoil the Apolline surface of coherence and harmony. More radically, this might suggest that sport requires an aesthetic language that is distinct to that of the arts (and especially the more traditional arts). Lacerda (2011) has begun to explore this by arguing for 'strength' as an aesthetic category.

The second issue that James's essay raises lies in his appeal to 'aesthetic' pleasure. If sport is pleasurable in this sense then it is something more than a mere entertainment or recreation. Philosophical aesthetics has linked the experience of beauty to the feeling of pleasure since at least the work of Shaftsbury (2000) and Hutcheson (2008) in the seventeenth and eighteenth centuries. As Ghose (1974: 68) notes, in everyday language and in the language of sports reporting, 'beauty' is frequently used as little more than an exclamation of 'private ecstasy'. As such, it would suggest little more than excitement or surprise – and a subjective one at that, which no one else need share. Yet for James, aesthetic pleasure is 'life enhancing' and, as such, has a weight and significance well beyond mere excitement or entertainment. The distinction is articulated by Kant. He differentiates the pleasure (*Lust*) that one experiences before an object of beauty from the mere agreeableness (*Annehmlichkeit*) that is derived from an object that satisfies sensual desires (see Kant 1952, section 3). A flower judged for its beauty yields pleasure, while an apple that is enjoyed for its flavour and for satisfying hunger is merely agreeable. Kant's point serves to emphasise the depth of the claim that an aesthetics of sport is making. In appreciating beauty, one is not indulging animal appetites – or, put more mildly, seeking mere entertainment – but rather engaging the rational and most dignified aspect of one's nature. This suggests that a genuine aesthetic appreciation of sport, as proposed by James, takes us well beyond sport as a merely entertaining diversion to touch upon the very dignity of what it is to be human – in James's terms, to experience sport is to have one's life enhanced.

The third strand that emerges from James's argument concerns the nature of aesthetic judgement and thus the role played by taste. A typology such as that derived from Kupfer, presented above, implies that aesthetic qualities are properties of the sport itself and, thus, that beauty or drama are akin to red or fast – qualities that can be perceived by any one with more or less well developed perceptual faculties. A more subtle position (and one that Kupfer may hold: see

Kupfer 1995: 398) entails either that aesthetic qualities are ascribed to the object in the act of tasteful judgement or that there is some interaction between the objective qualities of the object and the act of judgement and this interaction yields a perception of aesthetic qualities. Aesthetic qualities would not then be objective in any simple sense and the recognition of aesthetic qualities in sport would require of the spectator and even competitor some appropriate capacity to make judgements of taste.

While anyone with normally functioning sensory faculties can judge the sensible properties, such as its colour or motion, it is typically argued that the recognition of aesthetic qualities requires something more. This may be expressed as saying that aesthetic qualities are supervenient upon sensible properties (Sibley 2001: 52). Such supervenient qualities are recognised only through a judgment of taste. It may then be argued that, in judging something to be beautiful or pleasing and thus in exercising taste, one must take a distinctive stance towards that thing. One appreciates beauty only if one is within an aesthetic attitude. In Kantian aesthetics, this is an attitude of disinterestedness (Kant 1952: 50).[1] To exercise taste presupposes that one has no interest in the object judged. One does not desire that it should fulfil some pre-existing purpose or, indeed, that it has any extrinsic purpose. One brackets out all interest in its practical applications. Thus, an apple that is judged to be beautiful is so judged merely as a harmonious arrangement of colours, shapes and textures, and not as something edible. Such an account of aesthetic judgement poses two problems for the aesthetics of sport. Firstly, there is a danger of rendering the whole discipline trivial, for one may take an aesthetic attitude to (almost) anything. One may readily judge the beauty of apples, cars and mathematical proofs. That one can judge sport aesthetically is thus unexceptional, and potentially says nothing about the special quality of sport. Therefore, the second problem is to articulate what, if anything, is distinctive about the aesthetic appreciation of sport. Does sport, as it were, pose particular challenges for its aesthetic appreciation?

One approach appears, problematically, to sunder the sporting experience from the aesthetic experience. To judge sport in the same way that one judges any other potentially aesthetic experience – by adopting an attitude of disinterestedness – might fundamentally distort the experience of sport, precisely because it entails marginalising what otherwise might seem to be key elements of the sporting experience. An example that highlights this problem is offered by Eliseo Vivas (1959). In discussing the aesthetic attitude, he notes that he had once watched a hockey game in slow motion and, putting aside any interest in who was winning, he focused merely on 'the beautiful rhythmic flow of the slow-moving men' (Vivas 1959: 228). Vivas's claim is that, to treat hockey disinterestedly and thus aesthetically, one must bracket out precisely what makes hockey a sport: competition. Kovich (1971), explicitly addressing the relationship of art and sport, makes a similar claim. If athletes and spectators are made aware of the aesthetic aspects of sport, then they will become aware that 'the greatest significances of sports experiences can come, *not from the score*, but in man creating art in movement through the medium of sport' (Kovich 1971: 42 [emphasis added]). Ziff (1974) rejects the aesthetics of sport on precisely these grounds. If sport is essentially competitive (or at least involves the athlete in struggling to meet some physical challenge, such as climbing a mountain), to ignore that competition – and thus the score – in favour of the aesthetic entails a disinterest that ceases to take sport seriously *as* sport. For Ziff, sports therefore have no significant aesthetic qualities. Vivas, in fact, watches not an ice hockey game, but a slow-motion film. The implication is that hockey watched in the raw, as it were, is not aesthetic – the action is perhaps too violent or confused.

It may immediately be observed that certain sports do actually incorporate explicit aesthetic elements in their competition. These are Kupfer's 'qualitative' sports, including ice dance and artistic gymnastics, for example. Such sports are classified by Best as 'aesthetic sports', in contrast to 'purposive sports' such as tennis and soccer (Best 1974: 201). His point, echoing something of Ziff's argument, is that while a goal in soccer will count, whether it is hit majestically from 20 yards out or scrambled over the line in a goal mouth melée, it matters in gymnastics how a vault is performed. The contest in vaulting does not simply entail getting over the horse but, rather the vault is judged in terms of the very shaping and movement of the athlete's body. The vault must, in Kupfer's terms, have a certain 'quality'. To recognise that quality, the judges of aesthetic sports must cultivate a faculty of taste, much as would be attributed to the connoisseur of art works. That is to say that judgement goes beyond merely sensible properties, to the judgement of the aesthetic qualities that are supervenient upon them. Thus, a judge of figure skating must be able to discern not merely precisely quantifiable movements made by the athlete but also such aesthetic qualities as 'carriage', 'style and individuality/personality', 'projection' and 'unison, and "oneness"' (US Figure Skating Association 2012: 294).

Even in gymnastics and skating, however, the place of aesthetic judgement is strangely curtailed. Firstly, judges in these sports are rather more conservative than their artistic counterparts (Kuntz 1974: 11). The connoisseur has a greater freedom to debate aesthetic qualities and to welcome innovations in art works, while the judge of gymnastics or skating must all look for the same aesthetic qualities – and, crucially, the qualities upon which the competitors know that they will be judged. Put otherwise, it is not *sufficient* for an aesthetic athlete to be beautiful, for they must be beautiful in accordance with the rules and culture of the competition. The athlete will, consciously or otherwise, internalise the judges' expectations, thereby making their own performance aesthetic conservative, and necessarily so in order to compete effectively.

Secondly, it may be noted that one can watch, say, artistic gymnastics with no regard to the competition. As Kupfer suggests, it lends itself far more readily than most sports to being treated as something purely beautiful. Yet to do so is to distance oneself from the event *as* sport. The disinterestedness of the aesthetic spectator, taking no account of the competition has consequences for how they might respond to certain events. The gymnast tripping or dropping a piece of equipment would, for the disinterested spectator, spoil the event. The movements were not as beautiful as they might have been. However, for the sporting spectator, interested in the competition, such events are as significant as perfectly performed routines, for they impact upon the competition. The dropped piece of equipment entails lost marks and a change in positions on the leader board. Perhaps even more problematically, the aesthetic spectator is missing something fundamental to the gymnast's performance. They are missing the point, made above, that the gymnast is not simply striving to be beautiful – as a classical ballerina might – but rather to comply with the rules of the sport. The aesthetic spectator misses something of the discipline and thus significance of the athlete's movements.

It might be concluded that the aesthetic is indeed, as Ziff argues, irrelevant to purposive sports, and actually highly curtailed even in the case of aesthetic sport. In support of such a conclusion, Best (1974: 201) suggests, as self-evident, that a hockey player would rather 'score three goals in a clumsy manner' than 'miss them all with graceful movements'. Kupfer (1995: 394–5), however, offers a crucial counter-argument to Best. He suggests that an approach such as Best's presupposes that winning is the extrinsic purpose of a game. That is to say that the game is played to achieve the goal of a win and thus that scoring, however it is achieved, precisely because it contributes to the possibility of winning, is an instrumentally good thing to do. Kupfer suggests that this presupposition rests upon a confusion. Winning and scoring are not purposes *of* the sport but purposes *within* the sport. For Kupfer there are no external purposes of sport. That is to say that there is no purpose that exists independently of playing the sport. Only once one begins to play, acceding to the highly conventional rules of the sport – and thus crucially to rules that constitute the particular sport as the sport it is – does one acquire a purpose. Purposes are constituted within the sport, not prior to it. But, more subtly, the implication here is that a sport makes possible a multiplicity of purposes, and not just the single purpose of winning/scoring.

A rich sense of playing well recognises the range of human action that is made possible by the sport and celebrates it. To play well will entail that an elegantly executed goal is indeed better than a scrambled one, just as a game characterised by fair play is better than one marred by bad feeling and fouls. Kupfer (1995: 390–1) suggests that the reduction of sport to the supposedly extrinsic purpose of winning is little more than a reflection of professionalism and the commercial pressure on professional teams to win. The aesthetic would therefore seem, in Kupfer's hands, to offer something more than the brute entertainments or recreations of commercial sport. A well-played game is, as James suggests, life-enhancing, yielding an aesthetic pleasure that touches upon the very dignity of what it is to be human.

Yet such remarks, however noble in tone, remain somewhat vague in content. Again, Edgar's (2013) focus on the relevance of modernist aesthetics to sport may be significant. An aesthetics that takes sport seriously *as* sport – so one that does not disinterestedly bracket out elements of competition – must take into account the suffering and violence that underpins much sporting experience. Even if Vivas cannot cope with an ice hockey game as an aesthetic experience unless its complexity and violence has been stripped away in a slow-motion film, such a game may nonetheless be an aesthetic and richly meaningful experience, if viewed appropriately – and crucially, not as a harmonious classical drama.

Substance may be given to these arguments by turning away from the issue of sport's aesthetic qualities, in favour of an examination of the relationship between sport and art. At the core of debates about this relationship lies the argument that art can say something about the world. Those who seek some degree of identity between sport and art are at their most plausible when they argue that sport, like art, can express something about the world.

Sport and art

It was noted above that C. L.R. James (1983: 195) argues that sport should be seen as one of the arts, and does so on the grounds that sport, like art, yields aesthetic pleasure. This argument echoed by a number of more recent philosophers of sport, including Wertz (1985) and Welsch (2005). Best (1974) and Kupfer (1995) reply that this approach rests upon a fundamental confusion between the 'artistic' and the 'aesthetic'. While it may be accepted that sport, like almost anything else, can be judged aesthetically – and as such does indeed yield aesthetic pleasure – it does not then follow that it is one of the arts.

In accusing Wertz and others of conflating the aesthetic and the artistic, Best is suggesting that they are appealing to what is known as the 'aesthetic definition of art' (see Carroll 1999: 159). Here, art is defined as anything that yields aesthetic pleasure or, put otherwise, has aesthetic qualities such as beauty or grace. The inadequacy of this definition is revealed by noting that there are numerous objects and events – 'sunsets, cornfields, streetlamps, people' (Kupfer 1995: 48) – that are not art but nonetheless yield aesthetic pleasure. The argument does not end here, however. The definition of 'art' may be further qualified by holding that the status of art is ascribed only to objects and events that are intentionally designed to possess aesthetic qualities. This allows the examples of natural objects, such as sunsets and cornfields, to be dropped as red herrings. The defender of the association between art and sport may then point out that the participants in at least aesthetic sports – and, as noted above, perhaps well-played purposive sports – also intend their actions to have aesthetic qualities. Such athletes would then be akin to artists, who intend an aesthetic effect from their work. But still, the argument fails once it is recognised that there are objects created intentionally by humans to be beautiful, and yet are still not typically regarded as art. Pottery, cars and indeed streetlamps can be intentionally designed to be aesthetically pleasing, without thereby becoming art.

Best's (1978: 116) criticism of the aesthetic definition of art rests, therefore, upon the claim that the artistic must entail something more than just the recognition of aesthetic qualities in the object or event. This something more is the illusory or imaginary quality of art (Best 1978: 119). The imaginary quality of art is seen in Berenson's (1950) argument, noted above, that art works demand an imaginative response on the part of the audience. The everyday objects and events that confront the audience, be they people in costumes carrying props on a stage or stretched canvases covered in pigments, have to be actively interpreted as art works, and their subject matter has to be imaginatively reconstructed in that audience's mind. The actor who stands upon the stage is not Hamlet, they are merely playing Hamlet and the audience must recognise this distinction between actor and character both to understand that they are watching a play and to begin to interpret what the play may be about. In contrast, Best argues (1978: 117–18), there is no analogous distinction in sport. There is no distinction between an athlete and the role or position they are playing.

If an actor falls ill on stage (as once I saw happen to Michael Pennington while playing Hamlet), this illness is not transmitted to his or her character (and in this particular instance, the play was halted while Pennington recovered and then continued as if nothing had happened for, in the play, nothing had happened). Conversely, Hamlet dies, and yet the actor playing him survives unharmed for tomorrow evening's performance. Best's point is that, in the case of the athlete, there is no such divide. If the quarterback breaks his leg, Joe Theismann, playing in that position, also breaks his leg. Hamlet's death is imaginary but there is nothing imaginary about an athletic injury. While the audience to *Hamlet* must be aware that it is the character and not the actor, who dies, a sport's spectator who is indifferent to the quarterback's broken leg, because it has happened only to a quarterback and not a real person, would be disturbingly adrift in their understanding of what is happening.

The importance of this analysis lies in the justification that it gives to the claim that an art work, unlike a sporting event, can be about something – art has the possibility, in Best's (1978: 117) phrase, of being 'the expression of a conception of life issues, such as contemporary moral, social and political problems'. Best's paradigmatic art work here appears to be Picasso's *Guernica*, a work that is expressive of the traumas of the Spanish civil war (Best 1978: 117). A sporting event may betray or be symptomatic of moral, social and political problems. Here, one might consider the Louis/Schmelling bouts as symptomatic of political tensions between the democracies and Nazi Germany; or the 1956 Hungary/USSR Olympic water polo final and the Soviet invasion of Hungary that year. Yet a sports match cannot express those issues. Expression presupposes the artist's intentional composition of the art work and as such the intentional construction of a work that has imaginary content. This content is made available to the audience through the material and perceptible medium of the art work, but only in so far as the audience can imaginatively reconstruct the art work out of that material base, and thus reflect upon its subject matter. While the athlete may intend their movements to be beautiful, they cannot, as an athlete, intend them to be expressive. Best (1978: 121) notes that the ice skater Toller Cranston lost marks in competition precisely because he sought to express 'his view of life situations' and, as such, failed to perform movements that were defined as beautiful and worthy of points within the rules of the sport – as well as in the expectations of the judges and his fellow competitors. While there may be beauty in a sports match, there is nothing that needs to be imaginatively interpreted. It is then meaningless, in Best's account, to ask what the sport is about.

Best (1978: 115) illustrates this with his own experience of watching Indian dance. His modest but significant claim is that, because he was unaware of the conventions that determine the precise meaning of the dancer's gestures, he was unable to respond to the dance as an art work. His response was therefore merely to a beautiful and thus aesthetically pleasing sequence of movements. Unaware of the appropriate conventions and intentions of the dancer, he is unable imaginatively to reconstruct the subject matter of the work and thus, for him, it was purely aesthetic and not artistic.

It is perhaps Best's claim that sport has no subject that has been most vigorously contested. In particular, philosophers such as Roberts (1992, 1995), Gebauer (1994) and Krein (2008) have appealed significantly to Nelson Goodman's (1978: 1–22) concept of 'worldmaking'. For Goodman, there is no possibility of an immediate experience of a real world. Rather, our worlds are always already mediated by descriptions, drawn from our sciences, mythologies and arts. We thus live in a plurality of possible worlds, because different descriptions will be relevant to different contexts and activities, and existing descriptions are always open to revision and development. So, for Goodman, art is essentially a resource for such redescription, or worldmaking. Roberts, Gebauer and Krein therefore raise the possibility that sport is also such a resource. While sport may not comment, in Best's sense, upon specific life issues, the athlete can still act as a 'strong poet' (in a phrase that Roberts [1995] borrows from Harold Bloom and Richard Rorty) and, as such, through their athletic actions, provide resources for re-describing, and thus expressing something about, the non-sporting world.

This argument may be outlined by firstly considering Best's contrast between the imaginary status of art, and the comparative reality of sport. The question of sport's reality has been much debated (see Fox 1982, Cordner 1988: 34–5). The special spaces and times within which sports matches occur, segregating them from everyday or non-sporting life, suggest that sport is unreal, at least in the sense that it is not a part of the normal course of our lives. Here, sports shares something with art, insofar as art too is typically segregated into theatres, concert halls and galleries. Such institutional configurations are nonetheless perhaps deceptive, leading too readily to an identification of sport and the arts. A more rigorous response to Best can therefore be derived from formalist accounts of sport (see Suits 1995). In the formalist account, what matters for the identity of sport is *not* the institutional setting of the actions but, rather, the constitutive role of the sport's rules. Thus, the sequence of movements that make up, say, the scoring of a try are largely meaningless outside the constitutive rules of rugby. Put otherwise, scoring a try is impossible outside the game of rugby. This entails that the spectator (and indeed the players and officials) must be aware of the rules of the sport to understand the actions occurring before them. Here, already, there is a parallel with Best's experience of Indian dance. Just as he is unaware of the rules that govern the meaning of the dancer's actions, so the spectator uninitiated into a particular sport may find the action before them meaningless. This action may nonetheless be beautiful and exciting – and thus be perceived aesthetically – but it will not be understood and appreciated as sport.

To accept this basic formalist account does not immediately undermine Best's position – and indeed his own argument is not overtly inconsistent with formalism. The injury to the quarterback is still real, in a way that the Hamlet's death is not, and is so despite the fact that the action he was performing at the time of injury could only make sense, say as a 'flea-flicker' play, within the rules and strategies of American football. Further, it may be argued that formalism reinforces Best's claim that sport cannot be about anything. The rules of sport serve as a syntax that determines the meaning of any given action only in relationship to other actions within the game. As such, sport seems to have no semantics – which is to say, no way of referring beyond itself to the non-sporting world. Kupfer was noted above as arguing that sport has no extrinsic goals. He sums up his position by borrowing Kant's definition of beauty as a characterisation of sport: sport is 'purposiveness without purpose' (Kupfer 1995: 405, Kant 1952: 80). Sport is a structured and disciplined activity, with rules that determine the meaning and legitimacy of a given action within the game, but no external purpose that could allow the sport to hook, meaningfully, on to the non-sporting world.

Formalism can, nonetheless, suggest how sport does have content. The rules of a given sport present a particular physical challenge for the athletes. The rules do not merely determine the objectives within the game (to beat one's opponent by scoring more goals or to climb a given mountain) but also delimit the conditions under which those objectives are to be achieved (such as scoring goals without touching the ball with one's hands or climbing mountains without certain mechanical aids). Consequently, the rules will specify the materials, equipment and technology with which the game is played. As such, the game is using – and also prohibiting – resources from the non-sporting world. It may then be suggested that sport is, in some relevant sense, about these resources. Cricket is about the interaction of a leather-covered cork sphere and a willow bat; dressage is about the training and disciplining of a horse and rider to perform certain movements and is thus more generally about the training and control of horses. Lawn tennis is skilled action upon grass, not clay. More generally, sport may be seen to play with our experience of time and space: consider here the different temporal and spatial experiences provided by sports such as basketball (see Elcombe 2007) and golf; with our sense of embodiment: consider body-building (Bell 2008) and, indeed, James's reflections upon the way in which the athlete body's movements are disciplined and shaped by the rules of the sport – or free will and fate – consider the mathematical precision of the snooker or pool table compared with the oval rugby ball and thus its promotion of the lucky bounce. Sport has been described as a 'moral laboratory' (see McFee 2000) and, here again, it may be suggested that the rules of the sport constitute an artificial space that forces the player to focus on certain moral temptations or challenges – such as dealing with the usually prohibited violence of the boxing ring or how easy it so often is to move one's ball in golf to a better lie, without being seen.

These illustrations can be easily supplemented, but the core point is that sport does not exist in utter isolation from is ambient culture. It draws into it self, and plays with material, technological and moral resources from that culture. Precisely because the rules of specific sports are constituted to highlight and focus upon different aspects of that culture, sports are not merely symptomatic of those cultures but are an imaginative reconstruction and expression of them. As such, sport may be considered to be 'worldmaking'. The descriptions of worlds current outside of the sport are embraced and refigured within the sport, thereby opening up new ways of describing, and thus making, those non-sporting worlds. This is, in effect, to argue that thanks to sport we can come to think differently of the capacities and nature of the human body, of gender and of age; of the way in which social interaction is organised; of what it is to have freewill and responsibility; of the relationship between the human being and animals or between the human and natural worlds, and so on. It is here that Edgar (2013) argues for a shift from the aesthetics of sport to a hermeneutics, and thus to a concern with its meaning and how that meaning is interpreted.

It may be noted that the above argument is grounded in a subtle shift in the analogy that is typically drawn between sport and art. It is tacitly assumed that a sports match is analogous to an art work, and much of the argument for the identity for sport and art rests upon this assumption. Here, it is being claimed that a sport is analogous to an art work – so that each sports match is akin to the performance of, say, a piece of music or a play. On such an account, it is the sportswright who is analogous to the artist – even if the sportswright is typically a combination of traditions and the committees of governing bodies, rather than an identifiable individual. As Krein (2008) recognises, new and alternative sports such as skateboarding, kitesurfing and snowboarding crucially open up new worlds – and not least through embracing new technologies and sporting spaces.

If the sportswright is the artist or composer, then the athlete remains a performer and interpreter. Cordner (1988: 33) thus notes the creativity of certain athletes, who find new ways of playing their sports, citing Arnold Palmer's attacking golf and Bjorn Borg's topspin in tennis (and on creativity in sport, see Lacerda and Mumford 2010). The constitutive rules of the sport do not determine the way in which it is played and this, as Roberts (1995) expresses the point, opens up the possibility of the athlete as strong poet. The point is not merely that the great athlete can achieve that which is denied the physically less able. It is rather that, in realising these achievements of skill and strength, of strategic nous and an awareness of space and time and, indeed, of maintaining dignity under pressure, the athlete poses a challenge to the way in which what it is to be human is described. The creative response to the athletic achievement thus makes a new world.

Concluding thoughts

It may be suggested that the increasingly rich work being done in the aesthetics of sport still does not close the gap between sport and art. Indeed, a significant essay by Elcombe (2012) does not argue that sport is one of the arts but, rather, explores the consequences of instituting 'art' as the dominant metaphor in our description of sport, and all importantly thereby replacing the currently dominant metaphor of 'war'. Welsch (2005) argues for an aesthetics of sport by grounding aesthetics in the experience and judgement of everyday life, rather than of art. While Welsch's arguments are not wholly convincing (see Satoshi 2009), Kreft (2010, 2012) following to some extent Buckley (2006) offers a more promising articulation of the aesthetics of everyday life, not least by situating the 'dramatic' as the core aesthetic quality of sport. This category of drama is not the mere application of drama to an event in everyday life but, rather, recognises that sport is a performance and, as such, is executed under special circumstances – and here both the institutional separation of the sporting event in an arena or stadium and its peculiar constitutional rules may be considered – that separate it from everyday life and give it a distinctive history and tradition (Kreft 2012: 228).

Sport may have aesthetic qualities but, as Kreft's argument demonstrates, it is important to identify and clearly articulate the qualities that are of relevance to sport as sport. Otherwise, an aesthetic concern with sport is in danger of being trivial or of distorting the true nature of sport. Sport presupposes the pursuit of a precisely defined physical challenge but, most significantly, further entails the acute possibility that the athlete may fail in this challenge. As noted above, with respect to the potential ugliness of much sport, if a competition is a genuinely sporting one, then there must be the possibility of losing to one's opponent. Non-competitive challenges, such as conquering a mountain or swimming an expanse of wild water, must similarly entail the possibility of failure if they are to count as sport. The risk of failure is fundamental to sport. To neglect this, as Vivas neglects the score of the ice hockey match so as to appreciate it aesthetically, is to miss the point of sport as sport. Certain sports can take this risk of failure to extremes, for failure may entail physical injury or death. The very reality that Best points to in the athlete's, as opposed to the fictional character's, injury ultimately may give sport a pathos and importance that art cannot rival. This unique character of sport explains both why it is not art, and why at its most profound it is rarely beautiful.

Note

1   On the tensions between the committed attitude of the fan and the aesthetic attitude of a 'disinterested' spectator, see Mumford (2012) and McFee (2013).

Bibliography

Aspin D. N. 1974. Sport and the concept of 'the aesthetic'. In *Readings in the Aesthetics of Sport*, edited by H. T. A. Whiting and D. W. Masterson. London: Lepus, 117–38.

Bell, Melina Constantine 2008. Strength in muscle and beauty in integrity: building a body for her, *Journal of the Philosophy of Sport* 35: 43–62.

Berenson, B. 1950. *Aesthetics and History*. London: Constable.

Best, D. 1974. The aesthetic in sport, *British Journal of Aesthetics* 14(3): 197–213.

——— 1978. *Philosophy and Human Movement*. London: George Allen and Unwin.

Buckley, Anthony D. 2006. Aristotle and cricket: drama in retrospect, *Journal of the Philosophy of Sport* 33: 21–36.

Carroll, N. 1999. *Philosophy of Art: A Contemporary Introduction*. London: Routledge.

Cordner, C. D. 1988. Differences between sport and art, *Journal of the Philosophy of Sport* 15: 31–47.

Edgar, A. 2013. Sport and art: an essay in the hermeneutics of sport. *Sport, Ethics and Philosophy*, 7(1): 1–171.

Elcombe, Tim L. 2007. Philosophers can't jump: reflections on living time and space in basketball. In Gregory Bassham and Jerry Walls (eds) *Basketball and Philosophy: Thinking Outside the Paint*. Lexington, KY: University Press of Kentucky, 207–19.

——— 2012. Sport, aesthetic experience, and art as the ideal embodied metaphor, *Journal of the Philosophy of Sport*, 39(2): 201–19.

Elliot, R. K. 1974. Aesthetics and sport. In *Readings in the Aesthetics of Sport*, edited by H. T. A. Whiting and D. W. Masterson. London: Lepus, 107–16.

Fox, R. M. 1982. The so-called unreality of sport, *Quest* 34(1): 1–11.

Geakin, Geoffrey and Maasterson D. W. 1974. The work of art in sport, *Journal of the Philosophy of Sport* 1: 36–66.

Gebauer, G. 1994. Sport, theatre, and ritual: three ways of world-making, *Journal of the Philosophy of Sport* 20–1: 102–6.

Gerber, E. G and Morgan, W. J. (eds) 1979. *Sport and the Body: A Philosophical Symposium* (2nd ed.). Philadelphia, PA: Lea and Febiger.

Ghose, Z. 1974. The language of sports reporting. In *Readings in the Aesthetics of Sport*, edited by H. T. A. Whiting and D. W. Masterson. London: Lepus, 57–68.

Goodman, N. 1978. *Ways of Worldmaking*. Indianapolis, IN: Hackett.

Hohler, V. 1974. The Beauty of Motion. In *Readings in the Aesthetics of Sport*, edited by H. T. A. Whiting and D. W. Masterson. London: Lepus, 49–56.

Hutcheson, F. 2008 [1725]. *An Inquiry into the Original of our Ideas of Beauty and Virtue*. Indianapolis, IN: Liberty Fund.

Hyland, Drew. 1990. *The Philosophy of Sport*. New York: Paragon House.

James, C. L. R. 1983. *Beyond a Boundary*. London: Serpent's Tail.

Kant, I. 1952 [1790]. *Critique of Judgement*, translated by C. J. Meredith. Oxford: Oxford University Press.

Kovich, M. 1971. Sport as an art form, *Journal of Health, Physical Education, Recreation* 42(8): 42.

Krein, K. 2008. Sport, nature and worldmaking, *Sport, Ethics and Philosophy* 2(3): 285–301.

Kreft, Lev 2010. Aristotle and cricket, *Proceedings of the European Society for Aesthetics* 2: 265–77.

——— 2012. Sport as drama, *Journal of the Philosophy of Sport* 39(2): 219–34.

Kuntz, Paul G. 1974. Aesthetics applied to sports as well as to the arts, *Journal of the Philosophy of Sport* 1: 7–35.

Kupfer, J. H. 1979. Purpose and beauty in sport. In *Sport and the Body: A Philosophical Symposium* (2nd ed.), edited by E. G. Gerber and W. J. Morgan. Philadelphia, PA: Lea and Febiger, 355–60.

——— 1995. Sport – The Body Electric. In *Philosophic Inquiry in Sport* (2nd ed.), edited by W. J. Morgan and K.V. Meier. Champaign, IL: Human Kinetics: 390–406.

Lacerda, T. O. 2011. From Ode to Sport To Contemporary Aesthetic Categories of Sport: Strength Considered as an Aesthetic Category. *Sport, Ethics and Philosophy* 5(4): 447–56.

——— (ed.) 2012. Sport and aesthetics, *Journal of the Philosophy of Sport* 39(2): 183–320.

Lacerda, T.O. and Mumford, S. 2010. The genius in art and in sport: a contribution to the investigation of aesthetics of sport, *Journal of the Philosophy of Sport* 37(2): 182–93.

Lowe, B. 1977. *The Beauty of Sport: A Cross-disciplinary Inquiry*. Englewood Cliffs, NJ: Prentice Hall.

McFee, G. 2000. Sport: A moral laboratory? In *Just Leisure: Policy, Ethics and Professionalism*, edited by M. McNamee, C. Jennings and M. Reeves. Eastbourne: Leisure Studies Association: 153–68.

—— 2013. Making Sense of the Philosophy of Sport. *Sport, Ethics and Philosophy* 7(4):412–29.

Morgan, W. J. and Meier, K.V. (eds) 1988. *Philosophic Inquiry in Sport* (2nd ed.). Champaign, IL: Human Kinetics.

Mumford, S. 2011. *Watching Sport: Aesthetics, Ethics and Emotion*. London: Routledge.

—— 2012, Emotions and aesthetics: an inevitable trade-off? *Journal of the Philosophy of Sport* 39(2): 267–79.

Roberts, T. J. 1992. The making and remaking of sports action, *Journal of the Philosophy of Sport* 19: 15–29.

—— 1995. Sport and strong poetry, *Journal of the Philosophy of Sport* 22: 94–117.

Shaftesbury, 3rd Earl of [Cooper, A. A.]. 2000 [1711]. *Characteristics of Men, Manners, Opinions, Times*, Cambridge Texts in the History of Philosophy, edited by L. E. Klein. Cambridge: Cambridge University Press.

Sibley, F. 2001. *Approaches to Aesthetics: Collected Papers on Philosophical Aesthetics*, edited by J. Benson, B. Redfern and J. Roxbee Cox. Oxford: Oxford University Press..

Satoshi, H. 2009. An aspect of undoing aesthetics: on W. Welsch's aesthetics of sport, *Aesthetics* 13: 11–21.

Suits, B. 1995. The Elements of Sport. In *Philosophic Inquiry in Sport* (2nd ed.), edited by W. J. Morgan and K.V. Meier. Champaign, IL: Human Kinetics, 8–17.

Thomas, C. E. 1974. Toward an experiential sport aesthetic, *Journal of the Philosophy of Sport* 1: 67–91.

US Figure Skating Association 2012. *The 2012 Official US Figure Skating Rulebook*. Colorado Springs, CO: US Figure Skating Association.

Vivas, E. 1959. Contextualism reconsidered, *Journal of Aesthetics and Art Criticism* 1(2): 222–40.

Welsch, W. 2005. Sport – viewed aesthetically, and even as art? In *The aesthetics of everyday life*, edited by A. Light and J. M. Smith. New York: Columbia University Press: 135–55.

Wertz, S. K. 1985. Representation and expression in sport, *Journal of the Philosophy of Sport* 12: 8–24.

Whiting, H. T. A. and Masterson, D. W. (eds). 1974. *Readings in the Aesthetics of Sport*. London: Lepus.

Ziff, P. 1974. A fine forehand, *Journal of the Philosophy of Sport* 1: 92–109.

6

BIOETHICS AND SPORT

Silvia Camporesi

Elite sport has long been the laboratory for the introduction of biomedical technologies aimed at health optimization and performance enhancement (Hoberman 1992). In parallel, the body of the elite athlete has been the locus of experimentation of these technologies. Now, more than ever, with the advancement of biomedical technologies, elite sport is an arena where ethical questions are raised by the application of these technologies to the human body. Such questions arising at the intersection of elite sport and ethics are addressed in this chapter.

This chapter is divided into five sections: direct-to-consumer genetics for talent identification in sport; issues of confidentiality, disclosure and conflict of interest in sport medicine (including examples of return to play issue); gender issues in sport, specifically the case of Caster Semenya and subsequent discussion of the guidelines for eligibility with women with hyperandrogenism; the role played by technology in the Paralympics: essential for performance, or performance enhancement? I conclude with a discussion on future directions for research at the intersection of sport and bioethics. I eschew discussion of doping (see Chapter 21) and genetic technologies (see Chapter 23) that are discussed elsewhere in this volume.

Direct-to-consumer genetics for talent identification in sport

In the last 5 years, the United States has witnessed a boom of direct-to-consumer (DTC) companies that sell online genetic tests for sports performance or related traits. At least seven companies, including X Factor Sports Training, Atlas Sports Genetics, Geneffect and another company aptly named Warrior Roots, are available on the internet (Roth 2012). The prices for these tests vary between US$80 and US$200. These affordable prices have been made possible by the ever-increasing lower cost of whole-genome sequencing, which in turn was made possible by the new developments in sequencing approaches usually referred to as the 'next generation sequencing'.

It is not exactly clear how many people use these tests, because such data are proprietary (Brooks and Tarini 2011) but we can speculate that (at least) several thousand parents and coaches use them. The products offered vary. Some companies test for a group of what they call 'performance-enhancing polymorphisms' (PEPs), others only for one trait (Koboldt *et al.* 2013). Each of them tests for the alfa-actinin 3 (ACTN3) polymorphism, which was the first PEP to be demonstrated to have an association with the formation and function of skeletal muscles. Yang *et al.* (2003) found that both male and female elite sprinters have a significantly higher frequency of the functional 477R genotype, where R stands in place of an arginine 'R' rather than a stop codon in the ACTN3 gene. Alfa-actinin belongs to a large family of actin-binding proteins, where actin is a fundamental component of the contractile unit of muscle fibres. Polymorphism in ACTN3 is thought to contribute to the heritability of fibre-type distribution in the muscle, where type-I muscle fibres are slow-twitch fibres that use aerobic metabolism and are used in endurance races, whereas type-II muscle fibres are fast-twitch fibres that use anaerobic metabolism to create energy and are used in sprints (Berman and North 2010).

The test for the 'ACTN3 sports gene' is sold as a genetic 'power and speed performance test' and, as we can read on the website of Atlas Sports Genetics,[1] with the aim of giving 'parents and coaches early information on their child's genetic predisposition for success in team or individual speed/power or endurance sports'. They suggest that the results of the tests will be 'valuable in outlining training and conditioning programs necessary for athletic and sport development'. As argued by Caulfield (2011), these tests are examples of the widespread phenomenon of the exploitation of science or, using his neologism, of 'scienceploitation', defined as the 'exploitation of legitimate fields of science and, too often, patients and the general public, for profit and personal gain' (Caulfield 2011: 4). A case in point for science-ploitation: the tests for ACTN3 variant claim to assess the predisposition to athletic ability and prowess, whereas the ACTN3 gene accounts for only two per cent of the total variance in muscle performance (Eynon *et al.* 2011). There is also a general remark to be made about the wide discrepancy between the aim of research into genetics and sports and the claims that these DTC companies typically make. On the one hand, the aim of research in genetics and sport is to identify the influence of genes within the performance environment, whether it is in deter-mining risk of injuries or indicating predispositions to talent. On the other hand, we saw above what kind of far-fetched claims certain companies are making about the predictive power of their tests. This shift from experimental or therapeutic applications (the aim of research in genetics and sport) to enhancement intervention (the aim of the DTC genetic tests for athletic performance) must address substantial scientific problems, not least the extrapolation of data obtained under different experimental designs. Aggressive marketing claims like those made by DTC companies represent a clear overstatement of the predictive ability of the tests. Moreover, the tests offered by DTC companies do not address the problem of 'externality' – the fact that the results obtained on a set of subjects (for example, elite athletes in the case of ACTN3) are being applied to a completely different set of subjects; that is, children. Profound as these epis-temological challenges are, there are yet more problems with these tests. Although many genes and allelic variants have been tentatively associated with performance-related traits, these asso-ciations have not reached a conclusive level. As Roth (2012) pointed out: 'This is not a judgment against the existing science, but rather a recognition of the infancy of the field of exercise and sports performance genomics' (Roth 2012: 250). Moreover, these tests pose the potential problem of false negatives, with unwarranted exclusion of individuals from certain sports on the basis of the results of these tests. Moreover, genetic tests for predictive purposes, such as talent identification for performance, are potentially in breach of the Council of Europe's Bioethics Convention Article 12 (McNamee *et al.* 2009: 341). The European Society of Human Genetics (ESHG) has also expressed concerns regarding the possibly inadequate consent process in which individuals are enrolled in research conducted by the DTC compa-nies with their samples or data. The ESHG recommends that a separate consent procedure different from the consent procedure for research should be implemented (European Society of Human Genetics 2010). In addition, there are specific problems of confidentiality and consent in elite sports medicine, also highlighted by McNamee *et al.* (2009) and by Rudnik-Schoeneborn (2012):

> Following the guidelines of the ESHG commercially available tests for genetic variants in the context of general health purposes, lifestyle and sport performance should only be offered if the clinical utility and validity of the analysis is proven, if informed consent is given, and if privacy and confidentiality are secured
>
> *(Rudnik-Schoeneborn 2012: 17)*

It seems, therefore, that these kinds of tests present scholars, scientists, policymakers and practitioners (such as coaches) serious food for thought concerning the meaning and significance of sports for children, especially elite sports and talent development systems. Youth sports should not be framed exclusively as goal-directed activities (directed to victory). Sports at developmental levels must be understood differently from what it is for the amateur or professional athlete. The meaning of sport for the child must be pluriform: to stay healthy, to enjoy the company of friends, to enjoy the discovery of the possibilities of one's own body, to learn how to relate with a team, to learn the importance of rules, and so on (Sherwin 2007, Sandel 2009). It does not have to be, nor should it necessarily be, related to talent scouting and talent development (Camporesi 2013).

Issues of confidentiality, disclosure and conflict of interest in sport medicine

Elite athletes find themselves at the nexus of a web of interest that has repercussions for traditional issues in clinical research as they are translated to elite sport context, such as confidentiality, disclosure, and conflict of interest (Nixon 1993). At the core of these discussions seems to be the concept of the conflict of interest, which is explicated in different manifestations, as rehearsed below. Conflicts of interest originate when the athlete's short-term health, their ability to compete and their long-term health are not promoted by the same medical intervention.

Disclosure and confidentiality

In sports medicine, a distinction needs to be made between an athlete's personal physician, a team physician, a physician performing a pre-contract fitness test and a national team physician, although at times these roles are represented in the same person (Holm *et al.* 2011). For example, the team doctor is an agent of the club or team and, as such, has a contract and duties towards the team. Sports doctors are *de facto* employees (of the team, of the athletes) and athletes find themselves at the centre of a conflict of interest between the ethical norms of the medical profession (the patient's best interests first) and the ethical norms of sport medicine (excellence, victory first), where often short-term-health goals, such as a too-swift return to play are privileged over long-term health goals. In addition, more often than not, the athlete's income is controlled by their employer (team, sponsor) and the degree of control that the athlete has over the decision to play or compete may be very limited (Holm 2007).

While, in most cases, the dual nature of the obligations of the sports doctor (towards the athlete and towards the team) is understood by the athlete, there may be cases in which sensitive information is disclosed by the athlete to the sports doctors who find themselves then in a conflict between the duty of care towards the athlete and the duty to disclose sensitive and relevant information to the team doctor. Anderson *et al.* (2008) reports that 50 per cent of the doctors in their survey thought that their duty of care towards the athlete was the overriding consideration, and decided not to disclose this sensitive information to the team, therefore *de facto* breaching their contractual obligations to their employer. It seems that there is no consensus on what doctors should do in such conflict of interest dilemmas, which seem to be unavoidable in the current structure, where the sports physician is employed by the team or club and, as such, has an obligation to them. One possible solution, at least to make things more transparent, is the proposal put forward by (Holm *et al.* 2011), who suggested that the contract between athlete and club should always contain information about disclosure.

According to Holm (2007), the only possible long-term solution to the conflict of interest dilemmas inherent in elite sport is a drastic change in the economic and financial relations in the sport matrix. Such changes would ensure that sports physicians would no longer find themselves in the position of being employed by a team or sport association, and that the athletes would consequently not find themselves torn between their long-term health goals and their short-term gains for the team and for their athletic career. Even in this changed sport matrix, though, there would still be incentives to keep at least some unethical practices secretive to preserve exclusive use and competitive advantage. I discuss a possible solution to this problem in the final section of this essay. Another possible solution in this vein would be not only to have a contract between the sports physician and the team or club and the athlete and the team or club but also between the sports physician and the athlete, thus leaving less room for misunderstandings.

Concussions and return to play issues

Cases of athletes who opt for a swifter return to play at the expense of their long-term health are countless. One recent example is Kobe Bryant of the Los Angeles Lakers, who recently publicly challenged teammate Dwight Howard to play through a torn labrum in his shoulder: 'We don't have time for [Howard's shoulder] to heal', said Bryant.[2] Cases like these abound because high-performance athletes are focused more on their athletic achievements now than their future health status later. They adopt therefore a 'win at all costs attitude' as described by Krumer *et al.* (2011) that discounts future health for current athletic success (Camporesi and Knuckles 2014).

There is more than one ethical issue at stake in return to play considerations. One hinges on the respect of the patient's autonomy: to what degree should we let athletes exercise their autonomy and make decisions that could potentially be very harmful for their long-term health? How much risk taking is to be afforded to individuals in the context of elite sport? Are there specific reasons intrinsic to the context of elite sport for which we should limit the rights of athletes to accept risks? It should of course be stressed that decisions of return to play are often taken under a considerable pressure and, in the short-term, athletes may feel like they have no other choice but to return to play as soon as possible to avoid jeopardizing their future career. This point brings us back to the discussion of discounting future health for short-term gains. What is the role of the sport physician in a case where athletes should not return to play for their own benefit, but there is a pressure from the team or club for them to do so?

One issue that has been much discussed is when athletes may return to play safely following concussions. This is an especially serious issue because of a possible link between concussions and chronic traumatic encephalopathy or early dementia in former elite football players, hockey players and elite wrestlers. American football has been at the centre of a strident public debate in the last couple of years, owing to the recent wave of suicides among college footballers after concussion-related permanent traumatic brain injury, also known as chronic traumatic encephalopathy (CTE).[3] Concussion is defined as an event that occurs when the brain hits against the skull as a consequence of the application of force (Hecht 2002), although, as McNamee and Partridge (2013) have shown, while several global concussion statements have been issued, there is lack of universal consensus on concussion management, owing to the absence of a universal definition for concussion or mild traumatic brain injury and the presence of conflicts of interest, which have been noted above.

CTE is also referred to as 'dementia pugilistica', because elite boxers were the first known to develop the syndrome following repeated blows to the head.[4] In CTE, repetitive trauma initiates progressive degeneration of the brain tissue. The abnormal form of the protein tau, also found in Alzheimer's disease-affected individuals, is also found to accumulate in the brain of individuals with CTE. These pathological anatomical changes in the brain do not start taking place immediately after concussion but, typically, years after the last brain trauma or at the end of athletic career reference. The degeneration of the brain is associated with a plethora of symptoms – from progressive memory loss to impaired judgment, impulse control problems (often manifested as aggressive behaviour), depression and finally to dementia (McKee *et al.* 2009). In addition to these difficulties, there is no treatment and no definitive pre-mortem diagnosis, as the only definitive diagnosis is made at autopsy (Saulle and Greenwald 2012). By the end of 2012, thousands of former elite football players had been filing lawsuits against the US National Football League (NFL) accusing the League of hiding information about the long-term harms derived from concussions on the field of play.[5]

As in all diseases, genetic factors also contribute to the development of CTE. In particular, the apolipoprotein epsilon 4 allele (ApoE4) has been strongly associated with Alzheimer's disease and is now thought to have a possible role in the development of CTE (McKee *et al.* 2009) In an editorial, Gandy and DeKosky (2012) raise the question of whether screening for ApoE4 allelic variant could help to identify individuals at a higher risk of developing CTE following concussions either on the field of play (for athletes) or on the battlefield (for military personnel). They also conducted a preliminary survey among experts in the fields of Alzheimer's disease, traumatic brain injury and CTE regarding the value of introducing ApoE genotyping. The consensus resulting from the poll was clear: most of the interviewees agreed that it was premature to introduce ApoE genotyping, for several reasons. These included the lack of a systematic registry, screening or genotyping of at-risk individuals and the fact that most existing data on ApoE4 and dementia risks are healthy controls in their mid to late life, so these results could be extrapolated to athletes at risk of CTE, whose exposure may begin during adolescence (Gandy and DeKosky 2012). Savulescu and Foddy (2005: 29) have criticized the value of mandatory screening on the basis of its illiberality: 'We should educate, not involuntary test or restrict the freedom to choose what we do with our lives, including what risks we take'.

There is need for a much more substantive ethical discussion of concussion in sport, as argued by McNamee and Phillips (2011) and McNamee and Partridge (2013). The uncertainty of the safety of return-to-play decisions after a concussion needs to be recognised and disclosed to the player-patient. It is possible that only the threat of mass torts (as they are continuing in the USA from former NFL players) will drive a change in attitudes in elite sport. Policy and practice changes must be confronted by, for example, NFL rules regarding lawful head contact (e.g. in tackling) and helmet design and other prevention strategies. This will not be easy. In contact sports such as American football, ice hockey or rugby, 'hard hits and head collisions are more than simple aspects of the game; they are part of the sports' identity' as put by Saulle and Greenwald (2012: 7) and also a facet of marketing and media commodification. A successful prevention strategy requires a complex approach involving all stakeholders – from coaches, to players, to team doctors, to referees and the public (Saulle and Greenwald 2012) In addition, as noted by Goldberg (2009), 'No helmet can prevent the brain from striking the interior of the cranium upon the application of adequate force'. But, unless the 'culture' of these sports is changed from within, and athletes do not feel that they have to act as heroes and be 'patched up' for competition disregarding completely their future health, nothing is going to be changed.

Gender issues in sport: a critique of IAAF and IOC policies on hyperandrogenism[6]

Following the debacle surrounding Caster Semenya's case (Camporesi and Maugeri 2010), on 1 May 2011, the International Association for Athletics Federation (IAAF) issued its new policies on the eligibility of female athletes to compete in the female category (International Association for Athletics Federation 2011), although the Federation claimed that they were not specifically aimed at Caster Semenya. To briefly rehearse her case, in August 2009, Caster Semenya, the then 18-year-old South African runner, won the women's 800-metre race at the Berlin World Championships in Athletics with a time of 1 minute 55.45 seconds, with a margin of almost 2.5 seconds. The victory sparked rumours that she was not really a woman. On the basis of these rumours, the IAAF triggered an investigation that lasted for 11 months, while depriving Caster of her medal and banning her from competition. In July 2010, upon appeal, the IAAF cleared Semenya for competition and her Berlin victory was allowed to stand (Karkazis et al. 2012).

The regulations require female athletes who do not fall below the limit of 10 nmol/L of testosterone, as defined by IAAF regulations (IAAF 2011: 12) must undergo androgen-suppressive therapy for up to 2 years to reduce the level of testosterone before they may compete as females. Note that the burden of proof for demonstrating that female athletes with hyperandrogenism do not derive a competitive advantage from the excess testosterone rests with the athlete (IAAF 2011 para. 6.6). The preface to the regulations states: 'The difference in athletic performance between males and females is known to be predominantly due to higher levels of androgenic hormones in males resulting in increased strength and muscle development' (p. 1). The declared policy goal, hence, is not to determine whether someone is 'really' a woman, along the lines of the now-discontinued sex-testing policies (Heggie 2010) but to assess, instead, whether high levels of androgens (hyperandrogenism) confer any significant advantage to women displaying this condition.

The advantage or, better, the 'unfair advantage' thesis is the pervasive assumption underlying the construction of female categories in elite sports. Paragraph 6.5 of the IAAF regulations states this quite clearly:

> The Expert Medical Panel shall recommend that the athlete is eligible to compete in women's competition if:
> (i) she has androgen levels below the normal male range; or
> (ii) she has androgen levels within the normal male range but has an androgen resistance such that she derives no *competitive advantage* [emphasis added] from having androgen levels in the normal male range.
>
> *(IAAF 2011: 12)*

The idea that an extremely complex trait like athleticism can be reduced to one single biochemical component, and in a way that markedly discriminates between 'males' and females', is not uncontroversial. That is because there is no robust scientific evidence showing that successful athletes display higher levels of testosterone than less successful ones (Karzakis *et al.* 2012). If one assumes, for the sake of discussion, that higher levels of testosterone do indeed confer an athletic advantage, it can nevertheless be argued that the ensuing medicalization of athletes with hyperandrogenism is unwarranted.

As explained above, the rationale underlying the IAAF and International Olympic Committee (IOC) policies is that setting a limit on the levels of androgens would compensate for the 'unfair competitive advantage' of female athletes with hyperandrogenism and would achieve a 'level playing field'. But is this a plausible scenario in elite sports? As I have argued before (Camporesi and Maugeri 2010), singling out and setting a limit on hyperandrogenism from other biological variations that may confer a genetic advantage is, to say the very least, an inconsistent policy: there are plenty of other genetic variations that are not regulated by IAAF and, even though advantageous for athletic performance, are not considered unfair. One famous example is provided by Finnish athlete Eero Mäntyranta, who won two gold meals in cross-country skiing at the 1964 Winter Olympics in Innsbruck. It was later determined that Mäntyranta had primary familial and congenital polycythaemia, a rare genetic mutation characterized by an elevated absolute red blood cell mass and a consequent increase of 25–50 per cent in his blood oxygen carrying capacity (Tucker and Collins 2012). Certainly, such an increase could provide Mäntyranta with a competitive edge.

Cases like Mäntyranta's are hardly rare among elite athletes. Endurance athletes, in particular, have been shown to have mitochondrial variations that increase aerobic capacity and endurance (Ostrander *et al.* 2009). Acromegaly, a hormonal condition resulting in large hands and feet, is especially prevalent among basketball players.[7] There has also been speculation that Michael Phelps, winner of eight gold medals at the 2008 Beijing Summer Olympics, has Marfan syndrome, a rare genetic condition affecting connective tissues that results in long limbs and flexible joints, an obvious advantage for a swimmer.[8] Another example – this time not only speculated – was Flo Hyman, a world-class volleyball player, who had, post-mortem, demonstrated Marfan syndrome, which explains her tall stature and long arms, obviously also giving her an advantage in volleyball (Bostwick and Joyner 2012). In her case, it is also noteworthy that Marfan syndrome also caused aortic dissection, leading to her death during a match. All these examples (and there are many more reviewed in Ostrander *et al.* 2009) show that elite athletes derive advantages from a range of biological variations and hyperandrogenism is no different in this regard. As pointed out by Claire Sullivan:

> The fact is the playing field [in elite sports] has never been level. There will always be genetic variations that provide a competitive edge for some athletes over others. We readily accept the genetic, athletic gifts that elite athletes possess without trying to find ways to 'level the playing field'.
>
> *(Sullivan 2011)*

In addition, even if we accept the premise that hyperandrogenism were to confer a competitive advantage, this would not imply that such an advantage would be unfair. As argued by Hämäläinen (2012): 'It is often implicitly assumed that the concept of advantage is unambiguous and unproblematic; only the parameters of fairness pose a challenge. This seems to be an unwarranted assumption'. Hämäläinen distinguishes between two kinds of 'advantage' in competition: 'performance' and 'property' advantage. The former is a relationship of superiority between performance numbers possessed by different athletes (or teams) and is defined as follows: 'A has a final performance advantage over B if A has a better final performance number than B'. Examples of performance numbers are the number of seconds in which an athlete runs a sprint or the numerical score that is the result of a football match. The latter is defined as 'A has an advantage over B in property X if A has a more favourable amount of this property X than does B', where properties are 'constituent parts of competitors and competition environment' (Hämäläinen 2012). One of the examples of property advantages offered by Hämäläinen is the oxygen-carrying capacity of Finnish cross-country skier Mäntyranta already quoted above. Owing to his genetic condition, Mäntyranta had a property advantage against fellow competitors, which in at least two occasions (the two gold medals won at the Winter Olympics in Innsbruck 1964), and probably many others, contributed to his success but that not necessarily, nor always, nor alone, implies a performance advantage. Following Hämäläinen, we could also say that Caster Semenya may have (under the assumption that a higher level of androgens results in a more athletic body) a property advantage. Even though Hämäläinen does not go on to analyse the distinctions between fair and unfair advantage, it seems that merely possessing a property advantage cannot possibly be classified as 'unfair', because, as we have seen above, that does not necessarily, always or alone result in a performance advantage.

Why, then, is the IAAF policy targeting hyperandrogenism among the genetic and biological variations that confer a property advantage? What about all the other genetic and biological variations that confer an advantage and which might be thought to disrupt the level playing field by IAAF? The fact is that all exceptional biological and genetic variations are considered part of what the elite athlete *is*, and of what makes sports competitions valuable, namely achieving excellence through combination of talent: the natural endowment of the athlete, and dedication: the effort in training and preparation that the athlete puts in to maximize what her talent offers. Consequently, all the biological and genetic variations found in elite athletes are deemed ethically acceptable because we think it is part of the meaning of sports to see individuals (elite athletes) with exceptional physical characteristics push their bodies to the limit to win in competitions and achieve world records.

It seems therefore particularly problematic that the IAAF and IOC policies single out hyperandrogenism from the other biological and genetic variations, the possession of which could also be classified as property advantages (and as such, we argue, not 'unfair'), as being outside the 'ethically acceptable' limits. The current IAAF and IOC policies on hyperandrogenism raise a fundamental issue of consistency and, as Sullivan (2011) has pointed out, they can "open a floodgate for potential opposition on other types of genetic variations such as height, oxygen carrying capacity, and lactate thresholds" (Sullivan 2011, p 414). If one desires consistency to be a fundamental feature of policies impacting on the life prospects and elite careers of many people, the IAAF/IOC guidelines on hyperandrogenism need to put forward a strong rationale for regulation on a plethora of other genetic variations.

The current policies not only raise a problem of consistency but also of discrimination against female athletes with hyperandrogenism. Since the rationale underlying the policies is that they aim to achieve a level playing field by setting an upper limit for a biological molecule that provides a competitive advantage, then the rationale should be applied not exclusively to the female category. Why is a similar threshold not set for male athletes too? Indeed, as the medical historian Vanessa Heggie pointed out:

> What the sex test effectively does, therefore, is provide an upper limit for women's sporting performance; there is a point at which your masculine-style body is declared 'too masculine', and you are disqualified, regardless of your personal gender identity. For men there is no equivalent upper physiological limit – no kind of genetic, or hormonal, or physiological advantage is tested for, even if these would give a 'super masculine' athlete a distinct advantage over the merely very athletic 'normal' male.
>
> *(Heggie 2010: 158)*

Singling out hyperandrogenism from all other genetic and biological variation seems therefore to be unwarranted. For the sake of consistency, either IAAF/IOC would have to ban from competition all athletes who derive a property advantage from biological variations or let everybody who is 'out of the ordinary', compete, Caster Semenya and other athletes with hyperandrogenism included. Thus, the IAAF and IOC policies discriminate against female athletes on a feature of athletic performance that many people think is crucial to athletic competition, which, borrowing from Murray, is both a 'celebration of and a challenge posed by our embodiment' (Murray 2009: 236). By doing so, we could say that they 'dis-embody' female athletes in competition and they not only fail to achieve the ideal of 'fairness' for which they aim but they also deprive female athletes with hyperandrogenism exactly of the possibility 'to test their [bodies'] capabilities and limits, and to integrate them with our will, intellect, and character' (Murray 2009: 237).

The role of biotechnology in the Paralympics

Technology can be understood as a 'human-made means to serve human interests and goals' (Cooper 1995). Elaborating on this definition, Loland (2009) defines sports technology as a human-made means of serving human interests and goals in or related to sport. In this section, I analyse the role of prosthesis technology for Paralympic athletes, considering the case of Oscar Pistorius and its implications for the construction of categories in the Olympics and Paralympics. We all have heard of the controversy surrounding Oscar Pistorius's case but for the purposes of the discussion below it will be important to rehearse some of the early details of his case (see also Camporesi 2008).

Oscar Pistorius was born on 22 November 1986 without fibulae and had both legs amputated below the knee when he was 11 months old. Pistorius runs with the aid of carbon-fibre artificial limbs produced by Icelandic company, Ossur, called 'Cheetahs'. In 2007 (South Africa, then Rome), Pistorius took part in his first international competition for able-bodied athletes. At that time, the IAAF temporarily allowed him to compete with able-bodied athletes, while performing tests on the prosthesis. The IAAF assigned to German Professor Gert-Peter Brüggemann (Director Institute of Biomechanics and Orthopaedics, German Sport University Cologne) the task of monitoring Oscar's performances and analysing the information, which the IAAF would then use as the empirical basis for its decision. According to his study, Pistorius's limbs use 25 per cent less energy than able-bodied athletes to run at the same speed and the prosthetic limbs developed an energy loss of about 9 per cent during the stance phase, compared with 41 per cent in the human ankle joint (Brüggemann *et al.* 2008). Based on these findings, Brüggemann concludes that Oscar is actually performing a '*different kind of locomotion at lower metabolic cost*' [emphasis added]. On the strength of these findings, on 14 January 2008, the IAAF ruled Oscar ineligible for competitions conducted under its rules, including the 2008 Beijing Summer Olympics. In the same year, the IAAF amended its competition rules to ban the use of 'any technical device that incorporates springs, wheels or any other element that provides a user with an advantage over another athlete not using such a device' (rule 144.2). The Federation claimed that the amendment was not specifically aimed at Pistorius.

Pistorius appealed to the Supreme Court of Arbitration for Sport (CAS), in Lausanne (since 1984, the place where international sports dispute are resolved). He travelled to America to take part in a series of further tests carried out at Rice University in Houston by a team of scientists including Hugh Herr and Rodger Kram.[9] In their point-by-point reply to the work by Brüggemann *et al.* (2008) Kram *et al.* (2010) argue that as there are no sufficient data to support the claim that Oscar Pistorius has an advantage, the conclusion should be that he does *not* have an advantage over able-bodied athletes. 'Until recently it would have been preposterous to consider prosthetic limbs to be advantageous, thus, the *burden of proof is on those who claim that running specific prosthesis (RSP) are advantageous*' (Kram *et al.* 2010, emphasis, added).

On the basis of these findings, on 26 May 2008, the CAS in Lausanne reversed the IAAF decision and ruled that Pistorius should be able to compete against Olympic athletes, since the IAAF 'did not prove that claim [of unfair advantage] to a sufficient extent' reference. To note that the verdict is limited only to the use of the specific blades in issue in this appeal (that is, were Pistorius to change the kind of running specific prosthesis he uses, he would have to go through the same testing regimen again). It is therefore a very contextualized decision that cannot be extended to other double amputees, who would also have to undertake the relevant biomechanical tests.

After the appeal to CAS, Pistorius was allowed to compete with able-bodied athletes and he was the first amputee to compete in track events at the Olympics Games in London 2012. To note, Pistorius competed also in the Paralympics in London, as his participation in the Olympics did not exclude him from participation in the Paralympics. It is necessary to contextualise Oscar Pistorius's case within a narrative of other athletes with a 'disability' who have competed in the Olympics. Oscar Pistorius is not the first case of an athlete with an impairment or 'disability' competing in the Olympics (Edwards 2008, Jespersen and McNamee 2008). He is 'only' the first amputee competing in track events at the Games. Other athletes with impairments who have created precedents include: the American George Eyser, who won a gold medal in gymnastics while competing on a wooden leg at the 1904 Games in St. Louis; the kiwi Neroli Fairhall, paraplegic, competed in archery in the 1984 Olympics in Los Angeles; Marla Runyan, a legally blind runner from the United States, competed in the 1500 metres at the 2000 Olympics in Sydney; South African swimmer Natalie du Toit, who in 2008 became the first amputee ever to qualify for the Olympics (Beijing), where she placed 16th in the 10-km 'marathon' swim (Marcellini *et al.* 2011).

Pistorius's case has been framed by the IAAF and the CAS in Lausanne, and by many bioethics scholars, in terms of 'fair vs. unfair advantage', 'disability vs. super-ability'. It had been claimed that the blades gave Pistorius an unfair advantage over the able-bodies athletes and that, on this basis, he should not be allowed to compete with able-bodied athletes (Edwards 2008). A first way to respond to the claim that the blades give Oscar an advantage is to dispute the claim that the blades do, in fact, provide him with an advantage; that is, to question the biomechanics study by Brüggemann *et al.* (2008), as Weyand *et al.* (2009) have done. This may be done by pointing out the fact that the blades also bring some disadvantages, including a slower initial acceleration compared with natural legs and decreased stability and balance compared with a natural leg. Indeed, Oscar faces a slow start, as he needs approximately 30 metres to gain his rhythm and he suffers from an unsure grip in the rain and headwind (Edwards 2008).

Suppose, for the sake of the argument, that the blades do indeed confer Oscar an advantage. If this were the case, would that be sufficient grounds to exclude him from competition? To answer this question requires a consideration of the role and value of biotechnology in elite sports. Burkett, a biomechanist and former Paralympic swimming world champion himself, has written extensively on the value of technology in sports. He argues that technology is in many cases 'essential for performance' in Paralympic sports. (Burkett *et al.* 2011) For example, there are specialised prostheses for athletes who compete in track and field throwing events such shot-put, javelin and discus, or in jumping events. Similarly, there are specialized wheelchairs to enable athletes to compete in the equivalent of rugby, tennis and basketball. All these technologies, while being essential for performance, are also designed as being performance enhancing. The two features seem to be inextricably intertwined. The same happens also with the bikes for elite cycling, which are also designed to enhance performance. The point with performance-enhancing technologies in sport seems to be a problem of standardization of the 'essential for performance-enhancing performance' technology; that is, there needs to be an upper limit or cut-off point (arbitrarily chosen among a series of possible upper limits) for the biotechnology, above which we decide the value of athletic performance, and our admiration for it, are severely impaired by the technology itself (Murray 2009).

In addition, considerations of equity of access to technology for athletes have to be taken into account, as argued by Burkett (2010). It should be noted, though, that neither IAAF nor the World Anti-Doping Agency is concerned about providing 'equity of access' to their athletes in terms for example of access to best coaching or training facilities. Indeed, the reality is that there is a wide disparity among elite athletes in terms of access to coaching and training facilities, and both these factors do make a difference to the overall performance of the athletes. Returning to the question, 'which one of the two conceptualizations ('essential for performance' vs. 'performance enhancing') should prevail in our assessment of the role of biotechnology on our athletic performance, Burkett (2010) argues that, given that a 'grey area' remains regarding how well an athlete is able to transfer any potential mechanical advantage into a real advantage, we should err on the side of the benefit of the doubt. This implies that we should probably favour technology being essential for performance, rather than performance enhancing (Burkett *et al.* 2011) In this sense, Pistorius is an example of a technological hybrid or a 'compound athlete' (Marcellini *et al.* 2011), for which the technology essential for performance becomes part of his embodiment and may also be a way of enhancing his performance. The main problem for evaluating the role of technology, for Burkett, remains the problem of *equity of access* as highlighted above.

It is plausible to speculate that more cases similar to that of Oscar Pistorius will come to the fore at the 2016 Olympics in Rio de Janeiro (for example, Alan Oliveira, Paralympic athlete, ran faster than Oscar Pistorius at the London 2012 Paralympics in both the 100 metres and 200 metres competitions, raising Oscar's anger and talk of unfair advantage and shattering the 100-metres world record at the International Paralympic Committee Grand Prix in Berlin in 2013.[10] Bioethicists in sport need to be proactive and should start reflecting now on the role of technology in the construction of categories in sport, as I highlight in the next and final section of this chapter.

Future directions in bioethics and sport

In this last section, I outline two areas in sport medicine in which I think that ethical reflection could and should contribute in the near future: the role of biotechnology in construction of categories in sport and the shared participatory responsibility in doping.

With regard to biotechnology and the categorization of sport, I have little doubt that there will be other cases like that of Oscar Pistorius and that philosophers of sport and medicine should be proactive in these debates. I agree with Gregor Wolbring that it is necessary to reframe the discourse surrounding Oscar Pistorius's case, if 'one wants to take on the challenge linked to the advances and impacts of new and emerging science and technology on sports' (Wolbring 2008). We have seen above how Oscar Pistorius's situation has been framed as a case of 'unfair advantage' provided by the use of technology. But is there another way to frame that case?

Steven Edwards (2008) has suggested that what Oscar Pistorius does is strictly speaking not running but something closer to '*high-velocity/cadence bounding*'. In other words, he suggests that *prosthetics alter the nature of the activity*. This point is similar to one raised by Brüggemann *et al.*

(2008), who stated that Pistorius performs a *"different kind of locomotion at lower metabolic cost"* and is also similar to the conclusion of the study by Weyand *et al.* in 2009, who performed a biomechanical study on Oscar Pistorius and concluded that:

> Perhaps our most striking result ... is that our amputee subject [Oscar Pistorius] could be simultaneously similar to intact-limb runners physiologically but dissimilar mechanically. Physiological similarity is most likely explained by the reliance of both transtibial amputee and intact-limb runners on the large groups of extensor muscles that act across the hip and knee joints. ... However, *running with lower-limb prostheses might have substantially altered the nature of their activity*'.
>
> *(Weyand* et al. *2009, emphasis added)*

Both biomechanical studies, therefore, hint at the fact that what Oscar Pistorius does may not be running but a different kind of 'locomotion' and that the blades have fundamentally altered the nature of the activity. Indeed, Wolbring points to an alternative classification based on the establishment of a new category for double amputees running on blades (Wolbring, 2012). He notes that Olympics events should be recategorized as follows: a) those based mainly on the biological performance of the athlete (for example, high jump); b) those based or depending mainly on external tools (such as the pole vault, skiing or bobsleigh). In this sense, the role of technology is seen as a demarcation line between the two types of events. Along these lines, one could compare bionic and wheelchair racing with the pole vault and other sports where athletes use external tools to move beyond species-typical functioning while comparing biological racing with the high jump. Since both the high jump and the pole vault are included in the Olympics, the argument goes, we could envisage having both 'high-velocity bounding' and biological running in the Olympics but in two different categories. In other words, going 'beyond species-typical functioning' would not be a reason to exclude amputee athletes from competing in the Olympics. Obviously, one would not allow a person with a pole to compete in the high jump competition but a separate event could be perfectly acceptable and not seen as doping, as all athletes would perform under the same parameters. What would be the defining features of this category of 'high-velocity bounding'? The question to ask becomes: is his movement sufficiently different from running (provided that running is a 'loose' category) to warrant putting in another category? Burkett (2010), already mentioned above for his research on the role and value of technology on athletic performance, also raises the same question in a more recent paper (Burkett *et al.* 2011), where it is observed, after Edwards (2008) and McNamee (2011), that the question: 'Is what Oscar Pistorius does really running?' is not a simple empirical question to be settled by biomechanical analysis alone (although Burkett thinks that biomechanical analysis should play an important role) but is rather a conceptual question, namely, which gaits should be thought of as constituting running? I agree with Burkett *et al.* (2011) that the answer to this question cannot be informed by biomechanics alone and that ethicists need more actively to play a 'creative role' in the construction of categories in sport (Camporesi and Maugeri 2010). This construction cannot be informed by sports science or medicine alone, as questions of fairness in competition inform the categories and demand an ethical reflection.

The second area in sport medicine about which I think there is space for original ethical reflection is an interpretation of the conflict of interest dilemmas highlighted in the first section through the lens of 'unregulated clinical research', which was first applied by King and Robeson (2007) to the context of elite sport and, more recently, in King and robeson (2013) and Camporesi and McNamee (2014), where the analogies between pharmaceutical 'guinea pigs' and athlete 'guinea pigs' were discussed. King and Robeson (2007) were among the first authors to highlight the problematic position of the athlete-patient, situated in a elite sport context where the introduction of performance-enhancing technologies can be regarded, in their own words, drawing a parallel from the clinical context, as 'unregulated clinical research' (King and Robeson 2007). King and Robeson note how well-understood problems in research ethics (such as vulnerability, voluntariness, undue influence, full disclosure, equitable subject selections, conflict of interest) become particularly problematic in elite sports contexts, as opposed to the more typical health, medical and scientific contexts in and through which research is already regulated. I believe that this analogy and critical interpretation of the two contexts can be a particularly useful framework within which to understand the exacerbation of traditional norms of research ethics that are translated to the context of elite sport.

One of the ethical issues that we highlighted in relation to elite sport in (Camporesi and McNamee 2014) as unregulated terrain of experimentation and clinical research, where athletes find themselves to be guinea pigs, is the lack of transparency and accountability in the elite sport context. Following Holm (2007), it can be argued that lifting the ban on doping and putting doping 'under a medical context' would not eliminate doping from elite sport but would lead to a two-tiered system of doping, where two practices would ensue: a) the open use of well-known performance-enhancing drugs, and b) the hidden use of other performance-enhancing methods to preserve a competitive advantage over fellow athletes. In practice, doping behaviours occur under pressure and athletes often feel they have no realistic alternatives to doped participation. This happens because, to maintain a competitive advantage in a system that praises a continuous breaking of records and of improvements, athletes feel that they have to participate in the doping behaviours or they will cease to be competitive. As a consequence, choosing not to participate in doping is possible (that is, there is always the way out of doping by choosing to get out of the system) but is seriously constrained. This alternative becomes extremely costly for the athletes, as in practice it amounts to ceasing being competitive or exiting the profession. On this point, the comment by Alex Zuelle, a former Swiss professional cyclist who rode for the Festina team and who was found positive for erythropoietin in 1998 (what became later known as the 'Festina affair') is particularly insightful:

> Everybody knew that the whole peloton was taking drugs and I had a choice. Either I buckle and go with the trend or I pack it in and go back to my old job as a painter. I regret lying but I couldn't do otherwise.
>
> *(Hamilton and Coyle 2013: 100)*

In light also of the recent doping scandals in the field of elite cycling that have shown that doping is a highly organised enterprise (Hamilton and Coyle 2013), I think it is necessary to broaden the perspective of the moral responsibility in doping, beyond the athletes as the only moral agents on which blame, resentment, indignation and other reactive attitudes can be directed, to include the different stakeholders in elite sports. As Jörg Jaksche, a former professional cyclist from Germany, said in a telephone interview:

> Each new doping scandal follows the same pattern ... When someone is caught, the system acts shocked and upset, declares its absolute rejection of doping and depicts the athlete as a black sheep that deserves to be slaughtered. After that, everything continues like before. But the fact is that they slaughter a scapegoat, not a black sheep, and nobody ever looks at the shepherd's responsibility. I'm talking about those in the higher levels, those who govern the sports and, most importantly, those who provide the money that fuels everything.[11]

For these reasons, an area in which I think bioethicists and sports philosophers should focus is in developing a viable concept of shared participatory responsibility for doping. Atry (2013) attempted a preliminary outline of a theoretical framework for broadening the scope of responsibility in doping behaviours (what he refers to as "participatory ethics"), drawing on Strawson's (2008) relational concept of agency, where moral agents are embedded within the social practice in which they participate. Within that particular social practice, agency is mediated through the practice of responsibility assignment, where we assign responsibility to others by making legitimate demands/claims/expectations on others. These demands/claims/expectations are mediated through "reactive attitudes" such as resentment, indignation, blame, praise and so on, which become the locus of the assignment of responsibility. As argued by Ashkan Atry, 'It seems reasonable to assert that the nature of asymmetries in power relations between individuals (e.g. coercion or manipulation) could significantly affect responsibility-seeking/assigning processes' (Atry 2013: 45–6) and therefore it is plausible to argue that responsibility should shift from athletes exclusively to the entire entourage comprising the sports doctors, the sponsors and the other team members who were the agents of the doping enterprise.

The key problem for ethical reflection is that consideration of 'social groups' or 'collectives' as moral agents are often assumed to be problematic. For this reason, much interdisciplinary work will be necessary to the future development of sport and bioethics scholarship.

Acknowledgments

I acknowledge permission to reprint in this chapter material which first appeared in section (i) of Silvia Camporesi and Michael J. McNamee, 'Is There a Role for Genetic Testing in Sports?' in *eLS*, 15 May. DOI: 10.1002/9780470015902.a0024203.

Notes

1 Atlas Sports Genetics; see www.atlasgene. com (accessed 7 October 2014).
2 Jackie MacMullan, 'Kobe Bryant pushes onward', *ESPN LA*, 7 February 2013. Available online at http://espn.go.com/los-angeles/nba/story/_/id/8924518/kobe-bryant-tries-push-los-angeles-lakers-frustration (accessed 7 October 2014).
3 Madison Park, 'College football player who committed suicide had brain injury', *CNN*, 14 September 2010. Available online at http://edition.cnn.com/2010/HEALTH/09/14/thomas.football.brain/ (accessed 7 October 2014); 'Head injuries in football', *New York Times*, 10 December 2012. Available online at http://topics.nytimes.com/top/reference/timestopics/subjects/f/football/head_injuries/index.html (accessed 7 October 2014).
4 The British Medical Association has campaigned for a ban on all forms of boxing since 1985.
5 Paolo Bandini, 'NFL concussion lawsuits explained', *Guardian*, 29 August 2013. Available online at www.theguardian.com/sport/2013/aug/29/nfl-concussions-lawsuit-explained (accessed 7 October 2014).
6 I acknowledge the intellectual contribution of Paolo Maugeri for this section.
7 Anna Katherine Clemmons, '7 Feet 7 and 360 Pounds, With Bigger Feet Than Shaq's', *New York Times*, 9 January 2008. Available online at www.nytimes.com/2008/01/09/sports/ncaabasketball/09asheville.html (accessed 7 October 2014).
8 Jessica Ryen Doyle, 'Michael Phelps unintentionally raises Marfan syndrome awareness', *Fox News*, 21 August 2008. Available online at www.foxnews.com/story/2008/08/21/michael-phelps-unintentionally-raises-marfan-syndrome-awareness (accessed 7 October 2014).
9 David Epstein, 'Fair or foul? Experts split over whether Pistorius has advantage', Sports Illustrated, 3 August 2012. Available online at www.si.com/more-sports/2012/08/03/oscar-pistorius-london-olympics (accessed 7 October 2014).
10 James Crook, 'Oliveira becomes fastest leg amputee on planet by shattering world record', *Inside the Games*, 15 June 2013. Available online at www.insidethegames.biz/sports/summer/athletics/1014683-

oliveira-becomes-fastest-leg-amputee-on-planet-by-shattering-world-record (accessed 7 October 2014).
11 Claudio Gatti, 'Looking upstream in doping cases', *New York Times*, 15 January 2013. Available online at www.nytimes.com/2013/01/16/sports/cycling/critics-take-a-look-upstream-in-doping-scandals.html?_r=0 (accessed 7 October 2014).

References

Anderson, L. (2008). Contractual obligations and the sharing of confidential health information in sport. *Journal of Medical Ethics*, 34(9): e6.

Atry, A. (2013). *Transforming the Doping Culture: Whose Responsibility, What Responsibility?* [Doctoral thesis] Uppsala: Acta Universitatis Upsaliensis. http://urn.kb.se/resolve?urn=urn:nbn:se:uu:diva-206607 (accessed 7 October 2014).

Berman, Y. and North, K. N. (2010). A gene for speed: the emerging role of a-actinin-3 in muscle metabolism. *Physiology* 25(4):250–9.

Bostwick, J. M. and Joyner, M. J. (2012). The limits of acceptable biological variation in elite athletes: should sex ambiguity be treated differently from other advantageous genetic traits? *Mayo Clinic Proceedings*, 87(6): 508–13.

Brooks, M. A. and Tarini, B. A. (2011). Genetic testing and youth sport. *Journal of the American Medical Association* 305(10): 1033–4.

Brüggemann, G. P., Arampatzis, A., Emrich, F. and Potthast, W. (2008). Biomechanics of double transtibial amputee sprinting using dedicated sprinting prosthesis. *Sports Technology*, 1(4–5): 220–27.

Burkett, B. (2010). Technology in Paralympic sport: performance enhancement or essential for performance? *British Journal of Sports Medicine*, 44: 215–20.

Burkett, B., McNamee, M. J. and Potthast, W. (2011). Shifting boundaries in sports technology and disability: equal rights or unfair advantage in the case of Oscar Pistorius? *Disability and Society*, 26(5): 643–54.

Camporesi, S. (2008). Oscar Pistorius, enhancement and post-humans. *Journal of Medical Ethics*, 34: 639

Camporesi, S. (2013). Bend it like Beckham! The ethics of genetically testing children for athletic potential. *Sport, Ethics and Philosophy*, 7(2): 175–85.

Camporesi, S. and Knuckles, J. A. (2014). Shifting the burden of proof in doping: lessons from environmental sustainability applied to high-performance sport. *Reflective Practice*, 15(1): 106–18.

Camporesi, S. and McNamee, M. J. (2014). Performance enhancement, elite athletes and anti-doping governance: comparing human guinea pigs in pharmaceutical research and professional sports. *Philosophy, Ethics, and Humanities in Medicine*, 9(1): 4. DOI. 10.1186/1747-5341-9-4.

Camporesi, S. and Maugeri, P. (2010). Caster Semenya: sport, categories and the creative role of ethics, *Journal of Medical Ethics*; 36: 378–9.

Caulfield, T. (2011). Predictive or preposterous? The marketing of DTC genetic testing. *Journal of Science Communication* 10(3): 1–6.

Cooper, D. E. (1995). Technology: Liberation or enslavement? *Royal Institute of Philosophy Supplement*, 38: 7–18.

Edwards, S. (2008). Should Oscar Pistorius be excluded from the 2008 Olympic games? *Sport, Ethics and Philosophy*, 2(2): 112–5.

European Society of Human Genetics (2010). Statement of the ESHG on direct-to-consumer genetic testing for health related purposes. *European Journal of Human Genetics* 18:1271–3.

Eynon, N., Ruiz, J. R., Oliveira, R. *et al.* (2011). Genes and elite athletes: a roadmap for future research. *Journal of Physiology* 598(13): 3063–70.

Gandy, S. and DeKosky, S. T. (2012). APOE e4 status and traumatic brain injury on the gridiron or the battlefield. *Science Translational Medicine* 4(134): 134ed4.

Goldberg, D. S. (2009). Concussions, elite sports, and conflicts of interest: why the national football league's current policies are bad for its (players') health. *HEC Forum*, 20(4): 337–55. DOI 10.1007/s10730-008-9079-0.

Hämäläinen, M. (2012). The concept of advantage in sport. *Sport, Ethics and Philosophy*, 6(3): 308–22.

Hamilton, T. and Coyle, D. (2012). *The Secret Race: Inside the Hidden World of the Tour de France*. London: Transworld.

Hecht, A. (2002). Legal and ethical aspects of sports-related concussions: the Merril Hoge story. *Seton Hall Journal of Sport Law* 12: 17–64.

Heggie, V. (2010). Testing sex and gender in sports; reinventing, reimagining and reconstructing histories. *Endeavour*, 34(4): 157–63.

Hoberman, J. M. (1992). *Mortal Engines: The science of performance and the dehumanization of sport*. New York: Free Press.

Holm, S. R. (2007). Doping under medical control: conceptually possible but impossible in the world of professional sports? *Sports, Ethics and Philosophy*, 1(2): 135–45.

Holm, S., McNamee, M. J. and Pigozzi, F. (2011). Ethical practice and sports physician protection: a proposal. *British Journal of Sports Medicine*, 45(15): 1170–3.

International Association for Athletics Federation (2011). *Regulations Governing Eligibility of Females with Hyperandrogenism to Compete in Women's Competition: In force as from 1st May 2011*. Monaco: IAAF.

Jespersen, E. and McNamee, M. (2008). Philosophy, adapted physical activity and dis/ability. *Sport, Ethics and Philosophy*, 2(2): 87–96.

Karkazis, K., Jordan-Young, R., Davis, G. and Camporesi, S. (2012). Out of bounds? A critique of the new policies on hyperandrogenism in elite female athletes. *American Journal of Bioethics*, 12(7): 3–16.

King, N. M., and Robeson, R. (2007). Athlete or guinea pig? Sports and enhancement research. *Studies in Ethics, Law, and Technology*, 1(1): 1941-6008. DOI: 10.2202/1941-6008.1006.

King, N. M., and Robeson, R. (2013). Athletes are guinea pigs. *American Journal of Bioethics*, 13(10): 13–14.

Koboldt, D. C., Steinberg, K. M., Larson, D. E., *et al.* (2013). The next-generation sequencing revolution and its impact on genomics. *Cell*, 155(1): 27–38.

Kram, R., Grabowski, A. M., McGowan, C. P., *et al.* (2010). Counterpoint: Artificial limbs do not make artificially fast running speeds possible. *Journal of Applied Physiology*, 108: 1012–14.

Krumer, A., Shavit, T. and Rosenboim, M. (2011). Why do professional athletes have different time preferences than non-athletes? *Judgment and Decision Making*, 6: 542–51.

Loland, S. (2009). Fairness in sport: an ideal and its consequences. In *Performance Enhancing Technologies in Sports: Ethical, Conceptual, and Scientific Issues*, edited by T. H. Murray, K. J. Maschke and A. A. Wasunna, 175–204. Baltimore, MD: John Hopkins University Press.

Marcellini, A., Fereza, S., Issanchoua, D., *et al.* (2011). Challenging human and sporting boundaries: the case of Oscar Pistorius. *Performance Enhancement and Health*, 1(1): 3–9.

McKee, A. C., Cantu, R. C., Nowinski, C. J., *et al.* (2009). Chronic traumatic encephalopathy in athletes: progressive tauopathy after repetitive head injury. *Journal of Neuropathology and Experimental Neurology* 68(7): 709–35.

McNamee, M. J., Mueller, A., van Hilvoorde, I., *et al.* (2009). Genetic testing and sports medicine ethics. *Sports Medicine* 39(5): 339–44.

McNamee, M. (2011). After Pistorius: Paralympic philosophy and ethics. *Sport, Ethics and Philosophy*, 5(4): 359–61.

McNamee, M. and Partridge, B. (2013). Concussion in sports medicine ethics: policy, epistemic and ethical problems. *American Journal of Bioethics*, 13(10): 15–17.

McNamee, M. and Phillips, N. (2011). Confidentiality, disclosure and doping in sports medicine. *British Journal of Sports Medicine*, 45(3): 174–7.

Murray, T. H. (2009). In search of an ethics of sport: genetic hierarchies, handicappers general, and embodied excellence. In *Performance-enhancing Technologies in Sports*, edited by T. H. Murray, K. J. Maschke and A. A. Wasunna, 225–38. Baltimore, MD: Johns Hopkins University Press.

Nixon, H. L. (1993). Accepting the risks of pain and injury in sport: mediated cultural influences on playing hurt. *Sociology of Sport Journal*, 10(2): 183–96.

Ostrander, E. A., Huson, H. J., Ostrander, G. K. (2009). Genetics of athletic performance. *Annual Review of Genomics and Human Genetics*, 10: 407–29.

Roth, S. M. (2012). Critical overview of applications of genetic testing in sport talent identification. *Recent Patents on DNA and Gene Sequences* 6(3): 247–55.

Rudnik-Schoeneborn, S. (2012). Genetic tests in sports medicine – many studies, little impact. *Genomics, Society and Policy* 8(1): 13–19.

Sandel, M. J. (2009). *The Case Against Perfection*. Harvard University Press.

Savulescu, J. and Foddy, B. (2005). Comment: genetic test available for sports performance. *British Journal of Sports Medicine* 39: 472. DOI: 10.1136/bjsm.2005.017954.

Saulle, M. and Greenwald, B. D. (2012). Chronic traumatic encephalopathy: a review. *Rehabilitation Research and Practice* 2012: 1–9. DOI: 10.1155/2012/816069.

Sherwin, S. (2007). Genetic enhancement, sports and relational autonomy. *Sport, Ethics and Philosophy*, 1(2): 171–80.

Strawson, P. F. (2008). *Freedom and Resentment and Other Essays*. Abingdon: Routledge.

Sullivan, C. (2011). Gender verification and gender policies in elite sport eligibility and 'fair play'. *Journal of Sport and Social Issues*, 35(4): 400–19.

Tucker, R., and Collins, M. (2012). What makes champions? A review of the relative contribution of genes and training to sporting success. *British Journal of Sports Medicine*, 46(8): 555–61.

Weyand, P. G., Bundle, M. W., McGowan, C. P., *et al.* (2009). The fastest runner on artificial legs: different limbs, similar function? *Journal of Applied Physiology*, 107: 903–11.

Wolbring, G. (2008). Oscar Pistorius and the future nature of Olympic, Paralympic and other sports. *SCRIPTed*, 5(1): 139–60.

Wolbring, G. (2012). Paralympians outperforming Olympians: an increasing challenge for Olympism and the Paralympic and Olympic movement. *Sport, Ethics and Philosophy*, 6(2): 251–66.

Yang, N., MacArthur, D.G., Gulbin, J.P., *et al.* (2003). ACTN3 genotype is associated with human elite athletic performance. *American Journal of Human Genetics* 73: 627–31.

7

EASTERN PHILOSOPHY

Jesús Ilundáin-Agurruza and Takayuki Hata

This chapter explores dominant millennial Eastern philosophical traditions and their connection to sport, understood to include games, physical activity, martial arts, and dance.[1] As diverging yet complementary perspectives, they help to interpret and understand sport. To adequately cover these traditions discussion assumes unfamiliarity and centers on main tenets, methodologies, practical applications, and relevance to twenty-first-century sporting concerns.

The first section examines Indian philosophy, introducing basic concepts that thread their way from early Hindu traditions through Buddhism and on to other Asian philosophies. Section two considers China's native Confucianism and Daoism and, briefly, Mahayanistic Chan (禪) Buddhism. Section three looks at Japanese philosophy in Zen (禅) Buddhism and martial arts. The fourth section discusses contemporary Eastern sport philosophy scholarship and future developments. Each historically organized tradition engages two themes that topically ground matters from a sporting perspective: the human body and its cultural role, and the relation between results and process. On account of its foundational role, theoretical explanation predominates in Hinduism, setting the stage for later developments where sport takes center stage.

India's Hinduism and Buddhism – paths of plurality and discipline

India's autochthonous philosophies and religions are Hinduism and Buddhism. Delving into Hinduism is necessary to understand Buddhism's reactionary stance, to grasp Hinduism's subsequent influence of other Asian traditions (through Buddhism), and is worthwhile for its own sake. Idiosyncratically, Hinduism lacks both, an organized institution to keep the faith and a founder. Humans did not write its original sacred texts, classified as *sruti* (what is heard). Rather, these are part of the very fabric of reality. This makes Hinduism inherently philosophical, encouraging a critical dialogue to the best explanation of reality that results in a diversity of *darshanas* (schools of thought).[2] This discussion engages three of its four historical periods, as these present the original ideas that the fourth, the *Scholastic Period* (fifth century CE to present), expounds upon.

The sacred *Vedas* establish the Vedic period (BCE 1500–500), the first Hindu era. Setting out cosmogony and basic moral tenets, these evolve from polytheism toward monotheism and monism. Interestingly, the *Rig Veda* raises the possibility of ignorance concerning ultimate questions: "None knoweth whence creation has arisen;/And whether he has or has not produced it:/He who surveys it in the highest Heaven,/He only knows, or haply he may not know" (Radhakrishnan and Moore 1973: 24), then questions the very existence of the gods in a different hymn (ibid: 34). This skeptic strain remains vibrant throughout Indian thought, and marks the philosophical tenor of the various schools as one of vigorous disputation character-ized by keen logical analysis and refined argumentative techniques. One issue concerns whether fundamental reality is an unchanging singularity or a shifting atomistic multiplicity. Johan Huizinga's *Homo Ludens* echoes this penchant for manifold stances and debates when it examines Vedic literature. After considering the ritualized question-and-answer competitions regarding cosmogony, Huizinga (1955: 107) states, "All we can say of these venerable texts is that in them we find the birth of philosophy ... in sacred play", for in the riddles that typify them "lurks the profoundest wisdom concerning the origins of existence" (ibid: 106). Thus, the playful yet sacred riddle is a methodological tool for soteriological knowledge – a learned way to salvation.

But it is the *Upanishads* – meaning "those who sit in front," disciples sitting next to teachers – that are distinctly philosophical, and provide the overall epistemic context to explain reality and find salvation. They conceptualize the basic tenets of Hindu metaphysics and ethics on which most *darshanas* agree. Ontologically, the *Upanishads* postulate *Brahman*, meaning "to grow," as absolute reality and transcendental ground of being from which everything arises. Its coun-terpart *atman*, means "breath," and refers to our true essence (which different *darshanas* interpret variously). Its nature and relation to *Brahman* – is it the same or different ultimately? – is robustly disputed. Ultimate reality and our nature, as two sides of the same coin for Hinduism, concen-trate philosophical disquisition as to which one should be given priority when seeking to answer both. The skeptical *Kena Upanishad* famously embraces paradox, "It is not understood by those who [say they] understand It./It is understood by those who [say they] understand It not," meaning that this is an inscrutable issue" (Radhakrishnan and Moore 1973: 42).

These disputations are not merely academic. Proper methodology and correct answers have direct relevance to Hindu ethics and our fate. The goal is *moksha,* the blissful liberation from the sufferings of this world – a soteriology This hinges on realizing that a veil of illusion shrouds life, *maya,* and entails an epiphanic realization summed up as *Tat Twam Asi,* "you are that" – *Atman* is *Brahman* (Radhakrishnan and Moore 1973: 67–70), else we remain trapped in *samsara,* the wheel of birth and rebirth. In other words, salvation is a matter of embodied epis-temic insight – existentially and corporeally lived, not merely intellectual – into one's true nature and that of reality, called *prajna*, transcendental wisdom. After millions of lifetimes – Hindu's conception of time is cyclical – *prajna* is realized by observing certain tenets meant to avoid ignorance, *avidya,* regarding the identity of self and reality. *Dharma,* "law" or "truth," the moral order and code to follow (duty) lays out these principles. Its counterpart, *Karma,* refers to the moral law that parallels the natural law of cause and effect. We reap what we sow: good actions result in more goodness in the world and, resulting in good habits, bring *moksha* closer; bad actions mean rebirth in *samsara.* Orthodox schools within Hinduism, *astikas* or "affirmers," embrace these concepts, whereas dissenting ones, *nastikas* or "non-affirmers," reject certain elements. However, all agree on the importance of bodily-lived wisdom.

Excepting divergent views to be discussed below, Hindu orthodox ontology proposes a dynamic mind-body unity at the psychophysical level, and a separate, transcendental Self eligi-ble for *moksha.* Put another way, we find an integrated psyche and soma, and a separate soul. As John Koller explains, the Self, autonomous and independent of this body-mind, is karmi-cally trapped; only release from the body-mind will result in liberation (Kasulis, Ames and Dissanayake 1993: 42–3). The preeminence of the Self established, the fact is that "the lived body-mind is of central importance in every system" (ibid: 43). That is, the mind-body complex becomes an integral part of a corporeal praxis of liberation. Practice in Indian culture is more important than theory, as Frits Staal (1993) points out, unerringly engaging bodily practices that involve *discipline*, e.g., ritual, recitation, chant, dance, and martial arts (ibid: 66). Staal looks in detail at *kalarippayattu*, a southwestern Indian martial art, and gymnastics movements around and on an 11-foot pole, the *malkhamb* (ibid: 73–84), and concludes that these activities are not physical in a Western sense (as subject for the sciences *qua* physical), but that they are capable of indefinite development towards a goal within our reach (ibid: 84).

The *Bhagavad Gita,* a text from the Epic period (BCE 500–300) which embodies the Hindus' sense as a people, is the clearest exponent of discipline. Part of the *Mahabharata*, it parallels the standing of the Gospels within the Bible, endorsing devotion to a personal god. Centered on the concept of *dharma*, it presents Arjuna's plight, a noble warrior remiss to wage war against his kinsmen. *Krishna*, god Vishnu's avatar, incarnates as Arjuna's charioteer to persuade him to wage war. Krishna thus asserts the primacy of doing our duty regardless of consequences: "He who does the task dictated by duty,/Caring nothing/For the fruit of the action,/He is a yogi" (Anonymous 2002: 62). As an uncompromising deontological stance, it rides on the aforementioned realization that all that exists is but an aspect of *Brahman*. It also reflects a dominant Eastern current where consequences and results are less important than acting rightly by fulfilling our duty. Forsaking the win when our duty lies in winning is problematic. As in Kantian ethics, defining duty is a thorny issue: Is running up the score morally permissible? Does this endorse a win-at-any-costs ethos? Whereas the former question is more difficult to address,[3] the latter can be met through the disregard for consequences it upholds. Unlike Kantian ethics, the agent's intentions are not paramount, which simplifies the equation (but elides issues of merit or justice). One reading suggests ignoring how our actions affect others: Arjuna is not supposed to bemoan the killing of his kinsmen; humiliating opponents should not be an issue. More interestingly, the poem's fundamental message emphasizes working "for the work's sake only [and where] desire for the fruits of work must never be your motive" (Anonymous 2002: 40). In other words, it is about detachment from ego and results. This can be interpreted as advocating caring about playing well, in accordance with duty, not just winning (unless the former is reduced to the latter). This is coherent with non-instrumental views of sport that, embracing its internal goods oppose zero-sum stances on competition that make of the game but a means to victory regardless of how it is achieved, i.e., broad internalism and "deep" conventionalism.[4] To inculcate the determination to abide "liberating duty," the *Bhagavad Gita* embraces *yoga*.

Yoga, meaning "yoke" or "union" (overtly of body and mind), is one of six *astika darhsanas* unfolding during the third or *Sutra* period (BCE 300–400 CE). There are four *yogas*: devotion, action, knowledge, and discipline, each a path to salvation. These are matched with the four temperaments of Hindu psychological views, and in turn cohere with the four Hindu life stages, goals, and castes. With an avowedly different purpose, this bodily cultivation of a higher ideal parallels Ancient Greece's own fostering of agonic sport, and predates Western monastic *askesis*, ascetic energy management. As a dualistic philosophy largely congruent with *Samkhya*'s metaphysics, *Yoga* seeks liberation through the realization that *atman* equals *Brahman*. It involves a cosmogonic dualism (not of body and mind): *purusha,* an absolute consciousness that transcends any given self, and *prakitri*, original and primeval matter. However, it still faces the same Cartesian problem regarding interaction between radically incommensurate substances. The *Yoga Sutras of Patanjali*, the formative text, focuses on *prakriti* as embodied consciousness through various methodologies, e.g., meditation and *asanas,* postures.[5] *Prajna's* liberating realization is achieved by learning "how to understand and control the different elements of the human person, both physical and psychical" (Harrison 2013: 66). Beyond successful *dhyana* or meditation, the highest state is *samadhi*, "a pure, "untainted" knowledge, complete in itself," that is not so much ecstasy or trance but calmness (Brannigan 2000: 132). In the West, yogic practices are ubiquitously adapted as meditative techniques, health-promoting activities, or even sporting practices themselves. However, the philosophical background is oftentimes excised, which leads to arguably poorer practices for potential self-reflection.

Given Hinduism's dialogic and critical nature, heterodox *nastikas* sprouted: *Jainism, Carvaka,* and the most influential, Buddhism. Buddhists accept Hindu views on *karma, samsara,* and the need for a moral law, but reject *Brahman/atman*. Buddhist *dharma* differs greatly, casting aside the caste system and embracing non-violence (which the *Jainas* first espoused). The heart of Buddhism is the four noble truths that Siddhartha Gautama, the historical Buddha, inferred after 49 days of fasting meditation: 1) there is *dukkha* – suffering, dependence; 2) *samudhaya* – desire, thirst, longing – causes *dukkha*; 3) But there is *nirvana* – cessation of the self that achieves emancipation from the cycle; 4) *magga* – the eight-fold path, built around ethical conduct, mental discipline, and wisdom – is the way to *nirvana*. To become a Buddha (anyone reaching *nirvana* becomes one) we must realize these truths and follow *magga*. Contrary to lore, this does not entail asceticism. The Buddha propounded the *Middle Way*, moderation in all things with neither austerity nor hedonism. The pursuits of many elite athletes requiring immoderate dedication might seem proscribed. But the tenet is rather adaptable, advising moderation in accordance to one's dispositions and abilities (Aristotle's virtue ethics are analogous). What would be excessive for one runner may be the right amount for another, given her talents and previous training.

Buddhism's goal is to help people exit *samsara*. Hence, it emphasizes personal responsibility: each individual must realize in a lived sense the verity of the four truths and pursue the path. Being an eminently practical system, it largely avoids metaphysics. For Buddha, metaphysical speculation is dangerous, which he compares to being gravely wounded by an arrow, yet trying to determine who shot it, what the person looked like, and so forth, rather than immediately caring for the wound: death will ensue before finding out (Rahula 1974: 14). Likewise, worrying overly about sport ontology is negatively superfluous for the actual practice of sport, what really matters is playing well such that our ego does not get in the way of the playing itself.

Nevertheless, Buddhism has three key metaphysical elements. The already discussed *avidya*: ignorance as constitutive of the world *as* experienced. Following Hindu soteriology, it postulates that ignorance keeps us in *samsara*. But, whereas the former's ignorance was concerned with the metaphysical constitution of self/reality, for Buddhism this is strictly ethical, pertaining to the nature of suffering and desire. The second is *anatman* or *anatta*, no self (which the *Carvaka* also deny). Our attachment to the idea of an enduring self and attendant psychological 'needs' account for our misery. For Buddhism, five aggregates constitute what we call 'self,' but, ultimately, there is no permanent substance or eternal soul. However, Buddhism is not nihilistic either. It simply neither asserts that nothing exists, nor proclaims the existence of an eternal self (Koller 1993: 51). Instead of substances, it postulates processes of experience analyzed phenomenologically under the aegis of *dependent origination* (all phenomena are interrelated and affect one another).[6] As Victoria Harrison (2013) points out, it is more accurate to think of a no-abiding self,[7] and that the real insight is to realize the causal chains at play in the creation of the 'self' (ibid: 94–5). In the end, the 'self' is constantly changing. Change, *anicca* or *anitya* as the impermanence of things, is the third tenet. There is no being only becoming. Because this entails change in terms of causal chains, the way to handle it is to stop the cause. Realizing that nothing lasts is a vital path towards right understanding and liberation.[8] This can be seen positively as generative change, where the body is not a dualistic entity but rather a holistic, "creative, unified and continuous process of becoming" as Koller argues (Koller 1993: 52). Phenomenological accounts of the body, such as Merleau-Ponty's (1964) or Maxine Sheets-Johnstone's (2011), are amenable to this framework. Later traditions refine and build on this triad, devising corporeal mindfulness practices – beyond intellectualism – to inculcating insights as incarnate experiences. The irony is that mindfulness, a method to shed desires and ego, is used in sport for ego-centered outcomes that strengthen the athlete's sense of self. As with yoga, excision of the philosophical context often means limited, absent, or even negative self-growth. However, while Western sport could embrace self-knowledge as sporting Socratic path, the East could learn better to appreciate athletic excellence.

Eventually, Buddhism split into two schools that basically agree on the fundamentals presented above. The *Theravada* (Eldest) school spread throughout South East Asia, positing as ideals wisdom and the *arhat*, an individual who, having broken the cycle of *samsara*, will not be reborn. The *Mahayana* (Great Vehicle) school's ideals are compassion and the *boddhisattva*, an enlightened person who chooses to remain to release all other sentient beings. Dispersing to China first, the next waypoint, Buddhism, subsequently arrived in Japan.

China's Confucianism, Daoism, and Chan Buddhism – *The* way toward harmonious community and self

China boasts three formative philosophies: native Confucianism and Daoism, and Buddhism,[9] which Bodhidharma brought in the 6th century CE. Three notions vital to understanding Chinese culture are its pragmatic character, the importance of social harmony, and *Dao* (道) as *arché* for cosmological understanding of reality and organizing principle for a life in harmony with nature.

Kongzi (孔子) (BCE 551–479), the Latinized version being Confucius, was a literati or scholar who reinterpreted tradition. Confucianism can be said to predate him in the sense that core ideas he writes about precede him. As he put it, "I transmit but do not innovate. I believe in and love the ancients" (Confucius 1979: VII.1).[10] But, as Fung Yu-Lan (1976: 40) writes, "while transmitting the traditional institution and ideas, [he] gave them interpretations derived from his own moral concepts". Kongzi's contribution is so powerfully creative and invigorating that his *Rujia* school is *the* referent point for later Chinese philosophy and beyond: contemporary East Asian views on community, where family comes first, are Confucian. The two guiding issues are the right way to live and right government. Thus, Kongzi embraces ethics and politics with the goal to redress what he perceives as degeneration in Chinese society by promoting harmony in people's lives and government as people's caring steward. Moreover, as Chan Wing-Tsit (Chan 1963: 15) puts it, "he believed in the perfectibility of all men". Crucially, Kongzi seeks to perfect his countrymen through a *virtuous* education.

While *Dao* stands as the ultimate guiding principle, *de* (德), often translated as virtue, but also meant to capture the *power* of the Way of things or *Dao*, is the keystone of his ethical and political views. For Kongzi, the way to the good life is through the cultivation of a virtuous character. In fact, this emphasis on cultivating oneself (*xiushen*, 修身) becomes a central feature of Chinese (and Japanese) culture. The *junzi* (君子) embodies this virtue; he is the superior man. Originally designating noble birth, Kongzi reinterprets it to refer to men who earn such honorific through actions and character.[11] It is limited to men; traditional Chinese society is patriarchal. The most critical amendment is to make the Confucian system gender inclusive.[12] *Junzi* is achieved through a set of virtues. Six stand out, of which three are key.

Foremost is *ren* (仁).[13] Rich in meanings, it is variously translated as humaneness, love, kindness, benevolence, compassion, and human-heartedness. As Van Norden (2011: 40) points out, it is composed of the character for person *ren* (人) (which is appositely a homophone) and that of 'two' *liang* (两), "suggesting this is a virtue manifested in relationships between people." This clearly underscores a strong communitarian facet. More apposite, *ren* refers to a holistic view of the person that amalgamates rational, aesthetic, moral and religious dimensions through the lived body, hence denoting "a psychosomatology," as Roger Ames (1993: 159–60) highlights. Next is *yi* (義), righteousness or justice, which for Kongzi means doing what ought to be done regardless of consequences; whether we succeed or not should not matter.[14] Similar to the view discussed in the *Bhagavad Gita*, it importantly differs in emphasizing intentions and not results (out of our control). *Li* (礼) refers to propriety, rites and rituals, which are the repository and source of the previous two virtues, and therefore essential for a harmonious society.[15] Ames (1993: 148) observes that such ritual practices never detached from the physical body shape and are shaped by the community (body, *ti* (体), and ritual *li* are cognates). That is, *Li* formalizes *ren*'s psychosomatic dispositions (ibid: 160). The other virtues are courage to follow through with what is right,[16] sincerity to elicit trust, and wisdom to ascertain the latter.[17] This is fertile ground to reflect on sport.

The community-minded element is primordial, as the virtues must add up to a better life under the aegis of a harmonious society. This is crucial for sports, overtly team sports but also more individualistic sports. Both entail committed, caring, sincere, and generous relationships among team members, fellow athletes, coaches, management, and supporting constituencies. These virtues are at the heart of flourishing, long-lived sport programs able to face success without hubris and adversity *sans* resentment. Crucially, this also applies to competitors and is evidenced in the etymology since "competition" is *com* + *petere*, Latin for "strive + together" (Hyland 2001: 81). Mirroring *ren*'s structural dynamics, it also implies a common social under-taking. This extends to sport's very ontological and ethical structure. As a practice, sport is inherently a social undertaking whose formal structure of constitutive rules and normative architecture correlate directly with *li*'s intrinsic respect for the tradition as it is corporeally formalized. This implies observance of said rules and internal goods.

Staying with the subject of community, for Kongzi virtue is possible only within a commu-nal context whose center is the family. He advocates a view where proper familial relationships based on filial piety dominate.[18] *Ren* in its full sense is a socially compassionate virtue that is physically cultivated and results in a communitarian vein. Communitarian philosophers echo this, in contrast with Western liberal and democratic ideals. They quarrel on the preeminence of justice as impartial for the latter, or the standards of excellence furbished by a community the former. In sport philosophy, this plays out between libertarian consequentialists, e.g., Claudio Tamburrini and Tännsjö Torbjörn (2005) who, building on John Rawls (1971), prize autonomy above all to the point of endorsing genetic enhancement, and those who critically readapt Alasdair MacIntyre's (1984) work, *pace* Michael McNamee (2008), who embraces a virtue-theoretic account that amends MacIntyre (particularly his anti-institutionalism), arguing that individuals must observe certain standards even when sporting results suffer.[19]

If Confucianism puts self-cultivation on the agenda as a sociopolitical affair, it is Daoism that makes of it an art of living.[20] The three Daoist sages are Laozi (老子), contemporary of Kongzi, Liezi (列子), who lived between the former two, and Chuang Tzu (庄子) (BCE 369–286). A crucial aspect of this enormously influential school is its focus on practical, enacted, "know-how" knowledge (even more than Confucians), rather than theoretical, propositional, "know that" knowledge. Epistemically, these two cognitive modes are irreconcilable, since the former cannot be fully reduced to a set of propositions, as anyone who has tried to teach how to ride a bicycle can avow. The wisdom to live a sagely fulfilling life is not found in logical and propo-sitional reasoning. For Chinese philosophers, and Daoists especially, what is characteristic is "the insistence that knowledge of the most important matters is, properly analyzed, of the former [practical], not the latter kind [propositional]" (Cooper 2003: 63–4). This is connected to their belief that the *Dao* (道) is ineffable, as the famous opening lines of Laozi's *Dao De Jing* (道德經) make clear, "The *Tao* (道) that can be told is not the eternal *Tao*; the name that can be named is not the eternal name" (Chan 1963: 139). Hence, the deeper teaching about *Dao*, and how to live in harmony with(in) it must be without words. The implication is that this knowledge must take place through corporeal practice as we live harmoniously in the midst of things: "such harmony is located within the individual [and is] sought both in the body and the emotions" (Harrison 2013: 134). This brings the analysis to self-cultivation and Chinese conceptions of the body that can be used to analyze sporting bodies.

It is telling that *xin* (心) refers to both heart and mind. For the Chinese, there is a psychosomatic unity of body and mind where reason and emotion are attuned in the best cases. Tu Weiming explains that self-cultivation "involves the full recognition that the body is the proper home for self-realization" (Tu 2004: 9). Martial arts and sports are privileged practices for such self-realization. Of the several ways in which the Chinese conceptualized the body, two are relevant: *shen* (身) denotes a lived body rather than a mere object,[21] and has the connotation of a self, and *xing* (形) refers to the form or shape of the body as a process, illustrated with the *yin/yang* (陰陽) dynamics, where it can only be understood by reference to the intellect (Ames 1993: 160–5). The former is pertinent for kinesthetic and phenomenological accounts, while the latter pertains to technical implementation of dynamic tactics the way a tennis player plans and executes shots, or techniques used by an archer for body relaxation and mind-quieting before releasing the arrow. For Ames these coalesce most meaningfully around *li* because it provides order and allows formalizing natural processes as rules of conduct where "integration represented by physical efficacy is a characteristic of the consummating person" (Ames 1993: 167). This aim is to become a refined person of polished mind-body. In contrast to Confucians, who work hard on polishing their character thus, the Daoists seek to work on themselves effortlessly.

This effortlessness is *wuwei* (無為), a doing without doing or effortless action that takes place spontaneously, paradoxical as that sounds. Also conceptualized as *weiwuwei* (為無為), doing without doing, it encourages us to allow things to take their natural course. Put differently, we act spontaneously. To echo Chuang Tzu, we are to wander freely and at ease in the midst of things (Chuang Tzu and Watson 1968: 29). If an athlete trains too hard, going beyond what his body can handle, he will become overtrained. His performance, health (injury is more likely), and emotional wellbeing will suffer. On the other side, an athlete who does not force the issue and trains listening to her body, pushing when she feels strong or holding back and resting when tired, will become stronger, healthier, and more wholesome. Chuang Tzu and Liezi embrace an enactive model of skill development in terms of superior states that mark achievement. To exemplify this with one story found in the *Liezi*,[22] where Liezi himself is a character:

> Lieh Tzu learned archery and, when he was able to hit the target, he asked the opinion of Kuan Yin Tzu [関尹子] on his shooting. "Do you know *why* you hit the target?" Said Kuan Yin Tzu. "No, I do not," was the reply. "Then you are not good enough yet," rejoined Kuan Yin Tzu. Lieh Tzu withdrew and practiced for three years after which again presented himself. Kuan Yin Tzu asked as before: "Do you know *why* you hit the target?" "Yes," said Lieh Tzu, "I do." "In that case all is well. Hold that knowledge fast, and do not let it slip."
>
> *(Lao-Tzu et al. 2013: 201)*

Liezi explains that we must seek the harmony of the body within, and determine the causal process that makes us hit the target. This principle applies to life generally, and even government (Lao-Tzu *et al.* 2013: 201–2). In other words, we must know the reasons for our actions. Why do we compete? Is it for fame, gold, or because we enjoy the activity? Unless we find out the true motivations – and some reasons are better than others – the activity is worthless. In these cases, the activities are bodily practices that are supposed to lead to an insight about our inner motivations, values, and reasons for acting. Eventually, a deeper understanding may result that for some could lead to enlightenment. This can be gradual, or sudden, as *Chan* Buddhism propounds.

Chan Buddhism grows in China from India's *Dhyana* tradition (it means 'meditation'), where the Chinese optimistic character transforms it. In the Middle Kingdom, much as Buddhism split earlier into two factions, there is a schism after the fifth Patriarch's choice of Hui Neng (惠能) as his successor over his foremost disciple Shen Hsiu (神秀). The former's Southern School emphasizes finding our original face, or true nature. It means that we realize how Buddha-nature resides in all things, thus erasing the boundary between self and non-self. Also known as the sudden enlightenment school, it supported the idea that one could reach *prajna* suddenly and at any point in life. The Northern School embraced a slow process of cultivation and revelation.[23]

Ultimately, both schools seek the realization of our unity with the universe, which results in true freedom to live. Whether this realization is sudden or a protracted process is largely academic. In the end, Buddhist views of self and attachment prove crucial to literally let go of any self-concerns. Enlightenment, salvation, *prajna*, or deep insight need to be lived and are a matter of praxis. Intellectually grasping the four noble truths or the unreality of the self (akin to accurate arrow shooting) is not sufficient when an Olympic medal is at stake yet ignorance as to the deeper 'why' of shooting the arrow prevails. Only truly selfless shooting will do. Reaching this state requires actual practice. Which practices and methodologies are most fruitful is explored next alongside Japanese samurai.

Japan's Zen Buddhism and *do* – ways of life and self-cultivation

Historically, Shinto (神道), Confucianism, and Buddhism share different aspects of Japanese cultural life. Shinto, the native religion, addresses practical aspects such as weddings, fertility, and births, and prescribes belief in *Kami* (神), sacred spirits that may dwell in natural phenomena (wind, rain, mountains, trees). Humans become *Kami* after death. Confucianism was particularly influential for the nobility and educated classes, and largely dictated political views, social mores, and ethical education. In the twentieth century, Watsuji Tetsuro's (1996) ethics blend Confucian, Buddhist and Western ideas as he develops the idea of *ningen* (人間) – "in between-ness of human beings" where "ethics prevails" (Watsuji 1996: 10–12). For him, we are defined *in* our relations with others much as sport establishes a dialectical relation among athletes, officials, and public. But as Heisig, Kasulis and Maraldo (2011: 43) write, "Buddhism has been the most influential in shaping how the Japanese have thought about the most difficult and universal questions of human existence". It also engages in intense, deep philosophical examination and debate. Integrating a Daoist temperament without transcendental metaphysics or Indian detachment, Japanese Buddhism developed into many different schools: Nichiren (日蓮), Pure Land, Shingon (真言), Tendai (天台) and, the most influential, Zen. Such plethora speaks more to different methodologies and favored sacred texts than to radical disagreement on basic tenets. Following Mahayanistic doctrine, all seek universal salvation, a departure from the original Indian view where *nirvana* comes individually and *eventually* after millions of lifecycles (Koller 2011: 45). For the Japanese, the body plays a crucial role in this process.

Kukai (空海) (774–835 CE), Shingon school founder and philosopher extraordinaire, writes that we realize "Buddhahood in *this* very body" (Staal 2011: 60; authors' italics), echoing *Chan* Buddhist views (Chan 1963: 428). Much as Buddhism is given a Japanese imprimatur, the views on the body and its role in the soteriological process are also amended. Paralleling Chinese views, there is also a complex Japanese somatic taxonomy. It eschews ontological categories for functional terms that reflect actual corporeal worldly inter*actions*. In addition to the idea of a balanced heart-mind, *shin* (心), some of those apposite for our purposes are: *shinshin* (心身), an integrated mind-body (the homophonous words refer to 'mind' and 'body,' hence the different kanji), *karada* (体) the Greek *soma* or anatomical body, and *shintai* (身体), the human lived body as acting. This level of discrimination makes clear the importance of and rich contexts and varied methodologies regarding the body in Japan.

Soto Zen (曹洞禅) patriarch Dogen's (道元) methodology (1200–1253 CE) entails seated meditation, *zazen* (座禅 or 坐禅), about which he writes, "sitting meditation is the molting of body-mind. It is not burning incense, worshipping [Buddha 仏陀]. It is only sitting [*shikan-taza*]" (只管打坐) (Yuasa 1987: 117–18). As Kasulis contrasts, Western approaches emphasize metaphysics, the problem of mind–body interaction, and assume their relation as fixed, but for the Japanese the issue is, "how the mind-body complex works and develops … the assumption [is] that the mind-body complex is capable of increasing levels of integration" (Kasulis 1993: 298). Yuasa Yasuo echoes this, combining classic Buddhist and twentieth-century Japanese views into an intricate and refined theory of the body (Yuasa 1993: 63–4).[24] The integration of a novice tennis player is far less developed than that of a Grand Slam winner like Rafael Nadal. To paraphrase and adapt to sport Kasulis question: isn't the Western philosopher's assumption strange, that the way in which mind and body are related is the same in both tennis players? (ibid.). Accordingly, Yuasa explains how in Japan the integrated mind-body, which at its most refined level is called *shinshin ichinyo* (心身一如), oneness of mind and body, paradoxically but efficaciously, uses discipline to instill the sort of spontaneity that leads to exceptional execution (Yuasa 1987: 200).[25] This unified mind-body is something to be refined and cultivated, mirroring the soteriological themes found in India and China.

Enlightenment is not intellectual; it is the integrated mind-body that is enlightened. Kasulis clarifies, "enlightenment establishes a profound relation between the self and world, a relation with both mental and physical dimensions" (Kasulis 1993: 303). The notion of enlightenment varies, as does the integration, depending on the school. It may be identification with *busshin* (仏心), or 'Buddha mind,' *sunyata* (Japanese *ku* "空") or "emptiness," or *muga* (無我) "no-self." These share a common thrust toward selflessness, differences being doctrinal nuances. For Nishida Kitaro, Japan's foremost twentieth-century philosopher and Kyoto school founder, mu (無), nothingness, suitably constitutes the hub of the matter (to echo Laozi's dictum that the emptiness of the wheel's hub is what makes it useful). Abe (1987: 46) finds that, for Nishida, "at the end of true Self, the Self attained nothingness or selflessness". When this happens concern for victory or defeat disappears, and the activity, which Nishida viewed as action-intuition takes over. This action-intuition deepens and enlarges our state of pure experience (a concept derived from William's James view of pure experience), and becomes a unifying activity (Nishida 1990: 32). Yuasa (1987: 200) calls this "pure action," and often results in better performances. The body is pivotal: Nishida asserts that "the self without the body would be just a ghost" (Nishida 1990: 192 fn. 24). Through our acting body, we become the activity and the activity becomes us the way two opposing teams become one unity of action the moment they engage each other. This acting unification does not happen by accident.

Uniquely, Japanese scholars bring together previous insights on body and practice under an explicit, formalized system that is both social and personal. It entails a multiplicity of practices, *do*, ways of cultivation, such as traditional martial arts, Zen garden design, or *sado* (茶道), the way of tea. Structurally the process is identical, the aim being progressive refinement of our abilities and cultivation of self-awareness through selfless dedication to the task at hand. Ideally, it is a lifelong undertaking called *shugyo* (修行), which originates in Buddhist practice. Inextricably intertwined with somatic processes, it requires long-term dedication and discipline to develop our talents. Each *do* has methodological particularities that amount to different paths to the same ultimate goal. That is, the process of corporeal self-cultivation is tailored. Some involve quiet meditation, others movement, and others coordination with a partner or tools. And yet, in its own way, when successful, each is not simply a means or merely a path, but an end, a destination. Kasulis (1993: 308) points out, regarding Kukai (空海), Dogen, and others, how praxis in this context "is not simply the path to enlightenment, but it is enlightenment itself."

Zen, Suzuki Daisetz explains, is "the Chinese way of responding to Indian thought as represented by Buddhism" (Suzuki 1993: 42). Because it fittingly brings together much of the preceding, only its unique features are highlighted, presented in the contexts of martial arts and contrasted with Western sport. Just as martial arts and sports take place in the concrete moment of animate action, "the truth of Zen really lies in the concrete things of our daily life," according to Suzuki (1964: 83). This is not tantamount to merely savoring more the wine. The experience of elusive *satori* – a new perspective that changes how we view the world – requires unrelenting discipline (ibid: 95). Moreover, it needs to be reenacted, analogously to competitive sport where we are only as good as our latest performance. The centuries old Japanese framework is designed to propitiate reoccurrence. Suzuki writes regarding masters' unorthodox methods that they "were designed to create in their disciples a state of mind which would more systematically open the way to enlightenment" (ibid.) *Do*, having developed alongside Zen, are such methods, some of which begin with the samurai (those who serve), who were originally *Bushi* (武士): warriors.

In Zen, Masters' injunctions are meant to fit the pupils' state of readiness to attain insight, and much as a *koan* (公案) riddle was designed for a particular disciple originally (later used as heuristic tool for other students), in martial *do sensei* (先生) or masters, as good coaches should do, fit teachings to individuals. Eugen Herrigel's account of his apprenticeship under Awa Kenzo in *kyudo* (弓道), the way of archery, is famed. It relates his six-year spiritual pilgrimage through bodily practice. Noticing Herrigel's strained ways, Awa's first instruction was on breath control (Herrigel 1989: 18–19). Awa writes, "In the beginning if you forget about focusing on your breath, you will easily lose concentration. Always keep your breath in your center" (Stevens 2007: 41). Breathing is a vital element in the process of realizing self-awakening in Eastern praxes. Sekida Katsuki extensively discusses breathing in his methodological and philosophical Zen treatise (Sekida 1985: 47–82). Hardest for Westerners generally is to realize that one shoots the arrow or runs the track with no thought of target or finish line *per se*. When Herrigel tries to come to grips with the idea that the arrow must shoot itself, he contends that he *is* ultimately aiming to hit the target. Awa tersely replies: "The right art is purposeless, aimless!" (Herrigel 1989: 31) For Suzuki, *satori* is an epiphany that comes at the end of our wits (Suzuki 1964: 60). Herrigel's path was marked by much vexation before the arrow finally shot itself (which is but another beginning) (Herrigel 1989: 60). What had to be taught through practice, being ineffable, was the lived experience of egoless performance called *mushin* (無心): no-mind. Buddhist monk Takuan Soho's lengthy letter to consummate *samurai sensei* (侍) Yagyu Munenori (he once killed six enemy samurai bent on slaying his lord) is a short treatise on *mushin* (Takuan 1986).[26] Contrary to superficial readings of it, *mushin* is anything but a mindless or passive state. Harking back to Buddhist *anatman*, it is a matter of a self that does not abide or rest anywhere (ibid: 21). In other words, we are completely focused yet our attention does not get caught up at any moment. Abiding in fear of missing the target, being cut by the opponent, or simply losing, makes the mind stop. This is the confused mind that freezes, deliberating when it should not; the right mind "does not remain in one place [it] stretches throughout the entire body and self" (ibid: 32). Of course, this does not imply that swordmasters are as accomplished spiritually as master Buddhist monks or the reverse, but in their own way they sport unparalleled mind–body integration. *Mushin* is sometimes associated with flow and other peak performance states, vernacularly referred to as "being in the zone." But whereas *do* are geared specifically to elicit it, in Western sports, particularly competitive or highly skilled manifestations more likely to result in flow moments, it is incidental and accidental to the objective of the sport, irrespective of its outcomes. Additionally, there are phenomenological differences between the two experiences due to the cultural and philosophical framework (Krein and Ilundáin 2014). There are other differences between Eastern martial arts and Western sports.

The West is wont to rely on psychological techniques, neuroimaging, and abundant verbal instruction; a top to bottom, mind to body approach (with a mixed record). Its training methodology also "aims at developing the body's capacity, or more specifically, the motor capacity of muscles in the four limbs … and does not include the spiritual meaning of training the mind's capacity (Yuasa 1993: 32). In the East, this is carried out through diligent and arduous repetitive training: the swordsman performs thousands of cuts. As Suzuki (1993: 121) and Takuan (1986: 25) point out, physical training, *keiko* (稽古), refines technique, and is necessary but not sufficient. The goal is not killing, hitting the target, or winning, but *shugyo:* "to advance in the study of the Way (Tao)" (Suzuki 1993: 132), because what needs to be 'killed' is the ego (ibid: 134). Obviously, the West embraces the training facet; for example, top swimmers do hundreds of laps a day, but, in the West, the "mental aspect" stops with the improved performance understood as result, while process, flow states, or self-knowledge are ancillary or ignored. *Do* beg to differ: results are anecdotal while integrated psychophysical state and self-awakening are primary (which come in different degrees depending on mastery level). Whether it works better or worse than the Western approach is beside the point, neither success nor a *satori*-like epiphany are assured. From a different perspective yet, this pertains to the process versus results entente. Traditional Japanese ways clearly side with the former.

Another difference between Eastern *do* practitioners and Western sportspersons concerns the former's goal – tied to *mushin* – of emotional temperance: "a master of the *bushi* way, like an accomplished Zen Meditator, is a human being who is not swayed by his or her emotions and can control them" (Yuasa 1993: 33). For sportspersons emotional control is subsidiary to performance. Sometimes losing one's control, a common occurrence for many professional athletes, results in pursuing victory through referee intimidation, unsettling opponents, or plain cheating (which just does not happen in *traditional* martial arts). Additionally, *shugyo* aims at education in the sense of bringing out the best, and the rich framework of Zen and *do* help inculcate the ethical and existential truths of Japanese culture. For Robert Carter, there is nothing like this in the West, although some such truths "are found in sports, as in the values called sportsmanship, or being a team player … but Westerners do not engage in sports to achieve spiritual self-transformation" (Carter 2008: 4). In this way, the Japanese stance is not aligned with predominant Western practices in high-performance sport or with instrumental uses of sport or physical activity as exclusively means toward health, entertainment, or financial gain.

Nonetheless, and while prevalent sportive mores warrant this assessment, there are meaningful exceptions where athletes engage in the sort of reflective exercise that results in comparable existential insights. Pace runner and writer George Sheehan's (1978) account of running's transformative power, world-class sailor Ellen MacArthur's (2005) account of her circumnavigation, ripe with keen and candid reflections, and philosopher-triathlete Richard Lally's (2012) essay on Dewey and self-cultivation through endurance sport that interweaves his experiences and philosophy. Sport is not structurally and conceptually condemned to existential opacity and epistemic self-ignorance. The *potential* for *satori*-like Socratic epiphanies is common to both *do* and sport. This process of cultivation instills an autotelic enjoyment of whichever activity we are engaged in, as it emphasizes process and living the present moment intensely (rather than extrinsic outcomes that so tempt people, whether these be money, fame, power, or simply self-satisfaction). Abe (1986: 48) has conciliatory words and a path to resolution. He states how sport can share in a *mushin*-like state if the emphasis is put on "the process of sports participation rather than mere victory". These are pillars on which philosophical stances that appreciate internal goods and communitarian values can build bridges.

Contemporary sport philosophy – present and future routes

One of the first Western sport philosophers to genuinely incorporate Eastern philosophy was Spencer Wertz, who considered the inner awareness of sport in the context of Zen Buddhism and Yoga (1977).[27] Drew Hyland (1990: 77–84) also discussed Zen Buddhism, though more perfunctorily and skeptical of its claims and applicability with regard to peak experiences. There is a dearth of sport philosophy scholarship by Indian scholars in Western academic journals. In China the discipline begins in 1976 in Taiwan and 1981 in the Mainland (Hsu 2010: 239, 245), but there is scant work in English. Leo Hsu is the most prolific Taiwanese sport philosopher in English, having written especially on the Olympics (Hsu 2008, 2009). Japan saw the philosophy of physical education predate the development of sport philosophy (Hata and Sekine 2010: 216). A group of academics created a section for sport philosophy in 1955 under the auspices of the Japan Society of Health and Physical Education. In 1978, the Japan Society for the Philosophy of Sport and Physical Education was founded (ibid: 218).

The following gives a concise but representative account of the fertile academic landscape in Japanese sport philosophy. Given the stimulus of the 1964 Tokyo Olympic Games, the topic of the Olympics is popular among Japanese philosophers, among whom Masumoto's (1998, 2004) work stands out. The body has received attention as well, with Takizawa's (2006) phenomenological and comparative writings, Yamaguchi's (2003) work on freedom and the human body, and Ishigaki's (1995) elucidation of sympathy. Relatedly, Endo (2005) considers physical education kinesthetically. Sekine and Hata (2004) have also examined the issue of doping. With regard to martial arts, and in addition to the aforementioned Abe Shinobu, Fukasawa (2014) has written a comparative essay on Nishida, empathy, and martial arts, while Oda and Kondo (2014) highlight the role of *zanshin* (残心) in *kendo* (剣道) for its unique emphasis on the spirit in which action is performed.

In terms of future developments, five themes to which Eastern philosophy can insightfully contribute stand out: 1) Gender studies, always contentious in a historically patriarchal culture. Kondo (1997) pioneered a philosophical assessment of them in Japan when he considered gender verification, and Takemura (2014) critically evaluates predominant sociological and anthropological studies while outlining key issues and making a case for philosophical inquiry. Similar studies on sport and gender in India and China would be ground-breaking. 2) A philosophical area that is burgeoning concerns the philosophies and sciences of the mind, which have taken a keen interest in the intersection between consciousness and mindfulness techniques. Eastern views of consciousness from all three traditions, grounded in psychophysical integration and passive and active meditative practices, as shown above, are ripe with potential revelations. 3) In this regard, whereas the West looks at average participants, the East focuses on elite performers (Yuasa 1993: 63–4). An East/West comparative and interdisciplinary study of high-performance sportspeople and superb *do* practitioners is long due. 4) Environmental studies can also greatly benefit from the unique contribution that an Eastern outlook can make from the perspectives of ethics and aesthetics. Engaging their traditional philosophies, which erase the boundary between self and other, and coupled to sporting activities' affordance of unique experiences provides critical stances from which to challenge current practices and generate a sense of stewardship toward the environment. And 5) genetic enhancement and transhumanism tantalize us and tempt us to overcome our sense of finitude and limitation. To this technological "shortcut" toward perfectionism Eastern views on the body, which view it not as property but connect it to a community, provide a sense of self and apposite duties and privileges that counterbalance the Promethean impetus.

Undeniably, Indian, Chinese, and Japanese philosophies bring alternative, unique, and insightful perspectives to sport and life. The dialogue on sport philosophy between East and West is just beginning.

Notes

1 Staying clear of polemics, we acknowledge the artificiality of specifically determining what is Eastern philosophy. Operant criteria are: a) conciseness; b) the fact that Indian and Sinitic cultures are formative for other Asian/Eastern philosophies; and c) Japan's rich philosophical engagement with sport (as it intersects the martial arts).
2 Instead of using diacritical Sanskrit marks to accent correct pronunciation, we approximate the latter by replacing them with the closest English phonetic equivalent.
3 By virtue of its very specificity. Nicholas Dixon's distinction between a strong and weak humiliation in "On Sportsmanship and 'Running Up the Score'" is insightful.
4 See the chapters on "Internalism" and "Conventionalism" in this volume. For original essays, see William Morgan (2012), John Russell (2007), Robert Simon (2007), and Cesar Torres (2012).
5 For key excerpts see Radhakrishnan and Moore (1973: 454–85).
6 See Chapter 12 in this volume on phenomenology. Buddhist phenomenology and European variants have noteworthy parallels. See Evan Thompson's (2008) "Neurophenomenology and Contemplative Experience."
7 This no-abiding self plays a key role in Chinese and Japanese martial arts, as shown below.
8 One may wonder, rightly, who or what gets liberated or chained back into *samsara* after death if the self is non-existent. For a possible answer to this conundrum see Rahula (1974: 33ff).
9 Unless quoting, transcription of Chinese names follows *pinyin* usage rather than the Wade-Giles system; e.g., *Dao* rather than *Tao*.
10 Following commentators, references to Kongzi are given using the books (roman numerals) and chapters (arabic numerals) as organized in the *Analects*. This facilitates cross-referencing with other translations, which is advisable, given Chinese language's terseness and subtlety. The bibliography lists alternative Chinese classical texts.
11 For junzi see: I, 2, 8, 14; II, 11,13; IV, 5, 24; VI, 16; IX, 3; XIV, 30, 45.
12 This applies widely to contemporary East Asian communitarian theory. See Daniel Bell's *Communitarianism* for a keen analysis of the Western and Eastern entente (concerning gender, see p. 32).
13 See, I, 3; IV, 2; VI, 28; X, 11; XII, 2, 5, 22; XVII, 4.
14 See, II, 4; IV, 16; XIII, 6.
15 See Chapter III *in toto*.
16 II, 24; IX, 29.
17 See II, 17; VII, 28; XIII, 3. For an insightful comparative evaluation of virtue see Heather Reid's "Athletic Virtue: Between East and West."
18 This results in ethical partiality to those we hold dear: we should care more for those closer to us, duty diminishing the further removed from us they are. Obligation is proportional to what one receives. See V, 16; XVII, 21 Mozi (fifth Century BCE) was a stern critic of Kongzi who advocated universal love on utilitarian grounds. Buddhism's has also a strong communitarian streak that favors compassionate, universal love.

19 See also Chapter 9 on ethics in this volume.

20 In spite of the name, Daoists do not have a monopoly on the *Dao*; it permeates Chinese culture to the core.

21 For a Western similar distinction in terms of *leib* as lived, vital and organic body, and *körper* as living or dead material body. See Henning Eichberg's *Bodily Democracy* (2010), pp. 262–6.

22 In the cases of Liezi and Chuang Tzu, their works are eponymously named after them.

23 The Rinzai (臨済) and Soto Zen (曹洞禅) schools in Japan mirror this respectively. Rinzai Zen (臨済禅) emphasizes *koans* (公案; paradoxical riddles), over *zazen*, (seated meditation), Soto Zen (曹洞禅) the reverse. In Rinzai, anyone may experience *satori* (enlightenment) as a sudden insight at some uncertain point; Soto (曹洞) emphasizes a long tenure of study and constant meditation before a gradual realization of *satori*. A number of methods that begin in China and fully develop in Japan (enlightenment through the body) are considered in the next section of this chapter.

24 See Shigenori Nagatomo's (1992) *Attunement Through the Body* for an extremely lucid account of Yuasa's views.

25 Following Japanese custom, family name comes first, then first name.

26 This is a text as complex as concise, and translation is complicated. For an excerpted alternative with substantial commentary, see Suzuki (1993: 97–115); see also Thomas Cleary's (2005) *Soul of the Samurai*.

27 The article is also included in his 1991 book, *Talking a Good Game: Inquiries into the Principles of Sport*.

References

Abe, Shinobu. 1986. "Zen and Sport." *Journal of the Philosophy of Sport*. 8: 45–8.

Abe, Shinobu. 1987. "Modern Sports and the Eastern Tradition of Physical Culture: Emphasizing Nishida's Theory of the Body." *Journal of the Philosophy of Sport*, 14: 44–7.

Ames, Robert T. 1993. "The Meaning of Body in Classical Chinese Philosophy." In *Self as Body in Asian Theory and Practice*. Edited by Thomas P. Kasulis, Roger T. Ames, and Wimal Dissanayake, 153–75. Albany, NY: State University of New York Press.

Anonymous. 2002. *Bhagavad Gita: The Song of God*. Translated by Swami Prabhavananda and Christopher Isherwood. New York: Signet Classic.

Bell, Daniel. 2013. "Communitarianism". In *The Stanford Encyclopedia of Philosophy*. Edited by Edward N. Zalta. Fall 2013 ed. Available online at http://plato.stanford.edu/archives/fall2013/entries/communitarianism (accessed 7 October 2014).

Brannigan, Michael C. 2000. *The Pulse of Wisdom*. Stamford, CT: Wadsworth.

Carter, Robert E. 1997. *The Nothingness Beyond God: An Introduction to the Philosophy of Nishida, Kitaro*. St. Paul, MN: Paragon House.

Carter, Robert E. 2008. *The Japanese Arts and Self-cultivation*. Albany, NY: State University of New York Press.

Chan, Wing-Tsit, ed. 1963. *A Sourcebook in Chinese Philosophy*. Princeton, NJ: Princeton University Press.

Chuang Tzu, and Burton Watson. 1968. *The Complete works of Chuang Tzu*. New York: Columbia University Press.

Cleary, Thomas. 2005. *Soul of the Samurai: Modern Translations of Three Classic Works of Zen and Bushido*. North Clarendon, VT: Tuttle.

Confucius. 1979. *The Analects*. Translated by D. C. Lau. London: Penguin Books.

Confucius. 2006. *The Essential Analects: Selected with Traditional Commentary*. Translated by Edward G. Slingerland. Indianapolis, IN: Hackett.

Cooper, David E. 2003. *World Philosophies: A Historical Introduction*. 2nd ed. Oxford: Blackwell.

Deshimaru, Taishen. 1982. *The Zen Way to the Martial Arts*. Translated by Nancy Amphoux. Penguin Compass: New York.

Dixon, Nicholas. 1992. "On Sportsmanship and 'Running Up the Score'." *Journal of the Philosophy of Sport*, 19: 1–13.

Deutsch, Elliot, and Bontekoe, Ron. 2004. *A Companion to World Philosophies*. Oxford: Blackwell Publishing.

Eichberg, Henning. 2010. *Bodily Democracy*. Abingdon: Routledge.

Elvin, Mark. 1993. "Tales of *Shen* and *Xin*: Body-Person and Heart-Mind in China during the Last 150 Years." In *Self as Body in Asian Theory and Practice*. Edited by Thomas P. Kasulis, Roger T. Ames, and Wimal Dissanayake, 208–89. Albany, NY: State University of New York Press.

Endo, Takuro. 2005. "Practical Consideration of a Bodywork Class: Developing the Physical Education Wherein we Feel the Inside of Bodies." *Journal of Sport and Physical Education Center*, 27, 11–29.

Fukasawa, Koyo. 2014. "The Potentiality of Empathy with Others in Competitive Sport: A Suggestion from Nishida's 'Pure Experience' and 'I' and 'Thou'." *International Journal of Sport and Health Science*, 12: 47–52.

Gwin, Peter. 2011. "Battle for the Soul of Kung Fu." *National Geographic Magazine*, March: 94–113.

Harrison, Victoria. 2013. *Eastern Philosophy: The Basics*. Abingdon: Routledge.

Hata, Takayuki, and Sekine, Masami. 2010. "Philosophy of Sport and Physical Education in Japan: its History, Characteristics, and Prospects." *Journal of the Philosophy of Sport*, 37: 215–24.

Hay, John. 1993. "The Human Body as a Microcosmic Source of Macrocosmic Values in Calligraphy." In *Self as Body in Asian Theory and Practice*. Edited by Thomas P. Kasulis, Roger T. Ames, and Wimal Dissanayake, 176–208. Albany, NY: State University of New York Press.

Heisig, James, Kasulis, Thomas, and Maraldo, John, eds. 2011. *Japanese Philosophy: A Sourcebook*. Honolulu: University of Hawai'i Press.

Herrigel, Eugen. 1999. *Zen in the Art of Archery*. New York: Vintage.

Höchsmann, Hyun, Guorong Yang, and Chuang Tzu. 2007. *Zhuangzi*. New York: Pearson Longman.

Hsu, Leo. 2007. "Chinese Olympics: Justification and Possibilities for Multicultural Interactions." *Acta Universistatis Carolinae, Kinathronpologica*, 43 (1): 85–93.

Hsu, Leo. 2009. "Olympism and Sport Culture Education: East Asian Approaches." *International Journal of Human Movement Science*, 3 (2): 5–20.

Hsu, Leo. 2010. "An Overview of Sport Philosophy in Chinese-Speaking Regions." *Journal of the Philosophy of Sport*, 37 (2): 237–52.

Huizinga, Johan, 1955. *Homo Ludens: A study of the Element of Play in Culture*. Boston: Beacon Press.

Hyland, Drew. 1990. *Philosophy of Sport*. New York: Paragon House.

Hyland, Drew. 2001. "Opponents, Contestants, and Competitors: The Dialectic of Sport." In *Ethics in Sport*, edited by William J. Morgan, Klaus V. Meier, and Angela J. Schneider, 80–90. Champaign, IL: Human Kinetics.

Ishigaki, Kenji. 1995. "An Essay on Performance-Reproduction: The Structure of Sympathy and the Method of Performance-Reproduction." *Journal of the Philosophy of Sport and Physical Education*, 17 (1): 39–55.

Ivanhoe, Philip J., and Van Norden, Bryan W. *Readings in Classical Chinese Philosophy*. 2nd ed. Indianapolis, IN: Hackett.

Kasulis, Thomas P. 1993. "The body – Japanese style." In *Self as Body in Asian Theory and Practice*, edited by Thomas P. Kasulis, Roger T. Ames, and Wimal Dissanayake, 299–320. Albany, NY: State University of New York Press.

Kasulis, Thomas P., Ames, Roger T. and Dissanayake, Wimal, eds. 1993. *Self as Body in Asian Theory and Practice*. Albany: State University of New York Press.

Koller, John, M. 1993. "Human Embodiment: Indian Perspectives." In *Self as Body in Asian Theory and Practice*, edited by Thomas P. Kasulis, Roger T. Ames, and Wimal Dissanayake, 41–54. Albany: State University of New York Press.

Kondo, Yoshitaka. 1997. "Amendment of Gender Verification Regulation in Sport." *Journal of the Philosophy of Sport and Physical Education*, 19 (1): 53–65.

Krein, Kevin and Ilundáin, Jesús. 2014. "*Mushin* and Flow: An East-West Comparative Analysis." In *Philosophy and the Martial Arts*. Edited by G. Priest and D. Young, 101–64. Abingdon: Routledge.

Lally, Richard. 2012. "Deweyan Pragmatism and Self-Cultivation." In *Pragmatism and the Philosophy of Sport*, edited by Richard Lally, Douglas Anderson, and John Kaag, 175–98. London: Lexington.

Lao-Tzu. 2009 [1875]. *Lao Tzu's Taoteching With Selected Commentaries from the Past 2,000 Years*. 3rd ed. translated by Red Pine. Port Townsend, WA: Copper Canyon Press.

Lao-Tzu, Chuang Tzu, and Lieh Tzu. 2013. *Tao: The Way – The Sayings of Lao Tzu, Chuang Tzu and Lieh Tzu*, translated by Lionel Giles and Herbert A. Giles, special ed. El Paso, TX: EL Paso Norte Press.

Laozi. 1998. *Tao Te Ching*. Translated by S. Mitchel. New York: Harper Perennial.

MacArthur, Ellen. 2005. *Taking on the World: A Sailor's Extraordinary Solo Race Around the Globe*. New York: McGraw-Hill.

MacIntyre, Alasdair. 1984. *After Virtue: A Study in Moral Theology*. 2nd ed. Notre Dame, IN: University of Notre Dame Press.

Masumoto, Naofumi. 1998. "Cultural Aspects of the Opening Ceremony of 1998 Nagano Winter Olympic Games: From Localism to Globalism." *Journal of the Philosophy of Sport and Physical Education*, 20 (2): 45–53.

Masumoto, Naofumi 2004. "Field Note on the 2004 Athens Olympic Games: Opening Ceremony, Cultural Program, and 'Olympic Truce'." *Journal of the Philosophy of Sport and Physical Education*, 26 (2): 73–83.

McNamee, Michael J. 2008. *Sports, Virtues and Vices: Morality Plays*. London: Routledge.

McNamee, Michael J. 2010. *The Ethics of Sport*. London: Routledge.

Merleau-Ponty, Maurice. 1964. *The Primacy of Perception: And Other Essays on Phenomenological Psychology, the Philosophy of Art, History and Politics*. Evanston, IL: Northwestern University Press.

Merleau-Ponty, Maurice. 2002. *Phenomenology of Perception*. London: Routledge.

Morgan, William J. 2012. "Broad Internalism, Deep Conventions, Moral Entrepreneurs." *Journal of the Philosophy of Sport*, 39 (1): 65–100.

Morgan, William J., Meier, Klaus V., and Schneider Angela J., eds. 2001. *Ethics in Sport*. Champaign, IL: Human Kinetics.

Nagatomo, Shigenori. 1992. *Attunement Through the Body*. Albany, NY: State University of New York Press.

Nishida, Kitaro. 1990. *An Inquiry into the Good*. Translated by Masao Abe and Christopher Ives. New Haven, CT: Yale University Press.

Oda, Yoshiko and Kondo, Yoshitaka. 2014. "The Concept of *Yuko-Datotsu* in Kendo: Interpreted from the Aesthetics of *Zanshin*." *Sport, Ethics and Philosophy*, 8 (1): 3–15.

Radhakrishnan, Sarvepalli, and Moore, Charles, eds. 1989. *A Sourcebook in Indian Philosophy*. Princeton, NJ: Princeton University Press.

Rahula, Walpola. 1974. *What the Buddha Taught: Expanded and Revised Edition with Texts from the Suttas and Dhammapada*. New York: Grove.

Rawls, John. 1971. *A Theory of Justice*. Cambridge, MA: Harvard University Press.

Reid, Heather. 2010. "Athletic Virtue: Between East and West." *Sport, Ethics and Philosophy*, 4 (1): 16–26.

Reid, Heather L. 2012. *Introduction to the Philosophy of Sport*. Plymouth: Rowman and Littlefield.

Russell, John R. 2007. "Broad Internalism and the Moral Foundations of Sport." In *Ethics in Sport* 2nd ed., edited by W. J. Morgan, 35–50. Champaign, IL: Human Kinetics.

Sekida, Katsuki. 1985. *Zen Training: Methods and Philosophy*. Boston, CT: Shambhala.

Sekine, Masami, and Hata, Takayuki. 2004. "The Crisis of Modern Sport and the Dimension of Achievement for Its Conquest." *International Journal of Health and Sport Science*, 2: 180–6.

Sheehan, George. 1978. *Running and Being*. New York: Simon and Shuster.

Sheets-Johnstone, Maxine. 2011. *The Primacy of Movement*. 2nd ed. Advances in Consciousness Research. Amsterdam: John Benjamins.

Simon, Robert. 2007. "Internalism and Internal Values in Sport." In *Ethics in Sport*, 2nd ed., edited by W. J. Morgan, 51–66. Champaign, IL: Human Kinetics.

Staal, Frits. 1993. "Indian Bodies." In *Self as Body in Asian Theory and Practice*, edited by Thomas P. Kasulis, Roger T. Ames, and Wimal Dissanayake, 55–98. Albany, NY: State University of New York Press.

Stevens, John. 2007. *Zen Bow, Zen Arrow: The Life and Teachings of Awa Kenzo, the Archery Master from Zen in the Art of Archery*. Boston, CT: Shambhala.

Suzuki, Daisetz T. 1964. *An Introduction to Zen Buddhism*. New York: Grove.

Suzuki, Daisetz T. 1993. *Zen and Japanese Culture*. Princeton, NJ: Princeton University Press.

Takemura, Mizuho. 2014. "Prolegomena to Philosophical Considerations of Sport and Gender: A Critical Consideration of Research in Japan." *Journal of the Philosophy of Sport*, 14 (1): 97–111.

Takizawa, Fumio. 2006. "The Present State of One's View of the Human Body in Japan: Analysis Based on a Phenomenological Viewpoint." *Journal of the Philosophy of Sport and Physical Education*, 28 (1): 39–49.

Takuan, Soho. 1986. *The Unfettered Mind: Writings of the Zen Master to the Sword Master*, translated by William S. Wilson. Tokyo: Kodansha.

Tamburrini, Claudio M, and Torbjörn, Tännsjö. 2005. *Genetic Technology and Sport: Ethical Questions*. London: Routledge, 2005.

Thompson, Evan. 2008. "Neurophenomenology and Contemplative Experience." In *The Oxford Handbook of Religion and Science*, edited by Philip Clayton, 226–35. Oxford: Oxford University Press.

Torres, Cesar. 2012. "Furthering Interpretivism's Integrity: Bringing Together Ethics and Aesthetics." *Journal of the Philosophy of Sport*, 39: 299–319.

Tu, Weiming. 2004. "Chinese Philosophy: A Synoptic View." In *A Companion to World Philosophies*, edited by Elliot Deutsch, and Ron Bontekoe, 3–23. Oxford: Blackwell.

Van Norden, Brian W. 2011. *Introduction to Classical Chinese Philosophy*. Indianapolis, IN: Hackett.

Watsuji, Tetsuro. 1996. *Watsuji Tetsuro's Rinrigaku: Ethics in Japan*, translated by Y. Seisaku and R. C. Carter. Albany: State University of New York.

Wertz, Spencer K. 1991. *Talking a Good Game: Inquiries into the Principles of Sport*. Dallas, TX: Southern Methodist University Press.

Wertz, Spencer K. 1977. "Zen, Yoga and Sports: Eastern Philosophy for Western Athletes." *Journal of the Philosophy of Sport*, 4: 68–82.

Yamaguchi, Junko. 2003. "An Inquiry into Physical Freedom as it is related to the Transfiguration of the Eye to Human Body." *Journal of the Philosophy of Sport and Physical Education*, 25 (1): 1–11.

Yuasa, Yasuo. 1987. *The Body: Toward and Eastern Mind-Body Theory*. Translated by S. Nagatomo and T. Kasulis T. Albany, NY: State University of New York Press.

Yuasa, Yasuo. 1993. *The Body, Self-Cultivation and Ki-Energy*. Translated by S. Nagatomo and Monte Hull. Albany, NY: State University of New York Press.

Yu-Lan Fung. 1976. *A Short History of Chinese Philosophy*. New York: Free Press.

8

EPISTEMOLOGY AND SPORT

Steffen Borge

Introduction

Epistemology has traditionally been understood as the study of knowledge. Among the central questions we find: what do we know, if anything? How do we come to know those things, if at all? Can we provide a satisfactory analysis of knowledge and knowing, or must we settle for less? Are there several distinct modes of knowledge and knowing, or only one? And so on and so forth. An epistemology of sport deals with such questions in the context of sport.

The first question I address is the question of how we can know that a certain activity is a sport and not some other social activity. This question is similar to the well-know problem of the criterion and invites the same sorts of solutions amended to a sport context. I show that to know sports we must first know play and how play opens a social space from which sport can emerge.

The next section is concerned with the question of ways of knowing in sport. Should we distinguish between two types of knowledge in sport – knowing-that and knowing-how – or else be persuaded by an argument in epistemology to the effect that all knowledge is of the knowing-that type? Orthodoxy in the philosophy of sport has it that one can and should distinguish between knowing-how and knowing-that. I show that the orthodox view that knowing-how is constitutively connected to successful performance and thus should be regarded as a distinct type of knowledge, can be defended as long as one acknowledges that the knowledge-how relation is somewhat more complex than previously thought. The question of how to understand the phenomenon of knowing-how or practical knowledge has been much debated in the philosophy of sport. The main battle line is drawn between those who think about knowing-how as involving some sort of information processing and those who do not. The latter camp argues that the knowing-how of the expert performer is an intuitive knowledge of what to do at any given stage of a competition or training session. When the expert performer is in the zone, he or she does not think about what to do or how to do it, but intuits it. I show that even though knowing-how at an expert level might at times come only with a specific phenomenological in-zone-awareness (as I have dubbed it here) and no consciously felt reflective deliberations, it does not follow that this phenomenological feel necessarily is a reliable guide to what goes on in the performer's mind.

In the last section, I address the topic of various modes of expert know-how in sport. Expert performers can experience a state of automatism with an in-zone awareness – where the sport performance seems to merely flow naturally and intuitively – but this is not the only state of automatism that an expert performer can find him or herself in. There is both conceptual and empirical ground for thinking that there is another category of expert performance that also involves states of automatism, but without the in-zone awareness. The category of zoned-out awareness of expert performance is introduced and defended in the last section. Furthermore, when we look closer at expert performance, we find that expert performance is more complex than being merely a species of automatism, whether that is with in-zone awareness or zoned-out awareness. Expert performers it turns out can also reflectively deliberate on what to do and how to do it, when performing at the highest level.

Knowing sports

When the Spanish conquistadors invaded what is today known as Mexico, they encountered "a religious ritual ... *danza de los voladores* (dance of the flyers) ... that survived remarkably intact because the Spaniards took it for an acrobatic display of skill" (Harris 2000: 113; see also Leal 1982). If we allow ourselves to distinguish between doing something for sport and something being a sport, where the former is understood as an unnecessary activity undertaken as diversion, entertainment, recreation or pastime, then it seems reasonable to say that the Spaniards mistook that which was a religious ritual for sport. Although the religious meaning of *danza de los voladores* is lost in the mists of time, the example suggests that we can distinguish between what there is for something to be sport or a sport (plural: sports), and judging something as sport or a sport. This observation might also serve as a reminder that any cavalier attitude towards the question of whether some activity is sport or a sport, or not, is misguided. In the same way as the Spaniards mistakenly judged *danza de los voladores* as sport, those who think that, for example, the game of chess is a sport might just be mistaken. Here, for the sake of brevity, I mainly focus on those practices and activities that count as sports, while leaving those practices and activities that are being done for sport, like sport fishing, sport climbing, and so on for another day. Nor do I spend any time distinguishing sports from games, but merely assume that while all sports are games, not all games are sports.

The ontological question of what it is for some practice or activity to be a sport belongs to the realm of metaphysics, whereas the closely related question of how we come to know, recognize, understand, and so forth, that some practice or activity is a sport, is epistemic. Obviously, the Spanish conquistadors in the example above applied some criterion or criteria of sport and got it wrong, but how do we come by a criterion or criteria of being sport or a sport? Though this question is somewhat different than the well-known problem of the criterion, it still raises similar worries and invites parallel solutions.

One can recognize cases of sports, only if one knows the criterion[1] or criteria for something being a sport, while one knows the criterion or criteria of being a sport, only if one can recognize cases of sports. In light of this circle and the threat of scepticism, one might be tempted to appeal to institutions of sport as a way of distinguishing between sports and non-sports.

An institutional theory of sport, however, is unlikely to help with the dilemma. Take, for example, Stephen Mumford's (2012) attempt to defend an institutional theory of sport. Mumford argues for a parallel between sports and art, and that the defence of an institutional theory of art holds for sports, but since the latter theory is circular, as admitted by its major proponents, this line in the philosophy of sport offers no way out of the dilemma (cf. Dickie 1974, 1984; see also Borge 2012).

It is also worth noting that the dilemma cuts deeper than the well-known debate in the philosophy of sport between formalists and anti-formalists. Proponents of a formalist position – a position primarily championed by Bernard Suits – attempt to either provide necessary and sufficient conditions for what it is to be a sport or else to define sports in terms of their formal rules (Suits 1967, 2005). To do that, the formalists assume that we already have in place a criterion or criteria of sports by which they can pick out sports that provides a foundation for evaluating the (relative) success of an analysis, or by which they can pick out which rule-governed activities are sports. Anti-formalists, like Graham McFee, Mike McNamee and others, dismiss formalism as futile and, instead, argue that all the phenomenon of sports allows is a family resemblance comparison of activities and practices (McFee 2004; McNamee 2008; cf. Wittgenstein 1953). This also assumes that a criterion or criteria of sports is in hand, since one must already know which objects of comparison are sports.[2]

Barring scepticism (which was what Sextus Empiricus originally opted for), Roderick Chisholm identified two answers to the problem of what and how we know (the problem of the criterion). On the one side, we have the *methodists* who argue that we can first explain how we know something (we have a method for knowing; that is, a criterion or criteria) and, on the other side, we have the *particularists* who argue that we can first explain what we know and from that extract a method for knowing; that is, a criterion or criteria (Chisholm 1982: 61–106). Both approaches, amended to our topic, are needed in an epistemology of sport. I will argue that the key to resolving the problem of the criterion within the epistemology of sport lies in a proper understanding of how the phenomenon of play fits into the world of sports. This is not to deny, as many philosophers of sport have pointed out, that sports need not be play nor need play be sports (see, among others, Suits 1988; Meier 1988; Schneider 2001).

There are many ways to draw a line between play and sports but, here, the most fruitful starting point is the observation that, while many non-human animals and infants and small children engage in social play, they do not engage in sports. Johan Huizinga tells us that 'animals have not waited for man to teach them their playing', Scott Kretchmar correctly points out that 'play is more primitive ... [and] exists and thrives with or without culture' and numerous field studies leave little doubt that non-human animals play (Huizinga 1950: 1; Kretchmar 2007: 1; Bekoff and Byers 1998; Pellegrini and Smith 2005). Non-human animals, like dogs (and canids in general), are able both to initiate and to maintain social play like competing for objects, play fighting or tug-of-war. Furthermore, other dogs that are presented with, say, the play bow, recognize this as play initiation or play maintenance (Bekoff 1995). This also facilitates other dogs' recognition of play, enabling them to join in. Similarly, pre-linguistic children can pick up on others' play behaviour as play (Reddy 1991; Nakano and Kanaya 1993; Legerstee 2005). Exercise play (running around, climbing, jumping, etc.) and rough-and-tumble play (play fighting, play chasing, etc.), are play activities that children at an early age spontaneously initiate, participate in and are able to recognize as play (Tomasello and Call 1997; Pellegrini 2009; Smith 2010). Ontogenetically, play comes before sports and, given the prevalence of play behaviour among non-human animals and assuming standard evolutionary theory, it is reasonable to assume that also phylogenetically play precedes sport in our development as a species (Pellegrini 2009; Smith 2010; Burghardt 2005). As is apparent from the research on play behaviour, both non-human animals and humans (infants and young children) can recognize and understand behaviour as play without having a criterion or criteria of play. We get to know play by recognizing particular instances of play. The particularist line of reasoning is correct for knowing play.

Owing to our natural ability to reliably distinguish play from non-play, we can acquire a criterion or criteria for something being play and this criterion or criteria, I suggest, forms a basis for sports.[3] Play carves out a social space that stands apart from the everyday world and everyday concerns like getting food, getting shelter, avoiding harm, etc. In this social space of play, actions are not directed towards useful ends (means for survival), nor do they have the same consequences as they do in everyday life (non-play circumstances). Sports spring out of the social space of play. The literature on play is diverse, but most theorists in the various disciplines that are engaged with the topic seem to agree on certain features being crucial for play (see Burghardt 2010). These include:

- Play is autotelic; i.e. it is done for its own sake.
- Play is not needed for survival or any other immediate purpose; i.e. it is unnecessary (although play might both phylogenetically and ontogenetically be very important and beneficiary).
- Play is non-serious; i.e. play actions are not meant to have nor have the same consequences as similar actions outside the play context.

In the philosophy of sport, the closest we come to a commonly accepted view on what are sports is Bernard Suits' understanding of sports as physical skill activities that are 'voluntary attempt[s] to overcome unnecessary obstacles' (Suits 2005: 55). Later, William Morgan refined and shortened up this definition to the basic idea of sports following a 'gratuitous logic' (Morgan 1994: 211). Although many philosophers of sport reject Suits' more elaborated analysis of games and sports, most accept that sports follow a gratuitous logic. A card-carrying anti-formalist like McNamee, for example, subscribes to the view of sports as 'characterised by a gratuitous logic involving, centrally, physical skills' (McNamee 2008: 19). The gratuitous logic of sports overlaps with the logic of play in that both are autotelic and unnecessary activities. The two differ in that in play the participants primarily aim at the continuation of play (this is one important aspect of being a non-serious activity), while sports have 'agonal qualities' where winning/losing or achieving/failing become an important part of the activity (McNamee 2008: 19).

The particularist position is that humans gain a criterion or criteria of play by being able to recognize actions as play. To see how having a criterion or criteria of play can pave the way for sport and sports it is useful to consider Kretchmar's distinction between tests and contests (Kretchmar 1988; Kretchmar and Elcombe 2007). A test is a voluntary undertaking of a specific task, which is not needed to fulfil everyday needs and it involves some kind of difficulty, where '[a] test simply become[s] unthinkable or unintelligent in the absence of such opposition' (Kretchmar 1988: 225). Doing something for sport is to do it as a test. Contests are shared tests, where that involves recognizing the other(s) as participating in the same test and having a procedure to decide which contestant was better (Kretchmar 1988: 227–8). Sports are contests. Put briefly, '[t]ests are designed to measure simple achievement, whereas contests are structured to assess superiority and inferiority' (Kretchmar and Elcombe 2007: 181). Tests produce achievements and failures, while contests produce winner and losers (although not always superior winner and inferior losers, see Borge 2010). Play, on the other hand, is not aimed at some end-result but rather the continuation of play, which sometimes leads to self-handicapping among nonhuman animals.

> In a play fight in non-human animals or children, the stronger or more dominant animal might actually use less advantageous strategies, inhibit his or her behavior, or otherwise act to keep the 'opponent' in the game. This ... can be readily seen when watching a large dog playing with a much smaller one. Here the objective of play may

be to keep the interaction going rather than quickly terminating it by the larger animal 'defeating' the smaller.

(Burghardt 2005: 90)

However, social play also appears to be a kind of proto-contest, in that '[m]ost social play involves competition, including pinning in rats, tug-of-war in dogs, and king of the hill in goats', where it emerges which animal is the stronger and the weaker (Burghardt 2010: 742). Having a criterion or criteria of social play gives you three important features of contests, such as sports; seeing the activity as autotelic and unnecessary, while having the ability to recognize other players. When a creature with such a criterion or criteria of social play is able to substitute aiming at the continuation of play with aiming at a specific end state of the activity, like crossing a line, overpowering a opponent, scoring a goal, etc., together with a procedure for deciding who count as best or the winner of the contest, then that creature has a criterion or criteria of sports and can engage in sports and recognize others as engaging in sports. In other words, when a creature is able to do that it creates a constitutive rule or rules, which turns play into sport and that sits well with Kretchmar's line that games and sports 'are the product of their constitutive rules' (Kretchmar 2007: 2; see also Kretchmar 2001). The criterion or criteria of social play forms the basis for a criterion or criteria of sport by which we can get constitutive rules of sport (Searle 1969, 1995).[4] Constitutive rules enable us to become sporting creatures and to know sports. It is a further question to decide which cognitive capacities enable humans to turn play into sports, while non-human animals are, as far as we know, unable to do that (although having a language of a certain level of complexity is one obvious candidate). Suffice to say here, we get to know sports by having a criterion or criteria of sports. The methodist line is correct for knowing sports.

Ways of knowing in sports

To know that someone plays a sport involves having a criterion or criteria for something being a sport, which, as it turns out, is the same criterion or criteria that makes the sport activity possible in the first place. If one holds that view, then one ought to expect that anyone that plays, say, football knows that they are doing that and also knows (to some extent) or has a certain grasp of the sport's constitutive rules (at least the most important ones). Nevertheless, this is not necessarily the case. Many young children have been thrown into the activity of playing football without having much, if any, grasp of the rules of the game. Still, for an activity to be football, someone connected to a particular training session or match must know the rules, even if, say, in the case of young children learning the game, the only one who knows the rules is the coach overseeing the training session or the referee officiating the match. Consider a case where we encountered an activity that looks physically indistinguishable from a football match but where no one knew any constitutive rules (of football as we know it) or saw it as an activity where one aims at certain end-states such as scoring goals or winning the match. Is it football? I suspect that we might be puzzled about what to say about this case, owing to the oddness of an exact football-lookalike but without knowledge or awareness of the constitutive rules of football and no aiming at scoring, winning, etc. If we were persuaded that the aforementioned elements were missing, we would not judge it to be a sport and also thus not football.

Football and other sports demand knowledge of (a certain amount of) the constitutive rules of the sports by players or someone else connected to a particular instance of a sport. Is anything more needed for knowing sports? The question 'Do you know football?' could at least be answered in three ways, assuming we exclude the possibility of answering this question as 'Have you ever heard about a phenomenon called football'. We can formulate these three interpretations of the question without using the words 'knowledge' or 'know':

- Are you acquainted with football?
- Do you understand football?
- Can you play football?

The first question connects with having a criterion or criteria for sports; that is, recognizing something as a sport. One could answer the question by saying 'Yes, but I don't know the rules' without any air of contradiction or oddness. On the other hand, someone who knows of football (who has heard of it or even seen it) but mistakenly believes that it is some sort of art performance, or, say, an elaborated, but mostly unsuccessful rainmaking ritual; that is, does not recognize it as a sport, does not know football.

Interpretation 1 seems to be minimally connected with having a criterion or criteria for recognizing football as a sport. The other two interpretations of the question presuppose that, and instead hone in on whether, the addressee has (a certain amount of) propositional knowledge about football, aka 'knowing-that' or has the ability or the skill to play football, aka 'knowing-how'. Another and somewhat different way to slice the conceptual cake, would be to say that interpretation 2 concerns theoretical knowledge, while interpretation 3 is about practical knowledge, and yet another way is to talk of declarative knowledge and procedural knowledge. Ever since Gilbert Ryle's (1949) *The Concept of Mind*, it has been standard in philosophy to think of knowing-that and knowing-how as two distinct ways of knowing (Ryle 1949: ch. 2). Pre-theoretically, one could envisage someone who knew every true proposition about football, so that it would be natural to say that he or she understood football while having no ability to play football and thus not knowing-how to play football. Ryle tells us that 'a fool might have all that knowledge without knowing how to perform' (Ryle 1946: 8). Conversely, many great footballers struggle to explicate their football abilities verbally; that is, their football skills (the latter would be lack of declarative knowledge). Anyone who argues that there is a distinct way of knowing-how that is not explainable, translatable or reducible to knowing-that (propositional knowledge) occupies the position known as anti-intellectualism.[5]

One way of understanding what knowing-how to play football amounts to, is to argue that it entails the ability to play football, and '[t]his "ability account" of know-how is often attributed to Ryle' (Fantl 2012: 6; see Hornsby 2012 for a diverging interpretation of Ryle's position). Philosophers of sport have not engaged much in Ryle's ability account of knowing-how (but see Aspin 1976; Carr 1979, 1981; Loland 1992: 61–2) but it is more or less taken for granted in the literature that sports are connected with skills. Given that having skills is to have certain abilities, it would not be far-fetched to say that most philosophers of sport (tacitly) accept or rely on a skill account of knowing-how in sports. Also, given our interest in sport, we need not worry about whether all knowing-how should be understood as the performance of abilities or skills. Rather, we can concentrate on the question of whether sporting skills (being a species of abilities) outruns propositional knowledge (as the anti-intellectualist position would have it) or else should be understood as a type of propositional knowledge (as the intellectualism position would have it).

Although Ryle's most explicit argument against intellectualism is his so-called regress argument, perhaps even more influential is his claim that '[p]hilosophers have not done justice to the distinction which is quite familiar to all of us between knowing that something is the case and knowing how to do things' (Ryle 1946: 4; Bengson and Moffett 2011: 11–12). This both challenges and shifts the burden of proof to the defenders of the intellectualism position. Pre-theoretically, the distinction not only makes sense but also seems obvious, and it would take some persuading to convince us otherwise. Nevertheless, Jason Stanley and Timothy Williamson have argued that all knowing-how is knowing-that. At the heart of their attempt to provide cases of knowing-how that amount to knowing-that lies an example from the world of sport.

> [A] ski instructor may know how to perform a certain complex stunt, without being able to perform it herself. Similarly, a master pianist who loses both of her arms in a tragic car accident still knows how to play the piano. But she has lost her ability to do so. It follows that Ryle's own positive account of knowledge-how is demonstrably false.
>
> *(Stanley and Williamson 2001: 416; see also Stanley 2011: 127–30)*

According to Stanley and Williamson, you can know how to perform a Beillman spin on the ice but not be able to do it; that is, knowing-how without ability. Conversely, David Carr has argued that you could have an ability to do something without knowing-how to do it: that is, ability without knowing-how. He writes that '[a] novitiate trampolinist ... might at his first attempt succeed in performing a difficult somersault, which, although for an expert would be an exercise of knowing how, is in this case, merely the result of luck or chance' (Carr 1981: 53; see also Carr 1979: 397).

While Fantl (2012) and Weatherson (2006) have argued that Ryle does not hold the ability view often ascribed to him, the above challenges remain, since it is common ground in the philosophy of sport that knowing-how to do a sport is connected to skills.

The first thing to notice is that whereas the philosophical debate on Ryle and knowing-how is centred on abilities and its connection to knowing-how, philosophers of sport focus on skills. This makes an important difference. Mimicking Carr's novice trampolinist, let us envisage that I, being a mediocre amateur footballer, in a moment of luck and some basic footballing skills, manage to bend it like Beckham. Obviously, I am able to bend it like Beckham, I actually did, and, *pace* Noë, it is not unreasonable to say that if I am actually able to it, then I have the ability to bend it like Beckham (Noë 2005: 280). On the other hand, there would be no temptation to say that I have the skill to bend it like Beckham and, thus, according to the standard way of thinking about this in the philosophy of sport, I do not know how to bend it like Beckham. The fact that luck was centrally involved prevents my bending it like Beckham from counting as knowing-how to bend it like Beckham (see Hawley 2003: 27–8).

Here, we find an important parallel between knowing-how and knowing-that, which, if these two are distinct ways of knowing, is expected. In the same way as luck prevents something from being knowing-how, Gettier cases taught epistemologists that luck prevents true justified belief from being knowing-that (Gettier 1963). Having a true justified belief that *p* does not ensure that the agent in question knows that *p* and, similarly, successful performance of *p* does not ensure that the agent in question knows how to *p*. The latter fact is reflected in philosophers of sports' emphasis on skills, which demands that the successful performance in some sport discipline is not accidental, not centrally based on luck, for someone to know how to do that sport.

Stanley and Williamson's (2001) ski instructor example, on the other hand, challenges the idea that knowing-how to do something entails being able to perform it. The example succeeds in showing that in cases of knowing-how, the agent in question who knows how to *p*, need not be able to perform *p*. Stanley and Williamson's take home lesson from the ski instructor example is that knowing-how to perform a complex ski stunt is knowing a fact about a way of perform-ing the complex ski stunt (Stanley and Williamson 2001; Stanley 2011). I will show, however, that that does not follow from their example. In contrast, Ryle believed that knowing-how entails knowing a way of performing the complex ski stunt, and that is true as long as we remember that it need not be the agent in question; that is, the person knowing-how to *p*, who is able or has the skills to perform *p*. Let us consider what it would take for knowing-how in this case to be nothing but knowing-that. Put bluntly, one should be willing to credit the ski instructor with knowing-how to *p* (how to perform a complex ski stunt), where the knowing-that *p* (a fact about a way of performing the complex ski stunt) is not in any way connected to the performance of *p* (performing the complex ski stunt). In the ski instructor case, this means that we should exclude the case where the instructor (like the pianist who has lost her arms) used to be able or had the skills to *p*, since in that case it is the fact that the ski instructor used to be able to perform *p*, which justifies us in crediting her with knowing-how to *p*. In the case where there is a physical disability, which has always prevented the ski instructor from perform-ing the stunt, one would justify the claim that she knows how to *p* by arguing that if she did not have this-and-this physical disability, then she would have been able or have the skill to perform the stunt (Hawley 2003: 20–2). This justification, however, is also connected to skilful (neither accidental, nor based on luck) performance of the complex ski stunt.

Finally, in the case where Stanley and Williamson's ski instructor has never been able or could be able to perform the stunt in question, one could argue that one would still be justi-fied in crediting her with knowing-how to *p*, as long as she is successful in using her knowledge of a way of performing the complex ski stunt to enable others to perform the stunt in a skil-ful manner.[6] Unfortunately, once again it is not the knowing-that *p* per se, which justifies us in thinking of the ski instructor as knowing-how to *p* but the fact that we can tie that proposi-tional knowledge to the skilful performance of *p*. What Stanley and Williamson need to say is that someone who is not able to skilfully *p*, has not been able to skilfully *p*, nor could be able to skilfully *p* and, furthermore, has never been able to enable anyone else to skilfully *p*, still, on the basis of entertaining a thought that *p*, knows how to *p*. Substitute *p* with 'to ski' and you get the claim that a ski instructor who is not able to skilfully ski, has never been able to skil-fully ski, could not skilfully ski and, furthermore, has never been able to enable anyone else to skilfully ski, knows how to ski, because she knows the relevant descriptions of or facts about skilful skiing.[7] This ski instructor looks a lot like Ryle's fool who has all the knowledge with-out knowing-how to perform (factually or counterfactually) or make others perform, and we do well in denying that such a ski instructor knows how to ski. We can conclude that know-ing-how is constitutively connected to performance, although the performance connection is more complex than Ryle seemed to think.[8]

Cognitivism, phenomenology and the varieties of sport performance

The question of skilful execution of sports and knowledge is not uncharted territory in the philosophy of sport (Ziff 1974; Steel 1977; Wertz 1978; Hyland 1990; Loland 1992). In later years, Hubert Dreyfus's theory of expert performance has been influential when philosophers of sport have thought about knowing in skilful sports movements. Dreyfus's Heidegger- and Merleau-Ponty-influenced line of reasoning is that top athletes' bodies know what to do at any given point in a sport, because '[a]n expert's skill has become so much a part of him that he need be no more aware of it than he is of his own body' (Dreyfus and Dreyfus 1986: 30; see also Heidegger 1963; Merleau-Ponty 1945). The Dreyfus line builds on the Heideggerian insight that humans do not first figure out the world and then decide to act in it but, rather, as infants and cognizers, we are thrown into a world we must cope with, making this world our own. Only later do we reach the cognitive sophistication of being able to think about the world more abstractly, to plan actions and so on and so forth. In Heidegger's own words, '[w]e are always already in a world' by coping with the world, and this coping always precedes reflective thinking (Heidegger 1988: 165). Whereas Heidegger was concerned with a phenomenological description of our everyday dealings with the world, Dreyfus turns his attention to expert performance, often by way of examples from the world of sport. It is in the latter respect that philosophers of sport have found him relevant (Breivik 2007, 2008, 2011; Eriksen 2010; Loland 1992; Moe 2005, 2007; Hopsicker 2009; Standal and Moe 2011).

Dreyfus's philosophy of skilled coping is a reaction to what is sometimes called classical cognitivism. The central tenet of cognitivism is the idea that the mind is computational; that is, the mind processes information. In its classic form, spanning from the cognitive revolution of the 1950s throughout the 1970s, the slogan was that the mind is a computer or a syntactic engine (Dennett 1981; Haugeland 1981). The sportsman is a information processer and 'the elite performer might excel because she/he (a) recognizes the stimulus sooner (perceptual processing), (b) has a variety of appropriate responses ready for execution (decision processing), and/or (c) issues movement commands more rapidly (effector processing)' (Wrisberg 2001: 7; as quoted in Moe 2005: 161–2). Thus, at least one important difference between Roger Federer and an lesser-skilled tennis player is a difference of degree, where the former is just a lot better at processing information relevant to performing in a tennis match. The cognitivist picture allows that the information processing in expert performance, perhaps, takes place at a subconscious and/or automated level.[9]

In contrast, Dreyfus takes the same difference between Federer and a lesser-skilled tennis player to be a difference in kind. Dreyfus presents a picture of skilful performance that is acquired in a stepwise fashion – from novice, advanced beginner, through competence and proficiency and finally expertise – and where the expert level of knowing-how is phenomenologically different in kind from the others (Dreyfus and Dreyfus 1986: 21–36; Dreyfus 2002: 368–72). Both the competence and proficiency level of, say, playing tennis, qualify as knowing-how to play tennis (and a case can also be made for the advanced beginner) but, whereas these know-how levels involve reflective deliberations on what to do, the expert's performance 'is ongoing and nonreflective', so that '[c]ompetent performance is rational; proficiency is transitional; experts act arationally' (Dreyfus and Dreyfus 1986: 31, 36). According to this picture, the expert performer, who is an elite athlete, does not calculate what to do; he or she just does it without thinking about it. Regarding the expert performance of a tennis swing, Dreyfus writes:

> [I]f one is expert at the game, things are going well, and one is absorbed in the game, what one experiences is more like one's arm going up and its being drawn to the appropriate position, the racket forming the optimal angle with the court – an angle one need not even be aware of – all this so as to complete the gestalt made up of the court, one's running opponent, and the on-coming ball. One feels that one's comportment was caused by the perceived conditions in such a way as to reduce a sense of deviation from some satisfactory gestalt. But that final gestalt need not be represented in one's mind. Indeed, it is not something one could represent. One only senses when one is getting closer or further away from the optimum.
>
> *(Dreyfus 2002: 379)*

Elsewhere Dreyfus tells us that '[w]hen one is bodily absorbed in responding to solicitations there is no thinking subject and there are no features to be thought' and, in more general terms, he states that 'the enemy of expertise is thought' (Dreyfus 2007: 358, 354; see also Graybiel 1998: 130; Ennen 2003: 314). Obviously, as the quotes above show, the expert performer is aware of his or her environment, while responding to changes in that environment in a non-reflective fashion. Let us call such awareness *in-zone awareness of knowing-how*.

According to Dreyfus, the phenomenology of the expert level offers a guide to understanding how someone is able to play, say, tennis, at an expert level. If, from the inside, it does not feel like you need to think about what to do, then you don't think about what to do. This line of argument, however, relies on the implausible of view that all thinking takes the form of explicit formulations and considerations of propositions, concepts or ways to do things (Ginet 1975: 6–7; McDowell 2007: 367–8; Stanley 2011: 23–4). Rejecting this part of the Dreyfus line, however, does not invalidate the idea that the expert level of knowing-how comes with a specific phenomenological feel. One can accept an in-zone awareness and its phenomenology, while remaining neutral as to how the minds of experts work or even allowing that experts think, but that the experts' thinking does not take the form of reflective deliberations.

Regarding the phenomenon of knowing-how to do sports, the expert level is, of course, marginal. Most, say, tennis players in the world that know how to play tennis are not Dreyfusian experts. Indeed, the phenomenology of the lesser-skilled sportspersons (as contrasted with experts of a field), who nevertheless know how to play some particular sport, remains a neglected area of the philosophy of sport.[10] Clearly, there is a 'what is it like to be' question to be asked about, say, mediocre tennis players with a not-so-good backhand, which might be as philosophically interesting as questions about the expert level. If Dreyfus is correct in thinking that expert performers do not reflectively deliberate on what to do during a game, while lesser-skilled sportspersons do, then the knowing-how of lesser-skilled sportspersons is distinctly different and deserves attention on its own merits. By reflective deliberation I mean that the agent in question not only thinks about what to do but also is aware that such deliberations take place. Also, if expert performers sometimes reflectively deliberate on what to do during a sports event, as it will be apparent that they do, then one would like to know whether there is a quantitative or qualitative difference between experts and lesser-skilled performers' reflective deliberations.

Modes of expert performances

At the level of expert performance that does not involve reflective deliberations, the in-zone awareness of Dreyfusian experts is not the only mode of expert performance. David Armstrong's classic example of the absent-minded long-distance driver qualifies as a case of expert performance that exemplifies another mode.

> If you have driven for a very long distance without a break, you may have had experience of a curious state of automatism, which can occur in these conditions. One can suddenly 'come to' and realize that one has driven for long distances without being aware of what one was doing, or, indeed, without being aware of anything. One has kept the car on the road, used the brake and the clutch perhaps, yet all without any awareness of what one was doing.
>
> *(Armstrong 1970: 76)*

The driver in a state of automatism perceives, or is aware of, the road. If he did not, the car would be in a ditch. But he is not currently aware of his awareness of the road. He perceives the road, but he does not perceive his perceiving, or anything else that is going on in his mind. He is not, as we normally are, conscious of what is going on in his mind ... The driver in the automatic state is one whose 'inner eye' is shut: who is not currently aware of what is going on in his own mind.

(Armstrong 1970: 78; see also Armstrong 1968, 1981)

The phenomenon described by Armstrong seemingly involves a similar sort of automaticity of action as that which is associated with Dreyfusian experts but the phenomena obviously differ. Presumably, in-zone awareness of knowing-how is rich in phenomenological feel, whereas the phenomenon exemplified by the absent-minded long-distance driver is devoid of it. Still, as Armstrong points out, there is awareness of driving the car, since it does not end up in the ditch. Let us call such awareness *zoned-out awareness of knowing-how.*[11]

First, zoned-out awareness shows that it is not the case, as philosopher of sport Jens Birch has argued, that 'all knowing how involves phenomenal consciousness' (Birch 2009: 43). Although the phenomenon of zoned-out awareness has so far eluded philosophers of sport, there are at least some possible candidates where we might find sport instantiations of the phenomenon. For example, consider a marathon runner who has broken away from the field by a considerable distance and who is concentrating on keeping a steady pace and rhythm, while running his or her own race. One can easily envisage such a marathon runner zoning out for stretches of the race. Similar considerations hold for other long-distance endurance sports such as cross-country skiing, race-walking or rowing. Obviously, further attention to and research on the phenomenon of zoned-out awareness with regard to knowing-how to do various sports, is needed before one draws any conclusion as to how often, if it all, athletes zone out when doing a particular sport. Still, the phenomenon seems worthy our attention. This gives us three distinct modes of knowing-how to do a sport:

- reflective awareness of knowing-how
- in-zone awareness of knowing-how
- zoned-out awareness of knowing-how.

Do all expert performances exclusively belong to the latter two categories? Concerning bodily awareness, it seems clear that in everyday life 'when I am engaged in the world, I tend not to notice my posture or specific movements of my limbs' (Gallagher 2003: 55). Also, regarding various types of engagement in sport much of 'the body [is] a background, a dark zone' (Breivik 2008: 349). Yet, that does not mean that it all resides in the dark zone when top athletes perform at their best. A case reported by Breivik suggests that the Dreyfus position is too strong (see also Hopsicker 2009; Eriksen 2010; and Breivik 2011, for other recent critiques of the Dreyfusian line):

After winning a gold medal in the World Championship in downhill skiing in Åre, Sweden, 2007, Aksel Lund Svindal thought he had made an almost perfect race, just with one small fault. After the race he was interviewed on Norwegian TV by the reporter Espen Graff.

Reporter: We talk about choosing the right line and the perfect run. Are you so well prepared that you go on autopilot or do you also think during the run?
Aksel Lund Svindal: I think during the run and − I think it is important to think during the run − so you do not doze off in a way.
Interviewer: Then what do you think?

Aksel Lund Svindal: I think about … work tasks … that is exactly how it is … I think about racing well and – there are a lot of small details and you need some pegs that make the details go as planned.

(Breivik 2007: 130)

Even in a high-speed race like downhill, Lund Svindal reports having reflective deliberations of this sort. This does not mean there are not also automatic subdoxastic motor skill states involved in Lund Svindal's performance, only that it is not all in the dark zone. Similarly, Diego Maradona reports that when he scored his famous solo goal against England in the World Championship in football, 1986, Mexico, he was keenly aware of the position of his fellow striker Jorge Valdano. In fact, Maradona was looking for an opening to pass to Valdano as he took on the entire English defence – 'I was waiting to pass the ball – the logical thing to do' (Maradona 2000: 129; for further considerations, see Aggerholm, Jespersen and Ronglan 2011). This is not surprising, since research suggests that expert performers have heightened reflective awareness of the unfolding of events in which they participate as the event unfolds (Chaffin, Imreh and Crawford 2002; Ericsson and Kintsch 1995; Sutton 2007; Sutton, McIlwain, Christensen and Geeves 2011).

The net effect of these considerations is that the phenomenon of knowing-how in general and knowing-how at an expert level, in particular, is more complex and many-faceted than the Dreyfus picture suggest. There are at least three distinct modes of knowing-how and it is furthermore clear that expert performance is not confined to just one of these modes. Philosophers of sport should opt for sport-specific considerations when theorizing about knowing-how in sports, while entertaining the possibility that expert sport performance can render 'the mind wandering in and out between conscious effort and control and automatic subconscious state' (Breivik 2007:130). This, I believe, is good news for philosophers of sport, since there is still much exciting work to be done in this corner of epistemology, which, hopefully, will broaden and deepen our understanding of sport.

Concluding remarks

I have approached the question of an epistemology of sport by first addressing the question of how we can know sports: that is, being able to recognize something as a sport, and have shown that we first need to address the phenomenon of play. The particularist line, I have argued, is correct for knowing play. While we gain a criterion or criteria of play by already being able to know play, we acquire a criterion or criteria of sport when adding agonal qualities to the criterion of play, thus transforming play into sport and enabling us to engage in and know sports. The methodist line is correct for knowing sport. Furthermore, there are various ways by which one can know a sport and one of them is knowing-how to play a sport. Orthodoxy in the philosophy of sport has it that knowing-how to play a sport is constitutively connected to skilled performance and I have defended that orthodoxy against recent attacks. The fallout of that defence is that it turns out that the performance-connection is more complex than previously assumed or argued. Finally, I have shown that there are several modes of knowing-how and that top athletes' sport performances (that is, expert performances) are not confined to only one mode, which suggests that further sport-specific investigations and research into knowing-how in sports are warranted.

Acknowledgements

I am most grateful to Marc Bekoff, Gunnar Breivik, Scott Kretchmar, Mike McNamee, Bill Morgan and Margrethe Bruun Vaage for comments and critique. Parts of this work was presented at Norwegian University of Science and Technology, Vitenskapsteoretisk Forum, August 2013. I am grateful to all the participants.

Notes

1   The problem of the criterion was first championed by Sextus Empiricus (2000: 72–3) and brought into new prominence in the twentieth century by Roderick Chisholm (1957: 30–9; 1982: 61–75).

2   Notice that the problem, which Suits (2005: 161–74) discusses in the appendix 'The Fool on the Hill' in the Broadview reissue of *The Grasshopper*, is different from the problem of the criterion as I have presented it here. Suits addresses what is know as the inquiry paradox as it is formulated by Plato in *Meno* (1997: 79–86) and which in the twentieth century was dubbed the paradox of analysis by G. E. Moore (1903). Chisholm's problem of the criterion and my adaption of the problem within the epistemology of sport concerns the source of knowledge – in our case the source of knowledge of sports and the question of how we can recognize something as a sport as opposed to another type of activity. The inquiry paradox or the paradox of analysis, on the other hand, is about the seeming impossibility of a conceptual analysis being both correct and informative. In his appendix, Suits worries that:

> [I]n constructing my definition, I permitted myself to use as data things that were games … [b]ut how could I possibly know these things in the absence of the very definition[?] … Had I really had one tucked up my sleeve all along[?]'.
>
> *(Suits 1978: 163)*

This lands him, according to himself, 'in Plato's fire' (ibid.). In other words, either one cannot start constructing an analysis of the subject matter and thus there cannot be a correct analysis of games, or else the analysis will not be informative, since Suits already had an assumed definition of games, when he started his enquiry and thus no conceptual analysis of games can be informative. Suits acknowledges that his 'trouble appeared to be the same kind of trouble that Meno tried to make for Socrates' (ibid.). There is no room here to go into Suits own arguments about how to deal with the paradox of analysis. Suffice to say, Suits is worried about 'Meno's dilemma' as 'an entirely sensible one to raise against the search for definitions' (Suits 1978: 164), while the problem of the criterion for sports, as I have painted it here, concerns how we could even be able to recognize something as a sport – *pace* the question of whether we could come up with a valid and informative analysis of sports.

3   This is not to suggest that there cannot be borderline cases between play and non-play, where we are uncertain about the status of the activities as play or non-play.

4   Searle's account of constitutive rules as contrasted with regulative rules and how constitutive rules make certain social practices or institutions possible, is the most well-known and widely discussed theory in the literature, although Searle himself claims that the distinction was 'foreshadowed by Kant's distinction between regulative and constitutive principles', while acknowledging Rawls's (1955) 'discussion of a related distinction' (Searle 1964: 55; Midgley 1959 also precedes Searle).

5   Another, although somewhat different, anti-intellectualism position in the philosophy sport is found in Peter Hopsicker's (2009, 2011, 2013) work, which builds on Michael Polanyi's seminal work on tacit knowledge (Polanyi 1974).

6   Notice that several philosophers of sport deny this possibility, arguing that 'sports and games are acquired by demonstration, and not by teaching in the sense of being told' (Steel 1977: 101); see Breivik (2014), fourth section, 'Practical Knowledge: Sport Philosophy and Knowledge: the Beginnings' for an overview of this line of reasoning.

7   Stanley tells us that the main thesis of the Stanley–Williamson view is that 'knowing how to do something is the same as knowing a fact … when you learned how to swim, what happened is that you learned some facts about swimming' (Stanley 2011: vii).

8   Christopher Winch (2013) has also argued – although not in the context of thinking about sport – for a more complex picture of knowing-how.

9   Stanley's intellectualist position also allows for this (Stanley 2011: 24, 173, 183–4).

10 For a take on such issues with regard to playing music, see Sudnow (2001).
11 I take it to be uncontroversial that the phenomenology of in-zone awareness is consciously felt. That, however, need not mean that zoned-out awareness is devoid of phenomenology. Clearly, the phenomenon of zoned-out awareness has no explicit, available for the mind's eye phenomenology but perhaps there could be a more subtle and implicit, more evasive in its characteristics, phenomenology associated with zoned-out awareness (for an attempt to elucidate such a phenomenology in connection to the phenomenon know as self-deception, see Borge 2003: 19–21).

References

Aggerholm, Kenneth, Ejgil Jespersen and Lars Tore Ronglan. 2011. Falling for the feint – an existential investigation of a creative performance in high-level football. *Sport, Ethics and Philosophy*, 5(3): 343–58.

Armstrong, David. 1968. *A Materialist Theory of the Mind*. London: Routledge and Kegan Paul.

—— 1970. The nature of mind. In C.V. Borst (ed.) *The Mind–Brain Identity Theory*. London: Macmillan, 67–79.

—— 1981. What Is Consciousness? In *The Nature of Mind and Other Essays*. Ithaca, NY: Cornell University Press, 55–67.

Aspin, David. 1976. 'Knowing how' and 'knowing that' and physical education. *Journal of the Philosophy of Sport*, 3: 97–117.

Bekoff, Marc. 1995. Play signals as punctuation: The structure of social play in canids. *Behaviour* 132(5–6): 419–29.

Bekoff, Marc and John A. Byers (eds). 1998. *Animal Play: Evolutionary, comparative, and ecological perspectives*. Cambridge: Cambridge University Press.

Bengson, John and Marc A. Moffett. 2011. Two conceptions of mind and action: Knowing how and the philosophical theory of intelligence. In J. Bengson and M. A. Moffett (eds), *Knowing How: Essays on knowledge, mind, and action*, Oxford: Oxford University Press, 3–55.

Birch, Jens E. 2009. A phenomenal case for sport. *Sport, Ethics and Philosophy*, 3(1): 30–48.

Borge, Steffen. 2003. The myth of self-deception. *Southern Journal of Philosophy*, 41(1): 1–28.

—— 2010. May the best team win! In T. Richards (ed.) *Soccer and Philosophy*. Chicago, IL: Open Court, 23–35.

—— 2012. Review of Stephen Mumford, *Watching Sport: Aesthetics, ethics and emotion*. *Sport, Ethics and Philosophy*, 6(3): 401–6.

Breivik, Gunnar. 2007. Skillful coping in everyday life and in sport: A critical examination of the views of Heidegger and Dreyfus. *Journal of the Philosophy of Sport* 34(2): 116–34.

—— 2008. Bodily movement – the fundamental dimensions. *Sport, Ethics and Philosophy*, 2(3): 337–52.

—— 2011. Dangerous play with elements: Towards a phenomenology of risk sports. *Sport, Ethics and Philosophy*, 5(3): 314–30.

—— 2014. Sporting knowledge. In C. R. Torres (ed.) *The Bloomsbury Companion to the Philosophy of Sport*. London: Bloomsbury, 195–211.

Burghardt, Gordon M. 2005. *The Genesis of Animal Play: Testing the limits*. Cambridge, MA: MIT Press.

—— 2010. Play. In M. D. Breed and J. Moore (eds) *Encyclopedia of Animal Behavior*, vol. 2. Oxford: Academic Press, 740–4.

Carr, David. 1979. The logic of knowing how and ability. *Mind*, 88: 394–409.

—— 1981. Knowledge in practice. *American Philosophical Quarterly*, 18(1): 53–61.

Chaffin, Roger, Gabriela Imreh and Mary Crawford. 2002. *Practicing Perfection: Memory and piano performance*. Mahwah, NJ: Erlbaum.

Chisholm, Roderick. 1957. *Perceiving*. Ithaca, NY: Cornell University Press.

—— 1982. *Foundation of Knowing*. Minneapolis, MN: University of Minnesota Press.

Dennett, Daniel. 1981. Three kinds of intentional psychology. In R. A. Healy (ed.) *Reduction, Time and Reality: Studies in the philosophy of natural science*. Cambridge: Cambridge University Press.

Dickie, George. 1974. *Art and the Aesthetics*. Ithaca, NY: Cornell University Press.

—— 1984. *The Art Circle: A theory of art*. New York: Haven.

Dreyfus, Hubert. 2002. Intelligence without representation – Merleau-Ponty's critique of mental representation. *Phenomenology and the Cognitive Sciences* 1: 367–83.

—— 2007. The return of the myth of the mental. *Inquiry*, 50(4): 352–65.

Dreyfus, Hubert and Stuart Dreyfus. 1986. *Mind over Machine: The power of human intuition and expertise in the era of the computer*. New York: Free Press.

Ennen, Elizabeth. 2003. Phenomenological coping skills and the striatal memory system. *Phenomenology and the Cognitive Sciences*, 2: 299–325.

Ericsson, K. Anders and Walter Kintsch. 1995. Long-term working memory. *Psychological Review*, 102(2): 211–45.

Eriksen, Jørgen W. 2010. Mindless coping in competitive sports: Some implications and consequences. *Sport, Ethics and Philosophy*, 4(1): 66–86.

Fantl, Jeremy. 2012. Knowledge how. In Edward N. Zalta (ed.), *Stanford Encyclopedia of Philosophy*. Fall 2014 ed. Available online at http://plato.stanford.edu/archives/fall2014/entries/knowledge-how (accessed 8 October 2014).

Gallagher, Shaun. 2003. Bodily self-awareness and object perception. *Theoria et Historia Scientiarum*, 7(1): 53–68.

Gettier, Edmund. 1963. Is justified true belief knowledge? *Analysis* 23: 121–3.

Ginet, Carl. 1975. *Knowledge, Perception, and Memory*. Dordrecht: D. Reidel.

Graybiel, Ann M. 1998. The basal ganglia and chunking of action repertoires. *Neurobiology of Learning and Memory*, 70(1–2): 119–36.

Harris, Max. 2000. *Aztecs, Moors, and Christians: Festivals of Reconquest in Mexico and Spain*. Austin, TX: University of Texas Press.

Haugeland, John. 1981. Semantic engines: An introduction to mind design. In J. Haugeland (ed.) *Mind Design: Philosophy, psychology, artificial intelligence*. Cambridge, MA: MIT Press, 1–34.

Hawley, Katherine. 2003. Success and knowledge-how. *American Philosophical Quarterly* 40(1): 19–31.

Heidegger, Martin. 1963 [1927]. *Sein und Seit*. Tübingen: Max Niemeyer Verlag.

—— 1988 [1927]. *The Basic Problems of Phenomenology*, trans. A. Hofstadter. Bloomington, IL: Indiana University Press.

Hopsicker, Peter. 2009. Polanyi's 'from-to' knowing and his contribution to the phenomenology of skilled motor behavior. *Journal of the Philosophy of Sport*, 36: 76–87.

—— 2011. In search of the 'sporting genius': Exploring the benchmarks to creative behavior in sporting activity. *Journal of the Philosophy of Sport*, 38(1): 113–27.

—— 2013. 'The value of the inexact': An apology for inaccurate motor performance. *Journal of the Philosophy of Sport*, 40(1): 65–83.

Hornsby, Jennifer. 2012. Ryle's *Knowing-how* and knowing how to act. In J. Bengson and M. A. Moffett (eds), *Knowing How: Essays on knowledge, mind, and action*. Oxford: Oxford University Press, 80–98.

Huizinga, Johan. 1950. *Homo Ludens*. Boston: Beacon.

Hyland, Drew A. 1990. *Philosophy of Sport*. New York: Paragon House.

Kretchmar, Scott. 1988. From Test to Contest: An analysis of two kinds of counterpoints in sport. In W. J. Morgan and K. V. Meier (eds), *Philosophic Inquiry in Sport*. Champaign, IL: Human Kinetics, 223–9.

—— 2001. A functionalistic analysis of game acts: Revisiting Searle. *Journal of the Philosophy of Sport*, 28(2): 160–72.

—— 2007. The normative heights and depths of play. *Journal of the Philosophy of Sport*, 34: 1–12.

Kretchmar, Scott and Tim Elcombe. 2007. In defense of competition and winning: Revisiting tests and contests. In W. J. Morgan (ed.) *Ethics in Sport*. Champaign, IL: Human Kinetics, 181–94.

Leal, Luis. 1982. Los voladores: From ritual to game. *New Scholar* 8: 129–42.

Legerstee, Maria. 2005. *Infants' Sense of People: Precursors to a theory of mind*. Cambridge: Cambridge University Press.

Loland, Sigmund. 1992. The mechanics and meaning of alpine skiing: Methodological and epistemological notes on the study of sport technique. *Journal of the Philosophy of Sport*, 19: 55–77.

McDowell, John. 2007. Response to Dreyfus. *Inquiry*, 50(4): 366–70.

McFee, Graham. 2004. *Sport, Rules and Values: Philosophical investigations into the nature of sport*. London: Routledge.

McNamee, Mike. 2008. *Sports, Virtues and Vices: Morality plays*. London: Routledge.

Maradona, Diego Armando with Daniel Arcucci and Ernesto Cherquis Bialo. 2000. *Maradona: The autobiography of soccer's greatest and most controversial star*. New York: Skyhorse.

Meier, Klaus V. 1988. Tricky triad: Playing with sports and games. *Journal of the Philosophy of Sport*, 15: 11–30.

Merleau-Ponty, Maurice. 1945. *Phénoménologie de la Perception*, Paris: Gallimard.

Midgley, Geoffrey. 1959. Linguistic rules. *Proceedings of the Aristotelian Society* 59: 271–90.

Moe, Vegard Fusche. 2005. A philosophical critique of classical cognitivism in sport. From information processing to bodily background knowledge. *Journal of Philosophy of Sport* 32: 155–83.

—— 2007. Understanding the background conditions of skilled movements in sport: A study of Searle's 'background capacities'. *Sports, Ethics and Philosophy*. 1(3): 299–324.

Moore, George Edward. 1903. The refutation of idealism. *Mind* 12: 433–53.

Morgan, William. 1994. *Leftists Theories of Sport*. Chicago, IL: University of Illinois Press.

Mumford, Stephen. 2012. *Watching Sport: Aesthetics, ethics and emotion*. London: Routledge.

Nakano, Shigeru and Yuko Kanaya. 1993. The effects of mothers' teasing: Do Japanese infants read their mothers' play intentions in teasing? *Early Development and Parenting*, 1(2): 7–17.

Noë, Alva. 2005. Against intellectualism. *Analysis* 65(4): 278–90.

Pellegrine, Anthony. 2009. *The Role of Play in Human Development*. Oxford: Oxford University Press.

Pellegrini, Anthony D. and Peter K. Smith (eds). 2005. *The Nature of Play: Great Apes and Humans*. New York: Guilford.

Plato. 1997. *Meno*. In *Plato: Complete Works*, edited by J. M. Cooper. Indianapolis, IN: Hackett.

Polanyi, Michael. 1974 [1958]. *Personal Knowledge: Towards a post-critical philosophy*. Chicago: University of Chicago Press.

Rawls, John. 1955. Two concepts of rules. *Philosophical Review* 64: 3–32.

Reddy, Vasudevi. 1991. Playing with others' expectations: Teaching and mucking about in the first year. In A. Whitten (ed.) *Natural Theories of Mind: Evolution, development and simulation of everyday mindreading*. Oxford: Blackwell, 143–58.

Ryle, Gilbert. 1946. Knowing how and knowing that. *Proceedings of the Aristotelian Society*, 46: 1–16.

—— 1949 [reprinted 2009]. *The Concept of Mind*. London: Routledge.

Schneider, Angela. 2001. Fruits, apples, and category mistakes: On sports, games, and play. *Journal of the Philosophy of Sport*, 28(2): 151–9.

Searle, John. 1964. How to derive 'ought' from 'is'. *Philosophical Review*, 73: 43–58.

—— 1969. *Speech Acts: An essay in the philosophy of language*. Cambridge: Cambridge University Press.

—— 1995. *The Construction of Social Reality*. New York: Free Press.

Sextus Empiricus. 2000. *Sextus Empiricus: Outlines of scepticism*, edited by J. Annas and J. Barnes. Cambridge: Cambridge University Press.

Smith, Peter K. 2010. *Children and Play*. Chichester: Wiley.

Standal, Øyvind F. and Vegard F. Moe. 2011. Merleau-Ponty meets Kretchmar: Sweet tensions of embodied learning. *Sport, Ethics and Philosophy*, 5(3): 256–69.

Stanley, Jason. 2011. *Know How*. Oxford: Oxford University Press.

Stanley, Jason and Timothy Williamson. 2001. Knowing how. *Journal of Philosophy*, 98(8): 411–444.

Steel, Margaret. 1977. What we know when we know a game. *Journal of the Philosophy of Sport*, 4: 96–103.

Sudnow, David. 2001. *Ways of the Hand: A rewritten account*. Cambridge, MA: MIT Press.

Suits, Bernard. 1967. What is a Game? *Philosophy of Science*, 34: 148–56.

—— 1988. Tricky triad: Games, play, and sport. *Journal of the Philosophy of Sport*, 15: 1–9.

—— 2005 [1978]. *The Grasshopper: Games, life and utopia*. Peterborough, ON: Broadview.

Sutton, John. 2007. Batting, habit and memory: The embodied mind and the nature of skill. *Sport in Society*, 10(5): 763–86.

Sutton, John, Doris McIlwain, Wayne Christensen and Andrew Geeves. 2011. Applying intelligence to the reflexes: Embodied skills and habits between Dreyfus and Descartes. *Journal of the British Society for Phenomenology*, 42(1): 78–103.

Tomasello, Michael and Josep Call. 2009. *Primate Cognition*. Oxford: Oxford University Press.

Weatherson, Brian. 2006. Ryle on knowing. *Thoughts Arguments and Rants*, 22 July [blog]. Available online at http://tar.weatherson.org/2006/07/22/ryle-on-knowing-how (accessed 8 October 2014).

Wertz, Spencer K. 1978. The knowing in playing. *Journal of the Philosophy of Sport*, 5: 39–49.

Winch, Christopher. 2013. Three different conceptions of know-how and their relevance to professional and vocational education. *Journal of Philosophy of Education*, 47(2): 281–98.

Wittgenstein, Ludwig. 1953. *Philosophical Investigations*. Oxford: Blackwell.

Wrisberg, Craig A. 2001. Levels of performance skill: From beginning to experts. In R. N. Singer, H. A. Hausenblas and C. M. Janelle (eds), *Handbook of Sport Psychology*. New York: Wiley, 3–19.

Ziff, Paul. 1974. A fine forehand. *Journal of the Philosophy of Sport*, 1: 92–109.

9

ETHICS AND SPORTS

Mike McNamee

Introduction

It might be said that there are some interesting points of similarity within philosophy gener-ally, and ethics more specifically, and the philosophy of sport and sports ethics. In 1982, the American philosopher Steven Toulmin (1982) wrote an article entitled 'How medicine saved the life of ethics'. The success or otherwise of medical ethics led Glenn McGee (2006), another leading American scholar, to write an editorial in 2006 asking 'Will bioethics take the life of philosophy?'. The titles of the essays are self-explanatory. There is little doubt that the devel-opment of sports ethics breathed new life into the philosophy of sport and has, for the last two decades, been the most dominant subject of published scholarship in the field. Whether its success will be seen to have eclipsed the parent subject or 'merely' invigorated it is something that cannot be evaluated *in media res*. What I take to be incontestable is that the philosophy of sport has flourished during this period, and has brought wider interest from philosophers outside sport and policy makers within it than has ever been the case hitherto and that has been due in large part to the rise of sports ethics as an academic subject. In this chapter, I chart the history of sports ethics scholarship, set out its main theoretical approaches and indicate future prospects.

History and philosophical influences

When setting out to chart the nature, history and scope of sports ethics, I was reminded of a celebrated philosophical joke, whose punch line has import for the present task. Ryle's (1949) classic, *The Concept of Mind*, included the idea of a category mistake: the misappropriation of an item(s) belonging to one category that is put in another. Ryle (1949) gives the example of a foreign visitor to Oxford or Cambridge University, who claims to have seen all the colleges, libraries, playing fields and so on, but states that they have yet to see the university. Of course these universities are no more than the sum of their various parts, not another building or insti-tution. The analogy with sports ethics is this: the typical list of items that comprise the category (doping, inequality, technology, fair play, and so on) are already to be discussed under their own headings elsewhere in this volume. One is left wondering: what else is there to sports ethics other than these constituent parts?

One could go back to Plato and Aristotle and note that they had already made observations about the place and limitations of gymnastics and athletics in the good life (Reid, 2012). A renewed scholarship of this area has been of recent interest (Dombrowski, 2009; Holowchack and Reid, 2011). Others have connected that early Greek scholarship with similar developments elsewhere in the ancient world (Reid, 2010; Ilundáin, 2014). The highly regulated states of affairs we now recognize as sports is usually attributed to Victorian Britain, and one finds considerable ethical reflection in texts of sports history (see, for example, Mangan, 1981; Mangan, 1987; Holt, 1989; McIntosh, 1979; Renson, 2009). In addition, but closely related to both ancient and Victorian sources, were the reflections of the Baron Pierre de Coubertin (De Coubertin, 2000), among whose voluminous writings was the concept of Olympism, the official ideology and philosophy of the International Olympic Committee, which is rich in ethical content. It too has spawned a significant scholarship (see Reid and Austin, 2012; DaCosta, 2006; McLaughlin and Torres, 2011; McNamee and Parry, 1998; McNamee, 2006; Parry, 2006; Walmsley, 2004) despite near universal criticism of its philosophical coherence.

In his 1983 review of the state of the art in sports ethics, Scott Kretchmar surveys no more than a handful of articles on cheating, sportsmanship (*sic*) and the work of Fraleigh and McIntosh, but little else. This, in itself, is comment on the then embryonic state of sports ethics scholarship. Perhaps the first sustained scholarship – a monograph in sports ethics, recognizable within the philosophy of sport – was Warren Fraleigh's (1984) *Right Actions in Sport*, produced in the halcyon days of the philosophy of sport's rise in the USA. As the title indicates, the book was a confluence of Fraleigh's twin interests in philosophy and physical education. Fraleigh's task was to set out a coherent and philosophically robust system of duties for participants and others engaged in sports. It is a classic in the field. It is important to note that the book attempted much more than an analytical account of the moral nature of sports. Fraleigh laid out a very clear normative vision which, if assented to, committed rational sportspersons and coaches to a system of duties within sports regarding their individual opponents and opposing team and entourage. In this sense, he offered an account of duties of those engaged but also an account of what *good* sports look like. Thus, the book embodies both deontological (a theory of ethical duties) and teleological (a theory of ethical ends, goals, or purposes) concerns. The import of the book, however, largely resided in its systematic and practical application of duties or obligations that were rationally founded in the nature of the sports contest.

Shortly after publication of *Right Actions in Sport*, a second classic in sports ethics was published: Robert Simon's (1985) *Sports and Social Values*. Again, the text arose in the context of American sports and scholarship. As with Fraleigh's groundbreaking book, Simon sought to move beyond the mere conceptual analysis of games, play and sport that had dominated the sole journal then dedicated to the field – the *Journal of the Philosophy of Sport* – and to entwine conceptual and normative analysis. Simon's book has been revised since then, but its essential structure and message stayed the same: drawing on legal and political contractarian theoretical precursors he argued that sports are a mutual quest for athletic excellence. The thesis has been widely influential in the scholarship of the philosophy of sport, not just in sports ethics.

For reasons that are difficult to comprehend, these books, although well received in the philosophy of sport milieu, did not initiate a step-change either within the subject or in cognate professions. This may have been due to the philosophical complexity of the volumes and the relative paucity of qualified personnel to teach the subject. In 1994, Angela Lumpkin, Sharon Stoll and Jennifer Beller produced a text in the subject, *Fair Play*, which was clearly aimed at the American undergraduate market and enjoyed widespread success there. Nevertheless, it was not until 1998 that another volume, *Ethics and Sport,* edited by Mike McNamee and Jim Parry in the UK, was published in the English language, to bolster the work that Fraleigh and Simon's monographs had begun. Unlike those monographs, the book was both theoretically and geoculturally diverse, drawing on contributions from philosophers of sport from around the world. As an edited collection, it was eclectic in the subjects and thus showcased the range of issues that the ethics of sport might address. It was critically well received and went on to spawn a book series that now comprises approximately 30 volumes, making sports ethics easily the most voluminous of the strands of philosophy of sport. Another feature of its impact was that, in the UK and around Europe at least, new modules at undergraduate and postgraduate levels were initiated. In addition, several further international anthologies have been published that evidence the robust health of this branch of the philosophy of sport (Boxill, 2003; Morgan, 2007; McNamee, 2010).

Finally, in the first decade of the twenty-first century, two new journals have been developed. *Sport, Ethics and Philosophy* (2007), published quarterly, and *Fair Play. Journal of Sport: Philosophy, Ethics and Law* (2013), published biannually in both English and Spanish languages.

To sum up this first section then, it strikes me that, both intellectually and institutionally, the philosophy of sport sailed through difficult waters between the mid 1980s and 1990s. After Toulmin's remarks quoted above, it seems fair to claim that ethics, if it did not save the life of philosophy of sport, certainly gave it much-needed oxygen.

The scope of sports ethics

The reach of sports ethics is far and wide. I chart only what I take to be the major issues that have been discussed, although the survey is admittedly brief and selective. Only those issues that have generated significant philosophical interest are noted, while it is recognized that there are important issues, such as children's rights, child abuse, deviance, homophobia, racism, and so on, that have tended to be more discussed in the sociological literature.

The dominant ethical theories that are found in the sports ethics literature have generally speaking been applied *mutatis mutandis*. That is to say, there are no outstanding examples of sports ethics scholarship that simply take a received ethical theory and mix with sports to deduce normative guides for action. Fraleigh's (1984) classic came closest to this. But even here, as was noted above, the book was a combination of deontology and teleology. Precisely how the theories were to be combined was not laid out in sophisticated methodological detail.

Taking inspiration from Fraleigh, and to a lesser extent Simon, the Norwegian philosopher Sigmund Loland (2002) attempted to combine a Rawlsian theory of justice and aspects of utilitarian philosophy to maximize the rational assent of interested parties in sports with specific regard to binding norms of fair play. Loland's programme is a strong one, drawing in large part its inspiration from the liberal political philosopher John Rawls' (1971) classic *A Theory of Justice*. Nevertheless, both Loland and Fraleigh attempt to develop an architectonic structure that will bind all competitors to norms or action guides. This struck many philosophers of sport as overly rationalistic. Some claimed that their underpinning universalism pays insufficient detail to the human agent, cultural differences and the powerful roles that sports institutions play in the shaping of sports.

There exist exceptions to this multi-theory method of stating a system of sports ethics. A small but important literature has developed from a utilitarian perspective and represents a more deductive application of a single moral theory to sports. The second, virtue ethics, is less deductive and more context-sensitive. It might be claimed that it too eschews a single vocabulary of ethical vision, incorporating ideas from other theories under its broad theoretical umbrella. I discuss them in turn.

Over the last 10–15 years, the philosophy of sport welcomed a new and vibrant pair of philosophers from Sweden who had not previously published in sports. Bringing instead their expertise in moral and political philosophy, Claudio Tamburrini and Torbjorn Tännsjö created considerable interest in their challenging ethical ideas by the strict application of consequentialism. Although Loland, before, had incorporated utilitarian ideas within his largely Rawlsian approach to sports justice, Tamburrini and Tännsjö separately published work that challenged widely held norms regarding sports. Two positions are especially noteworthy.

First, Tännsjö (1998) argued that our admiration for sporting heroes embodied a fascistic disposition, since it necessarily entailed contempt for the weak (that is, losing or lesser opposition). His line was challenged by his former doctoral student, Tamburrini (1998: 45), arguing that, 'The positive results for the public's admiration of sporting heroes seems to outweigh the eventual negative consequences of the practice'. Other scholars offered criticisms that did not rely on consequentialist readings (Holowchak, 2005; Persson, 2000). Secondly, Tamburrini has argued for the relaxation of anti-doping policy, technologization and some forms of cheating (including Diego Maradona's famous illegal and deceptive punching of the ball into the 1986 football World Cup final), sex equality in sport, and so on (Tamburrini, 2000; Tännsjö and Tamburrini, 2005). Controversial claims such as these, were defended according to utilitarian principles. Both scholars brought fresh impetus to sports ethics, attacking conservatism, promoting liberal-utilitarian defenses for controversial topics, and promoting a largely neglected ethical theory in and for sport. Two points are worth observing here. The first is that *ceteris paribus* one might think there was a significant opportunity to explore the possibility of the public provision of sports in those countries of the world where there was state provision of sporting opportunities or elite sports programmes, or sports where the state has intervened on grounds of harm prevention where utilitarian commitments to beneficence, impartiality, and maximization would have ready application. But discussion of such is thin on the ground (cf. McNamee *et al.*, 2001; Radford, 1988; Savulescu, 2005). Secondly, despite their utilitarian credentials and expertise, it is noteworthy how little empirical evidence is offered in defense of the positions so controversially proposed by Tamburrini and Tännsjö – and for an ethic predicated on empirical matters this is an important weakness.

Two key themes emerged from the ruminations of utilitarian writings that have broader import and they can be traced back to John Stuart Mill's founding ideas: the focus on individual liberty (usually expressed as autonomous choice or agent sovereignty) and the 'harm principle', whereby competent adults ought to have the freedom to choose pursuits that might be harmful to themselves though not to others. Certainly, these principles fuelled Tamburrini's more *laissez faire* attitude towards doping practices in elite sport (and others of a non-utilitarian persuasion, such as Møller, 2009). Crucially, however, these two ideas have been propounded by others who have not relied overtly on a utilitarian (or more generically consequentialist) theoretical framework. Notable examples include Davis (1993) and Dixon (2001), in relation to boxing, and Russell (2005) in pursuit of adventurous activities. It is noteworthy that with respect to the latter or, more generally, risky pursuits, Breivik (2007) has remarked that the circle of those affected negatively by the apparently risky choices of BASE jumpers is far greater than the individual jumper. Negative consequences must be considered to extend to the unhappiness (even misery) of family members and state-provided health care services in the case of dead or seriously injured jumpers. Again, however, actual data for such are sparse. And this, for a branch of applied ethics, can be considered problematic *qua* incompleteness and/or accuracy of the harms and benefits that are to be counted.

Perhaps the most significant volume of sports ethics literature has been published in broadly speaking in the domain of virtue ethics in sport (Arnold, 1997; Feezel, 2004; Gough, 2007; Holowchak and Reid, 2010, 2011; McNamee, 2008). Much of their inspiration, although not all, has come directly from Aristotle's writings or from contemporary philosophers heavily influenced by Aristotle such as Martha Nussbaum, Edmund Pincoffs and, most especially, Alasdair MacIntyre.

In his most celebrated book, *After Virtue*, MacIntyre (1981) articulated the necessarily social contexts in which virtue, the particular dispositions of good persons aimed at the living of good lives rather than the principles of right action, must be understood. Certainly, some authors have taken this general theoretical commitment (Morgan, 2006; Feezel, 2013) without drawing in detail on MacIntyre's specific thesis on the social practices and their constitutive goods and virtues. Others have attempted to provide a critical interpretation of the idea of sports *as* social practices whose existence is predicated on supra-subjective norms of excellence, supportive virtues (and corrosive vices) in the pursuit of internal goods that represent the inherent satisfaction and value of sporting engagement (Arnold, 1997; Dombrowski, 2009; Feezel, 2004; McNamee, 2008; Reid, 2012). Each of these authors, despite their differences, share a common concern that goods external to sport such as money, fame, media, and so on, continue to have a corrosive effect on sports – although not all agree on the extent nor indeed on the precise economic pathologies (Lasch, 1979; Walsh and Giuliannotti, 2006) that have brought them about. The insight is, of course, hardly unique to virtue ethical considerations.

Notwithstanding the widespread support for the idea that an emphasis on external goods might corrupt sports, serious concerns have been raised about the intelligibility of the idea of internal goods as related to sports. Little philosophical attention has been paid to the dual, and mutually opposed, functions of sports institutions to structure, administrate, promote and regulate sporting practices. Serious sports journalists and sociologists of sports have tended to take on the critical task of holding sports institutions such as the Federation of International Football Associations (FIFA) and the International Olympic Committee to task (see, for example, respectively, Jennings, 1996; Sugden and Tomlinson, 1998). More complex philosophical analyses of the political and economic (cf. Walsh and Giulianotti, 2006) criticism of unethical practices and governance failures at individual and social levels have not been as forthcoming. Equally, little virtue ethical consideration has been given to issues of corruption in sports, which appears to be the biggest threat to sports integrity outside doping.

Authority and expertise in sports ethics

Those who specialize in sports ethics are likely to be met with uncomfortable questions, which come in at least two forms. The first pertains to the value of the field, while the second has to do with a confusion as to its methods and aims. When members of the general public learn that philosophers discuss sport ethics for a living, they respond (not infrequently) with incredulity to the fact that this could be the object of a profession and not more fitting to a bar or after dinner conversation. Part of this response is a general assumption that subjectivism is the only possible ethical perspective in late modernity, and a more specific one that ethical issues in sports are something in which non-philosophers might have as equal a claim to authority as the philosopher or ethicist. The most generous view, under such assumptions, would be that any view is as good as the next one, and the least generous would be that those enamoured of a lifetime of sports participation would have greater authority than sports philosophers or sports ethicists.

A word about nomenclature is necessary here. The term 'ethicist' has gained international recognition in a number of domains in recent years. Professionally, this might be seen to be a good thing and, although I confess that I am not enamoured of it, I use it throughout the chapter. It appears to identify (at least in name) a person who has the relevant knowledge, competencies and expertise to claim this domain as their field. One philosophical concern is that this confers a kind of technical expertise such as might be had by an engineer, or a doctor, plumber or a mechanic. By contrast to the general public, an ethicist would be thought of as having relevant and developed knowledge base that the general public does not. Is this identification justifiable? Specifically, for present concerns, it might be asked why ought sports ethicists' voices be thought of as authoritative? What is the nature of their expertise that might afford them such authority?

One helpful way to proceed in thinking about this problem is to indicate, at least loosely, an epistemological scheme that set out what a sports ethicist ought to know in order to be considered a bona fide ethicist. What might that look like? Kretchmar (1998) argued that a sophisticated understanding of the nature of sports would be a necessary precursor. It would be more than merely difficult to appreciate the kinds of behaviours of athletes and players without some appreciation of the nature of the activity they were engaged in. Sports ethicists should possess, in addition a thorough knowledge of the relevant rules. An understanding of the well-known distinction between constitutive and regulative rules (Reddiford, 1985; Suits, 2005) and widely agreed upon auxillary rules (Meier, 1985) would be necessary as well. Sports ethicists would also need to possess sufficient knowledge of the (relevant) rules that prescribe and proscribe forms of sporting conduct. They would also require a developed capacity to reflect upon the normative dis/value of a given behaviour, which, in turn, depends on a reasonable familiarity with the kinds of formal and informal agreements that the rules allow, or as the case may be, disallow. It is difficult to see, based on these provisional remarks, whether there is a sufficient body of ethical knowledge required in sport to designate someone as an ethical expert or authority on these matters. Is it not the case, it might reasonably be asked, that most devotees of sports already possess the kinds of knowledge mentioned above?

We might then say that the kinds of knowledge possessed by the sports ethicist must be more than, or at least partly different from, that possessed by the philosopher of sport who does not specialize thus. We might call the former, philosophical appreciation of the conceptual features of sports: a form of systematic knowledge. Understanding, for example, the gratuitous logic of sports is not something even devoted and lifelong players and coaches are likely to have reflected upon or understood in any deep or meaningful way (Hardman and Jones, 2010). Then, of course, there are the various understandings of formalism, internalism, conventionalism or institutional theories of sport discussed elsewhere in this volume, which extend and deepen the insights of what it means to play a sport.

Thus far, the sports ethicist is no more than a philosopher of sport. I am not convinced that a deep and systematic knowledge of the rules or cultures of sports are required for most scholarship in the philosophy of sport. Yet these seem to be vital to the sports ethicist if they are to reflect conceptually and normatively on the modes of conduct that have been the object of discussion such as cheating, gaining unfair advantages, the voluntary suspension of fair play, exploiting covert technologies, deceiving officials by simulation (diving), and so on. Knowing what the ethos of the relevant activites are, what the sports' rules are and how they are (or might be) interpreted, would seem to be critical if one aspired, as sport ethicists do, to provide nuanced ethical evaluations thereof. In outline, we would have here the basis of theoretical and practical knowledge that might comprise the knowledge base of sports ethics and the claims to authority of the sports ethicist. But more needs to be said about the theory–practice relation here, and the kinds of each that might develop *de jure* authority in ethical discussions of sport.

Certainly, the sports ethicist will need to understand ethical theories and have a grasp of general argumentative strategies, such as assumption spotting, the making of invalid inferences, asserting conclusions that go beyond the premises, and so on. One particular challenge to ethicists is their knowledge of the relevant empirical data. In ethics, as opposed to many branches of philosophy, facts seriously alter our considerations of particular cases, even where there is agreement on general norms. So the technical knowledge of sports ethics required by the sports ethicist will comprise general philosophical techniques, particular knowledge of sports cultures and the relevant empirical literatures concerning issues like of sporting practices, harms arising from participation, what athletes actually think about the intrusiveness of anti-doping controls, prevalence of homophobic attitudes, and so on. It is the combination of this technical knowledge that, along with the philosophical acumen of the ethicist, can help culti-vate the practical wisdom that is necessary for authoritative guidance and intervention into the daily milieu of sports contexts such as sports administration, policy making, coaching and event organizing.

I suggested in the previous paragraph that one form of *techne* a sports ethicist must grapple with and master pertains to empirical data concerning ethical issues in sports. Now the ques-tion remains, in the light of the naturalistic fallacy (Moore, 1903), whether and how such data may be used in ethical argument. In the early days of analytical philosophy it was widely held that facts and values were distinct logical categories. Moore (1903) argued, following Hume (1978), that one could not infer normative conclusions from statements of natural facts. The idea found its way into a number of arguments concerning the ethics of doping, where certain substances or methods were argued to be unnatural and, by virtue of that determination alone, regarded as unethical. Such arguments were (perhaps a little too swiftly) brushed aside (Miah, 2000). While it is true that one cannot slide together what is natural with what is good, the idea that a particular behavior or body enhancement was un/natural still has some normative force, drawing on either the pervasiveness of a widely held value or a fact pertaining to the health or harm of the body. Rather, it is the naive deductive move from what is natural to its being thought thereby to be good that is problematic. Moreover, as legion philosophers have commented, the very idea that the generation of fact is somehow removed from all evaluative or normative scientific enquires is a crude positivistic assumption now widely discredited (Putnam, 2002).

So, the place of facts within (sports) ethical discourse cannot be swept aside as a piece of faulty logic. And it is worth observing that some sports ethical argumentation may properly progress without recourse to empirical data. For example, it is a widely shared concern whether sports are to be conceived of, taught and evaluated as inherently ethical practices (Carr, 1998). The issue may be evaluated at a conceptual level (Gough, 1995). Equally, there might be rele-vant facts unearthed in favour of or against such a contention (Stoll, 1999). The facts do not settle the matter. Nevertheless, it may be necessary, depending on the ethical issue in question, to marshal the relevant empirical data for or against a position. Careful conceptual work is always inevitable and may even cut the feet from under psychological and sociological research, which is conducted in ways that display naiveté as to the theory-ladenness of the research ques-tions and data (Carr, 1998; Gough, 1995, 1997; McNamee *et al.*, 2003).

Pace Fraleigh and Loland, I submit that what cannot be expected of the sports ethicist, *qua* ethicist, are technical solutions that are necessarily error free, or neutrality with respect to theo-retical commitments. In some fields, the received idea of expertise will belong to the person who can identify best practice solutions, as if these were uncontested. There will be tasks that a sports ethicist might undertake where s/he might identify weaknesses in sports rules, incon-sistencies with mission statements, of guiding values of sports institutions, ambiguities in the concepts employed in educational materials, and so on. This conception of the task is likely to be less problematic than offering substantive and positive revisions for sports practices, being largely negative in nature and employing the technical knowledge and abilities typical of a philosopher. Making positive recommendations, for example, to bring about more just allocation of prizes, fairer alignment of competitors, rules for the protection of vulnerable participants in children's sports, educational anti-doping materials for athletes, and so on, are more likely to be contested. Both represent deeply normative tasks, but it is likely that the conservatism of sports institutions and their often anti-intellectual character may render them deaf or blind (or both) to the kinds of sophisticated marshaling of evidence and argument that a sports ethicist can offer. And this conservatism is not merely a product of the commercialization of sports and the preservation of their interests. After all, Macintyre himself argues that those who are not immersed in the practices he uses as exemplars of social practices (a heterogeneous list that includes agriculture, architecture, making and sustaining family lives, politics, sports, and so on) are incompetent thereby to judge them. This problem has been recognized in the sports ethics (Brown, 1990; McNamee, 1995) and social theory/political philosophy of sport literature (Morgan, 1994), and has appeared in debates regarding internalism (Simon, 2000). But it is not yet clear how much or to what extent this is either a theoretical or practical problem, or indeed both.

Future prospects

None of us has the gift of clairvoyance but it is possible to discern the initial developments of four new directions in sports ethics. I briefly discuss them as follows: (i) the critical evaluation of ethics of particular sports (iii) the confluence of sports ethics and sports law; (iii) ethical critique of policy; and (iv) the rise of descriptive or empirical sports ethics.

First, while the last 20 years or so have seen a number of edited collections, whether themed or not, a natural development for the subject will be the development of in-depth collections focused on single sports or categories of sports, such as Paralympic sports, which have been widely neglected. Such collections already exist within the philosophy of sport in the case of football (soccer) (Richards, 2013) and cycling (Ilundain Agaruzza and Austin, 2010). The extent to which future volumes will be aimed at a popular philosophy market or a professional one remains to be seen. There is no principled reason why the development should not be in relation to the latter, although the former will clearly have more commercial appeal and may have more beneficial long-term effects in terms of widening the appreciation for the subject and drawing in a wider group of philosophers hitherto unpublished in the field.

Secondly, in some branches of applied ethics, it is notable that ethics and law are taught and researched together. Certainly this is the case in medicine. Within sports, however, there is no tradition for the conjoining of the two disciplines. Yet there are definite benefits relating to that confluence. The first is that sports ethics discussions are seen to have greater purchase. Members of sports institutions are more likely to sit up and take note when an ethical point made by philosophers is contextualized in a legal landscape. Partly this will be out of crude self-interest: after all, who wants to be sued for breaking (for example) laws on discrimination or unjust treatment, or for fraud (such as doping and athlete sponsorships)? Secondly, legal scholars of sport can, in principle, benefit from the precise arguments laid out by sports ethicists. I say 'in principle' here because the legal toolkit is not so very different from a philosophical one. There may be no reasons to suppose *qua* sports ethicists that their reflections will be *sui generis*. At the very least, one might expect there to be synergy between the two disciplines but, at present, the academic field of sports law is still in relative infancy and the profession has tended to grow in close relation to commercial practices (typically regarding employment contracts).

Thirdly, sports ethicists develop their work in the realm of policy critique to create a greater profile. For more than 20 years, a considerable literature on ethical aspects of Title IX legislation in the USA regarding equal opportunities sexual discrimination in athletics funding has developed (Boxill, 1993; Burke, 2010; Francis, 1993; Lopiano, 2007; Simon, 1993; Staurowsky, 2003). Recent years have witnessed a burgeoning literature in relation to anti-doping policy (Houlihan and McNamee, 2013; Møller, 2009; McNamee and Møller, 2011; Murray et al., 2009). Nevertheless, the area of ethical policy critique is something of a lacuna. The dangers of work in this field are that one's work quickly becomes dated in relation to the shifting sands of policy makers and revisions of the policies under discussion. Moreover, it may be difficult for ethicists to find matters of significant ethical depth to engage them fully. Yet the value of greater clarity and coherence within sports policy and greater ethical justifiability therein are not gains to be dismissed lightly.

Finally, I have said that there are times when good facts are simply necessary for good arguments in sports ethics. Sometimes these data will come from personal observation, at other times they will come (or ought to come) from rigorous social scientific examination. The latter is often referred to as descriptive ethics. Those doing descriptive ethics need 'hard' facts to develop their postures or policies on ethically challenging matters. Of course how 'hard' these facts are is a moot point. Nevertheless, descriptive ethics – yielding both qualitative and quantitative data – is something that sports institutions are likely to seek more frequently in the future as the field becomes more established and better known. The challenge for sports ethicists with training in (sports) philosophy will be to contribute philosophical depth to these discussions. The criterion of 'relevance' is not one automatically pursued by philosophers, whose problems have often been thought of as timeless. This 'one step removed from the world' approach is highly unlikely to impress research sponsors or sports institutions. Creating impact can lead to dumbing down of research. But the challenges may well be worth the risk.

The only danger attending this shift is that policy makers, educators, coaches, and others, privilege descriptive over normative or philosophically dense ethical enquiries. If this were to happen, we might very well find that descriptive ethics brings in its wake a situation pathological to those sports ethicists who want seriously to engage in ethical theorizing in the contexts of sports. But only the future will reveal that. What is clear is that the field of sports ethics is, at least in these early decades, flourishing and with every sign of a healthy long-term future.

References

Arnold, P. (1997). *Sport, Ethics and Education*. London: Bloomsbury.

Boxill, J. (1993). Title IX and Gender Equity. *Journal of the Philosophy of Sport*, 20(1): 23–31.

Boxill, J. (ed.) (2003). *Sports Ethics: An anthology*. Oxford: Blackwell.

Breivik, G. (2007). 'Can BASE jumping be morally defended?' in M. J. McNamee, (ed.). *Philosophy, Risk and Adventure Sports*. Abingdon: Routledge, 168–85.

Brown, W. M. (1990). Practices and Prudence. *Journal of the Philosophy of Sport*, 17(1): 71–84.

Burke, M. (2010). A Feminist Reconstruction of Liberal Rights and Sport. *Journal of the Philosophy of Sport*, 37(1): 11–28.

Carr, D. (1998). 'What Moral Educational Significance has Physical Education? A question in need of disambiguation' in M. J. McNamee and S. J. Parry (eds), *Ethics and Sport*. Abingdon: Routledge, 119–33.

DaCosta, L. (2006). A Never-Ending Story: The Philosophical Controversy over Olympism, *Journal of the Philosophy of Sport*, 33(2): 157–73.

Davis, P. (1993). Ethical Issues in Boxing. *Journal of the Philosophy of Sport*, 20(1): 48–63.

De Coubertin, P. (2000). *Pierre de Coubertin 1863–1937: Olympism: Selected writings*, edited by N. Müller. Lausanne: International Olympic Committee.

Dixon, N. (2001). Boxing, Paternalism, and Legal Moralism. *Social Theory and Practice*, 27(2): 323–44.

Dombrowski, D. A. (2009). *Contemporary Athletics and Ancient Greek Ideals*. Chicago, IL: University of Chicago Press.

Feezell, R. (2004). *Sport, Play and Ethical Reflection*. Urbana, IL: University of Illinois Press.

Feezel, R. (2013). *Sport, Philosophy and Good Lives*. Lincoln, NE: University of Nebraska Press.

Fraleigh, W (1984). *Right Actions in Sport: Ethics for contestants*. Champaign, IL: Human Kinetics.

Francis, L. P. (1993). Title IX: Equality for Women's Sports? *Journal of the Philosophy of Sport*, 20(1): 32–47.

Gough, R. W. (1995). On Reaching First Base with a 'Science' of Moral Development in Sport: Problems with scientific objectivity and reductivism. *Journal of the Philosophy of Sport*, 22(1): 11–25.

Gough, R. (1997). *Character is Everything*. Fort Worth, TX: Harcourt Brace.

Hardman, A. and Jones, C. (eds) (2010). *The Ethics of Sports Coaching*. Abingdon: Routledge.

Holowchak, M. A. (2005). 'Fascistoid' Heroism Revisited: A deontological twist to a recent debate. *Journal of the Philosophy of Sport*, 32(1): 96–104.

Holowchack, M. A. and Reid, H. (2011). *Aretism*. New York: Lexington.

Holt, R. (1989). *Sport and the British. A modern history*. Oxford: Clarendon.

Houlihan, B. and McNamee, M. (eds) (2013). *Anti-doping: Policy and Governance*. Abingdon: Routledge.

Hume, D. (1978) [1739]. *A treatise of Human Nature*. London: John Noon.

Ilundáin, J. (2014) Skillful Striving: Reflective cultivation of excellence, active pursuits, and embodied cognition, *Sport, Ethics and Philosophy*, 8(3–4) [special issue].

Ilundáin-Agurruza, J. and Austin, M. W. (2010). Cycling – Philosophy for Everyone: A philosophical tour de force. Oxford: Wiley-Blackwell.

Jennings, A. (1996). *The New Lords of the Rings: Olympic corruption and how to buy gold medals*. London: Pocket Books.

Kretchmar, R. S. (1983). Ethics and Sport: An overview. *Journal of the Philosophy of Sport*, 10: 21–32.

Kretchmar, R. S. (1998). Soft metaphysics: a precursor to good sports ethics. In M. J. McNamee, and S. J. Parry (eds), *Ethics and Sport*. Abingdon: Routledge, 19–34.

Lasch, C. (1979). *The Culture of Narcissism*. New York: Warner.

Loland, S (2002) *Fair Play in Sport: A moral norm system*. London: Routledge

Lopiano, D. A. (2000). Modern History of Women in Sports: Twenty-five years of Title IX. *Clinics in Sports Medicine*, 19(2): 163–73.

Lumpkin, A., Stoll, S. K. and Beller, J. M. (1994). *Sport Ethics: Applications for fair play*. St. Louis, MO: Mosby.

McGee, G. (2006). Will bioethics take the life of philosophy? *American Journal of Bioethics* 6(5): 1–2.

McIntosh, P. C. (1979). *Fair Play: Ethics in sport and education*. London: Heinemann.

MacIntyre, A. C. (1981). *After Virtue*. London: Duckworth.

McLaughlin, D. W. and Torres, C. R. (2011). A Moral Justification for a More Inclusive Olympic Program, *Olympika*, 20, 55–78.

McNamee, M. (1995). Sporting Practices, Institutions, and Virtues: A critique and a restatement. *Journal of the Philosophy of Sport*, 22(1): 61–82.

McNamee, M. (2006). Olympism, Eurocentricity, and Transcultural Virtues. *Journal of the Philosophy of Sport*, 33(2): 174–87.

McNamee, M. and Møller, V. (eds) (2011). *Doping and Anti-doping Policy in Sport: Ethical, legal and social perspectives*. Abingdon: Routledge.

McNamee, M. J. (2008). *Sports, Virtues and Vices: Morality plays*, Abingdon: Routledge.

McNamee, M. J. (2010). *The Ethics of Sport: A reader*. Abingdon: Routledge

McNamee, M. J. and Parry, S. J. (eds) (1998). *Ethics and Sport*. Abingdon: Routledge.

McNamee, M. J., Sheridan, H. and Buswell, J. (2001). The Limits of Utilitarianism as a Professional Ethic in Public Sector Leisure Policy and Provision. *Leisure Studies*, 20(3): 173–97.

McNamee, M., Jones, C. and Duda, J. L. (2003). Psychology, Ethics and Sports. *International Journal of Sport and Health Science*, 1(1): 61–75.

Mangan, J. A. (1981). *Athleticism in the Victorian and Edwardian Public School*. Cambridge: Cambridge University Press.

Mangan, J. A. (1987). *Manliness and Morality*. Manchester: Manchester University Press.

Meier, K.V. (1985). Restless Sport. *Journal of the Philosophy of Sport*, 12(1): 64–77.

Miah, A. (2004). *Genetically Modified Athletes: Biomedical ethics, gene doping and sport*. Abingdon: Routledge.

Møller, V. (2009). *The Ethics of Doping and Anti-doping: Redeeming the soul of sport?* Abingdon: Routledge.

Moore, G. E. (1903). *Principia Ethica*. Cambridge: Cambridge University Press.

Morgan, W. J. (1994). *Leftist Theories of Sport: A critique and reconstruction*. Champaign, IL: University of Illinois Press.

Morgan, W. (2006). *Why Sports Morally Matter*. Abingdon: Routledge.

Morgan, W. J. (ed.) (2007). *Ethics in Sport*. Champaign; IL: Human Kinetics.

Murray, T. H., Maschke, K. J. and Wasunna, A. A. (2009). *Performance-enhancing Technologies in Sports: Ethical, conceptual, and scientific issues*. Baltimore, MD: Johns Hopkins University Press.

Parry, J. (2006). Sport and Olympism: Universals and multiculturalism. *Journal of the Philosophy of Sport*, 33(2): 188–204.

Persson, I. (2005). What's Wrong with Admiring Athletes and Other People? in C. Tamburrini and T. Tännsjö (eds), *Genetic Technology and Sport: Ethical questions*. Abingdon: Routledge, 70–81.

Putnam, H. (2002). *The Collapse of the Fact/Value Dichotomy and Other Essays*. Cambridge, MA: Harvard University Press.

Radford, C. (1988). Utilitarianism and the Noble Art. *Philosophy*, 63(243): 63–81.

Rawls, J. (1971). *A Theory of Justice*. Cambridge: Harvard University Press.

Reddiford, G. (1985). Constitutions, Institutions, and Games. *Journal of the Philosophy of Sport*, 12(1): 41–51.

Reid, H. L. (2010). Athletic Virtue: Between East and West. *Sport, Ethics and Philosophy*, 4(1): 16–26.

Reid, H. (2012). Athletic Beauty in Classical Greece: A philosophical view. *Journal of the Philosophy of Sport*, 39(2):281–97.

Reid, H. L., and Austin, M. W. (eds) (2012). *The Olympics and Philosophy*. Lexington, KY: University Press of Kentucky.

Renson, R. (2009) Fair Play: Its Origins and Meanings in Sport and Society, *Kinesiology* 41: 15–18.

Richards, T. (ed.) (2013). *Soccer and Philosophy: Beautiful thoughts on the beautiful game*. Popular Culture and Philosophy, vol. 51. New York: Open Court.

Russell, J. S. (2005). The Value of Dangerous Sport. *Journal of the Philosophy of Sport*, 32(1): 1–19.

Ryle, G. (1949). *The Concept of Mind*. Oxford: Oxford University Press.

Savulescu, J. (2005). 'Compulsory Genetic Testing for APOE Epsion 4 and Boxing' in C. Tamburrini, and T. Tännsjö, (eds). (2005). *Genetic Technology and Sport: Ethical Questions*. Abingdon: Routledge.

Simon, R. L. (1985). *Sports and Social Values*. Englewood Cliffs, NJ: Prentice-Hall.

Simon, R. L. (1991). *Fair Play: Sports, values, and society*. Colorado: Westview.

Simon, R. L. (1993). Gender Equity and Inequity In Athletics. *Journal of the Philosophy of Sport*, 20(1): 6–22.

Simon, R. L.(2000). Internalism and Internal Values in Sport, *Journal of the Philosophy of Sport*, 27: 1–16.

Staurowsky, E. J. (2003). Title IX and College Sport: The long painful path to compliance and reform. *Marquette Sports Law Review*, 14: 95.

Sugden, J., and Tomlinson, A. (1998). *FIFA and the Contest for World Football: Who rules the people's game?* Cambridge: Polity.

Tamburrini, C. M. (1998). Sports, Fascism and the Market. *Journal of the Philosophy of Sport*, 25: 35–47.

Tamburrini, C. M. (2000). *The Hand of God. Essays in the philosophy of sport*. Göteborg: Acta Universitatis Gothoburgensis.

Tännsjö, T. (1998). Is our Admiration for Sports Heroes Fascistoid? *Journal of the Philosophy of Sport*, 25(1): 23–34.

Tännsjö, T and Tamburrini, C. M. (eds) (2000). *Values in Sport: Elitism, Nationalism, Gender Equality and the Scientific Manufacture of Winners*. London: E & FN Spon

Toulmin, S. (1982). How Medicine Saved the Life of Ethics. *Perspectives in Biology and Medicine* 25(4): 736–50.

Wamsley, K. B. (2004). 'Laying Olympism to Rest' in *Post-Olympism? Questioning sport in the twenty-first century*, edited by J. Bale and M. K. Christensen. Oxford: Berg, 231–42.

Walsh, A. and Giulianotti, R. (2006). *Ethics, Money and Sport: This sporting Mammon*. Abingdon: Routledge.

10

EXISTENTIAL PHILOSOPHY AND SPORT

Kenneth Aggerholm

Introduction

Existential philosophy is commonly associated with 'existentialism' and understood as a both cultural and philosophical movement in Europe in the 1930s to 1950s. Sartre (2007) was the first to label his philosophy with the term 'existentialism' but he is far from the only philosopher who has been occupied with matters of existence or, more precisely, what it means to exist as a human being. This has been the concern of many philosophers at least since the Ancient Greek philosophers. Furthermore, some philosophers who are commonly associated with 'existentialism', such as Heidegger, Marcel and Camus, explicitly repudiated the label. In this essay, I therefore attempt to clarify an understanding of existential philosophy that is not restricted to the particular understanding outlined and labelled by Sartre. To describe existential philosophy as an '-ism' can easily denote a certain view and particular (i.e. Sartrean) construal of human existence (Schacht 2012). But existential philosophy is not a school of thought with an agreed project and programme (like, for example, the logical positivism of the Vienna circle or the critical theory of the Frankfurt school). Moreover, it could be argued that existential philosophy is not a philosophical branch of its own but rather a subcategory to especially existential phenomenology, theology and existential psychology. This would be hard to deny since most, perhaps all, existential philosophers either declared themselves to belong to one of these traditions or have informed subsequent studies within these fields. In that sense, it would be more appropriate to consider existential philosophers as a family or perhaps a philosophical movement (Cooper 2012). Existential philosophy thus understood describes a number of philosophers with a shared interest in human existence.

I first give a very brief overview of existential philosophy, including the most central aspects and key ideas found in this tradition. I then outline central positions and topics in existential philosophy, through which I describe sources and ways in which existential philosophy has been, and prospectively could be, taken up in the philosophy of sport.

What is existential philosophy?

In her essay *What Is Existential Philosophy?* Arendt (1994, 173) described that: 'Modern existential philosophy begins with Kierkegaard. There is not a single existential philosopher who does not show evidence of his influence'. A very brief historical account of existential philosophy would therefore properly depart from the writings of Søren A. Kierkegaard (2012a–d) in the 1840s. From this, another central precursor of existential philosophy is the writings of Friedrich Nietzsche (1967, 1997a,b, 1999, 2001, 2006, 2007) in the 1870–80s. Even though Georg Brandes, a Danish literary critic, tried to introduce the writings of Kierkegaard to Nietzsche there is no evidence that any literary contact was made between them (Collins 1952: 17). There is, however, an intellectual affinity between them, and their passionate attempts to restore or save human existence from analytical, systematic and academic philosophy have in many and various ways been taken up by other existential philosophers. Among the most prominent of these were, on the German side, Martin Heidegger, Karl Jaspers and Martin Buber. In France, the existential ideas were especially taken up in the philosophy of Gabriel Marcel, Jean-Paul Sartre, Albert Camus, Maurice Merleau-Ponty, Simone de Beauvoir and Paul Ricoeur. Others commonly identified as existential philosophers include the Spaniard José Ortega y Gasset and Russian Lev Shestov. Many other philosophers could be added to the list, depending on how broad existential philosophy is understood to be. For example, the later writings of both Husserl and Foucault, with their attention drawn towards the 'life-world' and 'techniques of the self' respectively, could arguably deserve a place in the history of existential philosophy. The same could be said about philosophers such as Henri Bergson and Hannah Arendt. These authors wrote in very different cultural, historical and political contexts, and their conclusions were indeed very different and often directly opposed to each other. What unites them and makes them existential philosophers is rather their point of departure and the particular subject matter of their writings: human existence.

What is human existence?

From Kierkegaard onwards, existential philosophy has reserved the term 'existence' to describe what it means to exist as an individual human being; if one is a human being, then one is an existing individual. This has in various ways been presented as an alternative to other positions that neglect and objectify human subjectivity. Kierkegaard himself was in keen opposition to abstract philosophical systems, especially that of Hegel. He continuously insisted and humorously illuminated how speculation, abstraction, objective thought and systematic and formal answers cannot provide answers to what it is like to exist as an individual human being. Nietzsche's understanding of existence was in various ways in opposition to dogmatic value regimes, especially religion, as he argued for the elementary human power to transcend these. Heidegger's account of existence described, among others, an alternative to the instrumentalism and objectifying tendencies of modernism. Merleau-Ponty laid out his understanding of existence as a third term between the Cartesian dualistic understanding of human beings as mind (*cogitatio*) and physical matter (*res extensa*). Sartre and Camus were, apart from sharing these concerns, also occupied with arguing for the importance of human existence in opposition to totalitarian political systems at their time.

These examples can illustrate how existential philosophy has in various historical and cultural contexts been occupied with providing an alternative to objectifying tendencies. This general focus was most precisely coined in Sartre's (2007: 20) famous clarification of the metaphysical basis of existentialism: *existence precedes essence*. Even if this claim may be of a metaphysical kind, the understanding of human existence in existential philosophy is, however, anything but metaphysical. The ambition is not to clarify existence as an eternal, unchangeable and universal essence. Human beings are not considered as substances with fixed and essential properties. Existential philosophy is first and foremost concerned with *experience* in relation to the way or manner in which we exist. This does not mean, however, that nothing general can be said about existential matters. There is a universal *human condition* that is shared by any existing subject (ibid: 42–3). Two central aspects of this condition can be highlighted.

First, it is a basic condition for human beings to be *situated* in the world. This understanding of subjectivity as belonging to the world is most clearly expressed through the notion of *being-in-the-world*, which Heidegger (1996: 135) further described as a characteristic of *thrownness*. This renders the primary way of being a matter of 'being there', which is the literal meaning of his term for existence: *Dasein*. Acknowledging this, existential philosophy implies a refusal of intellectualism and rationalism. There is not an eternal world of ideas where we can find a secure stance at safe distance to the contingency of the world. Human beings are not considered as (transcendental or rational) subjects that stand before a world of objects. From this basic condition, it follows that we necessarily experience and live in relation to the presence of other people, to things and objects to cope with, to tasks and work to be done, to our physical body of flesh and blood, to our past and eventually to death. This is, in Sartre's (2003) terminology, the *facticity* of existence.

Secondly, in existential philosophy, the meaning of this world that we live in is not considered as given with the objective presence of these situational elements. Human existence is not determined by the situation; man is not an object in the world. A particular social or cultural situation, or a particular kind of (for example, sporting) activity may invite for and make possible certain kinds of values and meaning. But the situation is not a being in itself that determines the subjective experience; it is a being for the subject. This makes existential philosophy opposed to the philosophical positions of, for example, behaviourism, physicalism and materialism. Instead, existential philosophers consider it a basic condition to find our own way of being in the world and give meaning to our life. We are, as Sartre (2007: 29; 2003: 462) famously put it, *condemned to be free*. As I return to in the next section, there are, however, various accounts and descriptions of this condition within existential philosophy. For now, the important thing is that this understanding of human existence implies that it is a task for human beings to balance the existential relation between transcendence and facticity or, as Kierkegaard (2012d: 145) described it, between the existential modalities of possibility and necessity: 'The self is freedom. But freedom is the dialectical in the modalities of possibility and necessity'. This reveals the basic understanding of *human freedom* in existential philosophy: it is not a matter of being able to do anything; it is a synthesis of possibility and necessity where both are of equal importance; it is a matter of being free to commit and choose our own terms of engagement in our situation.

This human condition implies that human beings are not predefined as essence but defined by their actions. On this basis, Sartre (2007: 38–40, 54) defended his understanding of 'existentialism' as optimistic. However, this view does not necessarily make things easier. In existential philosophy *becoming* is primary to *being* and from this follow that it is a task for every person to 'become oneself' or, as Nietzsche (2007) put it, to 'become who you are'. This was also a primary concern for Kierkegaard, who insisted that the movement of existence forces us to give primacy to becoming and consider existence as a matter of *continuous striving*: 'Existence itself, to be existing, is striving' (Kierkegaard 2012a: 90). In addition to this, existentialism does not build on the ancient idea of a well ordered cosmos; we cannot expect the world to be meaningful from the outset. Rather, the world is full of ambiguity and contradictions, which can make existence arbitrary. Therefore, from time to time we are bound to experience an uncanny feeling of estrangement, alienation or disintegration. From an existential stance, however, the task of philosophy is not to eliminate or explain this incongruity through systems, reasons or causal laws (for example, metaphysical, psychological or physical). Existential philosophy is, rather, an attempt to embrace this ambiguity and look deeper into what it is like to live under this elementary condition.

Existential philosophy of sport

Against the background of this very brief clarification of the most fundamental structures of human existence, the following section introduces and describes some central positions and topics, together with brief descriptions of how existential philosophy has contributed, and potentially could contribute, to the philosophy of sport. Within this field, Slusher's classic 1967 publication, *Man, Sport and Existence*, is commonly acknowledged as the first to engage in existential considerations on sport. Gerber and Morgan's rich but often overlooked 1979 anthology, *Sport and the Body*, was among the first to include existential philosophers (such as Sartre, Jaspers and Marcel) and present more rigorous philosophical accounts of human existence in relation to sport. Since then, existential aspects have mostly appeared in articles within the *Journal of the Philosophy of Sport* (JPS) and *Sport, Ethics and Philosophy* (SEP), with the exception of Müller's (2008) German monograph, *Risikosport: Suizid oder Lebenskunst*, which presents existential views on death in high-risk sports, and my own book, *Talent Development, Existential Philosophy and Sport: On Becoming an Elite Athlete* (2014), where I present an existential phenomenological analysis of performance and development in elite sport as a contrast to instrumental approaches in this domain.

A common thread in this literature that I seek to preserve below is the recognition of inherent tensions and sometimes contrasting understandings within existential philosophy. The strength of existential philosophy in relation to sport is its ability to reveal a range of ways in which human beings can find meaning and value in sport, rather than providing a systematic, analytical or absolute account of sport. In this sense, existential approaches to sport is a contrast to analyses of value in sport through formal criteria (formalism), abstract principles or imperatives (broad internalism) or sociocultural context (conventionalism). Also, approaching sport through existential philosophy is not a matter of claiming any particular kind of activity to be more or less existential.[1] This is not to say that certain kinds of activity cannot invite or make possible certain kinds of meaning and value. But since athletes are always, in an existential understanding, free to relate to a particular kind of activity in a variety of ways, the experience and meaning of a sporting practice ultimately depends on the existential attitude of the athlete.

The bodily existence: condemned to meaning

The first position I want to highlight is the existential philosophy of Merleau-Ponty. The existential weight of his works should not be neglected, even if it has often been subordinated to his phenomenological investigations. A central idea that runs through the writings of Merleau-Ponty is that human existence can only be properly understood against the background of our primordial and pre-reflective relation to ourselves and to the world. This may not be something of which we are aware in everyday life, where it provides the background upon which figures can come to our attention. But this background, Merleau-Ponty argued, is not merely an instrumental relation. Instead, he attempted to describe how this primordial relation has its own mode of existence and how this should, in fact, be understood as existence as such. It was for this he reserved his particular notion of existence, the *body*:

> The natural world is the horizon of all horizons, the style of all possible styles, which guarantees for my experiences a given, not a willed, unity underlying all the

disruptions of my personal and historical life. Its counterpart within me is the given, general and pre-personal existence of my sensory functions in which we have discovered the definition of the body.

(Merleau-Ponty 1962: 385)

This pre-objective and bodily existence that adheres to 'the natural world' (*Umwelt*) represents Merleau-Ponty's suggestion for a third term between the psychic and the physiological, between being-for-itself and being-in-itself (ibid: 140, note 55). Far from denying the human ability to transcend our immediate, habitual and embodied relation to the world, Merleau-Ponty stressed that this is always secondary to our bodily 'being-in-the-world'. Rather than passively received stimuli (realism) or actively projected intentions (intellectualism), *meaning* is first and foremost co-constituted in lived and bodily experience. It is due to this corporeal existence that we are, as he (ibid: xxii) put it, *condemned to meaning* before we know it.

The phenomenological dimension of this bodily existence is extensively covered in the philosophy of sport (see Chapter 12) but it also has existential implications and, in that respect, it is important to notice that Merleau-Ponty's understanding of bodily existence in the natural world does not put us at safe distance from the 'ambiguous life' with all its 'fundamental contradictions' (ibid: 425). The pre-objective or phenomenal field is an 'ambiguous domain' (ibid: 73) and, since this primordial mode of being is lived rather than known, it can never become fully transparent to us. Mostly, our bodily relation to the world only becomes apparent to us in cases when our habitual comportment breaks down or when objectifying reflection interferes with our conduct. For the same reason, Merleau-Ponty drew on many pathological cases to describe our bodily existence. He analysed, for example, phenomena such as phantom limbs, aphasia, apraxia, agnosia and schizophrenia and, most famously, analysed the motor disorders of a German soldier (Schneider) who suffered a brain injury during the First World War. He also pointed to the reality of various ambiguous phenomena such as illusion and hallucination. In such cases, the normal functioning of the lived body and the ordinary lived relation to the world is obstructed. Merleau-Ponty argued that neither empirical or intellectual analyses can grasp the disorders experienced in such cases. Instead, he pursues what he terms 'an existential analysis' to interrogate the *meaning* of such cases: 'The study of a pathological case, then, has enabled us to glimpse a new mode of analysis – existential analysis – which goes beyond the traditional alternatives of empiricism and rationalism, of explanation and introspection' (ibid., 157). One thing, for example, that objective science cannot grasp is how difficulties and ambiguity related to movement and/or perception can sometimes be resolved by having *faith* in the immediate and bodily relation to the world. He describes this phenomenon as a primary, immediate, primordial and perceptual faith (ibid: 280, 305, 344, 375, 475).

Within the philosophy of sport, Connolly (2008) has built on this to show how a movement education-based embedded curriculum, consisting of various existential movement themes, can provide a relief from the experience of stressed embodiment in cases of autism spectrum disorder and can improve the bodily and social existence. Another fine example of perceptual faith can be found in the study of Jordbru *et al.* (2008). This study describes the paradoxical case of people who from one day to the next lose their ability to walk (conversion gait disorder). Such persons fit into neither somatic or psychiatric hospitals because the disorder can be located neither as an organic nor a psychic illness. Then what? As their article reveals, adapted physical activity can in such cases provide an alternative, which they describe as an existential approach. Treatment consists in the apparent paradox that using the body can help the patients to forget the body and, further, that forgetting the body improves the movement of the patients. Hence, this reconsideration of the relation between body and mind allows for an existential behavioural therapy in which the patients regain control of their body by actively becoming unaware of it. This, I think, could also have general relevance for athletes in sport (as a contrast to strategies of cognitive sport psychology) and such generalisation would be in line with the ambitions of Merleau-Ponty, who tried to reveal common structures of human existence through the pathological cases.

This was, for example, a central point he made from the case of the German soldier (Schneider) mentioned above, who could not point to a part of his body when asked to do so, but quickly moved his hand to the point where a mosquito was stinging him. Merleau-Ponty asked: 'But how is this possible? If I know where my nose is when it is a question of holding it, how can I not know where it is when it is a matter of pointing to it?' (Merleau Ponty 1962: 119) His answer to this question was that there is an existential difference between grasping and pointing. The first phenomenon, concrete movement, adheres to the existential modality of the actual, whereas the latter, abstract movement, is a way of standing in an embodied relation to the possible. This distinction describes two ways of expressing 'motor meaning' that can only be comprehended by existential analysis. I have, in various ways, made use of this distinction to describe how athletes in sport are capable of performing highly ambiguous expressions and movements such as feinting, deceiving, seducing, pretence and others (Aggerholm *et al.* 2011; Aggerholm and Ronglan 2012; Aggerholm 2013, 2014). Merleau-Ponty (1962: 128) describes this kind of abstract movements as a way of being bodily related to a 'virtual or human space' and this kind of expressive phenomena points to the next position I want to highlight here.

Choice and anxiety: condemned to freedom

This understanding of existence as adhering to the 'natural world' (*Umwelt*) was presented by Merleau-Ponty in 1945 as a critical stance towards, among others, Sartre's account of existence outlined in *Being and Nothingness* published two years earlier and defended in his 1945 lecture *Existentialism is a Humanism* (Sartre 2007). As these titles indicate, Sartre was mostly interested in 'the human world' (*Welt*), where the human beings have the power of bringing nothingness into the actual appearance of the world, for example by questioning, negations, denying or taking distance. This is based on his fundamental understanding of human existence as characterised by absence and lack rather than an essence predefined by human nature or God. From the outset, the human being is haunted by what it is not, Sartre claimed, and from this he argued that it is a human condition to pass beyond ourselves to become ourselves by bringing possibilities, meaning and value into the world. This is why existentialism in his understanding should be considered a *humanism*, and this is the first principle of his 'atheistic existentialism': 'man is nothing other than what he makes of himself' (Sartre 2007: 22).

To Sartre, the primary way in which this occurs is by *choosing projects*, in accordance with which the world appears in a particular and meaningful way. This choice and project is not necessarily known to oneself. When I leave home to go to work in the morning, or when an athlete goes to training every day, it is not a matter of explicitly choosing to do so every time. But that does not mean that the athlete and I are not responsible for it. We cannot explain or excuse our choices or actions with reference to an essence, be it physical or psychological. The actions rest on an original and fundamental choice that colours and shapes the actions and gives meaning to the existential situation.

This is, however, not just something human beings can choose to do now and then when we feel like it. It is not just a possibility among others, it is our original and primary way of being in the world. We are, as mentioned previously, condemned to be free; not because we can step away from our situation and turning our back on the necessities and facticity of the world, but because a human *situation* consists, in Sartre's vocabulary, in both *facticity* and *transcendence*. Freedom is the possibility of finding ones own meaning and choosing ones own values in one's actual circumstances by involving, engaging and committing oneself to ones situation. There are, for example, a range of external conditions that athletes cannot choose, such as the condition of the field, the rules, the weather, and so on. What they can, however, freely choose is their attitude to these conditions as they reveal their situation as, for example, worth handling, funny, tough, tragic, annoying, dramatic or amazing. This also goes for one's own physical condition. Sartre (2003: 476–92) paid considerable attention to how the experience of fatigue is not given with the physiological state of the body. Of course, it has a physiological component but it can be suffered in many ways, for example as unbearable, bearable or maybe as a means of getting in (better) shape. Thus, in Sartre's view existential freedom is to acknowledge this and choose one's own way of engaging in one's situation to find one's own existential meaning and value. I (2014) have used this understanding of human freedom to describe how young athletes can take up different existential attitudes to their practice and thereby reveal various kinds of meaning in sport.

The consciousness of this freedom, of this human possibility and the responsibility that comes with it, is accompanied by *anxiety*. Unlike fear, anxiety is not related to an intentional object, to 'something' of which one is afraid. It is a mood rather than an emotion: the uncanny inchoate feeling of facing the possibilities of existence that arise from non-being and realising that it is *my* possibilities. The important existential point that both Kierkegaard, Heidegger and Sartre make is that this is not simply something to get rid of, for example through psychological techniques of mental training. It is a more fundamental condition and, what is more, it is to be considered a positive source of existential growth. Existential philosophy can therefore inform an understanding where neglecting this elementary possibility of freedom would be to overlook a central and potentially constructive part of being human, not least in sport. Nesti (2011) has described how anxiety is an important theme for elite sport performers, as it involves taking responsibility and being oneself by choosing ones own terms of engagement rather than being guided by extrinsic values such as great rewards. He also argues that anxiety accompanies *authenticity*. Chapter 9 has already described Heidegger's notion of authenticity (*Eigentlichkeit*) and how the derived understandings of authentic engagement in sport has been taken up within philosophy of sport. The opposite of this would be inauthenticity (*Uneigentlichkeit*), where 'they' (*das Man*) condition subjective being through what Heidegger (1996: 114–30) classifies as distantiality (*Abständigkeit*), averageness (*Durchschnittlichkeit*) and levelling down (*Einebnung*). Hyland (1979) has suggested that his own experience from playing basketball can point to another position, because the uncanniness (*Unheimlichkeit*) of anxiety was not part of his orientation 'toward the possibility of the end of the game … I *was* at home in a way that I rarely feel at other times' (Hyland 1979: 99; his emphasis). He also argues, that basketball can teach us that authenticity is not an individual but situated phenomenon, part of which is 'being-with' others: 'The basketball game situation suggests that meaning of the sort that leads to authentic awareness of one's human being can occur in a context of encounter, an encounter which can even be a kind of opposition' (ibid: 99).

Sartre was also critical to the notion of authenticity and in general avoided using the term.[2] Instead, he paid attention to the existential danger of *bad faith* (Sartre 2003: 70–94). This is a complex phenomenon but, for the present purpose, it can be narrowed down to a pre-reflective comprehension of fleeing one's existential freedom; that is, of not balancing the existential synthesis of facticity and transcendence.[3] Thus, it can occur in two forms: when a person either sees his or her situation as: a) pure possibility (transcendence); or as b) pure necessity (facticity).

Culbertson (2005) has analysed the first form of bad faith in elite sports with 'parallel competition' (swimming, athletics and weightlifting). He argues that this can be seen as an arena that promotes bad faith, as athletes tacitly accept the constituent factors of improvement, enhancement, quantification and endless pursuit of records. This can make athletes neglect the physical limits to the capacities of human beings (facticity) as they strive for limitless progress (transcendence).

I (Aggerholm 2014) have reflected on the existential danger of the second form of bad faith in relation to the case of Andre Agassi. He won (almost) all there is to win in tennis but, in his biography, he (Agassi 2009) reveals how he hated playing tennis his entire career and only did it because his ambitious father pushed him into it. Hence, his engagement was determined by necessity; he never chose to play and he neglected finding his own meaning in his practice. Without judging if this is right or wrong it can point to the existential importance of choosing one's own engagement in sport if the sportive endeavours are to be meaningful for the athlete.

In relation to team sports, Ryall (2008) has analysed how 'being on the bench' can put athletes in a contradictory situation that they have only partly chosen for themselves. Hence, it can make athletes liable to find themselves in the second form of bad faith, where they neglect their own possibilities (transcendence) and see instead their situation as determined and fixed (facticity).

This points to how the human ability to flee from freedom can also be experienced in relation to *social roles*. Simply living up to what one expects or the duties and established imperatives without choosing to do so, without choosing the duties and functions as your own, would be a case of inauthenticity in Heidegger's terms and bad faith in Sartre's terms. Sartre's (2003: 82) famous example is the waiter in a café who has adopted a peculiar kind of conduct, namely the characteristic quick, rapid and eager movements of a waiter. This social role need not imply that he is insincere or in bad faith. That is only the case if he believes that he *is* this social role; that is, he takes it as a necessity. If he, on the other hand comprehends it as a freely chosen possibility and merely *plays* at being a waiter, hence plays his part in this social world, he would not be in bad faith. This cannot be determined from the outside; it all depends on his attitude to the social situation. Both Ryall (2008) and I (Aggerholm 2013, 2014) have argued that this is kind of role-playing can be an important and constructive part of being in a team for athletes in team sports.[4] Howe (2007, 2008b) has used the same distinction between being and playing a social role to reveal how athletes (and others) can play with their identity. In these texts, she has a special focus on gender and argues that play situations in sport, even if bad faith lurks close by in professional sports, 'offers an arena within which one can play out situational responses and find out who one "is" – that is, gather one's character by venturing oneself in the possibilities' (Howe 2008b: 570). Involvement in sport can, thus understood, present a valuable opportunity for free self-expression that can contribute to redefining the gendered self.

Conflict and resistance: the value of obstacles

Within the philosophy of sport Martin (2010; 2012) has interpreted Sartre's understanding of skiing and Camus' understanding of swimming as two contrasting modes of existential consciousness in sport. Apart from being a keen boxer, Sartre enjoyed skiing in the Alps. Apart from being a goalkeeper in football and famously describing how he learned most about morality from playing football, Camus liked to swim in the Mediterranean. These sportive interests, Martin argues, infiltrated their writings on human existence. I focus here on their writings, which also share a common view of the human condition, namely that it involves conflict and resistance.

Sartre's main concern in his descriptions of the relation to the world and other people can be summed up with his description of the original meaning of 'being for others' as *conflict* (Sartre 2003: 386). This element is present from his first descriptions of how the look of the other can cause a feeling of shame or guilt, to the various ways in which human relations to each other are essentially variants of a master–slave relation, which can be described in a continuum between sadism and masochism. In his later writings, he used the case of boxing as an example of this, where two persons are united in a binary praxis of antagonistic reciprocity (Sartre 1991: 5–6, 17–50). This antagonistic understanding of intersubjective relations has been criticised by many but, in sport, where relations to opponents are essentially constituted as an antagonistic relation, I (Aggerholm *et al.* 2011; Aggerholm 2013, 2014) have argued that his account can offer insight into the many ambiguous and deceptive ways in which the struggles with other humans occur, for example in the enactment of feints.

This understanding of relations to others can also be found in Sartre's descriptions of human relations to the world in general. He (2003: 604–7) offers the experience of being on an alpine slope as an example of how the human relation to the field changes as soon as one engages with it, for example as the sportsman establishes an appropriative contact with the field of snow. He highlights three ways in which this relation to the slope can occur: sliding, overcoming difficulty and gaining ownership. *Sliding* is action at a distance. It is the opposite of taking root and the ideal for sliding is to leave no trace and to avoid compromising oneself. The action of sliding only develops potentialities in a continuous process of creation where the sportsman appropriates the slope. Another aspect of appropriation is *overcoming difficulty* caused by the resistance of the snow. It is, as he argues, identical with the other (human being) and the master–slave relation appears again: the sportsman must overcome, conquer and master the elements with which he or she is confronted. Finally, the aim of appropriating the slope is to possess it and *gain ownership* in the relation to it. This is not an objective aspect of the relation or a matter of possessing the slope in itself. It is a desire to be related to a certain object in a certain relation of being, which involves creating a qualitative or symbolic relation of value to the slope as 'being in itself for itself', which can occur both through creation and destruction. These three aspects can describe central existential features experienced by athletes in sport.

Camus (1956, 2005) paid most attention to the second of these in his accounts of the existential experience of *resistance* and *struggle* in both *The Myth of Sisyphus* and *The Rebel*. In the former, he argued that the contradictions of existence, which Camus described as an incommensurable relation between man and the world resulting in the experience of absurdity, can be overcome in two steps: firstly, by embracing and becoming aware of the absurdity of the human condition; and, secondly, by choosing one's way of overcoming it or at least coping with it. In Camus' view, this kind of engagement is in contrast with various kinds of escapes, such as by killing yourself (suicide), by religious leaps towards eternal and transcendent values (Kierkegaard, Chestov and Jaspers) or by rationalising the contradictory human–world relation (Husserl). Instead, Camus considered three models that can inform ways of overcoming absurdity: by the passionate seducer (Don Juan), the theatrical and dramatic actor and, finally, by the striving and struggling conqueror. He also described the myth of Sisyphus as an image of the human condition.[5] To Camus, he is an 'absurd hero' because he is aware of his condition and embraces his fate and destiny: 'The absurd man says yes and henceforth his effort and struggle will be unceasing' (Camus 1967: 116, my translation). Sisyphus's attitude and way of engaging with his stone and his mountain can, in Camus' view, describe the apparent paradox that obstacles, difficulties and the eternal struggles that are part of human existence can, depending on the human attitude to it, be the source of meaning and value: 'Sisyphus teaches the higher fidelity that denies the Gods and raises rocks ... The struggle toward the summits is enough to fill a human heart. One must conceive of Sisyphus as a happy man' (ibid: 117, my translation).

This account of struggle and resistance in relation to necessary obstacles can throw light on how the unnecessary obstacles experienced in sport can be a source of existential value and meaning. Often Suits' (2005) account of *game playing* in *The Grasshopper* is taken to be a formal account. But indeed, as Hurka's clarifying introduction in the book highlights, it has an existential tenor (see also Hurka 2007). Suits argues that game playing is a supreme human (intrinsic) good, by which he understands: the activity most worth choosing for itself. It represents, as he argues, 'the whole of the ideal of existence' (Suits 2005: 154). People in Utopia, where all instrumental activities of human beings have been eliminated, would still choose to engage in 'the voluntary attempt to overcome unnecessary obstacles', which was Suits' (ibid: 55) short definition of game playing. Why? Suits' own reason is this:

> For in games we must have obstacles which we can strive to overcome just so that we can possess the activity as a whole, namely, playing the game. Game playing makes it possible to retain enough effort in Utopia to make life worth living.
>
> *(Suits 2005: 154)*

An existential interpretation of this could be that game playing is a kind of activity that balances the existential synthesis between necessity and possibility, between facticity and transcendence. In Utopia, where necessity and facticity is eliminated and everything is easy and possible, game playing can in an existential understanding provide meaning and value as it introduces facticity to existence, owing to its quality of difficulties, challenges and obstacles. What is more is that Suits goes on to argue that everything depends on the interest in and *attitude* to the activity. The lusory attitude is thus not only what makes game playing possible in a formal sense but also in an existential sense. What can appear as work or play when observed from the outside can just as well be a case of game playing if the person engaged with the activity has chosen to make the activity interesting by attempting to overcome unnecessary obstacles rather than seeking easy solutions.

Introducing the work of Ortega y Gasset to the philosophy of sport, Inglis (2004) has described how this contains very similar ideas. Ortega, in general, conceived of sports as profoundly expressive of the human condition as it is understood in existential philosophy because, as Inglis describes it, he 'sees sports as occupying a middle ground between the grinding seriousness of necessary labor and the wholly capricious nature of play' (ibid: 84). Hence, in his view, existence consists of both difficulties and facilities, and in a time when technological innovations tend to free us from labour and ease our paths (c.f. Suits' account of Utopia), sportive activities and athletic striving can in Ortega's view fill the existential void and allow us to spend time and effort in overcoming artificial problems, adversaries and difficulties (Ortega y Gasset 2002; Inglis 2004). This, on the other hand, is not an obligatory effort, as in necessary labour, but a freely chosen effort through practical engagement (Ortega y Gasset 1995: 42; Inglis 2004: 90). This makes the enterprise of sportspersons a way of fulfilling the 'poetic task' of life, where the 'difficult business' of athletic striving can be a way of making of oneself what one can, which can at the same time contribute to overcome the existential dangers of anguish, despair and alienation (Ortega y Gasset 1984: 96–7; Inglis 2004: 83–4).

These constructive accounts of effort and struggle hold important existential implications, the most central being that difficulties and challenges can be meaningful and valuable. This argument has more recently been taken up by Kretchmar (2006) in relation to physical education. In his view, it marks a contrast to 'easy street strategies' that involve introduction, information and entertainment. These neglect the value of commitment, time, effort and persistence as students engage with 'just right problems'. Playgrounds are, as Kretchmar argues, not something we suddenly find or discover; they grow as we are attracted by challenges and movement-related problem solving.

Stages on life's way: towards transcendent aspects of existence

What has been said about the 'human world' (*Welt*) here was in many ways anticipated by Kierkegaard. Even if he was essentially a religious thinker he had much to say about existence in general, which has informed many, if not all, subsequent secular existential philosophers. He drew a distinction between three existential spheres or stages of life: the aesthetic, ethical, and religious. The first two are most directly covered in *Either – Or* (2012b, 2012c). In the aesthetic realm, we find persons who seek pleasure, poetry, immediate interest and new possibilities. In the ethical realm, we find the responsible and committed person, who has chosen his or her project and way of living and is courageous enough to continuously live up to the duties and obligations that follow from this choice. Within these spheres of human existence, Kierkegaard poetically and humorously described many ways of finding meaning in one's situation and leading one's life. I (Aggerholm 2014) have drawn heavily on this and attempted a secular reading of Kierkegaard to describe various ways of revealing meaning that can be of relevance in elite sport. I do this through five key existential phenomena: wonder, question, expression, humour, and repetition. Each of these include various sub-phenomena (dwelling, admiration, interrogation, seduction, irony, contradiction, passion, striving and many others) and can clarify ways of approaching and relate to one's practice within one's particular sporting discipline. I argue that such phenomena can inform important ways in which athletes can find meaning and sustain a passionate engagement in sport.

It should not be neglected, however, that Kierkegaard's answers to coping with and overcoming, for example, existential struggles, anxiety and despair were indeed different from the authors above. He continuously drew attention to how the human world does not exhaust human existence. There is more to life (and sport) and Kierkegaard's answer to this transcendent aspect was of course religious. In general, the religious aspect of sport can be traced back to the Olympic gods in Ancient Greece and has been revived in Coubertin's Olympic ideas with reference to *religio athletae* and *religio atletica* (Parry 2007). This idea of making a non-theistic or civic religion of sport is still prevalent and the link to the transcendent is in particular reinforced in the symbols, narratives and rituals that feature an Olympic anthem, oath, flag, doves and flame (Robinson 2014: 245). But there can be various ways of understanding this transcendent aspect of human being and the description of this 'world above' (Überwelt) has come in many variants in existential philosophy. Kierkegaard's ultimate aim was to reveal how it is only through the relation to God that human beings can find relief from despair, or the 'sickness unto death', as he termed it. The movement in which this relation can be established is highly ambiguous and completely transcendent. It involves a movement between the infinite and finite and consists in coming away from oneself in relation to the infinite (God) and returning to oneself as a concrete and finite self (Kierkegaard 2012d: 146). This is not a matter of directing or raising oneself towards something transcendent in the world. On the contrary, it is a matter of internalising the infinite. You cannot tell from the outside whether a person has faith or not. In fact, Kierkegaard scorned the people in his time who claimed to be religious by showing the world how strong their faith was. He saw it as infinitely comic when people followed the religious writings in external expressions (Kierkegaard 2012a: 89–90). The religious is rather an internal matter and something the single one can only arrive at through *passionate interest*, or as he puts it, by being 'infinitely personally in passion interested' (ibid: 30). I (Aggerholm 2014) have argued that variants of this passionate interest can be found in sport as well, for example in the many personal, hidden and yet highly advanced rituals performed by many (possibly even most) athletes in relation to competition. Some of these can be religious and can include prayers but that is far from always the case. In general, they can be seen as instances of the highest passion, the enactment of which contributes in various and transcendent ways of enhancing their performance.

Another aspect of Kierkegaard's description of the religious sphere of existence is that truly becoming religious takes a *leap of faith*. To believe is not to grasp something objectively (which Kierkegaard took Hegel's speculative and systematic approach to imply). Rather, you must momentarily lose sight of yourself to stand in uncertainty on the 70,000 fathoms of water (Kierkegaard 2012a: 187). This involves a 'teleological suspension of the ethical' (ibid: 239–44) and in her paper 'Kierkegaard and Sport: Willing One Thing in Competitive Sports', Cindy White (2004) has asked the thought-provoking question, 'could sports be one of those powers that have such a grip in our corporate consciousness that we are forgetting what is good?' (White 2004, quoted in Watson and White 2007: 61) This is an excellent question that, in my opinion, could deserve more attention in philosophy of sport. It can throw light on the many cases where athletes violate the rules and fair play codes in sport and, at the same time, avoid ending with the conclusion that sport cannot be a venue for moral conduct. Kierkegaard can in this way inform ways in which sportive engagements can allow human beings to relate to a transcendent dimension of existence, for better or worse.

Heightening of human existence: the value of *agon* and *askēsis*

On the basis of these descriptions it may appear paradoxical to claim an intellectual affinity between Kierkegaard and Nietzsche, who famously declared that 'God is dead!' but, even if they had radically different understandings of the 'world above', both were eager to reveal how the human (all too human) cannot be the ultimate source of value. As an alternative, Nietzsche argued that the source of meaning and value should be related to *enhancement* or *heightening* (*Erhöhung*). He saw this as a constructive alternative to religion and nihilism, the latter of which he described as a passage, a danger and temporary condition (Schacht 2012: 118–21). Still, where should this heightening of human existence be rooted when the transcendent God is dead and humans are all to human?

A clue can be found just after his first announcement of God's death in *The Gay Science*: 'When may we begin to *naturalize* humanity with a pure, newly discovered, newly redeemed nature?' (Nietzsche 2001: 110, section 109). As this points to and, as Schacht (2012: 124) has argued, Nietzsche was concerned with reinterpreting human reality naturalistically to free human existence from the chains of morality and religion; values should be found by through a naturalistic reorientation. This, to some extent, takes us back to the 'natural world' but, for Nietzsche, the natural world is not a realm of equilibrium and co-existence (as in Merleau-Ponty's account). He was more interested in the activity of a tightrope walker performed high above the heads of the crowd. In *Thus Spoke Zarathustra*, he (Nietzsche 2006: 5) used the image of a tightrope walker performing high above the heads of the crowd to illustrate how human being is something that must be overcome, and how: 'Mankind is a rope fastened between animal and overman – a rope over an abyss' (ibid: 7). This quote can describe how the 'natural world' and the 'world above' are tightly linked in the philosophy of Nietzsche. The abyss under the rope between them is, of course, the human, all too human, endeavours that claim morality and religion as truth. It was to avoid this levelling down of the crowd (and priests in his time) that he stressed the human capacity to engage in higher endeavours related to the 'enhancement of life' and the becoming of the 'overman' (*Übermensch*).

This image of a tightrope walker who ventures to walk on this rope between animal and 'overman' is no coincidence. Grounded in and extending his 'value-naturalism' Nietzsche applies *aesthetic* and *artistic* concepts (such as style) to describe the rise of the higher and nobler human, the 'free spirits' and the 'overman' (Schacht 2012). He acknowledges only an 'artist-god', one that knows how to dance (Nietzsche 2006: 29) and, in general, 'only as an *aesthetic phenomenon* is existence and the world eternally *justified*' (Nietzsche 1999: 33, section 5, his emphasis). Furthermore, to guide the heightening of human existence the magnificent figures of the *Olympian gods* played a central role for Nietzsche. These represent an 'over-brimming, indeed triumphant existence, where everything that exists has been deified, regardless of whether it is good or evil' (ibid: 22, section 3). They incarnate a 'fantastic superabundance of life' who allow for spectators to catch a glimpse of their perfection as an 'ideal image of their own existence' (ibid.). Nietzsche thus uses the Olympian gods to describe an aesthetic or artistic theodicy, where athletes carve out a realm of 'complete and perfect existence' (ibid: 24, section 3) that makes the experience of pain and suffering endurable: 'Under the bright sunshine of such gods existence is felt to be worth attaining' (ibid.).

This aesthetic theodicy can also throw light on his understanding of heightening as the ultimate task for human beings. This concerns human experiential significance, a feeling of fullness and increasing strength, rather than advancement in, for example, order of rank (Schacht 2012: 126). To describe this movement upwards, Nietzsche pays special attention to two artistic powers or drives of nature: the Apollonian and Dionysian. The first embodies the power of moderation, self-control, individuality and respect for boundaries. The latter is the drive for excess, transgressing limits, destroying individuality and dissolving boundaries. Sportive engagement can on this basis be described as a synthesis of recognising your limits and transcending them. These opposite powers unite in human creation, for example in sport, and contribute to defying despair and rise instead towards the heights of existence. Two aspects of this, which are of special relevance for the philosophy of sport, can be highlighted: *agon* and *askēsis*. I (Aggerholm 2014) have argued for the relevance of considering these as sportive virtues within talent development.

Agon is the ancient notion for contest and competition, and the role of this in Nietzsche's philosophy has in recent years received increased attention (see, for example, Acampora 2013; Tuncel 2013). His most explicit account of *agon* can be found in the short essay, 'Homer's Contest'. In her analysis of this essay, Acampora (2013: 43–8) describes how Nietzsche celebrated Homer's account of contests as a model for human struggle. She argues that this was in particular due to the way that Homer's understanding of *agon* can: a) inform an exemplary revaluation of human existence; b) give a life-affirming, positive and tangible value to human existence; and c) contribute to an understanding of values as renewable because contests and agonistic arenas supply a medium and forum in and through which further revaluations can occur. Could the contests we find in sport be a venue for such life-affirming, continuous and renewable revaluation of human existence? Nietzsche would obviously affirm this and of special relevance to the philosophy of sport would, in this respect, be his interpretations of the original meaning of *ostrakismos*. This is related to the third aspect of *agon* above and it describes the core of Hellenic understanding of contest, which was not about finding a winner once and for all. That would exhaust the contest and leave matters settled; hence, it would not stimulate and motivate others to strive for excellence and would therefore not be a common good, which Nietzsche considered *agon* to be. Instead, he argued that the ancient and primary meaning of contests is its ability to provide a continuous source of meaning and value because:

one does away with an outstanding individual, so that once again the competing game of strengths may awaken: a concept that is hostile to the 'exclusivity' of genius in the modern sense, but presupposes that in the natural order of things there are always several geniuses, who mutually incite each other to act, as they also mutually hold themselves within the bounds of moderations.

(Nietzsche 1997a: 40)

A first thing that this quote reveals is how ostracism implies a dynamic game of strengths. Here again, we see that becoming outstanding has primacy over being outstanding and Rosenberg (2008) has argued for the value and relevance of this understanding of contest and competition in sport. She describes how ostracism can teach us that a good contest consist of a genuine battle between worthy opponents and how it, as a motivating force, can teach athletes to remain competitive rather than rest on their laurels because: 'Their laps of victory will last only until the next competition' (ibid: 280). More existential points have been raised regarding this view of contest (although not with reference to Nietzsche) by Fry (2011), who argues for the existential value of comebacks in sport and by Kretchmar (2012), who argues that true competition involves a 'willingness to play again tomorrow'.

A second aspect that Nietzsche highlights in the quote above is that ostracism involves both mutual incitement and moderation between competitors (cf. the Dionysian and Apollonian powers). This is important, because the understanding and meaning of sportive agon can easily change. Hoberman (1997) has, for example, described how Nietzsche's ideal of *agon* and 'great health' has been distorted by the scientizing and pharmacologizing of elite sport into biological experiments and instrumental measurement that neglect the limits of the human body. Holowchak and Reid (2011) have voiced other concerns about variations of agonism in modern sport, where it can turn into a restless 'panagonism' (several contests within each contests and potentially limitless progress) or 'commercial agonism' (promotion for external goods). Instead of abandoning agonism in sport on this basis (which would of course be absurd), Nietzsche's reflections on the ancient meaning of *agon* can reveal and highlight the positive value that contests can give to human existence. In relation to the existential dangers described here, it can remind us, as Acampora (2013: 202) argues, that transcending our limits (desire to win and achieve mastery) need not exclude or be opposed to holding oneself within the bonds of moderation (respect for the instituted standards of excellence). A good contest involves both. It is a process of agonistic exchange where a lack of desire to win or a neglect of the boundaries and limits of the agonistic arena that make the achievement of victory possible would both disrupt the good contest.

Another central aim for Nietzsche was to remove the ideal of *asceticism* from the moral and religious aim of denial or obligation (Nietzsche 1997b). As a contrast to this, he described how 'I also want to make asceticism natural again: in place of the aim of denial, the aim of strengthening; a gymnastics of the will ... an experiment with adventures and arbitrary dangers' (Nietzsche 1967: 483). This ambition points back to the original meaning of *askēsis*, which was exercise, practice and training, and the sportive tone of this quote points to how sport can be a suitable venue for this kind of ascetic endeavour. Sloterdijk (2013) has taken up this idea to argue for a 'de-spiritualisation' of religion, placing *askēsis* at the heart of his anthropology of *the practising life (das übende Leben)*.

In this, Sloterdijk draws heavily on Nietzsche's understanding of heightening and he argues that 'humans are inescapably subject to *vertical tensions*, in all periods and all cultural areas' (ibid: 12, emphasis added). Sport is, of course, no exception and, in this cultural area, he clarifies the vertical tension to consist of the two poles of excellence versus mediocrity. These are the decisive vectors of the human condition for athletes, the first of which attracts and the latter repulses. From this he clarifies the implications for our understanding of human existence:

> Only from the angle of the attractive forces acting 'from above' can one explain why and in what forms *Homo sapiens* ... was able to develop into the upward-tending animal ... Wherever one encounters members of the human race, they always show the traits of being that is condemned to surrealistic effort. Whoever goes in search of humans will find acrobats.
>
> *(Sloterdijk 2013: 13, his emphasis)*

This understanding of human existence thus condemns us, not just to meaning (Merleau-Ponty) and freedom (Sartre), but also to *effort*. This ascetic understanding of the value of sportive efforts to achieve excellence was also a central part of Coubertin's Olympism (see, for example, Parry 2007) and it rests on the Stoic ideals of resilience, endurance, perseverance, overcoming and self-discipline. From the earlier descriptions of Nietzsche's aesthetic and artistic account of enhancement and heightening it should be no surprise that Sloterdijk describes this kind of human endeavours through the figure of the acrobat. The term 'acrobatics' originates from the Greek *akros* (high) and baínein (to walk) and literally meant walking on tiptoe or walking in the heights (for example, on a tightrope). It is in this sense that Sloterdijk clarifies the acrobat to incarnate both the artistic and naturalistic aims of Nietzsche. It is the artistic 'overlord' and Sloterdijk describes how the generalised 'acrobatism' involves "a doctrine of the processual incorporation of the nearly impossible' (Sloterdijk 2013: 123). Human beings, in this view, can transcend and overcome themselves by practising; that is, through continuous striving and repeated attempts at reaching out for the nearly impossible. Monahan (2007) has argued that martial arts can be seen as a manifestation of this kind of Nietzschean self-overcoming. He draws, however, a distinction between this field of practice and the competition and aim for victory in other athletic pursuits, which, in his view, implies that training in competitive sport is conducted less for the sake of self-overcoming. From an existential stance and keeping the account of *agon* above in mind, I argue that this need not be the case. In fact, I think that a proper understanding of ascetic self-overcoming can prospectively contribute to a better understanding of the immense struggles of athletes in all kinds of sport.

Even if *askēsis* involves work on oneself with the aim of strengthening and self-overcoming it can, like *agon*, be considered a common good. It implies, as Sloterdijk (2013: 125) puts it, a 'superversion' of the existing and the ones who walk or have walked in the heights attract and urge others (for example, talented athletes) in the field to look up: 'The human of the "over" is the artiste who draws our gaze to wherever he is active. For him, being there [cf. Heidegger's *Dasein*] means being up there' (ibid: 116). I (Aggerholm 2014) have used this perspective to analyse the indispensable meaning and value provided by role models in sport. However, being up there or, rather, the repeated attempts at getting up there in the process of practising, is not without danger. Nietzsche's tightrope walker actually fell down and died and, in general, *risk* and death can, as Müller (2008) has pointed out, be seen as an inherent element of sportive existence. Within the philosophy of sport, Russell (2005) has explored how dangerous sports can contribute to self-affirmation by 'meeting and extending the boundaries of our existence' (ibid: 14). Ilundáin-Agurruza (2008) has analysed how the apparently (at least for non-Spaniards) absurd bull run through the streets of Pamplona, where thousands risk their lives, can through the lens of Nietzsche's and Ortega y Gasset's life-affirming views be seen to hold a significantly joyous existential value. He argues that such tangible risk and danger can, with them, be understood as a prerequisite and means for an enhanced and joyful experience related to the sportive and festive sense of life. Howe (2008a) has explored risk in 'remote sports' (that is, non-urban sports) from an 'ecosophical' viewpoint to argue that such activity can advance one's self-realization and can contribute to understanding of both self, nature and 'self-in-nature'. Finally, Breivik (2010, 2011) has studied the risk involved in skydiving, kayaking and climbing, and argues that facing danger and possible death in such extreme situations can make deeper existential structures visible to us in a salient way.

None of these authors discusses *askēsis* in relation to risk and even if Breivik touches upon the vertical element of such sportive endeavour, it is in a significantly different understanding of the vertical than the one found in Nietzsche and Sloterdijk, who, as mentioned earlier, saw verticality as an existential movement of heightening and enhancement. This vertical dimension of existence, so elementary present in sport, has in many ways been overlooked within the field of philosophy of sport. Many concerns have, however, rightfully been voiced regarding instrumental variants of this, as seen in the continuous striving for records and results (Loland 2000, 2001) and the technological and medical assistance provided for example by performance-enhancing drugs (Hoberman 1988, 1992; Culbertson 2007, 2011; Loland 2009). But the deeper existential value of striving towards the heights of sport and the enhancing 'work on oneself' involved with the efforts of practising in direction of this, has yet to be thoroughly studied. I (Aggerholm 2014) have argued that such considerations can inform a virtuous and existentially sustainable account of enhancement and striving for improvements in sport.

Concluding remarks

This chapter has attempted to present existential philosophy as a broad range of ideas, topics and perspectives, rather than a school of thought with an agreed project or unified account of human existence. From a common understanding of fundamental aspects of the human condition, it is a branch of philosophy with inherent tensions and contrasting understandings. I have given examples of how some of these have been used, and prospectively could be of use, within the philosophy of sport. Through this I have tried to illustrate how existential philosophy can contribute to nurture an eye for both existential dangers and values in sport.

It can contribute to reveal objectification of human subjectivity in sport and provides an alternative to approaches governed by, for example, instrumental or dogmatic values. It can also help to understand and avoid other existential dangers, for example when athletes neglect their situated freedom to focus exclusively on transcendence or facticity.

On the more positive side, existential philosophy can be a constructive lens through which many engaging aspects of meaning and value can come to notice. Sport is a domain filled with attracting existential phenomena and people engage in sport for many more or less explicated reasons. I have presented ideas from key existential philosophers to describe aspects of existential meaning experienced in sport that can both be embodied, chosen and transcendent. This has guided the description of various and sometimes ambiguous existential phenomena present in the world of sport.

Much more could, and should, be said about this layer of meaning that provides a source for excitement and sustains the involvement of sportspeople around the world. This chapter has suggested some points of departure for the future study of this topic, which might inspire scholars within the philosophy of sport to grant existential philosophy the attention of which it is worthy.

Notes

1 In contrast to this view, Atkinson (2010, 2013) has, for example, proposed 'post-sport' (fell-running and parkour) as an existential alternative to modern sport.
2 Sartre (2003: 552) found Heidegger's expressions of 'authentic' or 'unauthentic' dubious and insincere because of their implicit moral content.
3 It should be noticed here how bad faith resembles Kierkegaard's descriptions of despair, as a result of lacking either the finite or necessity, on the one hand, and infinity or possibility on the other (Kierkegaard 2012d: 146–57).
4 I further analyse this in relation to Sartre's (2004) later analyses in *Critique of Dialectical Reason*, where he introduced 'the pledge' as a collective counterpart to the existential choice in his discussion of a football team.
5 Sisyphus is punished by the gods to roll a huge stone up a steep hill but, before he reaches the top, the stone always rolls back down, forcing him to start over again and making his struggles an eternal (and in Camus' description an absurd) quest.

References

Acampora, Christa Davis. 2013. *Contesting Nietzsche*. Chicago, IL: University of Chicago Press.

Agassi, Andre. 2009. *Open: An autobiography*. New York: A. A. Knopf.

Aggerholm, Kenneth. 2013. "Express Yourself: The value of theatricality in soccer." *Journal of the Philosophy of Sport* 40(2): 205–24.

Aggerholm, Kenneth. 2014. *Talent Development, Existential Philosophy and Sport: On becoming an elite athlete*. Abingdon: Routledge.

Aggerholm, Kenneth, and Lars Tore Ronglan. 2012. "Having The Last Laugh: The Value of Humour in Invasion Games." *Sport, Ethics and Philosophy* 6(3): 336–52.

Aggerholm, Kenneth, Ejgil Jespersen and Lars Tore Ronglan. 2011. "Falling for the Feint – an Existential Investigation of a Creative Performance in High-Level Football." *Sport, Ethics and Philosophy* 5(3): 343–58.

Arendt, Hannah. 1994. "What Is Existential Philosophy?" In *Arendt: Essays in Understanding: 1930–1954*, edited by Jerome Kohn, 163–87. New York: Harcourt Brace Jovanovich.

Atkinson, Michael. 2010. "Fell Running in Post sport Territories." *Qualitative Research in Sport and Exercise* 2(2): 109–32.

Atkinson, Michael. 2013. "Heidegger, Parkour, Post-sport, and the Essence of Being." In *A Companion to Sport*, edited by David L. Andrews and Ben Carrington, 359–74. Oxford: Wiley-Blackwell.

Breivik, Gunnar. 2010. "Being-in-the-Void: A Heideggerian analysis of skydiving." *Journal of the Philosophy of Sport* 37: 29–46.

Breivik, Gunnar. 2011. "Dangerous Play With the Elements: Towards a phenomenology of risk sports." *Sport, Ethics and Philosophy* 5(3): 314–30.

Camus, Albert. 1956. *The Rebel: An essay on man in revolt*, trans. Anthony. Bower, NY: Vintage. (Originally published in 1951.)

Camus, Albert. 2005. *The Myth of Sisyphus*, trans. Justin O'Brien. London: Penguin. (Originally published in 1942.)

Collins, James. 1952. *The Existentialists*. Chicago: Henry Regnery.

Connolly, Maureen. 2008. "The Remarkable Logic of Autism: Developing and Describing an Embedded Curriculum Based in Semiotic Phenomenology." *Sport, Ethics and Philosophy* 2(2): 234–56.

Cooper, David E. 2012. "Existentialism as a philosophical movement." In *The Cambridge Companion to Existentialism*, edited by Steven Crowell, 27–49. Cambridge: Cambridge University Press.

Culbertson, L. 2005. "The paradox of bad faith and elite competitive sport." *Journal of the Philosophy of Sport* 32(1): 65–86.

Culbertson, Leon. 2007. "'Human-ness', 'Dehumanisation' and Performance Enhancement." *Sport, Ethics and Philosophy* 1(2): 195–217.

Culbertson, Leon. 2011. "Sartre on Human Nature: Humanness, transhumanism and performance-enhancement." *Sport, Ethics and Philosophy* 5(3): 231–44.

Fry, Jeffrey P. 2011. "Making A Comeback." *Sport, Ethics and Philosophy* 5(1): 4–20.

Gerber, Ellen W. and William J. Morgan, eds. 1979. *Sport and the Body. A philosophical symposium*. London: Henry Kimpton (Originally published in 1972.)

Heidegger, Martin. 1996. *Being and Time*, trans. Joan Stambaugh. Albany, NY: State University of New York Press. (Originally published in 1927.)

Hoberman, J. 1988. "Sport and the Technological Image of Man." In *Philosophic Inquiry in Sport*, edited by William J. Morgan and Klaus Meier, 319–27. Champaign, IL: Human Kinetics.

Hoberman, J. 1992. *Mortal Engines: The science of performance and the dehumanization of sport*. New York: Free Press.

Hoberman, John. 1997. "The Sportive Agon in Ancient and Modern Times." In *Agonistics: Arenas of creative contest*, edited by Janet Lungstrum and Elizabeth Sauer, 293–304. New York: State University of New York Press.

Holowchak, Mark, and Heather L. Reid. 2011. *Aretism, An Ancient Sports Philosophy for the Modern Sports World*. Lanham, MD: Lexington.

Howe, Leslie A. 2007. "Being and Playing: Sport and the Valorization of Gender." In *Ethics in Sport*, 2nd ed., edited by William J Morgan, Champaign, IL: Human Kinetics.

Howe, L.A. 2008a. "Remote Sport: Risk and Self-Knowledge in Wilder Spaces." *Journal of the Philosophy of Sport* 35(1): 1–16.

Howe, Leslie A. 2008b. "Self and Pretence: Playing with Identity." *Journal of Social Philosophy* 39(4): 564–82.

Hurka, Thomas. 2007. "Games and the Good." In *Ethics in Sport*, 2nd ed., edited by William J. Morgan, 21–34. Champaign, IL: Human Kinetics.

Hyland, Drew A. 1979. "Athletics and Angst: Reflections on the Philosophical Relevance of Play." In *Sport and the Body. A Philosophical Symposium*, edited by Ellen W. Gerber, and William J Morgan. London: Henry Kimpton. (Originally published in 1972.)

Ilundáin-Agurruza, Jesus. 2008. "Between the Horns: A dilemma in the interpretation of the running of the bulls – Part 2: The evasion." *Sport, Ethics and Philosophy* 2(1): 18–38.

Inglis, David. 2004. "Meditations on Sport: On the Trail of Ortega y Gasset's Philosophy of Sportive Existence." *Journal of the Philosophy of Sport* 31(1): 78–96.

Jordbru, Anika A., Ejgil Jespersen, and Egil Martinsen. 2008. "Conversion Gait Disorder – Meeting Patients in Behaviour, Reuniting Body and Mind." *Sport, Ethics and Philosophy* 2(2): 185–99.

Kierkegaard, Søren A. 2012a. *Afsluttende uvidenskabelig Efterskrift [Concluding Unscientific Postscript]*. SKS-E 1.7 ed. Søren Kierkegaards Skrifter 7. København: Søren Kierkegaard Forskningscentret. (Originally published in 1846.)

Kierkegaard, Søren A. 2012b. *Enten – Eller. Første del. [Either – Or. Part one]*. SKS-E 1.6 ed. Søren Kierkegaards Skrifter 2. København: Søren Kierkegaard Forskningscentret. (Originally published in 1843.)

Kierkegaard, Søren A. 2012c. *Enten – Eller. Anden del. [Either – Or. Part two]*. SKS-E 1.6 ed. Søren Kierkegaards Skrifter 3. København: Søren Kierkegaard Forskningscentret. (Originally published in 1843.)

Kierkegaard, Søren A. 2012d. *Sygdommen til Døden. [Sickness Unto Death]*. SKS-E 1.7 ed. Søren Kierkegaards Skrifter 11. København: Søren Kierkegaard Forskningscentret. (Originally published in 1849)

Kretchmar, R. Scott. 2006. "Life on Easy Street: The Persistent Need for Embodied Hopes and Down-to-Earth Games." *Quest* 58(3): 344–54.

Kretchmar, R. Scott. 2012. "Competition, Redemption, and Hope." *Journal of the Philosophy of Sport* 39(1): 101–16.

Loland, Sigmund. 2000. "The Logic of Progress and the Art of Moderation in Competitive Sports." In *Values in Sport*, edited by Torbjörn Tannsjö, and Claudio Tamburrini. London: Routledge.

Loland, Sigmund. 2001. "Record Sports: An ecological critique and a reconstruction." *Journal of the Philosophy of Sport* 28(2): 127–39.

Loland, Sigmund. 2009. "The Ethics of Performance-Enhancing Technology in Sport." *Journal of the Philosophy of Sport* 36(2): 152–61.

Martin, Andy. 2010. "Swimming and Skiing: Two Modes of Existential Consciousness." *Sport, Ethics and Philosophy* 4(1): 42–51.

Martin, Andy. 2012. *The Boxer and the Goalkeeper: Sartre vs Camus*. London: Simon and Schuster.

Merleau-Ponty, Maurice. 1962. *Phenomenology of Perception*, trans. Colin Smith. London: Routledge. (Originally published in 1945.)

Monahan, Michael. 2007. "The Practice of Self-overcoming: Nietzschean reflections on the martial arts." *Journal of the Philosophy of Sport* 34(1): 39–51.

Müller, Arno. 2008. *Risikosport: Suizid oder Lebenskunst?* Hamburg: Merus-Verlag.

Nesti, Mark. 2011. "Phenomenology and Sports Psychology: Back To The Things Themselves!" *Sport, Ethics and Philosophy* 5(3): 285–96.

Nietzsche, Friedrich. 1967. *The Will To Power*, edited by Walter Kaufmann, trans. Walter Kaufmann and R. J. Hollingdale. New York: Vintage.

Nietzsche, F. W. 1997a. "Homer's Contest." In *Agonistics. Arenas of Creative Contest*, edited by Janet Lungstrum, and Elizabeth Sauer, 35–45. New York: State University of New York Press.

Nietzsche, Friedrich. 1997b. *On the Genealogy of Morality*, edited by Keith Ansell-Pearson, trans. Carol Diethe. Cambridge: Cambridge University Press.

Nietzsche, Friedrich. 1999. *The Birth of Tragedy and Other Writings*, edited by Raymond Geuss, and Ronald Speirs, trans. Ronald Speirs. Cambridge: Cambridge University Press.

Nietzsche, Friedrich. 2001. *The Gay Science*, edited by Bernard Williams, trans. Josefine Nauckhoff and Adrian Del Caro. Cambridge: Cambridge University Press.

Nietzsche, Friedrich. 2006. *Thus Spoke Zarathustra*, edited by Adrian Del Caro and Robert Pippin), trans. Adrian Del Caro. Cambridge: Cambridge University Press.

Nietzsche, Friedrich. 2007. *Ecce Homo. How To Become What You Are*, trans. Duncan Large. Oxford: Oxford University Press.

Ortega y Gasset, J. 1984. *Historical Reason*. New York: W. W. Norton. (Originally published in 1940.)

Ortega y Gasset, J. 1995. *Meditations on Hunting*. Belgrade, MT: Wilderness. (Originally published in 1942.)

Ortega y Gasset, J. 2002. "Man the Technician." In *Toward a Philosophy of History*, edited by José Ortega y Gasset, Urbana, IL: University of Illinois Press. (Originally published in 1941.)

Parry, Jim. 2007. "The *religio athletae*, Olympism and peace." In *Sport and Spirituality. An introduction*, edited by Jim Parry, Simon Robinson, Nick J. Watson, and Mark Nesti, 201–14. London: Routledge.

Robinson, Simon. 2014. "Sport, Spirituality and Religion." In *The Bloomsbury Companion to the Philosophy of Sport*, edited by Cesar R. Torres, 245–61. London: Bloomsbury.

Rosenberg, Melinda. 2008. "Nietzsche, Competition and Athletic Ability." *Sport, Ethics and Philosophy* 2(3): 274–84.

Russell, JS. 2005. "The Value of Dangerous Sport." *Journal of the Philosophy of Sport* 32(1): 1–19.

Ryall, Emily. 2008. "Being-on-the-Bench: An Existential Analysis of the Substitute in Sport." *Sport, Ethics and Philosophy* 2(1): 56–70.

Sartre, Jean-Paul. 1991. *Critique of Dialectical Reason. Volume Two. The Intelligibility of History*, edited by Arlette Elkaïm-Sartre, trans. Hoare, Quintin. London: Verso. (Originally published in 1985.)

Sartre, Jean-Paul. 2003. *Being and Nothingness. An essay on phenomenological ontology*, trans. Hazel E. Barnes. London: Routledge. (Originally published in 1943.)

Sartre, Jean-Paul. 2004. *Critique of Dialectical Reason. Volume One. Theory of Practical Ensembles*, trans. Alan Sheridan-Smith. London: Verso. (Originally published in 1960.)

Sartre, Jean-Paul. 2007. *Existentialism is a Humanism*, trans. Carol MaComber. New Haven, CT: Yale University Press. (Originally published in 1946.)

Schacht, Richard. 2012. "Nietzsche: after the Death of God." In *The Cambridge Companion to Existentialism*, edited by Steven Crowell, 111–36. Cambridge: Cambridge University Press.

Sloterdijk, Peter. 2013. *You Must Change Your Life*, trans. Wieland Hoban. Cambridge: Polity.

Slusher, Howard S. 1967. *Man, Sport and Existence: A critical analysis*. London: Henry Kimpton.

Suits, Bernard. 2005. *The Grasshopper: Games, life and Utopia*. Toronto: Broadview.

Tuncel, Yunus. 2013. *Agon in Nietzsche*. Milwaukee: Marquette University Press.

Watson, Nick J. and John White. 2007. "'Winning at all costs' in modem sport. Reflections on pride and humility in the writings of C.S. Lewis." In *Sport and Spirituality. An introduction*, edited by Jim Parry, Simon Robinson, Nick J. Watson, and Mark Nesti, 61–79. London: Routledge.

White, Cindy. 2004. "Kierkegaard and Sport: Willing One thing in Competitive Sports." Paper presented at the First International Conference, Sport and Religion: An Inquiry into Cultural Values. June 24–26, 2004, St. Olaf College, Minnesota, USA.

11

FEMINISM IN THE PHILOSOPHY OF SPORT

Leslie A. Howe

A generous observer of the philosophy of sport might conclude that the effect of feminist theory on the field has been subtle rather than pervasive. In terms of published journal pages, the philosophy of sport lags significantly behind its sister fields of the sociology of sport and social philosophy in general. Nevertheless, the influence of feminist thought and political action here as elsewhere has been to press profound reconfigurings of the central values and conceptions of sport and of how these values may be best realised in a just society. I do not in this chapter offer an historical survey of either feminist theory or its appearance in the philosophy of sport; there are a number of these already extant.[1] Rather, I offer an outline of the major theoretical concepts and problems that have been pursued by feminist philosophers of sport, explore their philosophical underpinnings and attempt to make evident connections between issues. In particular, feminist philosophers of sport have been concerned with equality of access to sport and its personal and social goods, the relative values of difference and separation in addressing equality issues, autonomy and the definition of gender in and through sport and sexuality. These are by no means the only issues in sport that are open to feminist philosophical questioning but they are the ones that have taken up the most attention in the philosophical literature. Of these, by far the greatest share of attention, at least up to the mid 1990s, has been equality and so we begin at the beginning.

Equality of access to sport

Equality is a fundamental liberal value, more noted in its absence than its achievement. This has been and continues to be so in sport. Questions concerning women's equality with men in sport are complex, in part because the equality advocated can be applied in many different ways. Are two people equal if they can both compete for the same opportunities to compete further, even in a society where goods and the means to compete are unequally distributed? Or are they equal only if they each have the same real prospect of enjoying those goods? Women's sports have consistently been under resourced in comparison with men's and, despite various legislative measures, largely continue to be so. Much of the philosophy of sport literature has concerned such measures, particularly Title IX legislation in the USA. While Title IX concerns only a limited set of American jurisdictions, the debates around it have served to refine some questions of fair distribution of resources in a context where both equality of fundamental right and historical failure to honour that right in practice occur.

Jane English's article 'Sex Equality in Sports' (1978) is the plausible starting point for this debate in contemporary philosophy of sport. In it, she poses the question of what exactly constitutes 'equal opportunity' for women in sports. A common interpretation of equality is a blanket principle of non-discrimination. This is a formal principle that stipulates simply that all applicants for or recipients of some benefit must be assessed without reference to non-relevant characteristics; in this case, we must be sex-blind. As English argues, however, this is too weak a principle for the advancement of women's participation in sport. Insofar as women perceive sport as a male preserve they may lack incentive to pursue sport and, thus, some violation of purely formal equality may be necessary to bring about a more just distribution of benefits. Also, purely formal equality may not be sufficient to cope with a context in which the differences between men and women are permanent (physiological) rather than (entirely) socially based, albeit those differences are statistical rather than essential. That is, while any given woman may be stronger or faster than some number of men, *on average*, men are stronger or faster than women. Given this, reliance on a formal principle of equality such as non-discrimination on the basis of sex has a strong likelihood of reinforcing present inequalities and, unlike other social contexts where this principle may come into force, it is unclear how such inequalities may be overcome.

In sport, bodily differences matter; they directly affect how well one can carry out its constituent movements and thus whether one can succeed at them, all other things being equal. That is, muscle mass matters in strength sports, height in those in which the athlete must reach a specific span, and so on. These may not be decisive: fine motor control and learned technique may put one athlete ahead of another despite their respective inherited anatomical advantages or disadvantages, so that where sport-specific skill is equivalent, a talentless behemoth might do less well than a skilled sprite in a physical contest. Although size, or strength, or raw speed, or natural flexibility, and so on, may be decisive, this depends on the requirements of the sport in question. Given a social bias in favour of those sports that privilege predominantly male characteristics, however, women and women's sports are less likely to flourish.

The question of equal opportunity is thus inextricably linked with those concerning the masculine bias of much conventional sport. As Betsy Postow argues in 'Women and Masculine Sports' (1980), sports can be described as 'masculine' in a number of different ways, such as in: (a) requiring certain kinds of behaviours culturally identified as 'masculine'; or (b) attitudes likewise identified, as being (c) a vehicle of masculine gender identification, or (d) as defining athletic excellence in terms of developed capacities in which men have a statistical advantage over women owing to biological factors (1980: 52–3). Sports falling under (c) may be problematic in some ways but, while (a) and (b) are considered by Postow to be morally neutral; that is, there is no reason why women should not participate in these activities, 'masculine$_d$' sports ought, she argues, to be avoided (Postow 1980: 53–4). This is because participation in them perpetuates the image of 'general female inferiority which we have a moral reason to undermine' (ibid: 54). Instead, we should increase the availability of sports in which women have a statistical superiority or are, at least, not inferior, although those women who enjoy or are well suited to masculine$_d$ sports should continue to pursue them, presumably because doing so mitigates the conviction of women's 'general inferiority'.

On the other hand, if able women can compete with men, the reverse ought also to be permitted and this may have undesirable consequences for women's sport participation.

> In masculine$_d$ sports, allowing men to compete against women would expose women
> to a drastically reduced probability of receiving the moderately scarce athletic

resources, such as access to facilities and coaching, that go with making a team. This too seems unfair.

(Postow 1980: 55)

As Postow points out, equality of opportunity *qua* freedom from socially imposed restrictions on one's ability to compete seems to work against equality of opportunity *qua* probability, given the same level of effort, of actually receiving the benefits of the sport.[2] In other words, if we all have equal opportunity in the sense that we can all *compete* for the same goods, then those who are already advantaged in the means of competition will exclude those who are not. Where the goods are assumed to be scarce, that means not merely that the disadvantaged will do less well but that they will not do at all.

Because of considerations like these, English argues in favour of an equality for sport that specifically stresses equality of access to the basic benefits that sport offers to participants:

> Sports offer what I will call *basic benefits* to which it seems everyone has an equal right: health, the self-respect to be gained by doing one's best, the cooperation to be learned from working with teammates and the incentive gained from having opponents, the 'character' of learning to be a good loser and a good winner, the chance to improve one's skills and learn to accept criticism – and just plain fun. If Matilda is less adept at, say, wrestling than Walter is, this is no reason to deny Matilda an equal chance to wrestle for health, self-respect, and fun.

(English 1978: 270)

English goes on to declare that 'a society that discourages Matilda from wrestling is unjust because it lacks equal opportunity to attain these basic benefits'. While *prima facie* this seems a promising approach, it may not do as much work as English suggests, even if we accept its fundamental principle. That is, English's principle supposes that everyone ought to have access to the means of obtaining the basic benefits offered by sport, whether male or female, whether exceptionally competent or not. *If* basic benefits are of fundamental value then participation should not be dependent on whether one is sufficiently skilled to make the top-tier team but only on whether one is willing to participate and compete. Guaranteed access to *basic* benefits, however, does not guarantee access to the participant's *preferred* form of those benefits. That is, a society may accept English's principle but still restrict women's access to sports that some women may prefer to participate in, such as those that are considered the appropriate preserve of ('real') men and direct women into what it considers appropriately 'feminine' activities, ones that reinforce stereotypes about women's abilities and that restrict individual women's actual choices.

Difference and integration

Such an outcome might be the result of assuming that the ways to play constitute a naturally limited set, as, for example, if one were to suppose that any given sport, say hockey, could only be played in a particular way, and nothing else could count as hockey. This is even more restricting if it is assumed that these ways are all ways in which only one group (men) happen to play, not least because this then suggests that only men's sports could count as sport – because that is just what sport is. There are a number of possible responses to this. The most common in this period is to suggest a fragmentation of possible play situations. For example, skill classes are one way to deal with physical differences between competitors. As English points out, these

163

are more readily justifiable than sex segregation as they are determined by relevant character-istics and provide satisfying levels of competition. English (1978: 275–7) also calls for the development of new sports that are more suited to women's 'distinctive abilities'.

> The just society ... would contain a greater variety of sports than we now have, providing advantages for a wider range of physical types. The primary emphasis would be on participation, with a wealth of local teams and activities available to all, based on groupings by ability.
>
> *(English 1978: 276)*

The devising of sports specifically for women is advocated by a number of authors in this period and can be characterised as an expression of dismay at the exaggerated masculinity of modern sport, whether that is perceived as inherent to it or a contingent aberration. This masculinisation excludes women's participation in sport either by entrenching the social view that sport just is by definition masculine and thus women *ought not* participate, or by making any sport competition that features both sexes a mismatch that confirms the prejudice that women do not belong in sport. This is 'demonstrated' in an explicit way by the exhibition of lopsided scoring or by the deliberate or incidental infliction of physical harm on participating women. An historically popular and marginally more subtle technique that remains in force today is to demand that where women's sports exist at all, the participants exhibit male-deter-mined ideals of femininity. Thus, for example, the exaggerated emphasising of female sexuality in sports such as volleyball, the social expectation that strong female athletes demonstrate gender-identified emotional traits (crying, devotion to family, etc.) and that female athletes, especially in masculine-identified sports such as hockey or football, signal strongly their real or feigned heterosexual identity. How then is the feminist project of reinventing sports for women not a tail wagged by a masculinist dog?

The crucial point is the modifier 'male-determined'. The conception of sport as funda-mentally masculine presupposes a particular conception of 'masculinity' and concomitantly a particular conception of 'femininity'. These are exclusively dyadic (and hierarchical) concep-tions. They are ideological conceptions, which is to say that they organise experience rather than follow it and are thus largely impervious to actual empirical evidence. The phenomenon of women playing and succeeding at sport does not shake the conception but merely confuses unless it can be placed back into the organising structure of 'masculine' = male = physically active and superior/'feminine' = woman = physically passive and inferior. On this structure, women doing sport makes very little sense, unless (perhaps) they also do it 'like girls' (that is, badly) and women doing 'male' sports makes no sense at all (so there must be something wrong with them).

The liberal feminist project of androgyny to which many of the authors of this period refer was an attempt to counter this dyadic conception of humanity. 'Androgynism' here refers to a number of theoretical responses to the recognition that sex (one's anatomical, hormonal, and/or chromosomal arrangement) and gender (one's set of psychological traits and/or social behaviours socially identified as belonging to one sex or the other, supposing a binary classifi-cation) are not necessarily or irrevocably linked. In particular, androgyny functions as an ideal of human development in which human individuals are enabled to develop so-called 'mascu-line' or 'feminine' gender traits independently of their sex and as an expression of a more fully developed humanness than is available under the '"this" or "that" and no other' of dominant heterosexist-dualist normativity. The central observation supporting the conviction that all humans should be treated *as humans* and as free to develop and express whatever (morally acceptable) traits they choose is that there are no human traits that are possessed by all and only males or by all and only females. The androgynist ideal rests on this principle there is no essential masculinity or femininity. Rather, human traits are distributed through the population, with an, at most, statistical preponderance in one sex or the other. An ideal human society would be one in which any human individual could choose what traits to possess or realise in him or her self without regard to whether such traits were 'ideally' 'masculine' or 'feminine'. Indeed, in the best of all possible worlds, such designations as 'masculine' or 'feminine' would in time wither away, and we would recognise traits as simply and solely human.[3]

Thus, many of these authors, in advocating the development of women oriented or women-only sports, are *rejecting* the dyadic conception of 'femininity' and endorsing the view that women's participation in sport is a legitimate expression of their equal capacity for rational choice of embodied activity, but in a way that facilitates the de-legitimation of the dyadic conception.[4]

On an even broader level, and as hinted earlier, the feminist critique opens the question of sport itself. Many of the criticisms of conventional sport are not unique to feminism; for example, is sport best understood as barely restrained combat or, as Boxill describes it, as a co-questing after excellence (Boxill 1993–94: 25). Feminism brings to such questions a sharper perspective: not simply one involving a conflict of styles or tastes or a philosophically neutral dispute about definitions, but a matter of unwarranted discrimination rooted in false and unsupportable ideologies about the nature of masculinity, femininity and humanity in general. Our views about what sport is, and what characteristics are required for success in it, leans heavily on the degree to which sport figures in a set of ideological assumptions, including our conceptualisations of ideal femininity and ideal masculinity. Insofar as sport is implicated in a view of masculinity that is strongly opposed to femininity, and insofar as it is as such recruited in the attempt to preserve hegemonic strategies of masculine interpretation, women will encounter significant resistance to their participation in sport and even more so the recognition of their athletic endeavours as genuine *sport*. Thus, questioning the appropriate 'masculinity' of sport is not only critical to rethinking women's possibilities for participation but entails a reconsideration of the nature of sport itself. Although this has sometimes been put in dyadic terms (masculine agonism versus feminine relational support), to do so, it can be argued, merely reiterates this essentialist framework and moves too quickly past an opportunity for a more thoroughgoing reflection on sport as an intersubjective social practice.

This last observation brings us back to the question with which we began: sport is a social practice, so achieving equality in sport should be a matter of finding the right kind of social policy, one that finds the right balance between equality and justice. One of the problems with opting to treat everyone as the same: that is, interpreting the ideal of equality entirely in terms of an abstract policy of treating everyone (as) the same, rather than as a substantive social goal, is that it ignores the concrete inequalities with which participants come to the playing field. In the matter of sport, the inequalities are not (only) the anatomical and physiological differences between men and women, but the social contexts that prepare and shape the participants, that assess their performances, and that reward them differently for their efforts.[5]

Postow (1981) attempts to make something like this point in defending the segregationist point that women ought not to participate in the sort of male-preferential sports (football, baseball, basketball, tennis; that is, those that, in her characterisation, favour upper-body strength) at which they are statistically more likely to measure poorly against male participants because doing so will contribute to the view that women are naturally inferior. A number of commentators have responded to this by pointing out that such a conclusion is not a compelling reason for women to refrain from engaging in such sports; that is, that other people may form false opinions about whether women are naturally inferior or not as a consequence of women participating in sport is no moral reason for women to cease to engage in it; the error is on the part of the observer, not the women (Vetterling-Braggin 1981; Grim 1981). As Vetterling-Braggin explains,

> No matter what sort of case is invented, the image formed is either accurate or inaccurate. Because women have no moral reason to prevent the formation of anyone's truths and no moral reason to limit our own sports possibilities for the purpose of preventing the formation of someone else's falsehoods, we have no moral grounds for withdrawing from 'masculine' sports.
>
> *(Vetterling-Braggin 1981: 57)*

Postow's point, however, is that such sports are not in and of themselves objectionable; what is, rather, is their 'virtual monopoly on social recognition' (Postow 1981: 62) and that social facts like this one are often mistaken for natural fact.

The criticism that women's social circumstances are treated as if natural fact is one with a long historical precedent. In 1792, Mary Wollstonecraft (1995) argued, in *A Vindication of the Rights of Woman*, that keeping women from education in the use of their reason was what very conveniently allowed men to decry women as naturally frivolous and stupid and on that basis to bar them from what supposedly would only be a wasted education (Wollstonecraft 1995: 44). As John Stuart Mill (1970) also pointed out in 1869 in *The Subjection of Women*, it is a curious sort of natural fact that needs so many safeguards for its support (1970: 27). So here as well, if women fail (relatively) at 'male' activities such as sport because 'male' characteristics are required for success and women are prevented from acquiring them, as by training, what we have is a social artefact of women's 'inferiority', not proof of a natural fact that would hardly need social intervention to maintain if it really were a natural fact. Nevertheless, false though it be as fact, it is a bone to the dog of sexist prejudice.

Autonomy

Insofar as much of the discussion concerning women's participation in sport in the philosophical literature has been based in a liberal framework, it has approached these issues as fundamentally about equality and therefore also, although less explicitly, as a matter of personal autonomy. This especially stands out when the connection is made between women's equality and the right to be free of paternalist interference. Paternalism is an issue for women's sport when women are prevented from participating in certain sports or in integrated (mixed sex) sports on grounds of the possibility of harm to women. 'Harm' here may refer to a number of anticipated outcomes: physical harm, of which there may or may not be a reasonable expectation due to the particular activities involved; presumed likelihood of harm that is alleged to affect women in particular (for example, the belief that strenuous activity threatens a woman's capacity for maternity); social harms of various kinds (for example, muscles might make a woman mannish and thus unattractive to men); alleged moral/religious harms (for example, for women to expose themselves publicly in athletic clothing); or psychological harms (for example, sport makes women aggressive); and so on. These putative harms, then, may be exaggerated for women or unreasonably presumed to affect women more than men, or it may be thought that women ought to be especially protected from such harms., If, then, women are on the basis of one or another of these pretexts prevented from pursuing such activities, those who do so, it can be argued, are treating women as non-autonomous beings for whom decisions must be made by others.

At its basic level, liberal theory supposes that each individual is in principle rational and thus is able to rationally and, by dint of rationality,[6] freely organise his own affairs for himself, to decide for himself which of his interests he will act upon and in what way. Liberal feminists point out that 'his' is also 'her', that women are just as capable as men of rational self-determination. For any such (ideally) autonomous agent, it is an affront to his or her human dignity and fundamental liberty to be ruled by another where autonomy itself does not warrant such constraint, and arguably not even then. In Wollstonecraft's words,

> I love man as my fellow; but his sceptre, real, or usurped, extends not to me, unless the reason of an individual demands my homage; and even then the submission is to reason, and not to man. In fact, the conduct of an accountable being must be regulated by the operations of its own reason; or on what foundation rests the throne of God?
>
> *(Wollstonecraft 1995: 53)*

And later:

> The being who discharges the duties of its station is independent; and, speaking of women at large, their first duty is to themselves as rational creatures, and the next in point of importance, as citizens, is that which includes so many, of a mother. The rank in life which dispenses with their fulfilling this duty necessarily degrades them by making them mere dolls.
>
> *(Wollstonecraft 1995: 67)*

Thus, for women to be subject to much stricter controls over their activities than men on grounds of possible harm is differential paternalism, objectionable both because of the assumption of rational agential incapacity and the presumption that women are rationally defective in comparison with men.

This liberal-autonomy view is implicit in Angela Schneider's (2010) discussion in 'On the definition of "woman" in the sport context'. If men get to decide at the institutional level what sports women can do, how they are to be judged and to what extent they are to be funded, she concludes, 'then women have a legitimate grievance of not being treated with due respect' (Schneider 2010: 42). Moreover, women have the right, just as men do, to decide what risks of harm they will run. Subject to the normal limitations on every person's freedom, it is immorally paternalistic to decide, on behalf of another competent adult, what personal risks he or she can choose to accept (Schneider 2010: 43).

The issue here is two-fold: paternalism as such and the usurpation by one class (men) of another's (women's) right to determine for themselves not only what risks may reasonably be incurred, but what by what standards and ideals they are to be judged. Thus, the broader issues here are not only paternalism but control over self-definition. More prosaically, this includes how women should play in sport, what counts as a good performance, by what rules sportswomen are to be governed, and do women even get to play at all. If the 'ideal (sports)woman' is determined according to men's rather than women's own expectations and interests then women are not respected as fully capable agents. The strength of the argument is in its ruling out paternalism on the irrelevant basis of class membership (that is, prejudice), since all that matters for self-determination is humanity. In effect, paternalism can only proceed if the members of a class can be shown to be not fully human. The weakness of the argument is that the claim that it is (always) morally wrong to act paternalistically in relation to another human being rests on a highly abstract conception of the human; no one is such an ideal agent.

Separation, sovereignty, and bio-Amazons

So far, we have approached the question of equality primarily as that of women's inclusion in sport. Women are equally entitled to enjoy the basic benefits of participation and entitled to decide for themselves how, when and in what way to play. Many of the feminist authors writing in the philosophy of sport have argued against integration of men's and women's sport on the grounds that it is the best way of expanding women's participation while avoiding exclusionary effects of direct competition, although often at the same time accepting the value of at least some women competing with men. Michael Burke, in contrast, argues that segregation just protects the male gender from confronting the fact of overlap in performance between men and women, while women's acquiescence in the situation reflects a desire to remain within the strictures of heteronormativity (Burke 2010a: 130–1). Claudio Tamburrini and Torbjörn Tännsjö, more radically, argue that segregated sport is itself sexual discrimination and as such indefensible. There is, in fact, a divide between those who regard separate men's and women's sports as important for allowing women to participate freely, or at all, and those who argue that segregation simply bolsters masculine hegemony in sport, elevating and entrenching male dominance over governance and the cultural assumption of male epistemological authority (Burke 2010b: 20–1). Ironically, while the case for separation has often been made from a different feminist position, both sides of this debate have been argued from liberal humanist principles.

There are a number of reasons why women might prefer to participate in sport separate from men. Some of these are reactive in the sense that they are responses to defective social conditions. For example, one might prefer to perform motions that leave one vulnerable away from an objectifying gaze or the possibility that one might in some way be taken advantage of. In a society that mandates female appearance in terms of sexual attractiveness to males, appearing strong/weak, attractive/unattractive, carry meanings and thus possible responses that women may prefer not to negotiate for an hour or two. To some extent, women-only sport situations allow women to put the male-oriented world 'on hold'. Moreover, so long as one competes with only one's own sex, one need not be constantly measuring oneself against that other, although some measuring is inevitable (that is, someone will be faster than another, etc.). Success may be encouraged if one's genuine achievements are recognised as such rather than constantly downgraded as not as good as the very best.

Women may also prefer to avoid physical harm. While we have good reason to resist that disingenuous 'protection' of women from harm, particularly when it is not extended to men, it may also be the case that some proportion of women prefer to play sports that do not put them in harm's way. So, for that matter, do many men, but segregation may be a means of minimising certain kinds of avoidable harm due simply to size and to differing learned styles of play. There is also the particular kind of socially rooted conflict that can arise when women do better than the men with whom they compete. Tännsjö (2007: 347) rejects this as a good reason for segregation – men should just come to terms with it. Since, however, many men do not act with such aplomb, it can be a reason for a *preference* on the part of some women to avoid mixed sport, at least some of the time.[7]

Another, more positive, aspect of women-only sport is the freedom to develop one's own sport independently of whether men value the activity. Where the sport is indeed woman-developed, rather than delivered to women as a vehicle of masculinist demands on women's behaviour and appearance, its very separateness can be the means of women's autonomous self-expression and independent creativity. There is no reason to suppose that sports can only and must always be exactly as they have been established, which has largely been by and for men; other sports are possible and other ways of doing sport legitimate.

The prospect of a women-developed sport, however, challenges not only the possible definition of sport and of what it means to be a woman in sport; it also challenges political and economic models of sport and thereby raises questions about control of sport. Such questions are not strictly gender questions but they do inevitably arise in this context. In 'Gender Roles Roll', Pam R. Sailors (2013) describes the phenomenon of a player-created and regulated roller derby league which offers an example of the tensions that come into play in the simultaneous performance and parodic deconstruction of heteronormative femininity by the players. The league, however, as Sailors relates, faces the prospect of a kind of integration that is not necessarily advantageous to those already participating. As it has become more popular, pressure has increased on the league to allow men's participation and to 'go mainstream', that is, to tone down its parodic (and thus arguably gender-revolutionary) elements in favour of making it 'serious sport'; that is, more conformable to a dominant (and lucrative) conception of sport. In other words, the aim is to tame its radical nature and make it look like men's sports in order to enhance its commercial appeal to the same old market. As Sailors rightly points out, this is a question of control over sport; in this case, who owns the sport: those who created it or those who participate in it? But there is also the potential transition of an activity from being a practice with a specific set of meanings for the women participating (and spectating) because it is the product of their own creative self-expression to becoming a vehicle for the expression of others through women's bodies – in effect, back to where they were before devising this act of self-construction and determination. Thus, this serves as an example of the positive potential of the refusal of integration: in a social context where financial control and regulation of meaning is not in women's hands, it is sometimes preferable to be able to find some area of self-expression that is apart from that context, and sport is one possible avenue for that self-expression.

On the other side of the integration–segregation debate are Torbjörn Tännsjö and Claudio Tamburrini, who characterise sex segregation in sport competition as sexual discrimination and as therefore morally objectionable. In their view, sport should be completely integrated so as to ensure that the primary goal of sport is met, which is the identification of the best competitor. As Tännsjö (2007: 347) explains, '[i]n sports it is crucial that the best person wins. Then sexual differences are simply irrelevant'. It is important to recognise that, although many of Tamburrini and Tännsjö's remarks seem radical, they are simply at the extreme end of the same philosophical tradition as many (although not all) of the authors we have so far reviewed; their stance is libertarian rather than liberal, but begins in much the same place, with the ideally autonomous agent. We can see this in their advocacy of 'the inalienable right of the agent – the woman athlete – to decide for herself whether and when to undergo genetic modification' (Tamburrini and Tännsjö 2005: 191). This makes their characterisation of the views of authors such as Jane English as belonging to a completely different tradition from their own somewhat tenuous.[8]

Tännsjö states that sex discrimination (segregation) in sport is supposed to be justified 'on the ground that, *on average*, women perform less well than men in certain sports' (Tännsjö 2007: 349). He objects that it is hard to ascertain this 'fact' beyond a reasonable doubt, given its possible explanation as either a statistical accident or a consequence of socially constructed gender differences, which could eventually be abolished. He remarks that even if biological in origin, it is still only a *statistical* difference and thus is only indirectly relevant and thus not a valid basis for discrimination. In addition, sex segregation means that 'some women, who are not (statistically speaking) 'typical', perform better than many (most) men do. They do so because to a considerable degree they possess the characteristics that are crucial to winning, and possess more of these characteristics than do most men. Consequently, there are some rare women who perform better than most men in the sport in question' (Tännsjö 2007: 349). It is discrimination, then, when a highly competent woman is prevented from defeating a man on the ground that most women do not have the ability to do so.

Tännsjö dismisses the statistical justification for separate sports but it is worth noting that this is not how it has been used by liberal feminists. Rather, the circumstance that there is a statistical variation between but not an absolute or essential difference in traits and abilities between men and women has historically been deployed in the opposite direction. As Joyce Trebilcot (1975)[9] rightly points out, there is no trait that is shared by all and only men, or all and only women; sex and gender differences are merely statistical in this sense. The observation is then the basis for claims to the effect that women ought not to be excluded from professions or activities *just because* they are women as any given woman may be better equipped for those positions than a given man – which is the view that Tännsjö defends.

This does, nevertheless, help to clarify Tännsjö's philosophical intentions. Implicit in his argument is the claim that *individuals* are unjustly treated if they are treated as members of a group because group membership is irrelevant. The liberal individualist presumption is also present in Tamburrini and Tännsjö's (2005: 182) 'The Genetic Design of a New Amazon', which declares that the best way of dealing with sexual discrimination in sport is to 'offer women the possibility of becoming as strong as men' through genetic modification. The model of competition presupposed here is that of a completely open market. We cannot discuss the merits of Tamburrini and Tännsjö's conception of the market here, except to note its characteristically atomistic underpinning and the deep conviction that it ought not be interfered with. What is troubling about it, insofar as we restrict our attention to its application in sport, is their acceptance of market value as determinative of athletic value and the consequent flattening of questions of justice to what the market will offer. Thus, they argue that women ought not to receive an equal share of the scarce benefits of sport (payment, prize money, public recognition, media coverage) because their performances are not at the same level as men and have consequently less public appeal. To correct this 'society would have to interfere with market mechanisms by taking a share of male athlete's revenues and giving it to woman athletes' (ibid: 185). Such redistribution would be unjust and, they think, would reinforce women's bad self-image. Instead, women should be allowed genetic modification to produce physiques that would permit equal competition with men (in this unfettered athletic marketplace) as 'bio-Amazons' (ibid: 187).

The view of sport that comes out in Tamburrini and Tännsjö's contributions is one that is very much limited to a conception of sport as the production of results, and for professional sport, production of a commodity for which the market will pay, with lower price indicating lesser value. Consequently, they focus on English's discussion of scarce benefits but not at all on her discussion of the basic benefits or on the *activity* of sport itself. The claim that '[i]n sports it is crucial that the best person wins' is not argued for despite its centrality to the overall view. This is a point that some critics have fixed on as this is by no means a closed question, in philosophy or in practice, and, if true, would otherwise negate as sport any variety of it that is not intended to produce a decision as to who is the best – which is, arguably, the vast majority of actually practised sport. As Susan Sherwin and Meredith Schwartz (2005) point out in direct response to Tamburrini and Tännsjö, sports contests are always local and even where we are concerned with determining winners, a 100-metre race, for example, that does not include Usain Bolt is not thereby invalid. Moreover, sometimes the best do not win.[10]

Sherwin and Schwartz also raise two related concerns with Tamburrini and Tännsjö's (2005: 200) position: the conflation of equality with sameness and the assumption that 'existing male standards are an appropriate norm'. The problem here, as they explain, is the failure to question the standards currently in place, and the requirement that those who are outside that norm must conform to it in order to compete. If one already fits the norm (because it is one's own 'natural' description, and thus perhaps invisible) one is advantaged in the competition over those who are different. But an explicit defence is needed to make the case that male traits or accomplishments should be the norm rather than female. As Sherwin and Schwartz explain:

> Basing equality on the presumption of sameness is likely to disadvantage [those who are oppressed on the basis of some difference] by denying the reality and implications of their difference. Since some of these differences are important to the person's identity and self-conception, and others are beyond their power to change, the suggestion that they need to assimilate to the norm that arose in their absence based on standards appropriate to the dominant group may be both impossible and offensive.
>
> *(Sherwin and Schwartz 2005: 200)*

In the case at hand, then, there appears to be no reason to assume that a woman must, to achieve athletic excellence equivalent to that of a man, become a bio-Amazon, *unless* we also assume both that the male norm is the right one (one is only the best if one defeats the best *man*) and that athletic excellence is a matter of *winning*. As Simona Giordana and John Harris (2005) also point out, these assumptions are not necessarily true and thus require an argument that Tamburrini and Tännsjö (2005: 211) do not provide.

All this adds to some of the problems we might have in accepting the market model of equality. Again, as Sherwin and Schwartz (2005) argue, market standards are developed in a skewed social context. Relying on the market to solve inequalities fails to appreciate that 'the problem of oppression for women is not that men are 'naturally' superior and women are struggling to 'catch up' to the male ideal. The problem is that the construction of what is 'best' reflects male talents, and those activities that are perceived as female are systematically undervalued' (Sherwin and Schwartz 2005: 201). We can see this last point in Tännsjö's (2007, 353) dismissal of the notion that women's sports offer any unique value; instead, he suggests that whatever is good about them should simply be absorbed into the dominant (male) system.

Bodies and practices

Since the late 1990s, there has been a slow growth in feminist sport philosophy scholarship that explores issues other than, though significant for, questions of equality between men and women. These include issues around embodiment, selfhood, and sexuality, many of which were largely missing from earlier discussions. There has also been some effort to redraw the way in which we think about issues like equality; that is, to think not just about social policy but about the epistemological and ontological frameworks that structure our apprehension of gender, sexuality, body, and embodied meaning in the sport context from a broadly feminist and queer perspective.

Lisa Edwards and Carwyn Jones (2007, 349) have argued that both humanist and gynocentric feminism have failed to 'sufficiently recognise and challenge the dominant masculine ideology of sport', having concentrated instead on either securing equality within it in the first case or rejecting mainstream sport altogether as irredeemably masculinist in the latter. Neither of these approaches, they claim, are necessary, and neither is satisfactory. Instead, they propose a middle course that 'unpacks gender ideology more carefully, but also leaves intact and celebrates the non-ideological features of sport' (ibid: 349). They aim to take on the radical project of exposing the roots of sexist exclusion in sport without discarding it as a potentially inclusive and fulfilling social practice; in effect, they claim we do not have to give up on sport just because it has been so badly used, not least because the question of sport and that of ideology are distinct questions. But it is also important to see that sport *is* being badly used and *how*. The success that women have had is often presented in such a way as to persuade that women's battles for equality have been won, in sport as in business, politics, and education, but as Edwards and Jones (2007, 350) point out, sport remains one of 'the most significant showcases for the confirmation of gender and the gender hierarchy', presenting gender norms, especially masculinity, as natural and inevitable, and thus impervious to challenge or change.

Edwards and Jones argue that this problem and the previous approaches to it require a new approach that re-theorises subjectivity in non-dichotomous terms. Opposing the valorisation of masculinised ideals by simply substituting 'feminised' ones, they argue, only reinforces ideo-logically damaging conceptions of women.[11] Such conceptions are formulated in opposition to masculine ones and are, in any case, suspect but they also retrench the ideological expectation that women will be more interested in cooperation than competition, etc.[12] Consequently, they advocate a relational approach that recognises the mutually transformative operation of the allegedly distinct members of dichotomous pairs. Following Prokhovnik, Tuana, and Flanagan, Edwards and Jones (2007: 357–9) suggest that the classic dichotomies of much humanist and gynocentric feminist debate such as nature/nurture are much more dialectical (in the Socratic sense) than exclusively oppositional. The reason why we cannot settle such questions as what is 'natural' to men and women and what is 'social' is that there are no human traits that are either wholly natural or wholly social; they are all a bit of both, in varying degrees, and describ-ing them one way or the other will make more sense in one context and less in another. But, even if this could be settled, 'nothing necessarily follows from this. It is not the existence and developmental or biological antecedents of traits themselves as psychological entities that is contentious; rather the ways in which traits are celebrated, cultivated, valued and rewarded in our society' (Edwards and Jones 2007: 358). Our task, then, would be to consider how we choose which traits to value, and which practices exclude or oppress; in other words, how do our practices and values presuppose other values and practices, but also what epistemological and ontological short cuts they entail.

In explicating their 'soft gynocentric' middle way, Edwards and Jones (2007) suggest a McIntyrean approach to sport in which the value of the practice is to be found in the internal goods available through the particular practice and which do not depend on sex or gender, only on the means employed to pursue them. Thus, the 'purported masculine excesses of violence, cheating, commercialisation and aggression are pathological, not because they are traditionally masculine but because they are contrary to the "good sports contest"' (Edwards and Jones 2007: 361). Therefore we could say that sport is bad not because sport is inherently masculine but because it has been masculinised; that is, the practice has been distorted in such a way that the goods available through the practice have been restricted in a way not justifiable within the practice as such.

The question, however, is whether we can make sense of the concept of a social practice without presupposing the social values, traditions, and preconceptions that inform that practice. Just as the social and the natural interact in the construction of human beings as human and as male/female, etc., sport is an artefact of human interaction; change the interaction and the sport practice is also changed. Seeing this is important for challenging the notion that sport just is the way it is (that is, natural) and that this is why only men can be (naturally) good at it. But how then can we make sense of an idea of sport that is outside of all social context? The answer is that we cannot and, moreover, we do not need to. If sport is a social practice, access to the internal goods of that practice requires an understanding of the set of social meanings that are played out in it but, while these may not be infinitely reinterpretable, they are both highly malleable and remarkably resistant to singular fiat. In other words, no one gets to legislate the meaning of such social practices arbitrarily or in isolation, but neither practice nor meaning is fixed: it is subject to shifts both gradual and rapid, over time and locale. Thus, when a major sportswear company places prominent advertising at an Olympic Games that describes silver medal winners as 'first loser', it creates a dissonance with the silver medallist who considers herself to have *won* second place, but it also contributes to a reinterpretation of the meaning of that achievement as *failure*, a reinterpretation that also depends on other meanings embedded in sport practice. Whether we are persuaded by any given reinterpretation also depends on which meanings in the practice are salient for us, and this may depend on other groups of social meanings, as for example, ones having to do with gender and social roles. But the important point is that we are able, at least in principle, to interpret these meanings both despite and because of our commitments to other meanings. If not, we could not disagree about them except in ignorance. The silver medal winner understands perfectly well what the billboard says about her and her achievement and rejects it as not fitting the meaning that she places upon herself, her performance, and her sport; that is, she is able to translate between meaning-structures and practices, but this does not necessarily require that sport be in some fundamental way supra-social. By analogy, human languages differ considerably, and the meanings of individual words are determined within a language, and yet we are able, with some loss of meaning and gain of insight, to translate reasonably well between languages, and to talk about what is common to language(s). Sport, like language, is not a Platonic form, but there are some things we are able to say about sport, as about language, that are generally true of all or most sports. And that is all we really need.

Most of the authors we have surveyed so far present proposals that incorporate some degree of challenge to traditional gender roles and heteronormative expectations for women; that is, that women either must or inevitably will conform to traditional and quite rigidly dualistic norms of both gender and sexual expression, that women are and must be 'feminine' and men 'masculine' in traditionally and mutually exclusive respects. These challenges have been primarily about what are essentially public social roles: participation in ordinary public sport practices. Further challenges are presented by those exploring the boundaries of what constitutes bodily heteronormativity. The experience of embodiment in sport is an important area in the philosophy of sport, and there have been valuable feminist contributions in this area, most notably Iris Marion Young's landmark essay 'Throwing Like a Girl' (1980), which pulled together sport, feminist theory and Merleau-Ponty, and inspired many further feminist writers, the present author among them. Our concern here, however, is with a notable recent shift in focus away from policy issues and toward an interest in the social significance of the individual body itself as a site for performance, disruption, and regulation, and with the concomitant shift in emphasis from gender to sexuality.

One arena of disruption of heteronormative expectations regarding physical presentation is body modification. In sport, this can be readily seen in body-building. Ken Saltman (1998) describes both male and female bodybuilding as pushing masculinity and femininity, respectively, to their limits and, in the process, both maintaining and undermining gender norms. Bodybuilders engage in a set of practices of bodily care that replicate for men the experience and daily practice of women; even as they realise their corporeal instantiation of masculinity, as they become 'real men', they also become women by making themselves into objects of the male gaze and desire. 'The male bodybuilder's body parodies its own hyperbolic butchness as it transmutes into the feminine' (Saltman 1998: 50). Female bodybuilders, on the other hand, under pressure to distinguish their masculine-because-muscled bodies from those of men, employ exaggerated signifiers of femininity (breast implants and elaborate hair and make-up) to demarcate their difference. Yet these serve only to highlight the artificiality of these signifiers of gender (ibid: 53). Nevertheless, Saltman argues that the transformation of the men into full-body objects of sexual desire and of the women to positions and postures of masculine power and authority is subversive of heteronormative gender. 'Humanisation and objectification both lend themselves as ideological constructs to be utilised to maintain or contest dominance by one group over another. Here I point to the potentially liberatory appropriation of objectification by women' (ibid: 55).[13]

There are flies in this ointment, of course. Melina Constantine Bell (2008) also argues for the emancipatory potential of women's bodybuilding, but finds this limited by the reliance on judging standards that reflect a masculinist aesthetic of female beauty. Insofar as judging standards are based on the competitor's sexual desirability, she explains, that judgement is only to the effect that the competitor's physique is subjectively pleasing to the judge and 'not a claim to the universal validity of the judgement that her physique is *beautiful*' (Bell 2008: 43). The problem here is two-fold: that judges use a different aesthetic standard for men and women in that sexual attractiveness (subjective to the observer) is imported into the aesthetic judging of women as it is not in men, and the inappropriateness of such a measure in any case. Bell's view is that the correct aesthetic attitude is humanistic and gender-neutral: 'the beautiful bodybuilder appears, because she is, strong, physically and emotionally healthy, confident, dignified, proud, sovereign; neither domineering nor subordinated' (ibid. 60).

Rebecca Ann Lock (2010) raises an important element for the critique of heteronormativity in sport, not in respect of bodybuilding as such but in connection with the attitude to female dopers and particularly muscular female athletes. Lock's thesis is that the effect of the ban on doping has not been to stop it but to reinforce the gender order, particularly in respect of aesthetic values that are inherently lesbophobic (ibid: 112–13). Certain female athletes and some female dopers disturb the coherence and stability of the man/woman distinction by virtue of their enhanced muscularity (ibid: 120). What is especially pertinent here is the connection made between increased muscularity and diminished heterosexual attractiveness; what is really offensive about female dopers, it seems, is that they have made themselves ugly to men (ibid: 121). This disturbs heterosexual norms of attractiveness and of behaviour, and of the presumed natural sexual availability of women to men, and it opens the possibility for men of finding sexually attractive a woman who looks more like them than the norm dictates that they should.

This, then, is where the most significant risk lies, as it has throughout our discussion in this chapter. We began with questions about equality of opportunity framed in terms of the separability of sex and gender. In the intervening years, much philosophical discussion has challenged the coherence of these two categories. Thus, we need to question not only whether women ought to be enabled to do things traditionally considered 'masculine' or restricted to men, but whether terms such as 'woman' or 'man' describe anything real.[14] What it means to be a 'woman' or a 'man' in sport is not only about whether or how one plays sports but how sport shapes our conception of what we are as 'masculine', 'feminine', 'man', 'woman'. Consequently, there is a growing body of literature not only on the construction of gender identity through sport but also its role in the configuration or erasure of sexuality as identity. One important and prominent thread in this discussion concerns sex verification and the response to those individuals who do not fit absolutist presumptions of sexual binarism. Another concerns the role that sport plays or is constrained to play in defining sexualities and maintaining sexual identities. A number of authors have argued that sport is instrumental in teaching boys not only how to be 'men' but, specifically, heterosexual men, where this term is understood to include the additional and wholly unnecessary qualifications of heterosexist and (potentially) homopho-bic.[15] For women, sport's role in defining sexuality has been more complex: while at times providing an outlet for outlaw expressions of sexuality,[16] it has also frequently, in response to external and internalised pressures to appear squeaky 'clean', been more intolerant than its surrounding social context toward non-traditional expressions of either sexuality or gender.[17] Fear of being or merely seeming other than conventionally heterosexual continues to exert a distorting force on participants in both men's and women's sport; in women's sport, this not infrequently manifests as a hypersexualisation of women's presentation that severely under-mines the recognition of their achievements relative to those of their male counterparts.

Nevertheless, it could be argued that sport is, as Edwards and Jones (2007) suggest, not a practice that should be identified with such distortions of its inherent potential. Thus, I have argued[18] that sport's promise for the development of identity, including identities relating to gender and sexuality, is in its exploration of self through play. Sport need not impose rigid preconceptions of human possibility but can also open up previously unexplored horizons of self, identity and expression. This, in turn, suggests the potential for sport to provide an oppor-tunity for subversive play, play that rewrites the player and the observer. This is the sort of change that is provoked by the practices described by Saltman (1998), Lock (2010) and Bell (2008), and by those sportspersons who, instead of waiting for mainstream sport to catch up, have opted to devise their own means to play in the ways they need to, as in the case of gay and lesbian sports movements. In doing so, all these players demonstrate not only the perme-ability of gender norms, but of sport practices. Sport is not fixed; its norms are fluid – as are the identities of the humans who realise them.

There is a sense in which all of the problems before us in this essay have been about iden-tity. Many of the issues raised in these pages could be interpreted in terms of what *sport* is, but an even deeper level of questioning is at stake in the challenge to make sport inclusive of women and of all those who do not fit into the distorting frame of traditional sex and gender binarisms. The viciousness of some responses to women's participation certainly suggests that more is at stake than participation in the activity alone.[19] The presence of women in sport, fully equal and self-determining, is not simply or even primarily a threat to male power as such, although it has this consequence. Nor is it simply a matter of those with privilege being unwill-ing to redistribute scarce resources or benefits more fairly. It is about who we are and who we think we are, who we are willing to contemplate and to risk being. Women in sport challenge identities that depend on men's *exclusive* access to sport and to the valorisation that attends it. In doing so, they reconfigure not only women's possibilities for identity but men's as well. That is the promise and the risk.[20]

Notes

1 See, for example, Joy De Sensi (1992) and Edwards and Jones (2007: 351–6).
2 See Simon (1993–94) and the commentaries of Boxill (1993–94) and Francis (1993–94) in the same volume, for a detailed analysis of these permutations of institutional interpretations of equality.
3 See Trebilcot in Vetterling-Braggin (1982); also Postow (1980) and Grim (1981).
4 See Howe (2003, 2008).
5 See, for example, Howe 'Being and Playing' (2007).
6 Following Locke, *Second Treatise on Civil Government* (1988: 3). Of course, utilitarians such as Mill follow a different, if parallel, line.
7 Tännsjö may be right about this aspect of the *morality* of the situation but the reality of it, speaking as well as one who has experienced these reactions both verbally and physically, is that there are some battles that one sometimes prefers not to have as the price of *play*.
8 English is characterised by Tännsjö and Tamburrini (2005: 183–4) as a 'gender essentialist feminist',

which would ordinarily indicate a view that there are essentially masculine and essentially feminine characteristics; this would be difficult to square with the claim that the differences between men and women are statistical. In addition, at least some of the proponents of separate sport are also proponents of androgyny, which is also a development of the same general tradition. Tännsjö, in any case, regards the statistical difference as irrelevant. See Sailors (2014) for a recent analysis of English's article that deals more exactly with her arguments concerning segregation.

9 Trebilcot (1975). This essay is reprinted in Vetterling-Braggin (1982), together with a number of essays by additional authors who also take up this point.

10 Sport may be better characterised as about the pursuit of excellence; this does not always entail winners in every competition. Sport, in this author's view, has to do with the activity that may *also* allow one to determine who is best, perhaps only on that day, in that place, and so on, but the activity is what makes this possible and meaningful. Tamburrini and Tännsjö's view of sport is instrumentalist and would downgrade participation and subjective experience as, at best, secondary.

11 For a nuanced analysis of such a project, see Paul Davis' 'The Ladies of Besiktas' (2012).

12 See, as antidote to this view, Mary Vetterling-Braggin's report that many women actually find totally cooperative sport frustrating and unappealing (1983: 128–9).

13 With respect to sexualisation, see Paul Davis (2010), for a strongly developed perspective.

14 The literature on this subject is fairly vast but Judith Butler is a possible starting point. See *Gender Trouble* (1990), *Bodies That Matter* (1993), 'Imitation and Gender Insubordination', (1996), *Undoing Gender* (2004).

15 For example, Messner and Sabo (1990), McKay, Messner and Sabo (2000), Brian Pronger (1990, 1999).

16 See, for example, Griffin (1998) and Lenskyj (2003); see also Howe (2007).

17 See, for example, Rogers (1994).

18 Howe (2003, 2008, 2011).

19 A good example of this is detailed in Jones and Edwards (2013); see also Howe (2007).

20 One could develop a Sartrean-de Beauvoirean argument here to the effect that resistance to the possibility inherent in this situation, in favour of clinging to the solidity of being promised by traditional 'masculine' and 'feminine' categories, is a form of bad faith – but that is for another occasion.

References

Bell, Melina Constantine. 2008. 'Strength in Muscle and Beauty in Integrity: Building a body for her'. *Journal of the Philosophy of Sport* 35(1): 43–62.

Boxill, J. M. 1993–94. 'Title IX and Gender Equity'. *Journal of the Philosophy of Sport* 20–21: 23–31.

Burke, Michael. 2010a. 'Could a 'Woman' Win a Gold Medal in the 'Men's' One Hundred Metres? Female sport, drugs, and the transgressive cyborg body.' In Paul Davis and Charlene Weaving (eds), *Philosophical Perspectives on Gender in Sport and Physical Activity*. London: Routledge, 129–40.

—— 2010b. 'A Feminist Reconstruction of Liberal Rights and Sport'. *Journal of the Philosophy of Sport* 37(1): 11–28.

Butler, Judith. 1990. *Gender Trouble: Feminism and the subversion of identity*. New York: Routledge.

—— 1993. *Bodies That Matter: On the discursive limits of sex*. New York: Routledge.

—— 1996. 'Imitation and Gender Insubordination', in *Women, Knowledge, and Reality*, Ann Garry and Marilyn Pearsall (eds). New York: Routledge, 371–87.

—— 2004. *Undoing Gender*. New York: Routledge.

Davis, Paul. 2010. 'Sexualisation and Sexuality in Sport'. In Paul Davis and Charlene Weaving (eds), *Philosophical Perspectives on Gender in Sport and Physical Activity*. London: Routledge, 40–54.

—— 2012. 'The Ladies of Besiktas: An example of moral and ideological ambiguity?' *Sport, Ethics, and Philosophy* 6(1): 4–15.

De Sensi, Joy T. 1992. 'Feminism in the Wake of Philosophy'. *Journal of the Philosophy of Sport* 19: 79–93.

Edwards, Lisa and Carwyn Jones. 2007. 'A Soft Gynocentric Critique of the Practice of Modern Sport'. *Sport, Ethics, and Philosophy* 1(3): 346–66.

English, Jane. 1978. 'Sex Equality in Sports'. *Philosophy and Public Affairs* 7(3): 269–77.

Francis, Leslie P. 1993–94. 'Title IX: Equality for Women's Sports?' *Journal of the Philosophy of Sport* 20–21: 32–47.

Giordano, Simona, and John Harris. 2005. 'What is Gender Equality in Sports'. In *Genetic Technology and Sport: Ethical questions*. Claudio Tamburrini and Torbjörn Tännsjö (eds). London: Routledge, 209–17.

Griffin, Pat. 1998. *Strong Women, Deep Closets: Lesbians and homophobia in sport*. Champaign, IL: Human Kinetics.

Grim, Patrick. 1981. 'Sports and Two Androgynisms.' *Journal of the Philosophy of Sport* 8: 64–8.

Howe, Leslie A. 2003. 'Athletics, Embodiment and the Appropriation of the Self'. *Journal of Speculative Philosophy* 17(2): 92–107.

—— 2007. 'Being and Playing: Sport and the Valorisation of Gender'. In *Ethics in Sport* (2nd ed.), William J. Morgan (ed.). Champaign, IL: Human Kinetics, 331–45.

—— 2008. 'Self and Pretence: Playing with Identity'. *Journal of Social Philosophy* 39(4): 564–82.

—— 2011. 'Convention, Audience, and Narrative: Which play is the thing?' *Journal of the Philosophy of Sport* 38(2): 135–48.

Jones, Carwyn and Lisa Louise Edwards. 2013. 'The Woman in Black: Exposing sexist beliefs about female officials in elite men's football.' *Sport, Ethics, and Philosophy* 7(2). 202–16.

Lenskyj, Helen Jefferson. 2003. *Out on the Field: Gender, sport, and sexualities*. Toronto: Women's Press.

Lock, Rebecca Ann. 2010. 'The Doping Ban: Compulsory heterosexuality and lesbophobia'. In Paul Davis and Charlene Weaving (eds), *Philosophical Perspectives on Gender in Sport and Physical Activity*. London: Routledge, 112–28.

Locke, John. 1988. *Two Treatises of Government*. Peter Laslett (ed.). Cambridge: Cambridge University Press.

McKay, Jim, Michael A. Messner and Don Sabo (eds) 2000. *Masculinities, Gender Relations, and Sport*. Thousand Oaks, CA: Sage.

Messner, Michael A. and Don Sabo (eds) 1990. *Sport, Men, and the Gender Order: Critical Feminist Perspectives*. Champaign, IL: Human Kinetics.

Mill, John Stuart. 1970. *The Subjection of Women*. Cambridge: Cambridge University Press.

Postow, B. C. 1980. 'Women and Masculine Sports.' *Journal of the Philosophy of Sport* 7: 51–8.

—— 1981. 'Masculine Sports Revisited'. *Journal of the Philosophy of Sport* 8: 60–3.

Pronger, Brian. 1990. *The Arena of Masculinity: Sports, Homosexuality, and the Meaning of Sex*. New York: St. Martin's.

—— 1999. 'Fear and Trembling: Homophobia in Men's Sport.' In Philip White and Kevin Young (eds) *Sport and Gender in Canada*. Oxford: Oxford University Press, 182–96.

Rogers, Susan Fox. 1990. *Sportsdykes: Stories from on and off the field*. New York: St. Martin's.

Sailors, Pam R. 2013. 'Gender Roles Roll'. *Sport, Ethics, and Philosophy* 7(2): 245–58.

—— 2014. 'Mixed Competition and Mixed Messages'. *Journal of the Philosophy of Sport*. 41(1): 65–77.

Saltman, Ken. 1998. 'Men with Breasts'. *Journal of the Philosophy of Sport* 25: 48–60.

Schneider, Angela J. 2010. 'On the Definition of 'Woman' in the Sport Context'. In Paul Davis and Charlene Weaving (eds), *Philosophical Perspectives on Gender in Sport and Physical Activity*. London: Routledge, 40–54.

Sherwin, Susan and Meredith Schwartz. 2005. 'Resisting the Emergence of Bio-Amazons'. In *Genetic Technology and Sport: Ethical questions*. Claudio Tamburrini and Torbjörn Tännsjö (eds). London: Routledge, 199–204.

Simon, Robert L. 1993–94. 'Gender Equity and Inequity in Athletics'. *Journal of the Philosophy of Sport* 20–21: 6–22.

Tamburrini, Claudio and Torbjörn Tännsjö. 2005. 'The Genetic Design of a New Amazon'. In *Genetic Technology and Sport: Ethical questions*. Claudio Tamburrini and Torbjörn Tännsjö (eds). London: Routledge, 181–98.

Tännsjö, Torbjörn. 2007. 'Against Sexual Discrimination in Sports'. In *'Ethics in Sport'* (2nd ed.). William J. Morgan (ed.). Champaign, IL: Human Kinetics, 347–58.

Trebilcot, Joyce. 1975. 'Sex Roles: The Argument from Nature'. *Ethics* 85: 249–55.

Vetterling-Braggin, Mary (ed.). 1982. *'Femininity', 'Masculinity', and 'Androgyny': A modern philosophical discussion*. Totowa, NJ: Rowman and Allenheld.

Vetterling-Braggin, Mary. 1983. 'Cooperative Competition in Sport'. In *Women, Philosophy, and Sport: A collection of new essays*. Betsy C. Postow (ed.). Metuchen, NJ: Scarecrow, 123–31.

Vetterling-Braggin Ramsey, Mary. 1981. 'One Form of Anti-Androgynism'. *Journal of the Philosophy of Sport* 8: 55–9.

Wollstonecraft, Mary. 1995. *'A Vindication of the Rights of Man' and 'A Vindication of the Rights of Woman'*. Sylvana Tomaselli (ed.) Cambridge: Cambridge University Press.

Young, I. M. 1980. 'Throwing Like a Girl: A phenomenology of feminine body comportment motility and spatiality'. *Human Studies* 3: 137–56.

12

PHENOMENOLOGY AND SPORT

Irena Martínková

Introduction

Phenomenology arose as a critique of an 'objective' approach to the world. The founder of phenomenology, Edmund Husserl, tried to deal with both everyday and scientific assumptions about the world that have been taken for granted. He aimed at first-hand examination and accurate description of lived experience – of structures of consciousness with their correlated phenomena. Since sciences explain the world in an objectivist way, phenomenology can help us to see the world from a different point of view.

Recently, the phenomenological way of thinking has made its way into the philosophy of sport and is becoming increasingly used. While analytical philosophers of sport usually cover topics that concern the concept of sport and its various aspects, phenomenologists draw attention to the athletes and to a wider scope of examining their participation in sport. Phenomenology also brings new concepts, such as, for example, intentionality, consciousness, perception, time, space, authenticity, movement, skilful coping and the body, that have been neglected or underestimated in the analytical tradition.

What is phenomenology?

Phenomenology is a philosophical movement founded by the German philosopher Edmund Husserl at the beginning of twentieth century, which describes phenomena and their appearing to a subject. It is important to emphasise that phenomenology is not one theory, however, but a group of theories that arose partly through reflection on and improvement of the ideas of its predecessors, and the development of their theories so as to change not only the theories but also the phenomenological method itself.

Thus, the 'phenomenological method' differs with respect to the great authors of phenomenology, such 'continental' philosophers as Edmund Husserl, Martin Heidegger, Maurice Merleau-Ponty, Jean-Paul Sartre, Jan Patočka and others. However, the unifying idea as suggested by Husserl – 'Back to the things themselves!' (Husserl 2001: 168) – can speak for all of them, despite its being often misunderstood. For the father of phenomenology, Husserl, 'things' means 'things as experienced' – that is, they are appearances (to a subject), such that there is no 'thing-in-itself' behind these appearances.

The word 'phenomenon' demands some explanation, since it sometimes causes misunderstanding. The word itself comes from the Ancient Greek word *phainomenon*, which translates as 'appearance'. Sometimes scholars in the social sciences have understood phenomenology to mean the scholarly description of concrete appearances. Yet phenomenology is interested in phenomena (appearances) as empirical phenomena only to the extent that they are correlations of the structures of our experience. This approach stems from the idea that an appearance always appears to some subject. What phenomenology is especially interested in are 'deep phenomena' (Patočka 1996: 46) or the 'phenomenological conception of phenomenon' (Heidegger 2001: 31), which are not self-evident appearances but, at first, rather concealed modes of being that shape our existence and that need to be brought to light.

The main contribution of phenomenology, therefore, lies in an examination and description of the structures of human experiencing, together with the things experienced that are their correlates. In other words, in phenomenology, we look *at* (and describe) what we normally look *through*. Instead of looking through our humanness at the world, we look at our humanness, to try to give an account of what we are, how we experience and the nature of this experiencing. Thus:

> When we do phenomenology, we are not simply participating in the world, dealing with things in our normal everyday way – rather we are taking a step back in order to contemplate what it is to be a participant in the world, and how things present themselves to us.
>
> *(Sokolowski 2000: 48)*

The claim is that understanding the way that we experience is what gives us the basic ground for all of our knowledge.

Phenomenological research proceeds primarily by an examination of one's own being; that is, the being of the phenomenologist. The aim of the phenomenologist's examination of his own being is not to describe the uniqueness of himself as a particular human being but, rather, to arrive at a description of a universal human mode of being (existence), from which stems the connection of phenomenology to the philosophy of existence and existentialism, which serves as a gateway to describing the modes of appearing of things. This 'subjective' approach is inevitable, since it is my own experiencing with which I am most familiar, which makes it a primary resource for phenomenological investigations.

Thus, with respect to the description of the human being, phenomenology does not offer a description of a person's unique traits. It is not a particular 'me' that is examined but, rather, the aim is to attempt a universal first-person account of being human. Phenomenology investigates subjectivity but it is not a form of solipsism or subjectivism. It investigates the first-person perspective but its results are not particular-personal but universal-personal. So, even though phenomenology emphasises *subjective* experience, it is not concerned with *personal* experience as such – it looks for what is true of every human being's experience. It tries to make general statements, not individual or particular observations, nor collections of or 'syntheses' of individual subjective reports.

Consider, for example, one of the Heideggerian characteristics of human existence or 'existentiale'– 'understanding' (Heidegger 2001). We humans are always in some situation and always have some understanding of it, whatever it may be, no matter whether we are a European man or an American Indian woman. Whatever our differences as empirical human beings, all of us share this essential feature of human beings: that we humans *understand*. This does not have to be any particular or deep kind of understanding but just an everyday kind of understanding (that we all have) that I more or less know who I am and what to do in my everyday existence (practical understanding). It is not possible to imagine a human being who is without some kind of understanding. If I do not understand some particular thing, this is possible only within an already existing more-or-less deep understanding. 'Understanding' is part of what makes us human. And this is a feature that distinguishes human beings from other entities, such as instruments, objects, or animals. Phenomenology is interested in such modes and structures of the being of entities, and not in the particular qualities of the particular entities themselves, nor in the unique way in which I understand a specific thing.[1]

The kind of truth that comes out of phenomenological analysis is *apodictic*; that is, necessary truth, truth that could not be otherwise. The truths that phenomenology arrives at may look trivial and basic – and maybe they are. But this does not mean that they are useless and do not require articulation. On the contrary, we often lack an understanding of these basic truths or do not take these basic insights seriously enough, which may compromise our understanding of ourselves and other things. This is why phenomenology is so important. Nevertheless, anyone's conclusions are open to criticism and, like anyone else, Husserl or Heidegger or Merleau-Ponty could be wrong in some or all of their views – indeed, they criticize each other. However, if and where they may be wrong, this must be demonstrated with respect to our experiencing. Since such accounts are presented as universal, this ensures that they are testable against each individual's personal experience. That is to say, when presented with some account of how a thing is presented to us in experience, we can each of us ask ourselves: 'Does this insight resonate with my experience?' In this way, such accounts are meant to refer to the experience of each and all of us as humans. If the given account by a particular philosopher does not resonate with our experience, it is open to us to reject it, and up to us to provide a better account, which itself will be testable against the experience of all of us as human beings.

Although phenomenology concentrates on human experience, it is obviously not possible to neglect phenomena that appear to the subject. Consequently, the correlation between the experiencing subject and the phenomenon is of special importance. A phenomenological phenomenon is 'the experiencing together with the experienced'. Thus phenomenology discusses the disclosure of things in the world and describes how the experiencing subject perceives things, how identities are constituted, how we humans are in the world and how we understand the world.

Some phenomenologists, especially those in the Husserlian tradition, also focus on the essences (essential structures) of various phenomena. Phenomenology does not explore these in an empirical way (that is, reaching a universal through what we have already experienced as such and which has not been falsified so far) but in an eidetic way. This means that, while phenomenology never abandons appearances on the empirical level, it does not rely solely on them. Rather, it aims to uncover their *eidos* (a form, a structure, that is necessary to them) by creative imaginative variation (by 'eidetic' variation) – and thus its results are 'eidetic universals' (Sokolowski 2000: 179).

> We try to move beyond empirical to eidetic universals, to necessities and not just regularities. In order to do so, we move from perception into the realm of imagination … We try to push the boundaries, to expand the envelope of the thing in question … However, if we run into features that we cannot remove without destroying the thing, we realize that these features are eidetically necessary to it.
>
> *(Sokolowski 2000: 178–9)*

What we discover in this way is not a figment of our imagination but a necessary feature that can be found in the empirical world and confirmed by common sense. However, this is not an approach unique to phenomenology but, rather, is an approach used generally in philosophy for exploring and clarifying concepts – a kind of a conceptual analysis (Zahavi 2003: 38ff.). While this investigation of phenomena does not exhaust phenomenology, it is important to mention it here, since it is the source from which empirical research that calls itself 'phenomenological' often stems (for example, empirical phenomenology, or interpretative phenomenological analysis, which collect such empirical data and that are sometimes mixed with phenomenology – see later section 'Phenomenology and sport sciences'). This enterprise goes back to Husserl and his eidetic analyses, rather than to the later phenomenologists, who did not examine phenomena correlative to human experiencing in such detail as did Husserl.

Recently, phenomenology has also been taken up by some analytical philosophers, who have used some of its ideas to bring new light into discussions within the analytical tradition. Phenomenology has proven useful, for example, in the philosophy of cognitive science (see Dreyfus and Hall 1982). Similarly, Shaun Gallagher (2005) has used ideas from phenomenology for his theory of embodied cognition, describing body awareness, self-consciousness, perception and social cognition. Further, with respect to social cognition, he has developed themes such as direct perception within an intersubjective context (Gallagher 2008), empathy (Gallagher 2012) and many others. While drawing mainly on Husserl and Merleau-Ponty, he also interprets and reinterprets their ideas through his own approach, while also developing further their distinctions, such as Merleau-Ponty's notions of body image and body schema (Gallagher 2005).

Some phenomenological concepts of major importance for sport

The first phenomenologically oriented essays in philosophy of sport can be traced back to the early days of philosophy of sport, to the early 1970s, but the phenomenological perspective has only begun to make a deeper impact on the philosophy of sport from the beginning of the twenty-first century. In this section, I introduce some of the most important phenomenological themes and works within philosophy of sport – and I restrict myself to examples of literature that are to be found on the international scene; that is, to books and articles in major journals of philosophy of sport in the English language.

The book often taken as the first work related to sport that was written within the field of phenomenology and the philosophy of existence, is *Man, Sport and Existence* by Howard Slusher (1967). Even though using some ideas from the philosophy of existence, this book does not fully engage with the phenomenological tradition and nowhere sets out or discusses the central concepts of the central phenomenologists, despite infrequent and cursory references to philosophers such as Husserl, Heidegger, Sartre, Jaspers, and so on. Slusher himself refuses the title of 'existentialist' for his work. He says in his preface that the book is 'one man's interpretation of sport' (Slusher 1967: xvi) and the index does not even include the word 'phenomenology'. In any case, this book might be understood as a forerunner of phenomenological thinking within the philosophy of sport, introducing some important ideas with respect to sport, such as the body, death, anxiety.

The first book within English-language philosophy of sport devoted purely to the introduction of the phenomenological method, *Phenomenological Approaches to Sport*, was published in 2012, based on a special issue of the journal *Sport, Ethics and Philosophy*, edited by Martínková and Parry (2011b). The book presents various examples of phenomenology with respect to sport, revealing its nature and meanings in ways that have not been developed in the analytical philosophy (of sport) and that go beyond the reach of sciences. The book includes papers that present and discuss ideas of the most important phenomenologists, examines some of their central concepts and applies them to particular issues in sport. Some of the papers from this issue are discussed in the following section, in which I present some phenomenological themes that are especially appropriate to the philosophy of sport.

Skilful coping

The theme most relevant to the concerns of the phenomenology to sport is skilful coping, which is closely linked to the theme of habit. Analyses of habit are already described by Husserl but they have not been acknowledged much so far, since they are mostly discussed in his posthumously published texts (see Moran 2011). Presently, the discussions of skilful coping most often come from Heidegger's *Sein und Zeit* (2001: section 14ff.) within the analyses of our common everyday practical understanding (readiness-at-hand, *Zuhandenheit*) and being of things that are understood in this way – as an instrument (*das Zeug*), demonstrated with the famous example of hammering. Later, it is discussed by Merleau-Ponty (1945) within his analyses of motility and motor intentionality. Heidegger's analyses are further developed especially by Dreyfus (2004), who explains how skilful coping develops from the novice to a virtuoso, but also discusses this theme within the context of more complex analyses of the human being. Skilful coping can be described as fluent and proficient dealing with various everyday tasks, without focusing on the process but just relying on the body and instruments. On the contrary, learning or re-learning a skill usually demands a focus.

Since skilful coping is such an important topic in the philosophy of sport, it has been discussed in several articles. Skilful coping, exemplified with Brazilian Jiu-Jitsu, soccer and baseball, has been analysed by Hogeveen (2011), who differentiates between Husserl's descriptions of how things appear to consciousness and Heidegger's highlighting of the primary understanding that arises within our common absorbed dealing and coping with things – which is of practical concern, without reflection upon things and without much self-awareness. However, Heidegger only presupposed the role of the body in this regard – and this is what Merleau-Ponty focused on. The body understands what is to be achieved and can do so through habits. In Merleau-Ponty's (2004: 169) words: 'We say that the body has understood and habit has been cultivated when it has absorbed a new meaning, and assimilated a fresh core of significance'.

Skill acquisition is also explained by Standahl and Moe (2011), who describe the Merleau-Pontian distinction between background capacities and foreground attention and who differentiate between *everyday coping* skills, when movements are performed at the margins of awareness, being a background for other activities and *skills of athletes*, where the focus on movements is at the centre of awareness. Aggerholm, Jespersen and Ronglan (2011) put skilful movement into a wider perspective, highlighting its context as an intersubjective encounter (in a game of football), with the complex example of the feint and discussing deception and creativity within it.

Some authors in philosophy of sport use both analytical and phenomenological perspectives. For example, Moe (2005) uses the philosophy of Searle and Dreyfus to show the limits of classical cognitivism (the information-processing approach) in explaining intentional movements in sport, and suggests an approach through understanding embodiment and its background knowledge.

Embodiment

Phenomenology, with its critique of the 'objective' scientific approach and its questioning of the nature of first-person human experience, opened a new way of examining human embodiment. To illustrate this new approach, two German words are sometimes used: *Körper* and *Leib* (Husserl 1952). The word *Körper* depicts the body as an object. The word *Leib*, often translated as 'the lived body', stands for embodiment as experienced from within human existence. However, *Körper* and *Leib* are not contradictory concepts. Rather, *Körper* is correlative to *Leib* as the perceivable body; that is, the body conceived in terms of how we perceive it.

The lived body is a complex and fleeting phenomenon, enabling many different conceptions, such as those described by Maurice Merleau-Ponty (1945, 1964), Jean-Paul Sartre (1943), Michel Henry (2000) and others. In short, the lived body can be described as 'my' own body (the inverted commas around the word 'my' mean that my body is not always in my 'hands', because I am also partly in the 'hands' of the body). The lived body is at the centre of human existence, for it is only through the body that human existence is situated and open to the world. According to Merleau-Ponty, our existence happens between 'a double horizon' (background) of the body and the world (Merleau-Ponty 1945: 117) as well as 'a double horizon' of the past and the future (ibid: 277). These double horizons of body and world, past and future, enable a specifically human space and time, which, however, is not empty, but inhabited and filled with personal projects. The body enables an individual perspective of the world, an orientation within it, a perception of things in it, movement within it, and action within it – doing things, accomplishing various tasks and dealing with other people.

In his later work, Merleau-Ponty introduces the notion of 'the Flesh' (*la chair*), that expresses the complex intertwining of the experiencing body and things in the world (the sensate and the sensible), which are not to be thought of as separate (Merleau-Ponty 1964).

A phenomenological understanding of the body is finding its way to various disciplines – it has made an important contribution to the philosophy of health, enriching the medical paradigm with new insights (for example, Toombs 2001), as well to education (for example, Kelan 2009), and it also has potential for the philosophy of sport. Within philosophy of sport, the body has not as yet become a key theme, as it has in phenomenology itself (Merleau-Ponty 1945). Most work has been devoted to trying to grasp what has been written in phenomenological philosophy, especially by Merleau-Ponty, and applying it to sport, rather than trying to develop existing theories further.

Embodiment is discussed by Meier (1975, 1988). Both of these papers differentiate between the Cartesian dualism of the body and mind and the concept of the body as developed by Merleau-Ponty. While accusing contemporary philosophy of sport of being replete with restatements of Cartesian dualism, he acknowledges the potential of a phenomenological approach to the body as a fruitful direction for the philosophy of sport. Meier's 1988 paper is included in the collection *Philosophic Inquiry in Sport* (1988), edited by Morgan and Meier, which includes a section on 'sport and embodiment', including several papers based in phenomenology. Apart from Meier's paper, there are original papers by Sartre (1988) and Marcel (1988) and a paper by Schrag (1988), who describes the lived body on the basis of Sartre, Marcel and Merleau-Ponty, differentiating it from a scientific understanding of the body as an object. Later, Breivik (2008) investigates our bodily existence in general and relates it to sport (especially football), through selected phenomenological concepts of Heidegger (the importance of practical understanding), Merleau-Ponty (bodily intentionality), Todes (the human intentional body in the spatiotemporal field) and O'Shaughnessy (proprioception), and discusses their contribution to embodiment.

Authenticity

Authenticity is a term most often associated with the philosophy of Martin Heidegger and his classic work *Sein und Zeit* [*Being and Time*] (2001). This term characterizes the overall mode of our understanding, which conditions the way we live our lives. According to Heidegger (2001: 146), we can understand our own existence as well as things in the world in either an authentic or an inauthentic mode.

Inauthentic understanding means following the dominant norms of a social group, often without much thought. Heidegger (2001: section 38) calls this 'falling' – being attracted towards things and tasks in the world, while being unaware of our 'selves' – of who we are. This is an understanding into which one is socialised through living in a society, which one accepts. Heidegger (2001: section 25ff.) calls this mode of understanding '*das Man*' (translated as 'the they' in English) – and it means understanding and living as 'they' usually understand and live.

On the other hand, authentic understanding, according to Heidegger (2001: 129) means understanding the self on the basis of who I am as a human being. This should not be confused with 'my own unique perspective' but, rather, it describes a genuine self-understanding, based on an understanding of what a human being is. Only a considered understanding of my 'existence' will enable an explicit understanding of human being, that will in turn enable a conception of *who I originally² am as a human being*. This, in turn, enables an adequate understanding of things and beings in the world. Understanding authentically means not being fooled by various human interpretations (including one's own 'socialised' interpretations of oneself). This is especially important with respect to one's finitude, understanding of which is crucial for our understanding of our own being (Heidegger 2007: 162).

Authentic understanding leads to a more 'human' existence, since it arises from the very human source of my own being – it helps one to focus on what is meaningful in his or her life. This is important for all spheres of one's life, including sport. With a more adequate understanding of the self comes more adequate sport practice. An understanding of the human being can also help us to design individual sports in a better way – so that sports are designed so as to support our humanness, rather than being designed to feed our curiosity (to see new records, etc.), to seek worldly ends, etc. (Martínková 2013). This resonates with idea of Olympism and de Coubertin's (2000: 163) conviction that self-knowledge is the 'be-all and end-all of physical culture'. Phenomenology can help a great deal in this respect.

Within philosophy of sport, authenticity is addressed by Standish (1998), within the context of skilful coping and the tendency of sport to 'a particular kind of everydayness' (ibid: 268). There is, however, a chance to find 'the palest shadow of the ultimate finality' (ibid. 268) through sport failures or in dangerous sports. Authenticity is also presented by Jirásek (2007), who, within a wider take on Husserl's and Heidegger's phenomenology, focuses especially on an authentic experience and its manifestation in various kinds of movement activities. Breivik (2010) discusses Heideggerian concepts of authenticity and inauthenticity with respect to skydiving. He describes the disruption of the everyday world that happens during one's first jump, leading to anxiety and awareness of death and to a glimpse of authenticity and then he describes how, on becoming proficient, the skydiver gradually inhabits the world of skydiving. This is a neat description of our tendency to be 'falling' into the world – following skydivers' aims, dealing with the usual equipment and fulfilling routine tasks, and forgetting about our own self. This nicely describes the tendency to be inauthentic, even in a context such as skydiving, in which most participants probably believe that their skydiving is the most authentic part of their existence.

Time

From its beginnings, time has been one of the key themes in phenomenology and it has contributed significantly to our understanding of the concept of time. Time is usually conceived as linear, objective, homogeneous and measurable, characterized by an axis divided into past, present and future – the present is seen as a point between the past and the future. And so time is characterized as an axis that can be divided into a myriad of moments or units of the same duration, each following successively. Time conceived as such refers back to Aristotle and was further developed with the rise of science.

However, the phenomenological conception of time is rooted in human experiencing (that is, our consciousness of time) and objective time is explained as derived from this 'experienced' time (for example, Heidegger 2001: section 78ff.).

For Husserl (1973: section 31) each new 'now' is a result of an original, primal impression, while from moment to moment its content, unchanged, slides into the past and is retained. However, what changes is its 'mode of givenness', since each new now succeeds it and pushes it away. The now is thus experienced as not being isolated from the past and the future. Each now slips into the past, being retained, and this is how we are conscious of the past, while each now is also open to what is coming, and this is how we are conscious of the future. For example, while writing this text, I experience it in the modes of the now (what I am writing right now), which is slipping into the past (retention), and which is directed to the future (protention). After having finished the whole paper, all of this is retained and if I want I can recall (re-present) the text in my actual now (the present). Without retention I could not remember anything. Husserl's analysis of time deeply influenced Heidegger (whose salient title is *Being and Time*), Sartre and Merleau-Ponty, among others.

While objective time constitutes and regulates the practice of most existing sports, the contribution of phenomenology lies in showing how time is experienced by athletes, which can help us to understand the practice of athletes in a more adequate way. This theme has been developed by Morgan (1976a), who discusses the futural modality of *training* and *sport*, following on Heidegger's highlighting of analysis of time, especially as it explains the future, since our understanding of our 'being-towards-death' and therefore of our present mortality are important for authentic existence. He distinguishes the inauthentic, instrumental, open-ended, futural orientation of training, in which an athlete forgets about himself, with sport that manifests a distinctive (non-everyday) projection of the future – which is closed rather than opened. Morgan refers to 'an opening of possibilities and a staking of the limits in which and by which these possibilities are to be realized' (ibid: 423) and which 'offers no guarantee of a future reckoning or rectification' (ibid: 425). This manifests the athlete's future as finite, and that determines how the athlete grasps his/her possibilities. In his later paper, Morgan (1978) explores more deeply the concept of lived time within training, emphasizing training as planned activity, characterized by its linear direction towards a determined end. Martínková and Parry (2011c) contrast two conceptions of time within sport – time as linear and as experienced – and discuss the problems that athletes experience through constraints arising from the various ways of employment of linear time in sport (linear time having various functions in constitutive and regulative rules).

Movement

Movement is an important theme in the philosophy of Jan Patočka. According to Patočka, our 'original'[3] understanding arises from the experience of the self as a primordial dynamism – a dynamism thrusting itself into the world. I 'originally' understand myself as an experiencing being – as living my own life, giving meaning to entities and dealing with them. Patočka conceives the human being as this movement, which can be seen as a novel expression of Heidegger's account of temporality (Patočka 1998: 132, 155). When Patočka says that the human being is movement, he is making an ontological point. This characteristic of the human being demands the usage of a dynamic terminology, such as life, existence, performance, energy, flowing stream and current, rather than a static one, such as substance, object, and so on.

Within this dynamism, Patočka (1992: 231ff.) distinguishes 'overall human movement' and 'partial and individual movements'. The overall life movement gives meaning and direction to every partial movement that the human being makes. Importantly, movement is visible only in relation to something static. According to Patočka, this 'something static' is not some immobile basis of the human being (such as Aristotelian substance) but, rather, something that the human being 'refers' to – a referent. 'Referent' means the horizon for all the partial movements of the human being; it is that to which movement relates and which itself is immobile (Patočka 1998: 149). Thus, though the human being *is* movement (a *kin-anthropos*, see Martínková 2011), not everything moves. In his work, Patočka shows three different referents with respect to the essential possibilities of human existence that can be realized. On the basis of these referents, he distinguishes three movements of human existence – the movement of acceptance, the movement of defence and the movement of truth (Patočka 1992, 1996). 'The movement of acceptance' is the foundational layer – the movement of growing into the world. This movement gradually changes into 'the movement of defence', which characterizes the area of everydayness, in which the human being is dispersed in his/her individual projects that sustain his/her existence. Finally, 'the movement of truth', means the transcendence of everydayness to a more authentic existence. These three movements differ from each other in terms of their overall meaning for the human being. Each of them then grounds all partial (concrete) movements of the human being (Patočka 1992, 231ff.).

While the ontological concept of movement may seem distant and too wide for the philosophy of sport, it is very important, since it puts the human being in the full perspective of his whole life. Then, if we wish to understand an individual movement (single act) of a specific human being, or the meaning of one's participation in sport in a more adequate (holistic) way, it helps us to interpret it with respect to this overall movement of human existence – because a single movement or set of movements is always only a part of a wider whole, and separating them from this wider whole brings on some kind of reduction.

Within philosophy of sport, this understanding is developed in the paper 'Anthropos as Kinanthropos' (Martínková 2011), which discusses both Heidegger's and Patočka's concepts of movement and derives conclusions for a non-reductive understanding of athletes' movement in sport. Patočka's understanding of movement is also applied to Olympism by Martínková (2012), describing two possible directions for human development through sport, labelled by Coubertin's metaphors: fair and temple.

Ethics

Phenomenology is primarily ontology and as such it is a description of the basic structures of experiencing of the human being. However, phenomenology can offer ideas for sport ethics too. There is the potential for ethics in Heidegger's notion of authenticity. Authentic understanding means an adequate understanding of ourselves, and as such it is a basis for becoming responsible for one's own life as well as for a more adequate understanding of others. This is important for athletes' participation in sport itself, as well as for thinking about the logical structure of sports and the possibilities for its change towards a more humane and ethical sport. Further, ethics is explicitly discussed in Sartre – especially in his concept of the human being, which binds together freedom and responsibility (Sartre 1996).

Sartre's ethics is discussed by Morgan (1976b), who argued that Sartre's claim that the ego arises only through reflection (existence precedes essence) has important implications for morality, namely, that moral values are rooted in our essential free nature. But since we necessarily live with others, we also need to recognize the freedom of others. Applied to sport, rules both constitute and regulate the activity – but truly to do so, they need to be freely accepted by the athlete. Without this understanding, sports rules tend to be understood as objective laws, which bring about conduct that is not based on free will, which further allows sport to be an instrument for exploitation for one's own interests – destroying both sport and humanity. Our essential free nature, as developed by Sartre, is also discussed by Culbertson (2011) with respect to transhumanism and the ethics of performance enhancement (especially genetic transfer technology) in sport. However, the ethical aspect of phenomenology has not been much discussed in philosophy nor in philosophy of sport, and so there is potential for further exploration.

Further topics

Of course, there are also other important topics within philosophy of sport that draw on phenomenology. On the most general level, Martínková and Parry (2011a) present key concepts of phenomenology and Müller (2011) gives an overview of selected themes within the development of phenomenology and existentialism and their relation to sport. Regarding various individual themes, Hughson and Inglis (2002: 4ff.) show the difference between the abstract and practical (lived) concepts of space on the basis of (mainly) Merleau-Ponty's analyses, in order to discuss play (especially with respect to football). Play is also discussed by Vannata (2008) and Zimmermann and Morgan (2011). Here, most authors draw especially on Husserl and Merleau-Ponty, while Eugen Fink's work *Spiel als Weltsymbol* (1960) is rarely mentioned. Hogen(ová) (2009) addresses athletes' anorexia by differentiating the Cartesian view of the body from the phenomenological one (especially as discussed by Husserl and Heidegger), introducing various phenomenological concepts, such as, for example, *epoche*, the Husserlian concept of time, and bodily intentionality. Breivik (2011) discusses risk in nature sports. Morgan (1993) uses phenomenological analysis for discussing sport as a religious experience. Kretchmar (2013) discusses competition within the frame of Husserl's eidetic analyses, noticing its similarity to conceptual analysis. Another important theme of phenomenology – intersubjectivity – is presented by McLaughlin and Torres (2011). Vannatta (2011) uses Husserl's philosophy to discuss the relevance of instant replay in football, concluding that 'perception of movement in lived time is optimally perceived in lived time' (ibid: 341).

Phenomenology and sport sciences

We can find the word 'phenomenology' used not only in philosophy (of sport) discourse but also within the area of qualitative research in some (sport) sciences, such as, for example, (sport) sociology and psychology (for example, Willig 2008). In this context, phenomenology is understood as a scientific method, calling itself empirical phenomenology, interpretative phenomenological analysis, and so forth. This is understandably a reaction of these researchers to the kind of depersonalized science that is abundant in (sport) research, trying to highlight the individual person (athlete) and this field of research is growing.

The important issue to be noticed is that the connection between philosophical phenomenology and these empirical modifications is not unproblematic. Philosophy and empirical sciences ask different kinds of questions and therefore the methods differ, as well as the outcomes. While, in philosophical phenomenology, the inquiry aims mainly at the description of the structures of how we as human beings experience ourselves and the world, empirical psychology and sociology that claim to be inspired by phenomenology are aimed at particular experiences in the specific understanding of individual people.

Another problem is that some of these same researchers think that they are doing phenomenology simply because their work is supported by reference to some philosophical sources that precede the description of empirical methods. While it is also presently generally agreed among empirical researchers who call themselves phenomenologists that phenomenological philosophy is the primary source of their empirical research (Finlay 2009), there is a problem with the relationship between these two discourses, which are, as previously noted, of a fundamentally different kind. This does not mean, however, that this form of empirical phenomenology in the sport sciences is without merit, but rather that it needs to be applied with thorough knowledge of the method, and in a critically sensitive way. As Zahavi (2010: 14) says: 'It is important to encourage the exchange between phenomenology and empirical science, but the possibility of a fruitful cooperation between the two should not make us deny their difference'.

Greater clarity would be achieved if empirical researchers stopped using the term 'phenomenology' to describe their work, in the style of Marton's (2004) 'phenomenography', or if they made it clear that they are just 'inspired' by phenomenology (although here we should still expect some explicit account of what difference it makes to the research methodology adopted). It is rare to find empirical work that genuinely applies phenomenological philosophy, addressing important topics from within their discipline in a philosophical way. One exception is R. D. Laing's (1960) development of the concept of 'ontological security' within psychotherapy – a description of human being that helps to explain certain 'pathologies', in a way that would otherwise be impossible.

Conclusion

The main contribution of phenomenology is its view of the human being from the first-person perspective, its emphasis on the character of human experiencing, and its attention to the human situation. Phenomenology thus brings new aspects and topics from human life to the fore. These are, for example, the importance of self-understanding and the meaning of one's life, the importance of transience and mortality, freedom and responsibility. Also, some topics relevant to sport receive fresh treatment from this new perspective, sometimes producing a new account – such as, for example, in discussions of the human body and movement, action, spatiality, time, skill, and so on.

Within sport philosophy, phenomenology helps us to take a fresh and wider grasp of the human being within sport and enables us to overcome a generally reductive approach. Let me emphasise that this does not mean that we should become subjectivists but, rather, that this is an approach that takes the human being seriously with respect to his/her experiencing and being-in-the-world. A failure to pay attention to human existence in its wholeness is reductive, and such approaches may well prove inadequate and inefficient for analyses that concern the human being in or outside of sport. Within the context of sport, a phenomenological account of human being puts a different emphasis on the athlete. It does not make the mistake of over-emphasizing the performance and its result, but rather it points towards emphasizing the importance of clarity of self-understanding without which meaning and significance recede, and the athlete's understanding of their participation in sport is diminished.

Notes

1 For more on this topic, see Martínková and Parry (2011a).
2 'Original' understanding in this context means the kind of understanding that characterizes the primordial human way of understanding, even though it is first and mostly inexplicit (Patočka 1998).
3 See note 2.

References

Aggerholm, Kenneth, Jespersen, Ejgil and Ronglan, Lars Tore. 2011. Falling for the Feint – An Existential Investigation of a Creative Performance in High-Level Football. *Sport, Ethics and Philosophy* 5 (3): 343–58.

Breivik, Gunnar. 2008. Bodily Movement – the Fundamental Dimensions. *Sport, Ethics and Philosophy* 2 (3): 337–52.

Breivik, Gunnar. 2010. Being-in-the-Void: A Heideggerian analysis of skydiving. *Journal of the Philosophy of Sport* 37 (1): 29–46.

Breivik, Gunnar. 2011. Dangerous Play with the Elements: Towards a phenomenology of risk sports. *Sport, Ethics and Philosophy* 5 (3): 314–30.

Culbertson, Leon. 2011. Sartre on Human Nature: Humanness, transhumanism and performance enhancement. *Sport, Ethics and Philosophy* 5 (3): 231–44.

De Coubertin, Pierre. 2000. Philosophy of Physical Culture. In *Pierre de Coubertin. Olympism. Selected Writings*, edited by N. Müller, 163–5. Lausanne: International Olympic Committee.

Dreyfus, Hubert. 2004. What Could Be More Intelligible Than Everyday Intelligibility? Reinterpreting Division I of *Being and Time* in the Light of Division II. *Bulletin of Science, Technology* and *Society* 24 (3): 265–74.

Dreyfus, Hubert and Hall, Harrison. (eds) 1982. *Husserl, Intentionality and Cognitive Science*. Cambridge, MA: MIT Press.

Fink, Eugen. 1960. *Spiel als Weltsymbol*. Stuttgart: Kohlhammer.

Finlay, Linda. 2009. Debating Phenomenological Research Methods. *Phenomenology and Practice* 3 (1): 6–25.

Gallagher, Shaun. 2005. *How the Body Shapes the Mind*. Oxford: Clarendon.

Gallagher, Shaun. 2008. Direct Perception in the Intersubjective Context. *Consciousness and Cognition* 17. 535–43.

Gallagher, Shaun. 2012. Empathy, Simulation and Narrative. *Science in Context* 25 (3): 355–81.

Heidegger, Martin. 2001. *Sein und Zeit*. Tübingen: Max Niemeyer Verlag.

Heidegger, Martin. 2007. Phenomenological Interpretations with Respect to Aristotle: Indication of the hermeneutical situation. In *Becoming Heidegger: On the trail of his early occasional writings, 1910–1927*, edited by T. Kisiel and T. Sheehan, 155–84. Evanston, IL: Northwestern University Press.

Henry, Michel. 2000. *Incarnation, une Philosophie de la Chair*. Paris: Seuil.

Hogen, Anna. 2009. Cartesian Bodies and Movement Phenomenology. *Sport, Ethics and Philosophy* 3 (1): 66–74.

Hogeveen, B. 2011. Skilled Coping and Sport: Promises of phenomenology. *Sport, Ethics and Philosophy* 5 (3): 245–55.

Hughson, John and Inglis, David. 2002. Inside the Beautiful Game: Towards a Merleau-Pontian phenomenology of soccer play. *Journal of the Philosophy of Sport* 29 (1): 1–15.

Husserl, Edmund. 1952. *Ideen zu einer reinen Phänomenologie und phänomenologischen Philosophie. Zweites Buch: Phänomenologische Untersuchungen zur Konstitution*. The Hague: Martinus Nijhoff.

Husserl, Edmund. 1973. *The Phenomenology of Internal Time-Consciousness*. Bloomington, IN: Indiana University Press.

Husserl, Edmund. 2001. *Logical Investigations*. London: Routledge.

Jirásek, Ivo. 2007. An Experience and Heidegger's Analysis of Authentic Existence. In *Sporting Reflections: Some philosophical perspectives*, edited by H. Sheridan, L. A. Howe and K. Thompson, 154–70. Oxford: Meyer and Meyer Sport.

Kelan, Elisabeth. 2009. Moving Bodies and Minds – The Quest for Embodiment in Teaching and Learning. *Educational Philosophy and Theory* 41 (1): 39–46.

Kretchmar, Scott. 2013. A Phenomenology of Competition. *Journal of the Philosophy of Sport* 39 (1): 1–15.

Laing, Ronnie D. 1960. *The Divided Self: An existential study in sanity and madness*. Harmondsworth: Penguin.

McLaughlin, Douglas W. and Torres, Cesar R. 2011. Sweet Tension and its Phenomenological Description: Sport, intersubjectivity and horizon. *Sport, Ethics and Philosophy* 5 (3): 270–84.

Marcel, Gabriel. 1988. If I Am My Body. In *Philosophic Inquiry in Sport*, edited by William J. Morgan and Klaus V. Meier, 107–8. Champaign, IL: Human Kinetics.

Martínková, Irena. 2011. Anthropos as Kinanthropos: Heidegger and Patočka on Human Movement. *Sport, Ethics and Philosophy* 5 (3): 217–30.

Martínková, Irena. 2012. Fair or Temple: Two possibilities for Olympic sport. *Sport, Ethics and Philosophy* 6 (2): 166–82.

Martínková, Irena. 2013. *Instrumentality and Values in Sport*. Praha: Karolinum Press.

Martínková, Irena and Parry, Jim. 2011a. An Introduction to the Phenomenological Study of Sport. *Sport, Ethics and Philosophy* 5 (3): 185–201.

Martínková, Irena and Parry, Jim (eds) 2011b. Special Issue: An Introduction to the Phenomenological Study of Sport. *Sport, Ethics and Philosophy*. 5 (3).

Martínková, Irena and Parry, Jim. 2011c. Two Ways of Conceiving Time in Sports. *Acta Universitatis Palackianae Olomucensis. Gymnica* 41 (1): 23–31.

Martínková, Irena and Parry, Jim. (eds) 2012. *Phenomenological Approaches to Sport*. London: Routledge.

Marton, Ference. 2004. Phenomenography. In *Educational Research, Methodology, and Measurement: An international handbook* (2nd ed.), edited by P. J. Keeves, 95–101. New York: Pergamon.

Meier, Klaus V. 1975. Cartesian and Phenomenological Anthropology: The radical shift and its meaning for sport. *Journal of the Philosophy of Sport* 2: 51–73.

Meier, Klaus V. 1988. Embodiment, Sport, and Meaning. In *Philosophic Inquiry in Sport*, edited by William J. Morgan and Klaus V. Meier, 93–101. Champaign, IL: Human Kinetics.

Merleau-Ponty, Maurice. 1945. *Phénoménologie de la Perception*. Paris: Gallimard.

Merleau-Ponty, Maurice. 1964. *Le Visible et l'Invisible*. Paris: Gallimard.

Merleau-Ponty, Maurice. 2004. *Phenomenology of Perception*. London and New York: Routledge.

Moe, Vegard Fusche. 2005. A Philosophical Critique of Classical Cognitivism in Sport: From information processing to bodily background knowledge. *Journal of the Philosophy of Sport* 32 (2): 155–83.

Moran, Dermot. 2011. Edmund Husserl's Phenomenology of Habituality and Habitus. *Journal of the British Society for Phenomenology* 42 (1): 53–77.

Morgan, William J. 1976a. An Analysis of the Futural Modality of Sport. *Continental Philosophy Review* 9 (4): 418–34.

Morgan, William J. 1976b. An Analysis of The Sartrean Ethic of Ambiguity as The Moral Ground for The Conduct of Sport. *Journal of the Philosophy of Sport* 3: 82–96.

Morgan, William J. 1978. The Lived Time Dimensions of Sportive Training. *Journal of the Philosophy of Sport* 5: 12–26.

Morgan, William J. 1993. An Existential Phenomenological Analysis of Sport as a Religious Experience. In *Religion and Sport*, edited by C. S. Prebish, 119–49. Westport, CT: Greenwood.

Morgan, William J. and Meier, Klaus V. (eds) 1988. *Philosophic Inquiry in Sport*. Champaign, IL: Human Kinetics.

Müller, Arno. 2011. From Phenomenology to Existentialism – Philosophical Approaches Towards Sport. *Sport, Ethics and Philosophy* 5 (3): 202–16.

Patočka, Jan. 1992. *Přirozený Svět Jako Filosofický Problém* [*The Natural World as a Philosophical Problem*]. Praha: Československý spisovatel.

Patočka, Jan. 1996. *Heretical Essays*, translated by E. Kohák. Chicago, IL: Carus.

Patočka, Jan. 1998. *Body, Community, Language, World*, translated by E. Kohák. Chicago, IL: Carus.

Sartre, Jean-Paul. 1943. *L'être et le Néant: Essai d'ontologie phénoménologique*. Paris: Gallimard.

Sartre, Jean-Paul. 1988. The Body. In *Philosophic Inquiry in Sport*, edited by William J. Morgan and Klaus V. Meier, 103–5. Champaign, IL: Human Kinetics.

Sartre, Jean-Paul. 1996. *L'Existentialisme est un Humanisme*. Paris: Gallimard.

Schrag, Calvin O. 1988. The Lived Body as a Phenomenological Datum. In *Philosophic Inquiry in Sport*, edited by William J. Morgan and Klaus V. Meier, 109–18. Champaign, IL: Human Kinetics.

Slusher, Howard S. 1967. *Man, Sport, and Existence: A critical analysis*. Philadelphia, PA: Lea and Febiger.

Sokolowski, Robert. 2000. *Introduction to Phenomenology*. Cambridge: Cambridge University Press.

Standal, Øyvind F. and Moe, Vegard F. 2011. Merleau-Ponty Meets Kretchmar: Sweet Tension of Embodied Learning. *Sport, Ethics and Philosophy* 5 (3): 256–69.

Standish, Paul. 1998. In the Zone: Heidegger and sport. In *Ethics and Sport*, edited by M. J. McNamee and S. J. Parry, 256–69. London: Routledge.

Toombs, S. Kay (ed.) 2001. *Handbook of Phenomenology and Medicine*. Dordrecht: Kluwer.

Vannatta, Seth. 2008. A Phenomenology of Sport: *Playing* and passive synthesis. *Journal of the Philosophy of Sport* 35 (1): 63–72.

Vannatta, Seth. 2011. Phenomenology and the Question of Instant Reply: A crisis of the sciences? *Sport, Ethics and Philosophy* 5 (3): 331–42.

Willig, Carla. 2008. *Introducing Qualitative Research Methods in Psychology* (2nd ed.). Maidenhead: McGraw-Hill/Open University Press.

Zahavi, Dan. 2003. *Husserl's Phenomenology*. Stanford, California: Stanford University Press.

Zahavi, Dan. 2010. Naturalized Phenomenology. In *Handbook of Phenomenology and Cognitive Science,* edited by S. Gallagher and D. Schmicking, 3–19. Dordrecht: Springer.

Zimmermann, Ana Cristina and Morgan, John. 2011. The Possibilities and Consequences of Understanding Play as Dialogue. *Sport, Ethics and Philosophy* 5 (1): 46–62.

13

PHILOSOPHY OF MIND AND SPORT

Paul Davis

Introduction

Philosophy of mind is a vast subject, covering the criss-crossing areas of consciousness, subjectivity, personhood, personal identity, thought, cognition, action, emotion, free will and responsibility, transcendence, authenticity and death. It has interfaces with, *inter alia*, psychology, philosophy of psychology, moral philosophy, philosophy of language, theories of human nature, philosophy of religion, feminism and the philosophy of sport. Luminaries and major influences include Plato, Descartes, Wittgenstein, Hegel, Spinoza, Brentano, Husserl, Heidegger, Sartre, Merleau-Ponty, Davidson, Putnam, Lewis, Strawson, Nagel, Searle, Dennett, Flanagan, Chalmers, Clark and Hurley.

Nagel advises that 'philosophy is not like a particular language. Its sources are preverbal and often pre-cultural, and one of its most difficult tasks is to express unformed but intuitively felt problems in language without losing them' (Nagel 1986: 11). Stephen Priest (1991) expresses such intuitively felt problems about the mind by offering two sets of predicates, one tacitly implied in calling something 'mental' and the other tacitly implied in calling something 'physical'. Priest does not mean to suggest that 'all are correctly implied or that all of them are implied in all people's usage, only that many are implied in many people's usage' (Priest 1991: 212). Those in the former, mental set include temporal, private, incorrigible, internal, one, free, active, I, sacred, indivisible, unextended, without shape, invisible, intentional and subjective; those in the latter, physical set include spatiotemporal, public, corrigible, external, many, determined, passive, other, profane, divisible, extended, with shape, visible, non-intentional and objective.

This chapter first outlines some approaches in the philosophy of mind, before proceeding to some of their manifestations in the philosophy of sport.

Dualism

If dualism is true, the implications of many people's language use to which Priest avers are largely correct. Dualism is the theory that there are two and only two kinds of stuff: physical stuff, which is extended in space and is the bearer of physical properties, and mental stuff, which is unextended and is the bearer of mental properties. The physical and mental are irreducibly different. For dualism, a person is a mind and a body, although most dualists hold that a person is essentially a mind and merely has a body. If this is true, it is logically possible that a person continues to exist after their body has ceased to exist.

Dualism's most vaunted proponents are Plato and Descartes. For each, the person, again, is identified with the immaterial soul, which contingently *has* a body. Plato, indeed, champions physical education ultimately for the health of the immaterial soul (Reid 2007).

The most celebrated of Plato's arguments for dualism is probably the recollection argument, which is that the knowledge we have is recollection of what we were acquainted with in a prenatal state. This is dialectically continuous with Plato's theory of forms, which is that the world of sensible particulars is an approximation to perfect, quasi-mathematical, non-spatiotemporal universals, which are, in turn, the only genuine objects of knowledge. Christianity is routinely taken to have imported Plato's dualism, including his hostility to the flesh.

The best known of Descartes' dualist arguments is an epistemological one, elicited by Descartes' method of radical doubt: I can doubt that my body exists but I cannot doubt that I exist, therefore I am not my body. Another, the argument from conceivability, is dialectically equivalent but invokes the Cartesian notion of clear and distinct ideas: to form a clear and distinct idea of myself, I do not need to think of my body and to form a clear and distinct idea of my body I do not need to think of myself, therefore my mind and body are distinct. Descartes' conclusion that he is essentially a thinking thing – an immaterial mind – is expressed in his famous cogito: 'I think, therefore I am'. For Descartes, there is something it is like for human beings to be hungry, in pain, and so on, and we are acquainted with this immediately and from the inside, as opposed to discovery through observation.

The most prominent objection to dualism focuses on the putative causal interaction between extended material stuff and unextended immaterial stuff: how can states of something immaterial bring about states of something material, and vice versa?

It might be, however, that this objection is not the anti-dualist *coup de grace* perfunctorily assumed. Reality cannot be intelligible through and through. Explanations need to terminate in unexplained states of affairs ('brute facts') and there is no *a priori* reason why the dualist's psychophysical interaction could not be one of them. On Hume's doctrine of causation, indeed, no causal connection is 'intelligible', for it makes no sense to posit any sort of necessary connection between cause and effect. And even if we do – as we surely should – acknowledge a disturbing oddity in the notion of a very precise set of physical processes uniquely generating immaterial states, it is not obvious that such causal relations would be more mysterious than some accepted or entertained, or that there is a less problematic alternative.

Moreover, it might be that the most powerful reasons for entertaining dualism do not involve any of the more ambitious Platonic or Cartesian architecture or arguments but are the quotidian grounds of consciousness, intentionality and rational thought. According to a landmark definition, something is conscious if and only if there is something it is like to be the thing, *for the thing*. And intentionality is the 'about-ness' of many mental states, for example hoping *that*, believing *that*. How could either of those properties of the mental be physical in nature? (Where are they located?) And how could rational thought be reduced to the behaviour of any set of physical processes? The first of those grounds inscribes Sorrell's 'innocent Cartesianism', defined by: (i) the idea that there is essentially something it is like to have sensations; (ii) that the best way of understanding some mental states may be by reference to what it is like to be in them; and (iii) modesty in claims about the intelligibility through theory of mind-body union (Sorrell 2005: 93–4).

Materialism

Monism is the theory that only one type of stuff exists. One version is materialism (also called 'physicalism'), the theory that all that exists is physical. Mental states are therefore physical states. Materialism too has a distinguished history, stretching back to at least the fourth-century BC and Democritus, who believed that everything that exists is composed of indivisible physical objects he called 'atoms'. Sixteenth-century English philosopher Hobbes also believed everything that exists is finally physical in nature. His argument is significant for its consequences for the nature of persons and the resultant intelligibility of posthumous personal survival. He argued that if we talk about a soul travelling or burning, for instance, we are talking about a process whose intelligibility depends upon its happening to something physical. This motif can be applied also to the question of how immaterial persons could be individuated and distinguished: if John and Tom are each divested of material properties, then 'where' (spatial language again) does Tom end and John begin, and how does one know that one is talking to John and not Tom? (And how can they even talk or hear?)

Modern materialism's simplest version is the mind–brain identity theory, which proposes contingent psychophysical identities (for example, 'pain = c-fibre stimulation') for 'occurrent states'. The identities are considered contingent because the mental term does not *mean* the same as its physical co-referent but picks out the same, essentially physical thing. Kripke (1980) challenges the notion of a contingent identity and asserts, moreover, that the essential nature of a state such as pain is how it feels to the subject (compare Sorrell) and not an observable physical state.

The mind–brain identity theory offers a dispositional analysis of intentional states (such as beliefs), which it casts as actual or potential behaviour; for example, to believe that it is raining is to be disposed to take one's umbrella if one goes out. This account echoes Ryle's (1949) landmark treatment, typically known as behaviourism (although he disliked the label), which rejects the so-called 'ghost in the machine' and argues instead that mental concepts logically refer to dispositions to behave in certain ways. In a more complex version of materialism known as anomalous monism, Davidson (1980) rejects an exhaustively dispositional account of intentional states on the ground that any such reduction always needs an irreducibly mental remainder (for example: 'provided he notices that …').

Anomalous monism sees mental states as physical states but holds that there are no laws on the basis of which mental phenomena can be explained or predicted. Psychophysical identities are not type–type but token–token and the causal laws which finally subsume the mental are to be found at the level of the physical. This has elicited the objection that in anomalous monism, the mental *as mental* does no causal work, expunging the mental of the autonomy and efficacy which Davidson wishes to preserve.

The principal objections to materialism are, again, the oddity of conceiving consciousness, intentionality and rational thought as physical in nature.

Idealism

Idealism is the monist theory that all that exists is mental. Therefore, the world that we take as physical is essentially a manifestation of the mental. Its two most eminent exponents are Hegel and Berkeley.

Hegel proposed that reality is a historical process in which spirit (*Geist*), which can be taken as consciousness, goes through a series of phases of increasing self-knowledge, culminating in complete knowledge of itself. He sees the 'world spirit' manifest in historical epochs such as the

'Greek world', 'Roman world' and 'German world'. In religion, spirit comes close to self-knowledge but falls short because of its reliance on image and analogy. It is the role of Hegelian philosophy *inter alia* to close this gap. In absolute knowing, reality is self-consciousness: consciousness and what exists are absolutely identical.

Hegel's system is dense, complex, and contentious. However, he arguably has substantial importance for the philosophy of mind through his recognition of the social and historical aspects of consciousness, which may be cast also as recognition of intimate connections between subjectivity and objectivity. The idea that consciousness is social and historical (as well as cultural and political) defines later thinkers, such as Marx, Nietzsche, Foucault and Bourdieu, and has significant influence on discussions within the philosophy of sport.

The key move in Berkeley's idealism is his definition of physical objects as 'collections of ideas', which he reaches via shrewd criticism of his predecessor Locke. To exist is to be perceived (*'esse est percipi'*). God assures the regularity and coherence of our perceptions, Himself perceiving everything at all times.

Berkeley's recourse to God has a 'rabbit in the hat' quality. Also, he seems to confuse the vehicle and object of perception: we need mental content to perceive physical objects but does it follow that the physical objects are themselves mental content?

Double-aspect theory

Double-aspect theory is the theory that the mental and physical are properties of an underlying reality which is neither mental nor physical. Seventeenth-century philosopher Spinoza is one exponent, arguing that consciousness and size are the two aspects of one substance, which can be thought of as God under its conscious aspect and nature under its extended aspect.

Twentieth-century philosopher Russell proposed that the mental and physical are secondary to the more fundamental category of events (neutral monism). Mental events are events in the brain but can also be subsumed under psychological laws for the purpose of psychological explanation. They are intrinsically neither mental nor physical. These categories would be supplanted in a completed science by causal laws concerning events.

To accept that things happen but not to anything, for example, something physical or mental, is monstrously counterintuitive (albeit that would not falsify it). Also, Russell (1970: 292) argues that what we ordinarily perceive is a part of our own brain, which exposes him to an objection which echoes that faced by Berkeley: we might need our brains to perceive but is it our brains we are perceiving? (And what if we could perceive our brains on a screen? Is that perception of one's brain another part of one's brain?)

A more recent exponent of double-aspect theory is Strawson (1959). Here, the concept of the *person* is given logical primacy, with priority for neither the mental nor physical. The subject of consciousness is the whole person, which is essentially something to which mental and physical properties are equally applicable. Moreover, we may identify persons only if we can identify their bodies, and one can ascribe states of consciousness to one's self only if we can ascribe them to others. This echoes Wittgenstein's (1953: 243–358) private language argument – routinely regarded as a refutation of the preceding Cartesian model of human mental states – according to which the identification of conscious states in one's own case requires a public background ('an inner process stands in need of outward criteria'), otherwise the distinction between getting it right and merely seeming to get it right disappears. Strawson illustrates the nuances of his own position in the case of depression: there could not be depression if it was never shown but, equally, there could not be depression if it was never felt. Both first-person experience and third-person behavioural criteria are necessary for the concept to have a use.

Strawson takes questions about subjectivity and objectivity to be prior the traditional mind–body problem. This carries echoes of Hegel, noted above, and phenomenologists such as Sartre, Heidegger and Merleau-Ponty, which are discussed below.

Personhood, emotion, language and value

The (corporeal) person enjoys equivalent primacy in the work of Charles Taylor (1985, 1989). Here, it also has a normative import, in turn structurally related to human emotion, language, agency, intersubjectivity and a specifically human consciousness defined by the capacity for 'strong evaluation'; that is, the articulation of the value attaching to our emotions, desires and volitions. This articulation may express affirmation or rejection of these emotions, desires and volitions, betraying commitment to the sort of person one is or wishes to become.

Sports philosopher McNamee (2008: 28–39) tries to iron out what he sees as a wrinkle or two in Taylor's approach. For instance, is self-understanding and self-evaluation as strongly linked to articulacy as Taylor makes out? Might emotions genuinely open one's conception of the good life, but without particularly robust, self-aware articulation? There are consequences for sport, some of which get mileage later.

Functionalism and cognitivism

Functionalism is an approach which has had huge influence in recent years. It is the theory that a mental state is a functional state, individuated or picked out through its causal relations. For instance, a sensory input and behavioural output may be the respective cause and effect of a mental state, which is therefore identified through this cause and effect. (Mental states are also causally related to one another.) This definition obviously allows for unconscious mental states, to which functionalists are hospitable. It also allows for a range of ontologies of the mind; it is consistent with, for instance, dualism and materialism, since it is noncommittal with regard to the kind of stuff in which its functional states are realised. There are two sources of functionalism. One is the mind–brain identity theorist Armstrong (1980), who accepts the behaviourist connection between the mental and behaviour but denies that it is identity. Instead, mental states are the cause of behaviour. The other source is the development of artificial intelligence, which led Alan Turing (1950) to develop his 'Turing test' of intelligence: if one asks a human and a computer a set of questions, without being able to see either, then inability to distinguish the sources of the answers means that the computer is intelligent.

The immediately preceding idea generated cognitivism, sometimes called strong artificial intelligence, which is the theory that running a program is sufficient for having a mind. This was challenged by Searle (1981) in his Chinese room experiment. Here, a non-Chinese speaker sits in a room following a program in his own language, which tells him which answers, written in Chinese, to send out for each Chinese question sent in to him. He matches the input questions and output answers perfectly. But he has no idea what they are about. Therefore, there is, Searle asserts, no genuine intentionality in the Chinese room but only a simulacrum, which might serve purposes that we have. Searle thinks this demonstrates that running a program is not sufficient for having a mind. (For Searle, the biology of the brain matters, challenging the ontological neutrality of functionalism, and results in his approach being called biological naturalism.) The most popular counter-argument is the systems reply, which deems that complexity matters: if we make the system much more complex, then genuine mentality emerges out of the set of subsystems. This idea inscribes Dennett's (1991) and Flanagan's (1992) book-length treatments of consciousness.

A more fundamental problem with functionalism might be that it downplays the subjective, experiential aspect of mental states. For instance, could pain play its functional role if it did not hurt?

Phenomenology

Phenomenology is heterogeneous but is fairly conceived as an enquiry into essences, an attempt to return, in Husserl's slogan, 'to the things themselves'. Phenomenology asks what it is like to be human for the human. Husserl is usually regarded as the first phenomenologist. His approach is primarily descriptive, prescribing 'bracketing' ('epoche') of ourselves from the natural world and of our 'natural' beliefs about the latter (for example, its objective reality) in order to uncover, by 'transcendental reduction', a presuppositionless description of the contents of experience – a pure transcendental consciousness. This project echoes Hegel's attempt to describe consciousness (*Geist*) just as it appears to consciousness.

Some regard Husserl's 'pure transcendental' consciousness unattainable, because of the preceding dependence of consciousness upon more objective features. (Sociologically inclined phenomenologists are among them, as we see later.) This pressured Husserl to reorient towards a theory of intersubjectivity using the concept of the *Lebenswelt* – the common-sense life-world of everyday experience. The preceding concept of intentionality ('about-ness') is also key to Husserlian phenomenology, casting human subjectivity as essentially directed outwards towards something other than itself. Heidegger strengthens this perspective by defining the human being, *Dasein*, as 'being in the world', entailing that description of the contents of consciousness is fundamentally interpretative, in turn precluding the Husserlian ambition of 'bracketing'. Heidegger's approach is therefore sometimes called 'hermeneutic phenomenology'.

Existential phenomenology, articulated in Sartre, De Beauvoir and Merleau-Ponty, responds to a putative limitation in Heidegger by centralising the body in human experience. Here, man is a 'body-subject' or incarnate consciousness. Where Husserl focuses upon the intentionality of the mind, Merleau-Ponty highlights the intentionality of the body: 'my body appears to me as an attitude directed towards a certain existing or possible task. And indeed its spatiality is … a spatiality of situation' (Merleau-Ponty 2002: 114–15).

The supersized mind

Our trajectory so far starts with a putatively individual, immaterial, thinking consciousness, before enlistment of the brain, organism, person, other persons and the environment (including social and cultural elements). A recent approach to cognition extends this trajectory in an intriguing way. Influenced by recent, transformative technological developments, it is defined by the parity principle, which is that,

> If, as we confront some task, a part of the world functions as a process which, were it done in the head, we would have no hesitation in recognising as part of the cognitive process, then that part of the world is part of the cognitive process.
>
> *(Clark 2008: 222)*

Therefore, props such as computers, phones and apps are part of the cognitive process and not mere causes of it. If the parity principle is sound, then a notebook in which a goalkeeper keeps notes of opponents' penalty-taking habits is part of the cognitive process, since we would immediately deem 'straight' memorising part of the cognitive process. The equivalent applies to 'epistemic actions' (Clark 2008: 222): the golfer's simulation of a putt (not Clark's example) is part of the cognitive process, since we would count purely private rehearsals and re-rehearsals in the same way. The parity principle is therefore known as the hypothesis of extended cognition (HEC) or simply EXTENDED. It is challenged by those who think it goes too far and by those who think it does not go far enough. The former adhere to the hypothesis of embedded cognition (HEMC), which in turn divides into BRAINBOUND (Adams and Aizawa 2001) and ORGANISMBOUND (Rupert 2004). The latter champion the cognitive significance of cultural practices (Hutchins 2011) (among which is sport). Clark (2011) has pleaded guilty to neglect of culture's cognitive significance.

Emotion and strong evaluation in sport

Sport is apt for strong evaluation. Emotions, desires and volitions around sport may be interrogated and subsequently affirmed, modified or rejected. The recent flowering of alternative sport forms (sometimes called 'lifestyle' sports), for instance, results in part from rejection of putative psychological, emotional and ideological characteristics of conventional sport; for example, hyper-competitiveness, hypermasculinity, and a mechanistic paradigm. The extent, however, to which such evaluation must be articulated is, again, a moot point.

Many debates within the philosophy of sport are undetachable from strong evaluation. For instance, McNamee (2007) challenges the affirmation of the 'genetically modified athlete' (see Miah 2004). He asks: (i) How much attention should we devote to our bodies in the effort to optimise our capacities? (ii) How much control should we allow physicians to exercise over our bodies? (iii) What ends should determine what counts as a sufficiently healthy body? (iv) What limits should we observe in our efforts to improve our bodily performance and remove causes of suffering? (ibid: 191) These questions are obviously key to the question of performance-enhancing drugs too.

Sportspersonship is also undetachable in McNamee's (2008: 37–9) view from strong evaluation. It is exemplified by the 'athlete, player or contestant who is able to act in ways that are either: (1) the effects of strong evaluation; or (2) the product of strong evaluation' (ibid: 37). Again, McNamee moderates the importance of articulacy, therefore allowing that young children and those of very limited capacity for self-critical awareness can be credited with sportspersonship. Indeed, McNamee relates an autobiographical anecdote which reinforces the aptness of emotion for rational evaluation and the perils of setting the bar of strong evaluation too high: invited to an international competition festival in the West of Norway for disability skiers, he found that pity for the athletes figured among his emotions. However, disability sport colleagues instructed him out of that emotion on the ground that it implied a wrongly privileged position of himself as able-bodied. Moreover, the disability skiers McNamee saw are, he asserts, capable of sportspersonship – 'they may have appreciated, recognised, taken on board the exemplars of courageous, honest, tenacious competitors and imitated their conduct so as to make it their own' (ibid: 38).

Fry (2003) also aligns himself with the preceding cognitivist view of emotion. We can, like McNamee (above), change our emotions by changing our evaluations of the relevant objects; conversely, we can 'talk ourselves into' emotions which do not tally with our sincere view of the object. Therefore, we can embody a lack of emotional integrity. Fry (2003) offers several examples from sport. The first concerns gymnastics coach Bela Karolyi, who, according to Joan Ryan, routinely feigned emotion by dramatically throwing tantrums over one's gymnast's score in the hope of influencing the score of the next (Ryan 1995: 199). These emotions were feigned – if Ryan is right – because Karolyi did not share the evaluative judgement constitutive of the genuine emotion. The second involves Knute Rockne, coach of American football at the University of Notre Dame. Before a game in 1922, he pulled a crumpled telegraph message from his pocket and lied that it was from his 'hospitalised and very ill' son (and team mascot) and contained the plea 'Please win this game for my Daddy'. Notre Dame won the match and were debriefed at an Indiana train station by a rudely healthy Billy Rockne rushing up to greet them. The third involves the same coach and the 'win for the Gipper' speech. George Gipp was a former Notre Dame player and the speech, given at halftime in a game against the army eight years after his death, supposedly sketches a poignant deathbed scene between Rockne and Gipp. The players who heard Rockne's speech became feverish. Rockne, however, was not present at Gipp's death and we do not know if the purported conversation between Rockne and Gipp took place. Coherence is absent at several levels: reality versus story, truth versus evaluative judgement, and possibly actual mental state versus feigned emotion.

Fry notes too that equivalent questions of emotional integrity apply to athletes who work themselves into hatred or anger towards opponents. To that one might add sport fans who cultivate a (culturally sponsored) poison and spite towards opposition players, fans, towns, countries, and so on.

Fry's final examples involve the intent of eliciting emotions of self-assessment, such as shame, guilt, humiliation and pride. By Ryan's preceding account, gymnastics coach Karolyi once gripped a pupil by the back of the neck and walked her to her mother's car, calling her 'pathetic' and 'no good'; called another a 'pregnant cow' as she began puberty; called another a 'pregnant spider'; and called another on 'overstuffed Christmas turkey'. Ryan accounts for this behaviour simply: it got results. Numerous hopefuls left 'disillusioned and often broken' (Ryan 1995: 206). Fry argues that while there might be a proper place for some cultivation and manipulation of emotion, such as positive imaging, encouragement and measured criticism, the preceding examples are unacceptable, since they involve 'a shallowness, which itself displays a lack of integrity' (Fry 2003: 33).

Consciousness in sport performance

Consciousness is, again, a key topic in the philosophy of mind, with functionalism in particular enthusiastic about unconscious mental processes. Particular ideas and contributions, for example Ryle's dispositional treatment, Polyani's theory of tacit know-how, Dreyfus' model of skill development, theories of 'being in the zone', 'peak experience' and the flow theories of Csikszentmihalyi and Jackson (1999) dovetail with this perspective and suggest that, at the elite level in particular, there is no room for conscious thinking. McNamee (2008: 31) touches on the implausibility of this, and Breivik (2013), following Birch (2011), argues that the truth is much more complex and involves elite athletes who are conscious and consciously thinking during performance. Breivik powerfully argues, specifically, that: (1) conscious and deliberate practice goes on at the expert level; (2) decisions about 'next moves' can be made consciously or unconsciously, with pivotal decisions sometimes accompanied by a heightened consciousness; (3) conscious attention counters the hazards (such as self-indulgence) of the 'flow'; (4) in some sports there are attentional control points that need to be regularly checked; for example, in river kayaking, one needs to look for waterfalls and drops; (5) elite athletes often have crucial mental pictures of movements ('gestalts') and recognise the 'proper feeling' when they conform to it; and (6) when athletes go on 'automatic pilot', consciousness moves to a higher level, overseeing patterns and decisions. Breivik's treatment in fact echoes Sutton's (2007) compelling account of the diffuse saliences of consciousness for batting in cricket. The former concludes that 'the feeling of what it is like to give a good performance … is one of the most phenomenal feelings one can have' (ibid: 104). In this, Breivik slightly outruns Arnold's observation that 'each sport's own distinctive structure offers different experiential possibilities, e.g. contrast tennis and cycling; for many competitors, these awakening and excitatory psychosomatic rhythms become part of the contest's intrinsic enjoyment' (Arnold 1985: 6).

The immediately preceding discussion reflects some key discussions in the philosophy of mind, evoking (among others) Descartes, Wittgenstein and Dennett.

Phenomenology in the philosophy of sport

Klaus Meier laments in a seminal philosophy of sport anthology (Morgan and Meier 1988) that 'the philosophy of sport is replete, both in theory and practice, with implicit and explicit affirmations of Cartesian dualism, despite occasional assertions to the contrary' (ibid: 97). He, in turn, elevates the method of (existential) phenomenological analysis and the figure of one of its seminal exponents, Maurice Merleau-Ponty. Twenty-three years later, an issue of *Sport, Ethics and Philosophy* (in 2011) is devoted to phenomenology and dotted with Merleau-Ponty, as well as early phenomenological co-excavators Husserl, Heidegger and Sartre. (For brief summary of phenomenology's strands and illustrations of their applications to sport and physical culture, see Allen-Collinson 2011: 300–3.) Studies within sport and physical culture influenced by the approach include Morley's (2001) study of breath control in yoga and Moe's (2004) exploration of the processes of skill acquisition in sport. And the title of Nesti's (2011) essay in the 'phenomenology' issue of *Sport, Ethics and Philosophy* paraphrases Husserl's imperative about the 'things themselves'.

Breivik (2008) details Heidegger's conception of being in the world and asserts its preceding putative limitation. The human subject is tied to the world in a primordial manner ('originary transcendence'), the most primary of which is 'the practical mode where things are discovered in their functionality or instrumentality' (ibid: 340). Heidegger writes that 'in our dealings we come across equipment for writing, sewing, working, transportation, measurement' (Heidegger 1962: 97). This quality of objects is their 'equipmentality'. We immediately see whether things can be used for some purpose. This quality in objects is sometimes called their 'affordances' and is, according to Gibson, what an infant begins by noticing (Gibson 1986: 134). Heidegger's next step is to observe the contextual quality of equipmentality, by which a piece of equipment is dependent upon 'a totality of equipment' (Heidegger 1962: 97). This entails an outward reference to an equipment structure, such as 'ink-stand, pen, ink, paper, blotting pad, table, lamp, furniture, windows, doors, room' (ibid: 97). Breivik illustrates this in the case of football:

> In the street the football pitch refers to the uneven loosely demarcated field, the improvised goal posts, the players on the two teams. From this … we can move up to the … Champions' League game … But in both cases the football itself … is meaningless unless understood in relation to other pieces of equipment, to feet and goal posts, in a larger reference structure.
>
> *(Breivik 2008: 340–1)*

Heidegger's next step is to show how equipmentality is constituted essentially in relation to a practice. For instance, the carpenter uses the hammer to hammer in nails to fasten the planks, and so on, and to finish the house so that people can live the life they want. We end up with the deepest life goals (*Sorge*). Heidegger's picture of instrumental justification in the ultimate service of intrinsically valuable goods echoes Aristotle centuries earlier (Aristotle 1998: I.1), and finds echo in the philosophy of sport through Suits' reflections on sport, leisure and seriousness

(Morgan and Meier 1988: 46–8). Breivik again reinforces the point with an example from football:

> The football … goalposts … corner poles, the other players and so on get their meaning … as part of the practice of playing football. The football player kicks the ball *in order to* pass it to the other players … *in order to* get closer to the opponent's goal … *in order to* score more goals than the opposing team … *in order to* win the match … *in order to* become the best team over a season, *in order to* succeed in a career as a football player, *in order to* lead a good life.
>
> *(Breivik 2008: 341)*

Heidegger and his inflections of phenomenology have formidable influence in the philosophy of sport. Prior to the immediately preceding tribute, Breivik offers a critical examination of the application of Heidegger's views on skilful coping to everyday life and sport (Breivik 2007). The same contributor offers a Heideggerian analysis of skydiving, which sees it as a condition of 'being in the void' (Breivik 2010) and sustains his Heideggerian bent in taking us towards a phenomenology of risk sports (Breivik 2011). Again, the preceding issue of *Sport, Ethics and Philosophy* contains an essay by Irena Martínková (2011) on Heidegger and human movement, and hermeneutic phenomenology is employed by Ryba (2008) to examine young athletes' experiences of figure skating. The Heideggerian Dreyfus, in turn, figures in Breivik (2007) and Moe's (2005) critique of cognitivism in sport, to which we return.

The deficit in Heidegger's analysis, as Breivik (2008: 341–2) asserts, is the concrete human body, which presents itself only indirectly. Heidegger describes how the hammer is possible only against the background of purposes, 'but he does not discuss how the hand that holds the hammer likewise is possible only on the background of a body with its postures, capacities and tasks' (ibid: 341). Breivik sees a double background: a bodily *Dasein* and a world of equipmentality. Extending his football illustration, Breivik notes that it is not enough to document the in-order-to references of purposes and goals but that it is 'also necessary to take notice of the foot as part of a body with its structure, postures and capacities' (ibid: 341). Breivik urges that the body is discovered equiprimordially with the world.

This is where existential phenomenology comes in. As Meier puts it,

> man's mode of insertion into the world is the body; it is his foundation in existence … The body is not simply another object in the world, rather it is 'an anchorage in the world'; it is man's mode of communication and interaction with it.
>
> *(Morgan and Meier 1988: 96)*

Breivik illuminates with another football illustration: players' movements and positions are defined by the movements of the ball and other players, and good players can read the situation before the ball is played (Breivik 2008: 342). This species of engagement leads Merleau-Ponty to talk of 'motor intentionality', a dynamic attitude in which it sometimes feels as if the task to be performed autonomously generates the action. At the same time, Merleau-Ponty considers that we 'transcend into' equipment, a characterisation recognisable to the elite sport performer, described by Breivik as 'totally unified with their equipment' (ibid: 344). The epistemic ramifications of wielding a tennis racket figure in a Merleau-Ponty-seasoned essay (Morris 2002).

Yet, for Merleau-Ponty, the body in a sense disappears: it is 'the darkness needed in theatre to show up the performance' (Merleau-Ponty 2002: 115). The body is the 'silent cogito'. And this might signpost a limitation, of interest to sport philosophers particularly, in

Merleau-Ponty's oeuvre. Shusterman has pointed out that Merleau-Ponty has very little to say about conscious somatic sensations, such as kinaesthetic or proprioceptive feelings (Shusterman 2005: 151). Neglect of these would be an oversight for the philosophy of sport.

Sociologically inflected phenomenology: commerce, nation and media

Critical sociologists Hughson and Inglis (2002) had, six years before the preceding Breivik essay, moved towards a Merleau-Pontian phenomenology of 'soccer play'. In the process, they affirm an augmentation of Merleau-Ponty different from and complementary to that suggested by Shusterman and Breivik. Any notion of a 'pure' phenomenological account of experience is misplaced (Hughson and Inglis 2002: 9–13). Footballers and the game of football, for instance, are 'always submerged within conditions of socioeconomic power'. Therefore, an account of power must be built into a phenomenological analysis. Hughson and Inglis acknowledge that others have already begun this augmentation. Bourdieu, Lefebvre, Bale, Eichberg and Giulianotti help Hughson and Inglis to conclude that,

> the phenomenology of the soccer experience today is … necessarily an exercise in analysis of the development of capitalism in a globalizing epoch, as much as it is concerned with the minutiae of play embodied within the corporeal frames of single players.
>
> *(Hughson and Inglis 2002: 12–13)*

Hemphill (2005) alerts us to the intra-team relational quality of a footballer's on-field subjectivity, suggesting that Hughson and Inglis' 'player-body-subject' is the 'team-player-body-subject' (Hemphill 2005: 111). Hemphill also heightens Hughson and Inglis' sociological inflections of footballer phenomenology with the help of MacIntyre's (1981) practice/institution distinction and recognition of how commercial, national and media pressures might inscribe the lived subjectivity of the elite player in particular (ibid: 112–13). The latter pressures, indeed, might come into tension with the elite player's identity as team player.

Sociologically inflected phenomenology: gender

Another influence upon the sociological augmentation of Merleau-Ponty is Iris Marion Young (1980). Young argues, in a classic essay, that the different movement patterns and body comportments of males and females are social facts to be explained in terms of gendered power. The male is socially constituted to be the active body-subject of Merleau-Ponty's casting, while the female is socially constituted to be a passive body-object. This results in radically different ways of experiencing one's body in space and explains the fact that the male's act of throwing involves projection of the entire body into space, while the equivalent female act uses far less of a body which is not projected into space. Hughson and Inglis transfer this account to football by contrasting the heading of the typical male and female player: the former will move forward relatively fluidly to meet the ball, while the latter is liable to move awkwardly towards the ball or even avoid taking the ball on the head through an expectation of pain which the male is more liable to discount (Hughson and Inglis 2002: 10–11).

Young, Hughson and Inglis help to scaffold Allen-Collinson's (2011) feminist phenomenological treatment of the woman in the running body. Allen-Collinson swiftly distances feminist phenomenology from any 'pure' experience, by asserting, like Young, that it acknowledges 'the powerful influences and constraints of social structure upon lived experience, and the corporeal specifics of bodies that are located in time and culture' (ibid: 299). Allen-Collinson uses a feminist sociological phenomenology to give a phenomenological account – contoured by the flagship concepts of description, epoche, reduction, essences and intentionality – of the physically and symbolically vulnerable female runner.

Phenomenology, Searle and classical cognitivism in sport

The phenomenological approach is fused with the more analytical approach of Searle in Moe's (2005) philosophical critique of classical cognitivism in sport. The computer processes information according to certain program or rule structures and cognitivism argues, again, that the human mind operates similarly. This has led to the cognitivist notion of the 'cognitive unconscious', supported within the cognitivist paradigm by contemporary research on, as Moe again puts it, 'the automaticity of perceptual-cognitive and motor skills, subliminal perception, implicit memory and hypnosis' (ibid: 162). And, again, Baars' analysis suggests that conscious processes are comparatively 'computationally inefficient', since they show a high number of errors, low speed and mutual interference when set against their unconscious counterparts (Baars 1998: 74ff.). This model has heavily influenced sport research and sport coaching. In sport psychology, the preceding conscious processes are referred to as controlled processing and the latter automatic processing. This distinction, which seemed to account for expert behaviour in terms of automatic, unconscious processes (contrast Breivik's preceding treatment of consciousness in performance), naturally became vital to sport scientists and coaches, who were concerned to understand how movements became automatic. Enter the notion of a motor programme, which can be conceived as an abstract representation, which is more sophisticated in more skilled athletes, and which fades from consciousness as the athlete reaches a certain skill level. Coaches were therefore liable to see their role involving the facilitation of unconscious motor programmes.

Moe's critique of cognitivism in sport comes down to two questions. First, do athletes process information? Second, are the intentional movements of athletes governed by motor programmes; that is, by abstract representations in the form of internalised rules or muscle commands? Moe answers that considerations from phenomenology and Searle suggest negative answers. The former considerations invoke Merleau-Ponty, Heidegger and Dreyfus. For Dreyfus, there is nothing in our everyday consciousness to suggest humans process atomistic bits of information. As Moe paraphrases, 'the carpenter and the soccer player experience immediately what the hammer and ball are and how they can be used, because these objects are, to quote Heidegger, "always already" an integrated part of their background' (Moe 2005: 164–5). Is the brain an information-processing device, then? Searle, again, has argued that 'information processing' is a humanly created, observer-dependent abstraction: 'a physical state of a system is a computational state only relative to the assignment to that state of some computational role, function or interpretation' (Searle 1992: 210). If Searle is right, the brain does not *intrinsically* process information.

Cognitivism might also court an infinite regress. Dreyfus offers the example of language skills: if the human is a system that processes bits of information in relation to program or rule structures,

> one must not only have grammatical and semantic rules but further rules ... to recognise the context in which the rules must be applied. Thus there must be rules for recognising the situation ... But if the theory then requires further rules in order to explain how these rules are applied ... we are in an infinite regress.
>
> *(Dreyfus 1991: 203–4)*

And Moe applies this insight to soccer: if cognitivism is true, then the player needs rules for how to kick and run, but also rules to show where the rules are applied, and further rules to show ... (Moe 2005: 169). Dreyfus stops the regress by situating our skills in an immediately meaningful practice and coping bodily background that cannot be rule governed. The background of Searle has affinity with the coping bodily background of the phenomenologists. The background is neurophysiologically caused and defined by Searle as 'the set of non-intentional or pre-intentional capacities that enable intentional states to function' (Searle 1995: 129). The background can, therefore, be 'causally sensitive to the forms of rules ... without actually containing any beliefs, desires or representations of those rules' (ibid: 141). Searle returns to sport, providing the case of the improving baseball player who begins by learning a set of rules, principles and strategies, and eventually 'develops skills and abilities that are ... functionally equivalent to the system of rules without ... containing any representations or internalisations of those rules' (ibid: 142).

Moe commends the marriage of phenomenology and Searle for its abolition of the cognitivist's regress, its abandonment of representation in the performance of high-level skill, and its reinforcement of the fact that embodied human beings have the tendency to get 'a maximal grip on the situation' (Moe 2005: 176–7). It is wise to juxtapose this approach with Breivik and Sutton's preceding discussions of the role of consciousness in performance.

The future

This contribution is an inevitably limited discussion of the philosophy of mind in the philosophy of sport. There are significant omissions, for example, free will (see Carr 1999 and Davis 2001), bad faith (see Culbertson 2005) and religion (see Scarpa and Carraro 2011). Of the areas covered, there is reason to expect the influence of existential phenomenology to continue. This might be particularly so in the case of its sociologically inflected applications. Commerce and gender are among the sites of exploration and might we expect to see, for instance, race and disability figure in phenomenological treatments?

The thorny status of consciousness in the philosophy of mind, alongside the preceding recent contributions to the philosophy of sport literature, probably portends further discussion of consciousness in the philosophy of sport. Slightly overlapping discussions are those defined by strong evaluation and emotion, which – naturally and healthily – never go away. Unexamined sport is, like the unexamined life, not worth it, and there is never a shortage of qualities in sport in need of the probing lens of strong evaluation.

One topic which has involved some strong evaluation in the recent literature is that of sport fandom (see, for instance, Dixon 2001; Russell 2012). One recent contribution (Mumford 2012) has also proposed a theory of unconscious mental oscillation, to account for the capacity of partisan spectators to appreciate opposition excellence and has also published a book-length treatment of watching sport (Mumford 2011). We can expect the constellation of discussions about fandom to continue apace. More specifically, a sociologically inflected phenomenology of fandom seems viable.

References

Adams, F. and Aizawa, K. 2001. The bounds of cognition. *Philosophical Psychology* 14 (1): 43–64.

Armstrong, D. 1980. The nature of mind, in Block, N. (ed.) *Readings in the Philosophy of Psychology*. London: Methuen.

Allen-Collinson, J. 2011. Feminist phenomenology and the woman in the running body. *Sport, Ethics and Philosophy* 5 (3): 297–313.

Aristotle. 1998. *The Nichomachean Ethics*, translated by David Ross. Oxford: Oxford University Press.

Arnold, P. J. 1985. Aesthetic aspects of being in sport: the performer's perspective in contrast to that of the spectator. *Journal of the Philosophy of Sport* 12: 1–7.

Baars, B. J. 1998. *A Cognitive Theory of Consciousness*. Cambridge: Cambridge University Press.

Birch, J. E. 2011. *In the Synaptic Cleft: Caught in the Gap Between Neurotransmitter Release and Conscious Experience in Sport*. Doctoral thesis, Norwegian School of Sports Sciences. Available online at http://brage.bibsys.no/xmlui/handle/11250/171313 (accessed 6 November 2014).

Breivik, G. 2007. Skilful coping in everyday life and in sport: a critical examination of the views of Heidegger and Dreyfus. *Journal of the Philosophy of Sport* 34 (2): 116–34.

—— 2008. Bodily movement – the fundamental dimensions. *Sport, Ethics and Philosophy* 2 (3): 337–52.

—— 2010. Being-in-the-void: a Heideggerian analysis of skydiving. *Journal of the Philosophy of Sport* 37 (1): 29–46.

—— 2011. Dangerous play with the elements: towards a phenomenology of risk sports. *Sport, Ethics and Philosophy* 5 (3): 314–30.

—— 2013. Zombie-like or superconscious? A phenomenological and conceptual analysis of consciousness in elite sport. *Journal of the Philosophy of Sport* 40 (1): 85–106.

Carr, D. 1999. Where's the merit if the best man wins? *Journal of the Philosophy of Sport* 26: 1–9.

Clark, A. 2008. *Supersizing the mind*. Oxford: Oxford University Press.

—— 2011. Finding the mind. *Philosophical Studies* 152 (3): 447–61.

Culbertson, L. 2005. The paradox of bad faith and elite competitive sport. *Journal of the Philosophy of Sport* 32 (1): 65–86.

Csikszentmihalyi, M. and Jackson, S.A. 1999. *Flow in Sports: The Keys to Optimal Experiences and Performances*. Champaign, IL: Human Kinetics.

Davidson, D. 1980. *Essays on Actions and Events*. Oxford: Oxford University Press.

Davis, P. 2001. Ability, responsibility and admiration in sport: a reply to Carr. *Journal of the Philosophy of Sport* 28 (2): 207–14.

Dennett, D. C. 1991. *Consciousness Explained*. London: Penguin.

Dixon, N. 2001. The ethics of supporting sports teams. *Journal of Applied Philosophy* 18: 149–58.

Dreyfus, H. L. 1991. *Being-in-the-World: A Commentary on Heidegger's Being and Time. Division I*. Cambridge, MA: MIT Press.

Flanagan, O. 1992. *Consciousness Reconsidered*. Cambridge, MA: MIT Press.

Fry, J. P. 2003. On playing with emotion. *Journal of the Philosophy of Sport* 30 (1): 26–36.

Gibson, J. J. 1986. *The Ecological Approach to Visual Perception*. Hillsdale, NJ: Lawrence Erlbaum Associates.

Heidegger, M. 1962. *Being and Time*, translated by J. Macquarrie and E. Robinson. San Francisco, CA: Harper.

Hemphill, D. 2005. Deeper inside the beautiful game. *Journal of the Philosophy of Sport* 32 (1): 105–15.

Hughson, J. and Inglis, D. 2002. Inside the beautiful game: towards a Merleau-Pontian phenomenology of soccer play. *Journal of the Philosophy of Sport* 29 (1): 1–15.

Hutchins, E. 2011. Enculturating the supersized mind. *Philosophical Studies* 152 (3): 437–46.

Kripke, S. 1980. *Naming and Necessity*. Cambridge, MA: Harvard University Press.

MacIntyre, A. 1981. *After Virtue*. Notre Dame, IN: University of Notre Dame Press.

McNamee, M. 2007. Whose Prometheus? Transhumanism, biotechnology and the moral topography of sports medicine. *Sport, Ethics and Philosophy* 1 (2): 181–94.

—— 2008. *Sports, Virtues and Vices: Morality play*. London: Routledge.

Martínková, I. 2011. Anthropos as kinanthropos: Heidegger and Patočka on human movement. *Sport, Ethics and Philosophy* 5 (3): 217-30.

Merleau-Ponty, M. 2002. *Phenomenology of Perception*, translated by Colin Smith. London: Routledge.

Miah, A. 2004. *Genetically Modified Athletes*. London: Routledge.

Moe, V. F. 2004. How to understand skill acquisition in sport. *Bulletin of Science, Technology and Society* 24 (3): 213–24.

—— 2005. A philosophical critique of classical cognitivism in sport: from information processing to bodily background knowledge. *Journal of the Philosophy of Sport* 32 (2): 155–83.

Morgan, W. J. and Meier, K.V. 1988. *Philosophic Inquiry in Sport*. Champaign, IL: Human Kinetics.

Morley, J. 2001. Inspiration and expiration: yoga practice through Merleau-Ponty's phenomenology of the body. *Philosophy East and West* 51 (1): 73–82.

Morris, D. 2002. Touching intelligence. *Journal of the Philosophy of Sport* 29 (2): 149–62.

Mumford, S. 2011. *Watching Sport: Aesthetics, ethics and emotion*. London: Routledge.

——— 2012. Moderate partisanship and oscillation. *Sport, Ethics and Philosophy* 6 (3): 369–75.

Nagel, T. 1986. *The View From Nowhere*. Oxford: Oxford University Press.

Nesti, M. 2011. Phenomenology and sport psychology: back to the things themselves! *Sport, Ethics and Philosophy* 5 (3): 285–96.

Priest, S. 1991. *Theories of the Mind*. London: Penguin.

Reid, H. 2007. Sport and moral education in Plato's *Republic*. *Journal of the Philosophy of Sport* 34 (2): 160–75.

Rupert, R. 2004. Challenges to the hypothesis of extended cognition. *Journal of Philosophy* 101 (8): 389–428.

Russell, B. 1970. *An Outline of Philosophy*. London: Routledge.

Russell, J. S. 2012. The ideal fan or good fans? *Sport, Ethics and Philosophy* 6 (1): 16–30.

Ryan, J. 1995. *Little Girls in Pretty Boxes: The making and breaking of elite gymnasts and figure skaters*. New York: Warner.

Ryba, T. 2008. Researching children in sport: methodological reflections. *Journal of Applied Sport Psychology* 20 (3): 334–48.

Ryle, G. 1949. *The Concept of Mind*. Chicago, IL: University of Chicago Press.

Scarpa, S. and Carraro, A. N. 2011. Does Christianity demean the body and deny the value of sport? *Sport, Ethics and Philosophy* 5 (2): 110–23.

Searle, J. R. 1981. Minds, brains and programs, in Hofstadter, D. and Dennett, D.C, *The Mind's I*. London: Penguin.

——— 1992. *The Rediscovery of the Mind*. Cambridge, MA: MIT Press.

——— 1995. *The Construction of Social Reality*. New York: Free Press.

Shusterman, R. 2005. The silent, limping body of philosophy. In *The Cambridge Companion to Merleau-Ponty*, edited by T. Carman and M. B. N. Hansen, 151–80. Cambridge: Cambridge University Press.

Sorrell, T. 2005. *Descartes Reinvented*. Cambridge: Cambridge University Press.

Strawson, P. 1959. *Individuals: An essay in descriptive metaphysics*. London: Routledge.

Sutton, J. 2007. Batting, habit and memory: the embodied mind and the nature of skill. *Sport in Society* 10 (5): 763–86.

Taylor, C. 1985. *Philosophical Papers: Volume 1, Human Agency and Language*. Cambridge: Cambridge University Press.

——— 1989. *Sources of the Self*. Cambridge, MA: Harvard University Press.

Turing, A. M. 1950. Computing machinery and intelligence. *Mind* 59 (236): 433–60.

Wittgenstein, L. 1953. *Philosophical Investigations*, translated by G. E. M. Anscombe. 3rd ed. Oxford: Blackwell, 1967.

Young, I. M. 1980. Throwing like a girl: a phenomenology of feminine body comportment, motility and spatiality. *Human Studies* 3 (2): 137–56.

14

PRAGMATISM AND THE PHILOSOPHY OF SPORT

John Kaag

Introduction

The philosophy of sport cropped up in a rather inhospitable environment. In the 1960s, sport enthusiasts remained largely unconvinced that philosophy could tell them something new about the experience and meaning of physical activity. And the philosophical mainstream remained almost wholly unconvinced that it should spend its analytical powers investigating something as mundane as sport. In its early years, the philosophy of sport worked against the growing tide of analytic philosophy that asked increasingly narrow philosophic questions and answered them in a way that only professional philosophers could understand. If this was the be-all and end all of philosophy, then sport enthusiasts were right to worry about viability of a philosophy of sport.

The discipline of philosophy, however, had some outliers who still believed that philosophy, at its best, should help people – not just philosophers – think through the business of living, and that this business included cultural processes and trends that defined modern life. These thinkers often traced their intellectual roots to classical American philosophy, and more particularly, to the pragmatism of John Dewey, William James, and C. S. Peirce. There are many ways of defining this philosophical movement, but one of the most basic tenets of pragmatism is the position that truth is to be judged on the basis of its practical consequences. This is the core of what Peirce and James developed as the "pragmatic maxim." Along these lines, pragmatism insists that philosophy be "world-ready" by attending closely to human experience and aiming to enrich it (see Kaag, 2009). This may sound good to many readers, but pragmatism's experiential approach was generally out of synch with twentieth-century analytic philosophy. So pragmatism was largely pushed out of the philosophical mainstream after World War II; its concentration on real-world problems and solutions did not mesh with the hyper-specialization of the philosophical analysts. However, as William Morgan and others observe, this made pragmatism very well suited to the needs of the philosophy of sport (see Morgan, 2000, 2007). American philosophers such as Richard Rorty, John Smith, John J. McDermott, Thelma Lavine and Paul Weiss had ties to pragmatism and created a space for philosophy to investigate the intricacies of twentieth-century culture, which included a wide array of sport activity. Morgan suggests that Rorty, especially, opened the door to the philosophy of sport with his insistence that "philosophy is always parasitic on, a reaction to, developments elsewhere in culture and society" (Morgan, 2000). One of the social developments of the twentieth century was the growing interest in sport, so of course philosophers could and should attend to this trend. Paul Weiss (1969), with his seminal *Sport: A Philosophical Inquiry*, was among the first to do so in any thorough way, which was one of the reasons that he was appointed as the first president of the International Association for the Philosophy of Sport in 1972.

As Morgan mentions in passing, Wiess's intellectual heritage was decidedly pragmatic (ibid.). Wiess's place in the history of American pragmatism has often been understated, but it should not be. Weiss was a student of Alfred North Whitehead at Harvard in the 1920s and, with Charles Hartshorne, worked his way through the papers of C. S. Peirce, the originator of an important strand of pragmatic thought. The fruits of this labor between 1931 and 1935 was the *Collected Papers*, a six-volume set of Peirce's (1960) writings remained the most valuable trove of primary literature in American pragmatism for more than half a century. Weiss was also a doctoral advisor to Richard Rorty, and was most likely responsible for Rorty's surprisingly kind evaluation of Peirce's work. All of this is to suggest that the birth of the philosophy sport as a discipline is inextricably bound to a figure that was very much part of classical American pragmatism. *Sport: A Philosophic Inquiry* (Weiss 1969) defined the landscape of the philosophy of sport for many years and continues to outline many of its most fertile themes. A great deal of work has been done in the philosophy of sport since 1969, but Weiss strikes upon a number of abiding topics in the current discipline. His seminal work – chapter by chapter – also lays out the issues and questions that have always guided American pragmatic thinkers. Indeed, the mere term "inquiry," the word that Weiss uses to describe his project, is at the heart of pragmatism; and Weiss remains faithful to the meaning of the term. Inquiry, in a Peircean or Deweyan sense, is the process of exploring hypotheses, making contextual generalizations and testing these generalizations against the bumps and bruises of experience to see if they hold up. Notably, this is not a view from nowhere philosophy (Morgan, 2007). As Rich Lally has argued (Lally, Anderson and Kaag, 2012), the activity of sport itself can be viewed as this type of inquiry, but Weiss takes the meaning of inquiry to heart in this first attempt at articulating the philosophy of sport. He wrote a draft of *Sport* and sent it out to sport enthusiasts, coaches, players, experts, and other philosophers (among them Richard Bernstein, another contemporary pragmatic thinker). He received feedback and then started from scratch, revising the book from beginning to end. The result, like all effective pragmatic inquiries, delivered Weiss and his readers to a number of beliefs about the nature and meaning of sport. One of these beliefs, however, is unstated and will be made explicit in the coming pages of the chapter: Weiss' seminal work on the philosophy of sport reflects most of the dominant themes of American pragmatism as developed by William James, C. S. Peirce, John Dewey, George Herbert Meade, and Jane Addams.

This chapter, which focuses on the relationship between pragmatism and the philosophy of sport, is structured around these themes, ones that Weiss takes up in his various sections of *Sport*: meliorism and perfectionism, habit formation and embodiment, self and community, feminism and anti-essentialism. Weiss, however, does not exhaust the ways in which these pragmatic lines of thought could be extended in the philosophy of sport. Recently, many other scholars have done valuable work to tie the philosophy of sport even more closely to pragmatism. So, while Weiss' book outlines the way in which the philosophy of sport might draw on the resources of pragmatism, it is necessary in the course of the discussion to highlight the contemporary research on pragmatism and the philosophy of sport. In many cases, this research was conducted by the contributors to the edited volume entitled *Pragmatism and the Philosophy of Sport*, published in 2012 (see Lally, Anderson and Kaag, 2012). The chapter concludes with a critical evaluation of recent work in pragmatism and the philosophy of sport that centers on theoretical issues of realism that Michael Burke has expressed in the last decade.

Meliorism and growth ("concern for excellence")

Weiss opens *Sport: A Philosophic Inquiry* with a chapter that suggests that sport's widespread appeal can be traced to a very basic "concern for excellence." This concern resonates with pragmatism's "meliorism" and gestures toward a type of perfectionism that runs through the writing William James and C. S. Peirce. In *Pragmatism*, William James (1995) elaborates on the pragmatic maxim, suggesting that the point of philosophy is not to provide concepts that mirror or correspond to reality, but rather, study the ways in which concepts and beliefs set a "program for more work, and more particularly as an indication of the ways in which existing realities may be changed." This is an important addition to the earlier discussion of the pragmatic method because it suggests that pragmatism is not simply interested in getting discrete results (pragmatism is often mischaracterized as a crass instrumentalism in this way), but rather focused on the process of effecting positive change in the lives of individuals and their communities. This focus is known as pragmatic meliorism.

As Scott Stroud (2009) observes, James's principle concern is about the way that ideas make practical changes, and more specifically, practical improvements, to the world in which we live. The task of life according to James is to become better than we currently are: better thinkers, better citizens, better runners, jumpers, swimmers, and bikers. James's meliorism – following Ralph Waldo Emerson and other transcendentalists – holds that this sort of progress takes many forms and is possible for every human being, not merely the elite few. According to Weiss (1969), sport activity should be understood along these melioristic lines, as a way for many, many people to pursue excellence in their daily lives.

For most pragmatists, athletes, and philosophers of sport, it is the pursuit of excellence (rather than the achievement of any particular excellent outcome) that is truly worth talking about. Weiss (1969) notes that "Most men have no athletic stature, but many of them participate in sports frequently and with great enthusiasm". But why? William James's philosophy begins to provide a good answer. As Gerald Myers suggests, James believed that "truth is in the making;" the verity of any concrete belief is always only ever provisional and dependent upon an ever-changing context (see Myers, 1986: 302). This does not mean that progress is impossible, but it does mean that our accomplishments – as thinkers and doers – are moments in a dynamic process and are always opportunities for greater refinement. This is an experiential fact that most athletes know with bone-jarring clarity; for many of them sport activity is primarily about practice rather than discrete victories. Doug Hochstetler, in his essay "Process and Sport Experience" articulates this point nicely and argues that pragmatism's process-oriented approach can shed light on the processes of sport activity (see Hochstetler, 2003).

Scott Kretchmar's work in the philosophy of sport reflects similar intuitions, especially the stance that games and sport activity have an aesthetic value that transcends the particular outcomes of victory or loss (see Kretchmar, 1989, 2000). His 2008 article, "Gaming Up Life," (Kretchmar, 2008) draws the writing of Bernard Suits into relation with William James's "What Makes Life Significant" in order to explain the value of struggle in sport activity. And, in the spirit of William James, Kretchmar writes:

> It is possible then that redemption for an activity that produces the frame-induced sting of defeat will be found more in chance, imprecision, hope, and the desire to play again tomorrow … Even if gracious intent on the part of the winner is not required by any offer of a rematch, "playing again tomorrow" is still a very rational and civilized thing for both winners and losers to do.
>
> *(Kretchmar, 2012)*

Drawing on the concept of "thirdness" from Peirce's philosophy, Tamba Nlandu makes a related point in describing the unifying ideal of sportsmanship and the spirit of the game (see Nlandu, 2008). Similarly, Jill Tracey, in her contribution to *Pragmatism and the Philosophy of Sport*, entitled "Living the Injury: A phenomenological inquiry into finding meaning, argues that the partial achievement of such ideas, and meaning-making more broadly, is always done in the midst of the bumps and bruises of life (see Tracey, 2012). This is place where obstacles can be faced but also where progress can be made.

This sort of strenuous progress is at the heart of pragmatic inquiry. It stands in contrast (although not in a mutually exclusive way) to early forms of perfectionism and growth that have defined classical American thinking. For example, Douglas Anderson, who has written extensively on virtually all of the American pragmatists, suggests that the growth that comes with endurance sport can be understood in terms of the humanizing project laid out by transcendentalists such as Henry David Thoreau and Ralph Waldo Emerson. According to Anderson, such physical activities "allow us to realize and re-create ourselves … [and through these activities] we bring our full range of powers and energies to life – we become fully human" (Anderson, 2001: 141). Transcendentalist interpretations of endurance activity differs from a certain pragmatic approach to sport to the extent that this latter take "envision[s] a more Spartan-like goal of preparing a hearty society to face the difficult contingencies of their booming industrial culture" (Hochstetler and Hopsicker, 2012). Pragmatism risks becoming fixated with the notion of progress, a danger that Anderson sidesteps with his use of the transcendentalists. Hochstetler and Hopsicker, however, contend that the pragmatic conception of growth put forward by John Dewey is not synonymous with crass understandings of instrumental progress. They write:

> For Dewey, growth is a continual project, never a particular fixed state or endpoint to be achieved. It is the antithesis of stagnation. He defined growth as 'the ability to learn from experience; the power to retain from one experience something which is of avail in coping with the difficulties of a later situation.
>
> *(Hochstetler and Hopsicker, 2012: 122)*

Throughout the growth process, individuals cultivate habits and a certain degree of plasticity. These habits, writes Dewey, "take the form both of habituation, or a general and persistent balance of organic activities with the surroundings, and of active capacities to readjust activity to meet new conditions" (Dewey, 1944: 44). When individuals stake their claim on endurance sport, for example, they develop this commitment through a series of daily decisions (ibid.).

These "daily decisions" are not made on the basis of discrete successes or failures, but for the sake of ongoing meaning-making embodied in particular habits and shot though with a particular quality of feeling.

Habit formation and embodiment

Many scholars in the philosophy of sport have followed Weiss in his observation that habit formation plays a central role in sport activity. Athletes are not born with good judgment. Rather, efficacious judgment develops over time in the context of practice, through activities that instill good habits. As Will Durant summarizes Aristotle: "We are what we repeatedly do; Excellence, then, is not an act but a habit" (Durant, 2005: 61). Peirce and his fellow pragmatists come out of this Aristotelian school of thought and hold the crucial role of habit in human flourishing. Applying this point to the philosophy of sport, Weiss remarks:

> Good practical judgment is a habit of using good common sense – which is to say, a habit of using reasonable suppositions regarding what is and is to be, and consequently deciding what one is to do, and when and how. The habit is acquired in large part through the course of daily living; it is accentuated in training and stabilized by practice.
>
> *(Weiss, 1969)*

Weiss's discussion reveals something important about the philosophy of sport and the way in which its assumptions converge with those of pragmatism. Judgment is never the product of some disembodied mind. This may seem obvious to every athlete, but many thinkers in the history of philosophy have had trouble grasping the point. Ancient thinkers like Plato and modern ones like Descartes and Kant generally denied that judgment arose from bodily processes and practices, and maintained a strict dualism between the body and the mind. Classical American pragmatists, along with Continental phenomenologists, however, objected to this sort of dualism, arguing that cognition was continuous with bodily practices. The habits of thought and judgment had to happen somewhere, and that somewhere were bodies like ours. William James (1995), who founded empirical psychology with his *Principles of Psychology* in 1890, was one of the most vocal proponents of this position. Recently, philosophers of sport have begun to extend James' insights into embodiment and habit formation, arguing that the process of habituation that James articulates in his psychology maps rather neatly onto the process of becoming a seasoned athlete (see Kaag, 2006). Weiss sets the stage for this work in his description of sport practice:

> The wisdom that the athlete needs is schematically present in him because of what he did in the past. By going through comparable acts again and again under controlled condition, he builds up the power of quickly estimating what a situation demands and how he is to behave in it.
>
> *(Weiss, 1969)*

Peirce and James both maintain that habit provides a type of heuristic shorthand for handling difficult situations, and what seems like a single moment of virtuosity is always, or at least usually, a product of the ongoing process of habit formation. In turn, Weiss (1969) writes: Without habit, [the athlete] will be forced to spend too much time in deliberating and experimenting when he has to be right, fast."

It is worth noting that while habit often delivers athletes to satisfying outcomes with surprising speed, it often does not. In these cases, habit cannot negotiate the newness of experience. This is a fact that pragmatists, especially Peirce and James, readily acknowledged. In Peirce's language, experience happens as a "series of surprises." Henry Bugbee, who was not a pragmatist *per se*, but whose "inward morning" provides deep pragmatic insights into the nature of embodiment and meaning-making, was also pointedly aware of the difficulty of fitting rigid habit to the various contours of experience (see Bugbee, 1999). Elsewhere, I have focused on Bugbee's description of rowing to draw out the pragmatic theme of novelty and adaptation and relate them to the psychology of William James. Modern philosophers of sport, such as Drew Hyland, address similar forms of athletic adaptation via the field of phenomenology (see Hyland, 1984, 1990).

Self and community

Being a good athlete is never simply an issue of developing individual excellence through individual practice. Sport, and therefore the philosophy of sport, reveals the way in which individuals develop good habits in the midst of wider communities, communities that also take on certain habits and dispositions. In terms of athletics, such communities are represented by teams, leagues and conferences; the philosophy of sport is interested in the way in which individuals participate in, and define themselves by, these wider communities. This is a focus that pragmatists have always explored and it is one that sets them apart from many in the history of philosophy who have held that the interests of the community stand in marked contrast to the interests and development of individual selfhood (one could think of the longstanding debates between traditional liberals and communitarians). Weiss was perhaps the first philosopher of sport to underscore the way in which the success or failure of individual athletes turns on the situation of team play, the communal context in which athletes perform. He does so by drawing on the pragmatic sociology of George Herbert Mead and John Dewey, stating,

> Since each player assumes a particular role and internalizes all the other roles [of team play] within himself point forcibly made by George Herbert Mead – blurs the distinction between himself and the others as helping to produce the outcome and as constituted by it.
>
> *(Weiss, 1969)*

Weiss is quite good on this pragmatic point, that selfhood is not atomistic, divorced from the development of wider environs, but is instead co-constituted in a transaction with his or her situation. This is what Weiss calls pragmatism's "contextualism." Daniel Campos has elaborated on this point, explaining the way in which fans and players interact to form soccer teams with unique dispositions and personalities. His analysis is explicitly pragmatist and draws from Peirce's discussion of personality, the unifying principle that underlies the relational unity between ideas (see Campos, 2012). Similarly, Tim Elcombe argues that agape is the proper way to understand effective coaching in his "Agapastic Coaching: Charles Peirce, Coaching Philosophy and Theories of Evolution" (Elcombe, 2012). Mead and Peirce were not the only pragmatic thinkers to argue that community was vitally important to the creation of individual selfhood. William James's (1995) notion of the "social self" in his *Principles of Psychology* and the work that Josiah Royce did in moral psychology at the turn of the century reinforced this point.

Two contemporary scholars, Mat Foust and Brent Crouch, argue that Royce's conception of loyalty provides a useful lens to examine modern sports figures such as LeBron James and Hope Solo (see Foust, 2012; Crouch, 2012). Royce is often excluded from treatment of pragmatism, more frequently characterized as an idealist. But he understood his own philosophy as a type of practical idealism that tried to wed the integrity of ideals with the variety of human experience. His philosophy of loyalty (developed in the first years of the twentieth century) aimed to explain how individuals could embody collective ideals and how these ideals, in turn, shaped the formation of individual selfhood. Foust and Crouch suggest that this philosophy goes a long way in explaining how sport teams function. In Crouch's case, however, he ultimately suggests that Royce's model does not adequately explain the situation of Solo or her role on the 2007 women's Olympic soccer team. Crouch points to another American pragmatic thinker, Jane Addams, to supply a type of care ethics that might better address the troubled relationship between Solo and her team.

Interestingly, Crouch's critical assessment of Royce's thought – and the estimation of its shortcomings – mirror the evaluation that Weiss makes concerning pragmatic contextualism in *Sport: A Philosophic Inquiry*. Weiss writes:

> Contextualist theories, such as those advanced by G. H. Mead and John Dewey [here, we could add Royce's philosophy of loyalty] … are admirably suited to describe the athlete in relation to his body, his equipment, his situation, or in a contest or game. But their very success points to a serious inadequacy. The theories are not able to explain how it is that some men [or in the case of Solo, women] are not well adjusted too these, or why it is that they are not willing to rule-regulate everywhere.
>
> *(Weiss, 1969)*

Crouch (2012), following Weiss, makes the point that work in the philosophy of sport can enrich and revise the standard interpretation of the American pragmatic canon. In some important cases, pragmatism needs to be brought into the present day and tailored to fit new realities.

Pluralism, feminism, and anti-essentialism

In principle, pragmatism is pluralistic. If pragmatism aims to understand and enrich human experience, then it cannot be too choosy about what sorts of experience it starts from. Therefore, pragmatism should be inclusive and open to the experience of individuals who have been traditionally marginalized in society and in the history of philosophy. Here, we see meaningful overlap between social justice movements and pragmatism, and indeed American thinkers such as Jane Addams, Charlotte Perkins Gilman, John Dewey and Alain Locke, who all understood pragmatism's meliorism as extending to the situation of minorities and the under-privileged. What does all of this mean for the philosophy of sport? It means that a pragmatic approach to the philosophy of sport should be interested in the way that sport activity affects and is affected by gender, race, ethnicity, and ability. Pragmatists should remain sensitive to the way that sport is not a one-size-fits-all phenomenon and should be wary of the way that the philosophy of sport can devolve into a sort of ablest mentality.

When we look at Weiss's *Sport: a Philosophic Inquiry*, we see him making gestures in these directions, particularly in his treatment of women in sport. These gestures are undoubtedly insufficient (they were being made in 1969, three years before Title IX was passed into law), but they give pragmatic philosophers of sport a starting point in creating a feminist-friendly philosophy of sport. Weiss opens his discussion of women athletes with the question, "Are women athletes to be viewed as radically and incomparably different from men or as comparable with them, both as amateurs and professionals." That this is a question at all for a philosopher in 1969 is significant; that Weiss opts for the latter option (that women and men deserve to be compared when it comes to many aspects of sport activity and opportunity) is a step in the right direction, but more certainly deserves to be done along these lines, work that Weiss himself is often reticent about taking up. Indeed, many feminist sport philosophers railed against his analysis of the relationship that women athletes have to their bodies (see Young, 1980).

Historically, sport has been a gendered activity. It was thought that men and women were essentially different – that they possessed radically different natures – and therefore the activities they engaged in were to be radically different as well. This idea results from what is commonly known as "gender essentialism." Gender essentialism holds that what it is to be a man and a woman is circumscribed by nature and that there are natural differences between the sexes that express themselves as necessary differences in behavior. Pragmatism, with its emphasis on practice and transformation through experience, tends to reject all forms of essentialism. There is no fixed and immutable character that defines men and women and therefore the experience of sport should be equal for and open to gender. At many points in his analysis of women athletes, Weiss supports this stance, explaining that women's general absence from the field of sport can be attributed to their being prohibited from practicing certain activities. As a remedy, Weiss states, "A woman must train and practice if she is to become an athlete … women can improve the functioning of their bodies. This is best done through exercise. And it can be helped through a vital participation in games" (Weiss, 1969). Weiss is not always consistent, however, when he continues to explain the physical training that he has in mind for women athletes: "Their training follows the same general procedures followed by men, with account of course being taken for their difference in musculature, strength, attitudes toward exhaustion, injury and public display" (see Weiss, 1969).¹ Here, Weiss steers off course, belying the very essentialism that pragmatism hopes to eschew. Pragmatists would suggest that dispositions – such as an attitude toward exhaustion and public display – are not essential or biologically determined, but socially defined and reinforced. This position is stated quite clearly in Jane Addams' work with immigrant population in Chicago at the turn of the nineteenth century. Differences in behavior, according to Addams, could almost always be traced to differences in cultural circumstances and context. Indeed, her educational project at Hull House was geared at changing this context for hundreds of underprivileged women in the Chicago area; her success suggested that nurture, not nature, largely determined the potentials of human beings. Weiss and other earlier philosophers of sport occasionally miss this point. At other times, Weiss maintains, in good pragmatic form, that women avoid sport because they "are more firmly established in their roles as social beings, wives and mothers" and therefore have little time for the self-cultivation that can occur in sport activity (ibid.).

In the decades that followed the writing of *Sport: A Philosophic Inquiry*, philosophical work was done in the midst of the debate surrounding Title IX, which supported pragmatist-feminist commitments. In terms of theoretical sophistication, Iris Marion Young's "Throwing Like a Girl" (first published in *Human Studies* in 1980) is unmatched. Young analyzes "feminine" bodily comportment, underlining the ways in which women come to feel inhibited and objectified in bodily processes such as sport performance. This theoretical work has been imported directly into the philosophy of sport, most recently by Leslie Howe in "Play, Performance, and the Docile Athlete" (2007) and by Joan Grassbaugh Forry (2012) in her valuable contribution to *Pragmatism and the Philosophy of Sport*. Here Grassbaugh Forry ties the writings of Shannon Sullivan and those of John Dewey into relation with the feminist scholarship in the philosophy of sport. What is significant in reference to the earlier discussion of habit formation is that Sullivan and Grassbaugh Forry explain the way that habits are constitutive of personhood, and that restrictions on certain actions (like the prohibition against women participating in certain sports) significantly interferes with the formation of women as flourishing individuals (see Tännsjö, 2000; Postow, 1983; and Howe, 2007).

Pragmatism as theoretical intervention

To this point, pragmatic themes have been used to analyze a number of topics in the philosophy of sport. This approach is the one that Weiss and a number of contemporary philosophers of sport have used to employ the insights from the pragmatic canon. In my opinion, it is the most appropriate way to use pragmatism in the philosophy of sport, since it grounds discussions in the experience of athletes and their wider communities in order to enrich and understand this experience. There is, however, another way of using pragmatism that has gathered speed in a number of disciplines including the philosophy of sport.

Recently, many disciplines such as international relations, sociology, and anthropology, have turned their attention inward toward the status of the disciplinary claims that they make, to the basic metaphysical and epistemological assumptions that they make in the course of their investigations. Recently, the philosophy of sport has made a similar move to examine itself and its foundational beliefs abut the nature of sport. This, in turn, generates hot debate between scholars who take sides that, at least in the philosophy of sport, have been characterized as "realist" or "anti-realist." This debate boils down to a disagreement about the status of knowledge claims and the ability to make such claims in reference to particular experiential situations. Can one make claims about a situation if he or she is not in the particular context in question? How can one get perspective on a situation if he or she is in the midst of it? Are there objective facts or values about the phenomenon of sport? These questions have been voiced for years in the history of philosophy. Indeed, the realist/anti-realist debate is a very old one and has taken many forms in the history of philosophy. Sometimes it is called the realist–subjectivist debate. At other points it is referred to as the difference between realism and nominalism. In any event, pragmatism, which emerged at the end of the nineteenth century was intimately familiar with all of these debates and attempted to intervene in the metaphysical and epistemological squabbles. It is therefore of little surprise that contemporary disciplines see pragmatism as a way of ending their in-fighting by providing middle-range theories that have normative weight but are also subject to some revisions (much like habits). This mediating role of pragmatism is on display in political science and international relations theory (see Kaag and Kreps, 2012).

Unfortunately, with perhaps the exception of Giacobbi *et al.*, scholars in the philosophy of sport have not understood pragmatism as making this sort of theoretical intervention in their field of study (see Giacobbi *et al.*, 2005). Instead, some writers, like Davis and Dixon, come too close to equating pragmatism with the linguistic turn of Richard Rorty and therefore dismiss it as nominalist and unable to make reliable normative claims. According to Davis, the papers in the philosophy of sport that draw on Rorty's philosophy: "confine themselves to describing the process by which change occurs in sport, without making any normative judgments about whether any particular change is desirable or justified" (see Burke, 2006). To be clear, this is a criticism that has always circulated around Rorty's work and the philosophy of sport risks rehashing some very detailed debates that have already taken place in contemporary epistemology and metaphysics. Michael Williams' *Unnatural Doubts* (1995) is particular good on the way that Rorty's philosophy borders on idealism and nominalism, the very sort that classical pragmatists like Peirce took pains to avoid. Michael Burke has defended Rorty from this critique in a way reminiscent of Richard Bernstein's attempt to save Rorty from being characterized as a relativist (see Burke, 2006).

While Burke's project is generally well founded, I hope that a pragmatic philosophy of sport avoids getting bogged down in the attempt to save pragmatism from itself. Pragmatism often erred and, as Anderson (2001) points out, when it does it is best simply to own up to its shortcomings (in Anderson's case, it is better to use the transcendentalists than the classical pragmatists for certain ends). Pragmatism is not a sacred canon that deserves to be defended at all costs. Rorty was more nominalistic than James and much more nominalistic than Peirce, both of whom held that experience should hold a central place in any philosophical outlook. And Peirce, at least, thought of himself as a realist. This is to suggest that pragmatism should not be regarded as an inviolable whole, but rather as a diverse canon that can and should be used for different purposes. For example, Rorty might be more nominalistic than Peirce, but he is arguably more attuned to culture and social–political realities than Peirce ever was. This might make Rorty rather unhelpful when it comes to analyzing meaning and bodily comportment (something Peirce and James are quite good on) but extremely helpful in shedding light, for example, on the way that advertising affects the supposedly eternal Olympic ideals. And this difference in emphasis is fine.

There is a great deal of secondary literature on pragmatism and the differences of interpretations on the writings of pragmatic thinkers. There is little need for other disciplines to repeat this interpretative work and every need for them to acquaint themselves with the literature that is already out there. This is not to chastise philosophers of sport; contemporary pragmatists working on exegetical and interpretive projects are often wholly unaware of the developments in adjacent and potentially friendly fields of study. Today, pragmatists often neglect sport and writing about sport, and pragmatism as a disciplinary subfield is "thinner" (to use a Jamesian expression) and less interesting because of this neglect. Unfortunately analytic philosophy, with its desire to parse reality with fine and rigid distinctions, has a certain allure (and respect in this academy) and it often attempts to pull both pragmatism and the philosophy of sport into its wake. It is my hope that together pragmatism and the philosophy of sport can resist this draw.

Acknowledgements

I would like to thank Matt Minigell for his assistance in the research and formatting of this chapter.

Note

1 For a detailed treatment of Addams feminism, see Hammington (2006). Scholars interested in the relationship between pragmatism and feminism should consult Charlene Haddock Seigfried (1996).

References

Anderson, Douglas. (2001). "Recovering Humanity: Movement, Sport and Nature." *Journal for the Philosophy of Sport*, 28(2): 140–50.

Bugbee, Henry. (1999). *The Inward Morning*. Athens: University of Georgia Press.

Burke, Michael. (2006). "Response to Dixon and Davis: Answering Realists With Antiepistemological Pragmatism." *Journal of the Philosophy of Sport*, 33(1): 78–99.

Campos, Daniel. (2012). "Peircean Reflections on the Personality of a Futbol Club." In *Pragmatism and the Philosophy of Sport*, Richard Lally, Douglas Anderson and John Kaag (eds). New York: Lexington, 33–46.

Crouch, Brent. (2012). "Gender, Sports and the Ethics of Teammates." In *Pragmatism and the Philosophy of Sport*, Richard Lally, Douglas Anderson and John Kaag (eds). New York: Lexington, 105–15.

Durant, William. (2005). *The Story of Philosophy*. New York: Simon and Schuster.

Elcombe, Tim. (2012). "Agapastic Coaching: Charles Peirce, Coaching Philosophy and the Theories of Evolution." In *Pragmatism and the Philosophy of Sport*, Richard Lally, Douglas Anderson and John Kaag (eds). New York: Lexington, 89–104.

Foust, Matt. (2012). "Where Should LeBron's Loyalty Lie? Where Should Ours? In *Pragmatism and the Philosophy of Sport*, Richard Lally, Douglas Anderson and John Kaag (eds). New York: Lexington, 77–88.

Giacobbi, Peter R., Jr., Poczwardowski, Artur, and Hager, Peter. (2005). "A Pragmatic Research Philosophy for Sport and Exercise Psychology." *Sport Psychologist*, 19(1): 18–31.

Grassbaugh Forry, Joan. (2012). "Towards a Somatic Sport Feminism." In *Pragmatism and the Philosophy of Sport*, Richard Lally, Douglas Anderson and John Kaag (eds). New York: Lexington, 125–54.

Hammington, Maurice. (2006). *The Social Philosophy of Jane Addams*. Champaign, IL: University of Illinois Press.

Hochstetler, Douglas. (2003). Process and sport experience. *Quest*, 55(3): 231–43.

Hochstetler, Douglas and Hopsicker, Peter Matthew (2012). "The Heights of Humanity: Endurance Sport and the Strenuous Mood." *Journal of the Philosophy of Sport*, 39(1): 117–35.

Howe, Leslie. (2007). "Play, Performance, and the Docile Athlete", *Sport, Ethics, and Philosophy*, 1(1): 47–57.

Hyland, Drew. (1984). *The Question of Play*. Lanham, MD: University Press of America.

Hyland, Drew. (1990). *Philosophy of Sport*. Ann Arbor, MI: Paragon House.

James, William. (1995). *Pragmatism*. Dover Philosophical Classics. Mineola, NY: Dover.

Kaag, John. (2006). "Paddling in the Stream of Consciousness." *Journal of Speculative Philosophy*, 20(2): 132–45.

Kaag, John. (2009). "Pragmatism and the Lessons of Experience." *Daedalus*, 138(2): 63–72.

Kaag, John, and Kreps, Sarah. (2012). "Pragmatism's Contributions to International Relations Theory." *Cambridge Review of International Affairs*, 25(2): 191–208.

Kretchmar, Scott. (1989). "On Beautiful Games." *Journal of the Philosophy of Sport*, 16: 34–43.

Kretchmar, Scott. (2000). Moving and Being Moved: Implications for practice. *Quest*, 52: 260–72.

Kretchmar, Scott. (2008). "Gaming Up Life." *Journal of the Philosophy of Sport*, 35: 142–55.

Kretchmar, Scott. (2012). Competition, Redemption, and Hope, *Journal of the Philosophy of Sport*, 39(1): 101–16.

Lally, Richard, Douglas Anderson and John Kaag (eds) (2012). *Pragmatism and the Philosophy of Sport*. New York: Lexington.

Morgan, William. (2000). "The Philosophy of Sport: A Historical and Conceptual Overview and a Conjecture in Regard to Its Future." In *Handbook to Sport Studies*, J. Coakley and E. Dunning (eds). London: Sage, 204–11.

Morgan, William. (2007). "Why the View from Nowhere Gets Us Nowhere in Our Moral Considerations of Sport." In *Ethics in Sport*, W. Morgan (ed.). Champaign, IL: Human Kinetics, 85–102.

Myers, Gerald. (1986). *William James: His life and thought*. New Haven, CT: Yale University Press.

Nlandu, Tamba. (2008) "Play Until the Whistle Blows: Sportsmanship as the outcome of thirdness." *Journal of the Philosophy of Sport*, 35(1): 73–89.

Peirce, C. S. (1960). *Collected Papers of Charles Sanders Peirce*. Charles Hartshorne and Paul Weiss (eds). 3 vols. Cambridge, MA: Harvard University Press.

Postow, Betsy C. (ed.) (1983) *Women, Philosophy and Sport: A Collection of New Essays*. Metuchen, NJ: Scarecrow.

Seigfried, Charlene Haddock. (1996). *Pragmatism and Feminism: Reweaving the social fabric*. Chicago, IL: University of Chicago Press.

Stroud, Scott. (2009). "William James on Meliorism, Moral Ideals, and Business Ethics." *Transactions of the Charles S. Peirce Society* 45(3): 378–410.

Tännsjö, Torbjörn. (2007). "Against Sexual Discrimination in Sports." In *Ethics in Sport* (2nd ed.). William J. Morgan (ed.). Champaign, IL: Human Kinetics, 347–58.

Tracey, Jill. (2012). "Living the Injury: A phenomenological inquiry into finding meaning." In *Pragmatism and the Philosophy of Sport*, Richard Lally, Douglas Anderson and John Kaag (eds). Lanham, MD: Rowman and Littlefield, 155–74.

Weiss, Paul. (1969). *Sport: A Philosophic Inquiry*. Carbondale, IL: Southern Illinois Press.

Williams, Michael. (1995). *Unnatural Doubts: Epistemological realism and the basis of scepticism*. Princeton, NJ: Princeton University Press.

Young, Iris Marion. (1980) "Throwing Like a Girl: A Phenomenology of Feminine Bodily Comportment Motility and Spatiality." *Human Studies* 3: 137–54.

15

THE RADICAL CRITIQUE OF SPORT

Lev Kreft

In this overview, radical critique of sport is understood as critical theory of sport set in the framework of allegedly agonistic and tragic crisis of humanity, where sport has, if not the main, then an extremely important place among those pillars which support existing state of affairs. Four radical critique cases of different cultural, geopolitical, and philosophical origin were selected for examination: Ljubodrag Simonović (Serbia), Roman Vodeb (Slovenia), Jean-Marie Brohm (France) and Douglas Kellner (USA). Because of its connectedness with the 1960s, the most important aspects of the New Left legacy to radical criticism of sport (ideology, alienation, manipulation) are identified in all four cases; global media spectacle is presented as a universal target of radical criticism; and the curious attitude towards emancipation of body, gender and lesbian, gay, bisexual, and transgender (LGBT) is exposed. From indebtedness of radical critique of sport to Marx and Marxism, appearance of the most quoted Marx's metaphor "opium of people" is analyzed. The next, and final, presentation concerns a radical criticism of Olympism. In conclusion, some contradictions of the radical critique of sport are discussed.

Introduction

Modernity and modernism

At the peak of his glory, Louis the Great, or the Sun King, had just one problem: what would happen to his empire after his death. He decided to give the dauphin (his heir) the best education possible. One of the people in charge was Jacques-Bénigne Bossuet, who had to teach the dauphin about his responsibilities to humankind and its universal history, from the Creation to his father. Starting with divine providence as the motor of eternal human progress, he wrote a textbook in which, in spite of all troubles and catastrophes, one can discover that the flow of human history climbed to more and more perfect heights, to reach the highest point of all times with Louis the Great and keeping doors open for further progress under his heir and successor. Bossuet's book on universal history appeared in 1679. During the early 1670s, members of the French Royal Academy were involved in a quarrel between the ancients and the moderns. On the surface, it was a struggle between those who claimed that art was not part of progressive history, because its ideal models were already produced by the ancients, and those who believed that new works of art could be much better than old works, because those who come later knew the ancient past, but also their own present, which the ancients could not. But the essence of this quarrel was the claim that there never existed a greater and better empire of more magnificent and more beautiful art than under the reign of Louis the Great: this kind of argument silenced the ancients, and the moderns won the quarrel.

These two stories demonstrate what modernity and modernism are about. Modernity is the present, which is, at the same time, the most progressive point of all human history, and a springboard for further progressive expanding in space and time. Modernism is a praise sung of such a present and its future potentials: an ideology of modernity. The twentieth-century crisis of belief in modernity changed the ideology from modernism to postmodernism. Whatever the change, we doubt today that it should necessarily be for the better.

Sport is a child and a part of modernity, especially with its inclination to constant expansion in records. The Olympic idea, at least up to now, is a rare example of the ideology of modernism untouched by postmodern skepticism.

Critique and critical theory

The notion of critique occupies a central place in the philosophical logic of modernity. The first person to use and develop it into concept and method was Immanuel Kant. Between his and our philosophical critique, there are many steps which went in different directions. To find the radical critique of sport, we follow the path which brings us from Kant to Marx and from Marx to the Frankfurt school and critical theory.

Kant's philosophical problem was how to confirm that three fundamental abilities of human mind are possible sources of the progress of humanity, developing of secure knowledge of the world of nature (pure reason) and of the reign of human action (practical reason), and then turning the field of nature into a homeland of human freedom (judgment) (Kant, 1914: 7–42). To achieve this, he decided to criticize all three abilities apiece, with the aim of limiting their competences inside borders within which they can operate sovereignly. The purpose was to avoid their use outside the territory covered by their sovereign power, and to avoid conflicts of these abilities over territories of their competence. The end of critique was to put the movement of enlightenment and its philosophy, after decades of conflict between rationalism and empiricism, on sure ground again. From such a solid ground, enlightenment, engaged with the emancipation of humankind, could progress further.

At the beginning of the nineteenth century, after the French revolution and Napoleon's defeat, German reality was still far below standards of its philosophy. The Hegelian left, a group of young radical philosophers, used Hegel's dialectic against its systematic totality to put forward the German claim for unity and emancipation. Karl Marx, then 23 years old, accepted the idea of emancipation, but criticized political emancipation as dissatisfactory: political emancipation is emancipation of the state from people. To reach the state of human emancipation, more radical change is needed than just a political change – a universal change in everyday practice where human beings must become the highest criterion of all social relations (Marx, 1970). The highest point of his radical critique was later articulated as a critique of political economy, where revealed contradictions of capitalist production become a weapon in the hands of workers organized as an international proletariat. Numerous critical theories came forward to heal the conflicts in capitalist society, but Marx's was the one which influenced critical theory the most.

Adherents, and those who were influenced by critical theory, are already in a third and fourth generation. The first generation started after the First World War as an Institute at the Goethe University in Frankfurt am Main, and is thus called the Frankfurt school (consisting of

Max Horkheimer, Theodor W. Adorno, Herbert Marcuse, Leo Löwenthal, Erich Fromm, among others). Departing from Marxist orthodoxy, they critically reflected upon: 1) the failure of social democracy which, instead of acting internationally against the First World War, supported the imperialist ends of their national bourgeoisies; 2) the failure of post-war revolutions, which left only the Russian revolution in power. That capitalist imperialism was the reason for the war, and its actual winner, was general the post-war opinion. In critical circles, which, before the war, still believed that capitalist society could be humanized by modern art and culture, this idea was now abandoned: modern culture was part of the problem, not its solution. The Frankfurt school still favored Marxist criticism, but with more emphasis on a critique of the superstructure than a critique of political economy. From their point of view, the proletarian revolution had its moment after the First World War and lost it. The existence of "socialism in one country", the Soviet Union, did not impress them as it did many others, and their contribution to the critique of Stalinism is no less important than their criticism of Nazism and fascism. As enemies of Nazism, and as Jews, they had to leave Germany, and, after few years in Paris, they settled in the USA until the end of the war. Their position, that the Second World War came as the solution to the economic crisis of capitalism, together with totalitarian political systems, troubled the Frankfurt school and critical theory thereafter. They claimed that totalitarianism was not something attacking modern liberal society from the pre-modern past, but its own product, emerging from the instrumental reason and from the tendency to construct (and in social practice, to control) the instrumentalised totality of natural, human and social life. Another crucial problem was why there was no revolution against this totality. Turning their backs on the critique of political economy, they developed a critique of ideology, alienation and manipulation. This included the third fundamental tenet of their criticism: liberal society, presumably the opposite of totalitarianism, developed totalitarian tendencies through mass culture and its practices of pacification of social conflicts without resolving them. It is in this promised land of entertainment where sport also belongs – but sport became a target of critique only later, with the second and further generations of critical thinkers.

The ideas of the Frankfurt school circle, known earlier just to a few specialized intellectuals and critical thinkers, became a much broader intellectual movement during the 1960s. Here, the ideas described above became public property, and started to mix with many other theoretical movements and philosophical ideas. This hybridization developed into the 1970s, when many different versions of critical theory appeared, which included elements of post-structuralist philosophy, cultural studies, other versions of Marxist tradition, theoretical post-modernism, theoretical psychoanalysis, and others. It is as hard to describe what is common to all these different versions, as it used to be difficult to say what is essential for Marxism and who therefore are genuine Marxists a few decades ago – including the inconclusive debate about the Marxist character of critical theory itself. As a consequence, there is no longer a unified critical theory, but a collection of differences and hybrids. Their family resemblance, however, comes more from the 1960s than from its first generation founders.

Radicalism and radical critique of sport

Radicalism is a certain attitude of modernity that demands the elimination of present society, and the rebuilding of the world anew from its roots upwards. It offers just one choice, since there can be no turning back. A special kind of "radicalism in reverse" appears when one believes that crucial opportunities for revolution were lost. Critical theory, especially during first generation of the Frankfurt school, was such a reversed radicalism. The moment for radical change appeared after the First World War, when capitalism was in a shambles and revolutions ensued. But the moment was lost, revolutions were defeated, or were, in case of Russia, an isolated event which developed into a tragic caricature. Can one expect another revolutionary moment, and with it another chance? Perhaps not. In a world resistant to radical change, radical criticism assumes a tragic position: its criticism is true, but prospects of radical change are next to none.

Radical critiques of sport are not to be understood simply as any kind of strong criticism of sport, or simple rejections of sport as a humanly and socially harmful activity. It is critical theory of sport only when put in a framework of tragic and agonistic crises of humanity. In this chapter, I focus on the radical critique of sport that emerged when sport became a globalized, post-industrial, professional spectacle. Of course, there were critiques of sport before these developments, but I focus on contemporary radical criticism of sport as it developed after the 1960s, as a "fellow-traveler" in sport's global growth and success. To distance theoretical radicalism from simple rejection of sport (and from those cases where sport is incidental to radical critiques), I discuss those theories and their philosophies of sport that are "literally" radical. By that, I mean criticism which digs beyond the surface to criticize the assumed roots of sport and criticism, which, even more radically, dissects sport because it is viewed as a crucial product of the contemporary global crisis of humanity. Criticism of sport is a prevalent and heterogeneous phenomenon, but there are not many cases of criticism that are truly radical.

I analyze four cases of radical criticism of sport in this chapter: Ljubodrag Simonović, Jean-Marie Brohm, Roman Vodeb and Douglas Kellner. At a first glance, they belong to different national and cultural traditions: Serbia, France, Slovenia, and the USA, respectively, and represent nuanced intellectual modes and embrace differences in sport traditions as well. Their ideas cover much ground, but it has still to be admitted that, of all possible sources of critical theory of sport, a German example is missing from this selection.[1]

Ljubodrag Simonović (b. 1949, Serbia) had an impeccable professional basketball career, and in his heyday was one of the best players in Europe. At the 1972 Olympic Games, Yugoslavia lost to Puerto Rico in the second round; interestingly, at least two Puerto Rican players were found guilty of doping, but Olympic authorities decided to ignore their offences. In protest, Simonović protested that he did not want to continue with the tournament, and was expelled from the national team as a result. He concluded his professional basketball career in Bamberg (Germany) in 1978. After that, he obtained a Master's degree in law and a Ph.D. in philosophy. His radical position, besides the criticism of sport, includes anti-capitalism and ecological concerns, but he betrayed his critical outlook by supporting Milosević and Serbian nationalism, and homophobia.[2] I examine his critique of Coubertin's ideology and his analysis of professional athletes as little more than robots, ideologically shaped to serve the interests of capitalist profit making, below.

Jean-Marie Brohm (b. 1940, France) is Professor of Sociology at the University of Montpellier III (Paul Valéry). His academic career was devoted to radical critique, with a radical critique of sport as its main focus and self-definition. His criticism of sport started in 1968, during the student revolt, and he established a journal and a group called *Quel Corps* in 1975, which was active until 1997, when the group decided to end their activities. In 2002, Brohm became editor in chief of the journal *Prétentaine* (to gallivant, to gad about). His philosophical sources are Marxist-based, but not as much in critical theory as in Althusser's critique of ideology, and in Debord's criticism of the development of the modern public spectacle. His sources, however, include all the critical theoretical positions on the French stage, from psychoanalysis (Freud, Lacan, Reich) to post-structuralism (Foucault, and others). His position is different from that of Althusser, because Brohm, starting with the New Left and student protests, adheres more to the radical New Left than to traditional communist positions, which he criticized early on, to include Western humanistic Marxism and Soviet Marxism alike. His is a figure of the radically engaged academic intellectual typical for French culture, and an "official outcast" in sport and mainstream academic circles. Of his many works, I focus attention on his critique of Olympism, and his general overview of sport as the "opium of the people".

Roman Vodeb (b. 1963, Slovenia) started as an elite gymnast at national level, continued as gymnastic coach, and after ten years of coaching graduated from the Faculty of Sport at the University of Ljubljana, where he subsequently received a Masters degree in 1996. He then changed fields into social and human studies; after taking a Master's in sociology he produced a Ph.D. thesis on the psychoanalysis of sport, which was not accepted by the university authorities and was therefore never publicly defended (and thus not awarded). Nevertheless, he published books and articles, and became a sport commentator in journals and at TV stations. In 2007, he became an independent researcher and counselor. His work is based in Freud (and not on Lacan, as is the Slovenian psychoanalytical school, together with its most celebrated figure Slavoj Žižek), and Althusser's critique of ideology. His theoretical positions made him famous in Slovenia, while at the same time, resulting in his marginalization. I present his psychoanalysis of sport and critique of the unfinished transition from socialist to liberal ideology of sport in Slovenia.

Finally, Douglas Kellner (b. 1943, USA) studied philosophy at Columbia University, then in Germany (1969–71) and France (1971–72), where he became interested in the Frankfurt school of critical theory and French post-structuralist thought (Foucault, Deleuse, Baudrillard, Lyotard). His combination of critical and post-modern theory is blended with British cultural studies. Perhaps that is why he focuses on case studies as his main source of criticism. He spent the first period of his academic career at University of Texas (Austin; 1973–97). He then became Professor of the Philosophy of Education at UCLA. Beside his academic work, he is very active as a commentator of political processes in the USA, well known for his criticism of the Bush presidency, and for his intellectual activist writings on his personal blog.[3] His interests are spread widely, but are more or less connected with his core work: new media in context of contemporary capitalism. In 2006, he was included on a list of UCLAs radical leftists ("winning" third place), which was presented by right-wingers as softer version of McCarthyism's blacklisting. From his work, I examine his research on Michael Jordan and his Nike relationship, where he analyzes how sport images are built by media spectacles, and how these function as important moments of capitalist economy and society.

These authors, taken together, create a field of differences and similarities, of which two circumstances deserve to be stressed: the persistent presence of the ideas inherited from 1960s (New Left with the concepts of ideology, alienation and manipulation; new media spectacle and its criticism; emancipation of the body) and adherence to Marx's claim that religion is "the opium of the people" (Marx, 1970). To these two features, we will add radical criticism of Olympic ideology. What is now required is the setting of a context for their thoughts on sport.

Overview

The period of 1960s is more than two generations away, but the origin of both radical critique and sport as global phenomenon can be traced back to this period. Brohm and Kellner were actively involved with radical movements of the time: Brohm in France, as an activist of "New Left", and Kellner in the USA as a protester against the Vietnam War. Simonović was still following his professional basketball career, and Vodeb was too young to have been active. Nevertheless, each was influenced by the 1960s, at least in three respects, which are common to all four: (i) New Left theories and ideologies; (ii) the appearance of global media spectacles including sport spectacles; and (iii) the change in the body politic from asceticism to pleasure.

The New Left is the name given to those leftist ideologies and theories which differed from inherited social-democratic (including socialist and labor) and communist positions, which lacked intellectual coherence, and disappeared during the period of disillusionment of the 1970s and the post-modern cynicism of the 1980s. What persisted was its commitment to radical criticism, which was equally skeptical of Marxist, Western and Eastern orthodoxies, but was still influenced by both of them. Critical theory – with the famous Frankfurt school as its founder – was very important, but what most typified the times were numerous theoretical, ideological and political movements and sects. There were three main concepts elaborated in different ways: *ideology*, *alienation* and *manipulation*. These three concepts are still critical to their point of view.

Ideology, alienation and manipulation

Ideology is an old concept, coined by Destutt de Tracy in 1796 to signify the science of ideas. It was used against him and other liberal thinkers by Napoleon, who was also the first to use it in another, negative sense: false ideas based on wishful thinking and selfish interest. Marx explained that false consciousness is not false because ideologues are incapable of scientific analysis of reality, but because reality itself is – false reality: "To call them [people] to give up their illusions about their condition is to call on them to give up a condition that requires illusion." (Marx, 1970) In contrast to the Marxist conception, contemporary usage of "ideology" can be classified as either "neutral" (merely describing a system of ideas) or "biased", (designating false consciousness of a criticized object or one's opponents), or "dialectic" (designating illusions which are produced because reality itself is "ideological"; that is, a false reality that would be unbearable without ideological illusions). This shift is not always explicitly acknowledged and authors slide from one meaning to another in the radical critique of sport. Some authors explore this concept and develop its definition, other are satisfied with simply using it. Simonović is in the latter category. He does not explicitly apply the term, but his theoretical effort is meant to unmask Coubertin's reactionary ideology that runs through Olympism in his books about the Olympic deception of the "divine baron" Pierre de Coubertin (Simonović, 1988) and the philosophical aspects of modern Olympism (Simonović, 2002). In *Pobuna Robota* [Rebellion of Robots] (Simonović, 1981), the competitive nature of sport is described as an ideology of efficiency that turns athletes into robots. After 1989, he adhered to an anti-Western ideology, which was the dominant political ideological position in Serbia. Athletes' body movements, like everything else in culture, are not immune to ideological manipulation: "Body movement in sport is not an expression of natural or 'divine' being of human; it is a phenomenal form of anti-cultural and anti-existential spirit of capitalism" (Simonović, 2007: xx).

The other three critical theories are more developed. Jean-Marie Brohm attacks sport ideology in a similar way to Simonović, including the Olympic ideas (Brohm, 2008), and links Coubertin and Carl Diem to the rise of National Socialism. The Olympic Games and the International Olympic Committee, the latter a "self-perpetuating oligarchy" in sport similar to that of *Komintern* in communism (Brohm, 2008: 15) and are largely, in his view, ideological props. Following Marx, Brohm takes ideology to mean false consciousness, as confirmed by the title of one of the chapters from *La Tyrannie Sportive*: "La Fausse Concience Sportive" – sport's false consciousness) (Brohm, 2006: 129–42). Sport is not just another innocent game; it is, rather, "a pernicious ideological vision of the World" (Brohm, 2006: 115), which inverts all values by converting right into wrong and *vice versa*. That is what ideologies do: "a transposition of principle of reality into mystifying phantasmagoria under primacy of wishful thought, here as "magic" metamorphosis of capitalist society with its social conflicts, class struggles, destructive and self-destructive violence into exotic universe, charming and seductive, into oneiric oasis [a never-never land] with its mirrors, hallucinations, legendary heroisms and its mythological narrations" (Brohm, 2006: 115). This Philippic style is supported by theoretical elaborations, with three ideological mechanisms at work in the "Disneyland of sport" (Brohm, 2006: 131): the first is negation of any ideological distortion of sport that parades itself as apolitical (Brohm, 2006: 131); the second comes from a near-schizophrenic dissociation between ecstatic official sport discourses and a corrupt reality, which calls for even stronger ideologization (Brohm 2006: 135–6); the third mechanism is the production of performative discourse, which falsely presents sport as an autotelic and autonomous activity (Brohm 2006: 140). This is where sport becomes a kind of religion, and is expected somehow to solve the problems and contradictions of contemporary capitalist society of which it is just – an ideology; that is, false consciousness.

Roman Vodeb, who is extremely critical of sport ideology preached by the totalitarian priests of sport education, uses ideology in more neutral manner, starting from a combination of Freud's psychoanalysis, Foucault's analysis of power, and Althusser's critique of (spontaneous) ideology. Where and how do these three come together? Vodeb writes:

> Without the engagement of psychoanalysis, epistemological discourse on sport is dead – that is our belief, and that is why we have chosen an epistemological context for what we have to say. By linking Freud, Foucault and Althusser we want to hint at theoretical aberrations and nebulous ideas in which sportology [Vodeb's term of art for the sport sciences] has found itself today. Researchers are seduced by such aberrations, because they assume from the outset that there must be some close, even causal, relationship between sport and health. Thus, they ignore pleasurable experiences and other derivations of libido, which are, as they see it, responsible for the social etiology of sport. These fixations can be traced to sport ideology itself. On the one hand, sport ideology is to blame, because it sought to turn sport into an immaculate sacred cause; on the other, the spontaneous ideology of scientists – 'sportologists' is to blame, as it is nothing else but scientific ideology as philosophically exposed by Althusser.
>
> *(Vodeb, 2001: 306)*

Following Freud, each subject is bound by the principle of pleasure, and is thus looking for delight. Ideology is an invitation to join the "already delightful", which has been socially constructed to allow the subjects' pleasure. In liberal and democratic societies, these ideological invitations are forms of social control: subject to the pleasure principle in the guise of free choice. Not so in totalitarian societies, where choice is preempted by the state, which prescribes what kind of pleasure is obligatory, and which forbidden. On one side, Vodeb is introducing the concept of ideology as an inevitable atmosphere which emerges from the primal experience of the subject's position in its relationship to father and/or mother. From the other side, however, Vodeb wants to get to the truth (just as any traditional enlightened scientist would) and therefore tries to mark a line that separates scientific efforts from ideological. As a consequence, his main target is the spontaneous ideology of Slovenian sport scientists who, under transitional circumstances, still cling to the state ideology of sport because it gives them more powerful pleasure than its liberal opposite. Douglas Kellner understood ideology as contradictory field of false ideas, but also of utopian dreams. In Marxist tradition, his approach is nearer to Ernst Bloch than to critical theory, as he himself declared (Kellner, 2010). Bloch claimed that, in our culture, most artifacts and practices contain a mixture if ideology and utopian elements. This two-sidedness leads to the conclusion that even when we find elements of ideology (that is, errors and mystification, as well as the world-view of the ruling class), we have to search for utopian elements which deny ideology's right to rule in the same cultural artifacts and practices. Kellner follows this understanding of ideology in his research into sport culture as well.

The most important source of the concept of *alienation* is Hegel, who insists that *Geist* (spirit/mind) has to become estranged from its own self and to inhabit its opposite, but only to master its substance and then to overcome it. Still, an opposing account argues that our identity, previously solid and complete, is lost in alienation. In the 1960s, to become a "real" or "authentic" being was imperative. Alienation was the enemy, and this idea of alienation persists in radical critique: sport is seen as a field of total alienation of the individuals and especially of the masses, where our authenticity is lost. As we have already seen, Simonović does not elaborate his categories and concepts theoretically; he uses them as a weapon and as a tool of interpretation that sheds new, radical light on relations of contemporary sport. These relations are undoubtedly alienated. Play is, as he claims in accordance with Western Marxism and its humanist orientation, the ultimate form of being human. Sport *qua* play is a non-alienated form of human expression, but professional sport is, by contrast, alienated by virtue of its negation of play. Contemporary athletes are, therefore, largely alienated robots.

Roman Vodeb has another notion of alienation. The source of our human "essence" is rooted in the primal family situation, where principles of pleasure and reality conflict with the figure of the father. From this situation comes the urge to compete. Alienation means to turn away from reality and enter the world of pleasure. Athletes and artists turn away from reality. The world of pleasure is different for men and women, because men find pleasure in competition and victory, whereas women find it in beauty. Women are discriminated against in sport, claims Vodeb, but that happens because as athletes in men's sports, they have to become "male women". This radical picture triggered numerous attacks against his theory. His conservative psychoanalysis arrives at similar conclusions as Camilla Paglia (1992) did. She fights against the postmodern insistence on the exclusively social background of gender differences, and gets back to sex as an uninhibited and unstoppable natural power.[4] For both Vodeb and Paglia, competitiveness is a natural and authentic drive. Vodeb accepts that the state has to control society, because otherwise it will be unbalanced by these natural drives. What he finds unacceptable is the state issuing commands: "You have to do sport!" and "play sport to become healthy and reduce obesity". The state should instead facilitate sport and decisions to engage in it. To promote health as reason for sport means to alienate sport from its basic pleasures. If sport is not a free choice, and if it is done for health and not for pleasure, it is alienated activity.

Brohm and Kellner both have very elaborate concepts of alienation – but their positions are quite different. In *La Tyrannie Sportive*, Brohm (2006: 93–142) devotes the second section to alienation in sport. Sport is a "totalized" social fact (an expression taken from Marcel Mauss, 1966: 76). A social fact is called "total" when it appears in all social phenomena from religion and economy to culture and politics. That is what sport has become as a result of the global media, capitalist economy and oppressive state ideology, including "alienated mass psychology of sport spectacle with its mortifying violence" (Brohm, 2006: 84). The radical critique of sport functions against the grain of alienation and its pleasures. Brohm's critical theory is based on the Frankfurt school: contradictions cannot be resolved in soft theorizing about "good" and "bad", "right" and "wrong" sides of phenomena. These two sides are inseparable. In sport, this means that looking for a way out that would preserve the good of sport and remove the bad is impossible. The de-alienation of sport necessarily requires the deconstruction of sport. In this context, Brohm attacks the sport ideology of health, as Vodeb does, but for different reasons.

Vodeb wants to stress that sport has to be "unhealthy" because of its deep demonic forces; Brohm criticizes the competitive character of sport because of its dependence upon capitalist ideology, which, he argues, is the source of the ideology that sport is healthy activity.

The problem of alienation is not elaborated in Kellner's (2003) *Media Spectacle*. We get more insight from his article on "New Technologies and Alienation" (Kellner, 2006: 8) where we are confronted with the multilevel and manifold effects of a social transformation "either to produce forms of alienation or contribute to disalienation". Alienation of the sports spectacle and of professional sport stars is exemplified by Michael Jordan's position in the global business world:

> Indeed, Nike engages in superexploitation of both its Third World workers and global consumers. Its products are not more intrinsically valuable than other shoes but have a certain distinctive sign value that gives them prestige value ... While Michael Jordan tries to present himself as the embodiment of all good and wholesome values, he is clearly tainted by his corporate involvements with Nike in the unholy alliance of commerce, sports spectacle, and celebrity.
>
> *(Kellner, 2003: 82)*

There is, moreover, another side to observe:

> Although Jordan's contradictions and tensions were somewhat suppressed by his ideological halo, to some extent Jordan always was his own contradictions ... Michael Jordan's combination of athletic prowess and his association with fashion, cologne, and the good life always made him a potential transgressor of bourgeois middle-class family values and propriety. Although Jordan's family values images articulated well with the conservative ethos of the Reagan–Bush I era (1980–92), there was always an aura of threatening sexuality and masculinity in Jordan, who was a potentially transgressive figure.
>
> *(Kellner, 2003: 86)*

The sport spectacle, global business world, and media celebrity culture: all three meet in the figure of Jordan. What is interesting for our analysis is not just a fact that we have processes of alienation at work (in relations between the "real person" and its "media presentation", between media product and fascinated consumers, between sport and market values etc.), but the fact that we are not completely lost in estrangement, because all alienating processes contain disalienation as a possibility as well.

As a label for mass culture behavior, the concept of '*manipulation*' was more frequently used in the past than it is today. But it is not absent from the radical critique of sport. To take an example from critical cultural studies of sport, which does not belong to radical critique: in *Sport, Culture and Advertising: Identities, Commodities and the Politics of Representation* edited by Steven J. Jackson and David L. Andrews (2005), the authors make no mention of the concept of "manipulation," and one cannot even find the term in the book's index. In the editors' "Introduction," however, they cite the following crucial questions from Graham Murdock's article on corporate dynamics and broadcasting future: "We also need to ask who orchestrates these representations? Who is licensed to talk about other people's experience? Who is empowered to ventriloquize other people's opinions? Who is mandated to picture other people's lives? Who chooses who will be heard and who will be consigned to silence, who will be seen and who will remain invisible? Who decides which viewpoints will be taken seriously and how conflicts between positions will be resolved? Who proposes explanations and analyses and who is subject to them?" (Murdock, 1999: 28). Radical critique of sport, quite similarly, may not use the term itself, but it answers these questions in diagnostic terms that suggest both totalitarian manipulation, and the softer, manipulating kind characteristic of management.

Simonović points out conscious and direct manipulation in sport, from Baron de Coubertin onwards, because he sees elite competitive sport as form of manipulation designed to pacify the masses and massive conflicts of capitalist society. Now sport serves to neutralize the consciousness of those who would otherwise rebel against the system, and to turn athletes into obedient robots: "With the support of TV program human being itself is programmed, his behavior is guided and space of his freedom is framed" (Simonović, 1985: 17). Brohm agrees that professional athletes look like robots coming from the laboratory (Brohm 2006: 10), but he understands the manipulative function of sport in the context of Tocqueville's critique of democracy's potential to become democratic despotism; in which political economy's "invisible hand" is turned from an ideological into an ontological category; and in the context of sport as religion of the people. When he attacks the mainstream understanding of sport as "culture, integration, peace, liberty, brotherhood etc.," (Brohm, 2006: 14), he characterizes sport as "*servitude sportive*" [sport slavery] (Brohm, 2006: 15). Tyranny is sport itself, not some person or persons that construct a despotic society: it is a democratic society that allows sport to serve such a tyrannical social function. The result is the "massification of conscience", a process which blinds people to sport's negative features such as its sanction of violence. In sport, we are all equal, as members of stupefied crowds.

> With the acceptance of the universal value of the market, as represented by the "invisible hand," the European left in effect, promoted the "*ontologization* of the invisible hand". The invisible hand, Adam Smith's well-known metaphor, is now recognized as governing power. Sport is its most powerful machinery, which turns the invisible hand into an unmovable rock, upon which "mediatized manipulation" does its work.
>
> *(Brohm, 2006: 84)*

At the same time, sport becomes a secular religion, what Marx calls the "opium of people". I discuss this metaphor later in the chapter. Vodeb is one more step away from a "Wizard of Oz" understanding of manipulation, but on the other hand, he accepts manipulation as natural state of affairs. What manipulates us is an inevitable unconscious force. It "manipulates" us into sport as well, because sport is a domain of pleasure in competition. What he presents as social and political manipulation is limited to the transitional struggle between liberal and statist ideologies of sport. Kellner is focused on media spectacle, which "is becoming one of the organizing principles of the economy, polity, society, and everyday life." (Kellner, 2003: 1) Each of these basic structures of social life is turned into entertainment in which its traditional logic and purpose is obscured. He starts from Debord's (1994) idea that contemporary societies are "organized around the production and consumption of images, commodities, and staged events." (Kellner, 2003: 2) His focus is different, because "while Debord presents a rather generalized and abstract notion of spectacle, I engage specific examples of media spectacle and how they are produced, constructed, circulated, and function in the present era." (Kellner, 2003: 2)

The difference in approach is a difference in general theory. Debord presented his case as "society of spectacle", which is manipulating crowds with pleasurable recuperation, to pacify radical ideas and possibilities; Kellner's concrete analysis makes visible media culture as a field of conflicting and manifold tendencies. Manipulation becomes enculturation into contemporary society's basic values and into its way of life (Kellner, 2003: 3), as "a social system predicated on submission, conformity, and the cultivation of marketable difference." The manipulative character of media culture, however, is not monolithic: "Thus, the spectacle is always contradictory, ambiguous, and subject to reversals and flip-flops so that a political administration and celebrities can never be sure if they will be beneficiaries or victims of the vagaries of spectacle politics" (Kellner, 2003: 16). Manipulators turn into the manipulated, and vice versa. There is not a definite division of society into one and the other, and the system is not monolithic but open to reversals, which opens it to "détournement" [rerouting][5] – turning media culture against its manipulating intentions.

New media spectacle

To mark its distinction from the old media of books and movies, "new" media are still called "new" but they are not new any more. The 1960s were a turning point, when television, with the help of satellite broadcasting, became global, and when new technology enabled genuinely televised production. To be able to watch directly what is happening on the other side of the Earth at that very moment (or even on the Moon) was an attraction in itself; the ability to produce pure entertainment put television immediately on a pedestal as the most important medium.

The transmission of visual material in the home and family situation stimulated critical voices even in its early days, but when it became easily accessible and the most popular entertainment, these voices multiplied. A radical critique of spectacular entertainment came from Guy Debord. The first part of his "spectacle" critique was published in 1967, and his *Comments* in 1988 (Debord, 1998). The title of his 1967 work (*Society of the Spectacle*) has to be understood literally: his is not a theory of spectacles organized in society but a theory of society organized as a spectacle. Debord introduced three types of spectacle: concentrated, diffuse, and integrated. In the first type, spectacle takes the form of a totalizing portrait of power reflective of centrally planned and bureaucratically controlled societies; the second, diffused type, by contrast, typifies liberal democratic and market economy societies. Both kinds of spectacles mixed together produce an integrated kind of spectacle, that builds society without a way out of it. In 1988, a year before the fall of the Berlin wall, Debord put the difference between the two alternative systems (communist and capitalist) aside, so that all three kinds of spectacle function globally and locally as a triad of a spectacular social system of power with an occult controlling center. It is called "occult" since it is, as Claude Lefort[6] would put it, "the empty place of power" which nobody can occupy, but in Debord it represents all moves of power, including those of democracy, as ghostly and uncontrollable. To these three kinds of spectacle, Steven Best and Douglas Kellner (Best and Kellner, 1999) added another, fourth kind: megaspectacle. Megaspectacle represents global scandals – events such as the Gulf wars, the melodrama of the death of Princess Diana's, the terrorist attacks on the USA of September 11, 2001, the trials and travails of Lance Armstrong or Oscar Pistorius. These events are (re)produced in and by media culture, where, as Jean Baudrillard might say, reality is indiscernible: events do not happen in reality, they are always staged in hyperreality where it is impossible to differentiate between "real" and "virtual". Here is the difference between critical theories of spectacle, and radical theory: in radical theory, society itself is spectacle. Radical critique of sport recognizes sport as a constitutive moment of such a society.

Vodeb could not put sport spectacle in central focus, because he accepted from Freud a position that crowds do not behave much differently than individuals, and because he does not acknowledge the essential difference between direct and mediated presence. Simonović is similar. His attention is more on aggressive masses at stadia than on global media spectacle. He compares contemporary sport with Roman spectacles because they are both "death games"; he even composed an anti-ode for London Olympics: "The London Olympics: The Death Games" (Simonović, 2012). Another of his interests to do with spectacles concerns the passivity of watching television: free time turned into time of enslavement. Brohm claims that spectacular sport can be traced to the 1936 Olympic Games in Berlin:

> Finally, the Berlin Games were the first really modern Games. Organized with symbolic apparatus which belonged to the Nazis, they installed protocol which more or less persists up to now: release of pigeons, Olympic fire and its travel from Olympia, mass procession, official account of medals won by nation-states, etc. On the other hand, the Berlin Games were the first to profit from all the technologic innovations which consequently turned the Olympic spectacle into immense publicity show. With the Berlin Games, for the first time the world itself has been presented as a spectacle.
>
> *(Brohm, 2008: 50–1)*

Today, international competitions are the zenith of sport production, which is totally commodified in the process of universal spectacularization, and which puts "living commodities in the service of dead commodities" (Brohm, 2006: 10). His main target is sport as a crucial embodiment of global capitalism, and not spectacle as such. Sport spectacles are the most important part of the entertainment industry (Brohm, 2006: 103–4) that turns reality into a "mystified and mystifying phantasmagoria" – to borrow from the German philosopher Walter Benjamin:[7]

> the "magic" metamorphosis of capitalist society with its social conflicts, class struggles, destructive and self-destructing violence, into an exotic universe, charming and delightful, and into a dreamlike oasis with its mirrors, hallucinations, legendary heroes and mythological narratives.
>
> *(Brohm, 2006: 115)*

All these social functions turn sport spectacle into "inversion of the real" (Brohm, 2006: 119) and into "performative illusion" (Brohm, 2006: 140).

Media spectacle is one of Kellner's main concerns (the other two being critical theory itself, and research into post-modern technology and science). The title of the first chapter in his *Media Spectacle* (Kellner, 2003) defines his focal issue: "Media Culture and the Triumph of the Spectacle". Sport contributes to this triumph. What makes the difference in the otherwise long history of spectacle, from the ancient times of all cultures onwards, are new media and informational technology. On one hand, reality and life are transformed into "entertainment"; on the other, guiding figures of the post-modern global world are celebrities produced to (re)present basic values and to become valuable commodities themselves. His case studies are many and from different fields (McDonaldization, Michael Jordan and Nike, O. J. Simpson and his trial, the "X Files"). Sport spectacle is just one field, but not an unimportant one. The "public wedding" between Michael Jordan and Nike is interesting because Jordan "embodies the success ethics and the quintessential capitalist ideal of competition and winning" (Kellner, 2003: 64). He is (or was) the greatest athlete and global media spectacle, "combining his athletic prowess with skill as endorser of global commodities and as a self-promoter", which "calls attention to the extent to which media culture is transforming sports into a spectacle that sells the values, products, celebrities, and institutions of the media and consumer society" (Kellner, 2003: 63–4) Sport spectacles and their celebrities are the focal crossing point where the necessity of the reproduction of contemporary global capitalism is effected, and where all borders and limits between divided fields and realms of culture, politics, and economy become blurred. Kellner's approach has a recognizable post-modern touch. Still, his critical stance is stronger than his relativism. Because it became spectacle, sport is now part of the reproduction of the capitalist ethic. It is not just a replica of work, as Bero Rigauer argued in 1969 (Rigauer 1981). It is media spectacle which "attests to the commodification of all aspects of life in the media and consumer society" (Kellner, 2003: 66).

In their respective views on spectacle, all four authors have something in common: the spectacle appears at the same time as attractive entertainment and as means of social surveillance over masses. In *Downcast Eyes*, Martin Jay wisely put Foucault and Debord in the same chapter (Jay, 1993: 381–434): Foucault represents the critique of panopticon as an allegory of contemporary society, where everybody is put under the surveillance of Big Brother's eye; Debord's critique of spectacle as allegory of the same society, is one, by contrast, in which everybody is watching and nobody is living any more. To put Debord's and Foucault's approach in connection with each other, we have to step back to Marcuse's incorporation of Freud into critical theory. Marcuse introduced two new categories dealing with the pleasure and reality principles: repressive desublimation, and non-repressive sublimation. From this point of view, the panopticon and spectacle are not two different ways to establish control over society and its members, they are one: in spectacle, everybody wants to see and watch, but also to be seen and watched. What all four authors describe and analyze as sport spectacle's most important characteristic is repressive desublimation: by entertaining themselves, masses exert social surveillance upon themselves.

The body and sport

The 1960s are famous for the emancipation of bodily pleasure(s), sexual emancipation (including the women's liberation movement, the emancipation of lesbians and homosexuals, or, later, the whole LGBT community) and for opposition to all kinds of asceticism and repression of "natural needs". Yet the emancipation of sensual pleasures did not include sport: the intellectualist dismissal of sport as body practice is one important reason why sport was largely overlooked. But the arguments of critical theorists changed that. It was not the physical side of sport which was dismissed now, but its fetishistic metaphysical function in commodified and mediatized universe. In the radical critique, sport has not been seen as part of the emancipation of senses and of body, but as part of biopolitics, specifically, the exemplar of the disciplined body. We can still find traces of this characteristic in contemporary radical critique. But there is another, more curious, contradiction here. The emancipation of (sexual) pleasure was (and is) not without its own tensions. Mainstream emancipation, while attacking ascetic patriarchy, was still reduced to male emancipation and oriented towards male pleasures, so that female and LGBT emancipation had to attack traditional patriarchy and male emancipation at the same time. In radical critique, this conflict still matters. Sport is not criticized just for its functional position in perpetuation of capitalist order but for its attitudes toward male and female, and heterosexual and homosexual athletes as well. Of our four authors, two: Vodeb and Simonović, were, and still are, involved in a bitter fight with feminist and homosexual critical voices. There are traces of this problematic attitude in Brohm as well. Vodeb claims that women practice sport to please their symbolic father figure in an unnatural way, not to compete for attention in terms of their sexual attractiveness and beauty, but to turn themselves into physically competitive men. At the same time, he believes that sexual orientation is decisive for personal and social experience, so that homosexuals have a different position in sport than their heterosexual counterparts. Simonović's views are openly homophobic:

In contemporary capitalism, movements are created of growing numbers of homo-sexuals, which would, according to Marx's "humanism–naturalism", fall under the classification of degenerated sociability and, consequently, degenerated naturalness … In the homosexual relationship. The human body loses its genuine erotic dimension and is instrumentalized in an unnatural and inhuman way.

(Simonović, 2011)

In his criticism of the Berlin Olympic Games, where he argues how close the Olympic move-ment's leadership and Nazism really were, Brohm concludes:

This corporeal ideology of askezis [asceticism], of purity, of discipline, of conformity, of sacrifice, of suffering and of hierarchy is shared by sport and fascism, and is evidently in its instinctual basement closely bound with repressed or sublimated homosexuality.

(Brohm, 2008: 211)

This is not a new aspect of fascist and National Socialism's anamnesis, not even in connection with sportive body, but it is interesting that what appears in Vodeb's "orthodox Freudism" as the male character of sport, is here presented as sublimated homosexuality.

The difficulties with male–female and with LGBT in radical critical analyses of sport make it clear that some radical critiques of sport can generate consequences which are at very least problematic. Their appearance is a sign that some motives of radical critique of sport have noth-ing to do with enlightened criticism oriented towards emancipation and liberation.

Marx and the "opium of the people"

Karl Marx is undoubtedly one of the most influential radical thinkers. Surprisingly, in radical critiques of sport, the most cited of his concepts is his famous metaphor "opium of the people" found in the introduction to *A Contribution to the Critique of Hegel's Philosophy of Right* (Marx, 1970), which contemporary critics of sport seized on to establish that sport has become a substitute for religion.

Simonović mentions opium *for* and not opium *of* the people when he compares sport with the industry of death (Simonović, 2002). Sport spectacles are criticized as being similar to Roman spectacles. Contemporary rituals, according to Simonović, are at the same time rituals of death, and give rise to a new sort of mass religious movement which represents "flowers on the chains"; that is, consolation and substitute instead of real pleasure and happiness. Vodeb (2001) does not refer directly to opium of the people, but obviously considers desire and pleas-ure to have the same hallucinatory effect. Brohm (2006: 14) uses opium of people as one of his two most important theoretical categories (the other is false consciousness). "Really, the term opium of the people with its evident Marxian if not Marxist connotation has no meaning but in the language of Critical theory of sport," (Brohm, 2006: 22) where it occupies a place of "central significance: sport, opium of people" (ibid: 23). And then one of his typical tirades follows:

Indeed, sport as opium cannot be reduced to one of its multiple aspects – fanaticism, chauvinism, xenophobia, racism, anti-Semitism, sexism, hating opponents, hooligan violence, bellowing of fans, mass emotions, intellectual regression, spectacle of gladi-ators, taste for symbolic death executions, all these facets which I have tidily dissected, as it represents a synthetic totality of a kind called by Theodor W. Adorno "exhortation to happiness," "illusory pseudo-satisfactions because of which the established order still can survive," and precisely because they reinforce the established order by concealing exploitation, alienation, oppression and domination, are never discovered by positivist sociologists who belong to a pre-established social harmony and to already existing "values of sport culture".

(Brohm, 2006: 23–4)

For Brohm, sport is compared to religion because he believes that religion used to be, and sport now is the most dangerous enemy of the people. Kellner makes no such claim, but even he found something of religious significance in the sport spectacle:

Moreover, the sports spectacle is at the center of an almost religious fetishism in which sports become a surrogate religion and its stars demigods. For many, sports are the object of ultimate concern (Paul Tillich's definition of religion), providing transcendence from the banality and suffering of everyday life.

(Kellner, 2003: 69)

This preoccupation with the connection between religion and sport, and with linking this comparison to Marx's opium metaphor needs further elucidation. "The opium of the people" was not coined by Marx. It comes from the enlightenment critique of religion, when it was used for instance by de Sade in 1797 and Novalis in 1798. Marx is actually saying exactly the opposite: "For Germany, the criticism of religion has been essentially completed, and the criticism of religion is the prerequisite of all criticism" (Marx, 1970). When criticism of religion is completed, the critique of Hegel's philosophy of right can begin, leading to criticism of the human world, society and state. Religion is the opium of people, because it is "the fantastic realization of human essence since the human essence has not acquired any true reality" (Marx, 1970). Obviously, the critique of religion is not enough. Even more, critique "has plucked the imaginary flowers on the chain not in order that man shall continue to bear that chain without fantasy or consolation" (Marx, 1970). In the radical critique of sport, the order of things is the opposite. If critique of sport would be analogous with the critique of religion under Marx's terms, it would be dismissed as something which should be over and done with, so that critique of the actual reality and not of its phantasmagoric reflection – the critique of right and of political order (or later the critique of political economy) could begin. In the radical critique of sport, the status of this critique is, contrary to Marx, analogous to the critique of political economy.

How is it possible that, with the radical critique of such various cultural and philosophical backgrounds, the equation of sport and religion goes hand in hand with understanding of sport as fundamental pillar of global order? One of the reasons is the need to explain why people do not revolt against repression and exploitation. Another is a post-modern inclination to transfer the accent of criticism from "reality", which ceased to be clearly discernible, to images and their phantasmagorias, where flowers themselves are treated as chains. Marx and Engels (1976) had an answer to that in the first sentences of *The German Ideology*, mockingly describing the Young Hegelians' diagnosis of phantasmagoric and ideological rule which makes people blind to reality, and their proposals for various therapies:

The phantoms of their brains have got out of their hands. They, the creators, have bowed down before their creation. Let us liberate them from the chimeras, the ideas, dogmas, imaginary beings under the yoke of which they are pining away. Let us revolt against the rule of abstract thoughts. Let us teach men, says one, to exchange these imaginations for thoughts which correspond to the essence of man; says the second, to take up a critical attitude to them; says the third, to knock them out of their heads; and – existing reality will collapse. These innocent and childlike fancies are the kernel of the modern Young–Hegelian philosophy.

(Marx and Engels, 1976)

The problem with radical critique of sport is neither its radicalness nor its dubious use of Marx's notion of opium but rather its insistence on the imaginary and phantasmagoric side of sport and other spectacles of media culture as the only reality, which leaves them with just one and only "therapy": to knock these images out of people's heads.

The Olympics

The Olympic movement and the Olympic Games get no attention in Douglas Kellner's and Roman Vodeb's works, because Kellner's focus is on American sports spectacles and Vodeb's on the psychoanalytical substance of sport. Jean-Marie Brohm and Ljubodrag Simonović, on the other hand, have written books on Olympic ideology, and on the decisive influence of their founder, Baron Pierre de Coubertin. Coubertin was not a theoretical thinker. His works are rather an eclectic mixture with an accent on Thomas Arnold's pedagogy of sport, Le Play's positivism, and Herbert Spencer's evolutionism.[8] Both critics see Coubertin as a reactionary reformer who offered athletic placebos rather than genuine solutions to class conflicts, and sought instead to integrate exploited people into society, and to propagate fundamental bourgeois values (competition, hierarchy of success, military discipline, colonialism, nationalism and even racism), and who dangerously courted fascism and Nazism in his support for the 1936 Berlin Olympic Games, and in later expressions of his admiration and thankfulness for the Nazi regime and its leader. In both authors, these accusations are well supported by Coubertin's writings and statements, and the 1936 Games are just a tip of the iceberg of his beliefs about sport, not just a mistake or a casual step aside. If we put together their general diagnosis of sport's function in contemporary global capitalism, and Coubertin's reforming intentions, we arrive at a conclusion not offered by either Brohm nor Simonović: if Coubertin's intentions were to pacify conflicts of capitalist society, and to integrate masses into such society and its basic values with the help of sport, he was extremely successful, as both authors prove with their radical criticism of contemporary sport.

Final commentary

The source of modern philosophical critique can be traced to the Enlightenment. Its initiative was two-fold. First, at the beginning of the seventeenth century, critique was formulated in the name of reason and deployed to criticize all institutions, beliefs, and customs from the position of reason as the highest judge; in short, to substitute reason for unreason. Then, with Kant's approach to the crisis of enlightenment in the second half of the eighteenth century, philosophical critique started to criticize reason and other abilities of the human mind itself, not so much to dethrone reason as to make it stronger and sharper in accord with the limits of its ability. During the nineteenth century, social conflicts inspired many kinds of criticism, not all of them philosophical, and not all of them enlightened, but many of them radical in both a revolutionary and reactionary sense. The twentieth century added extreme criticism to all those versions in between. Making sport the main target of radical critique is still the exception rather than the rule. The analysis of these four cases confirms that the first kind of critique, which turns its object into an enemy to be unmasked, prevails over the self-criticism of critique itself: over Kant's moment of philosophical critique. This exposes two of radical critique's weak points, both bound up with the dialectics of criticism. The first one is a tendency to flatten the historical development and contemporary situation of global sport to expose its negative side, which leaves "knocking sport out of our heads" as the only solution. By contrast, a dialectical approach would have to accept that "alienation" deserves philosophical critique not only because it is "negative" with regard to human authenticity, but also because human authenticity is developed only through "alienation" and its conflicting and contradiction-riddled development. This means that the solution would lie not outside the criticized phenomenon but, rather, inside it. The second one is a consequence of the first: when one paints the masses enjoying their pastimes, for instance sport, as deluded – as if under the influence of an opiate – the only way out is to put them into detox. But how can the masses take such a significant step of their own free will? Put simply, they cannot. The radical critique of sport, confronted with this fact, cannot but patronize sport crowds and underestimate their critical abilities. But to underestimate people is the very opposite of enlightening them.

While criticisms of sport offered by radical critique are often well deserved, radical critique itself has to be criticized for its non-dialectical approach to social criticism and for its caricaturing sport spectators as doped and intoxicated masses. On the one hand, as in Vodeb, it can come too close to naturalizing the human inclination to seek pleasure, so that any effort to change how spectators act counts at best as crude (manipulative) social engineering. On the other hand, as in Kellner, it can come close to realizing the critical ideals of the enlightenment in its critique of critical theory, and its incorporation of cultural studies and postmodern approaches to the study of new media and new technologies (including new technologies of power and government). And yet, as in Brohm, it sometimes appears as merely angry invective directed at sport-absent philosophical self-criticism and dialectical understanding. And it even can, as in Simonović's writings, become simply extreme right-wing criticism and ideology. It is this confusing and convoluted mixture of radical thought that deserves critical scrutiny itself so that the legitimate criticisms of sport it does make are not lost sight of but become critically preserved. Philosophy of sport is a discipline that questions anything but the right of its object to exist. It criticizes bad sport and promotes good sport. The radical critique of sport criticizes the right of sport to exist, and therefore does not attack only what philosophy of sport says about sport but what it stands for; that is, the existence of its object itself. Consequently, the philosophy of sport and the radical critique of sport rarely meet in the same room and, when they do, they dismiss each other without profound philosophical argument. Philosophy of sport, even when it is criticizing its object, remains an eulogy of sport; radical critique of sport, even when it admits to the attractiveness of sport, wants to uproot and eradicate it. This article is an attempt to find a language of communication between them, so that an account of the radical criticism of sport is brought to the attention of the philosophy of sport together with what it has to offer as critically sound. At the very least, a familiarity with the critical theory of sport can help the philosophy of sport steer clear of ideological accounts of sport that overplay its utopian potential and underplay its harsher, dystopian side.

Notes

1   *Sport and Work* is one of the rare works in critical theory of sport translated from German (*Sport und Arbeit*; Rigauer 1969) into English (Rigauer 1981), and its main thesis that sport is not the other of work but its mirroring copy is well known. If one wants to find more information on the relation

between the Frankfurt School critique of sport, there is German monograph edited by the Brazilian scholar Alexandre Fernandez Vaz (2004). Another collection of German critical texts on sport was edited by Jörg Richter (1972), but, other than that of Bero Rigauer, the most interesting approach is that of Gerhard Vinnai (b. 1940) who published a book on football as ideology (Vinnai 1970) and edited a book on sport and class (Vinnai 1972). Bero Rigauer's book *Sport and Work* (1969, 1981) represents early German critical theory of sport at its best. The main addressee of the book is Karl Diem (1882–1962), the central figure of German sport and Olympic movement from the First World War to the first bid for Olympic Games in Munich, with the Berlin 1936 Games and his Nazi career in between. In his writings as ideologue and historian of sport and Olympic movement, Diem insisted on the fundamental difference between sport as a free-time activity, and work as a paid activity of necessity. Rigauer, on the contrary, argues that modern sport is structured as work, which means that sport does not differ from the repressive regime of work. In sport, the same idea of efficiency is applied as in factory working process broken down into smallest moves repeated on an on, best illustrated by Charlie Chaplin at conveyor belt in his last silent movie "Modern Times". On the other hand, sport is industrialized mass culture activity, which turns free time into a time of standardized mass consumption and ideological manipulation. After this seminal work, however, Bero Rigauer did not publish much about sport, and while critical examination of sport lives on in his and other German sociologists, his position, developing from critical theory towards figurational sociology of Norbert Elias, can hardly be called radical, and does not appear as a source in contemporary radical criticism of sport.

2   A younger generation of critical sport theorists, such as Milorad Gačević and Tamara Đorđević, has developed a radical critique of sport based on the biopolitical theories of Foucault, and the radical critique of capitalism in *operaismo* and Antonio Negri. Milorad Gačević graduated from the faculty for sport and physical education (University of Novi Sad); Tamara Đorđević achieved her Ph.D. at the faculty for visual arts (University of Arts in Belgrade).

3   His blog, called *BlogLeft: Critical Interventions*, is available online at https://groups.yahoo.com/neo/groups/blogleft/conversations/messages/56 (accessed October 13, 2014). He alsp has a well-developed personal website, available online athttp://pages.gseis.ucla.edu/faculty/kellner/flash/kellneraug8.swf (accessed October 13, 2014).

4   Paglia's main thesis, which concerns Western art, is that there is unity and continuity through the whole history of Western culture, without any fragmentation (as modernism and post-modernism seem to suggest), because Christianity never conquered pagan thought, which remains at work in artistic eroticism, in astrology and in pop culture (where, by the way, sport belongs as well). This pagan core of Western culture comes from two brutal pagan forces: sex and nature. This is where feminists should look for their starting point: both forces are embodied in the figure of the Mother. The title of this work (*Sexual Personae*) suggests that the artists of Western art history are natural, sexual pagan beings wearing cultural masks or social veils: society is artificial construction to prevent the catastrophic release of natural forces. Still, violence always comes out, because violence is a an indelible part of human nature. Sexual liberation is thus an oxymoron: sex is rather a demonic power of nature. Women need more repression to become socially sustainable beings, because their chthonic natural essence is stronger. Conteporaneity (the book was first published in 1990) is an epoch when pagan sex and violence burst out of suppressed state, and over into thin Christian alluvion.

5   *Détournement* is a technique designed by the Lettrist International and later accepted and developed by Situationist International during the 1950s as a subversive practice which is to reveal the wearing out and loss of importance of the old cultural spheres (Debord and Wolman, 1956).

6   Claude Lefort, a French philosopher known for his political philosophy, marked the difference between authoritarian/totalitarian/despotic political regimes, and democratic regimes, as a difference between occupied seats of power, and empty places of power (Lefort, 1986).

7   Walter Benjamin used this term, which also appears in Marx's analysis of the fetishism of commodities, to characterize the irrational forms of material presence of the commodified world found in the megalopolis environment of Paris of the nineteenth century, and its interiorization in the mass conscience of modern capitalist civilization: social reality is experienced as phantasmatic dream and state of intoxication. Those interested in Benjamn's notion of profane illumination can consult Benjamin (1999) himself, or the seminal study by Susan Buck-Morss (1989).

8   Thomas Arnold (1795–1842) was a well-known reformer of sport education as headmaster at Rugby School; Frédéric Le Play (1806–1882) was a French engineer, sociologist and economist with proposals for new organization of labor and for social reform, who was installed as ideological leader of Paris International Exhibition of 1855 by Napoleon III. Herbert Spencer (1820–1903) was a British

philosopher, biologist, sociologist and liberal politic thinker famous for coining the phrase "survival of the fittest", but whose synthetic philosophy is more than just pure philosophical Darwinism.

References

Benjamin, W. 1999. *The Arcades Project*. Cambridge: Belknap.

Best, S. and Kellner, D. 1999. "Debord and the Postmodern Turn: New Stages of the Spectacle". *Illuminations*. Available online at www.uta.edu/huma/illuminations/kell17.htm (accessed October 16, 2014).

Brohm, J.-M. 2006. *La Tyrannie Sportive: Théorie critique d'un opium du peuple*. [Tyranny of Sport: Critical theory of opium of people]. Paris: Beauchesne.

Brohm, J.-M. 2008. *1936: Jeu Olympiques à Berlin* [1936: Olympic Games in Berlin]. Waterloo: André Versaille.

Buck-Morss, S. 1989. *The Dialectics of Seeing: Walter Benjamin and the Arcades Project*. Cambridge, MA: MIT Press.

Debord, D. 1967. *La Société du Spectacle*. Paris: Buchet-Chastell.

Debord, D. 1998. *Comments on the Society of the Spectacle*, trans. Malcolm Imrie. 2nd ed. London: Verso.

Debord, D. 1994. *The Society of the Spectacle*, trans. Donald Nicholson-Smith. New York: Zone Books.

Debord, G., and Wolman, G. 1956. *A User's Guide to Détournement*. In *Situationist International Anthology*, K. Knapp (ed.). Berkeley, CA: Bureau of Public Secrets.

Jackson, Steven J. and Andrews, David L. (eds) 2005. *Sport, Culture and Advertising: Identities, Commodities and the Politics of Representation: Identities, commodities and the politics of representation*. Abingdon: Routledge.

Jay, M. 1993. *Downcast Eyes: The denigration of vision in twentieth century French thought*. Berkeley, CA: University of California Press.

Kant, I. 1914. *Critique of Judgement*, trans. J. H. Bernard. London: Macmillan.

Kellner, D. 2003. *Media Spectacle*. London: Routledge.

Kellner, D. 2006. "New Technologies and Alienation: Some Critical Reflections". In *The Evolution of Alienation: Trauma, Promise, and the Millennium*, L. Langman and Kalekin-Fishman D. (eds). Lanham, MD: Rowman and Littleford: 47–68.

Kellner, D. 2010. "Ernst Bloch, Utopia and Ideology Critique", *Vlaams Marxistisch Tijdschrift*, 44(2): 40–8.

Lefort, C. 1986. *The Political Forms of Modern Society: Bureaucracy, democracy, totalitarianism*, John B. Thompson (ed.). Cambridge: Polity.

Marx, K. (1970) [1844]. *A Contribution to the Critique of Hegel's Philosophy of Right*, trans. J. O'Malley. Oxford: Oxford University Press.

Marx, K. and Engels, F. 1976. [1845–46]. *The German Ideology: Critique of Modern German Philosophy According to Its Representatives Feuerbach, B. Bauer and Stirner, and of German Socialism According to Its Various Prophets*, trans. and ed. C. Dutt, W. Lough and C. P. McGill. Collected Works, vol. 5, ed. M. Cornforth *et al*. New York: International Publishers.

Mauss, M. 1966. *The Gift: Forms and function of exchange in archaic societies*, trans. I. Cunnison. London: Cohen and West.

Murdock, G. (1999). "Corporate Dynamics and Broadcasting Futures." In H. Mackey and T. O'Sullivan (eds), *The Media Reader: Continuity and Transformation*. London: Sage, 28-42.

Paglia, C. 1992. *Sexual Personae: Art and decadence from Nefertiti to Emily Dickinson*. Harmondsworth: Penguin.

Richter, J. 1972. *Die vertrimmte Nation oder Sport in rechter Gesellschaft*. Reinbek bei Frankfurt: Rowohlt.

Rigauer, B. 1969. *Sport und Arbeit*. Frankfurt am Main: Suhrkamp Verlag.

Rigauer, B. 1981. *Sport and Work*. New York: Columbia University Press.

Simonović, D. and Simonović, L. J. 2007. *A New World is Possible*. Belgrade: the authors.

Simonović, L. J. 1981. *Pobuna Robota*. [Rebellion of Robots]. Belgrade: Zapis.

Simonović, L. J. 1985. *Profesionalizam i/ili Socijalizam*. [*Professionalism and/or Socialism*]. Belgrade: Mladost, Krt, Univerzitetska Riječ.

Simonović, L. J. 1988. *Olimpijska Podvala "Božanskog Barona" Pjera de Kubertena*. [Olympic Fake of "Divine Baron" Pierre de Coubertin]. Nikšić: NIO Univerzitetska riječ.

Simonović, L. J. 2002. "Filozofski Aspekti Modernog Olimpizma". ["Philosophical Aspects of Modern Olympism"]. *Crevna Kritika*, November 27. Available online at www.crvenakritika.org/filozofija/82-filozofski-aspekti-modernog-olimpizma (accessed October 13, 2014).

Simonović, L. J. 2011. "Homosexuality". Available online at www.scribd.com/doc/74553311/Homosexuality (accessed October 13, 2014).

Simonović, L. J. 2012. "The London Olympic: The Death Games". Available online at http://ljubodragsimonovic.wordpress.com/2012/08/01/ljubodrag-simonovic-the-london-olympics-the-death-games (accessed October 13, 2014).

Vaz, A. F. 2004. *Sport und Sportkritik in Kultur- und Zivilisationsprocess: Analysen nach Adorno, Horkheimer, Elias und Da Matta*. Hannover: Afra-Verlag.

Vinnai, G. 1970. *Fussballsport als Ideologie*. [Football as Ideology]. Frankfurt am Main: Europäische Verlaganstalt.

Vinnai, G. (ed.) 1972. *Sport in der Klassengesellschaft*. [*Sport in Class Society*]. Frankfurt am Main: Fischer Verlag.

Vodeb, B. 2001. *Sport Skozi Psihoanalizo*. [*Sport Through Psychoanalysis*]. Ljubljana: ZRC.

16

RELIGION, THEOLOGY
AND SPORT

Gregg Twietmeyer

Introduction

The association between sport and religion is by most accounts an ancient one. The intermingling of sport and its precursors with religion can be found in numerous ancient cultures all around the globe. From the ancient Olympics, to the Meso-American ball games, to the fertility and initiation rituals of North American Indians (Guttmann, 2004), a plenitude of sport's religious associations are identifiable in the ancient world.

Modern sport is different in so far as it is widely regarded as a secular rather than religious phenomenon. Sport historian Allen Guttmann (1978) first argued that modern sport was inherently secular in his book, *From Ritual to Record*. His thesis is now so widely accepted that the notion that modernity "invariably strips" sport of its "religious associations" is simply assumed as fact. (Guttmann, 2004, p. 11). Guttman's point was neither to celebrate nor lament that fact, but merely to chronicle this change as one of several significant differences between ancient and modern sport. On the surface, the truth of this claim seems self-evident. Yet upon further analysis some weaknesses in the thesis become apparent.

Unfortunately, Guttmann's paradigm has been so successful that it has buttressed the view held by many in the academy that the connection between sport and religion is an interesting anachronism. Debate over the veracity of Guttmann's thesis has been essentially non-existent. As a result, the problems and opportunities related to the interplay of sport and religion are missed largely because religious ideas themselves are not seen as *intellectually* respectable in the academy. Even when they are respected, religious ideas are quarantined from public view or relegated to narrow academic specialization. The view that religious ideas and religious questions are the product of living traditions that address perennial human questions, including those faced in sport, has lost currency. Religion may have been important in the past. It may have historical import, but enlightened adults, so the thinking goes, simply know better.[1]

A sound philosophical reflection on sport and religion reveals several problematic elements in the conventional secular accounts. The weaknesses of secularization theory – the claim that modernity is *necessarily* secularizing – have too often been ignored. The plausibility of these secularist narratives relies to a large extent on cultural myopia, where a focus on the contemporary geopolitical configuration called loosely "the West" is taken for granted. Furthermore, this criticism of secularization theory can be applied specifically to sport.[2] The secularist narrative is open to two major criticisms. First, there is significant *historical evidence* that sport and religion continue to intermingle. Our experience of modernity – at least if we *look closely* – is replete with examples of the interplay of sport and religion. Secondly, and more importantly, there are significant *philosophical problems* with secularization theory.

What are these philosophical problems and how do they illuminate the topic of this chapter on sport and religion? In short, the philosophical problems revolve around the definition of "sport" and in particular the definition of "religion". For the label "sport and religion" assumes an understanding of each term, each of which, upon reflection, may not be justified. If unjustified then the conceptual structure upon which the demarcations of "sport" and "religion" stand may end up bringing confusion rather than clarity. In other words, the conceptual framework, upon which this essay rests as an essay about "sport" and "religion", may itself be flawed.

In turn, the examination and clarification of these problems should open the door to some opportunities. For insofar as secularization theory's grip on the modern academy weakens, scholars should become more amenable to seriously considering the place of religious and theological insights in sport philosophy. At the very least, problematizing the dominant secularizing narrative, should open scholars up to a reexamination of their assumptions regarding the meaning, place, sufficiency, timeliness and import of "sport and religion" in contemporary sport philosophy. Christian theological resources, for example, can help sport philosophers to better understand several key issues in the discipline including – but not limited to – our understanding of play and our understanding of human embodiment.

This chapter comprises three parts. First, I examine some of the key authors and positions in the philosophic and historical literature related to sport and religion. This sets up a foundation upon which to consider the second major goal of the chapter; to challenge two assumptions in the modern academy: the truth of secularization theory and the reality of the genus "religion," of which Christianity is said to be one of several species. Finally, the chapter ends with some personal speculations on how Christian theology could help sport philosophers understand play and embodiment.

I Sport and religion: The extant literature

The literature on sport and religion is voluminous. For the sake of clarity and brevity, therefore, I review here some of the important sources from the following basic categories; historical accounts of sport and religion, important theological texts devoted to sport, and finally important texts within philosophy at large. I briefly consider some of the relevant work done within the sub-discipline of sport theology at the beginning of section III, on sport, religion, and embodiment.

It should be apparent that my read of the "sport–religion" canon – like all others – is necessarily incomplete, contestable and idiosyncratic. Hence, the point of this literature review is to give readers several key jumping off points from which to further consider the topic.

Sport history

Stephen Miller's (2004) *Ancient Greek Athletics* is an excellent examination of the birth growth and enduring cultural import of Greek sport in the ancient world. Particularly noteworthy for sport and religion is Miller's careful examination of the cultic and sacral origins of Ancient Greek sport, including not only at Olympia, but at the Pythian, Nemean and Isthmian Games as well. Miller's dismissal of the trope that Christianity killed ancient sport because Christianity was anti-athletic or anti-body is also noteworthy. As Miller notes, the Christian-backed banning of the Games was predicated on the fact that Greek "athletics had always been tied to religion; every game was sacred to some god or goddess in the old Greek pantheon" (p. 6). It was paganism, not athletics, to which the ancient Christians objected. One other noteworthy work regarding the intersection of ancient sport and religion is Don Kyle's (1998) *Spectacles of Death in Ancient Rome*, which has chapters on Christian persecutions in ancient Rome, as well as fascinating discussion of the interplay of religious, ritualistic, and ideological forces in shaping the Roman understanding of death in the athletic arena.

Regarding comprehensive general histories and modern histories, there are several works worth noting. Two highly regarded general histories spend considerable time on the religious aspects of sport, Guttmann's (2004) *Sport: The First Five Millennia* and William J. Baker's (1982) *Sports in the Western World*. Baker (2007) also wrote *Playing with God*, a history of modern sport and religion, a generally solid text, which occasionally descends into over-simplification and statements regarding religion so sweeping as to border on caricature.[3] Others worth noting are Robert J. Higgs (1995) *God in the Stadium*, an examination of the integration of sport and religion, and Shirl Hoffman's (2010) *Good Game*, which again cautions against too close of a relationship between sport and Christianity. Both texts, although well written, deserve further critical treatment and analysis.

One of the most important things that sport history does for the sport philosopher, especially with regard to its ties to religion, is to complicate and broaden the conceptual schemata upon which philosophical reflection proceeds. An excellent example of what I mean can be found in Nancy Struna's (1996) *People of Prowess*, in which she recounts the myriad influences involved in the cultural transition from traditional to early modern conceptions and practices of sport, leisure and labor. Put briefly, Struna shows two important things. First, patterns of sport, leisure and labor have changed. Our conceptions and practices are historical, that is, temporally bound, and organically evolving. This is a key point, as will be seen, when we consider the concept "religion". Second, this shift from Catholic to Puritan conceptions of sport was not just a religious one, but rather involved a dynamic mix of forces. Theology, geography, class, and technology (such as clocks) all played a role in reshaping modern conceptions of work and leisure. For example, the Puritan commitment to work – at least in the New World – resulted from "both theology and their economic interests", for the "demands and rewards of work itself were greater in the New World" (p. 61). The point is simple. Theology was not the sole influence and the Puritan position, even if excessive, had an internal logic. Idleness in the New World could get you killed.[4]

Similarly, the Puritans were not anti-sport in the way they are so often caricatured. In fact, they endorsed "lawful practices," including "athletic contests, archery, and hunting, fishing, and fowling" (pp. 62–3). In turn, they condemned gaming (gambling) and animal baiting. Each of which remain today, to one degree or another, associated with vice. Again, the clear logic of the Puritan position, even if problematic, comes into view. → Puritans

Theology and spirituality

Theologians and theological texts are worth mentioning in the context of sport and religion primarily but not exclusively for the light they shed on conceptions of the human person and the nature and/or importance of embodiment. This is important simply for its intrinsic philosophic interest, but also because misunderstandings of religion are, as Stephen Prothero (2007) has shown, quite common. Just as Puritanism has been caricatured, so too has Christianity. For example, consider the following claim made in a recent sociology of sport textbook: "some church leaders felt that the body was inherently evil and should be subordinate to the spirit"

Augustine

(Woods, 2007, p. 257). To read, engage, and understand the great theological texts in the Christian tradition, not to mention the Bible itself, is to see that such a claim is misleading if not clearly mistaken.

The two most noteworthy theologians in the Western tradition are, of course, Augustine and Aquinas, both of whom were, to some degree, philosophers as well.[5] Augustine's works of note for sport philosophy include; the *Confessions* (1991), where he famously condemns the inhumanity of the Coliseum, *On Christian Teaching* (1997), where he points out that there are many senses – including nonliteral – of scripture, and *The City of God* (1958), where he states clearly that "it was not the corruptible flesh that made the soul sinful; on the contrary, it was the sinful soul that made the flesh corruptible" (p. 299).

One final speculation on Augustine should be made. In *On Christian Teaching*, he argues that the state of one's heart, not just the type of activity in which one is engaged, is what requires moral evaluation: "In all matters of this kind actions are made acceptable or unacceptable not by the particular things we make use of, but by our motives for using them and our methods of seeking them" (p. 78). The importance of this point for sport is two-fold. Augustine's insight reinforces the importance of virtue rather than mere legalism. Inherent evils exist, but so do culturally defined norms. They should not be confused. In such cases, what matters is not the "use made of things, but the user's desire" (p. 77). Furthermore, his point supports the need for the type of practical analysis necessary in any working model of broad internalism. For an examination of the "point and purposes that underlie the game" (Simon, 2010, p. 52), we must evaluate context and motives, rather than merely the prescriptions or prohibitions found in the rules. If an authority such as Augustine can be brought to the cause, even if only tangentially, so much the better for those who want to champion broad internalism as a *practical* philosophy.

Thomas Aquinas is of importance for a myriad reasons. In terms of his importance to sport and religion, he again, like Augustine, insists on the goodness of embodiment, and integrates Aristotle's holistic conception of the human person (known technically as hylemorphic dualism) into his account of religion. Aquinas argues for the integral nature of human embodiment consistently and vigorously in his monumental work the *Summa Theologica*, but it also shows up other places, perhaps most importantly in his *Commentary on First Corinthians* (Aquinas, n.d.) where he corrects a common Platonic mistake often attributed to Christianity: Salvation is not about "saving souls" in the sense of escaping the body but, rather, is about personal transformation through resurrection. This follows from his claim that body and soul are constitutive features of a single person:

> For it is clear that the soul is naturally united to the body and is departed from it, contrary to its nature and per accidens. Hence the soul devoid of its body is imperfect, as long as it is without the body … but the soul, since it is part of man's body, is not an entire man, and *my soul is not I.*
>
> *(Aquinas, n.d., p. 197 [emphasis added])*

Several non-Christian philosophers who also grappled with Aristotle and his hylemorphic conception of human nature are worth briefly mentioning including the Islamic thinkers Avicenna and Averroes, as well as the Jewish scholar Moses Maimonides. For solid introductions to these philosophers and how they fit into the Aristotelian tradition, see MacIntyre (2009) and Copleston (1993). Finally, Eastern Taoist thinking has also made important contributions and are considered in greater depth in section III of the chapter.

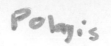

Philosophy

Given the ubiquitous influence of philosophy on religion, I again only point to a handful of significant sources, some of which reappear in greater detail in later sections. Two philosophically inclined works of sociology are worth mentioning in this regard. First is Johan Huizinga's *Homo Ludens* (1955), which argues that play is the root of culture. Man is not just a builder, nor a knower, but a player. Play, games, and sport are therefore worth serious attention. Second, is Peter Berger's (1969) *A Rumor of Angels*, in which he argues that play is itself an argument for the existence of a transcendent reality.

Leisure, The Basis of Culture by German Thomist Josef Pieper (1998) is another important text that makes religious claims about what leisure is and should be. Leisure is a stillness ultimately rooted in God. "Leisure is the disposition of receptive understanding, of contemplative beholding, and immersion – in the real" (p. 31). Leisure, rightly understood, is neither idle distraction, nor utilitarian efficiency. Our participation in sport has the potential to be both shallow and profound. If we are to experience such profundity, it will result from leisure, the "deepest root" of which "is worshipful celebration" (p. 55).

Finally, Michael Polayni's (1962) epistemology, found most comprehensively in *Personal Knowledge*, is important to sport and religion for two reasons. Polanyi's theory emphasizes the importance of skill, and the importance of fiduciary commitment. That is, all knowledge is built upon the foundation of personal skill and trust in authority. Polanyi's emphasis on skills relies on links between ritual, practice and apprenticeship, all of which can be found in both religious and sporting practices. Meanwhile, Polanyi's emphasis on fiduciary commitment makes room for a reconciliation of faith and reason by showing that belief not doubt is the ultimate source of knowledge. Sport philosophers have paid significant attention to Polanyi's focus on skills. See, for example, Peter Hopsicker's (2009) article in the *Journal of the Philosophy of Sport*. Further attention is needed on the implications of Polanyi's claim that all knowledge is rooted in belief and trust.

II Understanding religion

The definition of "religion" has always been problematic. In fact, the nature, history and definition of religion has been contested *vigorously* for at least the "past 30 years" (Nongbri, 2013, p. 2). Yet, there has been little to no attention paid to these issues among sport philosophers. Nevertheless, any sound understanding of "sport and religion" needs to take these debates over the meaning of "religion" into account. This is especially important since doing so will likely lead many to acknowledge that "religion" is, just like "sport", a contentious and thoroughly modern concept. As Brent Nongbri (2013) argues, "what is modern about the ideas of 'religions' and 'being religious' is the isolation and naming of some things as 'religious' and others as 'not religious'" (p. 4). In the pre-modern world, one's obligations to the divine were in fact communal, and permeated all aspects of society. Secularity is a modern idea.

In antiquity, the Latin term *religio* did not mean anything akin to a separate sphere of life regarding the gods or the transcendent, nor did it mean the genus for the species of different understandings or systems related to the gods or the transcendent. In contrast to those modern assumptions regarding religion, *religio* meant something akin to "a powerful requirement [or obligation] to perform some action" (Cavanaugh, 2009, p. 62). In fact, the ancients were much more likely to see alternative systems of belief as heresies rather than "separate religions". John of Damascus, for instance, "set a lasting precedent" when he classified Muslims "not as members of a separate religion but as Christian heretics" (Nongbri, 2013, p. 66). Since the concept

"religion" did not exist in the ancient world, this makes perfect sense. Theologian William Cavanaugh (2009) insists, "Ancient languages have no word that approximates what modern English speakers mean by religion" (p. 62). Given this fact, one might expect to find a dichotomy where religion has been problematic when applied to the ancient world, but fruitful when applied to the present. Yet again, things are not that simple. Even modern applications of the term religion are problematic.

As Cavanaugh (2009) points out, contemporary scholars have generally clung to either a substantive or functionalist definition of religion, neither of which are without problems. The "substantivist" view defines religion by the content or substance of its adherents' beliefs, while the functionalist defines religion by the import that a practice, institution or set of beliefs has in any given cultural context. For the substantivist, religion is about something – God, or the divine, or the transcendent – it deals with "ultimate reality." For a functionalist, religion is that to which we are most committed. It may be about God, but it may also be about the free market, Marxism, sports, or witchcraft. What matters is the sacral character of the devotion not the content of that devotion.

The substantivist view is often criticized for being either too narrow or too broad. It seems too narrow for instance, if one bases the substance of religion on "God". For this would seem to exclude things usually labeled as religions, such as Confucianism and at least some forms of Buddhism. To make sure that a substantivist definition is inclusive of more than monotheism, more generic language is often used. Yet, as one expands the substance of the belief to the divine or the transcendent, it becomes harder to exclude things not generally thought of as religions. It is hard, for instance, to argue that a shift to any sufficiently inclusive definition of a "transcendent" understanding of the substance of religion could exclude nationalism. "If transcendence can refer to any perceived reality that exceeds and unifies ordinary human experience of the material world, it is hard to imagine a better candidate for transcendence than the 'imagined community' of the nation" (Cavenaugh, 2009, pp. 103–4). Furthermore, the distinction between immanent and transcendent implicit in such thinking is itself problematic for many spiritual traditions.

These problems have led some scholars to reject the "substantivist" model in favor of a "functionalist" model. According to the functionalists, religion is not about content, but rather about commitment(s). That which holds our ultimate allegiance is our religion. It is from this point of view that some scholars have argued that "sport is the modern religion".

Arguments that sport is a religion are usually tempered by talk of the relation being analogical (Wann and Melnick, 2001, pp. 198–200). A similar qualification is the claim that sports are a "civil religion". Michael Novak (1994) explains the idea this way in his book *The Joy of Sports*, "Sports are religious in the sense that they are organized institutions, disciplines, and liturgies; and also in the sense that they teach religious qualities of heart and soul" (p. 21). From a functionalist point of view, sport, pleasure, money, power, Communism, or nationalism could all be – and often are – the object of religious devotion. This is because each can be seen as the object of our "ultimate concern" (Tillich, 1953). Yet, as Cavanaugh (2009) writes, "If nearly every ideological system or set of practices can be a religion, then calling something religious does not help distinguish it from anything else" (p. 106).

This brief discussion should point out the importance of examining the definition of religion for sport philosophy. For an article on the topic of "sport and religion" will take on very different meanings depending on the definition of religion assumed. In fact, if sport itself can – under a functionalist reading – be thought of as a religion, then the topic could be considered redundant at best or incoherent at worst.

In modern America, the concept "religion" is incongruent with pre-modern and non-Western spiritual practice. While we tend to think of religion as a matter of intellectual beliefs and private behavior, pre-modern "religion" – at least in terms of Christianity – was far more corporate, communal, and practical (ritualized).[6] Too often, the modern Western definition of religion starts with the assumptions of the Protestant Reformation. Scholars are apt then to try to shoehorn disparate practices from disparate cultures into a one-size-fits-all post-Reformation conception of religion. In practice, religion becomes "anything that sufficiently resembles modern Protestant Christianity" (Nongbri, 2013, p. 18). This is not to deny that Catholicism, or Buddhism, could fit into such a definitional structure, but rather to insist that the fit assumes a Protestant norm. As such, the structure itself in neither self-evident nor neutral.[7] Therefore, rather than search for an essence to religion, Cavanaugh argues that scholars should examine, "why certain things are called religion under certain conditions" (p. 119).

The fact that scholars (such as myself) struggle to discuss other spiritual traditions without using the word "religious" arises from the fact that our concepts and intellectual categories are culturally bound. Therefore they must be applied cautiously. That is not to say that there are no universals, but rather that sometimes we confuse a cultural construct for a universal. This point has purchase for sport philosophers trying to makes sense of the relations between sport and religion. First, our definition of religion is a choice not a trans-historical or trans-cultural reality. Our definition of religion is a choice, not in the sense of being an individual preference, but rather in the sense of requiring our personal loyalty and ideological commitment. All of us either implicitly or explicitly accept certain principles when we assent to any given definition of religion. "What counts as religion and what does not in any given context is contestable," insists Cavanaugh (2009), "and depends on who has the power and authority to define religion at any given time and place" (p. 59) Thus, the veracity of Guttmann's thesis – that modern sport is necessarily secularizing – may well hinge on the meaning of the vocabulary one uses. Or consider the fact that controversies over prayer in sport or "conspicuous piety" in sport (Feezell, 2013) hinge – to a large extent – on the assumption that sport is and should be a secular practice. Yet the sacred/secular dichotomy depends upon a vocabulary that only exists in the modern world. That is, modern sport is comparatively secular, because the sacred/secular dichotomy is itself *a product of modernity*. Furthermore, modern sport appears secular, as compared with ancient sport, because we only have the eyes to see things through the modern sacred/secular "religious" framework.

The quarantining of religious questions from academic discussion is not therefore inevitable, but instead relies on the maintenance of socially constructed dichotomies, such as religious/secular and public/private, that serve to maintain current liberal power structures. Even leaving aside whether such liberal structures are superior to other forms of political life – these distinctions may very well be warranted – the point remains that they are neither neutral, natural, nor inevitable. Thus, when sport philosophers acknowledge the volitional nature of the concept "religion", they promote more realistic appraisals of religion(s), they encourage intellectual tolerance, and they help scholars avoid the errors of anachronism.

If this is right it should be clear why the phrase "sport and religion" is itself problematic. For example, sport philosophers should avoid anachronistically imposing modern conceptions, ideas, and principles onto the past. The conception, for instance, that religion is a "private matter" while secular affairs are "public" is, independent of whether or not one finds it a good idea, a modern creation. As Talal Asad (2003) points out, "the supposedly universal opposition between 'sacred' and 'profane' finds no place in pre-modern writing" (pp. 31–2). Uncritically insisting on the application of our present conception of religion upon the past will only cloud our understanding of history.

Does all of this mean that scholars need to abandon the term "religion"? No, it is so deeply ingrained in our intellectual habits that trying to expunge it would likely cause as many problems as it would solve. However, it does mean that sport philosophers must broaden their field of vision when considering sport and religion. The bottom line is this: a close examination of the concept "religion" reveals that sport philosophers need to acknowledge that religion "is not simply found, but invented" (Cavenaugh, 2009, p. 58).

III Theology, play, embodiment

Sport and religion has received serious if sporadic attention in the philosophy of sport literature. The following developments are worth noting. The *International Journal of Religion and Sport* began publishing in 2009. Unfortunately, the journal has only published one more volume since then. Several anthologies of note have been published in recent years, including Parry, Nesti, and Watson's (2011) *Theology, Ethics and Transcendence in Sports* and Watson and Parker's (2013) *Sports and Christianity: Historical and contemporary perspectives.*

While there are myriad popular treatments of sport and religion, such as Phil Jackson's (1995) *Sacred Hoops,* systematic and academic book-length treatments of a sustained theological or religious argument as applied to sport philosophy are harder to find. Fortunately, this seems to be changing. Two books offering explicit theologies of sport have just been published: *The Games People Play: Theology, religion, and sport* by Robert Ellis (2014), and *A Brief Theology of Sport* by Lincoln Harvey (2014). Although it remains to be seen what enduring impact they will have, each is receiving praise from highly respected scholars in the field. Shirl Hoffmann, for example, says of Ellis (2014) that his book is "A must-read for anyone hoping to understand how sport fits within the Christian tradition" (back cover). Whatever the strengths or drawbacks of these texts, the trend towards an unapologetically theological approach to religion and sport rather than a merely anthropological, historical, or sociological approach, is a positive one.

I take the same theological approach when considering two ways that sport philosophy can benefit from examinations of sport and religion. As I consider the ways in which religion impacts sport and sport philosophy – in particular regarding play and the nature of the human person – I focus primarily on Christianity. This is for two reasons. First, given the conceptual difficulties of the general concept of religion here discussed, it is better to focus on specific spiritual traditions like Christianity. And, secondly, pragmatically, it is my own area of experience, belief and expertise. That said, I attempt to point out important insights or implications for sport found in other non-Christian spiritual traditions, for example – between play and the *Tao Te Ching.*

Sport, play, and God

Although the precise relationship between sport and play is a matter of contention, I follow Schmitz (1979) and claim that "sport is primarily an extension of play" (p. 22). As such, play must be taken into account in order to explore in what sense sport can be a religious phenomenon. I also think that Schmitz's further point that "Religion, art and play are rightly spoken of as ways of transcending the strictly natural world" (p. 25) provides yet another reason to see the connection between sport, religion, and play, in terms of play.[8] The following features of play seem apposite in this regard. The first concerns play's oft noted "uselessness". In a world so often driven by purposes, outcomes, and utility, play stands out for being superfluous. It is an autotelic practice in the sense that "the prize of play is play itself" (Meier, 1980, p. 25). The second aspect of play worth noting is its profundity. Although play has no instrumental purpose, or perhaps paradoxically because it has no such purpose, play seems to generate deep meaning. This experience has been described in various ways. Johan Huizinga (1955) says that

"play casts a spell over us," (p. 10) while theologian Romano Guardini (1994), insists that play is "life pouring itself forth without an aim, seizing upon riches from its own abundant store, significant through the fact of its existence" (p. 111). For Guardini, it is the embrace of purpose-lessness (its lack of an external justification or end) that gives play its depth and meaning. For meaning is not realized in the endless chain of extrinsic justifications, but rather "significance consists in [things] being what they are." Play reminds us that the highest things *are*; they have no need for justification. Existence is not, in the end, about purposes but rather meaning.

Play's uselessness and its profundity point to three important insights regarding "sport and religion". First, as sociologist Peter Berger (1969) suggests in *A Rumor of Angels*, play is experi-entially suggestive of the supernatural. It is a "signal of transcendence". Second, following Guardini, play has important implications for our understanding of worship. Finally, a proper understanding of play suggests, that sport philosophers can assert with *confidence* that sport should be pursued *in the spirit of play*. That is, the religious implications of play, ground and deepen one's claims regarding the normative status of the play spirit. The play spirit is not just phenomenologically interesting, or existentially important, as "one authentic choice among many", but rather philosophers can say with confidence that *we ought* to approach sport in the spirit of play.

As Berger (1969) argues, there are in the modern world "signals of transcendence". In addi-tion to play, our experiences of order, hope, damnation, and humor all point to the plausibility of the divine because each of these experiences suggest a purposeful reality transcending the chaotic and meaningless universe suggested by a materialistic understanding of reality.[9] These signs of transcendence are part of the common human inheritance and are therefore open to all. Berger's inclusion of play is built on Huizinga's insights regarding the separate time and space created by play. In play, we momentarily escape from the "'serious' time in which one is moving toward death".[10] In fact, Berger insists, "joy is play's intention" (p. 58).

Berger admits that although the experience of play admits of a religious interpretation it certainly does not demand it. Although the experience of play indicates strongly that we live in a meaningful world, the implications of that experience are open to interpretation. This admission of contingency may seem to weaken the power of the point, but in fact, it does not. For Berger only wants to allow for the credibility of the transcendent or religious interpreta-tion of play experiences. Of course, for those that have, or believe that they have had a play experience that points towards a divine reality, the experience is profound. The point is not to require belief but to *allow for it*. Again, religion and sport are linked through play. These signs of transcendence, including play, are proof of the plausibility and seriousness (in principle) of spiritual and religious interpretations of life. They are by no means proof of the truth of any of those interpretations. The rich world of play "cries out" for explanation and religious explana-tions of that experience should be taken seriously.

Acknowledging this experiential dichotomy (between those who believe and those who doubt) does not preclude one from advancing certain interpretations as true. Each side can hold their ground. It simply means one will be aware that other interpretations, even if mistaken, can be made in good faith.[11] One intriguing religious interpretation that could be fruitfully applied to the experience of play as described by Berger is the Christian idea of *prolepsis*, which theolo-gian Richard John Neuhaus (2009) defines as, "an act in which a hoped-for future is already present" (p. 14). In traditional Christian theology, for instance, both baptism and the Eucharist are understood as hints, or foretastes of the fullness of Christian life to come at the end of time. They are visible signs of God's grace at work in the world. Again, this type of experience is open to all, even if not all will interpret the experience the same way, even in non-religious contexts. As Neuhaus points out, most of us "have moments of encounter with the good, true, and beautiful in which we are moved to say 'Ah, it [heaven, the divine, truth itself] must be something like this'" (p. 228).

From this perspective, for those who understand their play experiences as a "signal of transcendence", play can point towards worship. For their play experience itself suggests a divine reality. That is, one's lived experience calls forth not only pleasure or joy or meaning, but also a profound sense of gratitude. Interestingly, at least if Guardini is correct, worship also points towards play. Guardini (1994) argues that worship suggests play because the liturgy is itself – at least when rightly conceived – a form of play and because play is hinted at in Scripture as an aspect of the Holy Trinity.

Suits' (1977) famous objection in *Words on Play* that worship or the contemplation of God can rarely be rightly understood as play does not hold up under scrutiny. He objects that: 1) All non-Utopian play must include the reallocation of resources; 2) Worship is not "purely autotelic" (p. 129), but instead usually involves some instrumental purpose. Both of these objections fail against Guardini's position. First, because, as Suits himself partially admits, time itself is an instrumental resource that must always be reallocated, and second because Guardini's (1994) conception of worship rightly understood is such that "In the liturgy, man is no longer concerned with himself; his gaze is directed towards God. In it man is not so much intended to edify himself as to contemplate God's majesty" (p. 110).

To defend this claim, Guardini draws a distinction between purpose and meaning. Purpose is about the subordination of "actions or objects to other actions or objects," (p. 106) while the meaning of an object   as mentioned previously – "consists in being what they are" (p. 107). Guardini then asks:

> Now what is the meaning of that which exists? That it would exist and should be the image of God the everlasting. And what is the meaning of that which is alive? That it should live, bring forth its essence, and *bloom* as a natural manifestation of the living God.
>
> *liturgy*   *(Guardini, 1994, p. 107 [emphasis added])*

Worship is about *blooming* in this sense. The liturgy is meant with the "help of grace", to grow human beings "into living works of art before God, with no other aim or purpose than that of living and existing in his sight" (p. 113). The liturgy is therefore about meaning not purpose. Worship, Guardini insists, is about play: "To be at play, or to fashion a work of art in God's sight – not to create, but to exist – such is the essence of the liturgy" (p. 112). In commenting on Guardini, theologian Robert Barron (2011) sums up the idea this way, "We play football and we play musical instruments because it is simply delightful to do so, and we play in the presence of the Lord for the same reason" (p. 173).[12]

These arguments reflect and reinforce the importance of my final point on play – that sport philosophers can and should confidently proclaim that sport is meant to be pursued in the spirit of play. In other words, theological ideas such as Guardini's are an untapped resource. Play is important – that is humanly significant. The sacral aspect of play reinforces and emboldens the declaration of some key realities in the world of sport. This is no small matter.

The most obvious and perhaps the most ignored example in the world of competitive sports is the fact that victory is fleeting. The dour ethic of workman-like obligation oft found in sport, which is built on an endless and insatiable pursuit of victory is not only miserable, it does not endure. Even if we secure victory, trophies tarnish, calendars and seasons roll over, and championships are forgotten. In contrast, the play spirit opens up sport to a reemphasis on process and not mere product. It opens up sport to the admission of human frailty (Skillen, 1998).

Although sport is non-trivial, and although the pursuit of victory is appropriate, the means of pursuit and the motivation for pursuing victory matter as much if not more than the end (victory). In pointing beyond itself, in prolepsis, a theological understanding of play reminds us of the vanity of placing our hopes in something as fleeting as victory. This is because the temporal points to the eternal. The experience is, from within the point of view of prolepsis, an intimation of beatitude; of being in the direct unmediated presence of God. As Saint Paul says, "For now we see in a mirror, dimly, but then we will see face to face" (1st Corinthians, 13:12, NRSV). Although winning and losing matter, they must be understood within the context of a larger understanding.

Consider for instance Stephen Mitchell's (Tzu, 1988) translation of the sixty-eighth chapter of the *Tao Te Ching*.

> The best athlete
> wants his opponent at his best.
> The best general
> enters the mind of his enemy.
> The best businessman
> serves the communal good.
> The best leader
> follows the will of the people.
> All of them embody
> the virtue of non-competition.
> Not that they don't love to compete,
> but they do it in the spirit of play (p. 68).[13]

The fact that play points beyond itself,[14] that it has a sacral aspect, allows for sport communities to emphasize and *defend* the non-instrumental aspects of the games. This sacral aspect can also help build the formal institutions necessary to protect the non-instrumental goods of play from competitive or commercial excesses, by creating and promoting a genuine concern for others. To the degree that this occurs, the play spirit can be said to foster human dignity (Twietmeyer, 2007). When play suggests that one's own life is actually meaningful, then by extension one see that all human lives are *actually* meaningful. It is not mere rhetoric but rather a profound and *experienced* truth. As such, a recognition of the sacral aspects of the play spirit creates a moral imperative in sport. In pointing beyond itself play demands personal responsibility. In short, play buttressed by its own anthropological and spiritual implications creates more room for the confident assertion of richer understandings of sport. To borrow from Guardini, it reminds us that sport is at its best when pursued for meaning rather than purpose(s).[15] Therefore, the *principle* of religious expression in sport should be received with a spirit of openness rather than suspicion, for it has the potential to be a strong force for good.

Sport, religion, embodiment

In this final section, I sketch the preliminary picture that I have been drawing of how certain religious insights can help sport philosophers address the perennial and perhaps preeminent issue in the field, that of the nature of the human person. As R. Scott Kretchmar (2005) argues, our conception "of human nature … is the foundation of everything we do" (p. 48). This is important for sport, physical education and kinesiology because our understanding of embodiment's role in human nature will deeply influence our conception of the import and possibilities of those institutions. For example, one might ask: to what extent is sport participation engaging the body or the person?

The most obvious example of how assumptions about human nature impact sport is the fact that a dualistic appraisal of education is unlikely to see "play, games and sport" as anything more than a tangential aspect of education (Kretchmar, 2005). Far too often, "play, games, and sport" have been devalued on the assumption that embodiment is a trivial or temporal aspect of human life. Furthermore, religion (Christianity in particular) has been advanced as the cause for the devaluing of embodiment in the West. Both claims are mistaken.

I want to speak, therefore, to some of the ways embodiment has been illuminated in Eastern spiritual thinking, as well as examine the Christian idea of the Incarnation and its implications. The overarching philosophical point of engaging both perspectives is this: religious traditions far from being uniformly suspicious of human corporeality can be and often are allies in the fight to defend the importance of human embodiment. If sport philosophers want to change the public's generally materialistic or dualistic conception of embodiment, they ignore these religious resources at their own peril.

In *Zen in the Art of Archery*, German philosopher Eugen Herrigel (1981) recounts his six years of travail in Japan attempting to master the art of archery. From a Zen perspective, Herrigel opines that archery is neither preparation for war, nor a sport, nor even really an art, but rather a spiritual exercise "whose aim consists in hitting a spiritual goal, so that fundamentally the marksman aims at himself, and may even succeed in hitting himself" (p. 4). This spiritual exercise is meant to develop (through the disciplines inherent in the practice) the ability to quiet the conscious self so that the embodied skills shine through unencumbered by calculation, worry or desire. The result is that the arrow can be said to shoot itself. The master's archery is "absolutely self-oblivious and without purpose" (p. 53). His shots fall "like a ripe fruit" (p. 53) falls from a tree.

When, after hours of practice and dedication, this "non-action" occurs, it is, says Herrigel, a tantalizing experience:

> But inwardly, for the archer himself, right shots have the effect of making him feel that the day has just begun. He feels in the mood for all right doing, and, what is perhaps even more important, for all right not doing. Delectable indeed is this state. But he who has it, said the Master with a subtle smile, would do well to have it as though he did not have it.
>
> *(Herrigel, 1981, p. 53)*

It is for this reason that ritual and repetition are so important. The skills are neither merely technical nor theoretical but living traditions born of apprenticeship. They are taught as part of a formal apprenticeship, which, in all likelihood, spans generations. Spiritual growth comes from right practice and is born from tradition. Although one lives in the moment, through the skill, this experience rests upon a historical foundation. This historical foundation is both personal and cultural. Zen spiritual insight is born of the embodied experience of archery, an embodied experience that relies on an interpersonal transmission of the central skills, habits, and dispositions of the practice.[16] The corporeal – in this instance at least – is anything but incidental to the spiritual life.

Yet Zen Buddhism is not the only religion that acknowledges the critical importance of embodiment. Christianity, as already noted, is not anti-body. Countless examples can be shown to demonstrate the point. Whether one consults the biblical texts, the great historical theologians such as Augustine or Aquinas, or simply considers the basic theological suppositions of the faith (such as creation, Incarnation, resurrection), it is clear that Christianity is a religion intensely interested in defending the goodness of human embodiment. In fact, this can be so clearly demonstrated that one can say with confidence that, "Although some Christians might claim that the human body is evil, it is an *un-Christian* belief" (Twietmeyer, 2008, p. 459).

To justify this claim, consider two sources, one historical, the other contemporary. The historical source is the great Protestant reformer Martin Luther, while the contemporary source comes from the work of the Lutheran turned Catholic theologian Adam Cooper. Luther argues forcefully in *On the Councils and the Church*, that Jesus is "true God and true man". That is, he was, in his human life, just as bound up in earthly realities as any other human person. With great poignancy, Luther then reminds his readers what this means:

> God did not derive his divinity from Mary; but it does not follow that it is therefore wrong to say that God was born of Mary, that God is Mary's Son, and that Mary is God's mother … She is the true mother of God and bearer of God … Mary suckled God, rocked God to sleep, prepared broth and soup for God, etc. For God and man are one person, one Christ, one Son, one Jesus.
>
> *(Luther, 1967, pp. 291–2)*

Luther's point is to reaffirm what was posited earlier, that Christianity is about a person not an idea.[17] God has become man. In the Incarnation, the spiritual invades the material world.[18]

More recently, Adam Cooper (2007, 2008) masterfully reviews the understanding of corporeality in the Hebrew Scriptures (Old Testament), the New Testament, as well as in several key figures from the Christian intellectual tradition. In examining these understandings of corporeality, he convincingly demonstrates the intelligibility of a "theological anthropology," an anthropology that sees the "human body as a kind of external, dynamic definition of both the human being and the visible image of God" (Cooper, 2008, p. 5). Cooper insists that "Perfected humanity, deified humanity, is always bodily humanity" (ibid.). Cooper beautifully points out the full implications of this insight:

> The Christian God is a God for whom immaterial or artificial representation will not do … A properly theological approach to the body involves asking what the body and the flesh mean, not first in their relation to mind or soul but above all in their most fundamental relation – which is to God. It is the conviction of the Christian tradition that the meaning of corporeality is an integral aspect of the meaning of the human person, a creature that bears in itself an inherent, irreducible relation to its creator.
>
> *(Cooper, 2007, p. 31)*

It does not take a great cognitive leap to see that this work could be adapted to or even in some cases directly applied to sport. Creation, the Incarnation and resurrection show that Christianity "is a religion deeply interested in the human body, since each body is a person, and each person a creature and image-bearer of God. In the three great mysteries of God's dealings with the universe – creation, incarnation, and resurrection – all material reality and especially spirited, sensible, sexed, and social human flesh, is radically implicated" (Cooper, 2008, p. 263). Although non-Christians may, of course, find these claims radical, they should nonetheless see that they are at very least worthy of philosophical consideration. Because of the limits of human knowledge, as well as the contentious nature of all genuine inquiry, Cooper himself insists on "the need for dialogue, conversation, criticism, and correction" (2008, p. 163). Although one may not find them personally compelling, one should defend the importance of allowing philosophers room for openly "dwelling in these mysteries" (Cooper, 2008, p. 263).

It has been the purpose of this chapter to establish the grounds for such a defense. First, by reviewing some of the relevant literature in the subdiscipline. Second, by calling attention to the importance of examining the definition of "religion". All too often philosophical analysis on the topic is undermined by faulty and or misleading assumptions regarding the nature and origins of religion. To date, sport philosophers' examinations have too often been superficial. Finally, I have asserted that there are two other principle areas of fundamental concern for those interested in the intersection of sport and religion; namely play and the nature of the human person. The point of focusing on these central concerns has not been to ignore other areas worthy of philosophic investigation (for example, prayer in sport), but rather to breathe new vitality into "sport and religion" in a way that a mere encyclopedic summary cannot. There are significant untapped resources available in both Christian and non-Christian spiritual traditions. Unfortunately, these resources are being misunderstood and under-utilized. Sport philosophy urgently needs a serious, sustained and broad engagement with both the nature of the concept "religion" as well as the specific spiritual traditions this concept is usually meant to represent.

Notes

1 Consider, for example, Richard Dawkins (2006) condescending evaluation of religious experience: "That is really all that needs to be said about personal 'experiences' of gods or other religious phenomena. If you've had such an experience, you may well find yourself believing firmly that it was real. But don't expect the rest of us to take your word for it, especially if we have the slightest familiarity with the brain and its powerful workings" (p. 92).
2 Further criticisms of secularization theory can be found in Asad (2003), Berger (1999, 2008), Cavanaugh (2009), and Jenkins (2007).
3 For example: "Dropping to a knee or pointing skyward after a touchdown, in full view of the television camera, presumably give God the glory. In fact, it calls attention to oneself. Ultimately, the Squad and the Me Generation play the same game. They are soul mates." While Baker's concern is legitimate, it would be made much stronger with qualifications. For instance he could have said, "*All too often*, it calls attention to oneself", which would have left room for authentic spontaneous acts of sincere worship, just as there can be authentic spontaneous acts of celebration.
4 Scarcity, for instance, often kept American colonists of any theological persuasion from recreation. "In short, like their contemporaries in the Chesapeake, migrants to the [Massachusetts] Bay Colony lacked the material culture to support a variety of recreations … horses and other domestic animals … were too few and too valuable to be used in sports" (Struna, 1997, p. 61).
5 However, they are hardly alone in having commented on things directly or indirectly relevant to a discussion of sport. Maximus the Confessor (2003, pp. 87, 92), for instance, a seventh-century Greek monk, argued that "The soul arises at conception simultaneously with the body to form one complete human being … There is no temporal hiatus of any kind within the nature itself or among the reciprocal parts of which it is constituted". Two other good repositories for citations related to sport or embodiment from the Church Fathers include, Alois Koch's (2012) essay, "Biblical and Patristic Foundations for Sport" and Ralph Ballou's (1973) essay, "An Analysis of the Writings of Selected Church Fathers to AD 394 to Reveal Attitudes Regarding Physical Activity."
6 "We should note, however, that that liberation [biblical criticism] signals a far-reaching change in the sense of 'inspiration' – from an authorized reorientation of life towards a *telos*, into a psychology of artistry whose source is obscure – and therefore becomes the object of speculation (belief/knowledge). It was a remarkable transformation. For in the former, the divine word, both spoken and written, was necessarily also material. As such, the inspired words were the object of a particular person's reverence, the means of his or her practical devotions at particular times and places. The body, taught over time to listen, to recite, to move, to be still, to be silent, engaged with the acoustics of words, with their sound, feel, and look. Practice at devotions deepened the inscription of sound, look, and feel in his sensorium. When the devotee heard God speak, there was a sensuous connection between inside and outside, a fusion between signifier and signified" (Asad 2003, pp. 37–8).
7 "The invention of Buddhism as a distinct religion was based on the discovery of Sanskrit texts that

could be used to trace the origins of disparate rites in Asia back to the figure of Gautama. Buddhism was born as textual religion on the model of Protestantism. Once this work was done, the actual living manifestations of these rites were understood by Western scholars as corruptions from the original spirit of the texts ... The Buddha was commonly presented – by Max Muller, among many others – as the 'Martin Luther of the East', a reformer who had rejected the ritualism of Hinduism to found a purely spiritual religion" (Cavenaugh 2009, p. 93).

8   Here again we see why "religion" is problematic. The assumptions of a transcendent/immanent framework are thoroughly theistic, as well as deeply if not exclusively Christian.

9   To put the other arguments all too briefly, the argument from order is based upon the universal human desire for structure over chaos, the argument from hope is based upon the experience that "human existence is always oriented towards the future" (Berger, 1969, p. 61), the argument from damnation is based upon the reality of evil and the tangible sense "that there are certain deeds that cry out to heaven" (p. 66), while the argument from humor is a result of the recognition of the limits of all human power (that is the "serious world"), as well as an "intimation of redemption" (p. 70).

10 Another source of liberation often found in play that is emphasized in Taoism is the freedom of "non-being"; that is, the freedom to live in the moment free of self-consciousness or reflective and paralyzing self-examination. "Less and less is done/Until non-action is achieved./When nothing is done, nothing is left undone" (Tzu, 1972, 50).

11 Such an admission need not descend into either syncretism or relativism. As the Catechism of the Catholic Church states: "The Catholic Church recognizes in other religions that search, among shadows and images, for the God who is unknown yet near since he gives life and breath and all things and wants all men to be saved. Thus, the Church considers all goodness and truth found in these religions as 'a preparation for the Gospel and given by him who enlightens all men that they may at length have life'" (Catechism of the Catholic Church 1993, Part one, Section two, Chapter three, article 9, para. 3, 843). Available online at www.vatican.va/archive/ENG0015/_INDEX.HTM (accessed October 14, 2014).

12 Guardini (1994) also claims that scriptural evidence for play is apparent. It can be found in a description of the second person of the Trinity – the Son – found in the thirtieth and thirty-first verses of the eighth chapter of the book of Proverbs: "I was with him, forming all things, and was delighted every day, *playing* before him at all times, playing in the world" [Emphasis Added] (p. 110). Guardini interprets these verses, traditionally understood by Christians to be reflections on the role of Wisdom in creation, in light of the first chapter of the Gospel of John, where it states that "In the beginning was the Word" (John 1:1, NIV). Guardini (1994) argues that the second person of the Trinity is the Wisdom by whom, as the Creed says, "all things were made". He created not out of necessity, but rather joy, as the "Son 'plays' before the Father" (p. 110).

13 Mitchell's translation has been criticized by some for being too loose; I am not qualified to offer either an affirmation or a defense of that charge. In either instance, Mitchell's translation sheds light on the point I am trying to make regarding play.

14 This idea of transcendence – of creation and our experience of it pointing beyond itself – was given profound theological expression in St. Augustine's *Confessions*: "Let these transient things be the ground on which my soul praises you (Ps. 145: 2), 'God creator of all'. But let it not become stuck in them and glued to them with love through the physical senses" (1991, p. 62).

15 One might argue that such a claim is too idealized. That it reflect the needs and desires of the philosopher rather than those of the sport practitioner. Don't the sport marketer, the sport parent and the sports fan all have purposes in mind (e.g. revenue, scholarships, accolades, championships)? I do not deny this point. My point is simple. Insofar as those purposes go they are justifiable, but they are by themselves insufficient. There is nothing wrong with profit, championships, etc. Nevertheless, a view of sport that reduces sport to its utility is a truncated, incomplete and ultimately unsatisfactory view. Instrumental goods are good but they are not – by definition – ends in themselves. "Man does not live on bread alone" (Luke 4; 4, NIV). Therefore, "although the stomach is good, there is much more to a human being than his stomach and much more to human life than filling it" (Twietmeyer, 2008, 457).

16 John Henry Newman makes a similar point regarding the interpersonal nature of spiritual conversion: "To the world indeed at large he witnesses not; for few can see him near enough to be moved by his manner of living. But to his neighbours he manifests the Truth in proportion to their knowledge of him; and some of them, through God's blessing, catch the holy flame, cherish it, and in their turn transmit it. And thus in a dark world Truth still makes way in spite of the darkness, *passing from hand to hand*" (Newman, 2007 [emphasis added]).

17 This same concern is given supreme visual expression in the charcoal drawing "Virgin Mary Suckling the Christ Child" by the renaissance artist Albrecht Dürer. The drawing beautifully captures the radical claim of the Incarnation.

18 "These two moments [the virgin birth and the resurrection] are a scandal to the modern spirit. God is 'allowed' to act in ideas and thoughts, in the spiritual domain – but not in the material. That is shocking. He does not belong there. But that is precisely the point: God is God and he does not operate merely on the level of ideas. In that sense, what is at stake in both of these moments is God's very godhead. The question that they raise is: does matter also belong to him?" (Benedict XVI 2012, 56–7).

Bibliography

Aquinas, Saint Thomas. n.d. *Commentary on the First Epistle to the Corinthians*, translated by Fabian Larcher. Available online at http://dhspriory.org/thomas/SS1Cor.htm (accessed October 13, 2014).

Asad, T. 2003. *Formations of the Secular: Christianity, Islam, Modernity*. Stanford, CA: Stanford University Press.

Augustine, Saint. 1958. *The City of God*, translated by Gerald G. Walsh, Demetrius B. Zema, Grace Monahan and Daniel J. Honan. New York: Bantam Doubleday.

—— 1991. *Confessions*, translated by Henry Chadwick. New York: Oxford University Press.

—— 1997. *On Christian Teaching*, translated by R. P. H Green. New York: Oxford University Press.

Baker, W. J. 1982. *Sports in the Western World*. Urbana, IL: University of Illinois Press.

—— 2007. Playing with God: Religion and modern sport. Cambridge, MA: Harvard University Press.

Ballou, R. B., Jr. 1973. "An Analysis of the Writings of Selected Church Fathers to A.D. 394 to Reveal Attitudes Regarding Physical Activity." In *A History of Sport and Physical Education to 1900: Selected topics*, edited by Earle Ziegler, 187–99. Champaign, IL: Stipes.

Barron, R. 2011. Catholicism: A journey to the heart of the faith. New York: Random House.

Benedict XVI, Pope. 2012. *Jesus of Nazareth: The infancy narratives*, translated by Philip J. Whitmore. New York: Image.

Berger, P. L. 1969. *A Rumor of Angels: Modern society and the rediscovery of the supernatural*. Garden City, NY: Doubleday Anchor.

—— (ed.) 1999. *The Desecularization of the World: Resurgent religion and world politics*. Grand Rapids, MI: Eerdmans.

—— 2008. "Secularization falsified." *First Things* (180): 23–7.

Cavenaugh, W. T. 2009. *The Myth of Religious Violence: Secular ideology and the roots of modern conflict*. New York: Oxford University Press.

Cooper, A. G. 2008. *Life in the Flesh: An anti gnostic spiritual philosophy*. New York. Oxford University Press.

—— 2007. "Redeeming Flesh." *First Things* (173): 27–31.

Copleston, F. S. J. 1993 [1950]. *A History of Philosophy. Volume II: Medieval Philosophy: From Augustine to Duns Scotus*. New York: Image Books.

Dawkins, R. 2006. *The God Delusion*. New York: Houghton Mifflin.

Ellis, R. 2014. *The Games People Play: Theology, religion and sport*. Eugene, OR: Wipf and Stock.

Feezell, R. 2013. "Sport, religious belief, and religious diversity." *Journal of the Philosophy of Sport* 40(1): 135–62.

Guardini, R. 1994. "The Playfullness of the Liturgy." *Communio* (Spring): 105–14.

Guttmann, A. 1978. *From Ritual to Record: The nature of modern sports*. New York: Columbia University Press.

—— 2004. *Sports: The first five millennia*. Amherst, MA: University of Massachusetts Press.

Harvey, L. 2014. *A Brief Theology of Sport*. Eugene, OR: Cascade Books.

Herrigel, E. 1981. *Zen in the Art of Archery*, translated by R. F. C. Hull. New York: Random House.

Higgs, R. J. 1995. *God in the Stadium: Sport and religion in America*. Lexington, KY: University of Kentucky Press.

Hoffman, S. J. 2010. *Good Game: Christianity and the culture of sports*. Waco, TX: Baylor University Press.

Hopsicker, P. 2009. "Polanyi's 'from-to' knowing and his contribution to the phenomenology of skilled motor behavior." *Journal of the Philosophy of Sport* 36(1): 76–87.

Huizinga, J. 1955. *Homo Ludens: A study of the play element in culture*. Boston, MA: Beacon Press.

Jackson, Phil, and Hugh Delebanty. 1995. *Sacred Hoops: Spiritual lessons of a hardwood warrior*. New York: Hyperion.

Jenkins, P. 2007. *The Next Christendom: The coming of global Christianity*. New York: Oxford University Press.

Koch S. J. and Alois. 2012. "Biblical and patristic foundations for sport." In *Sport and Christianity: A sign of the times in the light of faith,* edited by Kevin Lixey L. C., Christoph Hübenthal, Dietmar Mieth and Norbert Müller, 81–103. Washington DC: Catholic University of America Press.

Kretchmar, R. S. 2005. *Practical Philosophy of Sport and Physical Activity.* 2nd ed. Champaign, IL: Human Kinetics.

Kyle, D. 1998. *Spectacles of Death in Ancient Rome.* New York: Routledge.

Luther, M. 1967. *On the Councils and the Church. Volume 4 of Selected Writings of Martin Luther, 1529–1546,* edited by Theodore Tappert, 195–370. Philadelphia, PA: Fortress.

MacIntyre, A. 2009. *God, Philosophy, Universities: A selective history of the Catholic philosophical tradition.* Lanham, MD: Rowman and Littlefield.

Maximus the Confessor, Saint. 2003. *On the Cosmic Mystery of Jesus Christ: Selected writings of St. Maximus the Confessor,* translated by Paul M. Blowers and Robert Louis Wilken. Crestwood, NY: St. Vladimir's Seminary Press.

Meier, Klaus K. V. 1980. "An affair of flutes: An appreciation of play." *Journal of the Philosophy of Sport* 7: 24–45.

Miller, S. 2004. *Ancient Greek Athletics.* New York: Yale University Press.

Neuhaus, R. J. 2009. *American Babylon: Notes of a Christian exile.* New York: Basic Books.

Newman, John Henry. 2007. "Sermon 22. Witnesses of the resurrection." In *Newman Reader – Works of John Henry Newman.* Pittsburgh, PA: National Institute for Newman Studies. Available online at www.newmanreader.org/works/parochial/volume1/sermon22.html (accessed October 14, 2014).

Nongbri, B. 2013. *Before Religion: A history of a modern concept.* New Haven, CT: Yale University Press.

Novak, M. 1994. *The Joy of Sports: End zone, bases, baskets, balls and the consecration of the American spirit.* Lanham, MD: Madison Books.

Parry, J., M. Nesti, and N. Watson. 2011. *Theology, Ethics and Transcendence in Sports.* New York: Routledge.

Pieper, J. 1998. *Leisure, the Basis of Culture,* translated by Gerald Malsbary. South Bend, IN: St. Augustine Press. (Originally published as *Muße und Kult.* München: Kösel-Verlag, 1948.)

Polanyi, M. 1962. *Personal Knowledge: Towards a post-critical philosophy.* Chicago, IL: University of Chicago Press.

Prothero, S. 2007. *Religious Literacy: What every American needs to know – and doesn't.* New York: Harper Collins.

Schmitz, K. L. 1979. "Sport and play: Suspension of the ordinary." In *Sport and the Body: A philosophical symposium,* edited by E. W. Gerber and W. J. Morgan, 22–9. Philadelphia, PA: Lea and Febiger.

Simon, R. 2010. *Fair Play: The ethics of sport.* 3rd ed. Philadelphia, PA: Westview.

Skillen, A. 1998. "Sport is for losers." In *Ethics and Sport,* edited by M. J. McNamee and S. J. Parry, 169–81. New York: Routledge.

Struna, N. 1996. *People of Prowess: Sport, leisure, and labor in early Anglo-America.* Urbana, IL: University of Illinois Press.

Suits, B. 1977. "Words on play." *Journal of the Philosophy of Sport* 4 (1): 117–31.

Tillich, P. 1953. *Systematic Theology, Volume 1.* London: Nisbet.

Twietmeyer, G. 2007. "Suffering play: Can the time spent on play and games be justified in a suffering world?" *Quest* 59 (2): 201–11.

—— 2008. "A theology of inferiority: Is Christianity the source of kinesiology's second-class status in the academy?" *Quest* 60 (4): 452–66.

Tzu, L. 1972. *Tao Te Ching,* translated by Gia-Fu Feng and Jane English. New York: Vintage Books.

—— 1988. *Tao Te Ching,* translated by Stephen Mitchell. New York: Harper Collins.

Wann, D. L, and M. J. Melnick. 2001. *Sports Fans: The psychology and social impact of spectators.* London: Routledge.

Watson, N. J., and A. Parker. 2013. *Sports and Christianity: Historical and contemporary perspectives.* New York: Routledge.

Woods, R. B. 2007. *Social Issues in Sport.* Champaign, IL: Human Kinetics.

17

SPORT AS A LEGAL SYSTEM

John S. Russell

Sport incorporates the elements of a legal system. It is a rule-governed institution for regulating the conduct of human communities (the communities of individuals who participate in sports). It has legislators or legislative bodies (rules committees or gamewrights) that enact legislation (the rules of a sport). It has judicial officers whose role is to ensure that conduct is regulated according to those rules (referees, umpires and other officials charged with ensuring that the sports are played properly according to the rules). Such parallels suggest that our understanding of sport can be deepened by regarding it as a type of legal system. It seems worthwhile, then, to consider whether philosophical treatments of sport can be illuminated by drawing on legal theory and our experience of the operation of law in human societies. It has been just over 15 years now that a literature has emerged in sport philosophy that has examined these connections and begun to develop what might be called "a jurisprudence of sport" or, in effect, an account of sport as a legal system. Despite its recent appearance, this body of work has had a profound impact on sport philosophy and has important normative implications for the conduct of sport generally. This chapter critically surveys that literature and discusses its implications.

The attempt to understand sport as a type of legal system begins with two papers on adjudication in sport by Russell (1997, 1999). Russell noted that the distinction in law between judging "matters of fact" and "matters of law" has a parallel with umpires' and referees' decisions making calls and interpreting and applying rules. Judicial officials in both contexts, in sport and in law, are called upon to examine evidence to identify important facts and to make decisions about what the laws or rules are or mean and how they are to be applied. Russell used resources from law and philosophy of law in an attempt to clarify umpires' and referees' roles in these respects and, in particular, the nature of discretion they have with respect to making calls and application of rules. Russell regarded these two papers as presenting an outline of a theory of adjudication in sport (1999: 46n1).

It will be useful to organize the current essay into parts that consider judicial roles in sport with respect to matters of fact (or calls) and matters of law (understanding and applying the rules). Philosophical consideration of legal issues in sport extends beyond these two areas, but consideration of them leads to these other topics. It is also important to bear in mind important differences between the nature of law and adjudication in human societies and in sport. In particular, the progress that has been made in understanding the apparent nature of sport as a legal system allows us to sharpen the comparisons that legal theorists have often drawn from sport to illuminate the law of human societies. This is an interesting topic in its own right but it deserves separate treatment and will not be a focus of this chapter, although many of the issues that deserve discussion will be evident from ground covered here.[1] A complete account that describes sport as, or at least compares it to, a legal system should also say something about the nature of rules in sport and may also need to consider the relevance of the work of legal theorists in explaining the nature of rules. However, the nature and status of rules is a foundational issue in sport philosophy that extends beyond the current discussion, which will focus mainly on what appear to be legal institutions and practices in sport. While consideration of the normative content of sport, including rules, figure prominently, this discussion leaves aside consideration of basic questions about the specific nature and variety of rules in sport, despite their undoubted relevance to any jurisprudence of sport.[2]

Making the calls

Any systematic discussion of calls in sport should begin with a small philosophical puzzle (Russell 1997; see also Mumford 2006). By their pronouncements on events that occur during play, umpires in an important sense determine what the events are. That is to say, umpires' calls make facts. When the umpire calls a "strike" or an "out", this creates the fact that a "strike" is added to the count or the number of "outs" remaining in a game has been reduced. This is reflected in the famous saying attributed to baseball hall of fame umpire, Bill Klem "it ain't anything til I call it" (quoted in Russell, 1997: 21). The same idea is suggested in another Hall of Fame umpire Bill McGowan's reported statement to a batter who had protested a call: "If you don't believe you're out, read the morning newspaper!" (quoted in Russell 1997: 22). A puzzle arises because facts are neither true nor false. They simply are. (Propositions are true or false, not facts.) But clearly we do not want to say that we cannot challenge the truth or falsity of a call because it is a fact made by an umpire's pronouncement. That would let Klem and McGowan off the hook too easily. It would render meaningless the idea of "getting the call right" and trying to settle athletic contests as judged assessments of athletic skill. The solution to this puzzle is recognized by the philosopher of language J. L. Austin (1962). Austin noted that performative elements of language (those elements that use language to create social facts like "promises" or "outs" and "strikes") can be readily combined with declarative or descriptive statements which will be true or false. Austin noted that these are commonly combined in judicial-like pronouncements that he called "verdictives". Thus, a judge's finding of fact that an accused is guilty of murder creates the legal fact that the accused is guilty of the crime of murder, but the finding is also a declarative statement of fact and so can be true or false. This analysis applies straightforwardly to umpires and referees, as Austin himself recognized (1962: 152). Their calls, or findings of fact, create a sort of legal fact (a "strike" or an "out' is entered in the scorebook, or a goal is added to one team's score, etc.), but the umpire's finding may be true or false. He or she may have "missed the call" (that is, got it wrong).[3]

Using baseball umpires as an example, Russell describes the above puzzle and its solution to help to clarify the role and function of umpires and referees (these terms will be used interchangeably) in sport. Russell notes, however, that what is distinctive about umpires in sport as compared with judges in courts of law and many other contexts is that they are also *witnesses* to the events that they adjudicate (1997: 23–4). This has important implications for understanding the status of certain calls. In particular, it turns out that some classes of bad calls are not calls in any genuine sense and so should be open to review and change.

In particular, where an umpire either is not, or is prevented from, functioning as a judge or a witness, his or her calls cannot be regarded as genuine calls, even though they may have been made and are, so to speak, "on the books". Thus, an umpire who is prevented from making a call by a player's intentional deception, or a corrupt umpire's intentionally incorrect calls, or an umpire who in the heat of the moment makes a call on an event he or she did not witness but supposes has happened, is failing to meet some of the requirements of fulfilling the role of an umpire. Such calls should be regarded as having no genuine status as calls, much in the same way that we say that a paid-for mail-order Ph.D. is not a real Ph.D. or a flat soufflé is not a real soufflé (because they lack the functional elements of genuine Ph.Ds and soufflés). We might call these sorts of familiar judgments "dismissive judgments" (Kretzmann 1988), since they identify a purported instance of a particular kind (say, a mail-order Ph.D.) but dismiss it as not a genuine instance despite some appearances to the contrary. Thus, when a player deceives an umpire into making a bad call, for example, by "selling" a "phantom tag" or pretending to catch a trapped fly ball (that is, one that has hit the ground fractionally before being caught by the fielder), there is an attempt to prevent him or her from properly performing the function of an umpire by intentionally misleading or confusing him or her through deception as to what the evidence properly is. An umpire in this situation is prevented from performing his or her role by the player's deception. If he or she has a reasonable suspicion about this (perhaps because of the opposition's complaints and the circumstances), this is grounds for asking for help to review the call. Similarly, umpires who in the heat of the moment simply guess at calls or who think that they have made incompetent calls have good reason to believe that they have not functioned reliably as witnesses to an event. If so, they cannot regard their calls as having fulfilled a necessary element of their role as an umpire and should be prepared to seek help. Finally, corrupt umpires who fail to act impartially are not functioning as judges and their calls cannot be regarded as genuine judicial calls and should be set aside. In all these cases, we might apply something like the dismissive judgment "that is no call!" This has the air of paradox about it, because, of course, a call has been uttered and so appears to have been made. But since one of the necessary elements of being an umpire and making calls is missing (functioning as a reliable witness or as an impartial judge), the call's status as a genuine instance of its kind (like the flat soufflé or mail-order Ph.D.) is only apparent.

Russell's analysis (1997) opened discussion of when umpires should regard their calls as open to review and revision. His prescriptions seem modest in light of the reliance on various forms of replay and other electronic aids to umpiring that have become widely entrenched since this paper was published. Russell had little to say about technological aids to umpiring beyond acknowledging the issue and suggesting that replay for key plays was justified and that efficient conduct of games was a consideration in assessing how much further technological aids to officiating should be used (1997: 36–7n20). Nevertheless, Russell's proposals remain relevant. Nicholas Dixon (2003: 104–6) used the analysis to explain and justify the decision in the 2002 Winter Olympics to set aside the scores of a corrupt French figure skating judge and to award Canadian Figure skaters Salé and Pelletier gold medals (they had initially been awarded silver medals), and his argument applies generally to corrupt judging and refereeing scandals, which regrettably are far from unheard of in competitive sport (with refereeing in Olympic boxing taking centre stage recently [Sanneh 2012]). Russell's analysis can also arguably be extended to include instances where the behaviour of fans undermines impartiality; for example, when fan outbursts encourage "homer" calls. Where practicable, such calls should be reviewed on this analysis. Moreover, most of sport is played without benefit of replay and other electronic umpiring aids and will apparently continue to do so. Hence, the arguments that umpires should be prepared to review calls where they believe they have been deceived by participants into making bad calls or where they have reason to believe that their witness's reports are unreliable remain relevant. In either case, the rough test would be whether the umpire would be confident enough to offer his or her own observation of an event as evidence of what actually happened. If the answer is "no," help should be sought where this is practicable.

A rich literature has since emerged on the use of replay and other electronic aids to officiating. The leading contributions in this area are now Harry Collins' "The Philosophy of Umpiring and the Introduction of Decision-Aid Technology" (2010), Mitchell N. Berman's "Replay" (2011c, 2012), Tamba Nlandu's "The Fallacies of the Assumptions behind the Arguments for Goal-line Technology in Soccer" (2012) and Seth Bordner's "Call 'Em as They Are: What Is Wrong with Blown Calls and What To Do About Them" (2014). Collins (2010: 144n3) elaborates the same Austin–Russell framework for conceptualizing what umpires and referees do. He characterizes the performative aspect of the umpire's role as the umpire's "ontological authority" and the role of umpires as special witnesses as their "epistemological privilege. The ontological authority is grounded in their role as judges to make calls and their epistemological privilege is based in the belief that they will be trained, impartial witnesses who will ordinarily be in a better position than competitors to make calls. What has happened in recent years is that the epistemological privilege of umpires has been challenged in various ways by technology. Thus, television and event spectators, and even participants who have access to video review, are frequently in better positions to make calls than umpires are. This in turn has raised doubts about the extent to which their ontological authority should be preserved "leading to loss of credibility of the match official and the sport" (Collins 2010: 136). Collins distinguishes between two different types of technological decision aids, replays and "reconstructed track devices" (RTDs). The latter use television cameras to filter pixels in each frame to construct a path for a moving object to determine its location in space, say, as either inside or outside the service box in tennis. Information about the speed and composition of an object can also be calculated to determine the "footprint" it makes on contact with the ground, thereby to determine more precisely whether a ball is "in" or "out". Collins rightly points out that viewers often assume that RTDs are perfectly accurate, but as with all scientific measuring devices, there is a degree of (often disputed) uncertainty about this. Sports deal with this uncertainty differently. In cricket, Hawk-Eye technology[4] is sometimes used to assist an umpire's call on a "leg before wicket" infraction by calculating whether the thrown ball would have hit the wicket if it had not made contact with the batter's leg first. If the calculated trajectory falls within the machine's margin of error, the decision-making (ontological) authority remains with the umpire. In tennis, where Hawk-Eye technology is also used, no uncertainty is acknowledged, and the decision-making authority is removed from the umpires and the authority to make the call resides with the technology in the zone of uncertainty. Collins plausibly argues that use of technology in this latter way is unjust, since it encourages people to believe that justice is being done, when in fact this is not fully evident. The lack of acknowledgement of the limitations of Hawk-Eye technology delivers a sort of "false transparency". Rather, in some situations, we should acknowledge that even with the machine's assistance we simply do not know what is "in" or "out" when a call falls within a zone of uncertainty. Acknowledging this and retaining umpires' decision-making authority within such zones "would make it clear when and where nothing could *be sure to do* better than the human umpire" (Collins 2010: 142, original emphasis).[5]

Collins' discussion reflects a widely held view about the use of technological aids to umpiring, namely, that the on-field umpire's call should stand unless there is incontrovertible evidence that it is erroneous. Thus, the general conclusion to be drawn from his view is that where no call can be made that "is obvious to all" (Collins 2010: 143) as the correct one based on use of RTDs or other technological aids (such as instant replays), the decision should remain with the umpire. Versions of this approach are currently reflected in use of replays in many major sports, including professional (American) football, hockey, and baseball. Collins thinks that such an approach is mandated by considerations of justice. But all these claims can be challenged. First, it is not clear why the decision-making authority should be given to the umpires who made the initial call where the review does not provide fully definitive evidence to overturn a call. The problem is that all decision-making devices, including human umpires and RTDs and instant replay review, will have statistical "zones of uncertainty". It is entirely possible, and indeed likely, that on-field umpires' zones of uncertainty are larger than those of RTDs (or instant replay that is based on views of a dozen or more cameras that can manipulate speeds and other aspects of the images). Collins appears to acknowledge this (2010: 141). If umpires have, on average, greater zones of uncertainty, then other things being equal deferring to the best judgment of technologically aided calls with smaller uncertainty associated with them is simply deferring to the better measuring device (although neither is in a position to claim absolute authoritative superiority). If this choice is acknowledged and disclosed to participants and fans, there is no false transparency. Arguably, it is superior on grounds of justice as well, since it demonstrates that the most reliable efforts are used to recognize athletic successes. A qualification needs to be acknowledged, however. Since "zones of uncertainty" are statistical averages quantified over many different circumstances each of which has its own zone of uncertainty, in some circumstances on-field umpires may be more reliable (that is, have smaller areas of uncertainty). Such qualifications should be noted and incorporated where it is practicable. But this does not detract from the main point. There is good reason to defer to what we believe is, overall, the most reliable measuring device in the circumstances.

But Collins thinks that deference should be given to on-field umpires' decisions where there is uncertainty about what the correct decision should have been. His most striking claim is that "match officiating is not about accuracy it is about justice" (2010: 142). His comments in defence of this claim are brief but worth careful consideration:

> Accuracy and justice are not necessarily the same. For example, where an optimally skilled and perceptive umpire would consistently call the ball one way and an optimally accurate machine based on impact footprint would call it another, it is not at all clear that machine provides the appropriate call. Coherence with tradition and the way the non-technically assisted game is played may be more important so long as there is equity for all players.
>
> *(Collins 2010: 142)*

Collins may be correct that accurate umpiring decisions and justice are not necessarily the same thing in sport, but quite a bit of clarification and defence is needed for this claim. Match officiating does indeed seem to be about accuracy since, as we have seen, officials' calls are also witnesses' reports about what happened. Moreover, since competitive sport requires the measurement of relative competitive outcome, justice in competitive sport is directly tied to identifying competitive successes accurately. This explains why it is so important for umpires to get the calls right and to strive to learn to be reliable detectors of the on-field facts. It also explains why modern technologies have been adopted to assist adjudication in competitive sport: they can enhance accurate decision making and reinforce the appearance of impartiality in doing so. Thus, if optimally skilled umpires and optimally accurate machines disagree systematically on certain assessments of the facts, the best and fairest way of resolving the disagreement would appear to be to defer to the measuring device with the statistically greater reliability. Sometimes this may favour on-field umpires, although in increasingly many circumstances it will favour decisions supported by technological devices aids like Hawk-Eye and instant replays. This is a result that arguably all participants should find acceptable from the perspective of competition and justice. Justice would have the best chance of being done, and being seen to be done, in such circumstances. "Tradition" may play a role here, but at times it can be in conflict with justice.

Collins has an important, if partial, response available, however. He can point to the traditional role that human referees often play in managing games; for example, when they ignore calls to preserve the flow of a game or to avoid imposing an unjust penalty in certain circumstances (even sometimes for calls that are "obvious to all"), or when they make a call on uncertain evidence as a deterrent when the good conduct of a game needs to be preserved. Indiscriminate use of technological aids could thus end up changing the nature of many sports, not necessarily for the better and not necessarily in ways that would always preserve justice.[6] This is arguably a deeper concern than simply stating that "coherence with tradition" should be preserved. As we shall see, this point complements discussions below, including about the use of umpire discretion with respect to applying and interpreting rules. It does not, however, establish a complete defence of Collins' claim that deference should always be given to on-field umpires in the absence of evidence that should be "obvious to all" that a call needs to be overturned.[7]

An article that stakes out a position opposed to any use of in-game technological aids to umpiring is Tamba Nlandu's "The Fallacies of the Assumptions behind the Arguments for Goalline Technology in Soccer" (Nlandu 2012). Nlandu's arguments address the use of goal-line technology in soccer, but they can be applied generally to the use of technological aids to onfield officiating in all sports. He offers three arguments for opposing technological aids. First, he argues their use is driven mainly by "win at all costs" approaches to competition that are found in elite amateur and professional sport and that are inconsistent with a "play spirit ethic" that is the proper ideal toward which sport should strive. Second, he claims that it is a fallacy to assume that technological aids can be shown to affect game outcomes more than any other events that occur in a game. His view is that we have no reason to believe that umpires' decisions have a greater impact on the game than the players' and coaches' actions and decisions, and so use of technology is driven in part by a "scapegoating" of referees. Third, there is a mistaken belief that technology can eliminate most errors and ensure fairness of game outcomes. Nlandu's positive proposal is to educate athletes to take greater responsibility for assisting umpires make the correct calls (for example, reporting that a goal had been scored when the referee had failed to see it) and to take more responsibility to regulate the game themselves, as this would promote the appropriate play spirit and ethics education in sport while also de-emphasizing the role of referees and the potential for scapegoating them (p. 462–3).

Nlandu's argument for having participants share the responsibility of officiating is worth taking seriously (see Russell [2013], who comes to a similar conclusion via a different argument) But there is no reason to think this is inconsistent with some use of technological aids in some circumstances, for even people of good will may reasonably disagree or not be in a position to make accurate calls. Indeed, a judicious use of technological aids can arguably sometimes contribute to a play spirit and discourage scapegoating of referees when an important refereeing mistake may have been made but no one on the field can agree about this.

Nlandu's other arguments are challengeable as well. To begin with, it is not at all clear that technological aids must promote or encourage a corrupt win at all costs approach to sport. Indeed, it is reasonable to believe that a win at all costs approach will exploit umpires' limited ability to monitor all aspects of a game and thus they will fail to recognize or be taken in by various acts of deception and cheating. Technological aids can help prevent more of these activities from undermining fair competitive outcomes and may deter some of them. It is doubtful, for example, that certain types of cheating like baseball's "double squeeze cut play" would be attempted in any game that had video review.[8]

Nlandu's second argument is a counterfactual one. Thus, he says that a game of soccer "involves thousands of decisions made by players, coaches, managers, referees and even sometimes spectators" (2012: 458). As a result, there is no way of knowing whether "referee mistakes play a much more significant role in determining outcomes … than mistakes made, for instance, by players, coaches, and managers" (2012: 461). The inference to be drawn is that we cannot therefore say that the umpire's mistaken decision was more consequential to the outcome than any other error made by a participant, for if (counterfactually) a player or coach had made any number of different strategic decisions at other points in the game, the outcome could equally have been affected. If I am right that Nlandu has this sort of argument in mind, I doubt that it counts against assisting or changing umpires' calls through use of technological aids. The players and coaches are responsible for the choices and actions they take, including any strategic or other errors they make, so they should accept as fair the outcomes based on them. However, players and coaches can reasonably claim that an outcome may have been unfair if it was influenced by an erroneous call, since this means that the contest and its outcome are not the product of choices, actions, and omissions they are responsible for. The game is thus flawed to the extent that calls have been missed or mistaken. Their claims are stronger to the extent that the erroneous call occurs at a crucial point in a game and has a clear game-changing result, say, a winning goal scored by an undetected hand-ball in the last few seconds of a match.[9] It is certainly true that, had players made certain different choices, a different outcome would have resulted. But this is irrelevant. It overlooks the question as to whether the outcome that occurred was actually a reflection of the legal choices and actions or omissions of the participants – or whether a failure of officiating interfered with or "wrecked" the game in these respects. Another point is that umpires' erroneous calls can not only affect the fairness of outcomes, they can deny participants fair access to other scarce competitive goods (Russell 2013). Thus, an umpire who makes a bad call at first on the 27th out after a pitcher has retired 26 consecutive batters has denied the pitcher (and his teammates) a perfect game. Like competitive wins, personal achievements are also scarce competitive goods that should be fairly awarded. An example occurred in Major League baseball in June 2010, when umpire Jim Joyce wrecked Detroit Tiger Armand Galarraga's perfect game on a clearly erroneous call on the 27th out. Perfect games are extremely rare achievements in baseball. At that time, only 18 had been recorded since the modern Major League era began in 1900.[10] In this instance, there was no other outcome besides changing the call that would have produced a just outcome for the pitcher and his teammates. Nlandu is right that umpires are often wrongly "scapegoated" for what should more honestly be accepted as failures of athletes and coaches. But more argument is needed to show that umpires' failures should never be acknowledged and addressed on the field of play in soccer or other sports.

The most careful and thorough discussion of use of technological aids currently in the literature is undoubtedly Mitchell N. Berman's lengthy law review essay "Replay" (2011c). I cannot do full justice to Berman's rich and nuanced discussion. However, the essay should be the starting point now for discussions of use of technological aids to officiating, in part because it is mainly a ground-clearing exercise that is intended to set the terms for further discussion.

Berman helpfully sets out three separate questions that should be addressed: "(1) What calls should be reviewable?; (2) What should be the procedures for implementing review?; and (3) what should be the standard of review?"(2011c: 1687–8). Berman suggests that the answers to the first two questions are likely to be sport-specific because the practical costs associated with review are likely to be different for different sports (for example, time required for review, the effect the review has on continuity of play). The main part of his discussion addresses "the conventional view" that reversal of on-field decisions by umpires should occur only if there is "indisputable visual evidence" (or "IVE") to support this. Berman's discussion can be regarded, then, as a challenge to views like Collins' which give priority to on-field officials' decisions where there is any uncertainty about whether a call should be overturned. Following mainly the history and arguments for replay within the National Football League, Berman convincingly shows that arguments for the deferential IVE standard are substantially flawed and that the less demanding standard of "*de novo* review" would better serve the goal of error correction while not being unduly costly in loss of efficiency or respect for officials. (*De novo* review is when an appeal body, say, a higher court, makes a new decision as if no prior decision or trial had taken place. In the sport case, it would look at the available evidence, including the eye witness evidence of officials on the field, and make the decision that seemed most likely to be correct.)

Berman falls short, however, of endorsing *de novo* review, noting that it needs to respond to certain further objections that have either not yet been recognized or fully discussed. In particular, he thinks it is necessary to address the concern that all reversals may make sport less entertaining or satisfying because (1) overturning an umpire's decision may reduce the utility of those who lose out on changed calls (perhaps especially if the call is erroneously changed) more than it increases the utility of those who benefit from the corrected call; and (2) there may be a distinction between desert and entitlement that supports the idea that only blunders and not mere mistakes should be corrected. The former are manifestly mistaken calls that a competitor is entitled to have overturned, whereas the latter represent instances where a competitor deserves a different call but is not entitled to it. Thus, a pitcher might deserve a called strike on a pitch that was called a "ball" but may not be entitled to it. If so, only blunders reflect loss of entitlements and so should be corrected, but not mere mistakes. Berman does not appear to be sympathetic to either of these arguments, though he does not respond to them. Arguably, he overlooks the strength of his own arguments against IVE. There is scant evidence for (1). If *de novo* review reduces the number of overall errors without incurring other unacceptable costs (including the ones suggested by Collins), it is not unreasonable to think people will recognize that the best, impartial efforts have been made to get the calls right and live with the consequences without too much unhappiness. In some, probably very rare circumstances, a call may be overturned erroneously. Nevertheless, it is difficult to see why this should be sufficient to reject the case against IVE, and probably the only way to answer this question is to test by *de novo* review. Berman offers no clear grounds for distinguishing between desert and entitlement that seems to help here beyond suggesting it may be a character flaw to expect perfect justice and that just deserts should always be recognized.

If it is correct that Berman's arguments for reform are stronger than he acknowledges, the question then pressed is how far technological aids should be incorporated into competitive sport. A considerably more ambitious stand is taken by Seth Bordner (2014). Bordner argues that wherever it is technically practicable, we should make unrestricted use of technological aids. The goal of officiating should be "to get all of the calls right all of the time". If Berman's own misgivings about the strength of his position are put aside, it seems that we may be driven to a position like Bordner's. However, it is not clear that Bordner addresses objections suggested by Collins. I anticipate further productive discussion between all the points of view discussed so far. I have one related consideration to raise about this that that has not yet been directly discussed in relation to the use of technological aids, although it is suggested in Collins' work.

There may be instances where umpires' "errors" should be tolerated on athletic grounds. This is not because such errors can be competitive obstacles to be overcome as is sometimes argued, but because failures to enforce certain rules can actually add to and improve the nature of the athletic challenges a game presents. Bordner thinks that if machines can do a better job making calls, then they should be permitted to do it. Much of his discussion supports the use of electronic aids to call "balls" and "strikes" in baseball. However, in baseball the strike zone is rarely called as described in the rules. Indeed, it enlarges and contracts and changes shape depending on the level of skill of pitchers and hitters in a particular league, and there is also plenty of evidence that it changes depending on the count (Walsh 2007, 2010). As well, each umpire calls the zone differently, and so one of the interesting athletic challenges for pitchers and hitters is to adjust to an umpire's strike zone. The zone can also change during the game, for example, to improve its conduct (say, enlarging the strike zone to speed it up). Finally, it sometimes appears that umpires give any benefit of doubt on called strikes to the losing teams' batters in the final inning. This adds certain elements of athletic challenge and drama. I suspect, therefore, that there are some types of officiating "errors" that, if applied in an even-handed manner, can actually enhance the quality of the competition and the athletic challenges it presents. Similar points may be true about umpires' decisions not to call certain penalties late in games (discussed below). This is arguably not merely a matter of respecting tradition but of respecting the principles that underlie a competition, and it may mean that some calls should be respected even if technological review reveals an error is "obvious to all". Although further discussion is undoubtedly required, there are some good competitive and athletic reasons to think it would be a mistake to eliminate such elements from games through indiscriminate use of technological aids.

Two other notable papers about calls are Mark Hamilton's (2011) "The Moral Ambiguity of the Make-up Call" and Berman's (2011a) "Let 'Em Play: A Study in the Jurisprudence of Sport". Hamilton's paper discusses the apparent phenomenon in some sports of umpires' trying to correct mistaken calls by making proportionately compensating mistaken calls against the team that benefited from the initial error. Hamilton defines make-up calls as "the act of compensation for a questionable or bad officiating call by making a proportionately even call against the team that was aided by the first call" (Hamilton 2011: 212, 216–17). Hamilton argues that the best case for make-up calls treats them as a species of corrective justice, or roughly, the idea that people have obligations to repair harms they have caused (2011: 224). Make-up calls are thus instances of attempts to correct wrongful gains. In the case of competitive sport, the make-up call attempts "to keep the game in harmony" by restoring to a team or player what has been mistakenly taken away from them. However, Hamilton notes that that there are powerful arguments against make-up calls. Trading injustices seems morally questionable (it is controversial that two wrongs can make a right); make-up calls also appear to use players or teams as mere means; the practice is beset with uncertainty regarding what proper compensation amounts to, since the compensating call may provide either insufficient or excess benefit given its timing in a contest; and makeups create questions about the honesty and impartiality of umpires (2011: 216–17). We might add to this list that the practice it encourages of "working the umpires" (acknowledged by Hamilton) cannot be limited to laying the ground for make-up calls only. Hamilton concludes that make-up calls are "morally offensive … [and] are self-evidently immoral and compromise the integrity and impartiality of officials" (2011: 225).

The latter remark may be too strongly stated in light of the apparently conflicting moral considerations. But Hamilton's strong moral reservations seem well-founded on balance, as is his conclusion that the ethos of make-up calls in certain sports like baseball and basketball (and I would add hockey) is properly regarded as immoral. He proposes responding to this by becoming more accepting of the need to accept reversals of erroneous calls and by better training of umpires and more extensive use of technological aids (2011: 227). All this is consistent with much of what has already been covered here. Arguably, if Hamilton is correct that an ethos of make-up calls is immoral, it would also be appropriate to consider the proposals by Nlandu and Russell to call on participants, at least sometimes, to assist with making calls. The ethos of leaving these matters entirely to officials may be another tradition that deserves to be overturned on moral grounds and would further reduce the motive for make-up calls. Although having participants sometimes assist umpires may seem overly ambitious or unrealistic, it is worth recognizing that many sports have effective practices of having participants make calls (such as golf, ultimate, curling), and it used to be a more common practice in other sports (for example, tennis, including professional tennis).[11] The argument can be given straightforwardly on grounds of distributive and restorative justice: since athletic successes are scarce goods (for example, wins, strikeouts, hits, perfect games, championships), the team that benefits from an erroneous call is obtaining an undeserved scarce good. If the distributive justice argument is relevant, being the recipient of an umpiring error may be like finding a banking error in your favour (the apparent good fortune of a lucky windfall of a scarce good!) and having an obligation to disclose that error (Russell 2013).

Another important discussion of umpire discretion about calls is Berman's "Let 'Em Play: A Study in the Jurisprudence of Sport" (2011a). Berman attempts to justify the apparent practice of "temporal variance," or enforcing certain fouls (and sometimes other rules) less strictly toward the end of contests. Called fouls negatively affect opportunities and, according to Berman, can have more consequential effects later in a game as opposed to earlier in games because opportunities are running out. As a result, sometimes fouls called later in a game can result effectively in "over-compensation" for a rule violation. Berman has an extended defence of this view that includes careful discussions of probability and a complex conceptual apparatus, but the idea can be illustrated simply with an example. Awarding two free throws in the last second of a tied basketball game can amount to over-compensation, in particular, if the foul is given for an infraction that is tangential to determining the outcome of a contest (say, some minor body contact in basketball in the last seconds of a tied game).

The persuasiveness of Berman's position relies crucially (as he recognizes) on recognizing a role for principles in interpreting the rules in sport, in this case that athletic outcomes should be measured by relative display of the athletic skills a sport is designed to test (2011a: 1349). The role of principles in sport and in adjudication is an issue that will be taken up in the next section. I have two further observations to offer here.

Berman's arguments for temporal variance might be extended to justify other changes to umpiring practices, including proposals that may be in tension with his defence of temporal variance. Berman's focus is on fouls late in games that cause no or very little harm to an opponent's chances for competitive success. One might think penalizing such fouls is always over-compensatory and ask why they should be called at all. The idea that such penalties deter more serious fouling seems open to question, since the line could in theory be drawn consistently at another place where the penalties are appropriate. Berman says stricter enforcement early in games can be "easily defended" for its deterrent value (2011a: 1341). Maybe this is true, but the evidence deserves to be carefully examined (and it may be different for different sports). Moreover, a great deal of harmless fouling seems ignored generally in certain sports, including the sports Berman discusses. A more revisionist approach may be supported by standard legal practices of having the punishment fit the importance of the wrong or the harm caused, attempts to avoid falling afoul of the *de minimis non curat lex* doctrine in law (roughly, the law does not deal with trifles), and a simple commitment to the consistent application of the law.

Perhaps an even more pressing related question is whether Berman's reasoning supports enforcing certain rule violations *more strictly* late in games. For example, maybe referees in hockey or basketball, for example, should call certain obstruction-like fouls more closely later in games *to ensure* that sport-specific skills determine the outcome of games as time is running out. Purely inconsequential violations need not be called perhaps, but clear rule violations that are at all borderline as to whether they may influence outcomes should be assiduously called to encourage players to conduct themselves in ways that will do most to ensure that games are determined by superior game-specific athletic skills, particularly as opportunities to exercise those skills are running out at the end of a game.

The evidence that Berman collects for temporal variance could also be interpreted as being inconsistent with ensuring that games are determined by sport-specific skills (2011a: 1334–54). An explanation for temporal variance is that umpires prefer taking a more lenient approach to enforcement at the close of a game because they do not want to be seen to have too great an influence on the outcome of a game. Perhaps participants (and fans) also prefer that umpires adopt this practice because they would prefer to have available at the end of games an "anything goes" option for trying to win in order to preserve the drama of the contest. If such preferences are what is supporting temporal variance to any significant degree, we should be sceptical that umpires' willingness to "let 'em play" late in athletic contests means they are more likely to be determined by sport-specific skills. In fact, the contrary may be true, and if we want outcomes to reflect accurately players' relative display of skills, umpires should apply many rules more stringently than they currently do late in games. Or perhaps they should apply some rules more stringently and others more leniently at the end of games or perhaps throughout them. This is not a rejection of Berman's approach (it is arguably an extension of it), and I do not mean to defend the forgoing arguments. It suggests, however, that the possible implications of Berman's views merit further discussion. Arguably, temporal variance may sometimes reflect a conflict of values between sport as display and measurement of athletic skill and sport as dramatic contest. A consideration of this conflict may encourage more critical stances toward certain umpiring conventions. I suspect that further discussion would help to illuminate a theory of adjudication in sport and also deepen our understanding of specific sports and sport generally.

The discussion so far has overlooked the role of judging in aesthetic sports. Graham McFee initially discussed this topic in *Sport, Rules and Values* (2004: ch. 5) and has recently updated his position (McFee 2013). He has clarified the role of judging in aesthetic sports in part by contrasting it with what umpires do in refereed or umpired contests. He uses David Best's distinction between "aesthetic and purposive sports" (Best 1978) to mark the difference, respectively, between sports that are judged and sports that are umpired or refereed (for example, diving and figure skating are judged sports, whereas soccer and baseball are umpired or refereed sports). McFee notes that judged sports raise different questions about fairness of officiating, particularly since judging is driven by aesthetic value and may appear more subjective and less factual (a position that he challenges). He also notes that judging in aesthetic sports resembles refereeing more than may appear at first glance. These contributions represent foundational additions to the literature and introduce another area of scholarship in adjudication in sport.

Applying the rules

In his 1999 paper, "Are Rules All an Umpire Has To Work With?", Russell challenges the conventional view that umpires' sole source for making decisions are the rules of a game. He argues that this "ideology of games" reflects the vices of "legal formalism" that were noted by philosopher of law H. L. A. Hart (1961), in particular by overlooking the ineluctable indeterminacy of rules and the practical and moral necessity for the use of judicial discretion where rules fail to provide sufficient guidance by themselves or pose serious problems of injustice. Following Ronald Dworkin's (1978, 1986) theory of law and adjudication, Russell argues that certain principles are embedded in legal systems, including in sport. These principles are as much parts of the law as the rules, and so what is the law of a sport is a reflection of both principles and rules. Principles, in particular, can direct umpire decision making when the rules are significantly indeterminate or when their force indicates that the rules require amendment in some way. Thus, once we recognize the role and force of principles in legal systems, we must recognize that judicial officials have obligations to use those principles and that those principles can direct judicial discretion in determining what the law is. This will not lead to arbitrary decisions, since integrity is the supreme virtue of law and this requires that the law be interpreted in a principled and coherent way, looking at past practice and attempting to show it in its best light. Russell applies this idea to sport, using baseball umpires as an example: "We might try to understand and interpret the rules of a game, say, baseball, to generate a coherent and principled account of the point and purposes that underlie the game, attempting to show the game in its best light" (Russell 1999: 35).

This is quite abstract, of course. What might these principles be? Russell suggests the following key principle, which he describes as "the first principle of games adjudication": "Rules should be interpreted in such a manner that the excellences embodied in achieving the lusory goal of the game are not undermined but are maintained and fostered" (1999: 35).

Russell draws three other principles of adjudication from this principle (principles of competitive balance, fair play and sportsmanship, and good conduct of games). This is not intended to be an exhaustive list of principles of adjudication, and in fact Russell proposes some other principles as well.[12] He then shows how these principles are reflected in various disputed decisions by umpires and other rules officials from the history of baseball.

This analysis has had significant influence on sport philosophy generally. Robert Simon (2000) coined the term "broad internalism" to describe an account of sport that recognizes that normative principles are part of sport in addition to the rules, using this Dworkinian interpretivist analysis and the principles of adjudication as a principal support for this position. The position was offered as a competitor to formalist and conventionalist theories of sport and is now probably the leading account of sport in the literature. This discussion is not reviewed in this chapter, except to note that a Dworkinian approach to law in sport arguably must be informed by a general theory of sport, just as a theory of law must be informed by a theory of political morality (Russell 1999, 2011; see also McFee 2004: 110–11). Simon's article, in effect, takes up this suggestion. The discussion has since advanced further by noting the role of various moral principles that are internal to sport, all of which will of course be relevant to exercise of judicial authority and discretion in sport (Simon 2002; Russell 2004, 2007, 2011; Torres 2012).

Since a Dworkinian analysis of adjudication and law was developed in response to a legal positivist theory of law, it was to be expected that sport philosophers would present a legal positivist response to an interpretivist account of law and adjudication in sport. Although legal positivism is a theory of law and not a theory of adjudication *per se* (legal positivism regards law as constituted by certain social facts that do not include moral values as a necessary element), Patrick Lenta and Simon Beck (2006) later argued that virtues of efficiency, predictability, and respect for separation of powers are features of legal positivist approaches to law that can inform judicial practice. They argue this is preferable to a Dworkinian approach to adjudication in sport, which is too activist because it gives umpires and referees too much authority to meddle with the rules of games. They say Dworkinian referees threaten the advantages of predictability and efficiency involved in black letter (that is, literal and rigid) rule-following and represent a threat to the separation of powers between legislators and judges (or gamewrights and umpires).

Lenta and Beck's concerns about umpires' exercising too much discretion are understandable, but the importance of respecting predictability and efficiency were outlined in Russell's paper (Russell 1999: 34, 36, 40). Moreover, since Lenta and Beck agree that these virtues are not always overriding, it is not clear what the disagreement amounts to, particularly since they also recognize that positivists and Dworkinians can agree on how to deal with a well-known paradox in applying the rules of cricket that provides the case study that animates their discussion. Throughout his writings, Dworkin (1978: 37; 1986, 401) has recognized that respect for separation of powers is a principle that constrains adjudication. Russell's remarks reflected this as well (Russell 1999: 44), although he has acknowledged that they deserved to be developed more carefully (2011, 266). Respect for a doctrine of precedent also plays a similar constraining role in Dworkinian adjudication and can be exported to sport by recognizing precedents set by rulings of interpretation of rules by higher level officials and governing bodies. Even more importantly, however, Lenta and Beck's discussion overlooks the evidence for the normative principled foundations of sport and how they undermine the application of a positivist theory of law to sport and sport adjudication, since positivists reject the idea that legal systems have any inherent specific normative content. As Russell notes, sport, perhaps unlike municipal legal systems, appears to have an internally "fixed", principled constitution that includes various moral and other normative elements (Russell 1999: 39). Prospects for a legal positivist-inspired approach to law and adjudication in sport thus appear quite uncertain.

A similar but more sympathetic criticism of Russell's theory of adjudication in sport is presented by Berman in "On Interpretivism and Formalism in Sports Officiating: From General to Particular Jurisprudence" (2011b). Berman's qualified defence of formalism represents the most carefully argued response to Russell's Dworkinian interpretivist approach to umpiring adjudication. Berman's position is distinct from Beck and Lenta's in that he acknowledges a role for principles as internal to sport. He rightly observes, however, that while the law in sport includes principles, what the law is one thing and how far it should be enforced by judges is another. Thus, he suggests that a "formalist" theory of adjudication is reconcilable with interpretivism, in part because of the role certain principles internal to particular sports may play. For example, he suggests that some "honour sports" like golf may value rigid, black letter rule following as a sort of test of "self-abnegation" whereas other sports may value a "rules-lawyering" type of gamesmanship as an internal sport-related excellence (Berman 2011b: 187–9). (Rules lawyers "interpret rules in an overly literal sense or in such a way as to significantly reduce the thematic or logical aspects of a game").[13] A more pragmatic reason for defending formalism in sport is that umpires may do a better job of enforcement of rules if they take a formalist approach (2011b: 191). Given that what the law is in sport is a function of both rules and principles, formalism is thus, strictly speaking, a "second best strategy for epistemically limited officiators", although it is the best practically available strategy. It is not clear how far Berman means to defend such formalism. He says that "some degree of formalism in sports officiating may often be supported" (2011b: 178) but also that "formalism as a theory of adjudication is reconcilable with interpretivism as a theory of legal content" (2011b: 192). The first claim is a modest one that interpretivists should accept: sometimes black letter rule following is appropriate for all sorts of reasons. This discussion therefore focuses on the idea that formalism may be practically reconcilable with interpretivism as a matter of general practice.

Berman's arguments in defence of formalism are open to challenge on a number of fronts. About rules lawyering, it is difficult to think of an actual instance where it can plausibly be argued that this is a part of "the law or normative content of a sport " (2011b: 192). Berman thinks baseball represents an example, but the evidence supports the contrary. If rules lawyering were an internal part of baseball that justified a formalist approach to adjudication (because baseball recognizes "wily self-assertion" through exploitation of rules as a legitimate type of sporting excellence [Berman 2011b: 192]), then we should be surprised that decisions were overturned like the one in the famous "pine tar incident" (Russell 1999: 30–1) where umpires disallowed a potentially game-winning home run because some pine tar was covering the hitter's bat in a prohibited but non-consequential way, even though the rules could be stitched together and read this way. Moreover, this is consistently what happens when players attempt to exploit loopholes and other features of rules to their advantage, as Russell's baseball examples all show. The protests were all either addressed on the field or are overturned later in ways that follow from the principles of adjudication and Berman's similar "athletic principle" (Berman 2011b: 177). This distinguishes baseball from the examples that Berman gives of non-sporting games that explicitly permit rules lawyering. This strongly suggests that rules lawyering is not reflected in the internal principles or norms of baseball and that it should be treated with the utmost suspicion by adjudicators. Rather, the evidence supports the view that rules lawyering is a shrewd and sometimes desperate strategy to deny or nullify other players' deserved athletic successes by exploiting baseball's extensive and complex rules. It should thus be aligned with a morally-flawed "win at any cost" approach to competition (Russell 2013, 2014).

Berman's own example of umpire Dick Nallin's decision in 1932 to allow Yankee Tony Lazzeri to bat out of turn, which was overturned after the game was protested, is arguably not a matter of rules lawyering, since there was nothing merely formal or black letter about requiring this rule to be observed and overturning the umpire's decision. Tigers' manager Bucky Harris allowed the Yankees to make this mistake and then pointed it out to the umpire. This sort of "gamesmanship" (if it is that) is not obviously rules lawyering but merely an insistence that an opponent observe the rules in a way that is consistent with the principles of the game. Umpire Nallin should have known better. Knowing the batting order in advance is a key to defensive strategy in baseball (for example, often determining how the previous batter will be pitched to). Setting a precedent to the contrary would undermine this and raise questions about the need for a batting order. So upholding the rule had its basis in respect for something like the first principle of adjudication or what Berman calls "the athletic principle".

Berman is, however, correct that rules lawyering might be parts of some games. But there is another more general objection that any such introduction would face in sport. It is that the precedents it would set would often tend either immediately or over time to undermine, or render unrecognizable, a sport as a test of the athletic excellences it was designed to measure. As Russell (1999: 37) suggests, it is best regarded as a sort of "anti-game" strategy. Nevertheless, Berman (2011b: 187) is correct that some non-sporting games incorporate it and perhaps some sports could though this remains to be seen.

Berman's golf example is similarly open to question. One response is that formalism and a formalist approach to officiating actually interferes with the game of golf. There *should be* more exercise of discretion by officials in some situations and there should be a robust debate about certain rules in golf. Even with changes to rules to ensure that the game is properly a test of athletic excellence, there will still be plenty of room for golf to remain a test of honour and self-abnegation for the simple reason that the rules are complex, the game is expected to be self-officiated, and frequently only the players are in a position to know if a rule has been violated. Another response is that despite the apparently counterintuitive implications of some of the rules of golf in some circumstances, they nevertheless have a basis in ensuring that the game is really a challenge of the athletic skills that the game sets out to test. In a way, the expectations of officiating in golf are a challenge to the "let 'em play" approach that Berman defends elsewhere (2011a), but are grounded in the same principle that outcomes of games should be determined by who better displays the skills they were designed to test. Golf strives to do its utmost to ensure that outcomes in competition really are the product of the exercise of sport-related excellences by interpreting and applying the rules very strictly. It does not matter that a penalty late in a competition is more consequential to a player's prospect for success. Nor does it matter that certain penalties are for events that have the appearance of being inconsequential. What matters is that the entire competition should be judged consistently within the rules throughout and that everything be done so that we can be as confident as we can be that the winner really deserves the victory based on the athletic skill he or she displays *and* that the relative differences in skill between competitors is accurately measured. Perhaps golf should relax some of its rules and adjudicators should play a role in this, but this is consistent with recognizing that the consistent and meticulous application of rules in golf is appropriate and a model that perhaps should be taken more seriously elsewhere. Moreover, since golf is self-officiated, allowing golfers to exercise discretion about when rule violations are consequential and when they are not would present too great a conflict of interest for the competitors, and so the solution is to demand strict enforcement of the rules. All this is consistent with and supported by an interpretivist approach to adjudication that is focused on fostering a context where the excellences related to the game are maintained and fostered, or as Berman (2011b: 177) puts it "the outcome reflects the competitors' relative excellence".

Finally, it is not clear that formalism is the best practically available approach to adjudication generally. For example, if formalism should be taken as the proper approach to umpiring, then it would appear that Berman's (2011a) proposals in "Let 'Em Play" should be regarded with more scepticism than he acknowledges. Rather, it makes sense to acknowledge and discuss the principled basis for umpires to use discretion in applying rules, because they exercise that discretion *so very often* even where the rules are clear, as Berman shows in "Let 'Em Play," and as Russell suggests in his examples,[14] and as is evident in other umpired sports. Extensions of that discretion to resolve some further cases may make sense, and indeed are probably often occurring without comment. There are many good reasons for judicial restraint, but there will arise practical and moral necessities to exercise a limited (or a Dworkinian "weak") discretion. Where the boundaries are between judicial discretion and judicial restraint should be a lively topic of discussion in sport as it is in other contexts.

In "Fairness, Epistemology, and Rules: A Prolegomenon to a Philosophy of Officiating" (McFee 2011; see also McFee 2004: ch.6), Graham McFee advances a somewhat different Dworkinian framework for adjudication than the one defended by Russell. McFee is sceptical that it is possible to identify any "exceptionless" principles of adjudication that apply across sports. His view is "contextualist" in the sense that the principles in sport cannot be separated from the rules of a particular sport, which is to say that each sport will have something like its own principles that provide normative guidance along with its rules (McFee 2011: 234–5, 2004, 115–16). In defending this contextualist approach, McFee does not claim that the problem is with the abstractness of the principles of adjudication, "but rather that they are abstracted from actual decisions; and thus do not in themselves facilitate our coming to officiating decisions" (2011: 238). His idea is that the principles of adjudication are really just "derived after the fact ... where, having *made* the decision the umpires use these terms to explain or justify it" (2011: 239, original emphasis).

This is an interesting objection. McFee does not mean to press without qualification a common contextualist criticism that general principles are too abstract to be normatively useful (but see McFee 2004: 141–3). Also, I am sure that he is correct that umpires and participants can often look at a case and decide what is to be done without thinking carefully about what the principles might be that justify a decision. They may then look at what they have decided and explain their decision using principles like the first principle of game adjudication. But none of this shows that the role of these principles is limited to a sort of mere ex post facto rationalization of a decision. Umpires, and judges generally, want to know what led them to a conclusion. The principles that they identify are used to explain the normative basis for their reasoning, and thus support a role for the principles as internal to that reasoning, not abstracted from it. Dworkin's theory of law sought to explain this apparently key aspect of judicial reasoning, and to the extent that McFee rejects this position, it is unclear that he is really defending a Dworkinian account of judicial decision making in sport. In addition, the fact that umpires may not have explicitly recognized the role of such principles while they were deliberating (perhaps they talked about the importance of preserving the "spirit" or the "integrity" of the game, and so on, or perhaps they just *knew* what was the right thing to do) does not demonstrate that these principles were not at work. Moreover, once those principles are articulated, they may be used as guides in other relevantly similar contexts, although they may sometimes only amount to rough guides and new circumstances may shed further light on their meaning. The principles can also clarify the meaning and uses of frustratingly abstract terms like the "spirit of the rules" or "integrity of the game" that are often used to justify the exercise of discretion with respect to rules. In this way, what is going on reflects a clarification and deeper understanding of sport and specific sports and of judicial reasoning in sport. It is worth noting that, until very recently, there had been no serious discussions about umpires' exercise of discretion in sport, and there had been general scepticism that they have any such authority. Thus, we should see the principles of games adjudication as first attempts at contributing to a jurisprudence of officiating and look forward to further articulation of these and other principles.

A corollary to this is that McFee's account of umpires' decision making about rules seems obscure about how principles actually figure officials' reasoning. Again, the Dworkinian influence seems uncertain. Since rules and principles cannot be separated (cf. Dworkin 1978: 26) and umpires are to think contextually, the entire process seems intuitionist at its core. A problem with this approach is that it is unclear how disagreements about what should be done could be resolved without articulating what the deeper principles are that inform aspects of the disputants' reasoning and then examining the evidence to determine what weight, if any, should be assigned those principles in a particular context. This is, of course, a familiar problem with contextualist reasoning: its methodology may be too uncritical in its respect for authority or tradition. However, these are just problems, not refutations. The contextual nature of judgments involving principles deserves to be carefully considered, and the differences between the accounts described here "may be only one of nuance," as McFee (2011: 239) acknowledges. Nevertheless, we have not seen any compelling argument for rejecting a more traditional account of judicial reasoning.

Conclusion

Inquiry into the relationship between sport, law, and legal theory has emerged in recent years as a flourishing new area within sport philosophy. It has contributed importantly to the understanding not only of adjudication in sport but to the understanding of sport in general. Moreover, none of this work is of merely academic interest. The review presented here clarifies the grounds for the exercise of discretion by umpires and referees with respect to making calls and interpreting rules. These arguments support recent trends in officiating while also presenting noteworthy caveats to those trends and challenges to more traditional practices and conceptions of umpiring. The nature of judging in aesthetic sports has also been examined and clarified (a topic that tends to be further removed from the public spotlight and deserves careful consideration). Such contributions should be considered and taken into account by practicing umpires, referees, performance sport judges, and sport officials generally. Despite some cautions and disagreements, arguments considered here for review of judgment calls and use of technological aids have been illuminating and appear compelling and consistent with the best worked out conceptions of sport and of particular sports. As well, it is clear that umpires must acknowledge that the normative content of sport and what they do sometimes in upholding "the spirit" of athletic contests is informed by more than just the rules. Sport philosophers have developed specific, carefully supported proposals for what that extra-rule normative content might be. All this fits with and helps to inform trends in sport that have seen the role of umpiring change substantially in recent years. More change is likely on the way but will need to be informed by carefully considered evidence and reasoning. Officiating in sport is complex and fascinating, much more so than is commonly thought. A remarkable amount of progress has been achieved in making sense of this within a period of not much more than 15 years. It will be interesting to see what the next 15 years brings.

Acknowledgements

I am indebted to Harry Collins, Mike McNamee, Tamba Nlandu for comments which have helped to improve this paper. The errors remain my own.

Notes

1 See Russell (2011) for an attempt to explain some of the limitations of the sport–law comparison.
2 See Carlsen and Gleaves (2011) for a critical review of the literature on rules in sport philosophy. Sport philosophers' extensive work on the nature of rules in sport draws mainly on philosophy of language and has not yet been influenced by legal theory *per se*. See also McFee (2004).
3 Umpires' calls also have what Austin calls "exercitive force", which reflects the exercise of powers in light of the position an official holds (for example, the power to make a person out and thus to send someone off the field who has made an out). Austin (1962: 153) also recognizes that these performative elements can be bundled with descriptive statements. See Russell (1997: 23) for discussion.
4 Hawk-Eye cricket officiating system, Hawk-Eye Innovations Ltd. See the company website at www.hawkeyeinnovations.co.uk/page/sports-officiating/cricket (accessed October 14, 2014).
5 Collins' position is not meant to take a position on the use of video review in aesthetic judging; for example, in diving or gymnastics. The general issue of aesthetic judging in sport is addressed later in this chapter.
6 I am indebted to Harry Collins for clarifying that he meant "coherence with tradition" to include preserving the nature of the game and that use technological aids may unintentionally undermine this (personal communication, May 25, 2013). Technology may also undermine participant safety; for example, when umpires allow defensive players in baseball to miss bases on clear force outs to avoid injury (that is, so-called "vicinity plays").
7 See Royce (2012) for a more complete discussion of some of the elements of Collins' paper that appear in need of clarification. See also McFee (2004: 101–2) for other pertinent remarks about relying on technological devices.
8 In this case, under a two-umpire system with runners at second and third with less than two out, the batter lays a bunt down the first base line, the runner at third scores while the runner at second cuts across the infield in front of third base behind the field umpire, who will be watching the play to first and while the plate umpire is watching to see that the bunt remains fair. Two runs score on the

sacrifice because neither umpire can detect that third base was missed. Personal note: one of my philosophy of law students won a California state championship on this play. He reported that it was a controversial result – a near riot ensued.

9 See Berman's "Let 'Em Play" (2011a) for further development of this point (and discussed later in this chapter).

10 See Wikipedia "Perfect Game" and "Armando Galarraga".

11 Mike McNamee has reminded me that in the earlier times of "the gentleman athlete", matches were self-officiated by the captains of opposing teams. All these sorts of precedents suggest that we should be open to experimentation about sharing the burdens of officiating.

12 Later, Russell refers to the first principle of adjudication as "the internal principle" and contrasts it with another principle "the external principle" which recognizes the voluntary aspect of playing games. For Russell, these are the two most general principles that are internal to sport. See Hardman (2009) and Weimar (2012) for thoughtful discussions that express plausible objections to Russell's formulation of the external principle.

13 Definition from the website "Board Game Geek," quoted in Berman (2011b: 187).

14 The strike zone in baseball is probably his best example, but he could have mentioned "cheating" on balks and "vicinity plays" as others.

References

Austin. J. L. 1962. *How to do Things with Words,* edited by J. O. Urmson. Oxford: Oxford University Press.

Berman, Mitchell N. 2011a. "Let 'Em Play": A Study in the Jurisprudence of Sport. *Georgetown Law Journal* 99 (5): 1325–69.

—— 2011b. On Interpretivism and Formalism in Sports Officiating: From General to Particular Jurisprudence. *Journal of the Philosophy of Sport* 38 (2): 177–96.

—— 2011c. Replay. *California Law Review* 99 (6): 1684–744.

Best, David. 1978. *Philosophy and Human Movement.* London: Allen and Unwin.

Bordner, Seth. 2014. Call 'Em as They Are: What's Wrong with Blown Calls and What to do About Them. *Journal of the Philosophy of Sport.* Published online 1 May. DOI:10.1080/00948705.2014.911096.

Carlsen, Chad and Gleaves, John. 2011. Categorical Shortcomings: Application, adjudication and contextual description of game rules. *Journal of the Philosophy of Sport* 38 (2): 197–212.

Collins, Harry. 2010. The philosophy of umpiring and the introduction of decision-aid technology. *Journal of the Philosophy of Sport* 37 (2): 135–46.

—— 2012. Sport Decision-aids and the "CSI Effect": Why Cricket Uses Hawk-Eye Well and Tennis Uses it Badly. *Public Understanding of Science* 21 (8): 904–21.

Dixon, Nicholas. 2003. Canadian Figure Skaters, French Judges, and Realism in Sport. *Journal of the Philosophy of Sport* 30 (2): 103–16.

Dworkin, Ronald. 1978. *Taking Rights Seriously.* Cambridge MA: Harvard University Press.

—— 1986. *Law's Empire.* Cambridge MA: Harvard University Press.

Hamilton, Mark. 2011. The Moral Ambiguity of the Make-up Call. *Journal of the Philosophy of Sport* 38 (2): 212–28.

Hardman, A. R. 2009. Sport, Moral Interpretivism, and Football's Voluntary Suspension of Play Norm. *Sport, Ethics and Philosophy.* 3 (1): 49–65.

Hart, H. L. A. 1961. *The Concept of Law.* Oxford: Oxford University Press.

Kretzmann, Norman. 1988. Lex Iniusta Non est Lex: Laws on trial in Aquinas' court of conscience. *American Journal of Jurisprudence* 33 (1): 99–121.

Lenta, Patrick, and Beck, Simon. 2006. A Sporting Dilemma and its Jurisprudence. *Journal of the Philosophy of Sport* 33 (2): 125–44.

McFee, Graham. 2004. *Sport, Rules and Values.* London: Routledge.

—— 2011. Fairness, Epistemology and Rules: A Prolegomenon to a Philosophy of Officiating. *Journal of the Philosophy of Sport* 38 (2): 229–53.

—— 2013. Officiating in Aesthetic Sports. *Journal of the Philosophy of Sport* 40 (1): 1–17.

Mumford, Stephen. 2006. Truth-makers for Judgment Calls. *European Journal of Sport Science* 6 (3): 179–86.

Nlandu, Tamba. 2012. The Fallacies and Assumptions Behind the Arguments for Goal-line Technology in Soccer. *Sport, Ethics and Philosophy* 6 (4): 451–66.

Royce, Richard. 2012. Refereeing and Technology: Reflections on Collins' Proposals. *Journal of the Philosophy of Sport* 39 (1): 53–64.

Russell, J. S. 1997. The Concept of a Call in Baseball. *Journal of the Philosophy of Sport* 24: 21–37.
—— 1999. Are Rules All an Umpire has to Work With? *Journal of the Philosophy of Sport* 26: 27–49.
—— 2004. Moral Realism in Sport. *Journal of the Philosophy of Sport*. 31 (2): 142–60.
—— 2007. Broad Internalism and the Moral Foundations of Sport. In *Ethics in Sport*, 2nd ed., edited by W. J. Morgan, 51–66. Champaign, IL: Human Kinetics.
—— 2011. Limitations of the Law–Sport Comparison. *Journal of the Philosophy of Sport* 38 (2): 254–72.
—— 2013. Coaching and Undeserved Athletic Success. In *The Ethics of Coaching Sports: Moral, Social, and Legal Issues,* edited by Robert L. Simon, 103–20. Philadelphia PA: Westview Press.
—— 2014. Competitive sport, moral development, and peace. In *The Bloomsbury Companion to the Philosophy of Sport,* edited by Cesar R. Torres, 228–44. London: Bloomsbury.
Sanneh, Kalefa. 2012. Fixing the Olympics? Azerbaijan's Boxing Scandal. *New Yorker* August 2. Available online at www.newyorker.com/online/blogs/sportingscene/2012/08/olympic-fix-the-case-of-the-azeri-boxer.html (accessed October 14, 2014).
Simon, Robert L. 2000. Internalism and Internal Values in Sport. *Journal of the Philosophy of Sport* 27: 1–16.
—— 2002. Sports, Relativism, and Moral Education. In *Sport Ethics*, ed. Jan Boxill, 15–28. Oxford: Oxford University Press.
Torres, Cesar R. 2012. Further Interpretivism's Integrity: Bringing Together Ethics and Aesthetics. *Journal of the Philosophy of Sport* 39 (2): 299–319.
Walsh, John. 2007. The Strike Zone: Fact vs. Fiction. *Hard Ball Times* July 11. Available online at www.hardballtimes.com/main/article/strike-zone-fact-vs-fiction (accessed October 14, 2014).
Walsh, John, 2010. The Compassionate Umpire. *Hard Ball Times*, April 7. Available online at www.hardballtimes.com/main/article/the-compassionate-umpire (accessed October 14, 2014).
Weimer, Stephen. 2012. Consent and Right Action in Sport. *Journal of the Philosophy of Sport* 39 (1): 11–32.

18

METAPHYSICS AND SPORT

Stephen Mumford

Metaphysics

Metaphysics is the branch of philosophy that deals with the nature of things in the most general and abstract of terms. It thus considers questions such as what kinds of thing there are. But this is so general that the concern tends to be with categories of things rather than particular things. Hence, some of the fundamental questions concern the nature and existence of substances, properties and relations, time, causation, identity, natural kinds and laws of nature.[1]

To take by way of illustration the last item in that list of metaphysical notions, a scientist might consider what precisely the law of gravitational attraction is, aiming to find the right equation that describes the exact extent of attraction. But a metaphysician will ask in general what it is for something to be a law of nature. What conditions must something meet to qualify as a natural law? Science is concerned with particular things in their concrete instances and seeks to uncover the empirical facts about them. Thus science discovers and investigates what the specific laws are. But metaphysics, like almost the whole of philosophy, is fundamentally non-empirical and general. Just as one can ask in philosophy what, in general, is the good (in ethics) or what it is to know (in epistemology), so one can ask in metaphysics what it is to be a cause, a particular, or a property.

Metaphysics is one of the four main branches of philosophy, traditionally conceived, together with epistemology, logic and axiology (ethics and aesthetics). There is not, however, a very large literature that addresses explicitly the nature of metaphysics within sport. Introductions and surveys of the philosophy of sport will not always cover the area as a named subject matter. There are some exceptions, however. The first edition of Morgan and Meier (1988), in its first three parts, gathers together many key contributions to the discipline that have a metaphysical or ontological aspect: on the nature of sport, play and games, on sport and embodiment, and on play as revelatory of humanity's metaphysical nature. Hyland (1980) contains a chapter on mind and body in sport. A more recent introduction, Reid (2012), contains two chapters on the nature of play, games and sport.

Even though it is not always treated explicitly, however, there are a number of issues in sport that have a metaphysical aspect: indeed, some metaphysicians think that everything has a metaphysical aspect so sport would be no exception. More than that, however, it can be argued that sport has a very deep metaphysical nature and also that it reveals something profound about the metaphysical nature of human existence. The metaphysics of sport should not then be considered a peripheral special interest. Rather, philosophers of sport have a duty to uncover and advance the core metaphysical issues within sport. Doing so will provide an understanding of a very important form of human practice: one that arguably is central to the existential nature of humanity. If that is right, sport is as metaphysical as it gets.

What is sport?

As an example of the metaphysics of sport, let us take one of the biggest, and most basic, questions of all in the discipline. What is sport? There is a literature on this question, of course (see Morgan and Meier 1988, Pt. 1), but part of the point is to use the question to illustrate the different approaches we can take in trying to answer it.

A deflationary view of metaphysics would have it that in asking this question, we are involved merely in conceptual analysis: asking what it is that we mean by 'sport' or what is our concept of 'sport'. This is deflationary in the sense that, while many metaphysicians claim that they are talking about things in the world, this approach claims that all we can really consider is our conceptualisation of it. Instead of asking directly 'what is sport?', the metaphysical deflationist says we can only ask what is the meaning of the word 'sport'. This reduces metaphysics to linguistic conventions. There are reasons why some people still find such an approach attractive. Perhaps they think that the world as it is in itself is forever hidden from us, behind a veil of words. We cannot think about the things in themselves but only our own conceptualisations of them. Forebears of such an approach might be found in Kantian approaches to metaphysics (see Kant 1929 [1781]), that say the noumenal world of things-in-themselves cannot be experienced by us, or a Wittgensteinian approach would claim that 'the limits of my language mean the limits of my world' (Wittgenstein 1921: section 5.6).

But realist metaphysicians do not regard themselves as being limited to the asking of conceptual questions. Instead, inspired by Locke's (1975: III, vi, 6) discussion of 'essence', they seek the real essence of a thing: what it really is (what is a 'law', a 'cause', 'sport'). The ordinary concept of 'sport', for instance, might be messy and inconsistent, with no common usage or agreement. How much, then, is there to be gained from looking at how a term is used? Is not that just a matter for linguists or cultural anthropologists? Where would a metaphysician's interest arise, if at all, here? A thing could have a real essence irrespective of how people use words and it is the metaphysician's job to uncover this essence. Perhaps they might even be able to inform a more consistent use of our concept of sport, or whatever is the subject of investigation. Such a realist approach might best be thought of as Aristotelian in origin. Aristotle (1998), in his book *Metaphysics*, thought of metaphysics as first philosophy. It was first in the sense of being prior or fundamental to everything else, including logic and language. The latter two employ notions of truth and proposition that are themselves of a deeply metaphysical nature. Even the logic that we employ should be one that fits with the way we take the world to be.

Let us then tackle the question head-on of what is sport. The most famous answer to this question within the literature comes from Bernard Suits (2005). His account begins from the seemingly simple question of what it is to play a game, famously discussed by Wittgenstein (1953: sections 66, 67). After consideration of various possible definitions and objections, Suits' view is that to play a game is:

> to engage in an activity directed towards bringing about a specific state of affairs, using only means permitted by the rules, where the rules prohibit more efficient in favour

of less efficient means, and where such rules are accepted just because they make possible such activity.

(Suits 2005: 48–9)

Suits has a simpler statement of the same idea: game playing is the voluntary attempt to overcome unnecessary obstacles (Suits 2005: 55). He explicitly allows that this might not be what everyone means when they call something a 'game'. Nevertheless, that is what a game is.

This is not yet an account of sport. It is about playing a game. But we might think that there is some close relation. Perhaps all sport involves game playing though some games are not sport: tiddlywinks, for example. Our account of sport might include Suits' definition, therefore, but with something else added

What might that be? What turns a game into sport? There are various possibilities, such as that sports are more physically skilful than games (Suits 2007) or that they are conducted in a professional way. Unfortunately, it is very hard to find a single feature that all sports have and 'mere' games lack. Not all sport is professional, for instance. While it can be played professionally, there are many who engage in sports in an amateur way or just for fun. Similarly, it is not impossible to imagine professional tiddlywinks, bridge or chess players, even though these are considered to be 'only' games. And a game, such as the traditional tug-of-war, can be as physically demanding as a number of sports, even though it is not itself considered to be a sport.

This draws attention to another choice that we have to make in the way that we conduct metaphysics. I said that there was a realist view in which metaphysics was considered to be the search for essences. But one possible response, even from someone with a realist perspective, might be that some phenomena have no essence: and sport could be just such a thing (see Møller and Nauright 2003 for further essays on this topic).

The notion of an essence has been variously understood in metaphysics. Indeed, one deep metaphysical question asks what essence consists in. The basic idea, however, is that there is something that makes a thing what it is. If one considers the element gold, for instance, then the idea is that there is something (having 79 protons, for instance) that makes it gold. Metaphysics might be about finding such essences. However, it seems open that we allow that for at least some kinds of thing, there is no essence for that kind.

Where we think, for some phenomenon, that it is a kind with an essence, then we have a position known as essentialism. An essentialist about sport thinks that it has this sort of defining essence. But perhaps sport is one of the things that has no essence. With an institutional theory of sport, for instance, sports are games that have been given the status of sport by certain socio-historically contextualised institutions (see Mumford 2011: 5, 6; see also Ch. 4 in this volume). Games might have an essence, which Suits has described, but the additional element – that might with it comprise sport – does not. Rather, it suggests that sports are games that we have decided to treat in a certain way. If so, then the search for an essence of sport will be partly mistaken. What made something sport would be in a significant measure a socio-historical matter.

Even if that is true, there are still countless metaphysical issues to be found in sport. In this vein, we can ask questions related to sport such as what is fair play (see Loland 2002), what is a rule (McFee 2004), what is a foul, what is a game flaw (Kretchmar 2005), and so on. This does not rule out that the essence of some such phenomenon does contain an ethical or normative component, as fair play almost certainly does. And it does not rule out that there are deep metaphysical truths that sport reveals, about human existence for instance, even if this is not something that is the essence of sport in the Lockean sense. In the remainder of this chapter, therefore, I sketch some of the core metaphysical issues that ground sport: ones that we might consider central to its nature. These issues cluster around the notion of causation.

Causation in sport

Causation is one of the central issues of metaphysics generally: what it is for one thing to cause another (see Mumford and Anjum 2013). Causation is what connects distinct phenomena. Hume (2007a) called it the cement of the universe. We can see that, in sport, it is the absolutely vital metaphysical notion for without causation there could be no sport.

The competitor in sport is aiming to cause some distinct outcome. In golf, the golfer aims to get their ball in the hole. In football, they aim to get a ball into a goal. In weightlifting, the athlete seeks to raise a weight from the ground in a distinct fashion. In tenpin bowling, the aim is to knock down as many pins as possible with a bowling ball. These are all cases where the athlete aims to cause some event or state of affairs through their bodily movements using their skill, strength and technique. That humans are able freely to instigate chains of causation is why we call them 'agents', meaning that they are active with respect to the production of effects. The examples just listed are ones where the athlete exercises their causal powers on some object or tool: to swing the golf club in an appropriate way; to kick a football; to lift a weight, or to bowl a (bowling) ball. But there are many other sporting cases without such tools but, rather, where the agent is exercising causal powers purely within their own body. In the cases of high jump or long jump, swimming and running, the athlete does not cause some other object to move but moves only their own body. The relevant act, in such cases, is to move in a certain way, as fast as possible, as high as possible or as long possible, so as to bodily complete a required task (on bodily movement, see, for instance, Breivik 2008).

It is worth dwelling on just how crucial this notion of causation is to sport. Sport typically involves notions of winning and losing, based on some comparative measure: who crossed the line first, scored more goals, lifted the greatest weight, and so on. It makes sense to reward winners – and indeed pay attention to the actions of the athletes at all – only on the ground that the athletes are causally responsible for the outcomes that are produced. Hence, the goal scorer is congratulated only because they caused the goal to be scored and the weightlifter wins only because they lifted the most weight. Suppose there were no causation. Then anything could follow anything else. And then when one kicks a football, instead of it moving in a direction roughly 180 degrees to the kick, it could do something else completely, such as evaporate. Or it might do nothing at all. Action would then have no point. Its outcomes would be entirely unpredictable: and sport could not then be. A game of pure chance, such as coin-tossing, thus has no sporting merit, either in the playing or the watching, because a participant does not – indeed must not – cause the outcome in any remotely significant way.

What then is this metaphysical glue, which seems to bind one kind of event reliably with another and thus provides us with a basis for action? There are two traditional lines of thought that, despite being old, are still the main options. David Hume (1975, 2007b) argued that there was nothing more in the world than regularity or what he called constant conjunction. One type of event just happens regularly to follow another but there is no necessity or compulsion to it. The cause does not genuinely produce the effect, it is merely that the effect always happens to follow the cause. Humeans, such as Lewis (1973) continue to develop this insight. They think of the world as a mosaic or patchwork of unconnected events or facts, which have no necessary connections between them, but which can have an order in time. Some types of events are regularly followed by events of another type; others are not. Events of type A may always be followed by events of type B but not by events of type C. And if the world is just like this – call it a Hume-world – then the fact that A causes B and does not cause C is nothing more than the fact that the events form this pattern.

Because this is not thought to be sufficiently realist about causation, many other metaphysicians look back to an older, Aristotelian tradition (see, for example, Aristotle's *Physics* [1996]) in which the active causal powers of things are genuinely productive of their effects. It is not purely a matter of contingency what causes what, as Hume thought, but causes have a more intimate connection with their effects than with other events: they specifically dispose towards them. There are various anti-Humean theories of causation, of broadly Aristotelian origin, and we can call them all realist. The realist would point out, for instance, that Hume's regularity theory invites the problem of inductive scepticism, as he himself acknowledges. Given the lack of real connection between causes and effects, then the fact that all As known hitherto have been followed by Bs, cannot guarantee – or even make more likely – that future As will be followed by Bs. Hume does not deny that we form expectations based on our experience, but the expectation of what will follow future As is not a rational inference. And there is a further consequence, drawn by Groff (2013), that if Hume's theory is correct then an agent cannot claim true responsibility for anything that followed from their actions. In a Hume-world anything could have followed that action. Thus, although the kick of a ball was followed by that ball moving, there was no compulsion that it do so and thus the agent deserves no real credit (nor blame) for its subsequent movement. And Groff's view is that this account of causation effectively robs agents of their agent powers.

Needless to say, the metaphysics of causation is an area of continuing dispute. While the realist sees more to causation than a contingent pattern of events, the Humean asks what basis one would have for this conclusion. If we look to experience, all that we see is one event followed by another. We never see the connection between those events. Humeans thus claim that this additional force or compulsion that is supposedly productive of effects is fundamentally unknowable and we ought not, therefore, to speak of it. Whether causation really can be directly experienced, rather than merely inferred from constant conjunctions, is also a matter for debate. But if causation can be known, it is almost certain to be through our own bodies that we will know it, given that we are both causal agents, doing things, and causal patients, having things done to us (Mumford and Anjum 2011: ch. 9).

Empowered agents

Sport can now be understood as being grounded on – as a condition of its very existence – the exercise of the causal powers of the participants. It is thus premised on the idea of empowered agency, manifesting itself in clearly defined tasks that thus overcome, in Suits' terms, the unnecessary obstacles.

Such empowered agency requires a sophisticated set of skills. Speed alone, without intelligence, would not do it. One needs to know where to run, when to run and how to pace oneself over the full distance. Muscle power alone would not do it. One also needs to acquire specific techniques. And there are many sports that are played with the mind as much as the body, such as in cricket, football, basketball and rugby, where strategy and tactics have a significant impact on outcomes. What exactly the abilities are that ground agency is itself a huge area of debate because it leads us to the issue of free will (see Kane 2011). It seems that we are free agents, in control of our causal powers, and sport is premised on this fact. How there is room in the universe for free will, when so much seems controlled by physical laws of nature, is one type of question. But another is what specific abilities do agents have, that is the basis of their freedom, and which non-agents, such as tables and chairs, bats and balls, lack. All those abilities are likely to be essential to participation in sport. One must be appropriately in control of one's bodily powers in sport. One must be able to choose when to exercise them, in what degree and for how long. Hence, one must have abilities to form desires and intentions, decide between options, form strategies and plans, be aware of one's environment and obstacles to the achievement of one's goals, and so on.

Sport has an intimate relation with this notion of empowered agency because we can see sport as a way of encouraging through reward the maximum display of an agent's powers, pitting the powers of one competitor against those of another and measuring the greatest display. Humans are capable of running, jumping, lifting and swimming but sport is what spurs us on to display those powers to the maximum extent of which we are capable. For instance, each long-jumper manifests their power to jump, the jumps are measured and then the biggest manifestation of the power is rewarded. And by encouraging as big a display of powers as possible, sport has seen the development of those powers to an extraordinary extent. It seems unlikely, for instance, that anyone would have achieved a jump of eight-feet high without the encouragement within sport to develop such a capacity, requiring many years of training, for instance. And if one considers a sport such as football (soccer), we can see that a competent player must develop a host of abilities, where I am taking an ability, like a skill, simply to be a causal power that is useful for one's purposes. A footballer must be able to run, jump, head the ball, play a controlled and delicate pass, kick the ball hard, twist, turn, be strong, have awareness of positions within the field, and so on. This is a complex sport, measuring and encouraging several of the agent's powers.

The relationship between a causal power and its manifestation is a complicated one, which is a point that should be familiar to every athlete, even if they have not considered it in these terms. In training, one might produce a jump of a certain height in ideal conditions and yet be unable to reproduce it in competition. In other cases, some athletes find that their best performances come under competitive pressure. The key point is that a power can exist unmanifested, just as a vase can be fragile even though it is never broken, and thus an athlete may not succeed in manifesting the full extent of their ability. Sometimes an athlete or a team fails to manifest their superior skill level because something goes wrong on the day. Perhaps they have been weakened by a recent virus or are distracted psychologically. On other occasions, it may be pure bad luck that goes against them. Perhaps some event that is outside the control of any of the competitors could go one way or the other, with a huge effect on the sporting outcome. A ball might hit the post and spin into the goal, or spin away from it. Bad luck might see the stronger team nevertheless lose and thus fail to manifest their superiority.

However, while such luck is seen as all part of the game, we are very keen that both sides have an equal chance of benefiting or suffering from it. Each competitor or team must be given an equal opportunity to manifest their abilities. We sum up this idea with the metaphor of a level playing field. The level playing field is not about giving everyone the same chance of winning (handicap systems are more like this) but giving each an equal chance of showing their abilities. The level playing field is thus supposed to ensure that there is a good chance of an accurate measure of ability being taken. It is not always easy to judge what is fair in this respect. On striking the right balance between skill and luck in sport, see Kretchmar (2012).

What should be clear from all such examples is that while victory in sport is based on individuals and teams of athletes manifesting and having measured their causal powers, the determination of those victories is made comparatively. Hence, whether the manifestation of one's powers in an eight-foot jump is a winning jump is a matter settled only in relation to the other jumps that have been manifested. And in some sports, such as soccer again, opponents come into direct competition in which the aim is not simply to manifest one's powers to the best of one's ability but also to prevent opponents manifesting their own powers. In many sports this second – let us say negative – task cannot be legitimately undertaken: one cannot get in the path of an opponent's attempted high jump, for instance. But in what Kupfer (1983) distinguishes as directly competitive sport, such as in fencing, one does try to stop the opponent doing what they intend. And it is distinctive of powers that they admit of prevention or interference. An opponent might make a perfectly good lunge with their sabre but see it diverted from its path by a good parry.

It would seem, then, that the causes of a victory are not simply the winner having exercised their causal powers but also the absence of an opponent who could have done better or who could have blocked the power that the victor had exercised. A player might kick the ball to the goal, causing it to go in, but had an opponent been on the line and stopped it, it would not have been a goal. And an eight-foot high jump wins only because of the absence of someone jumping higher. Such considerations tempt some metaphysicians to believe that absences can also be causes. There are, however, reasons to be suspicious of causation by absence. An absence is nothing at all so how can it have causal powers? There really was no athlete jumping higher than the winner so how can that literal non-entity be causally efficacious in producing the victory? For such reasons, it might be best to say that while the absence of a better performance might be a necessary condition of victory – a *sine qua non* – that is not the same as causing it (Mumford and Anjum 2011: 173). Compare someone's birth being a necessary condition of their death: one would not say that it caused one's death.

If sport is so much a competition between the causal powers of human agents, it is hardly a surprise that the issue of enhancement of those powers is scrutinised so closely. It seems that the athlete is allowed to enhance those abilities naturally as much as they like: through training and diet, for instance. It is also the case that some simply have a naturally advantageous physique for certain sports, such as where height is an advantage in basketball. Two areas in which there is obvious concern, though, are doping and genetic modification of athletes, which are deemed to artificially enhance the competitively relevant causal powers (see Chapter 23).

Mutual manifestation

There is a further and highly significant consideration pertaining to the exercise of causal powers in sport. Typically, powers are exercised through mutual manifestations rather than individual athletes displaying their powers in isolation. This requires more explanation. In some cases, an athlete manifests their power in conjunction with some piece of equipment. An athlete may have a strong throwing arm, for instance, but the distance achieved in discus or javelin is also determined by the properties, such as aerodynamic properties, of the object thrown. It is hard to think of any sport in which athletes manifest their powers completely alone, that is, unaided. Even a runner runs faster and easier (for example, less injuriously) with good running shoes, the standard of which has shown clear improvement over time. In sport, the athlete seems perfectly entitled to use the best possible equipment they can get, sometimes within certain defined limits, and yet they are also entitled to full credit for the performance they achieve using that equipment. We do not award medals to the running shoes or the discus itself. Here it seems a case of athletes getting credit for choosing the most suitable equipment that enables them to manifest their powers to the utmost.

Sometimes the mutual manifestation occurs with a machine, as in the case of motor racing. The winner of the race is not determined solely by being the best driver nor by having the best car but by the two in combination. The car and driver have to work well together: what may be the best car for one driver might not be for another. But the quality of the car is clearly so important to the race outcome that there is indeed a constructors' championship as well as one for drivers. There can be dispute over whether some equipment gives an unfair advantage or not. Running shoes have not yet been a matter of controversy, although the prosthetic blades upon which Oscar Pistorius ran for a time were (Edwards 2008). Were those blades simply akin to running shoes or more an artificial enhancement of Pistorius's ability to run?

There are even cases in sport where the mutual manifestation is with a non-human animal, as in the case of horse racing or show jumping. Again, jockey and horse have to work well together. There may be a fast horse and a skilled jockey which, owing to differences in temperament, are an ill-suited combination. It seems important, however, that free human agency be at least a part of the mutual manifestation partnership that is being tested and measured in sport, which is why some may feel dubious about classifying jockey-less greyhound racing as a sport.

This notion of mutual manifestation is perfectly consistent with the way that many think that causation operates generally (Martin 2008: ch. 5). Effects occur when mutual manifestation partners come together. Hence, while we can think that the ice cools the drink or that the drink melts the ice, what we might have is a single process that is initiated when the ice and the drink come together in partnership but which could be described either from the point of view of the ice or of the drink. Causation in sport thus fits the model.

Parts, wholes and goals

The most significant case of mutual manifestation is in team sports, where the individual members must form a functioning mutual manifestation partnership with their team mates. The mutual manifestation partners here are other human beings, rather than equipment, machinery or animals. Success in team sports tends to come when the individual players can give themselves over to the whole such that they behave as a single cohesive unit, exercising its collective powers, rather than being a mere aggregate of the individual powers of the constituent players.

This raises metaphysical issues of wholes and parts and indeed holism versus reductionism. The reductionist view is that a whole is simply the sum of its parts. Add them together, duly arranged, and one has the whole. But another view is that the whole can be something more than a mere sum of parts. Someone who thinks this is called a holist or sometimes an emergentist. One might think that there is something more to a person, for instance, than just a collection of flesh and bones. One might even say that mental phenomena emerge from the otherwise purely physical cells and neurons of the brain.

When a sports team functions at its best, it is easy to think of it as an example of holism. Similarly, one could think of the team as having an emergent character not necessarily found at the level of the individual players. The coach's job might be to ensure that the team is indeed more than merely an aggregate of individual players by getting the team to play a certain way. Evaluations may differ but the German national football team is one that historically has been thought of as better than the sum of its parts. Certainly, they have had very good players but they have not necessarily been the very best individual players in the world at the time. And yet they have a fine track record of winning world championships. For this to happen, team members might have to be willing to give up their individuality to the whole: to make personal sacrifices and not play as they would usually play, for the good of the team. Bobby Charlton was thought to have done this in the 1966 World Cup Final where he did not shine because his role was limited to neutralizing Franz Beckenbauer. This was effective and the team as a whole benefited though Charlton's individual performance did not. The idea is that there are different roles that need to be played within a team and the individual player has to put this need first so that the team can become an organic whole. Brian Clough was a coach who was thought to be a master of taking relatively ordinary players and putting them together like a jigsaw puzzle into a whole that excelled, resulting in two European Cups won by a relatively small club.

What counts as the manifestation of powers for the complex wholes of team sports also becomes a complicated matter. During football, there are many individual contests, with players running, jumping, tackling and kicking. The players that compose the team are displaying their causal powers here. But it is whole teams that win, lose or draw, just as it is the whole team that scores a goal together. Certainly, one player gets the final touch before the goal but the team has put him or her in a position to do so. Indeed, individuals are not even allowed to play unless part of a team with a minimum number of players. Similarly, although a person needs eyes to see, it is whole persons who do the seeing, not the eyes. An eye on its own could do nothing. Thus, the power to win the game is a candidate for an emergent power, found at the level of the whole, where it is a mutual manifestation, belonging to the whole team, of the powers relevant to football. The actual victory is then determined when these collective, arguably emergent powers of team A are pitted against those of team B. Such considerations seem to apply to every team sport.

The stronger team – that is, the team with the greatest extent of this power – will tend to win though they need not always do so. Powers dispose towards certain outcomes but because they can always be prevented, there is no guarantee that they will succeed. As remarked above, the opposition is attempting to prevent a team from manifesting its powers, and a team may fail also through sheer bad luck. It can be argued that the interest of sport to participants and spectators crucially depends on the best team tending, but no more than tending, to win the game (Mumford and Anjum 2014). If sporting outcomes were necessitated – for instance, if the strongest team always won – then it would be dull to watch and pointless to play. The weaker team would know that they literally had no chance. But if the outcomes were completely contingent or random, sport would have no interest either. There has to be some connection between ability and outcome. The area of metaphysics that concerns necessity and possibility is known as modality. It is arguable that sport is premised on there being a modal strength than it less than necessity but more than mere possibility: an intermediate dispositional modality in which sporting abilities tend towards outcomes without guaranteeing them.

Powers, existence and inexistence

Given that sport is a voluntary attempt to overcome unnecessary obstacles, why do we bother to do it? Why tackle an unnecessary obstacle? That we appear to do so freely might reveal something very important about the human metaphysical core, as a number of others have suggested (see, for example, Fink 1960; Esposito 1974; Meier 1980). The thought is that in play we are performing an activity for its own intrinsic value to us; therefore, play (hence sport) reveals our true natures. In the case of sport, of course, many people participate in it for extrinsic reasons, such as to gain fitness, fame or riches. But the vast majority of us participate on an amateur basis and watch sport likewise for the simple pleasures it brings us.

That we freely play sport suggests that we want to exercise the causal powers the sport involves. And it is almost as if sport was invented for the very reason that we could do so in a relatively harmless way; as opposed to war or economic competition, for instance. It must be, therefore, that overall we find it pleasurable to exercise our causal powers and doing so the best of our abilities. A child will run and jump, for instance, just for the sheer unbridled joy of it. Sport regiments and codifies such activities but contains the same expression of freedom: to swim, to throw, to sprint to exercise all the best physical and mental powers at the agent's disposal. Such activities can be pure unalienated action (Algozin 1976), thereby revealing something of our authentic being. Perhaps it is because empowerment shows us that we are free agents that we find it such a pleasure. And someone who can jump 10 metres is more free that someone who can jump only 2 metres. The former has more possibilities open to them (see Esposito 1974) as they can do everything and more than the latter can do.

Returning to an earlier issue, it is through embodiment, it can be argued, that we are causally engaged with our world: that we are able to know causation first-hand. Suppose one is arm-wrestling an opponent. One attempts to push down the other's arm. Here, one is agent: exercising one's causal powers, aiming for a victorious outcome. At the same time, the opponent is attempting to prevent your victory. Here one is causal patient: having a causal power exercised upon one, aiming to prevent one's victory. In that bodily sensation, one proprioceptively encounters the active and passive sides to causation. And one feels that an exercise of one's power can be prevented or thwarted by a counteracting power in the opposite direction. Correspondingly, one feels a power acting on oneself that one can at least attempt to resist. Proprioception thus reveals direct experience of causation, in an argument going back at least as far as Thomas Reid in 1788 (Reid 1983). Arguably, it also reveals causation's irreducibly dispositional nature (Mumford and Anjum 2011: ch. 9). It gives us experience of a power tending in a direction but which can be counteracted.

We are rational embodied agents. Causation is our way of interacting with and hence engaging with other agents and the world around us. Being causally powerful is what it is to exist, to be real, according to a view in Plato (the Eleatic reality test from Plato's *Sophist* (1961: 247d–e), for how could something be real if it could make no possible difference to anything else?. To freely exercise powers is thus to be alive. Without any such an ability, one has ceased to be a person. With no causal powers at all, a thing has ceased to be. Sport thus reveals something of the essence of humanity and of existence generally.

Summary

I have tried to show that even though metaphysical issues have not figured prominently within the tradition of the philosophy of sport, they are nevertheless there and, what is more, they are at the very heart of sport. Indeed, it is hard to see how one could have a true grasp of the nature and existence of sport unless one is sensitive to its metaphysical foundation. I have indicated what I think this foundation to be and I have taken causation to be the central notion, given that it creates the possibility of human empowerment, both physical and mental, which sport is all about. For metaphysicians of a realist inclination, the claim that sport rests on a metaphysical basis should come as no surprise. Indeed, it is just an instance, as noted, of the Aristotelian view that metaphysics is first philosophy.

Note

1   See Mumford (2012) for a beginners' introduction and Le Poidevin *et al.* (2009) for detailed accounts of many of the issues discussed here.

Bibliography

Algozin, K. (1976) 'Man and Sport', in W. Morgan and K. Meier (eds) *Philosophic Inquiry in Sport*, Champaign, IL: Human Kinetics, 1988, pp. 183–7.
Aristotle. (1998) *Metaphysics*, trans. H. Lawson-Tancred, London: Penguin.
Aristotle. (1996) *Physics*, R. Waterfield (trans.), London: Penguin.
Breivik, G. (2008) 'Bodily Movement – The Fundamental Dimensions', *Sport, Ethics and Philosophy* 2: 337–52.

Edwards, S. (2008) 'Should Oscar Pistorius be Excluded from the 2008 Olympic Games?', *Sport, Ethics and Philosophy* 2: 112–25.

Esposito, J. (1974) 'Play and Possibility', in W. Morgan and K. Meier (eds) *Philosophic Inquiry in Sport*, Champaign, IL: Human Kinetics, 1988, pp. 175–81.

Fink, E. (1960) 'The Ontology of Play', in W. Morgan and K. Meier (eds) *Philosophic Inquiry in Sport*, Champaign, IL: Human Kinetics, 1988, pp. 145–57.

Groff, R. (2013) 'Whose Powers? Which Agency?', in R. Groff and J. Greco (eds), *Powers and Capacities in Philosophy: the New Aristotelianism*, New York, NY: Routledge, pp. 207–27.

Hume, D. (1975) [1739] *A Treatise of Human Nature*, L. A. Selby-Bigge (ed.), Oxford: Clarendon.

Hume, D. (2007a) [1740] 'Abstract of a Treatise of Human Nature', in P. Millican (ed.), *An Enquiry Concerning Human Understanding*, Oxford: Oxford University Press, pp. 133–45.

Hume, D. (2007b) [1748] *An Enquiry Concerning Human Understanding*, P. Millican (ed.), Oxford: Oxford University Press, 2007.

Hyland, D. (1980) *Philosophy of Sport*, St. Paul, MN: Paragon House.

Kane, R. ed. (2011) *The Oxford Handbook of Free Will*, Oxford: Oxford University Press.

Kant, I. (1929) [1781] *Critique of Pure Reason*, trans. N. Kemp Smith, London: MacMillan.

Kretchmar, S. (2005) 'Game Flaws', *Journal of the Philosophy of Sport*, 32: 36–4.

Kretchmar, S. (2012) 'Competition, Redemption, and Hope', *Journal of the Philosophy of Sport*, 39: 101–16.

Kupfer, J. (1983) 'Sport – the Body Electric', in W. Morgan and K. Meier (eds), *Philosophic Inquiry in Sport*, Champaign, IL: Human Kinetics, 1988, pp. 455–75.

Le Poidevin, R., Simons, P., McGonigal, A. and Cameron, R. (2009) *The Routledge Companion to Metaphysics*, London: Routledge.

Lewis, D. (1973) 'Causation', in *Philosophical Papers*, ii, Oxford: Oxford University Press, 1986: 159–213.

Locke, J. (1975) [1690] *An Essay Concerning Human Understanding*, Oxford: Clarendon Press.

Loland, S. (2002) *Fair Play in Sport: a Moral Norm System*, London: Routledge.

Martin, C. B. (2008) *The Mind in Nature*, Oxford: Oxford University Press.

McFee, G. (2004) *Sport, Rules and Values: Philosophical Investigations into the Nature of Sport*, London: Routledge.

Meier, K. V. (1980) 'An Affair of Flutes: an Appreciation of Play', in W. Morgan and K. Meier (eds) *Philosophic Inquiry in Sport*, Champaign, IL: Human Kinetics, 1988, pp. 189–209.

Morgan, W. J. and Meier, K.V. eds (1988) *Philosophic Inquiry in Sport*, Champaign, IL: Human Kinetics.

Mumford, S. (2011) *Watching Sport: Aesthetics, Ethics and Emotion*, Abingdon: Routledge.

Mumford, S. (2012) *Metaphysics: A Very Short Introduction*, Oxford: Oxford University Press.

Mumford, S. and Anjum, R. L. (2011) *Getting Causes from Powers*, Oxford: Oxford University Press.

Mumford, S. and Anjum, R. L. (2013) *Causation: a Very Short Introduction*, Oxford: Oxford University Press.

Mumford, S. and Anjum, R. L. (2014) 'A Tendential Theory of Sporting Prowess', *Journal of the Philosophy of Sport* 41 (3): 399–412.

Møller, V. and Nauright, J. eds (2003) *The Essence of Sport*, Odense: University Press of Southern Denmark.

Plato (1961) *Sophist*. F. M. Cornford (trans.) in E. Hamilton and H. Cairns (eds), *The Collected Dialogues of Plato*, Princeton, NJ: Princeton University Press, pp. 957–1017.

Reid, H. (2012) *Introduction to the Philosophy of Sport*, Lanham, MR: Rowman and Littlefield.

Reid, T. (1983) [1788] 'Essays on the Active Powers of Man', in R. E. Beanblossom and K. Lehrer (eds), *Inquiry and Essays*, Cambridge, MA: Hackett, pp. 297–368.

Suits, B. (2005) *The Grasshopper: Games Life and Utopia*, 2nd ed., Peterborough, Ontario: Broadview.

Suits, B. (2007) 'The Elements of Sport', in W. Morgan (ed.) *Ethics in Sport*, 2nd ed., Champaign, IL: Human Kinetics, pp. 9–19.

Wittgenstein, L. (1921) *Tractatus Logico-Philosophicus*, D. Pears and B. McGuiness (trans.), London: Routledge, 1961.

Wittgenstein, L. (1953) *Philosophical Investigations*, Oxford: Blackwell.

SECTION III

Key issues and themes in the philosophy of sport

19

COMPETITION

Paul Gaffney

The relationship between sport and competition

'Competition' and 'sport' are not coextensive terms. On the one hand, competition can be understood as the wider category, which suggests that competitive sport represents merely one instantiation of a basic type of human engagement. Indeed, it is not difficult to conceptualize many of our encounters with one another and many of our institutions as structurally competitive. In adversarial law, for example, two advocates are pitted against one another and successful litigation is measured directly by victories as much as by the achievement of justice or the determination of truth. In democratic politics, candidates must win elections to gain office, and then must 'win over' constituencies to implement public policy. In economics, competition is a defining feature of market capitalism, even if this ideal is only approximately realized in practice. Producers compete with one another for market shares, and there is even something of a contest between producers and consumers over the terms of their transactions. Finally, in cultural and intellectual arenas, we refer to a marketplace of ideas, which suggests – developing the economic metaphor – that contenders must survive a battleground of opposition and critique to be considered successful.

Competitive sport seems to share some features with these examples, which we might call 'institutional varieties' of competition. In each arena, there is an objective measure of success, a rival (or set of rivals) to confront, and an ineluctable logic to the confrontation: the success of one is, generally speaking, inversely related to the success of others. This basic similarity lends some plausibility to a remark by former Georgetown University basketball coach John Thompson: 'Life is *about* competition' (Gilbert, 1988: 88). One might feel an initial discomfort with this broad generalization because it appears to blur distinctions that are both obvious and important. For instance, whereas the institutional varieties provide structures to resolve some of life's inevitable and consequential struggles, competitive sports are generally contrived affairs that challenge their participants to overcome what Bernard Suits famously called 'unnecessary obstacles' (Suits, 2005: 55). But a moment's reflection reveals the inadequacy of this response, not only because the outcomes of sports do matter, at least to their participants, but also because the institutional competitions employ their own contrivances, such as formalized procedures and conventional standards of success. Indeed, following Thompson, it is not difficult to conceptualize much of modern life as a series of oppositional engagements within which we pursue certain scarce goods, such as power, money, favorable decisions, and glory. The stakes of the engagements differ, of course, but the logic and the psychology compare insofar as these structures create spaces wherein the combatants simply fight it out. And sport is one of those fights.

We can employ two strategies to understand the relationship among the varieties of competition. First, we can think of all of them as domestications of war, which suggests their intelligibility and moral value consist in their disposition to contain the basic problematic of the human condition. Competition of any sort, on this view, is simply regulated warfare. Viewed in this light, there is nothing particularly glorious or beautiful about what athletes do, even if we attribute some value to their efforts, nor is there a fundamental difference between an athlete's pursuit of glory, an entrepreneur's pursuit of money, or a warrior's pursuit of power. In modern professional sport we have, of course, ample evidence that argues for this reductive account. But the perspective is hardly new and would not seem to be entirely attributable, if at all, to increasing commercialization. George Orwell (1998) gave forceful expression to this understanding, partly because he feared the political manipulations of international sport, and partly because he distrusted the root of the competitive drive animating sporting contests. Sport, he famously said, is 'war minus the shooting' (p. 442). A similar sentiment is sometimes attributed to William James (1910), who coined the phrase 'moral equivalent of war', although he himself did not explicitly mention sport in his well-known essay. But many – both defenders and critics of sport – recognize in sport precisely what Orwell and James had in mind, namely, a surrogate for the experience of military exercise and engagement.

The second strategy would begin, so to speak, from the opposite end and would interpret all varieties of competition as better or worse approximations of sport. This view argues in effect that 'competition' belongs properly to sport (or perhaps, more generally, to games) and only analogously to the institutional varieties, and not at all to warfare, precisely because in sport the struggle itself is thematized as a locus of value and interest. Of course, participants in competitive sport strive earnestly for victory, but the character of the contest and even the difficulty of the struggle are embraced as intrinsic values. Philosophers sometimes describe sport as 'autotelic', which means an end in itself, both created and governed by 'constitutive rules' (Suits, 2005: 51) (formalism). In this sense, as I will explain below, competitive sport enjoys a kind of purity compared with the institutional varieties, because it need not make reference to, nor justify itself in terms of, the achievement of anything beyond its own activity. The institutional competitions, by contrast, involve a competitive element only as a structural mechanism, and their exercise does not guarantee achievement of the institutional ideals. Justice is not always served in adversarial law because one side might simply out-perform the other, just as bad policies and bad governments sometime win elections because of rhetorical superiority or personal charm. It should be noted that the purity or priority of sport is a conceptual point, although, in some respects, it might reflect historical developments as well. For instance, Stephen Miller (2004) has argued that some institutional principles, such as equal standing before the law, are actually lessons first realized at the Olympics Games and then adapted to institutional settings (p. 18).

Given these two understandings of the relationship among the varieties – which we might call respectively the 'war paradigm' and the 'sport paradigm' of competition – this chapter defends the latter. That is, it understands competitive sport to be the paradigmatic instance that makes intelligible all other varieties of competition. Reductive strategies, such as the one based on the war premise, ultimately fail because, in making all instances in principle the same, they under-appreciate the special goodness of sport and, at the same time, diminish the moral seriousness of the other endeavors.

On the other hand, as we consider the relationship between competition and sport, we can understand sport to be the wider term, given that much of what appears to qualify as sport is not competitive. We engage in many activities for the sheer pleasure of the physical exertion, for the camaraderie these activities occasion, for the health benefits, or for the aesthetic satisfaction that mastery of a skill provides, among many other satisfactions. Even those who intend ultimately to compete will spend a lot of time in non-competitive exercises. For example, soccer (football) players at every age and level will kick a ball around, just as baseball players will go out to play catch; a group of friends will meet for a morning jog, perhaps varying the route on a daily basis for sake of different scenery, and talking all the way; and tennis players will hit with a partner without concern for a score. There are countless other examples, and all would seem to be sporting activities in some important sense of the word. Admittedly, for some participants the non-competitive exercises gain their intelligibility from an eventual competitive engagement, so the tennis player will think about implementing her strokes into match play even as she hits with her partner, but for others kicking a ball around with friends is their whole experience of sport.

It is significant – not to mention troubling – that we often describe these non-competitive sporting exercises as something we do 'just for fun'. This suggests that competition somehow darkens an activity that was formerly playful, and thereby constricts or perhaps even corrupts its essential character. There is etymological and historical support for this understanding. 'Sport' derives originally from 'disport' (*dis* + *portare*), which means to carry away from or to divert, and therefore connotes a sense of liberation from the burdens of work and responsibility. Yet, as Steven Connor (2011) explains, the sense of 'sport 'has significantly altered in recent history: 'During the eighteenth and nineteenth centuries, and, for a time, as it remarkably seems, almost entirely in England, sport changed its meaning, and came to designate particular pursuits involving forms of physical competition governed by rules' (p. 23).

Thus emerges the familiar hybrid we know as competitive sport. The elements of this new form of life are still distinguishable, but it certainly seems that competitiveness is the dominant gene. That is, we would recognize the form even if there were there little or no evidence of the playful aspect, but we would exclude from this genre any activity that was not earnestly competitive. This may be primarily a matter of presentation, but the change is telling: whereas originally the countenance of sport was an exuberant, carefree smile, the modern expression – worn by the combatants and also, increasingly, by the coaches, fans, and various other stakeholders – is characteristically a scowl.

Scott Kretchmar (1975) distinguishes between tests and contests, both of which present 'counterpoint' challenges, although in logically different ways. A test stands before an adventurer as both 'impregnable' and 'vulnerable'; that is, it presents something difficult but not impossible to do (there would be no point if either of the two conditions were missing). For example, a mountain climber takes on her challenge because she believes the task to be significant in its own right, which implies that success is not guaranteed. A contest, as the word implies, occurs when two or more take on the same test, but not merely simultaneously:

> The transition from test to contest is the change from human singularity to community. Simply, it is finding someone with whom one can share a test. In addition, a commitment is made by each side to attempt to better the other's performance.
>
> *(Kretchmar, 1975: 27)*

This description contains some interesting elements. First, the contestants share something, which indicates that contesting is at some level a cooperative venture; and, second, the commitment to 'better the other's performance' trades on a rather fortunate ambiguity of the phrase insofar as a contestant attempts not only to outdo the other's performance but also, in the same effort, quite possibly to improve the other's performance. This is a theme that I develop below.

Kretchmar's analysis helps us outline a more precise taxonomy: 1) First, some sport is purely diversionary and playful, expressing tumultuous delight in movement and creativity; 2) second, some sport gains its intelligibility from a test of some sort, such as the completion of a marathon or the performance of a gymnastic routine, simply for its inherent value; 3) third, some sport is structured as a contest, which necessarily involves two or more participants pitted against one another and governed by constitutive rules. It is evident that the first category is non-competitive sport and the third category is competitive sport; the second category shares some features with both (for example, a runner who pushes herself to improve upon her personal best is competing with previous efforts). As I suggest later in this chapter, however, competition requires genuine otherness.

The foregoing argues that sport is a broad genus comprising a variety of expressions, even if the competitive expression seems to dominate our contemporary sports culture. Mindful of this context, the remainder of the chapter concentrates on the structure and meaning of competitive sport. Clearly something changes when we decide to keep score. Typically, we say that the game now 'counts' – a remark that implies both seriousness and quantification – and we are given to understand that the results will be a matter of public record, now and forever. The commitment to contest matters in a number of ways, but we should remember that the transition from non-competitive to competitive is not that from non-sport to sport, or from non-serious to serious, or from non-challenging to challenging.

Competition as relationship: Hobbesian and Hegelian understandings

I suggested above that we could understand competitive sport either as a domestication of warfare, or as the paradigmatic instance that makes sense of all the other varieties of competition. In philosophical terms, the first approach derives from Thomas Hobbes, the second from Georg Hegel. Both philosophers begin their account of human sociality with a primordial struggle but they understand the terms and the meaning of this struggle differently.

For Hobbes, the natural state of humankind is a universal war of all against all, a zero-sum struggle to survive and to acquire scarce goods. In *Leviathan* Hobbes (1999) lists competition, diffidence, and glory as the 'three causes of quarrel' and tells us that humans take no pleasure in each other's company without a 'common power to overawe them all' (Book I, ch. 13). His account would seem to imply that no value inheres in struggle *per se*; in fact, in the Hobbesian account it would be better if the other were simply not there. Although Hobbes' thought experiment has proven its value as a foundational political study, this last point indicates why it serves poorly as a model for competitive sport, since in sport we do not wish to eliminate our opponent. We need our opponent to be there and, even more, we need our opponent to thrive, at least to some extent, or else the activity ceases to have meaning. Of course, within the event the competitors' state of mind is simply to defeat one another, and the more soundly the better. But even here we must qualify the point: an easy victory is less than fully satisfying for someone seeking out a genuinely competitive engagement. We must also remember – recalling Kretchmar's point about the opponents agreeing to 'share a test' – that in sport the competitive fire burns within a cooperative endeavor. This is not domesticated warfare; it is not warfare at all.

As the above suggests, in competitive sport the antagonists are neither friends nor enemies, although they exhibit characteristics appropriate to both these interactions. In Warren Fraleigh's

(1984: 83–4) language, opponents are both 'facilitators' and 'obstacles'. They are 'friendly' insofar as they enter into a relationship, seeking a good not otherwise available. A competitor needs a worthy opponent; no one else in her circle – not her coach, not her trainer, not her fans, not the people who love her – can provide her with the satisfaction that she craves, precisely because they all want her to win. Her opponent, however, acts like an 'enemy' in the sense that she uses all her ingenuity to deny her the object of desire, and with no remorse whatsoever. A competitor deliberately sets out to frustrate her opponent (*qua* opponent), often employing deceptive strategies and exposing technical weaknesses in the effort. It is precisely because competitors do not want their opponents to enjoy the satisfaction of victory that victory, once achieved, is satisfying. Thus, the basic paradox of competition.

We can approach an understanding of this paradox through the 'Master and Slave' section of Hegel's *Phenomenology of Spirit* (1977). According to Hegel, the basic struggle of humankind is not for physical survival (as in Hobbes' materialistic vision), but rather for acknowledgement or recognition (*Anerkennen*), which transforms a 'subjective self-certainty' into an objective truth. That is to say, in the dialectical construction of spirit, self-consciousness requires recognition to assure itself of its own being. 'Self-consciousness exists in and for itself when, and by the fact that, it so exists for another; that is, it exists only in being acknowledged' (section 172). Acknowledgement must come from an adequate other, namely, another self-consciousness engaged in precisely the same pursuit to assure itself of its own objective truth. Because each side seeks something that it refuses to grant, a 'life and death' struggle ensues that ends only when one side gives up the quest in order to save its life. As Hegel explains, each self-consciousness attempts to gain dominance over the other through what he calls work (*Arbeit*), which can be the body, physical labor, power structures, or even (I am suggesting) the challenges of sport. The 'winner' of this struggle (the master) is acknowledged as free and independent, while the 'loser' (the slave) is forced to relinquish that claim.

The outcome, however, will be precarious and mutually unsatisfying: the slave does not at all succeed in gaining recognition, and the master finds the recognition provided by the slave inadequate precisely because it comes from an un-free self-consciousness. Each side, in different ways, finds itself dependent on the other, and thus the engagement fails to achieve its objective. But the imbalance proves to be merely a temporary stage because the slave finds dignity in the work he is forced to do and so prepares himself, with his new-found strength, to rise up against the master in search of his own recognition. Of course, the next stage in this dialectic will simply reverse the positions of the two antagonists, as the former slave will dominate his former master but find recognition from the 'new' slave to be inadequate and unsatisfying for precisely the same reasons the first recognition was inadequate. This back-and-forth dynamic continues, in principle, with only provisional resolutions.

The applicability of this paradigm to sport should be apparent. Hegel's theory of dialectic provides a structure according to which we can understand the reciprocally constructive engagement of competition. Although not every sporting event unfolds according to the pattern of the Hegelian dialectic, many of the best and most satisfying instances do. Some games, such as soccer or basketball, are structured in such a way as to permit a series of 'runs' of energy and execution, with one side and then the other gaining an upper hand. These reversals not only augment the dramatic appeal of the contest but also testify to the respective adequacy of the opponents, which makes the recognition eventually paid to the winner all the more meaningful. The contest ends – in principle if not in fact – when one side cannot respond and so must acknowledge the other's superiority. This is a bittersweet moment, even for the victor, because it signals the end of the contest and might come sooner than satisfaction requires. The winner enjoys his recognition even though it is somewhat qualified, because it comes from a loser; the loser finds disappointment in the outcome but has something to gain in a future meeting, because victory over the winner would appear to hold value. And so the competitive paradox is, on some level, irresolvable. Connor explains:

> The relation of opponency expresses this relation of reciprocity in struggle in the tightest possible fashion. Because the only way in which I can be free of my opponent is to overcome him, even though I cannot fully overcome him without revealing my dependency on the fact of his acknowledgement of my victory over him, my opponent is simultaneously the avenue to and ambushing of my free selfhood.
>
> *(Connor, 2011: 193)*

The ascendancy of the dialectic helps explain the fortunate ambiguity of the word 'better' in Kretchmar's account of contest. The opponents try to out-perform their adversaries to gain victory, but because each successive stage of the dialectic (which could be seasons, or matches, or even exchanges within an individual match or game) presents a new standard for the inferior position to match, the responses must improve upon what went before. Each side pushes the other to reach new heights, although the manner in which they push varies according to the structure of the particular sport, as I explain below. In an important sense, it is my opponent who improves my competitive excellence, confidence, and resiliency – all of which are positive or 'friendly' effects of the relationship – all while aiming to block and frustrate my efforts in this regard. As a matter of fact, it is probably no exaggeration to claim that if my opponent did not endeavor fully to block and frustrate my efforts, the 'friendly' benefits would be empty if not altogether absent.

The emphasis on competitive psychology suggests two considerations. First, one could claim that in competitive sport one competes ultimately against oneself, that the opponent merely objectifies the challenge of playing up to one's full potential. Such a description would effectively collapse the distinction (drawn by Kretchmar) between tests and contests and makes structural differences between sports less noteworthy. It would also seem to eliminate the need for an 'unfriendly' attitude toward the opponent, since the emphasis is now placed simply on doing well rather than doing better than. Some players and coaches provide anecdotal support for this approach when they report that they do not concern themselves with their opponents' strategies or mindsets, they simply try to 'play their game' and let the outcome be what it will be (although, as the next sections explains, this approach works better for some sports than for others). There would seem to be both advantages and disadvantages to this approach. On the one hand, the 'self-competition' approach might provide for a calmer and more focused psychology within the event, which might translate into a more effective performance. One could further imagine different motivations for adopting the 'self-competition' attitude: either that it helps me play better and therefore win more often, or it simply allows me to enjoy the activity more. On the other hand, it is apparent that the term 'self-competition' is something of a stretch, whatever psychological and competitive advantages it might have, because I am not other to myself and I can never be sure that I push myself as hard as an opponent would. The 'self-competition' approach seems vulnerable to the same criticisms that Ludwig Wittgenstein (2001) identified in his consideration of the possibility of private language, namely, that one cannot have epistemic certitude about the comparability of discrete experiences (sections 243–71). Unless one is measuring oneself against something objective, such as a clock, it would seem necessary for a competitor to be able to check himself against others to be sure his 'improvement' is not delusional. Robert L. Simon explains:

For one thing, an especially significant criterion of improvement is change in one's competitive standing when measured against the performance of others. Perhaps the best way of judging one's progress is to see whether one is doing better against opponents now than in the past.

(Simon, 2010: 29)

Ultimately, the suggestion that all competition is against oneself is a claim about the ontology of selfhood; it denies the constitutive role that another might play in the development of the self. By contrast, the present view argues for a relational ontology of selfhood, well-exemplified by sport: my opponent forces me to find a level of performance and even a dimension of myself that I did not know was there. Seen in this light, the competitive relationship reveals itself to be a positive and irreducible good.

Categories of competition and their respective psychologies

We should resist any reductionism that attempts to interpret all contests as tests, or vice versa. But it is important also to remember that there are a variety of contests, and this implies the second consideration about competitive psychology. Steven Skultety (2011) has argued that philosophers of sport typically emphasize a fairly narrow conception of competitive intentionality and then identify events that employ this psychology, which prejudices what qualifies as competitive sport. 'The result has been a heavy emphasis towards 'head-to-head' sports such as football or boxing, and subsequent generalizations that inadvertently neglect a wider range of competitions' (p. 434). Skultety proposes to begin with the various external structures of competition and then find the purposes and psychologies appropriate to them, rather than the usual method that works the other way around. Developing a distinction between performances and games originally introduced by Suits (2002: 33–4), Skultety (2011: 441) suggests two modes of assessment, 'standardized' and 'vis-à-vis', which determine the success of a performance. The former lends itself to judgment according to a set ideal – say a perfect score in bowling or a flawless gymnastics routine – whereas the latter indicates that the point is to outdo an opponent, whatever level that might require. In addition to this distinction, we recognize two ways in which competitors might interact: competitors can directly interfere with one another's actions, as in tennis or soccer, or they can perform parallel actions, as occurs in golf or in any racing event in which one remains in one's lane. Skultety distinguishes these as 'encumbered' and 'unencumbered' competitions. Taking these two distinctions together gives us four possible types of competition: 1) *vis-à-vis, encumbered competitions,* such tennis, basketball, and wrestling; 2) *vis-à-vis, unencumbered competitions,* such as swimming and track; 3) *standardized, unencumbered competitions,* such as figure skating and archery; and 4) *standardized, encumbered competitions,* such as bocce ball and billiards. These are all competitions, argues Skultety, but because they set different challenges for the participants and comprise different relationships it only makes sense that they would inspire different competitive psychologies. It would be very strange, to say the least, if a gymnast and a boxer were to approach their competitions with the same mindset. And yet we cannot deny that each engagement is, in its own way, intensely competitive.

Skultety provides an important corrective with this article, although he admits that some events do not fall neatly into his categories (for example, some sports, such as downhill mogul skiing, combine standardized and vis-à-vis elements), and it also would appear that the distinctions are not absolute. For example, the standards in a performance sport like diving might evolve as a result of vis-à-vis competitions, as the innovations of past performances will continually explore possibilities, which might make some elements mandatory in future programs. Similarly, the distinction between encumbered and unencumbered competitions might permit of some discussion. Skultety claims that in encumbered competitions the opponents 'affect one another's behavior' and in an unencumbered competition the opponents 'participate in the event without directly interfering with one another' (2011: 441). But this raises interesting questions about what it means to affect or interfere with another's actions in a sporting event. For example, in golf, which Skultety holds up as a prime example of an unencumbered sport, it is easy to see how one player could force the hand of another. Imagine a tournament coming down to the final hole, with the top two players separated by two strokes. Let us say the leader hits first and decides to play aggressively (perhaps imprudently); she hits a shot that carries over the pond in front of the green and sits with a 30-foot putt. At this point, the second player really has no choice but to try to carry the pond as well, because it is extremely unlikely that the two-stroke difference can be made up unless she gets up and down from where she lies in the fairway, and even then she will have to hope that the leader misses two putts. This example shows how both distinctions – between standardized and vis-à-vis, and between encumbered and unencumbered competitions – might be tweaked slightly to explain specific situations, although this does not detract from their general explanatory power.

The virtues and vices of competitive sport

It is no secret that many consider competition in all its varieties to be fundamentally problematic, and for a number of reasons: it operates (apparently) according to zero-sum logic, in which the success of one participant is inversely related to the success of others; it seems, for this reason, to encourage selfishness and aggression, which may spill over into violence, and it tends to put too much strain on rules, as competitors look for all possible advantages in the contest, sometimes at the expense of the regulations. As we saw in the first section, all of this might compromise the playful atmosphere of sport or even lead to problems beyond the scope of sport. Perhaps there is no solution to this tendency. As D. Stanley Eitzen (2001) remarks: 'Some believe that competition is the behavioral equivalent of gravity, a natural and inevitable force' (p. 235). In this section I address some concerns about the value of competition in sport.

There are two ways of exploring the problematic character of competition. First, we can approach it as an epistemological issue. An overemphasis on competitive results has a tendency to obscure other important facets of the event that a more sensitive observer would appreciate. Edwin J. Delattre (1976) argues that what really makes sport worthwhile are those intensely dramatic moments in a contest when everyone is fully put to the test: 'The best and most satisfying contests maximize these moments and minimize respite from pressure. When competition achieves this intensity it frequently renders the outcome of the contest anticlimatic, and it inevitably reduces victory celebrations to pallor by contrast' (p. 134). The epistemological mistake particularly characterizes partisan watchers of sport, those who are so intensely invested in the outcome of the event that they fail to acknowledge – or possibly even notice – the grace and beauty of the action, the various displays of virtue, the teamwork involved in organized plays, and countless other details, especially when they issue from the opposing side. Stephen Mumford (2012) draws a contrast between the 'purist' and the 'partisan' at a sporting event, and shows how they quite literally 'see' different events because they bring different sensitivities to the contest (pp. 15–24). His discussion persuasively argues that a preoccupation with winning and losing can actually limit an observer's appreciation of competitive sport. It is interesting to speculate that, ironically, modern sport culture encourages both devotion to and disrespect for the game, and for the same reason.

Second, we can consider the problematic character of competitive sport as a moral issue. Indeed, a plausible argument could be made that most of the bad effects of sport are caused by an overemphasis on winning and losing. Competitors naturally look for any edge in a contest, but if they do this without regard to other values, the overall appreciation of sport will suffer. The rules will then appear to be mere obstacles to a desired objective, rather than conditions that essentially create a desirable form of life, and the opponents will likewise seem to be enemies that need to be vanquished and silenced. These attitudes will manifest themselves in cheating and a total disregard for the principles of sportsmanship. For example, contestants with this attitude will try to gain advantages by altering the equipment of the contest, such as when baseball players cork their bats, or even by altering themselves, such as when they take banned performance-enhancing drugs. Even worse, arguably, is the regard the opponents develop for one another: any expression of joy by one's opponent, particularly at the moment of victory, will offend, and any opportunity to unnerve or even injure the opponent is taken. For example, consider the 'bounty' scandal in the National Football League, where an obsession with winning led some players and coaches to reward financially those teammates who caused serious injury to opposing star players. Of course, this is (fortunately) an extreme example, but it illustrates how pathological the thinking can become when the proper appreciation of competitive sport is lost. Nicholas Dixon summarizes:

> Putting winning and losing in a saner perspective may reduce the motivation to resort to cheating, distasteful forms of gamesmanship, and trash talking and other forms of taunting. And, while the desire to win is a necessary ingredient of competitive sport, realizing that winning is not the be-all and end-all of athletic excellence may help foster the cooperation that is part of healthy competition and prevent it from degenerating into alienation.
>
> *(Dixon 1999: 26)*

In addition to ugliness within the contest – as if that were not enough – we can also mention two spillover effects. First, the vices developed by the players within the competitive event might carry over into their non-sporting lives, so they tend to see every social encounter as an opportunity to demonstrate their superiority or to flout rules as they pursue their objectives. We often hear defenders of competitive sport celebrate the edifying effects of the activity, particularly on youth, but, if sport were driven by misplaced values, it would hardly surprise us that its effect would be deleterious. Secondly, we also witness the effect an emphasis on competition has on non-contestants, such as fans, owners, parents, and sponsors. They very often mimic the emotions and attitudes of the contestants: fans sometimes shout out personal and derisive comments at members of the other team, cheer injuries to opposing players, and even engage in violent displays following their teams' victories and defeats.

These are all problems, of course, but are they specifically *competitive* problems? In other words, do these bad displays spring directly from competition *per se*, or are they better understood as distortions of a genuinely competitive spirit? I want to suggest that, at least in principle, the problems outlined above – however paradoxical it might sound – evidence too little competitiveness rather than too much. Genuine competition is animated by what Suits (2005) calls a 'lusory attitude', which is a willingness to abide by constitutive rules that make the achievement of an ordinary task unnecessarily difficult. For example, in golf the 'pre-lusory' goal is to place the ball in the hole, but the game specifies the means through which one can legitimately accomplish this goal and thereby succeed in golf, which is the 'lusory' goal (p. 54). Competitors, therefore, simultaneously seek two things: victory (the objective of the endeavor) and challenge (the difficulty of the endeavor) – and are tenacious about both. A competitor really wants to win, of course, but also really wants to comply with the rules because they define the activity. Anyone who refuses to accept either of these conditions is not competing (no matter what the activity looks like). A cheater gives the appearance of competing but fails to accept the conditions of the contest; it makes no difference, in principle, if he picks up the golf ball and carries it to the green, or corks his bat to get an edge in his confrontation with the pitcher. Likewise, a competitor who engages in cheap gamesmanship, employs dangerous or illegal hits on the field, or otherwise denigrates the integrity of the opponent shows a profound misunderstanding of their relationship, and thereby undermines the prestige of the endeavor.

The lusory attitude logically implies that competitiveness is something like an Aristotelian virtue. Just as one cannot be too courageous, one cannot be too competitive – although we know, of course, what those descriptions intend to criticize. When people talk about 'too much courage' they really mean the vice of recklessness, which Aristotle (1962: Book II, cc. 6–9) describes as not courage at all. Similarly, when people describe someone as 'too competitive' they typically describe various personal vices that become manifest in a competitive context. Extreme competitiveness is not, for example, what explains the habit of throwing golf clubs to vent frustration over missed putts, or screaming at umpires to protest close calls; extreme competiveness is, rather, a kind of persistent vigilance in a contest in order to give oneself every opportunity to win, particularly on a tough day. It is a 'never give up' attitude in the throes of contest, a commitment to thorough preparation, and a genuine love for the lusory challenges (including the activity of the opponent) that define the sport. When things are going well, a true competitor senses her opportunity and moves in for the 'kill'; when things are going poorly, a true competitor hangs in there, looking for the moment that can turn the tide. As long as one is equally tenacious in upholding the constitutive rules and the spirit of the contest, one cannot be too tenacious in the pursuit of victory.

How does the virtue of competitiveness manifest itself? Consider an example recounted by William J. Morgan (2006), from the 1967 German International Tennis Championship. The final featured Hungarian Istvan Gulyas and Czech Jan Kukal. They were virtually tied late in a five-set match when Kukal was suddenly overtaken by severe leg cramps. The rules give an injured player a specific amount of time to recover and the opportunity to seek medical attention, but even after the allotted time, Kukal was unable to continue. Gulyas could have claimed victory at this point, but instead he petitioned the umpire to allow his opponent more time. More time was indeed granted, and Kukal came back and won (Morgan, 2006: 15–18). There are a number of ways of interpreting Gulyas's gesture. On the one hand, it seems to represent an exemplary instance of sportsmanship, patience, and generosity; on the other, it might seem foolish or even inappropriate for Gulyas to decline the victory, because he successfully campaigned to have a pre-established rule bent to accommodate an apparently less fit player, setting a problematic precedent. But it is hard to believe that his actions were motivated by pure unselfishness; he wanted to play the match out to have the satisfaction of a complete victory, and he wanted his opponent at more or less full strength. Once play resumed, we have to believe that he rediscovered his competitive fire and did everything he could to defeat Kukal – or else he was a fool. One could debate precisely how Gulyas's character was revealed in this incident, but I would suggest that the primary virtue is competitiveness, which manifests itself simultaneously as magnanimity and as self-interest, because that reflects the spirit of the lusory attitude and the meaning of the competitive relationship.

Some critics of competitive sport insist that even in its best instances – that is, when contests do not descend into violence, the players do not resort to cheating, or we do not see unsportsmanlike displays, etc. – one cannot deny that the zero-sum logic of competition presents insuperable conceptual difficulties, because the result of a contest is necessarily inequality. If 'competition' means anything, it means inevitably that someone will win and someone will lose, and so the dynamic tension between the 'friendly' and 'unfriendly' elements identified above will be resolved always in an unfriendly way. In response to this challenge, Simon (2010) presents a persuasive defense of the competitive engagement, emphasizing the cooperative basis presupposed by the antagonism and the intrinsic rewards of the confrontation. He defines competition as 'a mutual quest for excellence' (pp. 24–38), which nicely summarizes the moral appeal of the foregoing:

> Underlying the good sports contest, in effect, is an implicit social contract under which both competitors accept the obligation to provide a challenge for opponents according to the rules of the sport. Competition in sports is ethically defensible, in this view, when it is engaged in voluntarily as part of this mutual quest.
>
> *(Simon, 2010: 27)*

The key concept in this definition is mutuality, which implies not only simultaneity but also interactivity and reciprocity. If we employ Skultety's categories, we might say that sometimes I pursue excellence *with* you (typically in unencumbered or standardized competitions), but sometimes I pursue excellence *through* you (typically in vis-à-vis competitions).

This still does not completely resolve the issue of zero-sum logic, but it does mean that our successes are functionally inseparable, even if the results imperfectly express that. 'Although not all competitors can win, there is a sense … in which all the competitors in a well-played contest can meet the challenge and achieve excellence' (Simon, 2010: 29). We might say that a zero-sum structure creates an occasion for a host of non-zero-sum values, because only in a context in which it matters deeply whether one wins or loses would we recognize the heroism of an underdog's valiant although unsuccessful effort, the transcendent value of teammates joining purposes for a common good, or the 'sweet tension which seeks both continuation by further action and resolution by winning the point' (Fraleigh, 1984: 90). The outcome of a contest provides one measure of what transpires between contestants, but other values matter as well, as Dixon, Delattre, Simon, and others have pointed out. Furthermore, we must always remember that competitive sport is, for virtually all of its practitioners, a form of life rather than a single episode. We return to the game over and over – sometimes to defend and validate past successes, sometimes to reverse, or at least improve upon, past failures, and sometimes to begin a fresh narrative with a new opponent. Kretchmar (2012) makes the point well: 'For sportspersons, no game (aside from unusual circumstances) is the final game. No victory or defeat (apart from lopsided outcomes) offers a conclusive verdict. This pushes attention of competitors to the future, to the next chance, to the next inconclusive outcome. Hope, it would seem, is the lifeblood of the winner and loser alike' (p. 113).

Conclusion

Competition is a familiar form of human sociality, and sport is the paradigmatic instantiation. In competitive sport we deliberately set up encounters that are at once cooperative and antagonistic, and that test the human spirit as much as the body. Precisely because the structure is contrived, the engagement acquires meaning and moral significance; because the opposition is sincere, the relationship promotes respect and edification. Competitive sport is *about* nothing other than competitive sport; in principle, the antagonists seek out the struggle for its own inherent value and not as a means to any extrinsic reward. And thus we can say, without contradiction, that competitive sport is both playful and diversionary and yet deadly serious, in its own way. As Delattre says:

> It matters whether we win or lose. It also matters whether we play the game well or badly, given our own potential and preparation. It matters whom we play against and whether they are worthy of us, whether they can press us to call up our final resources.
>
> *(Delattre, 1975: 139)*

It is possible, of course, to misconstrue the nature of competition in sport, as well as the place of sport in society. These dangers are well-known and recommend our constant vigilance. But, rightly understood, the competitive dynamic in sport presents an opportunity for constructive human engagement, for moral aspiration and moral achievement, and for irreplaceable satisfactions. In its best instances competitive sport contributes significantly to the good life.

References

Aristotle. (1962). *Nicomachean Ethics*. (M. Ostwald, trans.) Englewood Cliffs, NJ: Prentice Hall.

Connor, S. (2011). *A Philosophy of Sport*. London: Reaktion Books.

Delattre, E. J. (1975). Some reflections on success and failure in competitive athletics. *Journal of the Philosophy of Sport*, 2: 133–9.

Dixon, N. (1999). On winning and athletic superiority. *Journal of the Philosophy of Sport*, 26: 10–26.

Eitzen, D. S. (2001). The dark side of competition. In Holowchak, M. A. (ed.). *Philosophy of Sport: Critical Readings, Crucial Issues* (pp. 235–40). Upper Saddle River, NJ: Prentice Hall.

Fraleigh, W. (1984). *Right Actions in Sport: Ethics for contestants*. Champaign, IL: Human Kinetics.

Gilbert, B. (1988). Competition: Is it what life is all about? *Sports Illustrated*, May 16, pp. 88–100.

Hegel, G. W. F. (1977). *Phenomenology of Spirit*. (Miller, A. V., trans.). Oxford: Oxford University Press.

Hobbes, T. (1999). *Leviathan*. Buffalo, NY: Prometheus.

James, W. (1910). The moral equivalent of war. *McClure's Magazine*, August, pp. 463–8.

Kretchmar, R. S. (1975). From test to contest: An analysis of two kinds of counterpoint in sport. *Journal of the Philosophy of Sport*, 2: 23–30.

—— (2102). Competition, redemption and hope. *Journal of the Philosophy of Sport*, 39: 101–16.

Miller, S. (2004). *Ancient Greek Athletics*. New Haven, CT: Yale University Press.

Morgan, W. J. (2006). *Why Sports Morally Matter*. New York: Routledge.

Mumford, S. (2012). *Watching Sport: Aesthetics, ethics and emotion*. New York: Routledge.

Orwell, G. (1968). *Collected Essays, Journalism, and Letters*. Vol. 4. New York: Harcourt, Brace, and World.

Simon, R. L. (2010). *Fair Play: The ethics of sport* (3rd ed.). Boulder, CO: Westview Press.

Skultety, S. (2011). Categories of competition. *Sport, Ethics, and Philosophy*, 5 (4): 433–46.

Spivey, N. (2004). *The Ancient Olympics: A History*. Oxford: Oxford University Press.

Suits, B. (2002). Tricky triad: Games, play, and sport. In Holowchak, M. A. (ed.). *Philosophy of Sport: Critical Readings, Crucial Issues* (pp. 29–36). Upper Saddle River, NJ: Prentice Hall.

—— (2005). *The Grasshopper: Games, Life, and Utopia* (2nd ed.). Peterborough, Ontario: Broadview Press.

Wittgenstein, L. (2001). *Philosophical Investigations*. (Anscombe, G. E. M., trans.). Oxford: Blackwell.

Further reading

Caillois, R. (2001). *Man, Play, and Games*. (M. Brash, trans.). Urbana, IL: University of Illinois Press.

Dombrowski, D. (2011). *Contemporary Athletics and Ancient Greek Ideals*. Chicago, IL: University of Chicago Press.

Elcombe, T. and Kretchmar, R. S. (2007). In defense of competition and winning: revisiting athletic tests and contests. In Morgan, W. J. (ed.) *Ethics in Sport* (2nd ed.). Champaign, IL: Human Kinetics, pp. 181–94.

Gaffney, P. (2007). The meaning of sport: competition as a form of language. In Morgan, W. J. (ed.) *Ethics in Sport* (2nd ed.). Champaign, IL: Human Kinetics, pp. 109–18.

Hundley, J. (1983). The overemphasis on winning: A philosophical look. In Holowchak, M. A. (ed.). *Philosophy of Sport: Critical readings, crucial issue.* Upper Saddle River, NJ: Prentice Hall, pp. 206–20.

Hyland, D. (1985). Opponents, contestants, and competitors: the dialectics of sport. *Journal of the Philosophy of* Sport, 11: 63–70.

Kohn, A. (1986). *No Contest: The case against competition* (rev. ed.) New York: Houghton Mifflin.

Kretchmar, R. S. (2005). *Practical Philosophy of Sport and Physical Activity* (2nd ed.). Champaign, IL: Human Kinetics.

20

DISABILITY AND PARALYMPIC SPORT PHILOSOPHY

Steve Edwards and Mike McNamee

Introduction

Relatively little attention has been given to what has variously been called sport for the disabled, sport for athletes with disabilities, sport for athletes with impairments or Paralympic sport, in contrast to the mainstream forms of sport for able-bodied persons. The heterogeneous nomenclature of the limited literature that exists betokens conceptual, ethical and political dimensions of debates for persons with disabilities. In this chapter, we focus on the development of these sport forms, with particular – although not exclusive – reference to Paralympic sports that comprise the quadrennial Paralympic Games. The Paralympic Games, organised by the International Paralympic Committee, are the analogue of the Olympic Games. Although their constitutive activities and the classifications of competing athletes within them are a matter of contestation and debate, they represent the most popular forms of sports for athletes with disabilities or impairments. Other forms and organizations are noted by way of context in the first section, before moving on to discuss issues of classification and identity, and the underlying conceptions of health, ability and disability itself.

Understanding the world of Paralympic sports first requires quite considerable investment in the philosophy and taxonomies and classifications concerning disability and impairment. Having discussed these conceptual issues, the chapter proceeds by discussing three of the most prominent ethical issues: doping (including 'boosting'), therapeutic use exemptions, fairness of competition, and elective amputation.

Historical landmarks for disability sport

The first disability sports group to mobilise themselves were deaf athletes (Tweedy and Howe, 2011). In 1888, the Berlin Sports Club for the Deaf was formed (Gold and Gold, 2007). It took more than a quarter of a century for the establishment of an international society for deaf athletes in 1922. In a move that foreshadowed later Paralympic Games, the first two International Silent Games were held following the 1924 Paris and 1928 Amsterdam Olympic Games (Tweedy and Howe, 2011). A decade later, in 1932, the British Society of One-Armed Golfers was formed (Brittain, 2010). The first systematically organised games for persons with disabilities occurred in the UK in 1948 and, when joined by Dutch athletes four years later, it can be said that the Paralympic movement began in earnest. Over time, the Paralympic Games have become parallel games and not merely as somehow lesser to their longer standing and illustrious counterpart, the Olympic Games. Just as the Baron Pierre de Coubertin was the spearhead for the development and internationalisation of the Olympic Games, it was Dr Ludwig Guttmann, a German-Jewish medic escaping the rise of Nationalist Socialism in his fatherland, who in 1948 inaugurated the Stoke Mandeville Games for athletes with disabilities, including athletes mainly from the UK but also the Netherlands. It is widely agreed that this was the birth of the Paralympic movement generally and the Paralympic Games specifically (International Paralympic Committee, 2011).

Today, new sports forms are being devised to test and perfect the athletic skills and character of athletes with a disability. While there is much that unites the different sports forms and their athletic contestants, there are genuine and interesting aspects of Paralympic sports that have gone relatively unnoticed by philosophers (Jespersen and McNamee, 2009). In able-bodied sports, the nature of contests, their organisation, rules and classification systems, have evolved over thousands of years from their Western roots in Ancient Greece. Paralympic sport, by contrast, is a relative newcomer to the world of elite sports. It has yet to probe, let alone resolve, many of the conceptual and ethical issues that arise therein. These issues relate across the whole spectrum of Paralympic sports, from the organisation of events, their marketing and promotion, to the more obvious dimensions of participation and officiating in them.

The contrast with Olympic sports in this regard ought not to be thought of as too sharp, however, especially in the light of the Beijing Games of 2008, which was the first time both Olympic and Paralympic bids were conjoined in the bidding process and brought the games much closer together in terms of organisation and promotion. This is not to say that conceptual and ethical issues are absent from the Olympic Games. Cheating, doping, and foul play – definitions of which presuppose some concept of justice – are everywhere to be found in just about all sports at elite levels. There is no reason to think that Paralympic sports would be an exception, human nature being what it is. Moreover, there remain thorny legitimacy issues regarding sex verification that give athletes, administrators, medics and philosophers problems. Nevertheless, these represent rather minor exceptions to the usual business of Olympic sports. It is, however, often far from clear at times who should be competing against whom in the Paralympic Games, as well as in disability sports in general. In Olympic sports, contestants are typically divided according to sex (for example, in athletics, field hockey and football) but also sometimes according to weight (for example, in boxing and judo). Why this is so is partly historical and partly logical. Sometimes the rationale is clear and justified while at other times it is not. At times, sex-segregated sports are organised on grounds of prevention of harm and, at times, this argument extends to competitions with same-sex contestants. At other times, sex is irrelevant to the performance of activity (for example, in equestrianism), where sex differences are thought not to offer unfair opportunities to win the contest. In Paralympic sport, by contrast, disputes as to who should compete against whom are almost ubiquitous. In this philosophical contribution, we therefore spend considerable time and attention marking conceptual distinctions as to the nature of disability, the arising issues of eligibility and classification that are at the centre of Paralympic sport. We then discuss three, among many, key ethical issues regarding doping, therapeutic use exemptions and healthcare rights for Paralympic athletes.

Issues of classification and eligibility

It is clear that all Paralympic athletes, in order to compete in the Paralympic Games, must have a disability (or more strictly speaking, an impairment) at the time of competition. Precisely who counts as being disabled is not at all clear. It is sometimes reported that around ten per cent of the world population may be considered disabled. Clearly, however, an appreciation of this statistic begs questions as to the criteria for what constitutes 'disability' itself. It is necessary therefore to consider some basic conceptual issues regarding who may be considered a 'Paralympic athlete'.

The International Paralympic Committee (IPC) states that a necessary condition of being eligible to compete in Paralympic sports is that the athlete must have an impairment and, importantly, that the impairment must 'lead to a permanent and verifiable activity limitation' (International Paralympic Committee, 2007, p. 10). This statement of eligibility employs key concepts – 'impairment/activity limitation' – that are central to the very idea of Paralympic sport. In this section, their meanings are unpacked.

Readers familiar with attempts to create a taxonomy of disability in general will recognise the terms 'impairment' and 'activity limitation' as deriving from a specific theoretical perspective. To appreciate the full significance of these terms, however, it is necessary to understand alternative and sometimes competing ways in which scholars and scientists have tried to capture the meaning and experience of disablement in ways that are theory laden. The first systematic attempt to create a taxonomy of disablement was undertaken by the World Health Organization (WHO) in 1980, in their publication *The International Classification of Impairment, Disability and Handicap* (ICIDH).

According to the ICIDH, disease is said to lead to impairment, which in turn can lead to disability, which can further lead to what was then described as a 'handicap'. Moreover, 'Impairment: In the context of health experience, impairment is any loss or abnormality of psychological, physiological or anatomical structure or function' (WHO, 1980, p. 27).

Impairments are said to arise at the level of parts of the body (WHO, 1980, p. 28). Thus, Oscar Pistorius properly contested Paralympic category T43, since, owing to a congenital disease, he was born without fibulae and consequently his legs were amputated just below the knee when he was 11 months old. Since lacking fibulae counts as an abnormality of anatomical structure, it is an impairment according to the WHO definition. Nevertheless, it should be noted that, according to the ICIDH taxonomy above, it may not follow necessarily that Pistorius should be classified as disabled; more is needed than the mere presence of an impairment. The ICIDH definition of disability holds that: 'Disability: In the context of health experience, a disability is any restriction or lack (resulting from impairment) of ability to perform an activity in the manner or within the range considered normal for a human being' (p. 28).

Whereas impairments arise at the level of 'body parts', such as organs, disabilities are said to arise at the level of the whole individual (WHO, 1980, p. 28). Thus, impairments are properly attributed to body parts and disabilities are properly attributed to persons. Continuing with the example of Pistorius, we can say that the relevant body parts include his legs but, if one were to attribute disability to him, this would occur at the level of the person – namely Pistorius himself – as opposed to one (or more) of his impaired body parts. Thus, one would say it is the person Pistorius that is disabled, not his legs, shins nor any other part of his body.

The idea of a disabled athlete

In what sense, if any, are highly performing Paralympic athletes to be thought of as disabled? Consider the case of Aimee Mullins, a double-amputee athlete and long-jumper who, in 1998, set world records in the 100-metres, 200-metres and long-jump. How is it that an elite sportswoman can be said to be disabled? Like Pistorius, she was born with fibular hemimelia and required transtibial amputation. Staying with the ICDH classification, it is evident that, without the use of prostheses she would be unable to carry out the normal human function of walking unaided. Specifically, Mullins would lack an 'ability to perform an activity in the manner or within the range considered normal for a human being' (ibid.). As with impairment, the definition of 'abnormality' (and normality itself for that matter) relied upon in the ICIDH is a biostatistical definition. This understanding of disability is often called, rather loosely, 'the medical model' (DePauw, 1997). It should be noted, however, that this is a somewhat crude essentialising of a variety of beliefs and norms about the nature of the human being in conditions of disease, health and illness, and that bringing them together under one label – although convenient – masks the inevitable heterogeneity of views belonging to medical professionals around the globe and crossing distinctions such as primary and secondary care, private and public health care, general practice versus high-tech medicine, and so on. Consistent with the ICIDH classification, the medical model of disability is predicated on the belief that there is a causal relationship between a person's impairment and their disability; it is therefore an outgrowth of the biomedical model of health. In a series of essays, widely regarded as classics in the philosophy of medicine, Christopher Boorse (1975, 1977) argued that health was conceptually the equivalent to 'normal functioning'. Health, within his theory, is understood as 'species-typical functioning' that occurs normally in the absence of disease or impairment. His account is deeply sympathetic to the medical professions' dominant self-understanding, techniques and ideologies. Moreover, it is positivistic in spirit. For Boorse, normal functioning is a matter of objective fact that can be determined without reference to the views of the person whose health or even, by extension their disability, is in question.

The WHO schema is in sympathy with the medical model and with Boorse's general theory. Thus, persons are considered normal or abnormal in relation to a reference class (human beings at the same stage of chronological development) who are conceived of as a class with a normal distribution of human functioning. So both Mullins and Pistorius would be described as disabled according to the ICIDH classificatory system. Hence, according to the schema above, disabilities are ultimately consequences of disease; disease leads to impairment, which leads in turn to disability.

The fourth category in the ICIDH (besides disease, impairment and disability), is handicap, which is defined as follows:

> In the context of health experience, a handicap is a disadvantage for a given individual, resulting from an impairment or a disability, that limits or prevents the fulfilment of a role that is normal (depending on age, sex and cultural factors) for that individual.
>
> *(WHO, p. 29)*

As mentioned, impairments are properly attributed at the level of *body parts* and disabilities at the level of *persons*, so it is said that handicap implicates a level beyond these, namely that of *social phenomena*. For, in contrast to the other two consequences of disease, this category makes explicit reference to social and cultural factors. The category 'disability' involves statistical comparison with other humans but not with reference to specific social or cultural norms. (Although the term 'handicap' is still used nowadays around the world, notably in Francophone and Scandinavian countries, in the English language, it is generally considered disrespectful.) For the WHO, a disability which 'limits' in the sense of 'hinders' 'the fulfilment of a role that is normal' amounts to a handicap. In the context of Paralympic sports, it is clear that amputee athletes have impairments that lead to activity limitations; for example, in their ability to run (unaided by prostheses). In the non-sports world, ambulatory limitations may be overcome by use of wheelchairs and, in turn, the use of ramps as opposed to stairs, and so on. The adaptation of the social environment has become more widespread, although is far from universal. It is, therefore, less clear that being unable to walk limits or hinders one's opportunities to fulfil a role that is normal to the degree that it once did. Nevertheless, one can appreciate that the WHO definition captures the viewpoint that those who cannot walk are, to a certain extent, handicapped in some way. Philosophers and sociologists have nevertheless, developed robust criticisms of the WHO definition (Oliver, 1990, 1996; Morris, 1991).

Indeed, critics (Oliver, 1990; UPIAS, 1975) have rejected completely the idea that disability and handicap are 'consequences of disease'. Commentators who promoted what became known as a 'social model' of disability argued against the medical model, that the causes of disability lie in the social environment and not in the individual person, as is presupposed in the WHO definition. Therefore, the ICIDH classification is itself considered to be deeply flawed. By locating the cause of disability in the individual concerned, the definition paints far too crude a picture of the relevant causal factors. However, it should be recognised that the WHO taxonomy has been key to the development of the Paralympic sports organisations, since its categories have been considered sufficiently robust to establish a way of comparing one athlete against another to ensure a fair competition – albeit it in a sometimes crude fashion (Howe and Jones, 2006).

Further, it is worth pointing out that the 'social model' of disability has itself been subjected to critique (Shakespeare, 2006; Harris, 2000). Critics complain that, just as the ICIDH may have overemphasised factors internal to the individual person to the neglect of social factors, in the causation of disability, the social model makes the opposite mistake; namely, by over-emphasising social factors and neglecting the significance of individual impairments. One might also add that it is difficult to see how the social model can easily encompass severe intellectual and sensory disabilities (French, 1993).

The international classification of functioning, disability and health

In response to criticisms of their earlier ICIDH, the WHO produced a subsequent version, which attempted to address some of the problems of the earlier one and used noticeably different terminology. The newer version is the *International Classification of Functioning, Disability and Health* (ICF) (WHO, 2001).

This new development should not be seen as a total rejection of the previous schema. One key similarity between the old and the new lies in its definitions of its three main categories. The old three-fold classification of impairment, disability and handicap is replaced with, impairment, activity limitations and participation restrictions. Previously, impairment (for example, an abnormality in anatomical structure, such as a missing spinal nerve) led to disability (inability to walk) and finally to handicap (such as an inability to work). The schema retains the part-whole-societal structure (WHO, 2001, p. 188), although the simplistic causal connection that some found in the ICIDH is now explicitly rejected in favour of a 'biopsychosocial' approach.

The three basic categories in the ICF are: 'Impairment is a loss or abnormality in body structure or physiological function (including mental functions). Abnormality here is used strictly to refer to a significant variation from established statistical norms (i.e., as a deviation from a standard population mean' (p. 190).

So, as was the case with the ICIDH, athletes with prostheses can be seen as impaired according to this definition for the same reason.

The disability dimension of the ICIDH, the 'person level' dimension, is defined thus:

> Activity limitations are difficulties an individual may have in executing activities. An activity limitation may range from a slight to a severe deviation in terms of quality or quantity in executing the activity in a manner or to the extent that is expected of people without the health condition.
>
> *(WHO, 2001, p. 191)*

The explicit reference to 'activities within the range considered normal for a human being' has been omitted here, yet there is a necessary appeal to some conception of normality against which limitations are to be understood: 'Limitations or restrictions are assessed against a generally accepted population standard' (p. 21). It is noteworthy that reduction in the quality of performance of an activity is mentioned explicitly within the definition. Thus, if a wheelchair athlete is capable of shooting an arrow in an archery contest, but, because of a condition which leads to muscular atrophy or loss of motor control (such as multiple sclerosis or cerebral palsy), can do this only seated from a wheelchair (as was the case with Neroli Fairhall in the 1972 Olympics), then one would also qualify as having an 'activity limitation'. By way of summary, then, according to this new definition, the term 'disability' has been superseded by the term 'activity limitation'. It is this term that is employed by the IPC in their literature (International Paralympic Committee, 2007), although its definition is stated more briefly than the WHO definition. According to the IPC, an 'activity limitation' refers to 'difficulties an individual may have in executing activities' (International Paralympic Committee, 2007). Thus, as mentioned earlier, one might hold that Mullins and Pistorius have an activity limitation, since, without their prostheses, both have difficulty walking as compared to a standard population.

The term 'handicapped' is no longer included in the ICF and is replaced by the term 'participation restriction', which is defined thus:

> Participation restrictions are problems an individual may experience in involvement in life situations. The presence of a participation restriction is determined by comparing an individual's participation to that which is expected of an individual without disability in that culture or society.
>
> *(WHO, 2001, p. 191)*

So, as with the ICIDH category 'handicap', it appears that a 'participation restriction' is determined by reference to the kinds of activities typically engaged in by one's standard peers, who become the reference class. If one is restricted from engaging in such activities, owing to 'impairments' or 'activity limitations', one is considered to suffer from a 'participation restriction'. This opens the door to participation in Paralympic sport.

Building on the critics of the 'medical model', the authors of the ICF make it clear that disability should not be conceived of solely as a problem of or for individuals (that is, their anatomical structure and functioning). The role of environmental factors is explicitly acknowledged thus: 'A person's functioning and disability is conceived as a dynamic interaction between health conditions (diseases, disorders ...) and contextual factors' (p. 10). To signal this, it is made explicit that the ICF involves a rejection of a medical model of disability, without embracing a social model. Instead, a model which recognises a role for both kinds of factors is adopted. As the ICF declares: 'a "biopsychosocial" approach is used' (p. 28) in this case. In other words, their approach – encapsulated in the definition – takes into account factors at each of the three-levels of analysis identified earlier. In summary, then, the new definition makes redundant the old terminology of impairment, disability and handicap.

Summary of the main differences between the ICF and the ICIDH

Although this chapter has thus far focused primarily on the WHO taxonomy of disability and its critics, it is important to signal the fact that disability is itself a hotly contested concept. An important alternative is proposed by Nordenfeldt (1983, 1993), who opposes simple biostatistical or positivistic understandings of both health and disability. Statistical norms play a key function in both WHO definitions and Boorse's philosophical theory. Nordenfelt is critical of such biostatistically based approaches because they fail to do justice to the values and priorities of the individual person.

To illustrate this, consider the former multiple world and Paralympic champion wheelchair athlete, Dame Tanni Grey-Thompson (2001, p. 8), who has remarked, 'I do not think of myself as disabled'. Or, again, consider Pistorius, who, according to reports (Edwards, 2008), refuses to park in parking spaces reserved for disabled people because he does not consider himself disabled. Nordenfelt's theory of disability lends some weight to their claims. His theory is that persons are disabled by virtue of their inability to *do* things that are important to them. Nordenfeldt labels these 'vital [personal] goals'. Thus, if leading a very active or athletic lifestyle is of paramount importance, to given individuals, and they are thus enabled (in addition to the activities of daily living), are able to fulfil their vital goals(s). Insofar as they are able to fulfil their goals, on Nordenfeldt's influential analysis, they would not be regarded as disabled. On this, more radical account, therefore, neither Mullins nor Pistorius (nor indeed wheelchair athletes) would be characterised as disabled.

According to Nordenfelt (1983, 1993), *typically*, disabilities stem from a combination of internal factors (such as impairments) and external factors (such as wheelchair-unfriendly public transportation systems). The most striking aspect of this approach to disability is the emphasis on the views of the person concerned.

Time and space do not allow a full account of Nordenfelt's approach but the description just given is sufficient to illustrate the central way in which it differs from the WHO approaches. Specifically, as indicated, it would certainly do justice to the kind of attitude voiced by Paralympic athletes and many others who would otherwise be classified as 'disabled' (by virtue of having impairment, plus an activity limitation, together with a participation restriction) according to the WHO definitions.[1]

Wolbring (2008a) poses a further and more radical challenge to all attempts to impose classificatory schema on human beings based upon appeals to species-typical function. Such taxonomies manifest forms of what he terms 'Ableism: a favouritism for certain abilities that are projected as essential while at the same time labelling real or perceived deviation from or lack of these essential abilities as a diminished state of being' (2008a, p. 31). The suggestion here seems to be that any attempt to taxonomise humans in terms of what they are able to do manifests a prejudice against those who are believed either to lack those abilities completely or to display them to a limited degree only. In spite of this general concern about the privileging of certain kinds of abilities, however, it is obvious that some kind of classificatory schema is necessary in Paralympic sport in order for meaningful competitions to take place.

As noted above, according to the eligibility criteria of the IPC (International Paralympic Committee, 2007) clause 5.2 'an Athlete must have an impairment that leads to a permanent and verifiable activity limitation'. It is not obvious that all Paralympic athletes have an activity limitation, still less a permanent one. As is well documented, many Paralympic sprinters are capable of achieving highly respectable times in some track events by the standards of able-bodied national-level athletes. Compare, for example, the world records for the wheelchair marathon. While Wilson Kipsang of Kenya has covered the 26.2 miles in an incredible 2 hours,

3 minutes and 23 seconds, the Canadian wheelchair athlete Josh Cassidy has covered the same distance in 1 hour, 18 minutes and 24 seconds, almost twice as fast.

A critic might say that there would be 'no contest' between the two. This must, however, be understood in conceptual terms. While there exist sports contests where able-bodied and disabled athletes co-participate, such as archery or equestrianism, it is not obvious where co-participation ought to be permitted. In the case of the London marathon, for example, the wheelchair event is started before the able-bodied event, although they cover an identical course. Co-participation might, however, cause considerable difficulties, owing to the forms of motility between both sets of athletes. Clearly, the space occupied by a wheelchair athlete is considerably greater than that by a runner. But co-participation in the same event would beg questions as to whether the participants were indeed sharing the same test (Kretchmar, 1975). Moreover, calling on Suits's (2005) notion of game playing, we can say that the wheelchair athlete is not using means permitted by the constitutive rules of athletics. In lay terms, it seems clear that the wheel chair athlete is rolling rather than running.

We can see that the WHO definition of activity limitations assumes that the activities referred to are unaided. Thus, it would indeed be the case that wheelchair and prosthetically assisted athletes are understood to have an activity limitation(s), where this refers to an activity such as 'walking unaided'. Moreover, an important consideration for athletes with disabilities arises when considering the permanence of the activity limitation. Clause 5.4 of the IPC Classification Code states:

> If an athlete has an activity limitation resulting from an impairment that is not permanent and/or does not limit the athlete's ability to compete equitably in elite sport with athletes without impairment, the athlete should be considered ineligible to compete.
>
> *(International Paralympic Committee, 2007)*

It is clear, then, that the permanence of the impairment is a necessary condition of an athlete's proper entitlement to compete in Paralympic activities according to the ruling body, the IPC. How is the concept of permanence to be understood and applied? One could imagine that athletes might be regarded as ineligible to compete because of progress in medical or prosthetic technology. Equally, developments in genetic and nanomedicine raise the possibility of growing missing or repairing damaged tissues, which can be grown or transplanted (such as nerve tissue or bone). If this is the case, then many severe impairments will in fact not be permanent (that is, irremediable) because there is the possibility of remedies for the impairment arising in the future.

Finally, it may be interesting to consider the possibility of integrating Nordenfelt's (1983, 1993) theory of disability with the IPC/WHO account of activity limitations. Recall that, according to Nordenfelt, one is disabled to the extent that one cannot, because of impairment, pursue one's vital goals. If it is the case that many athletes competing in the Paralympics are indeed pursuing their vital goals perfectly satisfactorily as they themselves see it, then – perhaps paradoxically – it follows they should not be thought of as disabled according to Nordenfelt's theory. Thus, the general impression that Paralympic sport is synonymous with disability sport would need to be abandoned. Instead, one would need to focus more on the notions of impairment and activity limitation, where the latter is understood to involve unaided activity. Indeed, it appears that this is the way that Paralympic organisations are heading (see also Howe and Jones, 2006, who anticipate the significance of a narrow focus on impairment and away from disability). Moreover, in addition to this potential to sever the conceptual link between

Paralympic sport and disability sport, some commentators think that the context of the Paralympics provide an ideal opportunity to develop the idea that human function can be enhanced by the use of technology. Running blades might come to be seen as very crude first steps along the journey to 'transhumanism' – that is an attempt to transcend the human biological form, and its constraints, completely via the use of increasingly sophisticated forms of biotechnology. Paralympic sport potentially provides the ideal vehicle for the transition from human, to cyborg (part human, part synthetic), to transhuman which some commentators envisage: some with apparent glee (see, for example, the website of the World Transhumanist Association) and some with dread (Wollbring, 2008b; Habermas, 2003).

Ethics and Paralympic sport

Unsurprisingly, ethical issues are plentiful in Paralympic sport, although they have not been discussed extensively within the philosophy of sport. We focus here on five ethical issues that are prominent in Paralympic sports. It is important to recognise that some of these are also issues in able-bodied sport (such as fair play and doping) but that there are also issues that are unique such as autonomic dysreflexia (or 'boosting' as it is commonly referred to) and elective amputation in order to gain eligibility to Paralympic sport or to enhance performance therein.

Equality, fair opportunity and fair play in Paralympic sport

All sports share the same 'gratuitous logic' in that they challenge athletes to overcome unnecessary obstacles (Suits, 2005). The overcoming of these difficulties or obstacles, which are created and preserved by the rules, is what gives sports their point and players their enjoyment. The underlying structure is that of a test which is shared by contestants in the form of a competition (Kretchmar, 1975). The rules that shape each sport are of two kinds: constitutive and regulative (Kant, 2007; Midgley, 1960; Searle, 1979). Constitutive rules define the activity (the size of the playing area; the duration of the activity; the composition and weight of playing equipment, and so on) while the regulative rules lay down what manner of means may be employed by contestants.

There is much dispute as to whether the rules alone create a structure of fairness within which contestants are able to engage in a mutual quest for victory (Simon, 1991) or whether rules are also necessarily reinforced by the ethos or prevailing set of unwritten norms as to how the activity should be engaged in (McFee, 2004). Clearly, both written and unwritten rules contribute to the fairness of the contest.

There are issues of equality that go beyond the nature of sports contest themselves. These relate to the treatment of individuals. Much has been made of the inequalities between Paralympic and Olympic sports. Athletes in Paralympic sport tend to be less well financially supported and rewarded, and enjoy less sports medicine and science support (Howe, 2009). Their media coverage, although it did improve for the Beijing Olympic Games of 2008, also falls far short of the Olympic Games, and this has immediate consequences for the funding of Paralympic sports and the profile of their participants. The 2012 London Paralympics included four sports (track and field athletics, rowing, swimming and table tennis) within the scheduling of the Olympic Games, which attests to the developing professionalism of Paralympic sport and recognition of the need to develop solidarity between the parallel games.

A further inequality that occurs outside of the Paralympic contest is found in the differences in access that Paralympians from varying countries to medical, sporting and technological resources. Take for example the case of severe spinal cord injured athletes who require the use of catheters. Clearly, those athletes coming from developing countries need to use and reuse catheters for much longer than their wealthier counterparts increasingly significantly the risk (and in fact, incidence) of infections (Mills and Krassioukov, 2011). Equally, the Italian wheelchair athlete and former Formula 1 driver, Allessandro Zanetti, is reputed to use a hand-racing wheelchair made by Ferrari that cost €50,000, which would be an unthinkable sum for most wheelchair athletes. Its lightness and durability offer a clear advantage to Zanardi over his competitors.

It is an open question as to whether and to what extent Paralympic sport should model itself on, for example, Formula 1 motor racing, where there are relatively tight parameters on equipment specification. In many technology-dependent sports, policy makers will have to determine the parameters of equipment not merely on grounds of fairness but also in terms of harm minimisation (or prevention), and also to ensure that talent and training win out over mere technological advances afforded disproportionally to athletes from more privileged backgrounds. Clearly, as with all sports, it is both undesirable and practically impossible to make all background conditions equitable.

In terms of fair play and fair opportunity to win, it should be noted that the diversity of classifications for Paralympic contests is intended to ensure that like athletes compete against like athletes. This is not always possible, and the history of Paralympic sport is replete with such disputes. In this regard, it is worth mentioning the incident that led to the expulsion of intellectually disabled athletes. During the 2000 Paralympic Games in Sydney, Spain won gold in the basketball competition. It was subsequently found that 10 of the 12 players were not intellectually disabled.[2] Clearly, the possibilities for cheating – intentionally gaining an unfair advantage by means of deception – are more widespread in Paralympic sport for those with intellectual disabilities because it is harder to determine their classification in comparison to athletes with structural impairments. The basketball case in Sydney was the trigger for an in-depth evaluation of the eligibility system for athletes with a disability, which proved to be wanting. For this reason, the IPC took action against the whole class of athletes with intellectual disabilities by banning them from the Paralympic Games. This decision was recently overturned and athletes with disabilities competed in the London Games of 2012, although they will have to prove eligibility via a new 'sports intelligence' test (BBC, 2009).

A final example of fair opportunity to perform arises when Paralympic athletes and Olympic athletes co-compete. There have been many instances where athletes with a disability have competed on equal terms with Olympic athletes, although, in that context, they were simply viewed as athletes (DePauw, 1997). Notably, DePauw cites Liz Hartel (post-polio), who won a silver medal in the equestrian dressage at the 1952 Olympics, and Jeff Float, a deaf swimmer, who won a gold medal in swimming at the 1984 Los Angeles Games. Similarly, a wheelchair archer, Neroli Fairhall, also competed in the 1984 Olympic Games; however, her disability became an issue as her alleged stability advantage was questioned by traditional upright archers. If the fair opportunity to perform (Loland, 2009) is an important principle across all sports, then the stability of the base of the archer will be important to determine if a significant unfair advantage arises between contestants.

A more recent case occurred in professional golfing when Casey Martin won the right to play on the highly lucrative United States Professional Golf Association (USPGA) tour. Martin required the use of a buggy (motorised cart) to move between shots. The USPGA argued that because Martin did not have to undergo the same physical test as able-bodied golfers who have to walk the course, he would gain an unfair advantage over his competitors. The issue became the subject of a legal dispute. In 2001, the Supreme Court in the United States held, by seven votes to two, Casey's legal right to use the golf cart in PGA tournaments. Ironically, he failed to make the cut at the final qualifying tournament to determine eligibility to the professional US Tour.

Doping and therapeutic use exemption certification

As noted above, the rules of sport have a dual structure, Paralympic or otherwise, that have to do with whether they play a constitutive or regulative role in the relevant sport. It has also been argued that there are auxiliary rules (Meier, 1985), which are special regulative rules that determine how contestants may prepare themselves. Rules regarding the use of performance-enhancing methods and substances (colloquially referred to as 'doping') are examples of such auxiliary rules.

It is recognised in Paralympics and Olympic sport that the right to fair opportunity to perform in sport is subservient to the more basic right to health care. There arise in sports occasions where the need for medication for a medically authorised condition, which is also performance enhancing, supersedes competitors' right to a fair contest. Contestants (or their medical support team) must ensure that there are no suitable alternatives that are not on the prohibited list of the World Anti-Doping Agency. They must apply for a therapeutic use exemption (TUE) certificate to legitimate their use of the banned substance or method. It is the athlete's responsibility to ensure that the TUE is up to date and that, for example in the obtaining of new inhalers for asthmatics, that their contents or delivery systems for the medication do not offend the list which is regularly updated. This responsibility is in effect a duty of care: all athletes must undertake to train and present themselves in competition in a manner consistent with the rules of Paralympic sport.

The presence of cocaine on the list has long been controversial because it is not performance enhancing and the evidence base on its harmfulness has been questioned in relation to other recreational drugs such as alcohol which are not proscribed. Moreover, athletes must also be aware of the condition of strict liability. In doping cases, anti-doping agencies are not required to prove guilt or the intention to dope. The mere presence of a banned substance suffices to constitute a doping offence and subsequent suspension from participation (McNamee and Tarasti, 2010). Take, for example, the case of Canadian Wheelchair Paralympian, Jeff Adams, who won gold in the 2000 Paralympic Games. Adams was found to have committed a doping offence, and, despite his protestations that a stranger in a nightclub had put cocaine into his mouth and that he had ingested it unknowingly, was found guilty of an anti-doping rule violation.

Another class of activity that has occurred, may still occur but which is banned by the IPC is that of so-called 'boosting'. In medical terms it is known as autonomic dysreflexia (Mills and Krassioukov, 2011) and it is claimed to be a form of self-harm. Boosting involves the athlete deliberately provoking a bodily response equivalent to an 'adrenaline rush', leading to increased heart rate and blood pressure. This may be done by a range of means, including self-administered electric shocks, intentionally withholding the release of urine or other forms of self-induced pain. The dangers are that, among other things, it can cause stroke or heart attack. In one sense, this looks categorically distinct from doping, since no extrinsic agents are used by the athlete, except in the case of electric shocks. Further, if a central function of classification in Paralympic sport is to reduce disadvantages that stem from the 'natural lottery', one might defend the practice by arguing that athletes with naturally low blood pressure are merely using their own bodies to compete on a par with those with naturally higher blood pressure. Alternatively, one could factor in the resting blood pressure of athletes in eligibility criteria and have two different events for the two categories of contestants.

Ethics, fairness and technology in Paralympic/Olympic sport

In the section on classification and eligibility above, the example of the South African runner, Oscar Pistorius, was used extensively. While he is far from alone in creating controversy in the history of Paralympic sport, his case provides an interesting and contemporaneous focal point for a consideration of whether and how technology may alter or even undermine the nature and goods (that is, those inherent aspects thought to be of value) of Paralympic contests and in his particular case, the possibility of shared competition between Olympic and Paralympic athletes (Burkett *et al.*, 2012; Edwards, 2008; Marcellini *et al.*, 2011; Wilson and Jones, 2009).

During the period prior to the 2008 Olympics in China, there was considerable debate over whether or not Pistorius should be allowed to compete, were he to make the required qualifying time for inclusion into the South African Olympic team. The main concern centred on whether or not his running 'blades' (prostheses) gave him not simply an advantage over other competitors but an unfair one. To substantiate or refute any such claim presupposes a robust definition of what counts as an unfair advantage, and that proved very difficult to produce. Moreover, although the debate took place in the context of consideration of his desire to compete in the Olympics, some cogent points can be raised in relation to his competing in the Paralympics too (for example, if it is true that the blades give him an unfair advantage in comparison to non-disabled runners, which excludes him from competition in the Olympics, perhaps it should follow that he should be ineligible to compete in the Paralympics too).

The kinds of advantages that the prosthetic blades were claimed to produce were mostly mechanical, attributable to the special properties of the blades. They are lighter than natural legs, more aerodynamic, and have reduced contact area with the ground when compared with natural legs. They may also give greater 'spring' than natural legs, thus leading to a longer stride. All these properties, it may be claimed, gave Pistorius an unfair advantage over athletes with natural legs (Jones and Wilson, 2009). It is somewhat ironic that Pistorius ended in second place to Alan Fonteles Cardosa Oliveira in the 400-metre event that he had been widely favoured to win. After losing, Pistorius remarked, 'If you look at videos from last year, Alan was shorter than me but now he's taller than me' (Paxinos 2012). A further irony here is that the reason Pistorius had employed shorter blades is because the Court of Arbitration for Sport had ruled that its judgment, allowing Pistorius to compete in the Olympic Games, was applicable *only* in relation to the specific blades tested. Clearly it would be impossible for an elite athlete to train with shorter blades for the Olympic Games and longer ones for the Paralympics, given the technical complexity of prosthetically assisted sprinting.

Even if one conceded that an advantage exists between and among competitors, one can still claim that it does not constitute an unfair advantage. (Nor, in the absence of rigorous evidence should we assume that Oliveira's longer prostheses gave him an unfair advantage). Suppose, for the sake of argument, then, that the blades do indeed confer an advantage. If this were so, would that be sufficient a ground upon which to exclude him? It is plain that advantages abound in sport. Current rules of competition do not exclude competitions in which some athletes have an advantage over others. For example, there are advantages that stem from the natural and social lotteries. These are not 'deserved', in that they are not earned. They are matters of historical accident. Thus, an athlete brought up in the high plains in Ethiopia might have an advantage over other athletes raised at sea level. An athlete raised in wealthy countries might be said to have an advantage over athletes raised in much poorer countries.

So some athletes are advantaged in relation to others because of factors over which they have no control. The arguments against allowing such advantages do not distinguish the kind of advantage (allegedly) possessed by one competitor from the advantages possessed by other athletes regarded as unproblematic – such as those regarding athletes from the high plains of Africa, or wealthy countries. For, just as the 'blades' might not be available to other athletes, so being born and brought up in a wealthy country is not available to other athletes. And of course, strictly speaking, the blades could be available to other athletes, were they prepared to have their lower legs amputated.

Elective amputation

There might be at least two sets of reasons why Paralympic athletes might elect to have amputation surgery. First, it has been claimed by some persons that this or that limb does not feel a 'part of them'. The idea of elective amputation is not a new one (Dyer, 2000). Generally, it is discussed in the medical and ethical literature under the guise of a body dysmorphic disorder (Eliot, 2003) or a body identity integrity disorder (Ryan, 2009; Müller, 2014). Such analyses identify an accepted disorder and subject it to a medical examination. Typically, there is no therapeutic indication to treat the limb as diseased. Rather, the elective surgery is better understood as a body modification, more precisely a 'self-demand amputation' (Sullivan, 2005). A second possibility is more problematic from the standpoint of regulatory bodies within disability and Paralympic sport. How should they view such a consideration? Moreover, it is not clear how clinicians should consider such an approach by athlete patients.

Two different approaches have been clinically identified that have application in disability sport generally and Paralympic sport in particular.[3] The first pertains to the elective (non-clinically indicated) amputation of part of the lower legs of a wheelchair athlete in order to lose weight and thus enhance athletic performance. If one is impaired to X degree in context Y, does it necessarily matter that one elects to have greater impairment X+1 in order that one may enjoy superior wellbeing in contexts Y+1? (McNamee *et al.*, 2014). Is this just another performance-enhancing method like specialised nutrition or calorific control? A similar issue has arisen in the case of a former army veteran whose ankle joints were damaged by an improvised explosive device, who, post-surgery, could still walk but only with some discomfort. Having witnessed the magnificent feats of amputee sprinters, he sought elective double amputation to become a disability sprinter.

To what extent are these requests ethically justifiable? There is no theory neutral answer here. Clearly, along the lines of the medical model, these requested interventions look very similar to requests to facilitate self-harm (perhaps even mutilation). Along the lines of Nordenfeldt's vital goals theory, it might appear that the athletes, post-successful amputation, might actually be flourishing. A further, political philosophical aspect is worth noting, too. If one assumes that the athletes are self-funded and that no one else is harmed, it can be argued that it is simply a matter of individual liberty that they be allowed to undertake elective amputation for such reasons as they (competently) see fit (McNamee *et al.*, 2014). In summary, however, one may distinguish the individual's desire for such interventions, and their permissibility. Nevertheless, it does not follow that disability sports' regulatory bodies should invite, condone or reject these persons from their competitions. It would be perfectly reasonable for them to deny access to such competitions on the grounds that their understanding of disability – whether congenital or acquired – need not include those who, in effect, create their own impairments.

Conclusion

In this essay, we have raised a number of conceptual and ethical issues that go to the heart of the idea of disability and Paralympic sports. The differences between different models of disease, health, impairment and activity limitations are substantial, and we have not attempted to cover all of them. We have indicated some clear differences between what is called the medical model, and one, more subjective, alternative. It is clear that the WHO definitions, upon which the IPC rely, and others such as those devised by Nordenfelt (1983, 1993) are profoundly different? This illustrates the highly problematic nature of what might seem to be a straight-forwardly clear concept, namely 'disability', and disability sports and Paralympic sport. We have also identified four issues that arise within disability and Paralympic sport: two that are merely modulated by the disability sport context and two that are *sui generis*. In discussing these cases, we have attempted to show how mainstream ideas from the philosophy of sport, together with the philosophy of medicine, bear upon disability and Paralympic sports for philosophers and policy makers alike.

Notes

1   The definition of disability and handicap given by Nordenfelt (1993, p. 22) is: 'A disability, as well as a handicap, is a non-ability – given a specified set of circumstances – to realize one or more of one's vital goals (or any of its necessary conditions)'.
2   Personal correspondence with a leading Paralympic scientist suggests that 60 per cent of the filed papers for athletes with intellectual disabilities were problematic. This suggests that the Spanish team was far from the only culprit here. Thanks to Prof Yves Van Landewyck.
3   With thanks to Dr Stuart Willick, who was indeed confronted by the requests that serve as examples in this section. A fuller discussion of these, and two further cases, can be found in McNamee *et al.* (2014).

References

BBC (2009). Disability sport. Intellectual disability ban ends. BBC Sport, 21 November. Available online at http://news.bbc.co.uk/sport1/hi/other_sports/disability_sport/8323369.stm (accessed 16 October 2014).
Boorse, C. (1975). On the distinction between disease and illness, *Philosophy and Public Affairs*, 5, 49–68.
Boorse, C. (1977). Health as a theoretical concept. *Philosophy of Science*, 44, 542–73.
Brittain, I. (2010). *The Paralympics Explained*, Abingdon: Routledge.
Burkett, B., Potthast, P. and McNamee, M. J. (2011). Shifting boundaries in sports technology and disability, is this equal rights or unfair advantage? A multidisciplinary analysis of Oscar Pistorius' Olympic Games eligibility, *Disability and Society* 26 (5), 643–54.
DePauw, K. P. (1997). The (in)visibility of disability: Cultural contexts and 'sporting bodies, *Quest*, 49: 416–30.
Edwards, S. D. (2008). Should Oscar Pistorius be excluded from the 2008 Olympic Games? *Sports, Ethics and Philosophy*, 2 (2), 113–24.
Eliot, C. (2003). *Better Than Well: American medicine meets the American dream*, New York: Norton.
French, S. (1993). Disability, impairment or something in between, in Swain J., French, S., Barnes, C. and Thomas, C. (eds), *Disabling Barriers, Enabling Environments*, London: Sage, pp. 17–25.
Gold, J. R. and Gold, M. M. (2007). Access for all: The rise of the Paralympic Games, *Journal for the Royal Society for the Promotion of Health*, 127, 133–41.
Grey-Thompson, T. (2001). *Seize the Day*, London: Hodder and Stoughton.
Habermas, J. (2003) *The Future of Human Nature*, Cambridge: Polity.
Harris, J. (2000). Is there a coherent social conception of disability? *Journal of Medical Ethics*, 26 (2), 95–100.
Howe, P. D. (2009). An accessible world stage: human rights, integration and the Para-athletic program in Canada, *Cambrian Law Review*, 40, 23–35.
Howe, P. D. and Jones, C. (2006). Classification of disabled athletes, *Sociology of Sport*, 23, 29–46.
International Paralympic Committee (2007). *IPC Classification Code and International Standards*, Bonn: IPC. Available online at www.paralympic.org/classification-code (accessed 16 October 2014).
International Paralympic Committee (2011). Paralympics – history of the movement. Available online at www.paralympic.org/the-ipc/history-of-the-movement (accessed 16 October 2014).

Jespersen, E. and McNamee, M. J. (eds) (2009). *Ethics, Dis/ability and Sports*, London: Routledge.

Jones, C., and Wilson, C. (2009). Defining advantage and athletic performance: the case of Oscar Pistorius, *European Journal of Sport Sciences*, 9 (2), 125–31.

Kant, I. (2007). *Critique of Pure Reason*, M. Weigelt (trans., ed.), Harmondsworth: Penguin.

Kretchmar, R. S. (1975). From test to contest, *Journal of the Philosophy of Sport*, 2, 23–30.

Loland, S. (2009). Fairness in sport: an ideal and its consequences, in Murray, T., Maschke, K. J. and Wasunna, A. A. (eds), *Performance Enhancing Technologies in Sports*, Baltimore: Johns Hopkins University Press, pp. 160–74.

McFee, G. (2004). Sport, rules and values. *Philosophical Investigations into the Nature of Sport*, Abingdon: Routledge.

McNamee, M. J. and Tarasti, L. (2010). Ethical and legal peculiarities in anti-doping, *Journal of Medical Ethics*, 36, 165–9.

McNamee, M., Savulescu, J. and Willick, S. (2014). Ethical considerations in paralympic sport: when are elective treatments allowable to improve sports performance? *PM&R*, 6 (8), S66–S75.

Marcellini, A., Ferez, S., Issanchou, D., De Léséleuc, E. and McNamee, M. (2012). Challenging human and sporting boundaries: The case of Oscar Pistorius, *Performance Enhancement and Health*, 1 (1), 3–9.

Meier, K.V. (1985). Restless sport, *Journal of the Philosophy of Sport*, 12, 64–77.

Midgley, G. C. J. (1959). Linguistic rules, *Proceedings of the Aristotelian Society*, 1960, 271–90.

Mills, P. B., and Krassioukov, A. (2011). Autonomic function as a missing piece of the classification of Paralympic athletes with spinal cord injury, *Spinal Cord*, 49 (7), 768–76.

Morris, J. (1991). *Pride Against Prejudice*, London: Women's Press

Müller, S. (2009). Body integrity identity disorder (BIID): Is the amputation of healthy limbs ethically justified? *American Journal of Bioethics*, 9 (1), 36–43.

Nordenfelt, L. (1993). On the notions of disability and handicap, *Social Welfare*, 1993, 2, 17–24.

Nordenfelt, L. (1983). *On Disabilities and Their Classification*, Linkopping: University of Linkopping.

Oliver, M. (1990). *The Politics of Disablement*, Basingstoke: Palgrave Macmillan.

Oliver, M. (1996). *Understanding Disability*, London: Macmillan.

Paxinos, S. (2012). 'We aren't racing a fair race': Pistorius furious after shock 200m defeat, *Sydney Morning Herald*, 3 September. Available online at www.smh.com.au/sport/we-arent-racing-a-fair-race-pistorius-furious-after-shock-200m-defeat-20120903-25908.html#ixzz2v0aGzqLe (accessed 16 October 2014).

Ryan, C. J. (2009). Out on a limb: the ethical management of body integrity identity disorder. *Neuroethics*, 2 (1), 21–33.

Searle, J. (1979). *Speech Acts. An essay in the philosophy of language*, Cambridge, MA: Harvard University Press.

Shakespeare, T. (2006). *Disability Rights and Wrongs*, London, Routledge.

Simon, R. (1991). *Fair Play*, Boulder, CO: Westview.

Suits, B. (2005). *The Grasshopper: Games, life and utopia*, 2nd ed., Toronto: Broadview.

Tweedy, S. and Howe, P. D. (2011). *Introduction to the Paralympic Movement*, Oxford: Wiley Blackwell.

UPIAS (1975). *Fundamental Principles of Disability*, London: Union of the Physically Impaired Against Segregation.

WHO (1980). *International Classification of Impairments, Disabilities and Handicaps*, Geneva: World Health Organization.

WHO (2001). *The International Classification of Functioning, Disability and Health*, Geneva: World Health Organization.

Wilson, C., and Jones, C. (2009). 'Defining advantage and athletic performance: The case of Oscar Pistorius', *European Journal of Sports Science*, 9 (2), 125–31.

Wolbring, G. (2008a). 'Why NBIC? Why human performance enhancement? *Innovation*, 21 (1), 25–40

Wolbring, G. (2008b). Oscar Pistorius and the future nature of Olympic, Paralympic and other sports. *Scripted*, 5 (1), 139–60.

21

DOPING AND ANTI-DOPING

An inquiry into the meaning of sport

Thomas H. Murray

In the *New York Times* of 7 April 1901 appeared an article under the title "'Dope' An American Term." The article noted that the word "is used most frequently as a term which implies impropriety, or at least the use of methods that do not come strictly within the provision of the rules." The rules referred to are those of horse racing; the practice of doping horses with the intent of boosting performance was said to be at least a decade old by then. English racing fans – and bettors – worried that American "touts" were controlling the outcomes of races with "dope" – "a mysterious something that made slow horses fast and cowardly horses brave."

A character known as "Doc" Ring, who frequented the New Jersey winter tracks, offered injections reportedly composed of nitroglycerin, cocaine, carbolic acid, and rose water. The "Doc" refused direct payment but had the owner place a bet on the horse in his name. When the horse won, he profited. When horses began showing permanent damage in the form of decayed bone and fractures, strychnine, capsicum, ginger, and other items, were substituted for the nitroglycerin. By the time the article was published, leading American racetracks were dispatching officials to watch over horses to deter doping. Whatever impact doping had on the horses, gamblers and bookmakers did not want to give up an advantage to someone who might have the "inside dope."

Human athletes, as far back as the Greek Olympics, are said to have employed potions in the belief that their performance would be improved. By 1904, the era of the *Times* article, an Olympic competitor had won the marathon using raw eggs, brandy and strychnine injections. According to the World Anti-Doping Agency's (WADA; 2014) brief history of doping, concern over stimulant use by athletes led the International Association of Athletics Federations (IAAF) – the international federation governing track and field events – to ban them in 1928. Synthetic hormones were making an impact on sport by the 1950s. In 1968, the International Olympic Committee (IOC) followed the lead of some international federations and instituted testing at both the Winter and Summer Games (World Anti-Doping Agency 2014).

Doping scandals since then are too numerous to list. Noteworthy incidents include the state-sponsored, scientifically administered programs of the German Democratic Republic, together with many allegations of positive tests covered up in multiple sports and nations. Among the most dramatic recent events were the repeated vehement denials by cyclist Lance Armstrong that he had ever engaged in doping, his denunciations of his critics, followed by the US Anti-Doping Agency's "Reasoned Decision," which laid out in detail Armstrong's deceptions and the intense pressures placed on his fellow cyclists to go along with the doping program he had organized (United States Anti-Doping Agency 2012). He eventually confessed, but many of his supporters felt betrayed and added their voices to those who had long been suspicious of him. Critics decried his ruthless treatment of those who had earlier threatened to expose him.

Not everyone agrees that Armstrong's use of erythropoietin (EPO), human growth hormone and other drugs, together with blood transfusions, was wrong. The author Malcolm Gladwell (2013), long a skeptic of anti-doping, wrote sympathetically of Armstrong, describing a "vision of sports in which the object of competition is to use science, intelligence, and sheer will to conquer natural difference." If doping is merely another application of science meant to maximize human performance, why should it be prohibited and its practitioners publicly shamed? Should athletes who submit themselves to transfusions, injections and hormonal manipulations be admired for their discipline and their willingness to accept the risks that follow?

The aim of this chapter is to illuminate the ethics of doping in sport by examining the principal arguments on either side of the doping debate. Anti-doping critics accuse it of a multitude of sins from conceptual confusion in its very foundations to morally unjustifiable paternalism to tactical missteps. The list of complaints is long and varied enough that critics do not always agree with one another or, on occasion, with themselves. Careful reading reveals a range of attitudes among anti-doping critics toward biomedical technologies in sport ranging from wary acceptance (typically, of those presumed not to endanger health) to warm embrace (of the sort exemplified by transhumanism).

On the other side, the primary arguments against doping in sport, and in favor of anti-doping strategies, fall into three main categories: to promote fairness, to protect health (or, alternatively, to prevent harm), and to preserve meaning.

Dictionary definitions of doping vary, but this chapter follows the lead of doping critics who often target the WADA, the organization charged by the IOC and other major sport organizations with updating the list of banned biomedical technologies. WADA's official definition of doping is in its Code, and is, not surprisingly, framed in language meant to be unambiguous and able to withstand the scrutiny of attorneys defending athletes accused of doping.

Article One of the Code provides the operational definition of doping: "Doping is defined as the occurrence of one or more of the anti-rule violations set forth in Article 2.1 through Article 2.10 of the Code" (World Anti-Doping Agency 2015). The violations listed include finding evidence of a prohibited substance in an athlete's sample, use or attempted use of a prohibited substance or method, refusing or evading sample collection, and avoiding out-of-competition tests by, for example, not letting the testing agency know where you will be. Other violations include tampering with samples, possessing, trafficking in, administering, or covering up evidence of prohibited substances or methods. Added to the list of violations in the revised Code for 2015 are complicity and prohibited association.

On what grounds is doping morally suspect? The current version of the revised Code includes an expanded account:

> Anti-doping programs seek to preserve what is intrinsically valuable about sport. This intrinsic value is often referred to as "the spirit of sport." It is the essence of Olympism, the pursuit of human excellence through the dedicated perfection of each person's natural talents. It is how we play true. The spirit of sport is the celebration of the human spirit, body and mind, and is reflected in values we find in and through sport.
> *(World Anti-Doping Agency 2015)*

Cynics may find this somewhat nebulous and excessively idealistic; and there is much to be cynical about the way elite sport is too often conducted. Individual athletes may be manipulated, exploited or exposed to excessive risks. People may use their association with athletes to enhance their reputation or their bank accounts. The expression "five-ring fever" has been used to describe the powerful desire for association with the Olympic movement. Cynicism, however, can become an excuse for not taking seriously whatever important values sports can serve. In any event, by this point it should be clear that any plausible definition of doping in sport: (1) will be implicated in some manner with technologies intended to enhance performance that sport has declared off limits; and (2) will require specification of *which* technologies to prohibit and *which* to permit. The definitional problem raises a complex issue in practical moral reasoning that must rely on two foundations. First, it must have a sophisticated appreciation of the practical realities that shape sport, including the pressures under which athletes function. Second, it should have a robust account of the values and meanings people find in and through sport sufficient to provide reasons to prohibit certain enhancement technologies but permit others. Let's see what the critics have to say.

Pro-doping and anti-anti-doping

The rather odd title to this section captures an important distinction in the criticisms of anti-doping programs. Some criticisms assume or assert directly that doping is either potentially a good thing in itself or, at least, not morally objectionable. We may call these the "pro-doping" arguments. At times the argument may concede morally problematic features to doping but then claim that similar features are common and routinely tolerated in sports. Many such arguments can be translated into the form "Doping is no different from …" followed by "Doping is therefore no worse than …"

The "anti-anti-doping" arguments on the other hand either concede that doping is morally objectionable or remain agnostic on that point (McNamee 2008a). Instead, they typically focus on the problems encountered in designing and executing anti-doping programs. They may focus on the rights and privacy of athletes, on costs, on the difficulty of catching those who flaunt the rules against doping, and on possible injustices in detection, adjudication and sanctions. It is not uncommon to find several of these arguments cobbled together in a single broadside against sports' efforts to curtail doping. Indeed, although one can find nearly pure examples of the pro-doping position, in many cases, the pro-doping and anti-anti-doping arguments are piled upon one another in the manner of throwing mud against the wall in the hope that something might stick.

A thought experiment clarifies the distinction between the pro-doping and the anti-anti-doping positions. Imagine a simple, cheap and foolproof method for determining whether an athlete had used a banned performance-enhancing technology. It detected all such uses without falsely implicating athletes who had not used them. And it did so without invading athletes' privacy or bodily integrity or causing notable inconvenience. This is at present a fiction, of course. If it ever came to pass, though, the anti-anti-doping arguments would lose their force, as they are premised on the burdens and fallibility of current anti-doping systems. Such arguments often rely on claims that athletes' rights are being infringed or that the consequences of anti-doping programs are negative on the whole. Pro-doping arguments, on the other hand, deny that there is anything wrong with doping; some celebrate it as a positive expression of individual liberty, of the human use of technology, or of a particular idea about the meaning of sport. They are not contingent on the alleged ethical or practical flaws with anti-doping programs, as are the anti-anti-doping arguments now to be considered.

Anti-anti doping

The practical difficulties and expense of organizing anti-doping programs have drawn abundant criticisms. The current system includes testing of athletes, laboratory analysis, adjudication, appeals, and sanctions. In recent years, a modest amount of funding has gone for research to, for example, improve laboratory techniques, anticipate new forms of biomedical enhancement, and understand athletes' experience of and attitudes toward doping. These activities require an administrative structure as well as a governance regime, both of which add further expense. Critics have suggested these resources could be used more productively in other ways, though the work of specifying in detail how such alternatives might function and what they would cost has not been done.

Critics of current anti-doping programs, the anti-doping lobby, face an important choice (McNamee 2008a). Either they do away with all efforts to prohibit all forms of doping, or they must draw a new line in a different place with different criteria. If all anti-doping programs are abandoned, then the expenses directly incurred by such programs will evaporate. Other kinds of expenses, however, may remain such as medical costs associated with the management and treatment of athletes using doping technologies. If, on the other hand, some forms of doping continue to be prohibited, many costs are likely to remain including administration, governance, research, adjudication and sanction enforcement. Whether testing remains will depend on the design of the particular program. Here again, we have few details.

The complaints are many and various; they cover the ground from the overall cost and effectiveness of doping control efforts, to concerns about athletes' privacy and a less than perfect system of adjudication, to proposals for reconceiving the goals of anti-doping as harm prevention and conceptual ambiguities that are said to make anti-doping incoherent.

Cost and effectiveness

Anti-doping tactics, particularly those requiring the collection and analysis of biological materials such as urine or blood from athletes, incur costs. Critics argue that the resources could be more usefully employed elsewhere (Kayser *et al.* 2005, 2007). Testing may be a deterrent but it is far from universally effective at detecting athletes who dope as the "Reasoned Decision" released by the United States Anti-Doping Agency (USADA; 2013) made abundantly clear. Lance Armstrong and his supporting riders used a variety of doping methods and successfully, for the most part, avoided testing positive. It is worth noting that many riders, including Armstrong himself in later interviews, regarded the system of ongoing monitoring known as the athlete biological passport to be a far more effective deterrent than testing for specific drugs or other doping technologies. Whether "gene doping," which can entail the modification of genes or of gene expression, would be detectable by current or future testing methods is at this time uncertain. In any case, anti-doping authorities now use a much wider set of strategies to deter doping. Armstrong himself was undone not by a positive test, but rather by overwhelming "non-analytical" evidence of his leadership of a sophisticated doping program.

The monetary cost of anti-doping programs should be seen in context. Professional, Olympic and other elite sports bring in huge amounts of money; anti-doping programs are small change in comparison. To the extent that anti-doping programs succeed at discouraging doping, there may also be savings in resources that would otherwise have to be used to deal with negative health effects caused by doping, though here some critics argue that the risks of doping are greatly exaggerated (López 2013). In any case, anti-doping does have an obligation to be attentive to its cost-effectiveness.

Privacy

Athletes asked to provide a urine sample to a doping control officer must endure "observed voiding" – that is, having someone watch as you urinate. Because many of the most potent drugs athletes use, such as anabolic steroids and EPO, are taken during training periods rather than immediately prior to competing, anti-doping programs have developed protocols for out-of-competition testing. The first challenge in testing athletes while they train is knowing where to find them. "Whereabouts" programs, which require athletes to inform anti-doping agencies where they will be for at least a part of each day, like observed voiding, are incursions on privacy. How serious an incursion, what athletes think about them, and whether the benefits justify the intrusion, are important matters.

Observed voiding does not appear to be the subject of widespread public complaints. Perhaps elite athletes become so accustomed to having other people measure, observe and manipulate their bodies that the doping control officer's gaze seems a routine part of an athlete's life. Perhaps also, athletes are familiar enough with the ingenious modes of evasion other athletes have employed including fake penises and purchased bags of "clean" urine that they acknowledge the need for such intimate observations.

Whereabouts reporting, however, has elicited much criticism. Kreft (2011) argues that whereabouts systems violate human rights and are intended to "safeguard the clean trademark of the sport business" by strengthening "the grip of business over labour: even when you are a star of the first rank, you have to know who is really in charge" (p. 160). Kreft dismisses athletes' support for whereabouts reporting, arguing that they have no choice if they desire to participate in elite sport. Studies assessing athletes' opinions, however, paint a more nuanced picture. Focus groups of Canadian and US athletes found unanimous support for out-of-competition testing, and for the testing to be "more stealth, less formulaic, more comprehensive (to include blood tests for example), and less predictable" to make it more difficult to avoid detection (Johnson *et al.* 2013, p. 13). The same study included a finding of special interest to readers of this handbook: "One participant even suggested having access to an on-call expert that the athletes could talk with about perfunctory and philosophical questions alike" (p. 12). A survey of Danish athletes (Overbye and Wagner 2013) revealed a mostly begrudging acceptance of whereabouts reporting. Some respondents even saw it as a complimentary acknowledgement of their elite status. But they also complained of its impact on their lives, the time it consumed, the feeling of surveillance, the fear of a warning, and reducing the joy they otherwise find in sport. Rather than blithely ignoring athletes' complaints, or discounting their reasons for tolerating something they both dislike and find necessary, we should pay attention to athletes' voices (Hanstad and Loland 2009).

Injustices

Justice should be a priority for all institutions, certainly for anti-doping whose mission is to foster fair competition. Like all human institutions, the pursuit of justice in anti-doping is an aspiration imperfectly fulfilled. In a recent plea for relaxing doping controls, the authors opened with the case of Michael Rasmussen, a prominent Danish cyclist who was kicked out of the Tour de France, they say, "on an allegation of doping (without evidence)" (Savulescu and Foddy 2011, p. 304). In January 2013, Rasmussen appeared at a press conference where he admitted to doping from 1998 until 2010, using EPO, growth hormone, testosterone, dehydroepiandrosterone (DHEA), insulin, insulin-like growth factor-1, cortisone and blood transfusions.

The forms of injustice of which anti-doping can be accused include treating like cases differently (for example, different sanctions for similar offenses), or treating different cases similarly (for example, leveling the same sanctions for inadvertent and intentional violations). Anti-doping codes generally attempt to accommodate the distinction between intentional and inadvertent use, but they also typically presume that athletes are responsible for whatever is found in their bodies. This is a rebuttable presumption, but the burden of proof that the use was unintentional falls on the athlete in whose body the prohibited substance was discovered. Lance Armstrong complained vociferously that his lifetime sanction is unfair because both teammates and competitors also doped and got off with suspensions of as little as six months. USADA (2012), the agency administering the sanctions, claims that he was both ringleader and enforcer of a highly sophisticated doping program, and that unlike others, he refused to cooperate in the investigation (USADA 2012). The adjudication and appeals process has been criticized for its standard of evidence (less than that required in a criminal proceeding) among other aspects.

The most common form of injustice in anti-doping is the failure to catch and sanction athletes who dope. This is both a defect and a design feature. Anti-doping agencies strive to avoid punishing athletes who have *not* violated anti-doping rules. Historically, they have set criteria and established procedures calibrated to insure that only genuine rule violators are sanctioned. As an entirely predictable consequence, an unknown number of violators escape detection. It is likely that those escaping detection far exceed the number caught each year.

Harm prevention as goal

One suggestion for how to respond to athlete's use of drugs such as steroids is to employ harm-reduction strategies such as needle exchange programs that have diminished disease transmission among heroin users. Kayser and Smith (2008, p. 87) proposed "making legal the use of drugs associated with low harm and testing health rather than testing for drugs." They argue that more athletes would use performance-enhancing drugs if they were legal and safe, and that this would make the playing field level. Holm (2007), from a game-theoretic perspective, argues that doping under medical control is very unlikely to have the benign impact its proponents describe.

Their proposal encounters practical and conceptual difficulties. First, what criteria will be used to decide which drugs are safe? EPO, the drug of choice for endurance athletes, carries a "black box" warning because of evidence that it increases the risk of death, stroke, heart attack, and blood clots in patients with kidney failure as well as more rapid tumor growth in patients with head and neck cancers (US Food and Drug Administration 2011). Anabolic steroids have a long history in sport, accompanied by a controversy over their impact on health with some commentators suggesting steroids' risks have been exaggerated (Hoffman and Ratamess 2006). Other scholars conclude that the risks are real (Sjoqvist *et al.* 2008).

Second, the focus on harm reduction appears to presuppose that the only valid grounds for opposing the use of performing enhancing drugs in sport is risk to health. Protecting health is certainly one reason for concern over drug use by athletes. But it is not the only objection. And their proposal does not, in any event, reduce the risk of harm, which becomes clear once we understand the contrast in the dynamics of drug addiction versus drugs in sport.

For one thing, making drugs legal and available to all athletes will surely increase population exposure to whatever drugs fall under the "harm-reduction" umbrella. If the drugs are truly harmless, and – another big "if" – if athletes do not take the "safe" drugs in higher dosages or in contraindicated combinations, or add other, unapproved drugs to the mix, then perhaps the proposal might reduce harm. But there are many reasons to be skeptical such a benign scenario will unfold.

The harm-reduction proposal rests on a fatally flawed analogy. Heroin users do not compete with each other to see who can get "higher." But that is precisely what athletes do. If particular drugs that enhance performance are permitted, they will instantly become the new minimum for any athlete who hopes to be competitive. And not all athletes will stop there. The same dynamics that drive some athletes to used banned performance-enhancing technologies will continue (Murray 1983). We can expect athletes to use dosages far in excess of the approved "safe" level and to combine "safe" drugs with banned ones in the continuing search for a competitive edge.

Conceptual ambiguities

Quite early in the debate over drugs in sports appeared the argument that no coherent distinction could be drawn between accepted practices to enhance performance and technologies that were banned (Brown 1980). Fost argued that the distinction between "additive" and "restorative" drugs was untenable; he advanced a similar claim about the distinction between drugs and food (Fost 1986). Many anti-anti-doping arguments adopt a similar strategy, describing a continuum of technologies affecting performance and arguing that at no place along this continuum can a conceptually coherent line be drawn.

This is a curious argument to make about sports, which continually draw lines along continua. Why is the goal in football (known in the United States as soccer) 8 feet (2.44 metres) tall and 24 feet (7.32 metres) wide? Why is the width not 48 feet (14.6 metres)? Surely that would lead to more scoring. When I suggested this change to a group of European scholars, they reacted in horror. Widening the net would diminish the goalkeeper's ability to block shots. It would make scoring much easier, as no goalkeeper could guard such a massive target. The goalkeeper's talents would effectively be nullified, kickers could be much less accurate and still score; the tension between the goalkeeper's athleticism and strategic savvy, and the striker's quickness, deceptiveness, and accuracy would dissipate. Now, if the goal were one-quarter of an inch (0.635 cm) wider or narrower, the game of football would not be radically altered. In order to have matches that display and reward the honed talents of would-be goal scorers and goal keepers, a line needed to be drawn somewhere along the continuum. It did not have to be at precisely 24 feet, but that distance works well for adults. Smaller goals are used for younger ages, for the same reason. To put the point more generally, sports must draw lines along a continuum in order to have meaningful play; all such lines must find their justification in the values and meanings that particular sport embraces. Baseball is especially proud of the continuity of its rules. Perhaps the most arbitrary measure in any sport is the distance between the pitcher's rubber and home plate: 60 feet, 6 inches (18.44 metres). Its origin lies in the early days of baseball as its rules were consolidated. It survives for the same reason football nets are 24 feet wide: it preserves the tension, in this case between pitcher and batter, that allows the display of athletic talents. When pitchers began to dominate in the 1960s, baseball responded not by increasing the distance to home plate but instead by lowering the height of the pitcher's mound from 15 inches (38.1 cm) to 10 (25.4 cm) inches. The aim was to restore the creative tension central to the game. Line drawing in sport may be "arbitrary" in the innocent sense that any particular line might have been drawn a bit to one side or the other without undermining the meaning of the sport. But when lines are drawn wisely, they are not "arbitrary" in any morally disreputable sense. Indeed, drawing lines to preserve meaning is an indispensable component of sport.

At times, new strategies, new types of players, or new technologies challenge where a sport has drawn its lines. Not surprisingly, as line drawing along continua is inherently challenging, it can be quite difficult to do it to everyone's satisfaction. Savulescu and Foddy (2011) compared technologies used to enhance endurance. Hypoxic chambers are not banned, while using EPO is prohibited, yet both increase the number of circulating red blood cells and both can enhance endurance.

Hypoxic chambers pose a hard case for defenders of anti-doping. What could justify treating them differently from drugs such as EPO? Loland and Hoppeler (2012) begin their defense of such differential treatment by noting that EPO bypasses the body's evolutionarily determined adaptations to the demands placed on it by training; instead, it directly manipulates certain physiological parameters. They describe EPO as a "short cut" that "trespasses, often in harmful ways, human phenotypic plasticity" (p. 352). They argue that "short cut" technologies nudge the locus of responsibility for improving performance towards experts and away from athletes. A core of their larger argument hinges on values and the meaning, or spirit, of sport: "The use of prohibited substances and methods overruns natural talent, reduces athletes' possibilities of developing sporting excellence as human excellence in virtuous ways, and contradicts the spirit of sport" (p. 352).

Ideas about values and the meaning of sport are important in understanding many, though not, all, of the criticisms from the anti-anti-doping camp. In the case of pro-doping advocates, the debate over values and meanings is all the more central.

Pro-doping

Pro-doping arguments fall into three categories: libertarian; transhumanist; and doping as a means to restore fairness to the genetic lottery that is sport. The libertarian strain appeared quite early in the debate (Fost 1986). As applied to sport, though, libertarianism seems particularly inapt. Its moral force rests most comfortably on purely self-regarding actions. But the use of performance-enhancing drugs in intensely competitive environments is profoundly other-regarding. My advantage is your disadvantage. Exercising my liberty can have a direct and disadvantageous impact on you. The response of an anonymous former elite athlete echoes the feelings of uncountable others facing competitors who doped:

> the syringes came out and I just felt at that stage very vulnerable and eh, I didn't feel that I could really mentally … that if I hadn't succumbed to it then, I didn't feel I'd actually be able to race that day.
>
> *(Kirby et al. 2011, p. 213)*

The libertarian argument fails to take into account the structure and dynamics of competitive sport, but it does not directly engage disagreements about values and meaning in sport quite the way the next two arguments do. Look first at transhumanist views of enhancement and sport.

Miah urges us to "celebrate the rise of a new age of genuinely superhuman athletes" in which we:

> recognize that what's important within sports is the degree to which athletes are competing on a level playing field, where everyone is free to choose the enhancements that best accentuate their performance. That is what the natural athlete should look like today.
>
> *(Miah 2008)*

This "natural" athlete, he proposes, could have surgically enhanced webbing between his fingers and toes, with genetic enhancement just around the corner. Miah predicts that current policies toward enhancement in sport are doomed to collapse: "As human enhancements become a constitutive element of broader social circumstances – and as enhanced adults give birth to similarly enhanced children – the concept of enhancement and of the natural human will become even more difficult to sustain" (Miah 2006, p. 318).

Optimism about technology and human enhancement is a core component of this world view. But it also incorporates ideas about meanings and values in sport. Miah asserts that we do not know what we want from sport, but then proceeds to tell us that we want world record breaking, extraordinary, superhuman athletes, and that enhancements will make the playing field both more level and more entertaining. Consider the following account of values in sport, in particular, what values should determine who wins:

> Far from being against the spirit of sport, biological manipulation embodies the human spirit – the capacity to improve ourselves on the basis of reason and judgment. When we exercise our reason, we do what only humans do … Sport would be less of a genetic lottery. The winner will be the person with a combination of the genetic potential, training, psychology, and judgment.
>
> *(Savulesu et al. 2004, p. 667)*

And, presumably, the best biomedical enhancements. Or, from the same article, this view of the meaning of sport: "in many ways the athletic ideal of modern athletes is inspired by the myth of the marathon. Their ideal is superhuman performance, at any cost" (p. 666). Tamburrini seems to agree:

> professional sport is now driven by a desire to expand the boundaries of what hitherto was considered to be humanly possible, even by jeopardizing one's own health … Banned doping substances and techniques are therefore obviously in accordance with the 'spirit' of today's crudely competitive, highly technified sports world, as they have everything to do with the essential purpose of the athletic contest: to expand the limits of our capacities.
>
> *(Tamburrini 2006, p. 203)*

Ideas like these are helpful in locating the underlying sources of disagreement over doping. If, as these and other authors argue, the meaning of sport is superhuman performance, then what makes us merely human is an obstacle to be overcome. And, because humans can choose to use technology to extend our powers in other spheres, employing biomedical enhancements in sport is simply an extension of our humanity.

Some suggest that biomedical enhancements are a legitimate means for correcting sport's moral defects, in particular, how sport favors natural, unearned talents. Tännsjö describes this point of view:

> It seems to be part of the ethos of sport that the winner of the genetic lottery, the person who, genetically speaking, is most fit, should also be the winner of the competition. This (Nietzschean) notion of justice or fairness is very different from, and even opposite to, the (more civilised) one we rely on in other contexts … in sport we should allow that people level out their inborn differences. We should allow all sorts of (safe) medical and genetic methods of enhancement of athletes. This would pave

the way for more exciting competitions and for the possibility that anyone who wants to do so can take part in them on equal terms. And at last we would come to grips with the problem of elitism in sport.

(Tännsjö 2005)

On this view, a person's unearned natural talents are a source of elitism and injustice in sport, and doping a possible way of leveling the playing field. Tamburrini predicts:

as genetic modifications probably will level out differences in performance capacity established by birth, athletes' initial conditions will be more equal than they are at present. Thus ... sport competitions will probably turn out to be fairer ... there will be more room for morality in this enhanced new (sport) world.

(Tamburrini 2007, p. 234)

The accusation that advantages provided by natural talents are unfair is a curious one for academics to make. Presumably, their institutions select the brightest faculty and students. To the extent that intellect, curiosity, and drive are either inherited or imbued through favorable environments and upbringing, those talents are likewise unearned; therefore, hiring faculty or selecting students is to that extent unfair. One fruitful approach for thinking about unfairness is to do as Walzer advises: by asking what goods are being distributed according to what principles in that particular sphere of human endeavor (Walzer 1983).

We could also turn to John Rawls, who used sports as a metaphor to explain how his theory of justice deals with unearned advantages. It does not rely on the principle of redress:

This is the principle that underserved inequalities call for redress; and because inequalities of birth and natural endowment are undeserved, these inequalities are to be somehow compensated for ... [but] the difference principle is not of course the principle of redress. It does not require society to try to even out handicaps as if all were expected to compete on a fair basis in the same race.

(Rawls 1999, p. 86)

The difference principle takes the unequal distribution of natural talents as a "common asset." Individuals "favored by nature" may benefit from their "good fortune" when "the basic structure can be arranged so that these contingencies work for the good of the least fortunate" (Rawls 1999, p. 87). Justice does not require that everyone be equally talented in all respects. But it does require attentiveness to the basic structures of society.

Rawls also provides a model in his fundamental approach, which endeavors to identify a framework of value implicit in a sphere of human endeavor and then to determine what the moral nature of persons must be in order for them to find value in such a sphere. In his work on justice this is a political conception, an account of our moral nature relevant to our role as citizens in a constitutional democracy. It is likewise possible to develop an account of a person's moral nature relevant to her or his role as a participant in sports (Murray and Murray 2011). Such an account requires identifying a framework of value implicit in sport. This cannot be accomplished simply by declaring what one believes sport is really all about. Rather, it requires an approach much like Rawls' reflective equilibrium, which embraces facts and arguments as well as moral observations and theories (Daniels 2013).

Good facts and enhanced scholarship on doping in sport

More than 30 years ago, philosophical scholarship in bioethics looked somewhat like contemporary work in philosophy of sport on doping. A rough distinction useful then might be helpful to current debates. To put it simply, some scholars used the issues in medical or bioethics as an opportunity to flex their philosophical muscles by, for example, exploring how a particular theoretical stance might be applied to a problem such as informed consent in research, the patient-physician relationship, or decisions at the end of life. This approach has been described as "top-down" bioethics (Murray 1987). However interesting philosophers may have found such work, it often failed to impress people faced with difficult practical decisions in the clinic or laboratory. A good part of the problem was the lack of understanding of the complex realities people faced. Context was a key to wisdom. A good way to consign one's scholarship to irrelevance was to get the facts wrong or fail to include centrally relevant realities.

An alternative approach appeared quite early in bioethics epitomized by the Hastings Center. It stressed interdisciplinary collaboration; a commitment to getting the facts right and attending to context; clear writing accessible to all with a minimum of specialist jargon; and a genuine engagement with difficult, complex problems intended not so much to display cleverness or erudition as to provide help to patients and research subjects, clinicians and researchers, and policy makers.

The debate over doping in sport is far more than a theoretical exercise. As a problem in practical ethics that affects not merely elite athletes but the many millions of people of all ages who participate in sport it deserves respectful consideration, including a firm grounding in facts wherever and whenever relevant.

At times the facts are about science or medicine. Atry *et al.* (2011) issued a call for less hype and more sophisticated discussions of the underlying science of gene doping; such discussions are too often simplistic and reductionist. Where credible, unbiased reviews are available on, for example, the risks of anabolic steroids or EPO, they should be favored over isolated studies that favor the author's point of view.

Athletes' lives and attitudes are referred to frequently. There is a growing empirical literature shedding light on how athletes experience and respond to doping. Boardly and Grix (2013) found that bodybuilders excused their use of performance-enhancing drugs on the grounds that they were *not* competing and therefore doing no harm to others. These bodybuilders understood that doping in a competitive setting is not, despite some scholars' claim, a "victimless" activity (Savulescu and Foddy 2011).

Lentillon-Kaestner *et al.* (2011) interviewed professional and aspiring professional cyclists who describe team physicians organizing and endorsing doping programs, sometimes lying, telling them they were taking vitamins rather than anabolic steroids and corticosteroids. The authors conclude: "as long as some cyclists take these substances, doping will be perceived, at the elite level, as essential to be able to keep apace with race leaders and to protect cyclists' health" (p. 8). That athletes see at least some of the banned drugs they use as protecting their health is a perception anti-doping agencies must take seriously.

Kirby *et al.* (2011) conducted intensive interviews with five athletes who had previously admitted to doping, guaranteeing them anonymity within the study. Several themes stood out. One cyclist described what happens when competitors are using effective performance-enhancing technologies:

> I got tired of being left behind and not riding at the ability that I know I am capable of on a level playing field ... I had a certain place in the peloton, and you know, over

the years I had lost that and it was not because of a lack of training and my physical talents.

(Kirby et al. 2011, p. 212)

Interviewees faulted their sport's governing body for failing to address doping. They stressed transparency and fairness, and welcomed extending sanctions to non-athletes who enable or foster doping.

Bloodworth and McNamee (2010) report on focus groups conducted among elite, mostly young, athletes in the UK. On the whole, these athletes strongly opposed doping citing health and inauthenticity as reasons. The authors note the importance of social sanctions and anticipated shame in shaping the athletes' attitudes to doping. A survey of elite Norwegian athletes revealed that they made a sharp distinction between vitamins and minerals on the one hand, and EPO, steroids and amphetamines on the other. Hypoxic chambers occupied an intermediate zone of acceptability. Interestingly, athletes were even more dismissive of EPO, steroids and amphetamines than the general public (Breivik *et al.* 2009). Surveys of the Swiss population and top-tier Swiss athletes showed growing awareness of doping and strong support for strict prohibitions and sanctions along with education and information programs (Stamm *et al.* 2008). Focus groups of promising young North American female triathletes found consensus that the biggest problem with doping was the unfair advantage it provided over athletes who did not dope. One athlete said that when doping is prevalent, "you get to the point where you have athletes on complete steroids, or whatever, just doing everything they can to win, killing their bodies to win. And then the sport isn't what it's meant to be like" (Johnson *et al.* 2013, p. 6). This study also found unanimous support for blood testing and out-of-competition testing.

Beyond the scholarly literature is a wealth of information on athletes' beliefs and attitudes. David Millar, a prominent professional cyclist who confessed to doping, told an interviewer: "It got to a point where it was almost easier for me to dope than not to," he says, pain clouding his face.

> Psychologically I just gave in, I couldn't fight it any more, it seemed like such a lost cause. No one seemed to care: not the team bosses or heads of the sport. Even the media seemed naive and blind to it all. So many things built to that point. It was an accumulation of little things, a deterioration of character and my ethical standards.
>
> *(Swarbrick 2011)*

Scholars should likewise be cautious in offering generalizations as to how people feel now or will feel about doping in sport. Tamburrini (2006), for example expresses confidence that "the direction in which sport is evolving at present suggests the public will increasingly accept doping" (p. 206). At present, evidence from surveys of the public show no such trend in acceptance. In his case for genetically enhanced athletes, Tamburrini offers a prediction about fans: "genetically enhanced athletes will perform at levels never dreamt of before, which most probably will increase the sport fans' fascination with the activity" (Tamburrini 2007, p. 234). It would be helpful to know on what empirical evidence this forecast is based.

In general, philosophy of sport's scholarship on doping would benefit from a more interdisciplinary approach that takes into account the dynamics of sport and, when facts of any kind are at issue, gathers and assesses dispassionately the relevant evidence.

Defending anti-doping

Three reasons stand out in defense of sport that does not resort to doping and, by extension, to effective and fair anti-doping programs that respect the rights of athletes. Critics challenge the effectiveness, fairness and respectfulness of current programs. But these are characteristics of programs, not justifications for their existence in the first place. Those reasons may be summarized as to:

- promote fairness
- protect health
- preserve meaning.

Promoting fairness

Anti-doping critics recognized quite early that doping would not be unfair if all athletes had equal access to drugs or whatever other biomedical technologies were being used (Brown 1980). Of course, as long as forms of enhancement are prohibited but at least some athletes seek the competitive advantage they bring, anti-doping programs have a role to play in promoting fairness. Whether to ban particular biomedical performance enhancements in the first place is not a matter of fairness. Justifying prohibitions falls to the next two reasons.

Protecting health

It was likewise clear early in the debate over doping that, with respect to mature adult athletes, a pure paternalist argument failed. Indeed, athletes viewed it as hypocritical to urge them to take serious risks in pursuit of their sport, but also to tell them not to use anabolic steroids or stimulants because they might hurt themselves. (Paternalist arguments remain cogent in the case of younger athletes.) Context matters greatly here: The dynamics of competitive sport press athletes not to give up a competitive advantage, including advantages conferred by biomedical enhancements (Murray 1983). This was made clear in conversations with athletes in the early 1980s and is resoundingly confirmed by social science research and by athletes' personal accounts. The act of doping is not merely a self-regarding act, against which the accusation of unjustified paternalism would be warranted. Doping affects the other athletes in the competition, either putting them at a disadvantage or pushing them to join in the doping. It may not be the same as a gun pointed at one's heart, but especially in the case of elite athletes for whom success at sport is central to their identity and flourishing, it seems fair to describe the phenomenon as "coercive." This is the first line of defense of anti-doping under the rubric of protecting health.

A second justification lies in the public health dimensions of doping. Public health is concerned with the health of populations, in this case both elite athletes and all other sport participants whose wellbeing might be affected by doping. This includes young and very young aspiring athletes as well as adult amateurs and "masters" – older athletes. A kind of contagion is likely to result. To the extent that elite athletes are permitted to use biomedical enhancements, it seems reasonable to assume that some, perhaps many, non-elite athletes will want to do the same. As doping becomes more prevalent in non-elite populations, more people are at risk of harm. Anti-doping skeptics proposing that only "safe" drugs should be permitted have to contend with several factors likely to make their widespread legitimation far from safe. For one thing, the dynamics of sport competition, the relentless quest by at least some athletes for a competitive edge, and the deep reluctance to surrender a competitive advantage, will result in permitted forms of doping becoming more or less required for all athletes at that level. Further, everything we know about human behavior and sport says that some athletes will use the "safe" drugs, and then pile on top of them whatever other biomedical enhancements they or their enablers believe will give them a further edge. The risks to health increase as more drugs are used in higher doses; drug interactions are more likely the more drugs get added to the mix. As for non-elite athletes, only the fortunate few are likely to have access to expert medical management, and many may seek out cheaper supplies of drugs with fewer guarantees they will be safe (Holm 2007). All in all, this is not an encouraging scenario for good public health.

Preserving meaning

The most interesting and challenging intellectual task facing the philosophy of sport on doping is to develop a robust account of the values people seek in and through participating in sport, and of the meaning of sport as a component of persons' flourishing (Schermer 2008). Bald declarations that sport is about superhuman performances, or that a desire to preserve what is valuable and meaningful in sport is a foolish pursuit of "purity" or a moralistic response to the use of drugs in culture are, frankly, unhelpful (Ritchie and Jackson 2013; López 2012).

Let me pose a challenge to the philosophy of sport community: What method(s) is (are) appropriate for elucidating values and meanings in sport? What criteria should be used in evaluating the coherence, validity, and moral persuasiveness of candidate accounts of values and meanings in sport? Addressing these questions seriously would, I believe, benefit discussions on ethics and sport broadly, and not merely on doping.

Earlier, I suggested employing a version of Rawls' wide reflective equilibrium: developing a values-based account of sport that incorporated as many relevant details as possible from individuals' perceptions of fairness and of why they participate, to social and institutional dimensions of sport, to the reality of human embodiment and human variation. A full account would be normative and not merely descriptive. It would include accounts of values and meanings in sport, and of persons as sport participants. All proposed accounts should be subjected to vigorous critical appraisal in the spirit of wide reflective equilibrium.

Loland has contributed to such accounts with his discussions of the place of technology in sport and his distinction between the structure of sports competitions (which includes comparing, measuring and ranking competitors) versus the meaning and value of sport. McNamee has likewise been developing an account of virtues in sport and the impact of doping in a variety of publications (McNamee 2008b, 2012; McNamee and Edwards 2006). Murray (2007) has also been developing such an account of enhancement in general and of the relationship of doping to values and meanings in sport around the central idea of sport as the virtuous perfection of natural talents in the quest for human excellence (Murray 2009). This account is meant to encompass sport and sports participants broadly, not only elite athletes.

How do these approaches differ from others in the philosophy of sport? Take the matter of fairness. Critics of anti-doping often recite the many differences among people that determine the outcome of sports competitions. Some are differences in opportunities and resources – easier access to good coaching, nutrition, equipment, practice areas, and more. Other differences, roughly the characteristics described as natural talents, are often rather simplistically described as "genetic" though most are likely complex expressions of interactions among genes, epigenetic processes, and intrauterine, physical and social environments. Nevertheless, it seems fair to describe most of these differences, as the critics do, as unearned. Of course, some people actively seek out more favorable circumstances and environments and presumably deserve credit for those initiatives. But the critics' central point remains: among the factors determining the outcomes of competitions many cannot be described as "earned" by the successful athlete. Other factors – their dedication, willingness to persevere and suffer, strategic cunning, and more – may count as earned. Some critics hail biomedical enhancements as a way to diminish the importance of unearned differences: "as genetic modifications probably will level out differences in performance capacity established by birth, athletes' initial conditions will be more equal than they are at present" (Tamburrini 2007). The underlying presumption is that success due to unearned differences is unfair. How well does that presumption stand up to other ways of thinking about fairness and unfairness in sport?

Paralympic competitors must often rely on equipment to be able to compete at all. Wheelchairs, prostheses, throwing frames and the like have the potential to give advantages to athletes. In response, IPC Athletics has had to be explicit about what it calls fundamental principles: safety; fairness (as in no "unfair advantage that is not within the 'spirit' of the event they are contesting"); universality (available commercially to all); and "physical prowess" described as "i.e., human performance is the critical endeavor not the impact of technology and equipment" (International Paralympic Committee 2014). The IPC is concerned with setting fair competitions that reward athletes' talents and dedication, not the technologies they employ. In the Paralympics, as in most sports, technology is seen as *enabling*, not determining, performance.

What then should we make of differences in natural talents, genetic or otherwise? Kayser *et al.* (2007) claim that "conventional sports ethics policies" treat inherited characteristics differently from doping. No argument there. "Conventional sports ethics policies," by which I assume they mean anti-doping programs, welcome and embrace the diversity of natural talents on the one hand and ban performance-enhancing drugs on the other. It is also true, as they say, that neither natural, inherited talents nor bodies enhanced by steroids, human growth hormone or EPO are "earned" by the athlete.

Basketball was the sport of my youth. Suppose that I challenge Lebron James, widely regarded as the most gifted current athlete in the National Basketball Association, to a game of one-on-one basketball. Suppose also that I have trained intensively for six months – just as hard as Lebron – for this match. I have worked as diligently to earn my conditioning and skills as he has. He's still going to overwhelm me: completely, resoundingly. It would be more farce than sporting competition. At barely 5 foot 11 inches, 170 pounds, in my 60s and with the arthritic knees to attest to a youth spent on cement and blacktop courts, it would be no contest. (Not that the match would have been any less uneven in my prime.) Today, at the top of my jump, you can slip maybe two credit cards under my foot. I would be lucky to get a single shot off without being blocked, or take two dribbles in a row before he stole the ball from me. The only way it might interest spectators would be as comic relief.

Now, according to Kayser *et al.* (2007), I have a right to complain that this contest was unfair. I worked as hard as Lebron (remember, this is a thought experiment). It just so happens that he is much taller, stronger, faster, and quicker than me. He is also more agile, leaps higher, with superior reaction time and better eyesight. And he is younger by nearly 40 years. These are all "unearned" advantages, like Eero Mäntyranta's abundance of red blood cells. If I challenged Lebron to a rematch a year later, devoting the year to relentless training while Lebron lounged in his recliner, ate donuts and watched television, the result would be the same. He is vastly more talented at basketball than I have ever been, even in my fantasies. So, if I take my inspiration from Kayser, I should be really steamed: This is *unfair*. I worked hard, he did not, but he still dominated me on the court.

By now, I trust that you see how ludicrous my complaint would be. There is no law of biology, or ethics, that demands that every talent be given out in equal measure to all persons, or that victory go only to the virtuous. Differences in natural, inherited talents are an inescapable, in fact, celebrated part of sport. When athletes talk of a "level playing field" they don't mean neutralizing all differences in natural abilities. But are all "unearned" differences – inherited abilities, equipment, drugs – ethically the same for sport? Only if you believe that the talents athletes are born with are morally indistinguishable from anabolic steroids, EPO and other performance-enhancing drugs. There is absolutely no contradiction in saying that sport values one kind of "unearned" advantage, and despises another. The way forward will be to decide whether conceiving of sport as valuing the virtuous perfection of natural talents, from the perspective of wide reflective equilibrium, is a more inclusive account than that offered by critics of anti-doping.

Bibliography

Atry, A., Hansson, M.G., and Kihlbom, U. 2011. Gene doping and the responsibility of bioethicists. *Sport, Ethics and Philosophy*, 5 (2), 149–60.

Bloodworth, A. and McNamee, M. 2010. Clean Olympians? Doping and anti-doping: The views of talented young British athletes. *International Journal on Drug Policy*, 21, 276–82.

Boardley, I. D. and Grix, J. 2013. Doping in bodybuilders: A qualitative investigation of facilitative psychosocial processes. *Qualitative Research in Sport, Exercise and Health*, 6 (3), 422–39.

Breivik, G., Hanstad, D.V., and Loland, S. 2009. Attitudes towards use of performance-enhancing substances and body modification techniques. A comparison between elite athletes and the general population. *Sport in Society*, 12 (6), 737–54.

Brown, W. M. 1980. Ethics, drugs, and sport. *Journal of the Philosophy of Sport*, 7, 15–23.

Daniels, N. 2013. Reflective equilibrium. In: E. N. Zalta, ed. *Stanford Encyclopedia of Philosophy*, Winter 2013 ed. Available online at http://plato.stanford.edu/archives/win2013/entries/reflective-equilibrium (accessed October 16, 2014).

Fost, N. 1986. Banning drugs in sports: A skeptical view. *Hastings Center Report*, 16 (4), 5–10.

Gladwell, M. 2013. Man and superman: In athletic competitions, what qualifies as a sporting chance? *New Yorker*, September 9. Available online at www.newyorker.com/magazine/2013/09/09/man-and-superman (accessed October 16, 2014).

Hanstad, D. V. and Loland, S. 2009. Elite athletes duty to provide information on their whereabouts: Justifiable anti-doping work or an indefensible surveillance regime? *European Journal of Sport Science*, 9, 3–10.

Hoffman, J. R. and Ratamess, N. A. 2006. Medical issues associated with anabolic steroid use: Are they exaggerated? *Journal of Sports Science and Medicine*, 5, 182–93.

Holm, S. 2007. Doping under medical control: Conceptually possible but impossible in the world of professional sports? *Sport, Ethics and Philosophy*, 1 (2), 135–45.

International Paralympic Committee 2014. *Athletics Rules and Regulations 2014–2015*. Bonn: IPC. Available online at www.paralympic.org/sites/default/files/document/131218164256138_2013_12%2BIPC%2BAthletics%2BRules%2Band%2BRegulations%2B2014-2015_digital.pdf (accessed October 16, 2014).

Johnson, J., Butryn, T. and Masucci, M. A. 2013. A focus group analysis of the US and Canadian female triathletes' knowledge of doping. *Sport in Society*, 16 (5), 654–71.

Kayser, B., Mauron, A. and Miah, A. 2005. Viewpoint: Legalisation of performance-enhancing drugs. *Lancet*, 366 Suppl 1, S21.

Kayser, B., Mauron, A. and Miah, A. 2007. Current anti-doping policy: A critical appraisal. *BMC Medical Ethics*, 8, 1–10.

Kayser, B. and Smith, A. C. T. 2008. Globalisation of anti-doping: The reverse side of the medal. *BMJ*, 337, 85–7.

Kirby, K., Moran, A. and Guerin, S. 2011. A qualitative analysis of the experiences of elite athletes who have admitted to doping for performance enhancement. *International Journal of Sport Policy and Politics*, 3 (2), 205–24.

Kreft, L. 2011. Elite sportspersons and commodity control: Anti-doping as quality assurance, *International Journal of Sport Policy and Politics*, 3 (2), 151–61.

Lentillon-Kaestner, V., Hagger, M. S. and Hardcastle, S. 2011. Health and doping in elite-level cycling. *Scandinavian Journal of Medicine and Science in Sports*, 22 (5), 596–606.

Loland, S. 2009. The ethics of performance-enhancing technology in sport, *Journal of the Philosophy of Sport*, 36, 152–61.

Loland, S. and Hoppeler, H. 2012. Justifying anti-doping : The fair opportunity principle and the biology of performance enhancement. *European Journal of Sport Science*, 12 (4), 347–53.

López, B. 2012. Doping as technology: a rereading of the history of performance-enhancing substance use in the light of Brian Winston's interpretative model for technological continuity and change. *International Journal of Sport Policy and Politics*, 4 (1), 55–71.

López, B. 2013. Creating fear: the 'doping deaths', risk communication and the anti-doping campaign. *International Journal of Sport Policy and Politics*, 6 (2), 213–25.

McNamee, M. J. 2008a. Anti-anti doping: Why scepticism doesn't cut the mustard. *BMJ*, 337, a584.

McNamee, M. J. 2008b. *Sports, Virtues and Vices: Morality plays*. Abingdon: Routledge.

McNamee, M. J. 2012. The spirit of sport and the medicalisation of anti-doping: Empirical and normative ethics. *Asian Bioethics Review*, 4 (4), 374–92.

McNamee, M. J. and Edwards, S. D. 2006. Transhumanism, medical technology and slippery slopes. *Journal of Medical Ethics*, 32, 513–18.

Miah, A. 2006. Rethinking enhancement in sport. *Annals of the New York Academy of Sciences*, 1093, 301–20.

Miah, A. 2008. Enhanced athletes? It's only natural. *Washington Post*, August 3, B1–B1. Available online at www.washingtonpost.com/wp-dyn/content/article/2008/08/01/AR2008080103060.html (accessed October 16, 2014).

Murray, T. H. 1983. The coercive power of drugs in sports. *Hastings Center Report*, 13 (4), 24–30.

Murray, T. H. 1987. Medical ethics, moral philosophy and moral tradition. *Social Science and Medicine*, 25 (6), 637–44.

Murray, T. H. 2007. Enhancement. In: B. Steinbock, ed. *Oxford Handbook of Bioethics*. Oxford: Oxford University Press, 491–515.

Murray, T. H. 2009. In search of an ethics for sport: Genetic hierarchies, handicappers general, and embodied excellence. In: T. H. Murray, K. J. Maschke and A. A. Wasunna, eds. *Performance-Enhancing Technologies in Sport: Ethical conceptual and scientific issues*. Baltimore, MD: Johns Hopkins University Press, 225–38.

Murray, T. and Murray, P. 2011. Rawls, sports, and liberal legitimacy. In: G. E. Kaebnick, ed. *The Ideal of Nature: Debates about biotechnology and the environment*. Baltimore, MD: Johns Hopkins University Press, 179–99.

Overbye, M. and Wagner, U. 2013. Experiences, attitudes and trust: An inquiry into elite athletes' perception of the whereabouts reporting system. *International Journal of Sport Policy and Politics*, published online May 9, 1–22. DOI:10.1080/19406940.2013.791712.

Rawls, J. 1999. *A Theory of Justice*, rev. ed. Oxford University Press.

Ritchie, I. and Jackson, G. 2013. Politics and 'shock': reactionary anti-doping policy objectives in Canadian and international sport. *International Journal of Sport Policy and Politics*, 6 (2), 195–212.

Savulescu, J. and Foddy, B. 2011. Le tour and failure of zero tolerance: Time to relax doping controls. In: J. Savulescu, R. ter Meulen, and G. Kahane, eds. *Enhancing Human Capacities*. Oxford: Blackwell, 304–12.

Savulescu, J., Foddy, B. and Clayton, M. 2004. Why we should allow performance enhancing drugs in sport. *British Journal of Sports Medicine*, 38, 666–70.

Schermer, M. 2008. On the argument that enhancement is 'cheating'. *Journal of Medical Ethics*, 34, 85–8.

Sjoqvist, F., Garle, M. and Rane, A. 2008. Use of doping agents, particularly anabolic steroids, in sports and society. *Lancet*, 371, 1872–82.

Stamm, H., Lamprecht, M., Kamber, M., Marti, B. and Mahler, N. 2008. The public perception of doping in sport in Switzerland, 1995–2004. *Journal of Sports Sciences*, 26 (3), 235–42.

Swarbrick, S. 2011. Cyclist David Millar tells of his battle with drugs. *The Herald (Scotland)*, September 13. Available online at www.heraldscotland.com/life-style/cyclist-david-millar-tells-of-his-battle-with-drugs-x.1123335 (accessed October 16, 2014).

Tamburrini, C. 2006. Are doping sanctions justified? A moral relativistic view. *Sport in Society*, 9, 199–211.

Tamburrini, C.M. 2007. What's wrong with genetic inequality? The impact of genetic technology on elite sports and society. *Sport, Ethics and Philosophy*, 1, 229–38.

Tännsjö, T. 2005. Hypoxic air machines: Commentary. *Journal of Medical Ethics*, 31 (2), 113.

US Food and Drug Administration 2011. Information on erythropoiesis-stimulating agents (ESA) epoetin alfa (marketed as Procrit, Epogen), darbepoetin alfa (marketed as Aranesp). Available online at www.fda.gov/Drugs/DrugSafety/PostmarketDrugSafetyInformationforPatientsandProviders/ucm109375.htm (accessed October 16, 2014).

USADA 2012. Statement From USADA CEO Travis T. Tygart Regarding The U.S. Postal Service Pro Cycling Team Doping Conspiracy, U.S. Postal Service Pro Cycling Team Investigation, October 10. Available online at http://cyclinginvestigation.usada.org (accessed October 16, 2014).

USADA 2012. Reasoned Decision of the United States Anti-Doping Agency on Disqualification and Ineligibility: United States Anti-Doping Agency, Claimant, v. Lance Armstrong, Respondent. Colorado Springs, CO: United States Anti-Doping Agency. Available online at www.scribd.com/doc/109619079/Reasoned-Decision (accessed October 16, 2014).

Walzer, M. 1983. *Spheres of Justice: A defense of pluralism and equality*. Basic Books.

World Anti-Doping Agency 2014. A Brief History of Anti-Doping. Available online at www.wada-ama.org/en/who-we-are/a-brief-history-of-anti-doping (accessed October 16, 2014).

World Anti-Doping Agency 2015. *World Anti-Doping Code*. Montreal: WADA. Available online at www.wada-ama.org/en/resources/the-code/2015-world-anti-doping-code#.VD_ei75fUQ4 (accessed October 16, 2014).

22

FAIR PLAY

Sigmund Loland

Competitive sport, both at high and lower performance levels, represents an ethically contested field. One the one hand, sport represents ideal values; fairness and equality of opportunity, mutual respect between participants, winning and losing with dignity, and human excellence. On the other hand, sport can be a cynical sphere and a struggle for prestige and profit by all available means; performance-enhancing drugs, corruption, and violence. How can the moral potential of sport be realized? What are sport's normative ideals? One classic response to these questions is a reference to the ideal of fair play. Here, I present a brief sketch of the historical background of the ideal and how the concept of fair play has been treated in the sport philosophical literature. In the main parts of the chapter, I discuss an updated interpretation of fair play of relevance in modern, competitive sport.

Fair play: background and interpretations

Ideals of fair and just conduct seem to have followed competitive games since their origins (Guttmann 1987). In the ancient Olympic Games, there was an emphasis on equality of opportunity. As compared with today, rule systems were rudimentary. Penalties for rule violations, however, were harsh, with significant fines and sometimes even public flogging (Wischmann 1962; McIntosh 1979). A true winner should express classic ideals of *agon;* striving at one's best to win, and of dignity and honour (Finley and Pleket 1976).

More direct historical roots are found in Anglo-Saxon culture (McIntosh 1979). Dictionary definitions refer to 'fair play' as just and honourable treatment, action or conduct. 'Fairness' associates what is impartial, disinterested and unprejudiced. Etymologically, 'fair' comes from Old English *fæger;* cognate with Old Saxon, Old High German *fagar,* Old Norse *fagr,* Gothic *fagrs;* terms that refer to what is attractive and beautiful (a fair day, a fair lady), as well as to what is considered just and honest and according to the rules.[1] The term 'fair' is found in church homilies around year 1200 referring to impartial and just conduct. In the late fifteenth century, Shakespeare used 'foul play' in his historical dramas.

Socioculturally, the fair play ideal is said to have developed from medieval chivalrous codes of conduct in games and battle and has survived over the centuries as part of the ethos of the privileged classes. At English public schools such as Eton, Harrow, and Rugby, ideals of fair play became significant in the education of young men for the future upholding of the British

Empire. Playing according to 'the spirit of the rules' and with honesty and effort were significant elements of the educational ideology of 'Muscular Christianity' (McIntosh 1979; Mangan 1981).

References to fair play were also used as an exclusionary mechanism by the upper classes to avoid 'professionals'; that is, people from the working classes, in 'their' sport. Amateur rules were justified by views that manual labour gave an unfair advantage and spoiled 'natural grace' and talent (Holt 1989). Others point to an extensive gambling tradition (Elias 1986). In eighteenth and nineteenth centuries, gambling was flourishing in Britain. Fairness, in the sense of equality of opportunity, was a cornerstone of the gambling business. Without a guarantees of a fair and unpredictable outcome, the very rationale for gambling would disappear.

Although development of the ideal of fair play can be linked to partial interests, its core reference seems to be basic moral ideals of equality of opportunity and good conduct. Today, the ideal is commonly accepted as a cornerstone of competitive ethics. Most sport organizations adhere to an understanding as proposed by the International Fair Play Committee:

> Fair play is a complex notion that comprises and embodies a number of values that are fundamental not only to sport but also to everyday life.
>
> Respect, friendship, team spirit, fair competition, sport without doping, respect for written and unwritten rules such as equality, integrity, solidarity, tolerance, care, excellence and joy, are the building blocks of fair play that can be experienced and learnt both on and off the field.[2]

This is, however, no strict definition. The formulations point to what are considered important attitudes and values but are of limited help in concrete dilemmas. Philosophically, a series of proposals have been made to better grasp and understand the fair play ideal.

Keating's 1964 *Ethics* paper on 'sportsmanship as a moral category' was pioneering in this respect. Keating distinguished between sport as amateur games and pleasant and playful diversion, from athletics with an emphasis on performance and competition. To Keating, generosity was the ideal of sport. In athletics, sportsmanship was defined by fair play, understood as the spirit and letter of equality.

McIntosh's *Fair Play: Ethics in Sport and Education* (1979) includes a historical review of interpretations of fair play and discusses social–psychological and educational studies of relevance. The philosophical part of the book appears as eclectic, with both utilitarian and Kantian interpretations, but has provided important inspiration to later work.

Among the first extensive and systematic philosophical volumes on the ethics of sport competition is Warren Fraleigh's (1984) *Right Actions in Sport: Ethics for Contestants*. Fraleigh develops a normative system of action guides expressing, more or less explicitly, interpretations of just and good sport contests. The analysis of rule violations and fouls (especially of the 'good' or the 'tactical' foul) has made a particular impact in the literature.

Robert L. Simon's *Fair Play: Sport, Values, and Society* (1991) and *Fair Play: The Ethics of Sport* (2015), co-written with Cesar R. Torres and Peter F. Hager, are case-oriented texts written on the normative premise of sport as 'a mutual quest for excellence in the intelligent and directed use of athletic skills in the face of challenge'. Simon construes fair play as 'commitments to the principles supported by the idea of ethically defensible competitions'.

Loland's (2002) *Fair Play in Sport: A Moral Norm System* is a systematic theory of the ideal of fair play inspired by social contract theory. A particular ambition is to present a detailed and upgraded interpretation relevant to the world of modern, competitive sport.

In several articles, Lenk (1964, 1993, 2002; Lenk and Pilz 1989) has discussed the varieties of fairness and fair play. Lenk makes a distinction between 'formal fair play' indicating adherence to the formal rules of the competition, and 'informal fair play' referring to attitudes and goals among competitors. Butcher and Schneider (1998) combine MacIntyre's (1984) concept of internal goods of a practice with empirical studies of the experiential qualities of autotelic activities and suggest and interpretation of fair play as 'respect for the game'.

A large number of articles and book chapters on the philosophy of sport touch upon fair play issues in more or less direct terms. Topics include rule violations and cheating, the use of performance-enhancing drugs, dilemmas of one-sided contests and so-called 'blow-outs', and reflections upon the role of merit, chance and luck in sport.[3]

How can the ideal of fair play be understood more explicitly? Does the ideal have a role to play in current, competitive sport, and if so, in what way? In what follows and with the help of relevant literature I propose a more detailed interpretation.[4]

Fairness in sport

Lenk's (1993) distinction between formal and informal fair play serves as a useful departure point. Formal fair play refers to an obligation on rule adherence. There is both a logical and a normative rationale behind the norm.

The common understanding of sporting rules is that they structure and define a competition, or at least that they define the framework within which competitors act. Searle's (1969: 33ff.) well-known distinction between constitutive and regulative rules informs the discussion. Constitutive rules are those upon which a sport is logically dependent and without which the sport would not exist at all. Football is defined in terms of rules against the use of hands, and rules that define what it means to score a goal. Tennis is defined among other things by the rule on allowing the ball to bounce only once on each player's court half, and by its particular point counting system. Regulative rules on the other hand regulate activities that are not a logical part of the game; rules on shaking hands before a football match, or wearing predominantly white clothing at the Wimbledon tournament.

General constitutive rule adherence, or what we may refer to as 'formal fair play', is a logical necessity for a sport to be realized at all. This, however, does not entail that constitutive rules have to be kept all the time. In sport, rule violations seem difficult to avoid. Sport practice includes for the most time extensive bodily movement that cannot be fully controlled. A soccer player may unintentionally touch the ball with her hands; a tennis player may stumble in a serve and step on court line; in basketball, body contact is proscribed but a game of basketball without body contact is hard to imagine. Hence, D'Agostino (1981) argues that a sporting game should be understood not only by its rules, but by the generally and socially accepted interpretation of the rules – by its ethos.

This leads towards a normative rationale of fairness. Voluntarily entering a competition can be seen as engaging in a kind of social contract with others of keeping the rules and norms of the practice (Loland 2002). We expect others to keep to their promises, and others expect the same from us. It seems unreasonable to expect ethos adherence from others without doing our fair share. The fairness idea can be given a more precise articulation. Fairness is a moral obligation on rule adherence arising when we voluntarily engage in a rule-governed practice (Rawls 1971). The premise is neo-Kantian: persons have infinite worth and should never be treated as means only, but always also as ends in themselves. This can be expressed by the following fairness norm:

- If voluntarily engaged, follow the ethos of the sport in which you take part!

The norm may seem intuitive and simple. At the same time there are challenges. Not every sport has an ethos worthy of admiration. How do we deal with an ethos that deviate significantly from the constitutive rules and allows for cheating, violence, and drug use?

According to Rawls (1971), fairness is a moral obligation arising under certain premises. Firstly, as indicated above, participants have to be voluntarily engaged. Secondly, the rule system or the ethos has to meet basic requirements on justice. If the rule system as a whole is unjust, the fairness norm is no more valid, and there is no good reason to engage in the practice. More specifically, we can say:

- If voluntarily engaged, follow the ethos of the sport in which you take part if the ethos is just!

When is a sporting ethos just?

Justice in sport

Ideas of justice structure rule systems in sport. Questions of justice often relate to the distribution of goods and burdens between individuals and groups – to distributive justice. At the societal level, the main discussion concerns the distribution of what Rawls (1971) labels primary goods: civil and political rights, liberties, income and wealth and the social basis of self-respect. Different ideological positions represent different distributive schemes. Competitive sport is less complicated. The distributive scheme is explicitly given in the rules. The characteristic social logic of competitions is to measure, compare and rank competitors according to the rule defined standard of performance (Loland 2002). How can this be done in just ways?

Aristotle's classic definition of formal justice serves as a common reference point. In Book V of the *Nicomachean Ethics* (Aristotle 1976), formal justice is defined as:

- Equal cases ought to be treated equally.
- Unequal cases may be treated unequally.
- Unequal treatment ought to stand in a reasonable relationship to the actual inequalities in question.

These norms are formal as they cannot be implemented in practice without qualification. Ideas of equality, inequality and unequal treatment vary between cultures, societies and social institutions and practices. To the nineteenth-century English upper class, only gentleman amateurs were considered eligible for sport. Up until the late 1990s, only men were considered eligible for competing in ski jumping. Although the circle of eligibility of sport participation is expanding, line drawing is still a challenge. What is fair and just when it comes to classification of competitors? Other discussions concern resources and technology. How much inequality in background resources between athletes is acceptable? What rules are required when it comes to standardization on equipment and technology?

Formal norms of justice have to be operationalized in terms of more concrete distributive norms (Perelman 1980). Consider that we are to distribute a certain sum of money between a certain number of persons. This can be done on the basis of equal distribution: each person gets the exact same sum of money. Distribution can also be carried out according to performance. A meritocratic scheme is what is usually found in sport. Other criteria can be 'effort' and 'progress' (as in physical education in school) and 'needs' (as in most civilized societies with a social welfare system). Finally, goods and burdens can be distributed according to social position. In medieval Europe, the noblesse and clergy were entitled to a certain part of the income of their subordinates. In most settings, we find combined distributive schemes. In physical education in schools, for instance, grades are based on a combination of performance, effort, and progress.

Distributive norms are ideal norms. They are implemented in practice by different kinds of procedures. Three kinds can be distinguished: perfect, imperfect and pure procedures (Rawls 1971). Perfect procedural justice realizes a distributive norm completely. An egalitarian scheme in the distribution of 100 Euros between four persons gives 25 Euros each. Usually, however, the realization of distributive norms is more complicated. Indeed, this is the case in sport. In outdoor sports, such as tennis or alpine skiing, wind and light conditions can be quite different for the participants. The point in these situations is to find the less imperfect procedure to reach the goal of the competition. Finally, there is pure procedural justice, in which there is no distributive norm to follow (Figure 22.1). The procedure itself guarantees a just outcome. The standard example is a lottery. If the lottery is carried out in the right way, each lottery ticket gives an equal chance of a win. The distribution of goods and burdens are based on a pure chance event and there are as many just outcomes as there are lottery tickets.

Equal opportunity to perform

The first part of the formal justice norm prescribes that equal cases are treated equally. Democratic societies are built on the idea of persons having equal worth and certain rights and liberties that cannot be violated. In public sport policies, one idea is that play, games and sport have had a significant role in a good life and in human flourishing. This is the premise of the policy principle of 'sport for all'. Everyone is entitled to possibilities of exercise and sport according to their own preferences and abilities.

The requirement of equal treatment does not, however, mean that everyone is to be treated equally. Individuals are different and individual inequalities may be ethically relevant in various ways. The physical education teacher assesses effort and progress, in addition to performance, when grading a student. In competitive sport, there is a purely meritocratic scheme in which goods and burdens are distributed on the basis of performance alone. In competitive settings, equal treatment refers to equality of opportunity:

- All competitors ought to be given equal opportunity to perform!

formal justice	norms for distribution	procedures
	egalitarian meritocratic according to effort according to need according to position or legal entitlement … combinations of the norms above	perfect procedures imperfect procedures
	pure	procedural justice

Figure 22.1 Overview of norms and procedures of justice

Implementation of this norm requires a criterion for distinguishing between relevant and non-relevant inequality. Beauchamp (2001: 372–4) discusses the ideal of equal opportunity and points to an interpretation that seems to be common in many ethical theories. In the sport setting, this applies as follows:

- All competitors ought to be given equal opportunity to perform by eliminating or compensating for elimination or compensation for significant inequalities between individuals that cannot be controlled or influenced by individuals and for which individuals cannot be held responsible.

At first sight, competitive sport seems fair in this respect. In running races, all competitors run the same distance on the same surface and they are timed with identical timing systems. Goals in football are awarded based on identical criteria for the two teams and the teams change pitch sides during half time to eliminate possible inequalities. Javelin throwers are given they same number of attempts and compete with standardized javelins. Usually, however, the norm on equality of opportunity is realized in imperfect procedures.

Equality in external conditions

A first challenge is tied to inequalities in external conditions. A wind at their back may give a long-jumper the necessary centimetres to win. A similar wind may reduce the length of a javelin throw. These are inequalities out of the control and influence of the individual. This is why there are limits for wind velocities when it comes to record setting in these sports. Rules are installed to avoid what are considered unjust inequalities to exert significant impact on performance. The rules, however, accept a certain variation in wind. One deals here with imperfect procedural justice.

In outdoor sport, in particular, complete equality in terms of external conditions is an unattainable ideal. In ski races, snow conditions vary. A soccer team can play the last half with a low evening sun in their eyes. A radical solution can be indoor sport facilities. Skating, handball and volleyball for instance are indoor sports.

Nevertheless, the discussion of outdoor sports concerns more than justice alone. Sport is not a scientific experiment with rigid requirements on validity and reliability of measurements and comparisons. Outdoor sports have other qualities that seem relevant. Changing wind, light and surface conditions may add complexity to skill challenges, and excitement. As long as these inequalities are controlled so that they do not exert significant and systematic impact, and as long as they are distributed in random ways, competitions can still be considered just.

Equality in personal characteristics

The norm on equality of opportunity does not only relate to external conditions. It seems unreasonable to match a heavyweight boxer with a lightweight one, owing to significant inequality in body weight. Men and women competing on the 100-metre sprint race provoke equality ideals. Again, the norm seems relevant and points towards eliminating or compensating for inequalities which individuals cannot control or influence in any significant way.

In combat sports, such as boxing and wrestling, athletes are classified according to body mass. The ability to develop speed is linked to genetic predispositions. Statistically, men have this predisposition to a larger extent than do women. Hence, in the 100-metre race, we classify according to biological sex. In children and youth sport, we classify according to age. In other words, non-controllable inequalities or what can be called 'biological absolutes' such as body size, biological sex and age and biological maturity levels are compensated for in sports in which these inequalities exert significant and systematic impact on performance.

A closer look at current classification systems, however, exposes irregularities. Why are there weight classes in combat sports but no height classes in basketball and volleyball? Is it not the case that, in these sports, height is a critical determinant of performance? Why are there sex classification in sports such as sailing, shooting and archery? Is it not the case that, in these sports, biological sex does not really influence performance?

Obviously, classification schemes have historical roots and have to be understood within the sociocultural contexts within which they have emerged. To enhance justice, applied philosophy has a role to play. Critical thinking can expose discriminatory schemes and create a basis for realizing the ideal of equal opportunity to a larger extent.

Equality in system strength

A third challenge for the equality norm, primarily in elite sport, is the existence of significant inequality in financial and technological resources behind an athlete or a team. The challenge concerns high-tech sports at all levels and all sports at elite levels. Heinilä (1982) labels this the totalization process of modern sport. Elite sport is a competition between extensive systems of human, scientific, financial, and technological resources. Heinilä's concern is what he calls 'the hidden validity' of sport and the decrease of individual responsibility for performance.

There are many examples from modern sport of system inequality. In cross-country and alpine skiing, technology and support systems exert significant impact on the outcome. During difficult snow conditions, help from waxing experts is crucial. In international elite soccer, the best clubs of England, Germany, Italy and Spain constitute an almost unbeatable group, primarily because of their superior economy and recruitment of the best talents (Walsh and Giulianotti 2007). In this way, sport mirrors general and what many consider unjust inequalities in society in general.

System inequalities violate the equal opportunity principle. These are inequalities that individuals and teams cannot influence or control in any significant way and for which they should not be made responsible. Of course, sporting institutions cannot be expected to change system inequalities at a societal and global scale. The role of sport, however, could be to reduce the impact of such inequalities within their competitive systems. Many measures can be taken. For instance, skiing could introduce strict standardization procedures. All competitors should have access to the same ski soles and the same conditioning expertise. In this way, the test is who is the better skier, and technology becomes no 'confounding variable'. In international team games, other solutions may work. For instance, each season each soccer team is given a certain amount of money to be spent on new players. The test then would be to use this resource in competent ways, which is a managing test requiring sport-specific knowledge and judgment.

Implementation of such measures is probably not an easy task. Ski manufacturers will, to a lesser degree, see the possibility of commercial promotion of their products. Many soccer players, coaches and agents will resist any scheme that leads to reduction of income. Still the struggle to reach the ideal of equal opportunity is an important one. Competitive systems that reflect and even reinforce general and unjust inequalities in society fail to meet basic, sporting ideals.

Relevant inequality: athletic performance

Requirements for equal opportunity are not goals in themselves but rather means towards ensuring evaluation of competitors according to a particular kind of inequality: inequality in athletic performance. The second part of the formal norm of justice prescribes that unequal cases can be treated unequally. How is this to be understood in competitive sport?

Sport performances are complex human phenotypes and the outcome of a high number of genetic and environmental influences from the moment of conception to the moment of performance. For the purpose of normative analysis, the analytical distinction between genetic and environmental factors is helpful.

Genetic factors are predispositions for developing the relevant phenotypes for good performances in a sport (Bray *et al.* 2009). A person with a good predisposition is usually characterized as a 'talent'. Talent in this sense is distributed in the so-called 'natural lottery' and based on inheritance.

Athletes develop their talent through gene–environment interactions. The extent to which talent can be enhanced by training is itself a genetic trait (Bouchard *et al.* 2001). Genes and environment interact in complex ways from the very first nurture via development of general abilities and skills to specific training and the learning of the particular techniques and tactics of a sport. To a certain extent, environmental influences are based on chance and luck (for instance, in the sense that a person with a talent for running is born next to a track and field facility with a good coach and in a social and cultural setting that values sport performance). To a larger degree, the influence from environment comes in the form of one's own efforts (the person realizes his or her talent over many years with hard training).

The key question is whether all kinds of inequalities linked to performance, including, for instance, those caused by performance-enhancing drugs, are of relevance in sports, or whether some inequalities ought to be eliminated or compensated for.

In the equality section, discussions were presented on why and how certain inequalities due to biological 'absolutes', such as body size and biological sex, should be eliminated or compensated for in some sports. The justification was the equal opportunity norm. One possible reason for such classification is a quest for uncertainty of outcome.

In general, one-sided contests are enjoyable neither to participants nor spectators. This, however, cannot be the only rationale. If this were the case, we could imagine all kinds of competitive set-ups, such as between humans and animals or between humans with very different performance capabilities adjusted for those with handicaps. This is not found in sports. Competitors of similar age and performance capabilities are matched to examine a particular kind of inequality. Classification schemes indicate that these are inequalities for which athletes can be held responsible and which are based on athletes' cultivation of particular human talents.

These ideas come close to what can be considered core values in competitive sport or what some refer to as 'the spirit of sport'. Philosophers articulate theses values in diverse ways. Some interpretations build on neo-Aristotelian and Kantian premises. Along the lines of Fraleigh (1984), Loland (2002), and Simon (2015), competition is considered an advanced form of cooperation in which individuals and teams do their utmost to out-perform each other while at the same time treating each other with mutual respect and as equals. Fairness and justice norms find support in the development of moral character or virtue (Morgan 2006; McNamee 2010). Training to realize one's talent takes will power, dedication and hard work. Competing well takes courage, concentration, doing one's best, and honesty and dignity both in victory and defeat. Murray (2007) pinpoints the idea by interpreting sport as not just any but the *virtuous* development of natural talent towards human excellence.

To sum up: athletic performance can be understood as a combination of talent (genetic predispositions for developing performance in sport) and the virtuous development of such talent. Inequalities in talent that individuals can influence by training are relevant to sport. Inequalities in talent that individuals cannot influence or control in any significant way and which exert significant and systematic impact on performance (biological 'absolutes' such as sex, body mass, age), should be eliminated or compensated for. This is done by classification. In the process of performance enhancement, development should not be based primarily on external assistance, expertise or biomedical technology, but primarily on the efforts of athletes themselves. Fair play implies a view of athletes as free and responsible moral agents in a virtuous pursuit of human excellence.

This interpretation has practical implications that can be exemplified with the debate over performance-enhancing drugs.

Performance-enhancing drugs in sport

In the public sphere, the use of performance-enhancing drugs implies a violation of what in most sports is a commonly accepted ban and is a violation against the fairness norm. Use of banned drugs is referred to as doping. This, however, is not a philosophical argument against performance-enhancing drugs. Justification of rules with reference to the wrongness of breaking them is circular and invalid. A second argument against such drugs is based on the risk of harm. Use of performance-enhancing substances can harm and even kill athletes and should be banned. Many sports, however, include the risk of harm. Hard training over many years often leads to injuries. So-called 'risk sports', such as downhill skiing, even include the risk of sudden death. Principled use of the harm argument could lead to the banishing of several sports. This seems unreasonable. There is a need for distinguishing between relevant and non-relevant risks of harm in sport.

Normative positioning in the case of performance-enhancing drugs requires a normative view or theory of sport. Brown's argument on paternalism has made impact in the literature (Brown 1984, 1990; Black and Pape 1997). The use of performance-enhancing drugs is not necessarily of value in sport but virtuous athletes are able to handle these choices in appropriate ways. Tamburrini (2000) and Savulescu *et al.* (2004) support this view and take a further step. Sport is considered a sphere for transcendence and continuous improvement and performance-enhancing drug use is an integrated part of its logic.

According to the World Anti-Doping Agency (WADA), however, the use of the most efficient and harmful variants of performance-enhancing drugs should be banned as they violate 'the spirit of sport'. In the WADA Code, the 'spirit of sport' is not really defined and the concept calls for clarification.[5] Murray (2007) and Simon (2015) exclude the use of performance-enhancing drugs from the sphere of human excellence. Loland and Hoppeler (2012) have combined biological insights in training with the norm on fair opportunity and developed this view in more detail. They define training as invoking the phenotypic plasticity of the human organism. This is a consequence of the specifics of the evolution of the human species. Accepting as relevant the innate adaptability to physical challenges coheres with the idea of developing natural talent. Most banned performance-enhancing substances exert qualitatively different effects, as they overrun the natural and evolutionary based complex stress and compensation reactions of the body. Hence, it can be argued that the use of such substances overruns talent, reduces the athlete's possibilities of developing natural talent in virtuous ways and contradicts 'the spirit of sport' and the development of human excellence. From this perspective, inequality in performance from the use of performance-enhancing drugs is non-relevant and should be eliminated. The position of anti-doping can be justified.

The use of performance-enhancing drugs in sport is a complex medical, sociocultural and ethical issue with no easy solution (Houlihan 1999). The argument above indicates that the issue goes straight to the core of our ideas of the values of sport. In the interpretation of fair play suggested here, there seems to be stronger arguments in favour of a ban on performance-enhancing drugs than for liberalization.

Unequal treatment

The third part of the formal justice norm prescribes a reasonable relationship between relevant inequality and unequal treatment. Above, I have discussed the relevant inequality in question: athletic performance. Based on their performances, athletes are awarded advantage in various forms: rankings, points, goals, and so on. In a similar way, lack of performance leads to no gain of advantage and to relative disadvantage. The following norm seems to be at work:

- In sport competitions, there ought to be a reasonable relationship between actual inequality in performance and unequal treatment in the distribution of (dis)advantage.

Are sport competitions just in this respect?

Competitive advantage

Athletic performances are measured in two main ways. In some sports, such as athletics, long jumping or weight lifting, athletes are ranked according to physical–mathematical entities; seconds, metres and kilograms. In other sports, performance is measured in units that are specifically defined in the constitutive rules of the relevant sport. Basketball players and rifle shooters compete for points, football and handball players for goals. This can be called 'sport-specific advantage'.

In sports with physical–mathematical performance measurement, there is a close relationship between performance and advantage. In running events in athletics, performances are distinguished by the one-hundredth of a second, in long jumping by centimetres.

In sports where performances are measured in sport-specific ways, the picture is less clear. Once in a while, even failed performance may give an advantage and successful performance can lead to loss. A technically weak shot on the tennis pitch may still hit the net and drop down on the right side. A brilliant passing shot may be one centimetre out and result in loss of a point. Sometimes, in ball games, the better playing team loses. Good and bad luck seem to play a more significant role with sport-specific advantages than what is the case of physical–mathematical measurements of performance.

Does this mean that sport-specific performance measurements are less just? This is not necessarily the case. Hager and Torres' (2005) discussion of points systems in rugby illustrates how different distributive schemes may increase (or decrease) fairness and justice in a sport. We have to distinguish between events that, by definition, cannot be controlled and predicted – as in a lottery – and good and bad luck that seem to be out of the control of those concerned but which, in principle, can be controlled with sufficient insight and skill. A good soccer player aims well and hits the inside instead of the outside of the post. Good tennis players rarely mis-hit and are usually rewarded for their good performances. The best athlete *usually* wins (Dixon 1999). Thus, golf legend Lee Trevino is attributed with the saying that 'the more I practice the luckier I get'.

The fact that sport-specific advantage units do not correspond completely to the quality of performance may challenge the norm on a reasonable relationship between the two. A goal in soccer is a goal, no matter the quality of the attack. As with the acceptance of certain inequalities in external conditions in outdoor competitions, the counter-argument is that sport is not a scientific experiment and that sport-specific measurements fuel sport with unpredictability and tension (de Wachter 1985). A certain reduction of strict meritocratic justice and certain openness to chance and luck adds excitement. As long as participants are voluntarily engaged and informed of the various ways of performance measurements in different sports, less-accurate sport-specific measurements are not unjust.

Penalties and reduction of advantage

There is another kind of unequal treatment in sport that is not linked to degree of performance but to lack of performance – to rule violations. Rule violations are sanctioned or penalized by reduction of advantage, by warnings and in severe circumstances, with expulsion from the competition. The proportionality of such reactions should be guided by the following norm:

*   In sport competitions there ought to be a reasonable relationship between actual inequality due to rule violations and unequal treatment in the distribution of penalty.

How is this norm followed in practice? Again, perfect procedures seem difficult. The point is to eliminate or compensate for advantage gained in an unfair manner. In this respect, sport has more or less refined procedures. A general distinction found in most rule systems is between non-intentional and intentional violations (Fraleigh 1984, 2003). A clumsy move in defence in handball may lead to pushing an opponent out of balance and a rule violation. A football player may accidentally touch the ball with his hands. A handball player may stumble and kick the ball. The fairness norm is violated. As long as the violation is unintentional, the rule violator cannot be morally blamed. The problem, however, is that an unfair advantage has arisen. Usually, such problems are solved by restoring the initial situation as far as possible and continuing with a fair competition. In ball games, for instance, rule violations lead to free kicks or free throws. It is more difficult to restore situations in which competitors or teams intentionally break the rules to gain advantage. Intentional rule violations come in different versions.

Cheating

The classic version is cheating; that is, breaking the rules with the intention of an advantage without being caught. Maradona's infamous hand-ball scoring against England in the 1986 World Cup is an paradigmatic example. Maradona's reference to 'the hand of God' was of little help, really. Both in the Argentine and in England there is probably a common understanding that intentionally breaking the rules is wrong.

In contrast to strategic deception within the ethos of a sport, such as feinting an opponent in a ball game, cheating is what Pearson (1973) calls 'definitional deception', as cheaters use means outside of the rule system of a sport. The logic at play is one of unfair exclusivity. Cheaters presuppose that most other participants adhere to the ethos of the competition. If all participants cheated, sport would not be possible at all. Cheating is contradictory to fairness and morally wrong. The cheater is a free rider who benefits from others cooperation without doing his or her fair share.

What should be the penalties? As with unintentional rule violations, a first step could be to restore the competition, to the greatest possible extent. In addition, the cheater can be morally blamed for his or her intentional attempt on deceit. Cheating calls for additional penalties, for instance in the form of a reduction of advantage or a warning. If cheating continues, cheaters should be expelled from the competition.

Professional fouls

Another category of intentional rule violations is so-called 'professional' or 'good fouls' (Fraleigh 1984). A competitor violates the rules intentionally and openly and accepts the penalty with the rationale of a long-term advantage for him or her, or for the team. A hockey player punches another player to avoid a goal and choose a two-minute penalty, with the idea that the team will benefit from the action. Or, in a more brutal version, a hockey player attacks the key player of the other team to eliminate the player from the game and accepts a penalty for an assumed long-term team benefit. What should be our reactions?

Brutality and violence are in clear contradiction of basic norms of mutual respect between competitors and a basic norm on avoiding unnecessary harm. These are severe violations and call for severe penalties, such as expulsion from the game. The reference to 'professional' indicates that these fouls seem to be accepted in sporting cultures. The usual argument is that the rule system is inadequate. Penalties do not fit the crime. If professional fouls are flourishing, rule systems need adjustments.

In most rule systems, however, there are loopholes and possibilities for exploitation. Even though there may be cases in which professional fouls can be morally defensible, in general, such fouls can be seen as expressions of a problematic sporting ethos in which competitors are concerned with the maximization of self-interest. A professional foul may sabotage a beautiful move and an exciting chance, a great performance. Is it not the case that the very concept 'professional foul' expresses a paradox? Competitions may turn into a game of what Torres (2000) calls restorative and not constitutive skills. The struggle becomes one of compensating for rule violations instead of cultivating performance.

In everyday life, we refer to professionalism as a sign of quality, knowledge and skill. Professional fouls express a lack of respect for opponents and sport in general. Perhaps a better use of the term 'professional' would be for it to refer to an athlete who respects his or her sport and plays hard but fair? Perhaps professional fouls can be seen as a form of 'unprofessionalism'?

Play-acting or 'diving'

A third version of intentional rule violations is what is called play-acting or 'diving'. A competitor acts as if he or she has been exposed to a rule violation, for example, a push, a punch or other irregular activity. The violation, however, has never occurred. In soccer, 'falling' within the penalty area to get a penalty and perhaps a red or yellow card for an opponent has been developed into an art for some players. In basketball, five fouls on a player gives reason for expulsion from the game. Some players are true experts in acting as if the player at risk has violated a rule, even if this is not the case.

If we accept the fairness idea, play-acting is a particularly problematic kind of rule violation. Not only does the play actor or his or her team gets an unfair advantage. Often the idea is to impose penalty on an innocent. Play-acting is a direct sabotage of the game. What is an appropriate penalty?

Firstly, as in the cases above, the initial situation ought to be restored to the greatest possible extent. Secondly, the play-actor can definitely be morally blamed and ought to get an additional penalty in the form of a warning or reduction of advantage. In extreme cases, play-acting ought to lead to expulsion from the competition.

The analysis and overview of the varieties of cheating (Figure 22.2) may serve as a general guide to the evaluation and development of awarding systems in sport and improve fairness and justice in these procedures.

Play

So far, I have discussed fairness in competitive sport or what can be called formal fair play (Lenk 1993). Fairness is generally understood as a moral obligation to follow the rules or, rather, the commonly shared ethos of the sport in question. For the obligation to arise, participants have to be voluntarily engaged and the ethos has to meet requirements of justice. I have discussed justice as institutional requirements to rule systems in sport. The obligation on fairness implies an obligation to promote justice in sport too.

Formal fair play is structured to realize what is morally right. Norms of fairness and justice do not, however, necessarily lead to what can be considered good games. A fair and just game may lack intensity and excitement, it may be uneven, it may lack meaning for those involved. The etymological roots of 'fair' indicate that fairness also points towards what is beautiful, admirable, unblemished and great – to what is morally good. A comprehensive understanding of fair play should say something of what characterizes good sporting competitions. The perspective is similar to what Lenk (1993) refers to as informal fair play.

What is 'informal fair play'? What characterize good sport competitions? There are many answers to what are the 'real' and 'proper' values of sport. What we may call the play tradition has exerted a significant role in the literature. Positive views on the values of play and autotelic activity are found in thinkers from Plato via Schiller to Huizinga, Sartre and to Csikszentmihalyi. In play, we are most truly human; play lies at the heart of culture; play offers moments of 'deep flow' and opens for self-realization. In the philosophy of sport, among others, Suits (1978), Meier (1988), Hyland (1990) and Morgan (1994, 2006) all discuss in a variety of ways the particular playful logic of sporting games.

The view of sport at its best as play seems relevant and significant. It has its critics, however. Huizinga (1955) was indeed critical of sport and strictly formalized competition encouraging instrumental attitudes. Radical or 'leftist' critics consider sport to be a reflection of degenerate capitalist society or 'a prison of measured time', to use Brohm's (1978) expression.[6]

	Unintentional violation	Cheating	Professional foul	Play acting
Restore	X	X	X	X
Penalty		X	X	X
Warning (degree of severity/harm)		(X)	(X)	XX
	Unintentional violation	Cheating	Professional foul	Play acting

Figure 22.2 Varieties of cheating: a moral taxonomy

It may be difficult to accept or reject categorically any of these views. Sport is a social practice and is open to interpretation and subject to change. The critical question is whether and possibly in what way sport can contribute to the ethically good? As a general point of departure, it seems reasonable to assume that competitions are considered good when participants (and spectators) get their motives or goals realized to the greatest possible extent. The intentional goals of the parties involved are, however, of great variety. Some are motivated by experiential qualities in the activity itself, such as experiences of joy, fun, mastery, challenge and excitement. Others have goals that can be realized only outside of the activity such as improving health, building up social networks and friendship, or winning to achieve prestige and profit. Most participants have complex goal structures. Which goals should be action guiding to realize ideals of informal fair play and good competitions?

The fairness norm prescribes that, if we are voluntarily engaged in a practice that requires the cooperation of others, we benefit from such cooperation and should therefore contribute by doing our share. In a similar way, it can be argued that if we are given the opportunity to realize our intentional goals in a practice by the cooperation of others, we ought to give others a similar fair chance to realize their intentional goals by our cooperation.

- Competitors ought to act in such a way that all parties concerned get their intentional goals realized to the greatest possible extent!

The fairness argument is based on a neo-Kantian understanding of persons as free and responsible moral agents. The norm above has typically consequentialist flavour. Norms are developed on the basis of their consequences.

For competitive evaluations of athletic performance to make sense, all parties have to make an effort and do their best. Competitions with participants without effort, or competitions with fixed outcomes, lose meaning. Elsewhere, I have described in more detail a consequentialist argument with participants with different combinations of external intentional goals (Win!) and internal intentional goals (Play fairly to win!) (Loland 2002). In competitions with participants with external goals, only the winner can be fully satisfied. In mixed competitions, the instrumentally oriented competitor with external goals has an advantage as he or she is willing to be ranked on top by committing rule violations and unfair play. Again, the chances for a high level of realization of intentional goals are limited. In competitions with competitors with internal intentional goals, a high degree of goal realization among all parties concerned can be expected. Whether one wins or loses, one can still have played to win. A first norm for good competitions then can be:

- Play fairly to win!

Even if all competitors keep the ethos of their sport and do their best, however, competitions may not necessarily turn out as good. One challenge is the risk for so-called 'blow-outs' (Dixon 1992). Uneven performance levels tend to reduce the possibilities of playing at one's best for all parties. If I play tennis with the top ranked Rafael Nadal, I may get a point or two but there is no real competition. On the other hand, if I play tennis with a player of even abilities and skills, both have a chance to win, there is a mutual challenge at the same level, we follow each other in points, games, and sets and we are uncertain of the outcome to the very end. Such a game is tight and often characterized as good.

Looking at how sporting games are organized and practised supports this idea. In children's game playing, uneven teams are usually adjusted and players change side to get the game going at its best. This idea is even more clearly expressed in organized sports. In the discussion of justice, classification of what we called biological 'absolutes' was discussed. Most sports also classify according to performance: in leagues, groups, series, tournaments and cup systems. The idea seems to be to cultivate competitions with even competitors and an uncertain outcome. Kretchmar's (1975) advice for good competitions is to search for members of our 'testing families'. An addition can be made to the norm of doing one's best:

•   Match competitors of similar performance potential to the largest possible extent!

These two norms of informal fair play aim to maximize realization of intentional goals among all parties concerned. Emphasis is put on the value of sport itself – on autotelic value. This again is an expression of a non-instrumental, playful or ludic attitude (Suits 1978). In other words, even a consequentialist approach accepting from the outset various normative views on sport seems to support the view of sport at its best as play.

As with the fairness norm, norms for play can be considered moral obligations for participants who are voluntarily engaged. Competitors are interdependent and interwoven in a mutual quest for excellence (Simon 2015). For a good competition to take place, each participant depends upon every other participant's honest effort as well as they depend upon his or her.

At a more general level, norms for play point toward more general values and towards a perfectionist tradition in ethics (Hurka 2007). If sport is realized in fair and just ways and competitors play by the rules in an honest effort to win, sport has ethical potential. In his formulation of what he calls the Aristotelian principle, Rawls (1971: 426) claims that human beings flourish when they 'exercise … their realized capacities (their innate or trained abilities)' and flourishing seems to increase the more such capacities are realized and the more complex they become. Honest efforts in competitions open for such flourishing. Norms for play can be linked to moral virtues and ideals of human excellence

Concluding comments

In this chapter, I have discussed various interpretations of the ideal of fair play. The ideal has long historical roots. It is argued that sporting games are inconceivable without at least a minimum understanding of equality of opportunity. In the systematic overview given here, the ideal of fair play is seen to include a formal part with norms for what is morally right, and an informal part dealing with the attitudes and efforts of participants and with what is morally good. With the help of relevant literature in the field I have elaborated on both the formal and informal parts.

Formal norms of fair play deal with fairness and justice. They are typically seen as obligations and justified within a deontological perspective, in particular within the social contract tradition. Fairness secures sport as an arena of primarily meritocratic justice. Interestingly, though, the discussion of athletic performance opens for a certain element of chance and luck. Competitions are not pure meritocratic practices, neither should they be compared to the rigid requirements on reliability and validity of the scientific experiment. This leads towards a reflection upon what makes good competitions.

Informal fair play norms deal with motives and goals among sport participants. An example is elaborated based on consequentialist reasoning on what maximizes expected realization of intentional goals among all parties engaged. A playful attitude, understood with the norms on playing fairly to win and to match competitors of even performance levels, came out strong. Play norms can be justified with ideals of perfectionism.

Norms for fair play as proposed here seem to be mutually supportive and, if elaborated, they seem to have considerable action guiding potential in sporting practice. The ideal of fair play is constitutive for sport to be ethically justifiable and a sphere for human excellence.

Notes

1 Dictionary.com definition: http://dictionary.reference.com/browse/fair play (accessed 17 October 2014).
2 International Fair Play Committee. 'The Essence of Fair Play'. Available online at www.fairplayinternational.org/fairplay/the-essence-of-fair-play#.UqWlwyhdOf4 (accessed 17 October 2014).
3 The more important works are collected in edited volumes such as in William J. Morgan and Klaus V. Meier's (1988) *Philosophic Inquiry in Sport*, in Jan Boxill's (2003) *Sports Ethics: An Anthology*, and in Morgan's (2007) *Ethics in Sport*.
4 By and large, the discussion follows the structure of Loland's *Fair Play – a Moral Norm System* (2002). In addition, the particular discussion on fairness and justice is based Loland's articles 'Justice in Sport: An Ideal and Its Interpretations' (2007) and 'Fairness and Justice in Sport' (2014).
5 World Anti-Doping Agency, 2015. *World Anti-Doping Code*. Montreal: WADA. Available online at www.wada-ama.org/en/resources/the-code/2015-world-anti-doping-code#.VD_ei75fUQ4 (accessed October 16, 2014).
6 For an overview and discussion of 'leftist theories' of sport, see Morgan (1994).

References

Aristotle (1976) *The Ethics of Aristotle. The Nichomachean Ethics*. London: Penguin.
Beauchamp, T. L. (2001) *Philosophical Ethics: An Introduction to Moral Philosophy*, 3rd ed. New York: McGraw-Hill.
Black, T. and Pape, A. (1997) 'The Ban on Drugs in Sport, the Solution or the Problem?' *Journal of Sport and Social Issues* 21 (1): 83–92.
Bouchard, C., Malina, R.M. and Pérusse, L. (1997) *Genetics of Fitness and Physical Performance*. Champaign, IL: Human Kinetics.
Boxill, J. (2003) *Sports Ethics: An Anthology*. Malden, MA: Blackwell.
Bray, M. S., Hagberg, J. M., Perusse, L., Rankinen, T., Roth, S. M., Wolfarth, B., *et al.* (2009). The human gene map for performance and health-related fitness phenotypes: The 2006–2007 update. *Medicine and Science in Sports and Exercise*, 41: 35–73.
Brohm, J.-M. (1978) *Sport: A Prison of Measured Time*. London: Ink Links.
Brown, R. M. (1984) 'Paternalism, Drugs and the Nature of Sports', *Journal of the Philosophy of Sport* 11: 14–22.
Brown, R. M. (1990) 'Practices and Prudence', *Journal of the Philosophy of Sport* 17: 71–84.
Butcher, R. B. and Schneider, A. J. (1998) 'Fair Play as Respect for the Game', *Journal of the Philosophy of Sport* 15: 1–22.
D'Agostino, F. (1981) 'The Ethos of Games', *Journal of the Philosophy of Sport* 8: 7–18.
de Wachter, F. (1985) 'In Praise of Chance. A Philosophical Analysis of the Elements of Chance in Sports', *Journal of the Philosophy of Sport* 12: 52–61.
Dixon, N. (1992) 'On Sportsmanship and "Running Up the Score"', *Journal of the Philosophy of Sport* 19: 1–13.
Dixon, N. (1999) 'On Winning and Athletic Superiority', *Journal of the Philosophy of Sport*, 26: 10–26.
Elias, N. (1986) 'The Genesis of Sport as a Sociological Problem' in N. Elias and E. Dunning (eds) *Quest for Excitement – Sport and Leisure in the Civilizing Process*. Oxford: Blackwell, 126–49.
Finley, M. I. and Pleket, H. W. (1976) *The Olympic Games: The first thousand years*. London: Chatto and Windus.
Fraleigh, W. P. (1984) *Right Actions in Sport: Ethics for contestants*. Champaign, IL: Human Kinetics.
Fraleigh, W. P. (2003) Intentional Rule Violation – One More Time, *Journal of the Philosophy of Sport* 30: 166–76.
Guttmann, A. (1987) 'Ursprunge, soziale Basis und Zukunft des Fair play', *Sportswissenschaft* 1: 9–19.

Hager, P. F. and Torres, C. R. (2007). 'Just evaluation systems in competitive sport', *Journal of Physical Education, Recreation and Dance*, 78 (7): 27–32.

Heinilä, K. (1982) 'The Totalization Process in International Sport', *Sportwissenschaft* 2: 235–54.

Holt, R. (1989) *Sport and the British: A Modern History*. Oxford: Clarendon.

Houlihan, B. (1999) *Dying to Win: Doping in sport and the development of anti-doping policy*. Strasbourg: Council of Europe Publishing.

Huizinga, J. (1955) *Homo Ludens. A Study of The Play-Element in Culture*. Boston, MA: Beacon.

Hurka, T. (2007) 'Games and the Good', *Proceedings of the Aristotelian Society* 80 Suppl: 237–64.

Hyland, D. A. (1990) *Philosophy of Sport*. New York: Paragon.

Keating, J. W. (1964) 'Sportsmanship as a Moral Category', *Ethics* 75: 25–35.

Kretchmar, R. S. (1975) 'From Test to Contest: An Analysis of Two Kinds of Counterpoint in Sport', *Journal of the Philosophy of Sport* 2: 23–30.

Lenk, H. (1964) *Werte, Ziele, Wirklichkeit der modernen Olympischen Spiele*. Schorndorf: Hofmann.

Lenk, H. (1993) 'Fairness und Fair play' in V. Gerhardt and M. Lämmer (eds), *Fairness und Fair Play*. Sankt Augustin: Academia Verlag.

Lenk, H. (2002) *Erfolg oder Fairness? Leistungssport zwischen Ethik und Technik*. Münster: LIT Verlag.

Lenk, H. and Pilz, G. A. (1989) Das Prinzip Fairness. Zürich: Edition Interform.

Loland, S. (2002) *Fair Play – A Moral Norm System*. London: Routledge.

Loland, S. (2007) 'Justice in Sport: An ideal and its interpretations', *Sport, Ethics and Philosophy* 1(1): 78–95.

Loland, S. (2014) 'Fairness and Justice in Sport' in Torres, C. (ed.) *The Bloomsbury Companion to the Philosophy of Sport*. London: Bloomsbury, 98–114.

Loland, S. and Hoppeler, H. (2012) 'Justifying Anti-doping: The fair opportunity principle and the biology of performance enhancement', *European Journal of Sport Science* 12 (4): 347–53.

Loland, S. and McNamee, M. J. (2000) 'Fair Play and the Ethos of Sports: An Eclectic Philosophical Framework', *Journal of the Philosophy of Sport* 27: 63–80.

McIntosh, P. (1979) *Fair Play. Ethics in Sport and Competition*. London: Heinemann.

MacIntyre, A. (1984) *After Virtue*, 2nd ed. Indiana, IN: University of Notre Dame Press.

McNamee, M. (2010) *Sport, Vices and Virtues: Morality plays*. London: Routledge.

Mangan, J. A. (1981) *Athleticism in the Victorian and Edwardian Public School: the emergence and consolidation of an educational ideology*. Cambridge: Cambridge University Press.

Meier, K. V. (1988) 'Triad Trickery: Playing With Sport and Games', *Journal of the Philosophy of Sport* 15: 11–30.

Morgan, W. J. (1994) *Leftist Theories of Sport: A Critique and Reconstruction*. Urbana, IL: University of Illinois Press.

Morgan, W. J. (2006) *Why Sport Morally Matters*. London: Routledge.

Morgan, W. J. (ed.) (2007) *Ethics in Sport*, 2nd ed. Champaign, IL: Human Kinetics.

Morgan, W. J. and Meier, K. V. (1988) *Philosophic Inquiry in Sport*. Champaign, IL: Human Kinetics.

Murray, T. H. (2007) Enhancement. In B. Steinbock (ed.) *The Oxford Handbook of Bioethics*. Oxford: Oxford University Press, 491–515.

Pearson, K. M. (1973) 'Deception, Sportsmanship, and Ethics', *Quest* 19: 115–18.

Perelman, C. (1980) *Justice, Law and Argument. Essays on Moral and Legal Reasoning*. Dordrecht: D. Reidel.

Rawls, J. (1971) *A Theory of Justice*. Cambridge, MA: Harvard University Press.

Rescher, N. (1995) Luck. The Brilliant Randomness of Everyday Life, New York: Farrar, Straus, Giroux.

Rigauer, B. (1969) Sport und Arbeit, Suhrkamp: Frankfurt am Main.

Savulescu, J., Foddy, B. and Clayton, M. (2004) 'Why We Should Allow Performance-Enhancing Drugs in Sport', *British Journal of Sport Medicine* 38: 666–70.

Searle, J. (1969) *Speech Acts. An Essay in the Philosophy of Language*. Cambridge, MA: Harvard University Press.

Simon, R. L. (1991) *Fair Play: Sport, Values, and Society*. Boulder, CO: Westview.

Simon, R. L., Torres, C. R., and Hager, P. F. (2015) *Fair Play: The ethics of sport*, 4th ed. Boulder, CO: Westview.

Suits, B. (1973) 'The Elements of Sport' in R. G. Osterhoudt (ed.) *The Philosophy of Sport*. Springfield: Charles C. Thompson, 48–64.

Suits, B. (1978) *The Grasshopper: Games, Life, and Utopia*. Toronto: University of Toronto Press.

Tamburrini, C. (2000) *The 'Hand of God'? Essays in the Philosophy of Sports*. Göteborg: Acta Universitatis Gothoburgensis.

Torres, C. R. (2000) 'What Counts as Part of a Game? A Look at Skills', *Journal of the Philosophy of Sport* 27 (1): 81–92.

Walsh, A. and Giulianotti, R. (2006) *Ethics, Money and Sport: This sporting Mammon*. London: Routledge.

Wischmann, B. (1962) *Die Fairness*. Frankfurt: Wilhelm Limpert-Verlag.

23

GENETICS, SCIENCE FICTION AND THE ETHICS OF ATHLETIC ENHANCEMENT

W. Miller Brown

Legacy of genetics and sports

Behind every sport is a story about genetics. Not a story about the science of genetics, or even a self-conscious awareness of the genetic basis of much that distinguishes athletes (as it does for the rest of us). But in the selection of players, in the rules of our games, and in the biases that sprinkle sports history, genetics lurks as a hidden factor. It is only in the past hundred or so years that the genetic basis of our athletic profiles and abilities has become evident. And only in the last 50 or so years have we imagined that we could begin to control the genetic determinants of athletic prowess.

This chapter reviews the prospects for genetic enhancement and its impact on sports. Several of the standard objections to enhancement of humans (whether athletes or not) are reviewed and found wanting. A further risk posed by the means of achieving such enhancement is deemed an important brake on further developments. The chapter concludes with some reflections on sports and the changes likely to result from enhancement projects in the wider population.

Our sports have always been segregated by the most significant genetic factor in human make-up: sex. Virtually all sports have, since the Ancient Greek games, been divided into those available to men and those available to women. With rare exceptions, this continues to be the case. Once in a while, a woman will ask to compete with men, and in a few cases, men, usually transformed by modern medicine phenotypically into women, will compete as women.[1] But in most cases, in sports we are almost two different species.

And in other respects as well, our sports are segregated by phenotypes whose basis is clearly genetic. By virtue of their different rules and objectives, sports present challenges of very different kinds that favor athletes with very different physical and mental abilities. Height and jumping are favored in basketball but not in gymnastics. Endurance and slow-twitch muscle fibers characterize long-distance runners and swimmers, but not sprinters or ice skaters. Bulk and musculature are an advantage in weight lifting and football, but not in mountain climbing and sailing. As a result of these differences in the demands of the sports, athletes largely self-select what sports they will participate in, honing their skills and developing their natural talents and traits to meet both the requirements of the sports and the relentless competition from other athletes. Of course, there are significant similarities in physical traits that different sports require, but our sports cater to the wide diversity of phenotypes (and their genetic foundation) that characterize our species.

The history of "sex verification" goes back at least to the 1930s when the International Olympic Committee (IOC) began questioning the sexual identity of athletes. Routine sex tests were mandated by the Committee in the 1990s, but discontinued after 1999. Individuals, however, are still being tested. But as our knowledge of the genetic basis of athletic abilities has increased, it has also generated much confusion and injustices (Levine and Suzuki, 1993).[2] The genetic basis of sexual differences in humans is complex and sometimes defects in the control mechanisms of sexual differentiation produce individuals with variations on the usual chromosomal features of men and women. One estimate is that one in 500 people have abnormal chromosomal traits that affect their biological sexual identities (Levine and Suzuki, 1993, p. 76). This signified to the IOC in 1991 that tests for abnormal X chromosomes could be used to segregate male and female athletes and prevent genetic males, whose testosterone was thought to promote greater muscle development, from competing with genetic females. Because of the complexities of genetic variations and their effects on phenotypic traits, and because of the indignities of their use, the tests have largely been discontinued. New rules and regulations by the IOC have done little to dampen the controversies, particularly in cases of hyperandrogenism (Karkazis, et al., 2012). The primary motive of their use, to prevent competition among athletes with widely different abilities due to differences in testosterone production, continues to prompt occasional genetic testing. The same motive lies behind tests for the use of exogenous hormones. But the policy issue of separating groups of athletes as male and female and its justification remains largely a relic of tradition.

There is, however, a fundamental difference between testing for genetic variation and testing for externally administered drugs such as steroids, growth hormone, and erythropoietin (EPO). Genetic variation is so far not something that can easily be created by the processes of contemporary biomedicine, although, in the opinion of some, it is not long to come. As a result, sports authorities have great difficulty deciding what to do about naturally occurring variations in human traits that are beneficial to athletic performance. For example, natural variation in levels of hemoglobin gives some people advantages in endurance sports such as cross-country skiing where oxygen transport is crucial.

Imagine a difficult case. Johan has autosomal dominant erythrocytosis that produces a (statistically) abnormal level of hemoglobin. This trait, together with rigorous training and the development of his skills, has enabled him to become a champion cross-country skier. Hans, however, has an average level of hemoglobin. He has found that taking synthetic EPO can boost his hemoglobin level to at least that of Johan and so he can, if he trains hard, effectively compete with him. Should Johan be allowed to compete, but Hans be excluded because he has used a forbidden substance to enhance his performance? Or should Johan be banned because he is a genetic anomaly whose natural traits give him an unfair advantage? Recall that the naturally occurring variation in X and Y chromosomes still forms the basis of banning athletes from some competitions.[3]

In other cases, we have chosen to ignore genetic-based variations in athletic ability such as height, strength, agility, coordination, intelligence, just as we have largely ignored the advantages of class, race, education, wealth, coaching, equipment, and medical care for the development and enhancement of athletic ability.

The controversies over the use of performance-enhancing drugs continue to rile our discussions of sports. But it is not often noted that the drugs in question are, in a sense, only first-generation enhancers. They typically act by supplementing naturally occurring substances in the body to boost various biochemical processes that can affect athletic performance. They promote muscle growth and reduce injuries, quiet muscle tremor, lower blood pressure, and increase oxygen transport from the lungs to muscles, and much more. Their types and effects are legion. The second generation will be drugs, already available for medical treatments, that directly trigger gene expression of proteins that will have similar effects on metabolic pathways and performance ranges. These techniques are already on the horizon. Third will be genetic modification of somatic cells, already being developed for treating genetic diseases, that are responsible for the same performance ranges. (Possibly in this category will be the use of stem cells to enhance organ growth and metabolic functions.) Fourth will be modification of gametes, sperm and ova, to provide for individuals who from birth possess enhanced biological endowments. Neither of these last two kinds of biomedical processes will be self-administered; and they will cloud the attribution of responsibility when they are chosen by others than those who benefit from them.

Anticipating such developments, a number of conservative commentators have railed at what they consider to be the dangers of enhanced athletes. Michael Sandel, in his book, *The Case Against Perfection* (2007, pp. 24, 35), claims that enhancement efforts will promote "a kind of hyper-agency, a Promethean aspiration to remake nature, including human nature" that threatens "the integrity of the game." He deplores the emergence of "bionic athletes." Leon Kass, chairman of the President's Council on Bioethics, made the startling claim that enhanced athletes are "getting their achievements 'on the cheap,' performing deeds that *appear* to be, but that are not *in truth*, wholly their own."(President's Council on Bioethics, 2003, p. 145)

Some of these expressions of concern are guided by an expectation that enhancement will be primarily for "positional advantages;" that is, for short-term advantages in competition that occur when some athletes, but not all, use enhancing techniques and so gain a competitive or positional advantage. As many writers have pointed out, such advantage is not likely to last since others will begin to use similar techniques, and so rebalance the competitive scene. Thus, if parents, hoping to have children who are successful in sports, promote their children's height through genetic or other means, their goals will be frustrated as soon as other children are similarly enhanced.[4]

There is some plausibility to this concern, although it clearly applies to many different factors in competition, such as training techniques, food supplements, coaching, and equipment modifications, to name a few. There is always a tendency in competition to seek advantages that are soon countered by imitation or alternative approaches to the game. But not all such efforts at positional advantage are superficial or temporary. Many may have longer-term benefits to the sport; they may enhance not only the players' competitive edge, but modify the sport in ways that increase its challenges and satisfactions. Furthermore, increasing the height, for example, of some people to make them more competitive may be a move to increased opportunity to participation by those who otherwise would fall short in the lottery of life. Techniques for achieving positional advantage may therefore, if widely shared, have the desirable effect of raising the level of ability of those who formerly were at a disadvantage thus increasing the distribution of competitive abilities and so the opportunities for participation.

Positional advantage is not the primary focus of critics of enhancement. They see athletes, perhaps rightly, as the most publically visible exemplars of their worries about genetic change, and sports as the embodiments of their fears. Their concern is rather that such practices may undermine our sense of authenticity, of personal identity, and even our sense of what is natural to our species, more generally in sports and elsewhere. And these objections, if sustained, would apply not only to enhancements aimed at positional advantages in sports, but also to "general purpose" traits such as enhanced immune systems, cognitive abilities, and emotional sensibilities, and a variety of physical changes in the patchwork of traits that characterize the legacy of natural selection. Some have even argued that the anti-enhancement efforts in sports is part of a more general "war on enhancement," motivated by the threat that enhancement technologies pose to those whose power and wealth rest not just on hard work, but on considerable luck and natural talent, neither of which is deserved or evenly distributed by the lottery of life. Should enhancement become widely available, thus leveling the playing field in society in general, and of sports in particular, the lucky would find their advantages, power, and wealth seriously challenged (Mehlman, 2009b).

This makes clear, therefore, that the wide and equable distribution of biomedical knowledge and engineering is uncertain. The availability of these technologies, should they be developed as some people imagine they will be, is an important matter of justice, probably on a global scale.

Accordingly, the challenge of genetic and other techniques of biomedical enhancement for sports comes not from practices aimed at athletes only, but from the quite general goal of enhancing the human species. And while the rules of sports are for the most part arbitrary, sports reside within a larger social matrix where enhancement technologies are likely to proliferate, driven both by the private interests of individuals and families, the commercial interests of pharmocogenetic enterprises, and the concerns of governments to maintain economic productivity and military effectiveness.

The case for enhancement

Many of the arguments that are made against the prospects of human enhancement echo those that are made against enhancement in sports. Indeed, the same critics of enhancement often use sports to illustrate their concerns. Michael Sandel (2007), for example, writes of "bionic athletes." A critical look at these arguments therefore accomplishes the double purpose of assessing the case against enhancement in general and against enhancement in sports in particular. In the end, it is the former that is likely to have the bigger impact on the latter.

Biomedical genetics and pharmacogenomic research are relatively new fields. Certainly, they postdate the discovery in the 1950s of the structure of DNA and rely heavily on the completion of the genome project in the 1990s. We are scarcely a generation into work in these areas that is prompting reflection on a "post human" future, a future that could result from deliberate manipulation of the human genome and our control of human evolution (Harris, 2007; Hughes, 2004; Buchanan, 2011a,b; Mehlman, 2012). On a less speculative level, we are already faced with a longer tradition of modifying human behavior with a pharmacopeia of astonishing variety. Largely rising out of treatments for medical conditions, drugs are now available for enhancing human behavior and are used widely in the military, in schools, in sports, and in our daily lives.

The drugs of choice on college campuses include Ritalin®, Adderall®, Prozac®, Zoloft®, Provigil® (modafinil), and others drugs, not to mention older standbys such as caffeine, antidepressants, synthetic hormones, and stimulants (Pence, 2012, p. 33). Moreover, the evidence is that these substances usually work, that they do indeed enhance the cognitive, physical, and psychological traits of people who use them, both those with diagnosed disabilities and those with more normal profiles. In sports, there is plenty of evidence that erythropoietin (EPO), human growth hormone, and many other drugs, including anabolic steroids, do effectively enhance athletic training and performance. We are probably witnessing the early stages of a large, unsupervised experiment in the pharmacological enhancement of human capacities. With the flourishing of stem-cell research and the prospects of genetic manipulation of both somatic and germ line cells in the human body to increase cognitive abilities, to improve our immune systems, to increase longevity, and to begin to remedy some of the worst results of our evolutionary history, we are indeed seeing the start of what may be profound changes in human life.

Biomedical research in these areas poses risks, but they also promise great benefits. It may be the case that failure to explore this research poses even greater risks to our future than does the research itself. We are in very early stages of this enhancement project, so it is not too early to look at its prospects. Still, we are not there yet, and so we might use a phrase of Allen Buchanan (2001, p. 22) to characterize it: the "ethics of science fiction." It is sobering to note the pace at which fiction is becoming reality.

I begin by examining several lines of criticism of human enhancement in sports that I believe are ill founded. I then turn to what I consider the real dangers of clinical research on human enhancement, dangers that reflect not so much on the ends of enhancement efforts, but on the means.

The nature of enhancement

Let me begin by commenting on the nature of enhancement.[5] Here, I focus on somewhat moderate claims, those changes that are more nearly within our grasp, given current levels of biomedical technologies, rather than on forms of radical enhancement favored by so-called "transhumanists" such Nick Bostrom (2010), Ray Kurzweil (2005), James Hughes (2004), (Agar, 2010).[6] Some enhancement of our immune systems, some increase in longevity, various increases in the ranges of cognitive, emotional and physical abilities seem to me likely in the foreseeable future. Immortality, uploading personalities into computers, the successful creation of cyborgs, and vast increases in cognitive and other abilities, seem to be far away.

But, first, there are a number of conceptual issues that need clarifying. Enhancements are generally understood to be improvements in normal capacities, or augmentations of normal abilities and traits that are typical of our species. Biomedical substances for performance enhancement in sports and colleges are familiar instances. But there are two problems that arise immediately with this broad characterization. First, how are we to distinguish such biomedical enhancements from other kinds of enhancement in a way that shows an ethically relevant difference? Second, can we distinguish biomedical enhancements from medical treatments of disease, disability and injury?

Consider the second problem, the distinction between treatment and enhancement (Frankford, 2007; Buchanan, *et al.*, 2001; Juengst, 2007, 2009). I am dubious that this distinction can be usefully maintained for several reasons. First, many treatments result in enhanced capabilities, not just repair of injury or remedying of illness. Second, much standard medical treatment is designed to enhance our ability to cope with our environment: vaccines boost our immune systems, beta-blockers improve our cardiovascular health, prophylactic antibiotics prepare us for microbial assaults, fluoridation of water strengthens teeth, and well-baby care prepares children for stronger responses to their environments. And, in the future, genetic medicine will both serve to remedy mutations causing disease, and to enhance at the same time our genetic profile. So we can anticipate two kinds of enhancement: bringing many people up to normal levels of ability or even up to the extremes of current natural variability, and also effecting improvements beyond current human levels.

But some people use the distinction to reject prospects for enhancement. Michael Sandel, a Harvard political philosopher, has made the claim that we should reject enhancements but not treatments on that grounds that "healing a sick or injured child does not override her natural capacities but permits them to flourish" (Sandal, 2007, p. 46). He seems to ignore the fact that one's natural capacities may be limited and their flourishing could be enhanced not only by curing illness but also by extending the range of their uses. The key word here is "override." Sandel writes as if enhancing would eliminate one's natural ability rather than extending its scope. If I have a natural ability to throw a baseball and extensive training extends that capability, we would not see it as being overridden, or that my enhanced skill is perverting nature. Further, enhancements, as well as treatments, may permit our abilities to flourish. For example, if we extended the human life span (an enhancement indeed) our natural abilities would have more time to flourish (Kamm, 2010; Brown, 2009).

But the first problem (distinguishing biomedical enhancements in a morally relevant way from other kinds of enhancements) suggests an even greater difficulty. Human history is in some ways the story of the development of practices and technologies that enhanced our abilities and capacities. Literacy, agriculture, economic and political systems, and inventions from the stirrup to computers are all enhancements of human powers.[7] These technologies have influenced our biology as well as modified our environments, for example, in the selection of lactose tolerance as adaptable to dairy farming and in the reprogramming of the microstructure of our nervous systems that accompanies literacy and numeracy. There is even some evidence that activation of the expression of various genes by environmental influences is heritable and so some environmental changes during embryonic development may have a profound effect on us.

Nature, human nature and the natural

Among the arguments against enhancement that figure most prominently in writings of conservative critics (such as Michael Sandel (2007), Francis Fukuyama (2002), Leon Kass (2000), and Jurgen Habermas (2003)) are ones that rely on concepts of the natural. Although there may be something valuable in their claims, they rest, I believe, on fatal flaws. Consider first the concept of nature.

The argument here (as we saw in the passage from Sandel) is that tinkering with nature, a kind of sacrosanct given, would not only damage the order of the world, but would deny in us a respect and appreciation for the given in our lives (or as Sandel refers to it, the "giftedness" of features of human life). In sports, the concern is that the creation of "bionic athletes" (Sandel's term) would produce athletes whose achievements mock the striving for excellence that characterizes the challenge of sports. Athletes' accomplishments would no longer be due to arduous training and flinty determination, but the artificial enhancements of biomedicine.

There is little that is persuasive in this view. Even with enhancements, athletic achievement would require the kind of effort, skill and training that is already the mark of great athletes, even those whose abilities and phenotype place them at a far extreme of the spectrum of human variation. Shifting that spectrum would scarcely reduce the need to develop whatever "given" is an athlete's starting point.

And, of course, we tinker with nature all the time. Indeed, when it comes to protecting ourselves against the forces of nature that damage and harm us, it is urgent that we do so. Modern medicine and public health, for example, are designed to modify the vagaries of nature that threaten our wellbeing. Whether we do so wisely and with good consequences does not depend on understanding any infringement of the givenness of nature, but on a careful examination of the results of our actions.

Nevertheless, these same writers often focus on our own natures as a basis for admonishing us not to undertake efforts to change these natures. Here, they rely on a long, controversial history of philosophical claims about human nature, first generated by Aristotelian essentialism, a history that offers little hope that their claims can be substantiated. Even Aristotle's vaunted rationality is no longer seen as the sole purview of humans.

The importance of an immutable or essential concept of human nature to those opposed to enhancement is that it might seem to offer a basis for ethical objections to any changes in that nature, and can be used as a standard for regulating participation in sports. Aristotle argued that what is good for humans is what is in accord with our natures. Accordingly, there ought to be a central place in our lives for the pursuit of rational activities such as philosophy. But the good and the natural are different categories and do not necessarily overlap. We know much in nature to be bad, and much that we value in modern medicine, for example, is far from natural.[8]

Contemporary evolutionary biology offers quite a different picture. We are a product of adaptation, of reproductive fitness to our environment (Buchanan, 2011a). And it is clear that not all of the traits we have acquired by natural selection are good ones. Our ability to reason is deeply flawed (Stein, 1996); our capacity for aggression and xenophobia are notorious; our arteries harden, our eyes weaken, our teeth decay, our bodies succumb to disease and are all too easily injured, our bipedal stance leads to hernias, backaches, and difficult childbirth. It only matters to mother nature that we survive long enough to produce children who themselves are likely to have as many defects. But it matters more to us. No moral objection follows, as far as I can see, to efforts to remedy our defects and to strengthen our better natures. So, too, for sports. Efforts to yoke sports to a concept of the natural has produced the very degrading morass of sex differentiation that has plagued Olympic officials (Karkazis *et al.*, 2012). We know enough, too, of efforts to discriminate among athletes based on race to be wary of any recourse to what is deemed natural.[9]

Psychological risks of enhancement

Critics (Sandel, 2007; Kass, 2000; Fukuyama, 2002) have argued further that enhancement threatens relatively stable features of human psychology. Included among these concerns is that such efforts will cater to a willful quest for mastery and thus reduce our sense of humility and tolerance for the frailties and limitations that are part of human life. But this is surely what athletes often strive to do: to master their sports, to develop their skills and capabilities far beyond the norms of human life.

Of course, even if it were true that the motivations of some who seek to enhance athletic achievement include a willful desire for mastery, Sandel does little to show that such a desire is incompatible with other virtues such as kindness, generosity, sportsmanship, and even a realistic sense of humility in face of one's limited ability to achieve greater levels of mastery. In any case, even if such a desire were deemed a vice, it does not follow that enhancements would be bad for us or that we would be better off without them.

Similarly, there seems to be no plausible case for concluding that efforts to enhance human life in general or athletic achievement in particular would inevitably lead to a loss of a sense of responsibility or solidarity or that it will undercut our "openness to the unbidden" (Sandel, 2007, p. 45). One can possess mastery without desiring to have it for its own sake; for example, developing mastery for the sake of goods that mastery makes accessible. One could master some things while remaining open to the unbidden in other areas, or even in an area one imperfectly masters. And even if mastery were an evil disposition, a kind of vice, seeking good results as manifestation of that mastery, say the cure of diseases, or the extension of human life, or great achievement in sports, would surely be morally permissible: bad people can do good things. We can be fully aware of what Sandel (2007, pp. 26–9) calls the "gifts" (or good things) of life, even being grateful for them, while seeking to improve them or augment them.

More generally, one might wonder how Sandel and other critics can single out biomedical enhancements for condemnation and not, by the same reasoning, condemn other forms of cultural enhancement which have included the mastery of writing, farming, mathematics, science, and an astonishing variety of technologies such as flight, computers, telecommunication, and medicine, which have greatly enhanced our abilities and arguably have changed us for the better. In sports, it is hard to find consistency in condemning biomedical enhancements and yet allowing the enhancements of diet, equipment, coaching, training, and the reliance on the unusual extremes of human phenotypes already central to elite sports.

Seeking mastery in their sports is a central trait of athletic accomplishment. There is little else so common to virtually all sports as the constant desire to improve even if it is only to improve one's own personal best performance. Seeking positional advantage is in some ways the heart of sports (Brown, 2001). Athletes do it by adjusting diet, modifying equipment, seeking better coaching, changing their training environments, and studying the processes of human physiology. They often do these things in the spirit of sport, often with increased effort, determination, and feelings of solidarity with their fellow athletes and a sense of responsibility to themselves, their fans, their teams, and the goals of their sports.[10] There is often pride in their achievements, but similarly a sense of their limits, a humility in face of the achievements of others that is not dampened by their efforts to do better.

Let us return to the criticism that enhancements that only achieve a positional or competitive advantage are immoral. Usually, this position is based on the fatuous, though true, claim that such efforts are frequently against current rules (Pence, 2012).[11] What is not noted is that it is precisely the rules themselves that are in question. More often it is noted that such efforts are potentially futile. If everyone tried the same things, no one could achieve a positional advantage. The favorite example is medical intervention to increase the height of children who either suffer from growth hormone deficiency or simply fall on the lower level of the normal height distribution curve (Sandel, 2007, pp. 16–19; Buchanan, *et al.*, 2001, pp. 115–16). If everyone were to be of roughly the same height, no one would benefit from the value our society places on height, although it would assure every one of the same opportunities that height may now confer on some. But this is not what the enhancement debate is primarily concerned with. Rather it is with what some have called "general purpose enhancements" that would be of value even if, perhaps especially if, everyone had them: increased cognitive abilities, more powerful immune systems, longer, healthier lives, and greater propensities to social cooperativeness. It is true that an unequal distribution of such enhancements would also create positional advantages and so raise serious questions of distributive justice. But if widely available, they would tend to create broader social benefits of productivity and creativity. There is nothing, so far as I can see, that morally privileges the normal which already includes an unequal distribution of traits as a result of the natural lottery of life (Bostrum and Ord, 2006). It is largely the individuals who far transcend what Norman Daniels (1985) has called "species-typical functioning" that fill the ranks of elite sports.

Finally, there is the claim that the enhancement project threatens to undermine our efforts to live authentic lives. Or even that it may undermine our sense of personal identity. Fears about inauthenticity are not new (Trilling, 1971; Taylor, 1991; Eliott, 1998). We will not benefit, it is claimed, from the hard tasks of coping with life's sorrows and limitations if these experiences are mollified by biomedical means.

Of course, there is not much evidence for any of these claims – except for the character transforming experiences of a non-biomedical kind: religious and political indoctrination, psychological trauma, education, and the profound influences of family and friends. So, yes, there is some basis for worry about personality-changing enhancements. But there is little justification for claiming that athletes would lose their ability to make authentic choices or to control those parts of their lives that are open to the rest of us. Just as in the case of other influences, if choices to use these enhancements follow from core traits of one's personality, if they were chosen voluntarily and with reflection, why would they not be authentic? It is true that we should value our best traits, that we should beware of radical and frequent efforts at self-transformation, but none of these concerns is unique to prospective biomedical interventions in the lives of athletes. Nor is inheriting exceptional traits, whether through biomedical intervention or not, a barrier to authentic living, though for all of us it does partly shape our identities as athletes and in other parts of our lives.

The real dangers of the enhancement project

The problem is that not all change is benign. Many of the objections I have discussed have shown little merit. Enhancement technologies are not new in human experience in general or sports in particular, or limited to biomedical processes. Nevertheless, there are salient differences in using new biological means to achieve the old ends of improving human life and athletic performance. I now want to consider some of the dangers inherent in these new technologies.

For the most part, the back door to enhancement research lies in the development of the treatment of disease and illness. In spite of my discounting the treatment/enhancement distinction as a good basis for drawing firm lines against biomedical enhancement research, it nevertheless offers the surest basis for assessing risk. Although they are fallible, and liable to the same pressures for fame and fortune as many medical enterprises, risk assessment protocols in therapeutic medicine offer a framework for discussion of the risks of biomedical enhancement. The problems I consider here are in regard to the means, not the ends, of the enhancement project. I return later to a renewed consideration of the how those ends will transform sports.

The risks of clinical research

Clinical research is the opening for enhancement medicine since many of the frontline procedures such as drug development to correct metabolic deficiencies and gene modification for serious diseases are likely to provide the techniques for both drug-based and genetic enhancement in sports. Unfortunately, the ethics of clinical research are far from straightforward. To show this, I want to consider briefly some of the categories of subjects that present the main ethical problems for clinical research. Our ethical precautions about their care can provide the matrix for the ethics of enhancement efforts in sports.

Almost all current medicine is directed toward treatment of people suffering from injury and disease, but what is learned in doing so is clearly a step toward enhancement medicine. In addition to adults, two other groups of subjects for this research are especially important: children and prenatal embryos and fetuses. A further category is research on germ line cells; that is, sperm and eggs.

My main concern is with the protections afforded such subjects, and what risks may be warranted in light of reasonable expectations of benefits. If we can proceed with such research with reasonable precaution,[12] the effects on sports may be significant.

Adults

The central problem for clinical research is determining when it is permissible to subject people to risky research for the benefit of others, either other people in the future or the researchers themselves (Wendler, 2012). The traditional solution to this problem is that subjects must give fully informed consent. This classic principle of autonomy faces the daunting task of overcoming much skepticism about the level of informed consent most subjects, and athletes in particular, are capable of achieving and so understanding what risks of pain and injury they may face.[13]

We currently, if reluctantly, allow subjects to participate from a variety of motives; for example, giving something back to society, seeking to benefit future generations, or as providing a form of personal charity. And of course, perhaps the strongest motive of all for those already desperately ill: The great likelihood of death if nothing is done at all. But we also place constraints on researchers: Some kinds of research are impermissible, even if subjects consent, because they are excessively harmful, degrading, or scientifically specious. The empirical problem is getting a good grasp of what the risks and benefits are so that people may judge when participation may on balance be a reasonable choice.

But let us suppose that we can cope with these problems. We redouble efforts to inform potential subjects, eliminating those who appear not to grasp the basic strategies of the research, particularly the risks of random assignment of test procedures and its implications for their own conditions, and allow that healthy subjects may sometimes grasp the potential harm they face and nevertheless accept it for altruistic or other reasons. We monitor research protocols through independent review agencies for types of research that are deemed morally impermissible. And we put into place strong regulations against using easily exploited subjects, regulations that protect the poor, needy, sick, uneducated, and deluded. We might even explore the possibility of allowing people to risk some dangers in return for significant benefits as we do in the workplace: financial payments, general health care, treatment for injury, and a measure of respect and protection from unnecessary danger.

And we regulate carefully other potential subjects that pose even more difficult ethical concerns: those who need emergency treatment, or who are comatose, senile, or terminally ill and so whose informed consent is not possible or not well-founded. Where the risk (or even imminence) of death or serious debility is great, consent can be obtained, and prospective benefits are considerable, there may be some cases of permissible involvement of such patients in non-therapeutic research. But we know enough of the horrors of unregulated research on such patients to be wary of any loosening of oversight and regulation of their care.

Children

If we are reasonably confident that we can allow research on adults, we can now turn to our concern for our children. Much of the dream of enhancement has to do with changes in our abilities to cope with and improve our interactions with the natural world and other people. And these changes are often conceived as beginning with modification of embryos, fetuses, and children. Here, too, there are standards of care and limits on permissible research that are useful guidelines.

Clearly, the requirements of informed consent that we saw were problematic even for adult volunteers now devolve onto surrogate or parental consent for children. There have been both successes and failures in gene therapy (Grady, 2012, 2013; Stolberg, 1999). Further research on gene replacement is advancing rapidly and it is likely soon to become widely available. Whether and how these techniques may affect athletic performance is not clear. The central challenge, however, is not likely to be their use for "positional advantage" but their ability to enhance "general purpose" capabilities for children who will subsequently embark on athletic careers.

In the United States, federal regulations on human experimentation are codified by what is called the Common Rule, based on a 1979 report (the "Belmont Report") by the National Commission for the Protection of Human Subjects of Biomedical and Behavioral Research. It has been adopted by 15 federal offices and agencies (US Department of Health and Human Services, 2009) The National Academy of Sciences also has extensive protocols on risk and benefits in research on children that mirror to some extent those for adults (Field and Berman, 2004). None of these regulations explicitly refers to enhancement experiments, but none explicitly forbids them.

Germ line research

Finally, we come to the heart of the matter. What changes to human germ line cells or gametes can be justified? It is these changes that could affect the general population, that portend the most likely changes in athletic prowess in the near future and so will most dramatically affect sports.

So far, as I have suggested earlier, these developments are mostly in the realm of science fiction, but the prospects of biomedical research in this direction are real. If genes can be inserted into somatic cells, they can be inserted into germ cells. If we can tinker with bacteria and plants, we can surely graduate soon to primates. Indeed, some fantasize about creating entire new chromosomes that will carry genes to power many enhancements of human capabilities. Once again, all of the arguments I have considered come into play: It is against nature; it threatens human nature; it will commodify us for the sake of research; it will threaten our ability to live authentic and humble lives; it will threaten to create a new species of superior post-human beings who may not care about the current sorts of people like us.

My sympathies are with those who reject these dire projections. But in light of my emphasis on the risk of harm, what harm in the short-term can come from biomedical germline research of this sort? If we could produce individuals with more powerful immune systems, more robust cognitive abilities, and greater capacities of empathy and social cooperation, who could object? But along the way to this self-controlled evolution, we are likely to make many mistakes. Iatrogenic mistakes (Stolberg, 1999) are surely not unique and similar unintended errors are likely to occur in any germline transfers of genetic material as well, although, as with many technologies, as our knowledge grows, these risks may significantly lessen.

One standard for precaution in this regard may be to consider acceptable risks as those equivalent to those if daily life or the risk of defects in normal births (Baruch, 2005). If, on the basis of animal studies and simulations, we could have reasonable expectations that efforts to produce enhanced individuals were no more risky than normal births, our research could be deemed acceptable, especially if we were persuaded that the likely benefits were great, just as we are with some of the risks of daily life. But this standard may set the bar too low, especially if we do not know how to provide for our mistakes – after they have been born.

Even if we accept a high level of risk, it needs to be offset by probable benefits. What are these? Are there any positive reasons to seek enhancements that outweigh the likely risks? Perhaps we are obligated to implement enhancements if possible to help insure human survival in face of global warming and social conflict, or to increase our inventiveness and creativity to cope with other problems. We may no more be able to afford not to seek enhancements than we can afford not to educate, or pursue technological innovation (Savulescu, 2001). But we must beware not to be driven by some vision of human progress that runs rough shod over the misery of those who will be harmed along the way.

So suppose we begin cautiously: We start by enhancing some particular trait, if we can do so safely, perhaps only to a level equivalent to the "highest" normal variation of that trait. Then we could move on to enhancements beyond the current maximum level of some trait such as memory or other cognitive abilities, immune responses, or empathic range.

For more extensive enhancements, a number of "cautionary heuristics" have been proposed to limit harm (Bostrum and Sandberg, 2010). These include targeting genes that function at the end of ontogenetic development, not ones activated early in embryonic development; intervening in ways that are limited to single individuals; intervening in ways that are reversible[14] and that entail no major morphological changes.

The basic issue is to protect future children (and athletes) from harm. So, here again, we must ask if the risk of harm is commensurate with the likely benefits that the genetic changes may engender. How much freedom should parents have to decide what risks and benefits are acceptable? What do parents owe to their children?

United States' law and tradition allow a great deal of freedom for parents to choose how their children will be treated. As part of a larger right to reproductive freedom, this control has been acknowledged (for example, in *Roe v. Wade*) to be extensive (Robertson, 1994). But it is not without limits. Drawing on legal precedents, and a long tradition of reproductive freedom, Maxwell Mehlman (2012, p. 168), an attorney and bioethicist at Case Western Reserve University, notes that, "Legally parents can do anything they want to their children so long as their actions do not amount to 'abuse' or 'neglect.'" He has proposed a general rule for governing biomedical efforts to effect germ line enhancements:

> Parents should be allowed to genetically engineer a future child except in ways that no reasonable parent would choose or that would expose the child to a substantial risk of serious bodily or mental harm or impairment that is not outweighed by the potential benefit to the child.
>
> *(Mehlman, 2012, p. 173)*

But how could such a rule be enforced? A variety of suggestions have flooded the literature. European countries have created state regulatory agencies and laws controlling various kinds of research. In the United States, in addition to guidelines such as those of the National Academy of Sciences, and federal agencies such as the FDA, the Belmont Report (National Commission for the Protection of Human Subjects of Biomedical and Behavioral Research, 1979), the *Federal Policy for the Protection of Human Subjects* (US Department of Health and Human Services, 1991) is the controlling policy. These guidelines are regularly applied, if not always assiduously, by institutional review boards that are federally mandated for all human subjects research. Ronald Green has suggested oversight by institutional review boards, and regulatory agencies like the Recombinant DNA Advisory Committee, established by the National Institutes of Health in 1974 (Green, 2007). Their rules were revised in 2007 and 2013 (National Institutes of Health, 2013). Allen Buchanan has proposed a "Global Institute for Justice in Innovation" both to regulate biomedical enhancement projects, and to insure that their results are fairly distributed throughout the world's populations (Buchanan, 2011b).

The future of sports

Clearly, we are groping in the dark, seeking both to foster biomedical research and to prevent the worst abuses we fear from it: harm to research subjects, unjust distribution of its risks to the poor and vulnerable and of its benefits to the rich and powerful.

In many ways we are like Otto Neurath's sailors, compelled to rebuild their ship at sea, plank by plank, out of its own best components, without benefit of dry dock (Quine, 1960; Glover, 2006). Our judgments about what values and traits to change, what ones to amplify, can only be based on the values and beliefs we begin with at present. But there need be no fixed nature, no standpoint outside our human experience, from which to begin, only the use of those qualities we now share, however limited and fallible they be.

Clinical research on biomedical enhancements under some of the conditions I have discussed is nevertheless, in my judgment, morally permissible and should continue. Research that is motivated by individual and family interests, corporate profit, government programs, and professional ambition is likely to go forward at a faster pace in spite of serious ethical deficiencies of inadequate consent, exploitation of subjects, and harm to individuals. But, barring major catastrophes of various kinds, enhancement projects have the potential to transform human lives for the better. Not soon perhaps; but it will come. In the end, it may be those enhancements that are our best bet to ward off catastrophe. And it is those enhancements that will have the major impact on athletic performance and sport.

Why not be satisfied with who and what we are? To accept our lot is clearly the message of the conservative critics of biomedical research and of those who fear changes in sports. One answer to this is that it is too late, and in any case, the research is scarcely distinguishable as a part of our long history of medicine in improving human lives. Another is that in spite of the evidence of our reproductive success in populating the globe and eliminating most of our competition, or perhaps because of it, we are a fragile species. Our best hope of continued survival may lie, ironically, in the evolutionary imperative of change, perhaps even change that renders our descendants quite different from us, but change that we cannot wait for nature to engineer. We must seek to make those changes ourselves so far as we can and consistent with our moral and ethical precepts. The great struggle will be to insure that these changes, like other new technologies, are fairly distributed to everyone, not limited to the rich and powerful. Likely our students today, and certainly their children, will know how it turns out.

I have only touched on the prospects for near-term biomedical enhancements. Some argue for more far-reaching developments resulting from biomedical control of human evolution. The result, they prophesy, will be transformation in the human species, new "bionic" athletics, the creation of "post-humans" or of a "transhumanist" civilization in which both new forms of animal life and of artificial life will proliferate and dominate. What place there might be for *Homo sapiens* in the long term is the subject of much speculation. So far such speculations belong largely to the realm of science fiction. But more modest changes are already available to us and will probably be a significant factor in the lives of our children and grandchildren. What will these changes in the availability of enhancement technologies do for the microcosm of sports, embedded as it is in the larger society where these changes will likely flourish?

After World War II, the development of concern for drugs in sports was strongly boosted by Cold War politics and the use of international sports competitions to further the ideological agendas of democratic and communist regimes. Anti-doping policies were also shaped by the "war" on recreational drug use (and its clandestine economic base) by the US government. Following actions by the US Congress in 1988 (and in later legislation) to criminalize the non-medical distribution and possession of steroids and human growth hormone, the war against doping in sports and the government's war on drugs merged (Mehlman, 2009b, p. 144). The police power of the state and the regulatory function of US Anti-Doping Agency (USADA; most of whose budget is funded by Congress) were partially combined. This merger raises sobering concerns not only for the autonomy of physicians to practice medicine, but for citizen autonomy as well.

Nevertheless, as we have seen, it is not likely that restrictions on enhancement technologies that arise out of medical research will foreclose their use by many people, though safeguards are clearly needed. There is even reason to believe that governments will find a compelling interest in allowing them to flourish. But limitations in sports are another matter. Regulation of enhancement techniques in sports, primarily at the present time of drug use, is largely voluntary, its support by Congress and international sports organizations notwithstanding. Because it is highly selective, it is also largely arbitrary. Sports organizations and national regulatory bodies like USADA can continue to control the conditions under which participants can play. And, of course, schools and universities will no doubt both follow professional sports organizations and attend to their special concerns with juvenile athletes. In short, whatever happens in the larger society, sports could for a time remain enclaves free of certain kinds of biomedical enhancement influences.

But if enhancement technologies proceed to develop at their current rate, and their use proliferates, then the larger society will change and bring a variety of pressures on sports to do so as well. I will not speculate on "bionic athletes," whatever these might be, or cyborg games, although I can imagine them. But I believe we have some basis for speculating on the gradual changes in sports that a change in our larger society would entail. Our sports have already changed over the years as various enhancement techniques have become available: new equipment and facilities, better coaching techniques, biomedical and psychological assistance in training and practicing, nutrition counseling, and the greater health and resources of the general population. But perhaps more important for some sports has been the active seeking and recruiting of potential athletes whose natural abilities and phenotypes place them at one extreme of human genetic variability. Variations in maximal oxygen uptake, types of muscle fibers, hematocrit levels, height, visual acuity, and coordination vary widely and can be identified as positional advantages for athletic competition. Several national sports organizations actively seek recruits for Olympic games from among those with ideal phenotypes for particular sports. The selections have produced profound changes in the sports themselves and effectively made the "playing fields" uneven for many people.[15]

A number of tactics are therefore open to sports organizations faced with a general population that embraces the enhancement technologies of drugs and genetic engineering. First is the old standby of divide and conquer. Just as participants are segregated by sex and size and sometimes by age and disability (although no longer by race), they could also be segregated into those who are the product of biomedical enhancements and those who are not.[16] The vast enforcement regime now being used by USADA and the World Anti-Doping Agency (WADA) would be needed to mark the boundaries between the two. But many enhancements will not be ones chosen by athletes, but rather chosen by their parents, so, like those with natural genetic variations or mutations, the athletes cannot be designated as rule breakers and outlaws (Schneider, 2005). Sports organizations will need to justify their exclusions from team rosters or simply set arbitrary cutoffs on certain genetic or physical traits for participants as is now done for hematocrit levels as a way of checking for use of EPO and for sexual traits. They will need to offer cogent defenses of such approaches to meet objections of arbitrary bias and exclusion.

Fearful of the changes that challenge such segregation, sports organizations can follow the usual last ditch stand: they can appeal to the "spirit of sport." WADA's appeal (quoted in Juengst, 2009) to this spirit as "the celebration of natural talents and their virtuous perfection" falls prey to several problems. Once again it appeals to a limited and normative concept of the natural. It cannot easily account for those whose inherited abilities are the product of the choices of earlier generations rather than their own. It has little to offer in clarifying the policies dealing with genetic variation that already advantage many athletes or disadvantage those deemed to be deviant from current norms. It seems further to have a very limited view of sport as characterized by competitive and hierarchical rankings, thus ruling out ice climbing, hang gliding, sailing, hunting, and many other forms of sporting activity. It falters in its prescriptive recommendation on a covert appeal to an essence of sport.

A more likely scenario is that sports will gradually change, embracing new ranges of ability and perhaps the welcome result that more and more people will have the capability of competing at a high level, no longer being limited by the vagaries of the lottery of life.

Notes

1 But not always: Herman Ratjen impersonated a female high jumper in the 1936 Olympics, possibly under Nazi influence, and lost! And in a few sports, for example as jockeys in horse racing, men and women participate together.

2 The recent case of Caster Semenya, who competed as a female middle-distance runner, is a case in point. See Wikipedia article: http://wikipedia.org/wiki/Caster_Semenya (accessed October 20, 2014); see also Karkazis *et al.* (2012).

3 The most well-known case is that of Finnish cross-country skier Eero Mäntyranta. See the Wikipedia article "Eero Mäntyranta": wikipedia.org/wiki/Eero_Mäntyranta (accessed October 20, 2014); see also Malcolm Gladwell, Man and Superman: In athletic competitions, what qualifies as a sporting chance? *New Yorker*, September 9, 2013. Available online at www.newyorker.com/magazine/2013/09/09/man-and-superman (accessed October 20, 2014); de la Chapelle *et al.* (1993).

4 There are ethical concerns as well; see Joel Feinberg (1980).

5 Virtually all the literature explores this concept; see, especially, Juengst (2007); Savulescu and Bostrum (2010); Harris (2007); Murray (2007).

6 See also Miah (2004) for a more moderate view.

7 Michael Jones, chief technology advocate at Google, claims, "effectively, people are about 20 IQ points smarter now because of Google Search and Maps." James Fallows, Google's Michael Jones on How Maps Became Personal, *Atlantic*, January 3, 2013. Available online at www.theatlantic.com/technology/archive/2013/01/googles-michael-jones-on-how-maps-became-personal/266781 (accessed October 20, 2014).

8 These and a number of related issues are discussed in Tolleneer *et al.* (2013).

9 Erik Juengst offers a useful review of some of these issues in Juengst (2009).

10 And for fame and fortune – professional athletes gain much in social status and wealth by their achievements.

11 Pence writes (p. 57), "I believe that the link between enhancement and cheating is the master philosophical question of all enhancement ethics."

12 I allude here to the so-called precautionary principle, originally formulated for environmental concerns and often extended to other activities whose risks are not known; Rio Declaration on Environment and Development, United Nations Conference on Environment and Development, Rio de Janeiro, June 3–14, 1992. Available online at www.unep.org/Documents.Multilingual/Default.asp?DocumentID=78&ArticleID=1163&l=en (accessed October 21, 2014).

13 Hans Jonas long ago struggled with this puzzle and concluded that upending our usual selection of research subjects could solve it; see Jonas (1974).

14 Some techniques for doing this have been developed by Nobel laureate Mario Capecchi of the University of Utah. See Green (2007) for a discussion of Capecci's work.

15 Since 1949, the average height of professional male basketball players has increased from 6 foot 4 inches to 6 foot 7 inches, and average weight by almost 25 pounds; see www.apbr.org/apbr-faq.html (accessed October 21, 2014).

16 Maxwell Mehlman (2009a) has suggested segregation of athletic performance by "natural ability" whether "inherited or installed" measured by "a sophisticated combination of phenotype and genetic markers" (p. 222).

References

Agar, N. (2010). *Humanity's End: Why We Should Reject Radical Enhancement*. Cambridge: MIT.

Baruch, S., Huang, A., Pritchard, D., *et al.* (2005). *Human Germline Genetic Modifications: Issues and Options for Policymakers.* Washington, DC: Genetics and Public Policy Center, 2. (quoted in M. Mehlman, 2012, p. 170).

Bostrum, N. and Ord, T. (2006). The Reversal Test: Eliminating Status Quo Bias in Applied Ethics. *Ethics* 116, 656–79.

Bostrum, N. and Sandberg, A. (2010). The Wisdom of Nature: An Evolutionary Heuristic for Human Enhancement. In J. Savulescu and N. Bostrum (eds), *Human Enhancement* (pp. 375–416). Oxford: Oxford University Press.

Brown, W. M. (2001). As American as Gatorade and Apple Pie: Performance Drugs and Sports. In W. J. Morgan, Meier, K. V. and Schneider, A. (eds), *Ethics in Sports* (pp. 142–68). Champaign, IL: Human Kinetics.

Brown, W. M. (2009). The Case for Perfection. *Journal of the Philosophy of Sport* 36 (2), 127–39.

Buchanan, A. (2011a). *Better Than Human: The Promises and Perils of Enhancing Ourselves.* Oxford: Oxford University Press.

Buchanan, A, (2011b). *Beyond Humanity? The Ethics of Biomedical Enhancement.* Oxford: Oxford University Press.

Buchanan, A., Brock, D. W., Daniels, N. and Wikler, D. (2001). *From Chance to Choice: Genetics and Justice.* Cambridge: Cambridge University Press.

de la Chapelle, A., Traskelin, A. L. and Juvonen, E. (1993). "Truncated erythropoietin receptor causes dominantly inherited benign human erythrocytosis," *Proceedings of the National Academy of Sciences of the U S A* 90(10): 4495–9.

Daniels, N. (1985). *Just Health Care.* New York: Cambridge University Press.

Eliott, C. (1998). The Tyranny of Happiness: Ethics and Cosmetic Psychopharmacology. In E. Parens (ed.), *Enhancing Human Traits: Ethical and Social Implications* (pp. 177–88). Washington, DC: Georgetown University Press.

Feinberg, J. (1980). A Child's Right to an Open Future, in W. H. Aiken and H. LaFollette (eds), *Whose Child? Parental Rights, Parental Authority and State Power* (pp. 124–53). Totowa, NJ: Littlefield Adams.

Field, M. J. and Berman, R. E. (eds) (2004). *The Ethical Conduct of Clinical Research Involving Children.* Washington, DC: National Academies Press.

Frankford, D. M. (2007). The Treatment/Enhancement Distinction as an Armament in the Policy Wars. In E. Parens (ed.), *Enhancing Human Traits: Ethical and Social Implications* (pp. 70–94). Washington, DC: Georgetown University Press.

Fukuyama (2002). *Our Posthuman Future: Consequences of the Biotechnology Revolution.* New York: Farrar, Straus and Giroux.

Glover, J. (2006). *Choosing Children: Genes, Disability and Design.* Oxford: Clarendon.

Grady, D. (2012). In Girl's Last Hope, Altered Cells Beat Leukemia. *New York Times*, December 10. Available online at www.nytimes.com/2012/12/10/health/a-breakthrough-against-leukemia-using-altered-t-cells.html?pagewanted=all&_r=0 (accessed October 21, 2014).

Grady, D. (2013). Cell Therapy Shows Promise for Acute Type of Leukemia. *New York Times*, A1, March 21. Available online at www.nytimes.com/2013/03/21/health/altered-t-cell-therapy-shows-promise-for-acute-leukemia.html?pagewanted=all&_r=0 (accessed October 21, 2014).

Green, R. M. (2007). *Babies by Design: The Ethics of Genetic Choice.* New Haven, CT: Yale University Press.

Habermas, J. (2003). *The Future of Human Nature.* Cambridge, MA: Polity.

Harris, J. (2007). *Enhancing Evolution: The Ethical Case for Making Better People.* Princeton, NJ: Princeton University Press.

Hughes, J. (2004). *Citizen Cyborg: Why Democratic Societies Must Respond to the Redesigned Human of the Future.* Cambridge, MA: Westview Press.

Jonas, H. (1974) *Philosophical Reflections on Experimenting with Human Subjects. Philosophical Essays: From Ancient Creed to Technological Man.* Chicago, IL: Chicago University Press.

Juengst, E. T. (2007). What Does Enhancement Mean? In E. Parens (ed.), *Enhancing Human Traits: Ethical and Social Implications* (pp. 29–47). Washington, DC: Georgetown University Press.

Juengst, E. T. (2009). Annotating the Moral Map of Enhancement: Gene Doping, the Limits of Medicine, and the Spirit of Sports. In Murray, T. H., Maschke, K. J., and Wasunna, A. A. (eds), *Performance-Enhancing Technologies in Sports: Ethical, Conceptual, and Scientific Issues* (pp. 175–204). Baltimore, MD: Johns Hopkins University Press.

Kamm, F. (2010). What Is and Is Not Wrong with Enhancement. In J. Savulescu and N. Bostrum (eds), *Human Enhancement* (pp. 91–130). Oxford: Oxford University Press.

Karkazis, K., Jordan-Young, R., Davis, G. and Camposi, S. (2012). Out of Bounds? A Critique of the New Policies on Hyperandrogenism in Elite Athletes. *American Journal of Bioethics*, 12(7), pp. 3–16.

Kass, L. (2000). The Wisdom of Repugnance. In G. McGee (ed.), *The Human Cloning Debate*, 2nd ed. (pp. 68–106). Berkeley, CA: Berkeley Hill Books.

Kurzweil, R. (2005). *The Singularity Is Near: When humans transcend biology.* New York: Viking.

Levine, J., and Suzuki, D. (1993). *The Secret of Life: Redesigning the Living World.* Boston, MA: WGBH.

Mehlman, M. (2009a). Genetic Enhancement in Sport: Ethical, Legal, and Policy Concerns. In Murray, T. H., Maschke, K. J., and Wasunna, A. A. (eds), *Performance-Enhancing Technologies in Sports: Ethical, Conceptual, and Scientific Issues* (pp. 205–24). Baltimore, MD: Johns Hopkins University Press.

Mehlman, M. (2009b). *The Price of Perfection: Individualism and Society in the Era of Biomedical Enhancement.* Baltimore: Johns Hopkins University Press.

Mehlman, M. (2012). *Transhumanist Dreams and Dystopian Nightmares: The Promises and Perils of Genetic Engineering.* Baltimore, MD: The Johns Hopkins University Press.

Miah, A. (2004). *Genetically Modified Athletes: Biomedical Ethics, Gene Doping and Sport.* London: Routledge.

Murray, T. H. (2007). Enhancement. In B. Steinbock (ed.) *The Oxford Handbook of Bioethics* (pp. 491–515). Oxford: Oxford University Press.

National Commission for the Protection of Human Subjects of Biomedical and Behavioral Research (1979). *The Belmont Report: Ethical Principles and Guidelines for the Protection of Human Subjects of Research.* Washington, DC: US Department of Health and Human Services.

National Institutes of Health Office of Biotechnology Activities (2013). *NIH Guidelines for Research Involving Recombinant or Synthetic Nucleic Acid Molecules.* Washington, DC: NIH. Available online at http://osp.od.nih.gov/office-biotechnology-activities/biosafety/nih-guidelines (accessed October 21, 2014).

Pence, G. (2012). *How to Build a Better Human: An Ethical Blueprint.* London: Roman and Littlefield.

Presidents Council on Bioethics (2003). *Beyond Therapy: Biotechnology and the Pursuit of Human Happiness.* Washington, DC: National Bioethics Advisory Commission.

Quine, W. V. (1960). *Word and Object.* Cambridge, MA: MIT Press.

Robertson, J. (1994). *Children of Choice: Freedom and the New Reproductive Technologies.* Princeton, NY: Princeton University Press.

Sandel, M. (2007). *The Case Against Perfection: Ethics in the Age of Genetic Engineering.* Cambridge, MA: Belknap.

Savulescu, J. (2001). Procreative Beneficence: Why We Should Select the Best Children. *Bioethics* 15, 413–26.

Savulescu, J. and Bostrum, N. (eds) (2010). *Human Enhancement.* Oxford: Oxford University Press.

Schneider, A. (2005). Enhancement of Athletic Performance. In Tamburrini, C. and Tännsjo, T. (eds). *Genetic Technology and Sport: Ethical Questions* (pp. 32–41). London: Routledge.

Stein, E. (1996). *Without Good Reason: The Rationality Debate in Philosophy and Cognitive Science.* Oxford: Clarendon.

Stolberg, S. G. (1999). The Biotech Death of Jesse Gelsinger. *New York Times Sunday Magazine,* November 28. Available online at www.nytimes.com/1999/11/28/magazine/the-biotech-death-of-jesse-gelsinger.html (accessed October 21, 2014).

Taylor, C. (1991). *The Ethics of Authenticity.* Cambridge, MA: Harvard University Press.

Tolleneer, J. Sterckx, S. and Bonte, P. (eds) (2013). *Athletic Enhancement, Human Nature and Ethics: Threats and Opportunities of Doping Technologies.* Dordrecht: Springer.

Trilling, L. (1971). *Sincerity and Authenticity.* Cambridge, MA: Harvard University Press.

US Department of Health and Human Services. (1991). *Federal Policy for the Protection of Human Subjects ("Common Rule").* Washington, DC: US Department of Human Services.

US Department of Health and Human Services. (2009). *Code of Federal Regulations, Title 45, Public Welfare, Department Of Health And Human Services, Part 46: Protection Of Human Subjects.* Washington DC: US Department of Health and Human Services.

Wendler, D. (2012). The Ethics of Clinical Research. In Edward N. Zalta (ed.), *The Stanford Encyclopedia of Philosophy,* Fall 2012 ed. Available online at http://plato.stanford.edu/archives/fall2012/entries/clinical-research (accessed October 21, 2014).

24

OLYMPISM – A PHILOSOPHY OF SPORT?

Heather L. Reid

The philosophy that underpins the Olympic movement is generally referred to as "Olympism," but it is far from clear exactly what Olympism is, where it comes from, and where it takes itself to be going. The purpose of this chapter is to explore those questions, beginning with a discussion of whether Olympism can legitimately be called a philosophy at all. The second question addressed is whether Olympism constitutes a philosophy of sport, or rather is a philosophy informed by sport – specifically, values intrinsic to sport which support the larger goals of the Olympic movement. One of these values is that of human excellence, but it can be hard to discern exactly what is Olympism's idea of human excellence. Olympism also touts the value of education through sport – specifically the educational value of good example, but it needs to be made clear what these examples are and how they are expected to educate. The values of justice and athletic fair play are also affirmed, but they face the challenge of diverse ethical views within international communities. This leads to the political ideal of a world community and the question of how the Olympics might promote it without falling into the traps of hegemony or homogenization. Given the movement's grand social and political goals, Olympism can appear inadequate as a philosophy. This inadequacy, paradoxically, may be the secret to Olympism's success.

Is Olympism a philosophy?

Before we can discuss Olympism as a philosophy of sport, we must first address the question of whether it *is* a philosophy of sport – or even a philosophy at all. If we think of Olympism expansively as a philosophy emerging from the ancient Olympic Games and the rich philosophical heritage of Greece (Nissiotis, 1979; Reid, 2006), we may conclude that it is one of the most important philosophies of sport in history. If we think of Olympism more historically as the eclectic and often-contradictory ideas of the French pedagogue, Baron Pierre de Coubertin (Loland, 1995; Chatziefstathiou, 2005, 2012), we may conclude that it is not a philosophy at all but, at best, an ideology that served the needs of the nineteenth-century revival, which has since become outdated and irrelevant (Bale and Christensen, 2004). And if we think of Olympism in practical terms, as a philosophy that must unite and guide the modern Olympic movement, with its massive global reach and ambitious social goals, we may conclude that it is hopelessly thin and vague – incapable of articulating clear principles or setting rigid guidelines, and therefore impotent to face such challenges as multiculturalism, globalization and environmental degradation (Segrave, 1988). It turns out, paradoxically, that Olympism's weakness as a philosophy may be its strength as an international philosophy of sport.

In his detailed examination of Olympism from the perspective of the history of ideas, Sigmund Loland (1995, p. 49) considers Olympism to be an ideology rather than a philosophy – that is, a set of beliefs designed to bring about a particular social order. That analysis is certainly consistent with the aims of Pierre de Coubertin, who was neither a professional philosopher nor a great intellectual – but rather an idealistic pedagogue seeking to organize an ambitious event for the tangible benefit of his French compatriots and, ultimately, all of mankind. Coubertin apparently coined the term 'Olympism' in 1894 during the run-up to the first modern Games of 1896, but he never seems to have completed his articulation of the philosophy. In 1936, the year before his death, he regretfully concluded that he had failed to define Olympism in an accessible way (Coubertin, 1939, p. 1). This "failure" may be due to the fact that Coubertin's idea of Olympism changed throughout his lifetime. The writings and speeches he left behind paint an eclectic and sometimes contradictory picture of his philosophical vision (Müller, 2000). But Olympism's "failure" to be rigidly defined would turn out to be the secret of its success. In an overview of the philosophical controversy surrounding Olympism, Lamartine DaCosta (2006, pp. 169–70) concludes that it should be considered a process philosophy – an ongoing philosophical conversation merely started by Coubertin and open to the contributions of subsequent philosophers. As a matter of practice, that is exactly what Olympism has turned out to be – a philosophical conversation about the value of sport for promulgating a particular vision of humanity and for achieving international social goals.

The foundational text of Olympism can be found in the Olympic Charter; specifically, the section that articulates six "Fundamental Principles of Olympism." Of these, only the first two are obviously philosophical. In fact, it is the first fundamental principle that declares Olympism to be a philosophy:

> Olympism is a philosophy of life, exalting and combining in a balanced whole the qualities of body, will and mind. Blending sport with culture and education, Olympism seeks to create a way of life based on the joy of effort, the educational value of good example, social responsibility and respect for universal fundamental ethical principles.
>
> *(International Olympic Committee, 2011, p. 10)*

Embedded in this statement are metaphysical and ethical claims about the nature of human beings and the kinds of lives they ought to live, as well as an assertion that there are (or at least should be) universal ethical principles of some sort. The second fundamental principle lays out Olympism's political vision: "The goal of Olympism is to place sport at the service of the harmonious development of man, with a view to promoting a peaceful society concerned with the preservation of human dignity" (ibid.).

This goal is political in the Aristotelian sense of being concerned with the community – in this case, the world community. The very assumption that the world should be a community is itself a political statement. More specifically, the Olympic movement here is declaring its political goal to be peace – something confirmed by the fourth item under the "Mission and Role of the International Olympic Committee," which is to "endeavor to place sport at the service of humanity and thereby to promote peace" (International Olympic Committee, 2011, p. 14).

To understand Olympism as a philosophy, however, we must go beyond its published "Fundamental Principles." We must examine the philosophical heritage of Ancient Greece as well as the enlightenment ideas that influenced the articulation of those ideals. We should also consider the symbols and sayings of the Olympic movement, such as the five interlocking rings, the Olympic motto: *citius, altius, fortius* (faster, higher, stronger), and the Olympic creed: "The most important thing in the Olympic Games is not to win but to take part." Finally, we must look at Olympic history; at the way the movement has behaved in light of its stated ideals. Olympism is, if nothing else, a living philosophy that has served and must continue to serve the practical needs of the Olympic movement for vision and guidance. And even if we successfully discern (or perhaps construct) a coherent philosophy from all of these elements, it is still unclear whether we will have a philosophy of sport.

A theory of sport?

What could we mean by a "philosophy of sport" in this context? Does the philosophy of Olympism offer, for example, a metaphysical account of sport? The International Olympic Committee (IOC) sets out criteria for inclusion of sports in the Olympic program, so there is, as Parry (2006, p. 21) notes, some meaningful debate about what an *Olympic* sport should be.[1] But this is not a discussion of what *sport is,* it is rather an eligibility discussion concerning which sports are appropriate for the Games, which is to say which sports are conducive to the goals of the Olympic movement – including such practical concerns as media-friendliness, commercial potential, and so on. What this shows is that Olympism is primarily a social and political philosophy of sport, one that considers how to use sport or what can be accomplished through sport, rather than a philosophy that seeks to define what is sport.

Even though Olympism does not define or even discuss the metaphysical nature of sport *per se,* its social goals dictate to a certain extent what sport *should be.* Indeed, if we take the expansive view of Olympism as a philosophy arising from the ancient Olympic Games, we may observe that practical social problems during that era gave shape to the configuration of sport as we know it. The initial problem for the ancient Greeks was how to select among competing claims to a social honor – a problem still common today and one very often resolved through a competition in which each candidate is given an equal opportunity and the reward is allotted according to merit. Places in college, contracts for work, even architectural designs, are frequently decided this way.

Since its origins around the eighth-century BCE, ancient Olympia had been a religious sanctuary – one where diverse tribes would gather to sacrifice to common gods. The honor of lighting the sacrificial flame would conventionally go to the highest ranking member of a given society – the king or primary ruler. But Olympia was a Pan-Hellenic sanctuary – one dedicated to all the Hellenes rather than any single tribe – and so there must have been multiple sovereigns making claims to this particular honor. What is more, from a religious point of view, it was important to choose an honoree who would be pleasing to the god in question – a god who was understood to transcend the social rivalries and hierarchies of mere mortals. This social problem seems to have been solved by running a race from the edge of the sanctuary to the sacrificial altar.[2] Equal opportunity, reward according to merit, public observation of the process – this set of foundational qualities endures in Olympic and non-Olympic sports alike.

Looking at the challenges faced by the modern Olympic movement, especially with regard to their selection of sports to be included in their program – these qualities remain central and they go beyond sport. Equality of opportunity may be enshrined in the rules of individual events, but it is difficult to achieve when observed from a global perspective. Not only do most Olympic sports have a Western heritage (judo and taekwondo are the only non-Western sports on the current program), global economic disparities exclude large numbers of people from expensive sports such as sailing and equestrianism. Sports like figure skating, track cycling, luge, and gymnastics, require facilities that are not available publically in much of the world. Other sports, such as skiing, cycling, and bobsled, are influenced by expensive technologies available to only a select few. Accordingly, Olympic participants from less wealthy countries and families are poorly represented in these sports, whereas sports requiring minimal facilities and equipment such as running, soccer, and wrestling boast a more geographically diverse slate of participants. This diversity is important to the Games' political goal of "a peaceful society concerned with the preservation of human dignity" (International Olympic Committee, 2011, p. 10).

Olympic sport cannot uphold the ideals of equal opportunity if social and economic disparities impede large numbers of athletes from participation in the first place. This lesson had been learned already in the ancient Olympic Games where aristocrats had hoped that athletic excellence would justify their social privilege, but the success of lower class athletes undermined this hope. So they attempted to gain competitive advantage with their wealth, first by hiring coaches and trainers and eventually by adding equestrian events in which the victory crowns were awarded to the owner rather than the rider or chariot driver (Reid, 2011, pp. 37–9). Stephen Miller (2004, p. 233) argues with much support that there is a connection between the equal opportunity inherent in sport and the birth of democracy in Ancient Greece. Although wealthy countries and individuals still try to buy competitive advantages in the modern Games, Olympism demands that sport be kept as free as possible from economic disparities. In fact, since 1981, the IOC has promoted a program called Olympic Solidarity, which distributes a proportion of Olympic television revenues to athletes and organizations in need, to live up to the ideal of equal opportunity and reward according to (athletic) merit – as opposed to wealth or social position.[3]

So, even if Olympism does not offer a metaphysical account of sport, the goals and ideals of the Olympic movement seem to dictate that Olympic sports must exhibit the principles of equal opportunity and reward according to athletic merit. These principles may seem to be guaranteed internally by the rules of sport, but in an international context they demand an effort to compensate for external social inequities, and to regulate or exclude sports which emphasize technology and financing at the expense of the human element. The Olympics may include sailing on the program, but the boats are identical and relatively inexpensive – in contrast to the Americas' Cup yacht race, which is as much a contest of wealth and technology as it is one of sailing.[4] It is only by applying the foundational sports value of equal opportunity – as symbolized by the common starting line and level playing field – beyond the contests themselves and in the larger global community, that Olympism can meet the contemporary challenges of the Games. Olympism does not proffer a theory about what sport is, but what sport is – in terms of its internal values and principles – shapes the contours of Olympism.

A theory of human excellence through sport

Another way to look at Olympism as a philosophy is as a theory of human excellence through sport, or as Lenk (1982) and Parry (1998) describe it, a philosophical anthropology. To be sure, Olympism is a humanistic philosophy. Its first fundamental principle says that Olympism "exalts" humanity as a "balanced whole" of the qualities of "body, will, and mind" (International Olympic Committee, 2011, p. 10). This particular language reflects the modern European metaphysical idea of persons as combinations of body, will, and mind, but it also emphasizes – contrary to the received opinion of the day – that these qualities should be balanced and that the emphasis should be placed on the whole. Ever since Rene Descartes's (1985) radical separation of body and mind in the seventeenth century, the emphasis had been put on mind rather than body. Descartes' famous statement, "*Cogito ergo sum*" (I think, therefore I am) promulgated an interpretation of humanity that not only took our minds to be more important than our bodies, but declared us to be *essentially* thinking (rather than playing, dancing, or even moving) beings.[5] Unsurprisingly, under this intellectual hegemony sport and physical education – as well as general health and fitness – were significantly undervalued. Coubertin was one of several pedagogues trying to fight this devaluation by re-emphasizing the physical dimension of our being.

"*Mens sana in corpore sano*" (sound mind in sound body) was among the favorite slogans of the pedagogical movement called Muscular Christianity. Its origins suggested a connection with ancient Greco-Roman world – which was in fashion at the time due to new archeological excavations and academic discoveries. Tapping into that sentiment was a great way to increase Olympism's appeal. In practical terms, however, the Roman writer Juvenal's coining of the phrase "*mens sana in corpore sano*" had nothing to do with the Olympic Games, sports, or even exercise. He was simply recommending a prayer (Young, 1996, p. 189). It was absolutely correct, however, to associate a holistic view of human excellence with the ancient world. Whether he knew it or not, Coubertin was tapping into a very rich philosophical tradition when he placed human excellence at the center of Olympism.

The Greek word for human (and other kinds of) excellence is *aretē*, and it is at the center of the most venerated ethical traditions of the ancient world. Starting no later than Socrates, and moving through Plato, Aristotle, and even the Roman Stoics, the cultivation of *aretē* is the central focus of a good life. Socrates chastises the Athenians at his trial for caring too much for wealth and not enough for *aretē* (Plato, *Apology* 29de), Aristotle defines human happiness (*eudaimonia*) as activity in accordance with *aretē* (*Nicomachean Ethics* 1098a), and the Stoics were said to believe that "nothing is good except for virtue."[6] Pythagoras, before all of them, had gone to the gymnasium in search of good students for philosophy, not least because athleticism had been long interpreted as a sign of *aretē* (Iamblichus 1818, p. 5). What the eighth-century BCE advent of the Olympic Games did was to generate the idea that *aretē* was not just a matter of noble birth, but could be acquired through training like athleticism. This training for virtue became the task of moral philosophy and indeed the Ancient Greek philosophers' methods of dialogue and dialectic are not far removed from athletic competition (Reid, 2011). Both sport and philosophy in the ancient world were understood as means of cultivating excellence.

What is more, this Ancient Greek and Roman notion of excellence was understood holistically as a quality that engaged body and mind. Although most ancient philosophers conceptually divided body (*sōma*) and mind/soul (*psychē*), they understood the *psychē* to be the origin not only of intellect and thinking, but also of locomotion and of life itself. *Aretē* was therefore an excellence of both body and mind, the source of the strong and beautiful movements associated with athletes. In Plato's famous political treatise, *Republic,* sport and exercise are prescribed explicitly for the health of the *psychē* (411e). Even famous Greek athletic statues like Myron's *Discus Thrower* are to be interpreted not as portraits of great physical specimens, but rather as the expression of *aretē through* the body (Reid, 2012). *Kalokagathia,* a concept combining beauty and goodness, is practically synonymous with *aretē* and is specifically associated with youthful athleticism (Martinkova, 2001).

So Olympism's exaltation of humanity as a "balanced whole," like the nineteenth-century slogan of "*mens sana in corpore sano,*" taps into a very rich and very relevant philosophy of human excellence, even if it does so inadvertently. In addition, this ancient tradition of virtue ethics meshes well with the Eastern philosophical traditions of Daoism and Confucianism, thereby shielding Olympism somewhat from the criticism that it is an irretrievably Eurocentric philosophy (Inoue, 1999). Likewise, by failing to spell out in much detail exactly what this ideal of humanity looks like – by failing even to list the particular excellences prized in human beings – Olympism also manages to transcend the limitations of a specifically historical philosophy.[7]

By exalting human excellence but keeping our minds open about the various ways it may be instantiated, the Olympic Games have managed to put a very diverse face on the conception of an excellent human being. Olympic Champions admired for their excellence include tiny females like Nadia Comenici and imposing males like Usain Bolt. They come from every human race, every socioeconomic class, and a variety of religious backgrounds. But they all have a common athletic excellence which "exalt(s) and combine(s) in a balanced whole the qualities of body, will and mind" (International Olympic Committee, 2011, p. 10). These few words and the Olympic Games' long history result in a theory of human excellence robust enough to carry philosophical weight, but not so clearly defined as to exclude the possibility of human excellence through sport coming from an unexpected place – perhaps even from a disabled athlete. Olympism's ideal of human excellence should tap in deeply to its ancient roots to find philosophical structure, but it should also look to the future with an open mind and heart.

A theory of education through sport

A third way to interpret Olympism is as a theory of education through sport. I say education through sport rather than sports education or even physical education to emphasize that the goal of Olympism is not primarily the acquisition of athletic skills or physical strength and fitness. Even from Pierre de Coubertin's perspective, physical education was a means to larger social and political goals (Chatziefstathiou, 2012). As we saw in the last section, the humanistic vision of Olympism aims at cultivating excellence and, as the first Fundamental Principle of Olympism states, it expects to do this at least partially through "the educational value of a good example." The Olympic motto and creed, meanwhile, suggest a pursuit of excellence (higher, faster, stronger) through participation (the important thing is not to win, but to take part). Superficially, these three things may seem contradictory. Is Olympism promoting education through spectatorship, playing to win, or mere participation? Is the example to be followed a champion, a gracious loser, or perhaps not a person at all but a particular kind of spirit exhibited through gestures of fair play?

The obvious interpretation of what Olympism means by a "good example" would be the Olympic athlete and specifically his or her display of excellence, which is thought to educate by inspiring others to strive for excellence, too. The stories of children taking to sport after watching the Olympics on television are legion and the idea is hardly new; in fact, Ancient Greek athletes performed the same educational function. Winners at the ancient Olympic Games earned the right to erect statues of themselves in the sanctuary at Olympia, sometimes they also commissioned poets like Pindar to compose victory odes that celebrated their glory. The odes and the statues intentionally idealized the beauty of the athletes and their feats because their social function was to celebrate the community's shared value of *aretē* – a quality which was thought to bring humans closer to divine perfection. Like the prize of the olive crown, which dries up and disintegrates quickly, human excellence is ephemeral and merely reflective of that of the gods – as Pindar (1997) put it famously, "a dream of a shadow is man" (*Pythain* 8, p. 97). Even today, Olympic victors represent – at least symbolically – such globally shared values as courage, self-discipline, and respect.

There is a danger, however, with the educational use of athletes as role models – one recognized even by Socrates who said that Athens should reward him for his educational services rather than rewarding Olympic athletes for their victories because their victories only made them think themselves better while his questioning actually made them better (Plato, *Apology* 36de). The Modern Olympic Games have had to deal with the problem of athletes whose virtues in the contest are not always reflected in their behavior outside of competition – Oscar Pistorius facing trial for murder comes to mind – and athletes who turn out to have gained their medals through dubious or illicit means, such as doping.[8] Marion Jones and Lance Armstrong are prime examples of this problem. The danger is not only that individuals some-times succeed in sport without actually having the virtues the victor is supposed to symbolize, but also the larger educational message that what *matters* is victory by any means and not the virtues associated with it.

Unfortunately, the ethos in many Olympic sports and even some national Olympic commit-tees is focused squarely on results or private rewards and only tangentially on the human excellences that give the medals their symbolic value.[9] This focus on results may be thought to represent the Olympic motto "*citius, altius, fortius*" described in the *Olympic Charter* as express-ing "the aspirations of the Olympic Movement" (International Olympic Committee, 2011, p. 21). It is also a phrase, as Loland (2001) points out, that seems to reflect fascination with records of progress common in Coubertin's era. But the motto need not be interpreted exclusively as a focus on results, or even more generally as the overcoming or outdoing of others. That latter interpretation would, as several philosophers have noticed, be at odds with the Olympic creed, which states:

> The most important thing in the Olympic Games is not to win but to take part, just as the most important thing in life is not the triumph but the struggle. The essential thing is not to have conquered but to have fought well.[10]

As sport philosopher Cesar Torres (2006, p. 243) observes, an enlightened understanding of Olympism – and athletic competition itself – requires that we see the Olympic motto and creed as compatible, even complementary. Meaningful participation in athletic competition implies a concern with performance and results insofar as these represent the goals of the contest itself. But it is the process of engagement in competition – the taking part, the strug-gle – that makes sport and even victory itself valuable. You can buy an Olympic medal on eBay but its purchase value is nothing compared with the value of actually winning it through good competition. Likewise, a competition may be won without struggle, through lack of good competition, or maybe just luck – as when Steven Bradbury won a gold medal in short-track speed skating at the 2002 Olympics because all the competitors ahead of him crashed into each other in the final turn (Baka and Hess, 2002). But this kind of victory lacks value – indeed it lacks the spirit of *citius, altius, fortius* – the athletic ethos of constantly improving and perform-ing as well as one can, whatever the result.

So Olympism's educationally valuable good examples are not limited to winners or even individuals. The entire spectacle of striving for excellence through fair competition itself, taking into account particular obstacles overcome and challenges met, qualifies as an educa-tionally valuable example. It is characteristic of the Olympic Games to celebrate athletes who overcome particular social and economic barriers. Even athletes who perform well below inter-national standards, such as Eric "The Eel" Moussambani, a swimmer from Equatorial Guinea, or Wojdan Shahrkhani, the first female Olympian from Saudi Arabia, are cheered by the crowds and feted in the media. Unlike world championships and most other competitions, the Olympic Games leave some room for athletes to participate who would not otherwise qualify based on performance. This practice entails, however, that some potential medalists will be left at home (as when one country has the top three athletes in a given discipline, but is only allowed to send one or two of them to the Games), and it provides strong evidence to counter the charge that Olympism cares only about performance. The IOC's emphasis on diversity and inclusion is itself an important educational example. Furthermore, encouraging and facilitating diverse participation produces a wide variety of role models. By failing to define its educational examples – even in terms of athletic success – Olympism allows for a conception of excellence valid around the world.

A theory of justice through sport

If Olympism is characterized, as many philosophers claim, by an effort to promote moral values through sport, its most important educational examples will not be athletes but actions – especially its own institutional behavior.[11] Although the first Fundamental Principle cites "respect for universal fundamental ethical principles," it does not specify what those principles are or how they are to be understood. Those who consider ethics to be culturally relative would deny the existence of universal principles, and indeed Olympism risks a kind of ethical imperialism if it understands Anglo-European principles to be universal.[12] Doing ethics in a multicultural environment requires some form of common ground and in the Olympic Games, sport provides the common ground. The primary ethical principle of sport is fair play, which the fourth Fundamental Principle of Olympism identifies, along with mutual understanding, friendship, and solidarity, as essential to the "Olympic spirit." If fair play can be understood as the ethical principle of justice applied to sport, Olympism may also be interpreted as a theory of justice through sport.

In Ancient Greek philosophy, justice is understood generally as the excellence appropriate to communities. It is the subject of Plato's utopian dialogue *Republic,* and it is discussed extensively by Aristotle in two books: *Nicomachean Ethics* and *Politics.* Although the concept of fair play seems specific to or at least derived from sport, it is relevant to justice understood as the excellence of communities because – as Alisdair MacIntyre's (1981) work has shown – sport *is* a kind of community. For one thing, sports are governed by rules similar to the way communities are governed by laws, and it is important both to sport and to communities that these regulations are well-formed, generally respected, and properly enforced. Democratic communities consider themselves to be ruled by law. In all communities, rules and laws should be constructed in such a way that excellence may be cultivated, expressed, and appropriately awarded. One of Olympism's primary ethical demands, we may conclude, is for the proper administration of the rules and regulations of sport. It is no mistake that Olympic athletes and officials take oaths in which they swear "to respect and abide by the rules" governing the Games.[13]

It would be a mistake, however, to reduce Olympism's conception of justice or fair play merely to rule adherence. After all, the fourth Fundamental Principle characterizes fair play as a "spirit" rather than a principle. In this it is not so distant from Ancient Greek ideas of justice as it may seem. Aristotle in particular took the concept of beauty (*to kalon*) to be essential to ethical social action. In the *Eudemian Ethics,* he describes justice as something beautiful and says that the good and beautiful person (*kaloskagathos*) does just actions in the community not because they provide any personal benefit, but simply because they are beautiful (1249a). The English word "fair" retains this aesthetic link between beauty and justice, although it often seems forgotten in contemporary discussions of fair play, which tend toward the technical and legalistic. For example, the advantage gained by hydrodynamic swimsuits in the 2008 Beijing Games was largely accepted because it violated no rules. It took a larger sense of justice for the International Swimming Federation to finally ban the suits in 2009, under pressure partly from the threatened boycott of Michael Phelps, who had arguably been the biggest beneficiary of the suits, winning eight gold medals in Beijing. Phelps' opposition to the suits was aimed at benefiting his sports community,[14] something Aristotle might have recognized as beautifully just.

If it is to be a universal ethical principle, justice in the Olympic community cannot depend on the legalistic authority of a single body – even an international body like the IOC. It needs to transcend individual and national interests to serve the common interests of the international sports community. This lesson was learned in ancient Olympia, which was a PanHellenic sanctuary, by definition the property of all Hellenes and therefore lacking a sovereign ruling authority – other than the god Zeus, whom all officials, athletes, and spectators were there to worship. The race, mentioned above, to select an honoree to light the sacrificial flame was a fair solution to the problem of competing claims to that honor, not least because everyone present could witness the contest and attest to its impartiality and the validity of its results. The open and transparent process seems to have had a unifying and pacifying effect on rival tribes who in most other contexts would address their differences through violence. One might even say the ancient contest had been conducted with "a spirit of friendship, solidarity, and fair play," that is to say, in the Olympic spirit, which cannot be dissociated from the aesthetics of justice.

The transparency required by this Olympic aesthetic of justice explains why "invisible" problems like doping and corruption are such a big threat to the Olympic Games. Unlike fouls committed in the contest, doping is a form of injustice that cannot be seen by the audience or even the officials without the aid of sophisticated scientific testing. Since those responsible for policing doping in sport often had a financial interest in preserving the illusion of justice; they usually acted not like Aristotle's *kaloskagathos* to preserve the intrinsic good of the community, but rather on the basis of lower motivations like avoidance of shame and accumulation of wealth. When doping cases were exposed – like Ben Johnson's after his victory in the 100 meter sprint at the 1988 Seoul Olympic Games – it was usually due to a courageous and sometimes insubordinate act by a single individual. It was not until 1999, when the doping problem was perceived to threaten the entire Olympic movement, that the independent World Anti-Doping Agency (WADA) was founded. About the same time, the text of the Olympic athletes' oath was changed to include the phrase, "committing ourselves to a sport without doping and without drugs." Only in recent years has this massive anti-doping effort begun to restore public confidence in the fairness of Olympic competition. Maintaining transparency may be seen as central to the goal of promoting Olympic justice.

Philosopher Claudia Pawlenka (2005) argues that fairness as a moral concept actually derives from sport. Given that sport is the common denominator for the multicultural Olympic community, it makes sense that a sport-inspired concept of justice should be its primary ethical principle. Furthermore, since the Olympic community must operate in the absence of a single authority, the democratic idea of the rule of law, exemplified by sport's close association with rules, is very promising. The Olympic understanding of justice must not be reduced, as noted, to rule adherence, however. In fact Olympism, as also noted, characterizes fair play as a "spirit" or attitude that includes community based concepts of mutual understanding, solidarity, and friendship. This characterization harks back to the aesthetic aspect of justice touted by Ancient Greek philosophy that demands transparency and community observation. In the London 2012 Games, this aesthetic conception of Olympic justice as a kind of spirit seems to have been employed by badminton officials who disqualified eight players for "not using their best efforts" in preliminary matches so they could gain advantageous matches in the finals (BBC, 2012). Olympism's theory of justice may indeed be derived from the principle of fair play that informs sport itself, but the concept turns out to be ethically robust while accommodating diverse cultural beliefs.

A theory of world community through sport

The attempt to create an international or indeed universal philosophy may be Olympism's most distinctive characteristic. The Olympic ideal of a world community is expressed in its symbol of five interlocking rings, which "represents the union of the five continents and the meeting of athletes from throughout the world at the Olympic Games" (International Olympic Committee, 2011, p. 21). The fourth Fundamental Principle of Olympism demands universal access to this world sporting community: "The practice of sport is a human right. Every individual must have the possibility of practicing sport without discrimination of any kind." (ibid., p. 10). The sixth Principle reinforces the point, "Any form of discrimination with regard to a country or a person on grounds of race, religion, politics, gender or otherwise is incompatible with belonging to the Olympic Movement" (ibid., p. 11). These very strong statements are at odds with Olympic history – which is riddled with exclusions based on race, creed, politics, and gender. Olympism's effort to provide some kind of coherent philosophy for an extremely diverse community – without capitulating either to hegemony or homogenization – is daunting. It should not be seen as trivial or quixotic, however, because this is the challenge posed by the phenomenon of globalization.

Globalization is the twenty-first-century version of a phenomenon that has appeared in the world before. It refers to advances in travel and communication technology which increased contact between people and cultures that were formerly more isolated from one another. In our current times, internet technology and air travel characterize the phenomenon, but developments in telegraph and train technology can be correlated with the inauguration of the Modern Olympic Games in 1896, and even the eighth-century BCE founding of the Ancient Olympic Games can be linked with expansion of shipping and trade in the Mediterranean. The link between the Olympic Games and such "world-shrinking" phenomena is that both bring diverse people together and challenge them to get along despite their differences. First of all this requires at least a temporary change of attitude – an effort to see oneself as part of a world community, what the ancients called "cosmopolitanism."[15]

Unlike cosmopolitanism, globalization is not an ideal. It is a phenomenon that brings with it the twin dangers of hegemony and homogenization, both of which challenge the Olympic Movement's goals.[16] Hegemony is imposition of the dominant group's values upon all others and in the case of the modern Olympic movement, the dominant group has historically been European and North American. Globalization, furthermore, tends to favor the wealthy and powerful. As Olympic scholar Jim Parry (2000) points out, this combination portends a perfect storm in which Olympism's world community risks becoming a giant Europe or United States, rather than a multicultural society. Charges of Eurocentrism or American dominance are accordingly common in the Olympic Movement, but as Mike McNamee (2006, p. 185) notes, the social practice of sport furnishes Olympism with a notion of universal human virtues which transcend distinctively Western values. A similar conclusion is reached by Nanayakkara (2008). Even if charges of Eurocentrism are overblown, however, Olympism demands that the movement fight against the risk of Western hegemony by striving for diversity in terms of its official sports, host cities, and organizations – not least the IOC itself.

Diversity is also essential to resist globalization's tendency toward homogenization – the elimination of differing styles and approaches not just in sport but in all kinds of social practices. Often this happens in the name of efficiency – a particular approach to a sport increases the chances of success and pretty soon everyone is using it. Complex sports like soccer can and do accommodate a variety of playing styles and approaches – indeed the great success of the Federation of International Football Associations' World Cup depends on the diversity of styles employed by the various national teams. As Sigmund Loland (2006, p. 147) observes, however, less-complex, record-type sports like the 100-meter dash do not allow for much diversity because the standards for performance are so strictly structured and defined. These sports have the tendency to become homogenized to the point that the athletes, their preparation, and even their styles all start to resemble one another. Very often they train together in one place under one or a few coaches, no matter the country they actually compete for at the Olympics. As we noted earlier, the emphasis on records and performance has its place in Olympism, but diversity is an equally important value and sports should be chosen and regulated in such a way as to promote it.

A special case of diversity very important to Olympism is that of women. Despite the exclusion of women from the ancient Olympic Games,[17] and Pierre de Coubertin's initial opposition to their participation in the modern Games, women have competed in every Olympics since 1900 and in the London Games of 2012, they competed in every sport on the program, making up 44 percent of all athletes (International Olympic Committee, 2013b, p. 1). The Olympic Charter, furthermore, defines one of the roles of the IOC as follows: "to encourage and support the promotion of women in sport at all levels and in all structures, with a view to implementing the principle of equality of men and women" (International Olympic Committee, 2011, p. 14). This commitment to female participation engages the issue of diversity in a special way because it can be just as easily interpreted as a case of cultural hegemony as prevention of sex discrimination. In many countries, females are not considered equal to males under the law and their participation in sport is discouraged. When the IOC pressures these countries to include females on their Olympic teams, are they demonstrating "mutual understanding with a spirit of friendship, solidarity, and fair play," or are they arrogantly forcing their own views on a minority?

The participation of women from conservative Muslim countries has been a particular concern for the Olympic movement. As William Morgan's (1998) essay on Algerian runner Hassiba Boulmerka shows, this issue engages issues of religion, culture, politics, and economics. Not only does the IOC's declaration of equality between males and females contradict traditional Muslim beliefs and laws, the uniforms required by many sports along with public display more generally is seen by many – male and female – to flout appropriate standards of female modesty.[18] What is more, the honor and reputation of a woman's entire family is often thought to depend on perceptions of her morality (Pfister 2010, p. 2946). For the London 2012 Olympics, the IOC pressured the Saudi Arabians to include female athletes in their team. The Saudis complied by entering a judoka but then threatened to withdraw when the International Judo Federation declared that she could not wear a headscarf in competition for safety reasons. Eventually, the athlete was allowed to wear a modified scarf that addressed – at least partially – the safety concerns. The episode illustrates the complexity of Olympism's commitment to non-discrimination and the challenge of building a world community through sport that does not amount to an empire. Olympism must provide a philosophical foundation from which to negotiate particular issues, without becoming so rigid as to work against the goals of the movement.

Conclusion

Olympism's goal of a "peaceful society concerned with the preservation of human dignity" (IOC 2011, p. 10) incorporates all of the interpretations we have surveyed in this chapter. Although Olympism does not offer a metaphysics of sport, the principles implied by the structure of sport – such as equal opportunity and reward according to merit – provide common ground and common values around which a flexible and adaptable philosophy can be constructed. Part of this philosophy is a theory of human excellence, which is tied closely to sport but not necessarily to victory or to any particular type of human being. Like Ancient Greek virtue ethics, Olympism promotes an ideal that is harmonious, holistic, and based on activity rather than status. Olympism also offers a theory of education through sport, both through participation and through the observance of good examples. Olympism's theory of justice derives from the sporting idea of fair play, incorporating both rule-based and aesthetic understandings of fairness. Finally Olympism promulgates an ideal of world community, characterized by non-discrimination and a commitment to mutual understanding, but also conditioned by the claim that sport is a human right. The Olympic movement must remain aware of the twin dangers of globalization, hegemony and homogenization, if it is to create a peaceful international community.

As the philosophical beacon for the Modern Olympic Games, Olympism is right to make sport its common denominator and to remain flexible enough to adapt to a constantly changing world. We might wish for a clearer and more robust Olympic philosophy, but such an articulation may in practice be less conducive to the movement's goals. Olympism is a philosophy of what can be achieved through sport, rather than a philosophy of sport *per se*. But the question of what can be achieved through sport just is the central concern of the philosophy of sport – an improved critical understanding of sport is valuable insofar as it enables us to improve our lives as human beings and perhaps even to promote "a peaceful society concerned with the preservation of human dignity" (International Olympic Committee, 2011, p. 10).

Notes

1 As Parry explains, the criteria for inclusion of a sport in the Olympic program (International Olympic Committee, 2007) are based on popularity and universality, but Coubertin also wanted the Olympic movement to contribute to the development of all sport. The debate about which sports should be included and why is accordingly complex.

2 This is the story told by Philostratos (*Gym.* 5). For a fuller discussion, see Reid (2006).

3 See "Olympic Solidarity Commission" *Olympic.org*. Available online at www.olympic.org/olympic-solidarity-commission (accessed online October 21, 2014).

4 Taking these principles seriously as tenets of Olympism means leaving behind Coubertin's narrow understanding of Olympism. Coubertin was not an advocate of equal opportunity – at least outside sport. Women and lower classes were at best discouraged and at worst excluded outright from the early Olympic Games.

5 The Latin formulation of this saying comes from *Principles of Philosophy* 1644: 1.7. The more popular text that makes the "cogito" argument is *Meditations on First Philosophy* 1.16-17.

6 According to some scholars this comment may be misleading, see Nicholas White's introduction to the *Handbook of Epictetus* (Epictetus, 1983: 7–8).

7 As is well known, the ancient Olympic Games excluded females, slaves, and non-Hellenes. The first Modern Olympic Games also excluded females and discrimination based on race, religion, class, politics, and disability have also been issues in the modern Games. The point is that Olympism should be based on ideals rather than historical practice.

8 Schneider and Butcher (1994) explain how doping conflicts with the ideals of Olympism.

9 National Olympic committees pay particular attention to the so-called medal count, not even considering the fact that this constitutes an unofficial and unfair competition, which clearly favors the larger and richer countries. For an interesting account, see Bernard and Busse (2004).

10 The Olympic creed does not appear in the *Olympic Charter* or on the current IOC website, but it is so frequently cited in discussions of Olympic history and ideals as to be considered part of Olympism.

11 As Derek Bok (1996) has shown, moral behavior (good and bad) is learned more by observing an institution's behavior than from the teaching or professing of theories.

12 Indeed European Rationalism, a movement that includes such philosophers as Rene Descartes and Immanuel Kant, took its philosophy to be universal since human reason is universal. But there are other ethical traditions, such as the Eastern philosophies of Daoism and Confucianism, which believe

ethical truths transcend rational expression. For a discussion of this problem, see Reid (2010).

13 Coaches and IOC members also take similar oaths. The text of the IOC member's oath can be found on p. 30 of the Olympic Charter. The athletes, officials, and coaches' oaths can be found in an IOC Factsheet (International Olympic Committee 2013a, p. 3).

14 This is, at least, suggested by Phelps' comments at the time; see Associated Press, FINA moves up body-suit ban. *ESPN Olympic Sports*, July 31, 2009. Available online at http://sports.espn.go.com/oly/swimming/news/story?id=4368338 (accessed October 21, 2014).

15 At the ancient Olympic Games, that larger community was that of all Hellenes, as opposed to particular tribes, and its purpose was to worship a common deity. The concept of a world community appropriate to the Modern Olympic Games also emerged in Ancient Greece with Diogenes, the fifth-century BCE Cynic philosopher, who is said to have coined the Greek term *cosmopolis,* which means "world community." The idea was later embraced by the Roman Stoic school, especially Marcus Aurelius, who envisioned the wellbeing of all mankind to be intertwined and advocated cosmopolitanism, an attitude of world citizenship. For a full account of Stoic cosmopolitanism in relation to Roman sport, see Reid (2011), chapter 9.

16 Nationalism and "insincere internationalism" are also threats; see Iowerth, Jones and Hardman (2010), and Morgan (1995).

17 Women were excluded from the Olympic Games, but not all of Ancient Greek sport and there is evidence that they competed in other PanHellenic games, such as those at Delphi, Isthmia, and Nemea. For female exclusion at Olympia, see Mouratidis (1984). For women in Greek sport, see Scanlon (2002) chapters 4–7. For the philosophical debate between Plato and Aristotle on the females and sport, see Reid (2011, pp. 64–8 and 77–8).

18 This is true not only for Islam, but for conservative communities within most major religions, including Judaism and Christianity. For more on concerns about female bodies at the Olympic Games, see Weaving (2013).

References

Aristotle (1984). *Complete Works*. Ed. Jonathan Barnes. 2 vols. Princeton, NJ: Princeton University Press.

Baka, R. and R. Hess (2002). Doing a "Bradbury"! An analysis of recent Australian success at the winter Olympic Games. In K. Wamsley, R. Barney and S. Marty (eds), *The Global Nexus Engaged: Past, Present, and Future Interdisciplinary Olympic Studies* (pp. 177–84). London, ON: University of Western Ontario Press.

Bale, J. and M. K. Christensen (2004). *Post Olympism? Questioning Sport in the Twenty-first Century*. London: Berg.

BBC (2012). Olympics badminton: Eight women disqualified from doubles, *BBC Sport*, August 1. Available online at www.bbc.co.uk/sport/0/olympics/19072677 (accessed October 21, 2014).

Bernard, A. and M. Busse (2004). Who Wins the Olympic Games: Economic Resources and Medal Totals. *Review of Economics and Statistics* 86, 413–17.

Bok, D. (1996). Can Higher Education Foster Higher Morals? In W. H. Shaw (ed.) *Social and Personal Ethics* (pp. 494–503). Belmont, CA: Wadsworth.

Chatziefstathiou, D. (2005). *The Changing Nature of the Ideology of Olympism in the Modern Olympic Era*. Doctoral Dissertation, Loughborough University, UK. Available online at https://dspace.lboro.ac.uk/dspace-jspui/handle/2134/2820 (accessed October 21, 2014).

Chatziefstathiou, D. (2012). Olympic education and beyond: Olympism and value legacies from the Olympic and Paralympic Games. *Educational Review*, 64(3): 385–400.

Coubertin, P., Baron de (1939). Les sources et les limites du progrès sportif. *Olympische Rundschau* 4, 1–2.

DaCosta, L. (2006). A Never-Ending Story: The Philosophical Controversy Over Olympism. *Journal of the Philosophy of Sport* 33, 157–73.

Descartes, R. (1985). *The Philosophical Writings of Descartes*. J. Cottingham, R. Stoothoff, and D. Murdoch (eds). 2 vols. Cambridge: Cambridge University Press.

Epictetus (1983). *The Handbook of Epictetus* (N. White, trans.). Indianapolis, IN: Hackett.

Iamblichus (1818). *The Pythagorean Life* (T. Taylor, trans.). London: Watkins.

Inoue, A. (1999). Critique of Modern Olympism: A Voice from the East. In G. Pfister and L. Yueye (eds), *Sports – The East and the West* (pp. 163–7). Sant Agustin: Academia Verlag.

International Olympic Committee (2007). *Factsheet on the Olympic Programme*. Lausanne: IOC.

International Olympic Committee (2011). *The Olympic Charter*. Lausanne: IOC, 2011.

International Olympic Committee (2013a). *Factsheet on the Opening Ceremony of the Games of the Olympiad*. Lausanne: IOC.

International Olympic Committee (2013b). *Factsheet on Women in the Olympic Movement*. Lausanne: IOC.

Iowerth, H., C. Jones and A. Hardman (2010). Nationalism and Olympism towards a Normative Theory of International Sporting Representation. *Olympika* 14, 81–110.

Lenk, H. (1982). Towards a Philosophical Anthropology of the Olympic Athletes and the Achieving Being. Ancient Olympia, Greece: *International Olympic Academy Report*, 163–77.

Loland, S. (1995). Coubertin's Olympism from the Perspective of the History of Ideas. *Olympika* 4, 49–78.

Loland, S. (2001). Record Sports: An Ecological Critique and a Reconstruction. *Journal of the Philosophy of Sport* 28, 127–39.

Loland, S. (2006). Olympic Sport and the Ideal of Sustainable Development. *Journal of the Philosophy of Sport* 33, 144–56.

MacIntyre, A. (1981). *After Virtue*. Notre Dame, IN: University of Notre Dame Press.

Martinkova, I. (2001). *Kalokagathia*: How to Understand Harmony of a Human Being. *Nikephoros* 14, 21–8.

McNamee, M. (2006). Olympism, Eurocentricity, and Transcultural Virtues. *Journal of the Philosophy of Sport* 33, 174–87.

Miller, S. (2004). *Ancient Greek Athletics*. New Haven, CT: Yale University Press.

Morgan, W. (1995). Cosmopolitanism, Olympism, and Nationalism: A Critical Interpretation of Coubertin's Ideal of International Sporting Life. *Olympika* 4, 79–91.

Morgan, W. (1998). Multinational Sport and Literary Practices and Their Communities: The Moral Salience of Cultural Narratives. In M. McNamee and J. Parry (eds.) *Ethics and Sport* (pp. 184–204). London: Spon.

Mouratidis, J. (1984). Heracles at Olympia and the Exclusion of Women from the Ancient Olympic Games. *Journal of Sport History* 11, 41–55.

Müller, N. (ed.) (2000). *Olympism: Selected Writings*. Lausanne: International Olympic Committee.

Nanayakkara, S. (2008). Olympism: A Western Liberal Idea That Ought Not to Be Imposed on other Cultures? In. K. Wamsley (ed.), *Pathways: Critiques and Discourse in Olympic Research, Ninth International Symposium for Olympic Research* (pp. 351–8). London, Ontario: University of Western Ontario.

Nissiotis, N. (1979). The Philosophy of Olympism. *Olympic Review* 136, 82–5.

Parry, J. (1998). Olympism at the Beginning and End of the Twentieth Century. *Proceedings of the International Olympic Academy*: 81–94.

Parry, J. (2000). "Globalization, Multiculturalism, and Olympism." *Proceedings of the International Olympic Academy*: 86–97.

Parry, J. (2006). Sport and Olympism: Universals and Multiculturalism. *Journal of the Philosophy of Sport* 33, 188–204.

Pawlenka, C. (2005). The Idea of Fairness: A General Ethical Concept or One Particular to Sports Ethics. *Journal of the Philosophy of Sport* 32, 49–64.

Pfister, G. (2010). Outsiders: Muslim Women and Olympic Games – Barriers and Opportunities. *International Journal of the History of Sport* 27(16–18), 2925–57.

Pindar. (1997). "Pythian 8." *Pindar: Olympian Odes, Pythian Odes* (W. Race, trans.) (pp. 95–7). Cambridge, MA: Harvard University Press.

Plato. (1997). *Complete Works*. J. Cooper (ed.). Indianapolis, IN: Hackett.

Reid, H. (2006). Olympic Sport and Its Lessons for Peace. *Journal of the Philosophy of Sport* 33, 205–13. Reprinted with revisions in K. Georgiadis and A. Syrigos (eds) (2009), *Olympic Truce: Sport as a Platform for Peace* (pp. 25–35). Athens: International Olympic Truce Center.

Reid, H. (2010). East to Olympia: Recentering Olympic Philosophy between East and West. *Olympika* 19, 59–79.

Reid, H. (2011). *Athletics and Philosophy in the Ancient World: Contests of Virtue*. Abingdon: Routledge.

Reid, H. (2012). Athletic Beauty in Classical Greece: A Philosophical View. *Journal of the Philosophy of Sport* 39, 1–17.

Reid, H. and M. Austin. (2012). *The Olympics and Philosophy*. Lexington, KY: University Press of Kentucky.

Scanlon, T. (2002). *Eros and Greek Athletics*. New York: Oxford University Press.

Schneider, A. and R. Butcher (1994). Why Olympic Athletes Should Avoid the Use and Seek the Elimination of Performance-Enhancing Substances and Practices From the Olympic Games. *Journal of the Philosophy of Sport* 20–21, 64–81.

Segrave, J. (1988). Toward a Definition of Olympism. In J. Segrave and D. Chu (eds). *The Olympic Games in Transition* (pp. 149–61). Champaign, IL: Human Kinetics.

Torres, C. (2006). Results or Participation? Reconsidering Olympism's Approach to Competition. *Quest* 58, 242–54.

Weaving, C. (2013). Smoke and Mirrors: A Critique of Women Olympians' Nude Reflections. In M. McNamee and J. Parry (eds), *Olympic Ethics and Philosophy* (pp. 130–48). Abingdon: Routledge.

Young, D. (1996). *The Modern Olympics: A Struggle for Revival*. Baltimore, MD: John Hopkins University Press.

25

PHILOSOPHICAL APPROACHES TO COACHING

Jeffrey P. Fry

Introduction

In this chapter, I analyze trends in contemporary philosophical reflection on coaching, and I point to some bold and perhaps, in the estimation of some individuals, unsettling future directions for philosophical thought and research. This is an invitation to consider potentially far-reaching ideas about minds, brains, and decision making in terms of their possible implications for a philosophy of coaching. These ideas challenge the default view, which involves a kind of "dogmatic slumber" reflected in the widespread, implicit acceptance of a pervasive "perennial philosophy."[1]

What is meant to by a "*philosophical approach to coaching?*" The question arises in part owing to the variety of ways, ranging from loosely to more restrictively, in which the word "philosophy" is used. Some people may deem it desirable for a coach to develop a philosophy with respect to coaching. But what is thereby intended in each case warrants clarification.

For analytical purposes, I distinguish between a *coaching philosophy* and a *philosophy of coaching*. By "coaching philosophy," I refer to an individual's reflective views on coaching as a strategic enterprise. Sufficient conditions for having a *coaching philosophy* will be met if, for example, an individual has developed views about the employment of game strategies under specified conditions, or of ways to motivate athletes to achieve desired outcomes. Thus, having a coaching philosophy in this sense will be closely related to instrumental or means–end reasoning.

By "philosophy of coaching," I refer to a further reflective distancing from coaching as a strategic practice; that is, to adopting a position that the coach is not precluded from adopting, and ideally will be conversant with, but which is the special purview of the trained philosopher. In developing a *philosophy of coaching*, philosophical tools and concepts are brought to bear on thinking about the nature and purposes of coaching. Empirical methods of investigation, such as those employed in the natural and social sciences, may also helpfully inform a philosophy of coaching. A philosophy of coaching need not be tied primarily to means-ends reasoning. Indeed, in this chapter I deviate from a purely instrumental approach to coaching.

When developing a philosophy of coaching, significant weight may be given to normative considerations. In particular, such considerations come to the fore in specifying the qualities of a good coach, or in unpacking what it means to possess coaching expertise. In part I of this chapter, I discuss the vexing issue of the good coach. This topic is challenging in part due to the ambiguity and vagueness that attach to the word "good." In addition, there is the challenge of determining the threshold for a "good enough" coach.

In Part II, I examine applications of ethical theories in contemporary philosophical accounts of coaching. This focus is fitting, given recent work in this area, and given that the ethical dimension suffuses other aspects of coaching (Simon, 2013: 48). In Part III, I focus on how metaphysics can inform a philosophy of coaching. In particular, I examine fundamental positions in the philosophy of mind and their implications for our understanding of coaching. I suggest that the practical orientations of coaches reflect simulacra of various stances in the philosophy of mind. In Part IV, I thematize further underdeveloped areas of consideration for the philosophy of coaching by considering epistemic competencies and limitations of coaches. I highlight this issue because the coach is entrusted with consequential decision making. Ethical considerations continue to loom in Part IV, under the umbrella of agent-centered concerns relevant to moral psychology.

I. The good coach

Who is the good coach, and when is the good coach *good enough*? These issues call for nuanced treatment. While a high definition picture of the good coach may elude us, it may nevertheless be possible to sharpen the image.

Why the good coach is hard to find

Any attempt to delineate precisely the necessary and sufficient conditions of a good coach faces significant challenges. In his classic book, *The Varieties of Goodness*, Georg Henrik von Wright (1996, p. 33) suggests that when we speak of "a good K" – teacher, chess player, carpenter, scientist, and so forth – we frequently mean to say that an individual is "good at" "some well-defined activity" named by a term. As von Wright (1996, p. 33) puts it: "The good K is a K, who is good at the proper activity of K's." So, a good teacher is good at teaching and a good chess player is good at playing chess. In this sense of "good," a good coach is good at coaching. But under what description do we identify someone as good at coaching? Is the goodness of the good coach a simple, unanalyzable property, only to be apprehended by intuition? Or are there rather recognizable, good-making qualities of a good coach? I adopt the stance that the process of identifying qualities of a good coach is not a hopeless task. Nevertheless, it is a more complex process than some acknowledge.

Consider first the close association in the minds of many of winning with being a good coach. Is being a winning coach a reliable marker of being good *at* coaching? Various considerations undermine confidence in this reliability. One consideration is the fact that coaches may resort to flagrant forms of cheating. It is true that cheating coaches can create the impression that they have won, and they may also gain the spoils of victory. Nevertheless, formalists will protest that cheaters never win insofar as they violate the constitutive rules of a sport. Indeed, formalists may deny that cheaters are even playing the game.

A second reason for being wary of assuming too tight of a connection between the good coach and the winning coach is that coaches can amass easy victories by scheduling weak opponents. Victories over non-competitive opponents do not guarantee that a winning coach is a good coach. On the contrary, predictably lopsided victories show that the athletes and coaches have not faced worthy challenges (Simon, 2013, p. 53). Again, possession of a winning record may not be a sufficient condition for being a good coach.

There are also reasons to doubt that winning is a *necessary* condition for being a good coach. As previously noted, the level of athletic talent on hand is often a major factor, even if it is not always the decisive factor, in determining who wins.[2] While coaches' contributions to winning may not be negligible factors, coaches have a limited role to play in athletic success. If you are short, slow, and can barely jump off the ground, any coach will face a formidable challenge in helping you to realize your dreams of being a professional basketball player.

Even if a coach assists in developing athletic talent, the outcome will reflect the bounded potentiality of the athletes. Furthermore, although a coach might be credited for recognizing and making efforts to recruit athletes with significant potential, the success of recruitment efforts may hinge on factors beyond a coach's control, such as proximity of the location of a team to an athlete's family, or even the kind of landscape or weather that an athlete prefers.

In the final analysis, if a coach is in charge of a team with negligible athletic ability, and yet the coach faces a schedule of opponents that are considerably more talented than the members of her own team, the coach may be exemplary under the circumstances, even if her team does not post a winning record. If these considerations are salient, then possession of a winning record may not be a necessary condition for being *good at* coaching.

Winning appears to be neither a sufficient nor a necessary condition for being a good coach. But this does not mean that, other things being equal, winning is irrelevant to good coaching. If athletic contests are viewed as tests of competitive excellence, winning is (*ceteris paribus*) evidence of athletic excellence. Likewise, especially in cases where athletic opponents are evenly matched in talent, coaches' contributions may tip the balance one way or the other, and thus in such cases winning may be evidence of good coaching.

Winning may be more loosely connected to being good at coaching than some might hold. A more fine-grained analysis of the good coach may reveal other factors relevant to good coaching. The individual who is *good at* coaching exhibits a version of what von Wright (1996, p. 32) refers to as "technical goodness." If the coach is technically proficient, the coach is skillful, even if this skill does not always translate into wins. Technical proficiency is exhibited in analyzing game situations and proposing effective strategies to meet challenges. Of course, the technically proficient coach will also need to be an effective communicator if these technical skills are to be efficacious. Other things being equal, this coach's athletes should enjoy a fair share of athletic success, but they will not necessarily win when the talent level of opponents is disproportionately higher. No doubt, this notion of technical goodness also captures an aspect of what it means to be good at coaching. But other nuances are also available, some of which require us to negotiate morally fraught terrain.

Georg von Wright (1996, p. 19) also identifies what he refers to as "instrumental goodness," which "is mainly attributed to implements, instruments, and tools, such as knives, watches, and cars." He (p. 20) glosses this usage by saying that "To attribute instrumental goodness to some thing is *primarily* to say of this thing that *it serves some purpose well.*" In a derivative sense, perhaps persons and their actions may be said to possess instrumental goodness. If so, then when coaches are evaluated in terms of whether they serve some purpose well, then the evaluation is in terms of instrumental goodness. Given a plurality of purposes, the coach may demonstrate instrumental goodness in various ways. A coach may be linked to such ends as producing victories, cultivating accomplished players and the rewards they gain, and generating familial and community pride.

By highlighting the instrumental goodness of coaches, however, we risk assimilating them to objects whose reason for existence as coaches is to serve our purposes. If these purposes are not fulfilled in any given case, this may lead to the unwarranted conclusion that the coach is a poor coach *simpliciter* (von Wright, 1996). In turn, a negative assessment of a coach in terms of instrumental goodness can be a source of stress that can plague a coach's sense of wellbeing, and can even lead coaches to deviate from ethical coaching practices in order to maintain a favored status and job security. In the context of considering the instrumental worth of coaches it is thus salient to invoke the Kantian prohibition of treating humanity simply as a means to an end.

Closely related to instrumental goodness is what von Wright (1996, p. 41) terms "utilitarian goodness" or "usefulness." He (1996, pp. 43–44) acknowledges that the terms "instrumental goodness and "utilitarian goodness" ("usefulness") are sometimes used interchangeably by philosophers. Nevertheless, he distinguishes between the two notions by pointing to the difference between the phrases "be good for a purpose" (related to usefulness) and "serve a purpose well" (having instrumental goodness), where in the latter case the thing in question is used in a way essentially connected with it. It is, however, difficult to distinguish essential from accidental purposes that a coach may serve. Again, as an illustrative example, consider the fact that some individuals may hold that being an effective recruiter is partly constitutive of what it means to be a good collegiate coach. But talent for recruiting may not be equally relevant at all levels of coaching. In addition, as I noted earlier, success in recruiting gifted athletes depends in part on factors beyond a coach's control. Finally, note that whatever has utilitarian goodness, like that which is instrumentally good, is conducive to being regarded as a means to an end, and therein lies a potential moral hazard.[3]

The morally good coach

As I have indicated, it is important to attend to the ethical treatment of coaches. This is arguably an underdeveloped theme in the philosophy of coaching. In addition to its intrinsic significance, ethical treatment of the coach, by example, sets a bar of expectation for the coach's own deportment. I now turn to the issue of the moral status of the coach, since a robust account of a good coach will also attend to the moral qualities of a good coach.[4]

While being a morally good coach may not suffice to make one a good coach overall, a thick description of a good coach will give prominence to this dimension. Being a good coach may not require sainthood, but the absence of a clear moral baseline as a qualification for a good coach is itself problematic. Of course, the term "morally good" is itself ambiguous. Is the morally good coach a person of principle? If so, which principles are worthy of a coach's commitment? Or is the morally good coach rather a person of virtue? If so, what virtues does the good coach exemplify? Is the good coach rather both principled and virtuous? How does being a morally good coach relate to being a good person or to being a morally good person overall? Such issues warrant more space than I can allocate to them in this chapter. But we should not merely assume agreement on answers to these questions.

Epistemic virtues of the good coach[5]

Mike McNamee (2011) argues that it is not sufficient to equip coaches with a professional code of conduct consisting of moral rules to follow. Rather, it is also imperative that coaches possess virtues. Among them, McNamee (2011) highlights trustworthiness as a core virtue. At the same time, Sigmund Loland (2011) argues that coaches need to be enlightened generalists, who possess various kinds of expertise, including knowledge of the sciences and moral wisdom. These two ideas are blended with the notion of a robustly good coach in the following syllogism. A robustly good coach is a trustworthy coach. A trustworthy coach is an enlightened generalist. Therefore, a robustly good coach is an enlightened generalist.

This line of reasoning suggests that the robustly good coach will possess and use epistemic competencies. This coach possesses not only skills (both in moral and non-moral terms) but also background knowledge that informs and enables those skills. The robustly good coach's repertoire of competencies include, but are not limited to, knowledge of the fundamentals and rules of the relevant sport, self-knowledge (a moral dimension of a coach's character), insight into the particular individuals with whom the coach interacts, and awareness of what human beings, and in some cases, nonhuman animals, are in general like. The robustly good coach also possesses know-how, which includes an ability to transmit knowledge to athletes.

The coach who is an enlightened generalist will also acknowledge his or her epistemic limitations. To quote former US Secretary of Defense Donald Rumsfeld, there are "known unknowns" and "unknown unknowns." Later in this chapter, I look at the role that inchoate factors play in coaches' judgments and decision making. For now, I issue a promissory note by asserting the relevance of epistemic virtue for a philosophy of coaching.

Summary

In sum, the nature of a good coach is complicated, and it is becoming more so. As our knowledge base evolves, so do the standards of proficiency in the vocations, including that of coaching. I have not exhausted the senses of "good" that may attach to the good coach. What has emerged is that a sufficiently robust conception of a good coach will be many sided. It will refer to a number of competencies – moral and non-moral competencies – which may, to be sure, be intertwined – but will also point out limitations of the coach, inherent and otherwise.

A good coach may or may not be hard to find, depending on what one means by a "good coach." These understandings must be articulated and debated. Much hangs in the balance, including the good name of the coaching profession.

II. Ethical theory in contemporary philosophy of coaching

Philosophical thought on coaching today evinces a variety of approaches, ranging from theoretical accounts to thick analyses of specific issues. One factor that figures prominently in various approaches is the role of the coach as moral decision maker. In what follows, I sample ethical frameworks as they are utilized in contemporary philosophical reflection on coaching.

Theoretical stances

Corresponding to a smorgasbord of options standardly discussed in surveys of ethical theories, contemporary philosophical thinking about coaching also evinces a range of normative stances. Perhaps it should come as no surprise that recent significant philosophical work on coaching has highlighted ethical concerns. Consider the fact that, in the introduction to their book *The Ethics of Sports Coaching*, editors Alun R. Hardman and Carwyn Jones (2011, p. 2) state: "Most, if not all, coaching exchanges have a moral dimension to them. This premise is predicated on the fundamental Kantian principle that all persons are first and foremost ends in themselves."

Robert Simon (2013) notes that there is intermingling of the moral dimension of coaching with other facets of coaching. He (p. 48) states: "Clearly coaching is a complex activity that involves a network of strategic, technical, personal and moral dimensions, all of which may be interconnected in particular cases." To illustrate this interconnectedness, consider the case of the benchwarmer, as discussed by Scott Kretchmar (2013). Benchwarmers typically work hard in practice and prepare their teammates for the challenges presented by game opponents. Should benchwarmers also participate during significant outcome-affecting periods of athletic contests?

Obviously, coaches' decisions about allocations of playing time are *strategic* decisions that influence the outcomes of games. These decisions also involve a *personal* dimension, insofar as athletes typically want to participate in meaningful ways. In addition, Kretchmar (2013) argues that there is a *moral* dimension to coaching decisions with respect to playing time. Kretchmar's approach to benchwarmers draws on a deontological framework that is also attentive to contextual matters, especially the age-level of the participants.[6] At lower levels of competition, Kretchmar (2013, p. 125) stresses "the rights to basic benefits," including "a right to learn and improve." As he also (2013, p. 122) writes: "The deontological side of my thinking privileges the rights of players over arguments of utility."

In a paper that I authored entitled "Coaching a Kingdom of Ends" (Fry, 2000), I also used a deontological, and explicitly Kantian framework, while addressing a number of scenarios faced by coaches. The Kantian approach employs a decision procedure that emphasizes universalizable maxims and treating persons as ends in themselves, never as mere means to ends (Kant, 1964). These considerations place normative constraints on coaches' decision making.

Even those who are favorably disposed to Kantian arguments may not view the Kantian framework as capturing all that is morally salient. Thus, Simon (2013, p. 48) contends that Kantian considerations provide a "moral baseline," but that coaching involves "complexities" that require good judgment.

Ethical approaches that complement or compete with a Kantian-style approach to ethics are readily found in the philosophy of coaching literature. For example, the search for a viable philosophy of coaching may lead to virtue-theoretic approaches that focus on character traits, context sensitivity, and practical wisdom. An illustrative example can be found in Mike McNamee's (2011) article entitled "Celebrating Trust: Virtues and Rules in Ethical Conduct." McNamee considers the limitations of rule-based ethical codes of conduct for coaches, and cites the need for virtues in coaching, especially the virtue of trustworthiness. This need is central, but by no means exclusively present, in youth coaching. He writes:

> Now the coach is someone in whom discretion is invested. Parents value their children more than just about anything in the world. When they entrust the coach with their children, they place within his or her sphere of influence a vulnerable person, one who can be damaged in a variety of ways. Yet they necessarily trust the coach as a professional.
>
> *(McNamee, 2011, p. 35)*

McNamee's discussion of trust points us towards the critical issue of scope. Over what domains must a good coach exhibit trustworthiness? Once again, Loland's normative portrayal of the coach as an enlightened generalist is relevant. But just how broadly should we conceive of the expertise of a good coach?

For those who, like virtue ethicists, emphasize practical wisdom and good judgment with respect to coaching Simon writes:

> Proponents of the view just articulated rightly point out that the coach must be a master of 'spontaneous response.' Making just the right substitutes, for example, just at the right time, or changing the defense just at the moment when the opponent is least likely to adjust to the change, call for good judgments in response to complex situations, not automatic application of strategic rules. Similarly, when the ethical

dimension of decision making is paramount, good judgment rather than the mastery of rules is key.

(Simon, 2013, p. 49)

He (2013, p. 50) points out that those who emphasize good judgment and practical wisdom should be prepared to give reasons for their judgments. He (2013, p. 51) further suggests that the use of a method of "reflective equilibrium" that moves back and forth between judgments in specific cases and a theoretical stance is appropriate.

In keeping with this stance, Simon (2010, 2013) has labeled his own approach as "broad internalism" or "interpretivism." He contends that a sporting contest is ideally a "mutual quest for excellence." This insight into the point of sport provides normative guidance. Against this background, Simon suggests that sports participants are not limited to constitutive and regulative rules of sport for practical guidance. Instead, a coach may also appeal to broad principles that are grounded in the basic idea of an athletic contest.

John Russell (2004, p. 94–5) provides an example that displays reasoning consistent with Simon's interpretivist approach. The example supports the idea of adjudicating sports in ways that allow relevant skills to be tested. In July of 1983, George Brett of the Kansas City Royals of Major League Baseball hit what might have ended up being a game-winning home run. The home run was nullified by the umpires after opposing team manager Billy Martin of the New York Yankees protested that Brett had smeared pine tar resin on an area of the bat proscribed by the rules. The Yankees won. Subsequently, American League President Lee McPhail, not wanting the game to be decided on a technical issue, reinstated the home run, and ordered the game to be replayed from that point. As a result, Kansas City proved victorious.

While appreciative of features of the interpretivist framework, William Morgan (2013, p. 75) argues that if it is not contextualized, the approach is ahistorical and thus deficient. Therefore, interpretivism must be "tweaked" in "a conventionalist way". He writes:

> But what I want to argue is that what is most needed when our normative predicaments require fine-grained normative judgments and responses from us is not so much the personal counsel of wise individuals but the collective counsel of the battle-tested social conventions of sport that shape, or so I will argue, so much of our understanding and appreciation of the purpose and value of competitive sports, to include the so-called practical judgments of coaches and players.
>
> *(Morgan, 2013, p. 63)*

According to Morgan, this takes place against the backdrop of social conventions from which there is no escape to a "view from nowhere." Again, he writes that:

> the principles that serve as the presuppositions of our normative inquiry into sports, as the basic premises of the arguments we formulate to justify our normative judgments to one another, are social conventions that do their justificatory work in a context-dependent manner as opposed to abstract principles that supposedly do their work in a context-independent manner.
>
> *(Morgan, 2013, p. 71)*

By virtue of a thickly textured conventionalism, Morgan (2013, p. 62–3) attempts to avoid the potentially ahistorical nature of some brands of interpretivism, and the abstraction of the Kantian-style account. He (p. 62) claims that his conventionalist brand of interpretivism, "while culturally and historically biased retains critical force nonetheless." One critical issue is whether Morgan's brand of conventionalism, given its relativistic nature, can sustain a "critical force" that is sufficiently robust.

Summary

Various ethical frameworks are in evidence in contemporary philosophical thinking about coaching. I have explored here only a representative few of these approaches. One might choose to adopt an eclectic approach that utilizes insights from a variety of frameworks. However, even as ethical theories are applied in the philosophy of coaching, the metaphysical underpinnings of these views are often left implicit and unthematized. This represents a lacuna in the philosophy of coaching. In what follows I make a modest contribution to filling this gap.

III. Why coaches need metaphysics

In this section on the philosophy of mind, I enter relatively unexplored territory for the philosophy of coaching. Some may hold that the considerations that I raise here are too ethereal for a philosophy of coaching. On the contrary, I argue that the default, dualistic view is of consequence, including ethical consequence, as are alternative positions. Furthermore, I contend that a general awareness of these issues will be included in the epistemic competencies of a coach who is an enlightened generalist.

The mind–body–coaching problem

Building on the work of Wilfred Sellars, Owen Flanagan (2002) distinguishes between two approaches to the mind: the "scientific image" and the widely disseminated "humanistic image," which Flanagan and Sellars link to "perennial philosophy." According to Flanagan (2002, p. ix.), components of the humanistic image include concepts of a "nonphysical mind, free will, and a permanent, abiding, and immutable soul." On this dualistic view, human agency works, as Gilbert Ryle (1949) put it, like a "ghost in the machine."

One does not often encounter explicit challenges to the humanistic image in the philosophy of sport literature, and I suspect even less so among coaches. Perhaps, at least in the West, the humanistic image is dominant among coaches, or even the default view. Therefore, it may be useful to consider coaching in the light of different philosophies of mind. A close examination of coaching may also reveal, in terms of practical orientations, simulacra of various philosophies of mind. I consider these practical orientations, and examine how explicit theoretical commitments to different philosophies of mind might have divergent implications for the theory and practice of coaching. What follows is by not an exhaustive treatment of possible approaches, but rather a sampling of views and potential implications.[7]

The "ghost in the machine"

The Cartesian view of the mind–body relationship is, of course, a dualistic one. The mind and the body are distinct substances. The essential attribute of minds is thought, while bodies are characterized by extension. Descartes claimed, infamously, that the mind and body interact via the pineal gland. Thus, there is a role for mental causation in connection with bodily behaviors. The mind is indestructible, indivisible, non-spatial, and free. Bodies share none of these features.[8]

In the practical orientation of coaches, we can detect elements that are consonant with features of the Cartesian framework. First of all, it seems that the reality of mental causation is widely accepted in sports. Consider the Zen-like aphorism attributed to former Major League baseball catcher and manager Yogi Berra: "Baseball is 90 percent mental, the other half is physical" (Encyclopaedia Brittanica, 2013). Or think about how often coaches rhapsodize about the importance of mental toughness, mental fatigue, and having a mental edge. These declarations suggest that a key to athletic performance is exercising mind over matter.

But many philosophers hold that all or at least much of this picture is an illusion. Furthermore, these contrary views are not necessarily tied to reductionist, materialist theories of mind. Adherents to a view called occasionalism claimed that God intervenes on each occasion to correlate occurrences of mental and physical events, without their causal interaction. Those who espoused a view called parallelism contended that God established from the beginning that the occurrence of certain mental events would correlate with and run parallel to the occurrence of physical events, again without the existence of a causal relationship between the correlated phenomena. If either of these views is true, then perhaps former collegiate and US Olympic men's basketball coach Bob Knight was incorrect when he suggested that God, given weightier matters to attend to, does not care about who wins in sports.

Another feature of the practical orientation of coaching, which is perhaps consonant with Cartesianism and other dualistic approaches, has a darker side. This is the sluggish pace at which coaches and sport administrators have acknowledged and responded to the issue of brain injuries in sport. No doubt, coaches have sent concussed athletes back onto playing fields after they have had their "bell rung" with the ironic admonition to "shake it off." After all, if the real you is immaterial and indestructible, what happens to your body may be of less consequence, and surmountable. That being said, in the United States, the issue of dementia among former National Football League players is finally capturing attention and may lead to changes in the game and to a ripple effect that will have a significant impact at various levels on the long-term health of athletes.

Finally, note one further implication of the Cartesian view. Each of us is essentially an invisible mind. This view conflicts with other frameworks that view us as essentially embodied beings. One such view is behaviorism.

Behaviorism and the "conditioning coach"

Behaviorism has two standard expressions (Searle, 2004, pp. 35–6). Classic methodological behaviorists focused on the study of behavior for methodological reasons. Mental phenomena were not considered proper objects of scientific study, given that they were purportedly unobservable, subjective, and ghostly. But behavior could be observed, tracked, replicated, and even manipulated to desired ends. Therefore, the mind was bracketed in favor of the more scientifically respectable investigation of behavior.

But logical behaviorists went further than this. They did not merely bracket the mind based on methodological grounds. In logical behaviorism the mind underwent an ontological reduction to behavior and dispositions to behave. On this view, when we refer to "mental" phenomena we mean behavior and behavioral dispositions.

In practice, there is much in coaching that has a behavioristic flavor. First of all, the idea of conditioning plays a prominent role in sport. One thinks first perhaps of the conditioning for physical fitness relevant to a given sport. But the practice of conditioning extends well beyond this in sports. The countless hours devoted to practicing a sport are exercises in conditioning to produce learned, desired behaviors. In the process, coaches mete out rewards to reinforce desired behaviors and sometimes take punitive measures in attempting to eliminate undesired behaviors.

Authoritarian coaches may even attempt to reserve the prerogative of thinking for themselves and have athletes follow scripts. Some coaches implore athletes simply to "react" to the situation they see in front of them. This approaches something like methodological behaviorism as a practical orientation. Shun the touchy-feely, spectral mental realm and focus on behavior and results.

Logical behaviorism has been widely disparaged (Searle, 2004, pp. 37–9). I do not rehearse these criticisms here, but consider what it would be like to adopt this theoretical orientation as a coach. The logical behaviorist coach need not be troubled with "what it's like" (to use Nagel's formulation) to be like Michael Jordan or any other athlete. Add-ons like qualitative states of subjectivity, including affective states, and mental causation will be close relatives of Cartesian "category mistakes," to use Gilbert Ryle's (1949) terminology. There is no ghost in the machine. Indeed, one may be tempted to say that there are only machines. In thoroughgoing behaviorism, we will be philosophical zombies, carrying on just as we do, but without qualitative states of consciousness – something like athletes in the zone, that is, the "twilight zone."

Let's get physical (metaphysical), or identity theory

Identity theory also takes an ontologically reductionist approach to mental phenomena. As with behaviorism, identity theory comes in two standard forms (Searle, 2004, pp. 41–3). "Type" identity physicalists reduce mental states to types of brains states, or states of the nervous system. The standard example, known now to be far too simplistic in its formulation, is that states of pain are identical to states of C-fiber firings. On the other hand, "token" identity theorists do not reduce mental states to types of brain states. Rather, they hold that each token mental state is identical to some token brain state or other.

Identity theory too has been subjected to numerous criticisms (Searle, 2004, 39–43). One criticism, to be elaborated on further below, is the charge of "neural chauvinism." Why need mental states be realized in, or identical to, brain states? A second criticism is that, as with behaviorism, the identity theorist is challenged to give an adequate account of *seemingly* qualitative, subjective features of consciousness. This is because, for the identity theorist, a full description of the physical facts leaves room for no remainder to be explained.

I have conjectured that coaches, if polled, would report dualistic views about the mind–body relationship. But what would a coach committed to identity theory and living out its implications be like? A pure reductionist would not worry about Cartesian minds, or irreducibly mental states. The coach would be concerned about bodies moving in desired ways across physical planes. He or she might also be more concerned than some kinds of dualists about brains, brain health, and the frailty of human existence.

Functionalism

Functionalists hold that mental states are "multiply realizable" (cf. Searle, 2004, pp. 43–4, 49–50, 58). This is the antithesis of neural chauvinism. According to functionalists, mental states are potentially realizable in a variety of mediums. For something to count as a mental state, (such as being in a state of belief or desire), it need only stand in the proper causal relationship to inputs and outputs. To take a standard example, perhaps then the thermostat has mental states. The functionalist need not ontologically reduce the mental realm to the physical realm (Searle, 2004, p. 58).

There is a detectable kind of, broadly speaking, practical functionalism that is exhibited in sport and coaching. An illustrative example is found in the practice of college coaches in the United States of revoking athletic scholarships. Athletes can be replaced by functional equivalents or even improvements. After all, the fillers of positions on teams are placeholders, who are multiply realizable. Today, these positions and the players who fill them are sometimes reduced to numbers. Thus, in basketball you are no longer a guard, forward, center, or just a plain basketball player. Instead, you are a "1" or a "4" or a "5." who performs a functional role. This phenomenon attains its highest level, or perhaps its nadir, in professional sports, where multiple realizability goes without saying. After all, it is not *personal*; it is just business.

What implications follow for a coach who is committed to functionalism as a theoretical perspective? As already suggested, functionalism has a kind of practical orientation – inputs, outputs, and internal states standing in causal relationships. To achieve felicitous results a coach will need to trigger causal states that lead to outputs of desired bodily movements.

"Strong AI"

The consideration of functionalism leads naturally to a discussion of computer functionalism and "strong artificial intelligence," (AI) a designation coined by John Searle (2004, p. 45). According to Searle's rendering of computer functionalism, the mind is to the brain (its wetware) as the program is to the hardware of the computer. Linked to this computational theory of mind is the Turing test. Alan Turing contended that if the answers given to questions addressed to a computer are indiscernible from the answers given in human responses, then the computer is intelligent. Searle's famous and much debated "Chinese room argument" is a foil to these views.[9] The upshot is that Searle contends that the digital computer of today does not understand anything. It deals in syntax or form, not semantics or meaning.

In the practical orientations of coaches, there are approximate parallels to our relationships to computers. In the case of the computer, the key is to program the machine to execute the desired computations. The results follow from adherence to algorithms. Likewise, there are coaches who function like programmers. Install the program in the athletes and let it run. They monitor the situation for viruses, including independent thinking and memes that might invade and disrupt the system. It is even the case that in American collegiate sport references to basketball and football *teams* have been replaced by references to the *programs*. Successful programs follow almost algorithmic formulae.

But what would it mean to coach in a manner consistent with a theoretical commitment to a computational theory of mind? One surprising result might be that not much would change. The programming is going on now. Even if coaches do not resort to invasive procedures such as brain surgery to instill their programs, their reach extends into athletes' plastic and hence malleable brains. Note an additional point as well. On Searle's reading of the implications of the computational theory of mind, neither coaches nor athletes need be concerned about self-understanding, or mutual understanding. In fact, to the degree that their minds function computationally, there is no understanding at all.

Finally, if "strong AI" is true, in the future "multiple realizability" may take on new meanings in sport. With developing technology, perhaps sports teams of the future will be constituted by intelligent robots. These athlete-bots may be highly coachable, given that they will be more easily programmed and thus more dependable than humans. Athlete-bots may take their place alongside sex-bots for the amorous, and companion-bots for the elderly. Perhaps the technological revolution that MIT professor Sherry Turkle (2011) argues is leading us to be "alone together" will reach its logical conclusion. We will simply be alone, or alone together with our bots. But perhaps coaches are already unwittingly preparing for this time by spending countless lonely hours cut off from other humans, pouring over videos of their own team's games and scouting opponents' tendencies.

Panpsychism

I must confess to finding elegance in panpsychism. The view is teeming with the mental as a fundamental feature of reality. The view has its contemporary proponents. Among them is Galen Strawson (2008). David Chalmers also flirts with it.[10] If you find the view that consciousness is at some level pervasive throughout the world spooky, there is no need to worry. Practical correlates of the view already find instantiations among coaches. I speak here of coaches who love the games they coach, and revere the players, equipment, playing fields, stadia, and perhaps at times even the game officials and referees. Borrowing a term from the theologian Karl Rahner (2010), we might refer to these coaches as "anonymous" panpsychists. These Buberian coaches have a personal, "I-thou" relationship with all aspects of sport.[11] They live and breathe sport. They are in a reciprocal relationship of give and take.

A coach with a theoretical commitment to panpsychism would have us entertain a revision of the standard view of physical phenomena, including in sport. In doing so, the pansychist coach might expand common conceptions of the significance of the material world.

Summary

I believe that the philosophy of coaching needs metaphysics, and in particular, the philosophy of mind. A broad awareness of the complexity of the issues should also form part of the knowledge base of the coach who is an enlightened generalist.

I have conjectured that most coaches would, if pressed, express a dualistic view of the mind–body relationship. At the same time, I have argued that simulacra of various philosophies of mind are also present in the practical orientations of coaching. Regardless of which philosophy of mind turns out to be the correct one, it will affect coaches directly. Coaches may turn out to be ghosts in machines. Coaches' mental states will be reducible or not to behaviors, brain states, or functional relationships, and the mental states of coaches, if they exist in an irreducibly mental form, will either be causally efficacious or, alternatively, as Searle (2004, p. 21) puts it, like the "froth on the wave".

Differing philosophies of mind do suggest divergent practical orientations towards coaching. So, let's get metaphysical about coaching.

IV. Coaching in a "cloud of unknowing"

I have examined numerous fundamental conceptions of the mind. But how do coaches utilize the mind to render judgments and make decisions? These questions point to further underdeveloped themes in the philosophy of coaching.

The notion that human beings are rational agents who, in varying degrees, judge and decide in terms of a rational analysis of costs and benefits has been challenged from a number of quarters. These challenges focus on ways that our judgments and decisions are shaped by factors outside of conscious awareness, such as brain states that prompt behavior without the mediation of conscious processes, situational influences on behavior, and heuristics and biases that can lead to systematic distortions of thinking. Serious engagement with these challenges could lead to a transformation of thinking about the nature of coaching, and especially of our understandings of the authority of the coach.

Coaching with the "new unconscious"

Is it desirable for a coach to know what he is doing and why he is doing it? If so, to what extent are these epistemic conditions realizable? Freudian notions permeate everyday conversation. It is commonplace to suggest that unconscious factors influence our thoughts, feelings, and behaviors. That being said, the Freudian unconscious, with its emphasis on repressed sexual desires, has been supplanted in the work of some psychologists by the "new unconscious," or what is referred to as the "adaptive unconscious." The extent of the role played by the unconscious is debated, but its handiwork is apparent, and fraught with potential implications for coaching. Consider various kinds of biases that coaches may exhibit. For example, coaches who coach their own children in the context of team sports may unconsciously extend favoritism to them. On the other hand, these coaches may unconsciously overcompensate in an attempt to be fair. Unconscious assumptions and motives may also lead coaches to make coaching decisions that exhibit racial or gender bias. In this regard, consider the practice of "stacking" players in positions accord to conscious or unconscious racial profiles. Finally, consider how biases may influence coaches' perceptions of athletic officiating or of their own competence.[12]

Psychologist Timothy Wilson (2002, p. 6) suggests that consciousness is not aptly conceived as the "tip of the mental iceberg," but rather as "the size of a snowball on top of that iceberg." He goes on to state:

> The mind operates most efficiently by relegating a good deal of high-level sophisticated thinking to the unconscious, just as the modern jumbo jetliner is able to fly on automatic pilot with little or no input from the human, 'conscious' pilot.
>
> *(Wilson, 2002, p. 6)*

He goes on to consider what it would be like to forego the operations that take place in the unconscious and to make our way through the world merely on the muscle of consciousness. According to Wilson, the results would be, to put it mildly, debilitating.

Psychologist John Bargh claims that the degree to which automatic processes hold sway rivals the degree of purity advertised for a bar of Dove® soap: 99.44 percent (cited in Kihlstrom, 2008, p. 161). Bargh writes that "most of a person's everyday life is determined not by their conscious intentions and deliberate choices but by mental processes that are put into motion by features of the environment that operate outside of conscious awareness and guidance" (Bargh and Chartrand, 1999, p. 462; also cited in Kihlstrom, 2008, p. 161).

Psychologist John Kihlstrom (2008) calls the emphasis on unconscious, automatic processes the "automaticity juggernaut." He argues that stronger claims made in behalf of automaticity may be true, but they have not yet been substantiated by evidence. Nonetheless, to the extent that factors outside of conscious awareness influence thoughts, feelings, and behavior, this is a relevant issue for the philosophy of coaching. This issue adds a further layer of complexity that affects not only a coach's ability to attain self-knowledge but also other parties' ability to know the "core" of the coach. In addition, this presents a challenge to the coach's ability to "read" athletes.

These issues raise questions about the processes by which coaches render judgments and decisions, especially when they must react quickly under pressure. They also pose questions for those whose philosophy of coaching emphasized practical wisdom, good judgment, and virtuous dispositions.

The situated coach

One does not live in a vacuum. We are always situated in contexts, which may function in an inchoate way until we direct our attention to them. Social psychologists, in particular, have emphasized how situations affect our behaviors without our awareness of their influence. In turn, some "situationists" have argued that character traits are neither as global nor as robust as some have heretofore held. Some psychological experiments that are used to buttress situationist claims have reached near-legendary status, such as the famous Milgram (2010) experiment.

We can debate the extent to which situations can influence behaviors while operating outside of our conscious awareness. But to the extent that they do, this has relevance for a philosophy of coaching. It does so because it implies that coaches must contend with a form of situationally induced epistemic opaqueness, since they are always situated in numerous ways, and they cannot be conscious of all of these factors at once.

We are familiar with numerous stories about coaches' gaffs, lapses, and ethical violations. To what should we attribute them? If the social psychologists are correct, we should beware of the fundamental attribution error, whereby we chalk up behavior to character traits. Instead, the psychologists tell us, we must consider the role of situations. In this regard, John Doris (2010, 205) warns of entering the "moral 'hot zone'" in which situational factors can overwhelm us. In a complementary vein, philosopher Gilbert Harman (2009) argues that we should be less concerned about educating for character, and more concerned about situating individuals for success.

Coaches often find themselves in the "moral 'hot zone'." Their responsibility is great, and their decisions are often made under pressure. While the rewards for winning can be significant, the repercussions of losing pose an existential threat. Indeed, outside pressures can make it seem as if winning and losing are the only relevant factors. This raises a fundamental question: How do we situate coaches for success more broadly defined?

Fast and slow thinking in coaching

Coaching shares features with other occupations. Coaches form judgments and render decisions under conditions of uncertainty, and often under the pressure of time. How should they proceed in order to produce sound judgments?

Research has been conducted on how people make decisions under relevantly similar conditions. Researchers vary on what they emphasize in the final analysis. This can be seen by juxtaposing the work of Gary Klein (1999) and Gerd Gigerenzer (2008), on the one hand, with the findings of Nobel Prize winner Daniel Kahneman (2011) and Amost Tversky on the other.

Klein (1999) has lauded "naturalistic decision making" employed in intuition. His findings come from studying in the field professional firefighters, nurses on neonatal units, chess masters, and others. Klein demystifies intuition and traces expertise to experience and pattern recognition. Gigerenzer's (2008) research focuses on the way we use "fast and frugal" heuristics in decision making. Under certain conditions, the results can be quite impressive.

On the other hand, Daniel Kahneman (2011) has emphasized the drawbacks of intuitive thinking and the use of the heuristics and biases method.[13] He claims that intuitive thinking can be derailed by various forms of systematic distortions. Algorithmic processes surpass intuitive thinking. Klein and Kahneman agree that claims that intuitive expertise works best where validity is high and under conditions of certainty.

Coaches embody a variety of decision making styles. At one end of the spectrum are coaches who emphasize sticking to carefully laid plans. At the other end of the theoretical spectrum are particularists, for whom each situation is unique, and who trust their intuitions.

Some coaches rely on quasi-heuristics. Consider the baseball manager who as a rule plays a right-handed pitcher against a heavily left-handed-hitting batting line-up, or the basketball coach who always orders a foul to prevent a potentially game-winning three-point basket in the waning seconds of a game, or who dictates that the basketball be placed in the hands of the player with the "hot hand." Or consider the football coach who always punts on fourth down. Some coaches cannot resist the idea that a favorite strategy will work, even in the face of contrary statistical evidence. It is like the optical illusion that we cannot help seeing, even when we know that it is an illusion.

On other occasions, an algorithmic-like approach is used. An example of this was Major League Baseball's Oakland Athletics, as chronicled in Michael Lewis's (2004) *Money Ball*. The Athletics used finely tuned statistical analyses to guide their baseball decisions.

What do these considerations suggest? First, coaches may be affected by biases that affect judgments and decisions. Second, for younger coaches, this suggests the importance of an apprenticeship, and working with experienced coaches.[14] Third, it is important for coaches at all levels to have colleagues whose alternative perspectives are respected and can represent an intrusion of reality.

The "hidden brain" in the game

Forming a backdrop for all of the considerations in Part IV has been the "hidden brain."[15] In his book *Incognito: The secret lives of the brain*, neuroscientist David Eagleman writes:

> The conscious you – the I that flickers to life when you wake up in the morning – is the smallest bit of what's transpiring in your brain. Although we are dependent on the functioning of the brain for our inner lives, it runs its own show. Most of its operations are above the security clearance of the conscious mind. The I simply has no right of entry.
>
> *(Eagleman, 2011, p. 4)*

He continues: "Whether we're talking about dilated eyes, jealousy, attraction, the love of fatty foods, or the great idea you had last week, consciousness is the smallest player in the operations of the brain" (Eagleman, 2011, p. 5).

Few seriously doubt the tight connection between the brain, on the one hand, and the mind and behavior on the other. The question is, how tight? Even if the precise mapping of neural correlates onto mental states eludes us, the idea that the nervous system is implicated is central.

I mentioned in Section I the vulnerability of the brain to injury. But another kind of vulnerability needs to be emphasized, having to do with the brain's plasticity. To the extent that coaches' interactions not only affect athlete's brains but perhaps also rewire them, this poses a new dimension of responsibility. This is what I have referred to as the "neuroethics of coaching" (Fry, 2013).

Summary

Part IV has emphasized factors that lie outside the conscious awareness of coaches, but which influence coaches' judgments and decision making. This lack of self-transparency points to the importance of the accountability of coaches, and suggests that, in the face of a modern-day cult of coaching, coaches, like all of us, are human, all too human.

Conclusion

There is much that is valuable in contemporary philosophy of coaching. At the same time, there are depths yet to be plumbed. This daunting task requires making connections across philosophical disciplines, and incorporating the empirical findings of the natural and social sciences. In this chapter, I have outlined a few directions that such inquiries and analyses might take. In doing so, I have examined coaching in the light of ethical, epistemic, and metaphysical considerations. These considerations take us beyond what I termed "coaching philosophies" to a full-blown philosophy of coaching. I also looked at social scientific and neurobiological considerations that ground our philosophical analyses in our social situatedness and embodied nature. This provided a context for coaching and the philosophy of coaching. In particular, it allowed me to reveal how what is experienced as manifest in coaching experience occurs against an inchoate background.

The philosophy of coaching as presented in this chapter is a many-layered discipline. Those with a pragmatic bent may be satisfied simply with what "works"; that is, that which secures a good win:loss ratio. But philosopher also seeks to understand. Taking this road will be unsettling for some, as it will challenge preconceived ideas that are widely shared. But as any coach worth her salt will know, the easy way is not the path to transformation and growth.

Notes

1 For an explication of "perennial philosophy," see Flanagan (2002), who in turn draws on Wilfred Sellars.
2 Phil Jackson coached professional basketball teams to a record 11 National Basketball Association championships. Still, only late in his coaching career did he emerge from a cloud of doubt about his coaching ability. Critics said that Jackson's teams should have won titles, given that players like Michael Jordan, Scottie Pippen, Shaquille O'Neal, and Kobie Bryant have filled his teams' rosters.
3 To some extent, the notion of instrumental goodness, as conceived here, has a natural home in sports. The members of a team and the coach depend on each other. There is a sense of instrumental goodness that applies to each one when each one is contributing to a common goal. However, when individual goals or goals of a sub-unit predominate, individuals become separated from a common purpose. When instrumentality becomes the primary criterion of evaluation, the temptation may be to view the members of the supporting cast as potentially replaceable "cogs in a machine." I am indebted here to Brian Schrag.
4 This is not to suggest that we should take it for granted that a coach will be either a role model in a normative sense or a "sage." See Feezell (2013).
5 I am indebted to Mike McNamee for prompting the way that I have framed the issue as one of epistemic virtue.
6 According to Kretchmar (2013), as participants grow older and advance through the ranks, the right to play meets the growing relevance of other factors. In particular, at the collegiate level, the pursuit of excellence assumes special relevance.
7 In elaborating on various positions in the next few pages, I am especially indebted to, and recommend, the introduction to the philosophy of mind by John Searle (2004). See also John Heil (2013).
8 See Searle (2004, pp. 6–27) for a succinct discussion of Descartes' views on mind and body.
9 See, for example, Searle (2002).
10 See Searle (1997), in which Chalmers stated that he was "agnostic" (p. 165) as to whether panpsychism was the correct position to hold, and added: "I do argue that panpsychism is not as unreasonable as is often supposed, and that there is no knockdown argument against it" ("Appendix": "An Exchange with David Chalmers," p. 166).

11 See Martin Buber's (1970) classic, *I and Thou*.
12 I am indebted to Mike McNamee for his helpful suggestions here.
13 Klein and Kahneman have had something of a rapprochement, and have even collaborated on a paper. But their emphases remain different.
14 Note the trend for even NBA head coaches to have a wizened veteran on the sidelines. For example, Phil Jackson had his Tex Winter.
15 I borrow the designation "hidden brain" from author and National Public Radio social science reporter Shankar Vedantum (2010).

References

Bargh, J. A. and Tanya L. Chartrand. 1999. The Unbearable Automaticity of Being. *American Psychologist*, 54 (7): 462–79.

Buber, M. 1970. *I and Thou*, translated by W. Kaufman. New York: Charles Scribner's Sons.

Doris, J. 2010. Persons, Situations, and Virtue Ethics. In *Moral Psychology: Historical and contemporary readings*, edited by T. Nadelhoffer, E. Nahamias, and S. Nichols. Chichester: Wiley-Blackwell, 197–209.

Eagleman, D. M. 2011. *Incognito: The secret lives of the brain*. New York: Pantheon.

Encyclopaedia Brittanica 2013. "Yogi Berra." *Encyclopaedia Brittanica*, October 30. Available online at www.britannica.com/EBchecked/topic/62684/Yogi-Berra (accessed October 22, 2014).

Feezell, R. 2013. *Sport, Philosophy and Good Lives*. Lincoln, NE: University of Nebraska Press.

Flanagan, O. 2002. *The Problem of the Soul: Two visions of mind and how to reconcile them*. New York: Basic Books.

Fry, J. P. 2000. Coaching a Kingdom of Ends. *Journal of the Philosophy of Sport*, 27: 51–62.

Fry, J. P. 2013. The Neuroethics of Coaching. In *The Ethics of Coaching Sports: Moral, social, and legal Issues*, edited by R. L. Simon. Boulder, CO: Westview, 151–66.

Gigerenzer, G. 2008. *Gut Feelings: The intelligence of the unconscious*. New York: Penguin.

Hardman, A. R. and Jones, C. 2011. *The Ethics of Sports Coaching*. Abingdon: Routledge

Harman, G. 2009. Skepticism About Character Traits. *Journal of Ethics*, 13, 235–42.

Heil, J. 2013. *Philosophy of Mind: A contemporary introduction*. 3rd ed. Abingdon: Routledge.

Kahneman, D. 2011. *Thinking, Fast and Slow*. New York: Farrar, Straus, and Giroux.

Kant, I. 1964. *Groundwork of the Metaphysic of Morals*, translated by H. J. Paton. New York: Harper and Row.

Klein, G. 1999. *Sources of Power: How people make decisions*. Cambridge, MA: MIT Press.

Kihlstrom, J. F. 2008. The Automaticity Juggernaut – Or, Are we Automatons After All? In *Are We Free: Psychology and free will*, edited by J. Baer, J. C. Kaufman, and R. F. Baumeiester. Oxford: Oxford University Press, 155–80.

Kretchmar, S. 2013. Bench Players: Do Coaches Have a Moral Obligation to Play Benchwarmers? In *The Ethics of Coaching: Moral, social, and legal issues*, edited by R. L. Simon. Boulder, CO: Westview, 121–36.

Lewis, M. 2004. *Moneyball*. New York: W. W. Norton.

Loland. S. 2011. The Normative Aims of Coaching: The good coach as an enlightened generalist. In *The Ethics of Sports Coaching*, edited by A. R. Hardman and C. Jones. Abingdon: Routledge, 15–22.

McNamee, M. 2011. Celebrating Trust: Virtues and rules in the ethical conduct of sports coaches. In *The Ethics of Sports Coaching*, edited by A. R. Hardman and C. Jones. Abingdon: Routledge, 23–41.

Milgram, S. 2010. Behavioral Study of Obedience. In *Moral Psychology: Historical and contemporary readings*, edited by T. Nadelhoffer, E. Nahamias, and S. Nichols. Chichester: Wiley-Blackwell, 179–86.

Morgan, W. J. 2013. Interpretivism, Conventionalism, and the Ethical Coach. In *The Ethics of Coaching Sports: Moral, social, and legal issues*, edited by R. L. Simon. Boulder, CO: Westview, 61–77.

Rahner, K. 2010. Religious Inclusivism. In *Philosophy of Religion: Selected readings*, 4th ed., edited by M. Peterson, W. Hasker, B. Reichenbach, and D. Basinger. Oxford: Oxford University Press, 588–96.

Russell, J. S. 2004. Taking Umpiring Seriously: How philosophy can help umpires make the right calls. In *Baseball and Philosophy: Thinking outside the batter's box*, edited by E. Bronson. Chicago: Open Court, 87–103.

Ryle, G. 1949. *The Concept of Mind*. London: Hutchinson.

Searle, J. 1997. *The Mystery of Consciousness*. New York: New York Review of Books.

Searle, J. 2002. Can Computers Think? In *Philosophy of Mind: Classical and contemporary readings*, edited by D. J. Chalmers. New York: Oxford University Press: 669-675.

Searle, J. 2004. *Mind: A brief introduction*. Oxford: Oxford University Press.

Simon, R. L. 2010. *Fair Play: The ethics of sport*, 3rd ed. Boulder, CO: Westview.

Simon, R. L. 2013. The Ethical Coach: An Interpretive Account of the Ethics of Coaching. In *The ethics of coaching: Moral, social, and legal issues*, edited by R. L. Simon. Boulder, CO: Westview, 41–59.

Strawson, G. 2008. Realistic Monism: Why physicalism entails panpsychism (plus appendix). From *Real Materialism and Other Essays*. Oxford: Clarendon.

Turkle, S. 2011. *Alone Together: Why we expect more from technology and less from each other*. New York: Basic Books.

Vedantum, S. 2010. *The Hidden Brain: How our unconscious minds elect presidents, control markets, wage wars, and save our lives*. New York: Spiegel and Grau.

von Wright, G. H. 1996. *The Varieties of Goodness*. Bristol: Thoemmes.

Wilson. T. D. 2002. *Strangers to Ourselves: Discovering the adaptive unconscious*. Cambridge, MA: Belknap.

Further reading

Cassidy, T., R. Jones and P. Potrac. 2009. *Understanding Sports Coaching: The social, cultural, and pedagogical foundations of coaching practice*. London: Routledge.

Clifford, C., and R. M. Feezell. 1997. *Coaching for Character*. Champaign, IL: Human Kinetics.

Jones, R., K. Armour, and P. Potrac. 2004. *Sports Coaching Cultures: From practice to theory*. London: Routledge.

Lyle, J. 2002. *Sports Coaching Concepts: A framework for coaches' behavior*. London: Routledge.

26

SPECTATORSHIP – WATCHING AND FOLLOWING SPORT

Carwyn Jones

According to Santayana "Athletic sports are not children's games; they are public spectacles ... Spectators are indispensable, since without them the victory, which should be the only reward, would lose half its power" (in McNamee 2008: 49). Goods like glory and honour in sport seem to depend on the presence of spectators. Spectators themselves might be watching sport for a variety of motives. One might think of spectatorship from a subjective and objective point of view. The first might consider the personal experience of the spectator, the psychological states of mind such as enjoyment and excitement which motivate them to watch sport. The latter might consider what role spectators play in sport more generally, what contribution they make to the practice of sport, how their behaviour affects our experience of sport. In this chapter, I discuss some token spectator types and pick out some key conceptual and ethical ideas therein. After briefly exploring the gambler, perhaps the original spectator at sports contests, who watches to see if his/her wager is successful, I discuss different conceptions and manifestations of the sports fan. The sport fan comes in various guises, but I focus on two types commonly referred to in the literature, namely the loyal and dedicated *partisan* whose allegiance is to a particular team and the *purist* who is looking to enjoy the spectacle of sport without a particular allegiance. I discuss the conceptual and ethical dimensions and interrogate the relative ethical merits of both types. Finally, I discuss the sporting patriot and the vices of excessive partisanship.

The gambler

A number of people watch sports because they have bet on the result. The very existence of some sports seems to depend on the fact that spectators gamble on the result; for example, horse racing or Kirin bicycle racing in Japan. Spectators may or may not form allegiances with certain performers (horses, jockeys, cyclists) but their main reasons for attending or for taking an interest in the activity is focused on their wager. They will experience tension, anticipation and risk, but only if they have placed a bet. More recently, the deregulation of the gambling industry in the United Kingdom and the development of the internet have opened up countless new opportunities to bet on sports. It is not merely the result that counts these days because individuals can bet on discrete features of contests such as the timing of the first goal, the exact score, who scores first, and almost any other aspect of the game.

Although some gamblers have encyclopaedic knowledge about their sport, their interest in it as gamblers is whether or not events unfold in a way that maximises the return on their stake. Some gamblers do not even need to watch the sport; they are simply concerned with the result. It is important for sport, and for the gambling industry, that the outcomes of contests (or certain elements within the contest) are not predetermined. [Although betting on sport might be seen as potentially corruptive and parasitic upon nobler endeavours, it played a significant part in the development of modern sport.] According to Elias:

> Greater emphasis on the enjoyment of the game-contest and the tension-excitement it provided as such, was to some extent connected with the enjoyment of betting which, in England, played a considerable part both in the transformation of "cruder" forms of game-contests into sports and in the development of the ethos of fairness…But the prospect of winning one's bet could add to the excitement of watching the struggle only if the initial odds of winning were more or less evenly divided between the two sides.
>
> *(Elias 1971: 101–2)*

Despite the partly historic positive role played by gambling in the development of sporting structures and the ethos of fair play, the presence of gambling in sport has a significant and potentially 'venal' (Walsh and Giulianotti 2007, 17) influence on the activity. The lure of money, the extrinsic rewards, can provide motivation for players to focus on priorities other than sporting excellence. Boxers have been paid to 'take a dive', horses have been 'nobbled' (disabling a racehorse, usually with drugs), referees have been bribed and players have thrown games. Match fixing is a serious and increasingly common corruption of sport, given the billions of dollars at stake in the gambling industry. Former Pakistan cricket captain Salman Butt was jailed for 30 months for his role in a conspiracy to manipulate events in a cricket match in England in 2010.[1] It could be argued that, in a game like cricket, the validity of the contest was not necessarily under threat or, at least, the risk was low in this case because the action (performing a sequence of 'no-balls' [illegal pitches] at a predetermined time in the match) would have little impact on the actual result. Nevertheless, he performed a certain sequence of actions at predetermined times such that a wager was won. [Manipulation of events within a contest but not necessarily affecting the result of the contest is known as 'spot fixing'.] There are other issues with gambling, of course. The Columbian football player Andrés Escobar was murdered in 1994 after inadvertently putting the ball into his own net (scoring an own goal), which contributed to his team's defeat. The motive for his shooting was allegedly related to gambling losses.[2]

Gambling in general, and in sport in particular, is normally a highly regulated activity and, for some, it can be a cause of great harm, financially and otherwise. It can become what Flanagan (2011) calls a 'process addiction'. John Daly (2007: 209), the American Golfer, estimates he lost US$55 million at casinos over a period of 15 years and many English Premier League football players are said to spend vast fortunes on gambling.[3] Gambling on sport can therefore provide the reason for taking an interest in certain activities (horse racing) and thus can sustain an arguably economically and culturally important social practice: it can also be an enjoyable addition to the sporting experience or can serve as 'just something to bet on' for gamblers largely indifferent to the nature and quality of the event. The presence of gambling in sport is, however, forever a threat to the integrity of contests but, increasingly (following the demise of tobacco and alcohol sponsorship in certain countries), betting companies provide significant sponsorship of sport; a kind of unholy alliance.

The fan

The fan is perhaps the most common watcher of sport who may or may not also bet on the result of the contest. Fans come in various guises. Some fans identify with a particular sport and more specifically with a particular team. In Europe in general, and in the UK in particular, there is a deep-rooted culture of supporting football (soccer) teams such as Manchester United or Barcelona. Such fans are often initiated into the culture of fandom from an early age and identify strongly with a particular club. This type of watcher is perhaps most commonly associated with team sports. There is another type of fan who watches individual sports, such as tennis. They may form allegiances to certain players on the grounds of nationality but they may equally be formed on the basis of an individual's skill, flair or personality. What both have in common is a primary concern for the victory of their team or player. Their experience of watching and their enjoyment is tied up in the fortunes of the player or team they are supporting. They are happy when they win, miserable when they lose.

The partisan fan ≠ purist

The concept of fan has received plenty of philosophical scrutiny in the literature (Davis 2012; Dixon 2007; Jones 2003; Mumford 2004; Russell 2012). A distinction has been drawn between two fan types, namely the partisan and the purist.

The partisan is a loyal supporter of a team to which she may have a personal connection or which she may have grown to support by dint of mere familiarity. The purist in contrast, supports the team that he thinks exemplifies the highest virtues of the game, but his allegiance is flexible (Dixon 2007: 441).

Partisan allegiance

A necessary condition of the partisan is that they have an allegiance to a particular team. There may be some partisans whose allegiance is to an individual player; for example, British tennis fans' allegiance to Andy Murray and previously to Tim Henman but, as Mumford (2012: 132) argues, this is a different type of allegiance because, in relation to an individual (as opposed to a team), one cannot be a part of 'that which I would support'. I do not focus on fans of individual sport or fans whose allegiance is to a national team in this section (the latter will be dealt with under the discussion of patriotism later in this chapter). Rather, I focus on partisan fans who identify with a particular team. A necessary condition of being a partisan is allegiance to a particular team but it is not clear whether any further necessary conditions can be identified. There may be some family resemblances but no additional essential features. At some point, every partisan's allegiance was formed (or perhaps evolved) but the genesis of the allegiance might differ from fan to fan. Local ties and or family loyalty are a common source but a good friend of mine and a passionate fan of Sunderland Football Club for over 50 years was initially attracted by the colour of the team's jerseys. Another friend decided at a young age to support the arch rivals of his brother's favourite team. According to Mumford (2012: 15), the reason for team allegiance can be random and, therefore, not rationally based: 'It seems, therefore, that the partisan often has no good reason for selecting one team to follow rather than another, other than some accident of circumstance'.

Although all fans have an allegiance, whose genesis might differ, they commonly demonstrate their allegiance or involvement in different ways. Some are official members of a club and attend every game, forsaking other commitments, some compose and sing songs and chants, some form supporters' clubs and fanzines, others may watch from a distance on television, some choose to emblazon themselves in the colours of the team or even permanent tattoos, others may demonstrate their allegiance more discreetly, and some may even propose to their partners or get married at their team's stadium and name their children after favourite players. According to Russell (2012: 24), forming sporting allegiances has evolutionary antecedents and is an expression of a human instinct to form attachments to groups. Additionally, he argues that humans are 'meaning-seeking creatures who pursue meaning largely through narratives' (ibid: 25). This helps to explain why fans follow teams in which their own narratives are intertwined with the narrative of the team they support. Experiences and memories are shared and recounted. Sights, sounds and smells are recalled, such as our first visit to the stadium, our first replica team kit and the smell of hotdogs. The fans' chronology can be measured in terms of the team's fortunes; for example: 'I can remember my daughter was born in 1986 because that's the year we won the cup' or 'I got married on the day we beat the Yankees'. For many fans, following a team is fundamental to the good life and one's mood reflects the fortunes of the team – we are happy when they win, sad when they lose and angry if they lose unjustly!

The good partisan

It is sometimes difficult to separate descriptive accounts of fans from conceptual accounts. As a matter of empirical fact, there are very different types of fans, all variously committed to their team. In the literature and in fan and media discourse, there is a sense that certain types of fans are normatively superior to others. The label given to the best type of fan depends on who is making the judgment but such labels include *loyal* fans, *real* fans, *traditional* fans, *ideal* fans, *good* fans, *true* fans, *dedicated* fans, partisans and moderate partisans. *Bad* types of fans might be referred to as *fair-weather* fans, plastic fans, fickle fans, fanatics and *extreme* fans. Claims and counter claims are made about club X's fans or sport Y's fans being better fans than club A's and sport B's fans. Are such criteria subjective? Does the amount of noise that a group of fans make really make them better fans? Are fans that create an intimidating atmosphere for the opposition and make the home field a 'fortress', superior in any way? Within fan cultures, the best fans should exhibit qualities like loyalty, commitment, passion and dedication evidenced in a variety of (sometimes dubious) attitudes and behaviours. Morris (2012) argues that most typical fan behaviour (shouting, cheering, chanting, and so forth) which is aimed at (or has the foreseeable consequence of) affecting the outcome of a contest in their team's favour (encouraging our team, disrupting theirs) undermine fairness and ought to be discouraged.

Yet despite what seems a prima facie rational objection to much of fan culture, others (beyond the confines of those cultures) argue that there are grounds, in fact normative grounds, for preferring one type of fan over others. The claim is that being a certain type of fan is better, not only subjectively in terms of self-actualisation and enjoyment as a fan but also objectively in terms of contributing to the wellbeing of clubs in particular and sports in general. One important quality (already mentioned above) that seems to be a fundamental criterion of the best type of fan is loyalty (Walsh and Giulianotti 2001; Dixon 2007). Dixon argues that fan loyalty is virtuous for at least two reasons. First, loyalty to a particular team is important because it sustains a team as a viable concern financially and otherwise. According to Morgan (1994: 236), 'the community specific to practices like sport is an internal good of its practice'. Walsh and Giulianotti (2001) argue that the internal good of community can only be generated by the presence of loyal fans. The absence of loyal fans is therefore considered to be potentially detrimental to the existence of particular teams (institutions) and ultimately to the sport itself. The second reason that Dixon gives that loyalty to sports teams is a virtue which trades on an

404

analogy with loyalty in romantic relations. His argument is that a fan's allegiance and loyalty to their team is similar to a romantic relationship with a beloved. Commitment over time to one's partner despite certain changes, and unwillingness to 'trade up' for someone better, are attributes shared by fans who stick by their team through difficult times (Dixon 2007: 445). For Dixon then, it is the partisan that exemplifies the important and admirable qualities of loyalty.

If we consider that a fan who embodies loyalty is preferable to one who does not, we might be claiming one of two things. We might be saying that the loyal fan has a virtuous disposition(s) and the presence of virtue is grounds for preferring this fan to others who lack such a virtue (Pincoffs 1986). Or we might be claiming that the loyal fan is fulfilling an obligation *qua* fan to be loyal. Let us take these one at a time. The virtue of loyalty in Aristotelian terms is a mean between two vices; the vice of indifference, or lack of commitment on the one hand (perhaps only supporting the team when things are good or even 'trading up' [Dixon 2007]) and the vice of blind loyalty on the other. That there is a vice of deficiency requires careful consideration because it is not so obvious why it is a vice not to form loyal attachments to a team. After all, it is a matter of choice whether we support teams and it might seem strange to accuse someone of a vice if they fail to exhibit the relevant levels of loyalty and commitment. The arbitrary nature of identification with a particular team, however, does not, according to Mumford (2012, 15), render "the allegiance, bond and attachment … lesser". Furthermore, fans are supporting an entity of which they are an important part. Nevertheless, Mumford fails to see why a lack of allegiance and loyalty to a team should be considered a vice or a failure to fulfil an obligation to one's peers. Russell (2012) is also sceptical about loyalty as grounds for preferring Dixon's partisan. The analogy of loyalty to a team with loyalty to a partner (beloved) does not, Russell argues, in itself show that fan loyalty is admirable in the same way. Although there are some parallels between the two types of loyalty, he argues that they are not significant or deep enough to warrant Dixon's conclusion. Fan relationships, he argues, are not genuine partnerships in the same way as romantic relationships because they do not involve the relation of a *we* that is destroyed if the relationship ends. He concludes that 'Relations of romantic love are so profoundly personal, immediate and reciprocal that they are fundamentally different from a partisan fan's frequently abstract and distant connections with a particular team' (Russell 2012: 20).

If we consider loyalty as a virtue some slightly different questions might arise. Crucially, we might enquire how such an obligation could arise. Both loyalty as a virtue and an obligation must stand in some relation to the role of being a fan. In other words, loyalty is admirable/obligatory in virtue of some role/function a fan might play and its presence better enables the fulfilment of that role/function. As mentioned above, there is a real sense among fan groups and in the literature that such roles, obligations or expectations exist and that a failure to meet them means one is not a fan at all. These might include levels of expected commitment, knowledge, passion and meeting the requirements of a variety of norms and conventions which are thought to be definitive of being a fan or a good fan. 'Best type of fans' purportedly engage in certain positive club-sustaining behaviour and refrain from behaviour that might undermine the fortunes of their club and sport. Such behaviour is thought to be connected in an important way to one's role as a fan. As mentioned above, the fan plays a role in sustaining the practice in many ways. Walsh and Giulianotti (2001) argue that the best type of fan has a significant role in the flourishing of practices and such fans contribute to the internal goods of sport in an important way. Moreover they argue that the connection between the fan and the club is a deeply rooted one, and in some cases 'the most committed groups of traditional fans view their support as a kind of unbreakable social contract' (ibid: 62). Moreover Giulianotti (2002, 33) argues that for some fans showing support 'is considered to be obligatory' because individuals 'have relationships with the club that resemble those with one's family and friends', a kind of unconditional bond stronger than the bond formed in romantic relations. It seems plausible, if fans have such an important role and/or are engaged in some form of reciprocal relationship with a club, that loyalty is indeed admirable and perhaps obligatory.

Russell sees an inherent confusion about talk of an ideal type of fan in this way, although there is no doubt that fans play a role; for example, the increasing fan base of Manchester United plays a *role* in their success. The fan's vocal and financial support has a causal role in the success of the team in particular and of the club in general. Conversely, fans unwilling to commit their time and effort to the ailing local club can have causal implications for its continued existence. Fans all have 'meaningful connections and attachments with each other and form a meaningful community through their common attachment to sport' (Russell 2012: 26). But this does not entail that they have a *role* in a more substantive sense. Unlike the role of judge or teacher, the role of fan does not require the recognition of 'certain moral obligations that are internal or intrinsic to any role they play or fulfil' (ibid: 18). In other words, there are no special role-related requirements or obligations which provide us with criteria for evaluating the moral conduct of fans. For Russell then, moral evaluation of fans character and actions 'is simply of their conduct and not of whether they are properly performing a role' (ibid: 18). Fans should adhere to principles like respect and common decency and should avoid the vices of excess, but the valorisation of loyalty, he believes, is more likely to be generative of vices than it is to insulate the fan from theses excesses.[4] I return to the vices of excess in later in this chapter when I discuss the patriotic fan. In the next section I explore the purist fan, which is often contrasted with the partisan mainly because they lack loyalty to a particular team.

The purist

The purist is often contrasted with the partisan, although, as we shall see, it is not a contrast that is universally endorsed. It is also worth noting that the difference between the two is perhaps better conceived in terms of the way they watch sport, or as Mumford (2012: 9) argues, what they see. The partisan and purist, he argues 'see a different game, even when they are present at the same event'. It is not possible to fully do justice to Mumford's claim here, but we can at least scratch the surface of such a distinction. We have already seen that the partisan is a fan of a team, whereas, according to Mumford (2012), the purist is a fan of a sport. Mumford's purist is different than Dixon's purist, the former having no preference for either team to win, but wanting both to excel, where the latter, Mumford claims, switches allegiance to the team which best exemplifies the excellences of the sport at any given point. Mumford's purist supports no team at all but wants to see the contest in all its beauty and drama. Such a fan wants to see the 'highest virtues of the sport succeed and be rewarded' (ibid: 14) but they are indifferent to which team displays those virtues. In fact, the ideal for the purist is that both display the virtues. Mumford (2012: 14) argues that 'A true supporter of the virtues of the sport could have no team allegiance because, in any game or passage of play, which team plays virtuously could alternate rapidly'. The purist is a different kind of fan; a fan of the sport, but who can 'love it as much as the partisan loves their team' (ibid: 14) with no allegiance to a team. The purist values the sport itself and 'and wants to see it played in the best way possible' (ibid: 16). When purists are unshackled from the concerns of the partisan for their own team, they are free to enjoy the full range of pleasures, especially the aesthetic pleasures, which may pass the partisan by.[5] According to Mumford (ibid: 17), 'A concern with the mere result looks a crude measure of the worth of a game' in comparison to the range of other qualities on display.

As we have seen above, Dixon and Walsh and Giulianotti argue that partisanship is a fundamental good of watching sport. It displays the virtue of loyalty and in so doing contributes to the flourishing of the practice community and therefore to the sport. Moreover, such attachment is important to get the full enjoyment from the game, the excitement, the tension, the competitive struggle. As such, the detachment of the purist is purportedly inferior both morally and in terms of the pleasure available from watching. Mumford (2012) defends the purist against such criticism. He denies that the purist exhibits vice by failing to form loyal allegiances and argues that wanting all teams to flourish and exhibit excellence 'does not seem like an especially vicious stance' (ibid: 16). Moreover, such a stance is less likely to lead to the vices that often accompany partisan support.[6] Neither does the purist's stance, according to Mumford, deny the possibility of experiencing the tension and excitement of the contest nor the psychological benefits such as esteem associated with 'belonging'. Mumford makes a case for the superiority of a purist stance in watching sport in terms of the broader range of aesthetic value available to the spectator. Such values, particularly when manifest by rivals, might be missed by the partisan. 'The purist is someone who has this aesthetic mode switched on most of the time, looking at the sporting contest aesthetically' (ibid: 57). They are watching sport for its own sake, for the demonstration of skill, the 'sweet tension of uncertainty of outcome' (Loland 2002), the effort and endeavour of the athletes, and not for any contingent pleasure a victory against arch rivals might bring. According to Mumford, the aesthetic experiences that the purist enjoys include beautiful body movements, the physical form of the athlete, poise, balance, precision, symmetry, rhythm, power, strength, the grace, elegance and fluidity of a skilled move, swiftness of foot, inventiveness, efficiency and complex tactical patterns.[7] Each sport is different; thus, there is a plurality of aesthetic experiences to be had.

There is no space here to offer a full defence of the purist stance in sport (Mumford makes an excellent and persuasive job of this) but I offer some remarks about the relative merits of the purist and the partisan. First, it seems to me that without the partisan fans there would be nothing for the purist to watch. The very spectacle of sport (team sport in particular) relies on individuals making a commitment to the team or club. The purist is in some way parasitic upon the efforts, commitments and loyalties of partisan fans. Without the partisans, there would be no practice community (or a significantly impoverished one), which generates the games, players and ultimately the aesthetic spectacle enjoyed by the purist and partisans alike. Walsh and Giulianotti (2001) are particularly concerned with a breed of fan they call *arrivistes*. The *arriviste*, they argue, comes to games through 'its mediation, such as on television, and employs that lack of personal engagement to create "distinction" (typically class-rooted) from those who are allegedly too parochial to read the game's fineries' (Walsh and Giulianotti: 65). The *arriviste* allegedly threatens the traditional partisan fans because of their increased capacity to fund their consumption.[8] Second is the question of the purists 'eye' for the aesthetic values. Walsh and Giulianotti argue that cultivating an appreciation of the game's intrinsic values comes through immersion in loyal fan (partisan) culture. The partisans are the ones likely to have developed the 'eye' for the game and it is precisely their (loyal fans) 'deep and socialized immersion in the sport, as expressed in part through support for the club and its players that makes possible a "purist" appreciation of the sport's laws, spirit and aesthetic codes' (Walsh and Giulianotti 2001: 65). Mumford's own biography is of partisan turned purist, and one might speculate whether his love and appreciation for the game of football were cultivated during his days as a partisan.

The patriot

While watching the 2012 Olympic Games taekwondo competition with my mother (who gets very excited and loud when watching sport), it dawned on me that she was cheering for, and verbally abusing, the wrong contestant. Given that a British competitor might be fighting in red in one bout, and blue the next, she had failed to recognise which competitor was British. When I pointed this out to her, she continued with her vociferous support and abuse but switched the targets without much pause. It is clear that, in that context, the only motivating factor for her support was patriotism. She knew nothing of the sport, nothing (not even the names) of the contestants, yet was fully immersed in watching the unfolding contest and felt great pride when the British fighter won. According to Dixon, a key element in patriotism in sport is that fans identify with their country's success on the playing field. For Dixon,

> Indeed, the sight of athletes giving their all when representing their country while being willed on by their adoring compatriots seems to be not only an exemplar of the virtues that sport makes possible but also a paradigm case of healthy, morally justi-fiable patriotism.
>
> *(Dixon 2001: 74)*

Patriotism in sport is familiar, and most global sporting events such as the football World Cup and the Olympic and Paralympic Games are contested between representatives of countries. Much has been written about sport, patriotism and national identity but perhaps Orwell's (2003: 196) description of international sport as 'mimicking warfare' encapsulates concerns about the potential for vice in international sporting contests. The vices with which Orwell was concerned are prone to appear not only among patriots but also among partisan support-ers more generally. The kind of vices that troubled Orwell are described by Davis as the 'fag end of masculinity' and include:

> Spiteful aggression; petty hatreds, enmities and grudges; pleasure in the pain and misfortunes of the other; childish one-upmanship; the worship of dominative strength and power, misogyny; homophobia; and the gamut of -isms, including sexism, racism, anti-intellectualism, philistinism, hooliganism and hedonism.
>
> *(Davis 2012: 5)*

In the context of international sport, we might add jingoism and xenophobia to the list. Earlier, I discussed the virtue of loyalty and the vices of excess and deficiency. Many of the behaviours and vices of concern here seem to be grounded on excessive loyalty, partisanship or patriotism. The corollary of this excess seems to be a moral disregard or a failure to respect opponents (play-ers, coaches, fans and, by association, nations). Dixon (2001) argues that often the excesses can manifest themselves in callous disregard for one's own athletes. Fans of the Brazilian football club Palmeiras attacked their own players at the airport following their loss in a cup competition.[9] Although there is broad agreement in the literature that respect is an important moral principle in sport, there is debate about what constitutes disrespect and what forms it takes.[10] Dixon (2001, 2007) argues that partisan support (either for club or country) need not take the excessive forms discussed above often reported in the media (and written about by sport historians, sociologist and ethicists). A moderate form of partisan support is the ideal and the moderate partisan or patriot neither manifests the vice of deficiency nor excess with respect to their allegiance.

The ideal attitude for fans, then, appears to be the tenacious loyalty of the partisan, tempered by the purist's realization that teams that violate the rules or spirit of the game do not deserve our support (Dixon 2007: 445).

One might propose 'purism' as an antidote to the partisan patriot, however, as suggested above, since the presence and commitments of patriots are arguably crucial to the existence and persistence of international competitions like the football World Cup and the Olympics.

Conclusion

Sport is watched at every level whether it be by the doting parent on the school field or the thousands crammed like sardines into the terraces at football grounds or the millions watching on satellite television. In this chapter, I have attempted to explore the conceptual and moral features of a few token types of spectators. As a matter of empirical truth, the felt experience of spectators and the strength and power of their involvement might vary greatly. It is claimed that although individuals can have radically different subjective experiences when watching sport, some forms of watching are thought to be normatively preferable to others on a number of grounds. Some claim that attachment to a team is necessary both to sustain sporting practices and to fully experience the excitement and competitive intensity of sport. Others dispute this claim, proffering an alternative detached aesthetic stance as the best way to experience the value of watching sport. Having too much of a concern with the victor, either because we have bet on their success or because we have a partisan attachment to the winner, can result in vice which can corrupt both the individual and the practice itself. What is certain is that watching sport can bring out the worst as well as the best in us, and keeping Aristotle's 'golden mean' in mind should help us avoid the vices of excess and deficiency.

Notes

1 See 'Salman Butt and Pakistan bowlers jailed for no-ball plot', *BBC News*, 3 November 2011. Available online at www.bbc.co.uk/news/uk-15573463 (accessed 23 October 2014).

2 See Barry Glendinning, 'World Cup: 25 stunning moments … No. 7: Andrés Escobar's deadly own goal', *Guardian*, 25 March 2014. Available online at www.theguardian.com/football/blog/2014/mar/25/world-cup-moments-andres-escobar-death (accessed 23 October 2014).

3 Professional Footballers' Association, 'Players "Using Loans to Fund Bets"', *TheFPA.com*, 24 October 2013. Available online at www.thepfa.com/news/2013/10/24/players-using-loans-to-fund-bets (accessed 23 October 2014).

4 See Jones (2003), who problematizes a romantic and perhaps uncritical view of certain fan groups as custodians of the game.

5 Mumford's (2012) key claim in his book is that sport has aesthetic value and the purist is a spectator who watches sport to enjoy and experience its aesthetic value.

6 In the next section, I outline an argument that such vices are contingently (historically) associated with partisan support but are not necessary associations.

7 Tännsjö (2001) argues that the very idea of admiring sporting heroes is morally dubious; in his words, it displays fascistic tendencies.

8 The *arriviste* and the traditional fan are sociological categories that can be mapped to a class structure, which Walsh and Giulianotti (2001) and Giulianotti (1999) argue is central to fan culture. Roy Keane infamously criticised sections of the Manchester United supporters, referring to them as the 'prawn sandwich brigade' – fans in corporate boxes. He is reported to have said, "I don't think some of the people who come to Old Trafford can spell football, never mind understand it'; see 'Angry Keane slates Man Utd fans', *BBC Sport Online*, 9 November 2000. http://news.bbc.co.uk/sport1/hi/football/champions_league/1014868.stm (accessed 23 October 2014). See Jones (2003) for a critical discussion of the conceptual validity of the distinction.

9 See 'Palmeiras Fans Attack Own Team', *SBS*, 8 March 2013. Available online at http://theworldgame.sbs.com.au/news/1143296/palmeiras-fans-attack-own-team (accessed 23 October 2014).

10 For example, McNamee (2003), Dixon (2008), Summers (2007) and Jones and Fleming (2007).

References

Aristotle (1980) *Nichomachean Ethics*, Oxford: Oxford University Press, (trans) W. D, Ross (updated J. O. Urmson and J. L. Ackrill).

Daly, J. (2007) *My Life In and Out of The Rough*. London: Harper Sport.

Davis, P. (2012) The Ladies of Besiktas: An example of moral and ideological ambiguity? *Sport, Ethics and Philosophy* 6 (1): 4–15.

Dixon, N. (2001) A Justification of Moderate Patriotism in Sport. In T. Tännsjö and C. Tamburrini (eds), *Values in Sport*. London: Routledge, 74–86.

Dixon, N. (2007) The Ethics of Supporting Sports Teams in W. J. Morgan (ed.) *Ethics in Sport*, 2nd ed. Champaign. IL: Human Kinetics, 441–50.

Dixon, N. (2008) Trash Talking as Irrelevant to Athletic Excellence: Response to Summers. *Journal of the Philosophy of Sport* 35: 90–6.

Elias, N. (1971) The Genesis of Sport as a Sociological Problem. In E. Dunning, (ed.) *The Sociology of Sport*. London: Frank Cass, 88–115.

Flanagan, O. (2011) What Is It Like to Be an Addict? In J. Poland and G. Graham (eds), *Addiction and Responsibility*. Cambridge, MA: MIT Press, 269–92.

Giulianotti, R. (1999) *Football: A sociology of the global game*. Cambridge: Polity.

Giulianotti, R. (2002) 'Supporters, Followers, Fans, and Flaneurs: A taxonomy of spectator identities in football'. *Journal of Sport and Social Issues* 26 (1): 25-46

Jones, C. (2003) The Traditional Football Fan: An ethical critique of a selective construction. *Journal of the Philosophy of Sport* 30 (1): 37–50.

Jones, C. and Fleming, S. (2007) 'I'd Rather Wear a Turban than a Rose': The (in) appropriateness of terrace chanting amongst sport spectators. *Race, Ethnicity and Education* 10, (4): 401–14.

Loland, S. (2002) *Fair Play in Sport: A moral norm system*. London: Routledge.

McNamee, M. J. (2003) Schadenfreude in Sport: Envy, justice and self esteem, *Journal of the Philosophy of Sport* 30 (1): 1–16.

McNamee, M. J. (2008) *Sports, Virtues and Vices*. Abingdon: Routledge.

Morgan, W. J. (1994) *Leftist Theories of Sport: A critique and reconstruction*. Urbana, IL: University of Illinois Press.

Morris, S.P. (2012) The Limit of Spectator Interaction. *Sport, Ethics and Philosophy* 6 (1): 46–60.

Mumford, S. (2004) Allegiance and Identity. *Journal of the Philosophy of Sport* 31 (2): 184–95.

Mumford, S. (2012) *Watching Sport: Aesthetics, ethics and emotion*. Abingdon: Routledge.

Orwell, G. (2003) The Sporting Spirit. In *Shooting an Elephant*. London: Penguin, 195–200.

Pincoffs, E. L. (1986) *Quandaries and Virtues, Against Reductivism in Ethics*. Lawrence, KS: University Press of Kansas.

Russell, J. (2012) The Ideal Fan or Good Fans? *Sport, Ethics and Philosophy* 6 (1): 16–30.

Summers, C. (2007) Ouch … You Just Dropped the Ashes. *Journal of the Philosophy of Sport* 34: 68–76.

Tännsjö, T, (2001) Is it Fascistoid to Admire Sports Heroes? In T. Tännsjö and C. Tamburrini (eds), *Values in Sport*. London: Routledge, 9–23.

Walsh, A. J. and Giulianotti, R. (2001) This Sporting Mammon: A normative critique of the commodification of sport. *Journal of the Philosophy of Sport* 28: 53–77.

Walsh, A. J. and Giulianotti, R. (2007) *Ethics Money and Sport: This sporting Mammon*. Abingdon: Routledge.

27

SPORT, COMMERCE AND
THE MARKET

Adrian Walsh

Introduction

Over the past 50 years, we have witnessed a revolution in the organisation and social understanding of elite sport. Elite sport has been commercialised. Top-level athletes have become
professionals who often receive remarkable levels of income and sporting events, such as the
World Cup, are multi-billion dollar exercises that attract enormous levels of sponsorship. Many
sports, such as cricket, have been substantially revamped in order to make them more appealing to mass audiences and, accordingly, more beneficial to sponsors and many clubs, such as
Manchester United, have become corporations in their own right.

Clearly, then, elite sport is in many cases a form of big business and its governing bodies are
ruled to a great extent by the laws of supply and demand.[1] Unsurprisingly, such commercialisation has not been without its critics. The penetration of business language into the
self-understanding of both sports administrators and sportspersons, seems to critics to be at odds
with the ideals properly associated with sport. Many sports were codified in a period of the
nineteenth century when the ideals of amateurism were at their most influential. One need
only look to the writings of the founder of the modern Olympic movement, Baron de
Coubertin, to observe highly romantic views about the fundamentally non-commercial nature
of sport properly pursued. The focus of contemporary sporting culture on the bottom line
would presumably horrify the good Baron. Equally, for many sporting enthusiasts – and this is
particularly true of followers of many team games – sport provides an escape from the mundane
realities of work and commerce that dominate our everyday lives. If the motivations of the
administrators of the club one supports, and the players who belong to that club, are too trans-
parently venal, this will undermine for many the meaning of the fixtures in which their team
engages. But equally, large-scale commercialised sporting events are among the most significant
cultural events of our age in most contemporary societies and that centrality has been brought
about, in large part, by their commercialisation.

The question, then, of the extent to which the commercialisation of sport should be
regarded in a positive light is highly contested. Those who endorse this commercialisation
point to the many benefits that have accrued to elite athletes, which enable them to pursue the
development of their skills while being financially rewarded, as well as the benefits to sports
fans who have excellent facilities in which to enjoy sporting events, excellent broadcasts to

entertain them and improved standards of play. Those critical of commercialisation, on the other hand, point to what they regard as negative consequences of the process, such as the disregard for non-commercial ideals that is so evident in many sports, the loss of connection with community meanings, the putative exploitation of athletes from developing nations and the apparent objectification of these elite sportsmen and women. While most of these critics do not wish to see money eliminated entirely from sport – although there are a minority who do – they do want constraints to be placed upon the degree to which market norms direct the development and operation of sport.

As should be clear from the preceding discussion, the central philosophical questions surrounding sport and commerce are ethical and political. In this chapter, then, the following questions, among others, will be investigated. The first of these concerns what the positive and negative features of the commercial revolution in sport might be. Secondly, could the influence of commerce undermine the spirit of sport? Might it actually corrupt sport? If so, how? Thirdly, does modern commercial sport involve exploitation in any real and significant sense? Next, should marketization be constrained? Are there some features or elements of sport that should be outside the bounds of the market? Finally, what role should the state play, if any, in policing the moral boundaries of the commercialisation of sport? In this chapter, I explore how different philosophers have responded to all of these questions.

Philosophical and economic literature on sport and commerce

Let us begin by considering the philosophical literature dealing directly with commerce and sport (which is not as extensive as one might perhaps expect). Three books that do explicitly explore the topic are Nick Hunter's *Money in Sport* (2012), Adrian Walsh and Richard Giulianotti's *Ethics, Money and Sport: This Sporting Mammon* (2007) and William Morgan's *Leftist Theories of Sport: A critique and reconstruction* (1994). The third of these works contains an extensive critical discussion of the incursions of the market into the world of sport, making use of Alasdair MacIntyre's moral distinction between the *internal* goods of practices and the *external* goods of institutions. According to Morgan, commercialisation involves moving sport from a practice into an institutionally governed activity. There are also more radical critiques from the 1970s, such as Paul Hoch's *Rip Off the Big Game: The exploitation of sport by the power elite* (1973) and J. M. Brohm's *Sport: A prison of measured time* (1978), which advocate the complete 'de-commercialisation' of sport.

While works dealing directly with commerce and sport are reasonably rare, there is an extensive literature on the ideals and values of sport, much of which has implications for commercialisation and hence provides theoretical grounds for limiting the range of the sporting market. Notable examples of this literature include Robert L. Simon's *Fair Play: The ethics of sport* (2004), Sigmund Loland's *Fair Play in Sport: A moral norm system* (2001), M.J. McNamee's *Morality Play: Sports, Virtues and Vices* (2008) and Scott Kretchmar's *Practical Philosophy of Sport* (1994).

Additionally, there is a more general literature on commercialisation and markets that can readily be applied to sport. On the left, there are various Marxist and socialist critiques of 'commodification' that reject money and the market entirely. These critiques typically concentrate on either: (i) the exploitation that capitalist social relations of production are said to institute; or (ii) the distortion of fundamental human activities in the search for further profits. There are also right-wing responses, predominant of which are the works of libertarians such as Robert Nozick, who emphasise the importance of consenting agents being able to trade as they choose, and if this involves an expansion of the market then so be it. In *Anarchy, State and*

Utopia, Nozick (1974) famously rejects the *very idea* of the state interfering in freely chosen capitalistic acts between consenting adults, and sport would be no exception to this rule. Between these two extremes, there are what we might call 'moral boundaries theorists' who argue, on a range of differing theoretical grounds, for constraining both what goods are available on the market and what kinds of things one might do with such goods when they are bought and sold on the market. Significant works here include Michael Walzer's *Spheres of Justice* (1983), Elizabeth Anderson's *Value on Ethics and Economics* (1993), Debra Satz's *Why Some Things Should Not Be for Sale: The Moral Limits of Markets* (2010) and Michael Sandel's *What Money Can't Buy* (2012).

Let us turn briefly now to the economic literature on sport. There is, in point of fact, a substantial literature on both the economics of sport and the social phenomenon of sport becoming a business. On the latter topic, it is possible to discover a remarkable amount of extant works with titles like *The Business of Sport, Football Inc.* and *The Sports Business*. The underlying philosophical view of these works is, unsurprisingly, utilitarian. The thought is the consequentialist one that we should assess the moral status of any social change in terms of its overall social outcomes and, in particular, in terms of its financial benefits. Again, unsurprisingly, most of these writers are very positive about the consequences of the commercialisation of sport, for it has led to an increase in the availability of sporting entertainments for fans, greater rewards for athletes and a general improvement in the skills exhibited in nearly all sports. Any criticism of commercialisation by such writers would be of the economic costs accrued from the provision of accompanying services by governments and of the cost to the community at large for the injuries that often are sustained by sports people. Hence, in so far as there is criticism by economists of commercialisation, it largely concerns the costs that are incurred to the community through the state provision of services required for the ongoing operation of large-scale sporting events. Beyond these utilitarian considerations, the economics literature is not particularly relevant to the questions we outlined in the introduction.

In the following sections, I explore some of the most significant normative issues surrounding the commercialisation of sport and which lead some to regard it with suspicion and, sometimes, outright hostility.

Access to the goods of sport

One common concern many have with commercialisation is that it has undesirable effects upon access for both participants in, and supporters of, sporting events. When considering the interests of spectators, the thought is that commercialisation leads to an increase in prices for entry to games in such a way that less wealthy members of the sporting community no longer have access to these goods (or at least their access is severely limited).

We see this kind of distributive concern expressed in Michael Sandel's book, *What Money Can't Buy*. Sandel discusses baseball, a game dear to his heart, which he has followed avidly since he was a young child. He notes how in recent years ticket prices have increased to such a level that it makes regular attendance more difficult for poorer members of the community. (Sandel also notes that the emergence of highly private corporate boxes affects the community atmosphere of large-scale sporting events). In Sandel's work, commercialisation of sport is seen as a genuine threat to what matters about sport because of the consequences it has for access.[2]

However, this distributive line of objection might equally seem odd to many – at least at first sight – for it might well be thought that the *relative availability* of sporting entertainment is an aspect of the impact of commercialisation that *supports* the case of the commercialisers. Present-day fans clearly have opportunities to view a great deal more sporting entertainment than was once the case; and sportsmen and women now have access to excellent training and playing facilities, the like of which earlier generations could only have dreamed. One might well run a utilitarian justification of commercialisation here to the effect that the great majority have far better access to sports events as a consequence of the commercialisation of sport.

What should we make of this? How might we resolve the apparent conflict between these two radically differing images of the distributive consequences of commercialisation. Has commercialisation been good or bad from a distributive point of view? I suggest that we can better understand the issues by considering some *normatively salient features* of the process of commercialisation itself.

Let us consider these in more detail. One of the most significant features of commercialisation, at least from the viewpoint of political philosophy, is that it transforms the system via which the valuable goods of sport are produced and distributed. Within a market system, access to a commercial good is (ideally) *contingent solely* upon possession of sufficient financial resources and this is just as true of markets in sporting 'goods' as it is elsewhere. In an important sense, the sports market is non-discriminatory in that access to, for instance, sporting events and activities, is not dependent upon one's ethnicity, religious affiliation or party membership.[3] However, market systems of distribution do in fact discriminate between those with financial resources and those without and, clearly, this is of considerable concern to many critics of commercialisation.

A second morally salient feature of commercialisation is that this process transforms the incentive structure associated with the production and distribution of goods. With the advent of a market system in sport, the profit motive comes into play and those organising sporting events now have an incentive to pursue either their own economic self-interest or that of the corporation for which they work, often to the detriment of the values that have traditionally been associated with sport. Under the profit motive, sport is organised so that the owners of sporting goods will realise maximum profits; if this means some of the less wealthy members of society are excluded, then so be it. It is not simply the fact that with the advent of commercialisation access is contingent upon wealth that is of moral concern, but that this contingency exists within a system where there is an incentive for those who organise sporting events to maximise their returns and, accordingly, this means there are pressures towards increasing prices.

It should be clear then how commercialisation might generate undesirable distributive outcomes. Whenever commercialisation leads to the exclusion from goods to which people previously had access, then this is, from a moral point of view, *prima facie* undesirable. (We might call this the 'objection from exclusion'). If commercial operators reap profits by increasing prices and in so doing access comes to be denied then this presumably provides genuine grounds for concern.

Commercialisation might generate other distributive 'pathologies'.[4] Many large-scale public sporting events were originally administered by, and expressive of the attitudes and ideas of, local communities. Yet, as the popularity of these events has increased, and they have become increasingly commercialised, these events are removed from their original roots. Sporting teams often lose touch with the communities that supported them and, thus, events that had been sites for the expression of local identity disappear. Local people find themselves no longer having a say in the decision-making processes of events and teams and, accordingly, it is often the case that local interests come to be ignored. So, for instance, Manchester United Football Club is administered as a corporation rather than as an institution that fundamentally reflects the ideals and interests of the people of Manchester. In some parts of the world, sporting franchises have shifted location entirely. Thus, for instance, the Montreal Expos basketball team played some of its home matches in Puerto Rico, before moving more permanently to Washington DC.

Presumably this 'objection from community identity' underpins some disquiet that many feel about commercialisation. At the same time, it must be said that it is doubtful that all of the blame here can be apportioned to commercialisation itself. Whenever a sport becomes highly popular and increases in scale, it is likely that community organisations will be sidelined, regardless of whether it is the state or the market that is responsible for the expansion.

A more plausible related line of objection is based upon the loss of the *inclusive democratic space* that sport once represented. It is not so much that people are excluded from sport that is the problem, as it is that many modern commercial sporting events – with their special seating for the wealthy and corporate boxes – undermines one of the great values associated with such events, namely the opportunity for people from "different walks of life" to encounter one another (Sandel 2012: 202). As Michael Sandel notes of the advent of corporate boxes in baseball, the loss of the class-mixing experience is a loss for both those looking down from the boxes as well as those not privy to such luxuries. The issue here is not so much with inequality as it with the loss of a shared experience. As Sandel notes of this phenomenon:

> Democracy does not require perfect equality; but it does require that citizens share a common life. What matters is that people from different backgrounds and social positions encounter one another, and bump up against one another, in the course of everyday life. For this is how we learn to negotiate and abide our differences, and how we come to care for the common good.
>
> *(Michael Sandel 2012: 203)*

The thinking here is that the commercialisation of sport – or at least certain aspects of that commercialisation, such as the stratification of seating – undermines the shared civic space that large-scale sporting events have traditionally fostered.

These, then, are some of the negative views about the consequences of commercialisation. However, if we reconsider the morally salient features of commercialisation we can also see why some might view the process less bleakly. The key features of commercialisation outlined involve both a transformation of the distributive mechanism and of the incentive structure. In general, one way to realise greater profits is to provide more services for more people at a cheaper price. Accordingly, if a commercial sports agency can increase the amount of entertainment available to the public then this is another strategy for increasing profits. In many cases, this has happened. There is a plethora of new sporting entertainment available to the general public that has appeared over the past 30 years. Although there remain dangers that where professional sports teams and leagues have their own viewing platforms, poorer members of society will be excluded from access, one consequence of this increased revenue is not only an improvement in the amenities for spectators but a vast improvement in the facilities and resources available for sportsmen and women.

The best outcome here would be if markets provided these extra services for both spectators and participants without excluding people from access (from price increases, for instance) to resources to which they previously had access. Obviously, this state of affairs is not impossible and will often be realised as a result of commercial agents pursuing self-interested outcomes. In the latter scenario, the community receives the benefits of markets without 'offending' against the objection from exclusion. Some proponents of commercialisation, however, might defend a utilitarian argument to the effect that if the great majority are better off through the provision of new sporting events, amenities and facilities, then we should not be concerned if a minority is excluded from access which they previously enjoyed. The claim would be that if overall utility can be increased via the commercialisation of sport then we should not concern ourselves with cases where a minority of less fortunate groups are made worse off. How one responds to this line of reasoning will, in part, be dependent upon whether one accepts the utilitarian claim that overall majority benefits can justify sacrificing the interests of the worst-off or whether one adopts a more 'Rawlsian' position in which such maximising is only acceptable if it makes the worst-off better off.

One final point to note is that determining whether access for all is the ultimate good of sporting development or alternatively whether maximising the breadth and quality of sporting events, facilities and amenities should be prioritised will be important consideration for any government bodies dealing with sport policy formation.

Meanings, motives and the ideals of sport

One striking – and often problematic feature of contemporary elite sport is the overtly commercial discourse of many athletes. When Michael Jordan famously declared, when asked about his new basketball team's chances in the National Basketball Association, that he intended to 'teach this franchise how to win', his description of the team (with the apparent emphasis on franchise rather than winning) seems remarkably removed from the language used by idealistic figures like Baron de Coubertin or even from that of many sportspeople 50 years ago. While one might naturally expect sporting companies, and perhaps sports administrators, to use the language of commerce, the language used by many elite athletes is indicative of the extent to which sport is understood as a business and, thus, reveals an apparent shift in both the *motives* of athletes and the *meaning* of sporting events which, one would imagine, would have been incongruous to earlier generations of athletes.

This brings us to another socially significant criticism of commercial sport. The idea is that such commercial understandings and attitudes are at odds with the ideals and motives internal to sport. This is the issue that I explore in this section. To what extent do the overtly economic motives of elite sportsmen and women, of businesses and of those who administer the game undermine the proper ideals of sport?

What, then, are the ideals of which we speak and, against which, some critics juxtapose contemporary commercialised sport? Typically, when critics talk in this way, it is clear that the *amateurist* ideals of the nineteenth and the first half of the twentieth century are animating their critique. Those ideals were explicitly anti-commercial and were focused on a vision that glorified sport for sport's sake. If sport is to be played in the right spirit, the central actors must, or so it is said, be driven by appropriate motives and not be primarily focused on financial gain.

The main problem with amateurism as the basis of critique – at least as it was usually explicated – is that it so imbued with a class bias towards the upper classes. Who, except the independently wealthy, can afford to devote themselves to the pursuit of excellence in sport without remuneration? (Further, although this might be a little unfair towards amateurism more generally, the English version of amateurism had explicit rules about the importance of those who were to be classified as amateurs not having worked manually in their lives.) It is not only the origins of the 'amateurist' discourse with which we should be concerned. Why think that being an amateur is a good in and of itself? We need to be able to say more about the ideals themselves and how money might transform the motivational structures of athletes. A plausible critique of the motives of contemporary sports men and women needs to answer these questions.

What ideals then should motivate sportsmen and women? Although there is no clear consensus in the philosophical literature on this – nor in the public discussion more generally – there are a number of plausible candidates, and these include: (i) fair play; (ii) the pursuit of excellence; and (iii) the exhibition of grace under pressure. The suggestion is that if a person is commercially motivated, these other motivations either disappear from their thinking or are swamped by considerations of 'Mammon'. An underlying assumption here is that these ideals are incompatible with commercial motives; hence, if an athlete is motivated by money alone, or his or her motives are dominated by financial gain, then he or she is unlikely to be motivated by, for instance, the pursuit of excellence.[5]

Critics of this view might well question whether it is true that commercial motives cannot co-exist with the aforementioned ideals, since reasons for acting are, after all, often over-determined. We regularly (and perhaps typically) have a range of reasons for pursuing any particular course of action. Why not think that sports motives can be similarly plural and include plural aims? Indeed, it is clear that many sports stars are, in point of fact, motivated both by money *and* other ideals such as breaking the world record in swimming and thus pursuing excellence.

That said, given that we value these ideals, if sport is engaged in solely for commercial purposes then something of moral significance will be lost. The question then will be about the extent to which sport played with money as one of the key motives will eventually come to be dominated by commercial motives. Is the commercial motive 'imperialistic'?[6]

Another plausible way of explicating what might be wrong with excessively commercial discourses would focus on the meanings associated with sport: the thought would be that 'commodified sporting talk' erodes the meanings associated with sport. The North American philosopher Elizabeth Anderson (1993), in her book *Value in Ethics and Economics*, provides a theoretical framework for such a critique. She argues that the normative significance of actions arises not so much from their consequences but in the values expressed in and of themselves. Sport has – and this is particularly true of many large-scale sporting events like the football World Cup – cultural meanings and a great deal of cultural and sociological work has been undertaken exploring those meanings. The pride that people take, for instance, in the performance of their nations in the Olympic Games or the European Football Championships is but one example. A proper analysis of such meanings is obviously well beyond the scope of this present chapter but acknowledging their existence in this context is important. Such meanings, while diverse, are not typically framed within what could plausibly be called an economic discourse. So when Michael Jordan calls his team a 'franchise', the very act, in and of itself, changes the meaning of the activity; equally, when sports commentators focus on the financial value of some event, as opposed to the significance of it as a sporting competition, again they express very different values than those many might regard as part of their real meaning. The argument here would be that there is a real danger of those meanings being lost within a commercial understanding of sport.

There are also pragmatic considerations that bear on this point. If it becomes too apparent that a particular sport has become fundamentally oriented towards profit making for sporting enterprises, then it is likely to undermine general public interest in it. Somewhat paradoxically, it might sometimes be the case that if a sport wishes to be financially successful it cannot be perceived too widely as primarily being about money. Perhaps this provides some constraint against the erosion of the expressive meanings of such sports. If this is true, then the cultural meanings expressed in sport might well be more secure against the incursions of commercial language than some critics are willing to acknowledge.

One problem with the focus on expressive meanings, however, relates to whether there is agreement about what those proper meanings are. It might be argued that the meanings associated with sporting events are very diverse and contested, and to suggest that markets are culpable for undermining specific ideals or meanings, is to privilege one set of meanings above other legitimate accounts. Further, it might be argued that if the meanings are sufficiently robust then they will survive any incursions by the market, or alternatively, meanings change all the time so why try to preserve one particular set. Finally, those of a more utilitarian bent might well argue that if the majority are better off overall through the advent of a more commercial discourse, then so much the worse for those expressive meanings that are lost through commercialisation.

The general point here then is that criticisms based on motives and meanings, while under-pinning a great deal of the discomfort many feel about commercialisation, do not provide uncontested or knockdown arguments against the incursion of money into sport. One question we should ask is whether such discomfort is justified and worth reflecting upon or simply reveals a nostalgic reaction against ongoing social change.

Let us turn now from attitudes towards sport to concerns with undesirable attitudes towards the athletes who play sport.

Exploitation and objectification

Another important set of moral worries about commerce and the commodification of sport invokes the concepts of exploitation and objectification. Let us begin with the idea of exploitation, which here involves primarily ethical and political concerns with the justice of contracts. Although one often hears talk of exploitation in sport, it is not immediately clear that elite level players are exploited – indeed it would seem extremely odd to describe sportsmen such as David Beckham or Usain Bolt as exploited – but, we must remember that famous and finan-cially successful athletes represent only a small proportion of those engaged in professional sport and their experiences and financial circumstances are atypical.

One striking feature of modern elite sport is the increasing professionalization of athletes. Such professionalization involves, among other things, the establishment of contracts between sports people and commercial sporting institutions (be they clubs, sports associations, sporting manufacturers or media companies). Professional contracts are an integral part of modern commercial sport. If we commodify sporting activity in this way, then clearly there are questions that arise regarding the justice of the contracts signed:

- What counts as a fair payment in such contracts? Should they be determined solely by the market?
- What kinds of contractual obligations can employers and other relevant commercial agents reasonably impose on athletes?
- To what extent should contracts signed under conditions of economic duress be regarded as binding?

Some contracts might well be regarded, with respect to their financial arrangements and the kinds of obligations they impose, as being exploitative.

So can some sporting contracts be regarded as exploitative? One rather radical line of response here would be that such contracts are *necessarily* exploitative and hence should be abolished (this might be part of a robust repudiation of commercialised sport). Traditional Marxists, for instance, would regard any wage–labour contract as exploitative, on the grounds that athletes are not paid the full commercial value of the acts they perform. Recall that, for Marx, labourers are exploited because they are not paid the total value of their productive activ-ity. Here profit (or surplus value) is understood as the difference between what a worker is paid and the real value of their work on the market. One might argue, then, following the Marxist line of reasoning, that sportsmen and sportswomen are exploited financially because their activity realises profit for sporting capitalists.

There are good reasons for thinking that, in the case of sport at least, this is implausible. It is difficult to view a sportsman such as David Beckham as a victim, even if he does not receive all of the value he creates. Also, such a view fails to acknowledge the possibility that capitalists might do anything useful when they engage in entrepreneurial activity or create anything of value.

At the other end of the spectrum are those advocates of the free market who hold that any contract engaged in by consenting adults is both morally legitimate and binding. As long as the contract is obtained through free bargaining in an open market, then the arrangement achieved is permissible. On this line of thought – which we find expressed most eloquently in the work of Robert Nozick – contracts are fair so long as they are negotiated under conditions of genuine mutual consent.[7] In the case of sport itself this would imply that:

- any contract to which an athlete consents is fair so long as the bargaining process does not involve coercion or blackmail
- given players and sporting associations engage in mutually consenting commercial bargains, then any interference by third parties is wrong.

This seems to ignore a number of significant facts, however. Firstly, there is the question of coercion. The Nozickian picture is undergirded by the assumption that, as long as both parties freely consent, regardless of the material circumstances, then any contract forged is morally permissible (Nozick 1974: 262–3). Nevertheless, one might plausibly argue that, for instance, extreme poverty sometimes leads one to engage in forms of what Michael Walzer (1983: 102) labels '*desperate exchange*'; that is, trades of last resort undertaken in desperate circumstances. Secondly, as a matter of historical fact, sportspeople have often engaged in desperate exchanges. The reasons for this are many and varied but part of the explanation is that many athletes are romantics for whom pursuing their sporting dreams is the most important, or indeed the only thing that matters in life. This leaves them far more vulnerable to unfair commercial offers. Further, many professional sports people come from underprivileged backgrounds, being born into either the lower classes in the affluent West or the Developing World. Their desperation to escape their extreme material poverty might well increase the likelihood of their accepting exploitative conditions.

If these criticisms of the free-market approach are correct, and one also does not wish to adopt a socialist or Marxist critique, then one needs to adopt a middle path according to which contracting itself is regarded as morally legitimate, but hold that *some* contracts can be exploitative. The questions that then need to be answered include: (a) how one might distinguish between a just form of contract for sports people from an unjust one and; (b) to what extent one will allow free-market bargaining to occur and to what extent should the state intervene to ensure minimal standards are met in setting payments and conditions. If we are to avoid exploitation in sport (given we regard exploitation as both possible and normatively undesirable), then presumably these are problems that need to be resolved.

Let us turn now to the problem of objectification. The idea here is that commercial sport *objectifies* athletes, especially those involved in team sports. It is commonly said that players who are bought and sold on the open market by sporting clubs, companies and advertisers are treated like cattle or like meat in a supermarket; that is, they are treated *instrumentally*. The kinds of practices towards which such criticisms are directed would include the trading of players that goes on between clubs in competitions such as the English Premier League in football or evaluations by businesses of the commercial value of athletes for advertising and for generating interest in a sporting event. In such cases, it is clear that the athletes in questions are viewed by these enterprises, at least in part, as means to financial profits.

We can tease this objection out in Kantian terms by talking of persons being treated as mere means.[8] The German philosopher Immanuel Kant (1724–1804) stressed in his ethical writings the importance of not treating people instrumentally. According to the second formulation of his 'categorical imperative' we should always treat persons as ends and never simply as mere means. This principle – which is often referred to as the 'principle of respect for persons' – emphasises ideals of dignity and respect, both of which are often lacking in commercial exchanges. The relevance of this to commercial sport and, in particular, our attitudes towards athletes, should be clear. When soccer players, for example, are bought and sold by clubs like Arsenal and Manchester United, we might well say that they are being treated as mere means or instruments for the realisation of profit. Their worth is understood, in such cases, in terms of their commercial value. Critiques of instrumental modes of regard, whether explicitly Kantian or not, underpin a great deal of the critique not only of commercial sport but also, more generally, of a whole range of capitalist exchanges.

Applying the respect for persons principle to commercial transactions should not be regarded as a misuse of this Kantian maxim. Kant is quite explicit in his writings about the danger of commercial exchanges and financial attitudes to the maintenance of the dignity of human beings. In the *Groundwork of the Metaphysics of Morals*, immediately following his enunciation of the categorical imperative, he claims that price and dignity are mutually exclusive. He writes that:

> In the kingdom of ends everything has a *price* or a *dignity*. If it has a price, something else can be put in its place as an *equivalent*; if it is exalted above all price and so admits of no equivalent, then it has a dignity.
>
> *(Kant 2012: 46)*

This is a very strong line of reasoning. If it were to be applied to sport, and we agree with the claim that dignity must always be maintained and dignity requires no price, then there could be no commercial or transfer systems for players. Its adoption would presumably lead to a prohibition on all commercial sport or at least those parts of commercial sport that involve ascribing a price to human beings. (We should note that the principle has been employed by applied ethicists in other areas of social policy to provide justifications for prohibitions on, for instance, the sale of human organs and of sex.)[9] Do those who oppose the objectification of athletes really want to eliminate money from sport so radically?

Not only is the price–dignity dictum very strong, perhaps impossibly so, but it also seems to be in considerable tension with the principle of respect for persons that does, when we reflect upon it, allow for use. There the concern is with treating persons as *mere* means – but the principle does not rule out treating as a means. This formulation of the principle allows for a *compossibility* (that is, a mutual possibility) between being treated as a means and being treated as an end. In this way, the principle implicitly acknowledges the myriad ways in which human beings use each other every hour of the day and in all our human interactions. What matters for Kant is that we do not treat persons as *mere* means but always regard them as ends in themselves. Accordingly, it would be more in keeping with the categorical imperative if the price–dignity dictum stated that we should not regard things with dignity merely to have a price.

This failure to recognise, when considering a wide range of forms of social life, the compossibility of instrumentally useful interactions with treating a person with dignity is symptomatic of much of the literature on objectification, which too often conflates usage with treating merely instrumentally. A better way to formulate the objectification objection would involve the claim that commercial sport is morally objectionable when it treats athletes as mere means to the realisation of profit. This reformulation allows for commercial exchanges so long as those exchanges do not involve athletes being treated as *mere* means to the realisation of gain. It does not necessarily involve a repudiation of all commercial arrangements in sport, nor does it make human social life in which we make use of each others' skills a miserable trough of moral vice.

Nevertheless, this leaves a further question unanswered. Does the commercialisation of sport, as a matter of fact, lead to athletes (at least in elite sports) being treated as mere means?[10] We might regard this, at least herein, as an open question. If commercialisation does lead to objectification – understood as treating as a mere means – then there would be a Kantian justification for rejecting commercial sport or, at the very least, rejecting those practices which encourage *purely instrumental* modes of regard? Some critics of commercial sport might argue that commercial sport, while not necessarily causing vicious objectification, has a strong tendency to do so. The suggestion would be that it is very easy to slide from commodity to mere commodity. If one holds that such objectification is undesirable, and it is true that there is a *strong tendency* for commercial sport to objectify, then we need to determine what measures need to be taken to prevent it. Does it require prohibiting some forms of commercial exchange (such as player markets) or does it simply mean that regulatory measures need to be instituted to ensure that such objectification does not arise? For those who take this line of criticism seriously, there is a need to determine, then, how likely it is that commercialisation gives rise to objectification and, if there is a strong tendency towards these undesirable modes of regard, how it might be prevented.

Of course, many would reject this objectification critique. First, some critics might deny the claim that commercial sport encourages any objectification of athletes whatsoever. To the contrary, placing dollar values on athletes is a way of recognising their worth. Via monetary valuation and valuing we show our esteem and appreciation for the athletes themselves. Alternatively, it might be argued that we should not be concerned that commercial organisations regard athletes instrumentally (if indeed they do), if those athletes are being handsomely rewarded. On this line of reasoning, being objectified is not the worst fate that might befall a sportsperson.

Another way of responding would be to query whether any commercial transaction could be regarded as morally vicious if it is freely chosen by all parties concerned. A Nozickian would presumably argue that moral equality requires that all parties be treated as free to engage in commercial transactions as they see fit. As long as any commercial relations or contracts to which they agree are not coerced through force or fraud, then one cannot make moral judgements about the actual content of the contract nor about the attitudes of those contracting towards one another.

Finally, one might adopt a consequentialist utilitarian approach to the problem. Critics could argue that even if one grants, for the sake of argument, that athletes are objectified in some pernicious manner via commercialisation, that nonetheless the overall benefits that commercial sport generates for the community at large and, ultimately, for the players themselves, outweigh the harms.

Regulation and sport: the role of the state in constraining commerce

Lurking in the background of all of these debates is the vexed question of the state's involvement in preventing harms from commercialisation. If some form of commercialisation is normatively undesirable or has normatively undesirable consequences, then should the state intervene? Does the state (or a relevant sporting authority) have a legitimate role to play in constraining the activities of commercial entrepreneurs involved in sport?

There are a number of different policy approaches that the state or publicly paid sporting administrators might pursue here. (Note that, from this point on, I refer simply to the 'state' but assume that this includes non-governmental sporting authorities, such as the commissions and committees that run various sports). One option open to such authorities is to place some sporting activities or goods completely outside of the market; that is, to turn them into what Michael Walzer (1983: 97) referred to as 'blocked exchanges'. Alternatively, sporting administrators and government bodies might adopt a less radical approach in which buying and selling is simply regulated rather than prohibited. A third (and less radical yet again) policy approach would be to engage in programs of *moral education* that aim to prevent normatively undesirable outcomes in sport via widespread promulgation of instruction on the potential harms of commercialisation. This third strategy would not involve direct intervention but instead would exhort athletes, administrators and business people to avoid certain practices which would, for instance, objectify or exploit others sportsmen and women.

The question before us concerns the extent to which the state should be involved in *determining* what sporting goods should be available on the market and *regulating* how goods that are commercially available should be bought and sold or finally institute moral education programmes oriented towards blunting the 'claws of the market'. We should also note, before proceeding any further, that a wide variety of practices aimed at lessening the effects of the market are already in place. In some sports, we find vigorous regulations have been instituted. For instance, some leagues have, with the aim of preventing the richer clubs buying the best players on offer, established 'salary caps', which set an upper limit on the sum total that clubs can pay their players. The English Premier League, by way of contrast, has no such salary cap in place.[11] The point here is simply that there is currently a great variety in terms of the market-constraining practices in place.

Intervention of the kind outlined above is, unsurprisingly, controversial. There are many who hold that the state has no role to play in constraining the market in sport (often because of a more general animus against state intervention in the market). We have already encountered the work of Robert Nozick (1974), whose book *Anarchy, State and Utopia* is arguably the most philosophically sophisticated account of a view that is widely held and according to which the state should not interfere in commercial arrangements, beyond providing the background legal conditions which make such transactions possible. Nozick's general rationale is that the state has no right to interfere in capitalistic acts between freely consenting adults. Accordingly, if an athlete freely chooses to sell a certain service to a commercial agent, then the state should not attempt to prohibit or regulate the content of any contract to which they agree. The Nozickian would regard the idea of regulating sport to prevent, for instance, objectification or exploitation, as an unjustifiable violation of individual liberties. Again, the institution of a salary cap to prevent larger more financial clubs dominating competitions for long periods of time would also be regarded as illegitimate.

At the other end of the political spectrum are those who would, in order to avoid the pitfalls of commercialisation, strongly advocate government regulation of commercial sport. For such thinkers, what is required is an *extension*, to certain commercial practices in sport, of the kinds of regulatory and prohibitionist policies that are currently practiced to limit the influence of drugs in sport. It is implausible to think that sport will, in the near future, be free from commercial interests and thus the real question for such theorists becomes how the excesses are best constrained. Such a critic might, for instance, regard the domination of sport by the most financially well-off clubs to be undesirable and thus advocate the introduction of salary caps into all elite team competitions. Such a critic might advocate a ban on the trading of players on open markets or perhaps wish to limit the influence of player agents. More generally, he or she might defend limits being placed upon the amount of control that commercial interests can have in the development and administration of sport. All of these are but mere examples of the measures that anti-commerce advocates might adopt.

What would warrant the implementation of such practices? Their justification is to be found partially in the kinds of criticisms of commercialisation outlined earlier (although that list is not intended as being exhaustive), combined with a belief that the state has a right and a duty to prevent excesses perpetrated by the 'realm of Mammon'.[12] The thought is that it is not enough simply to acknowledge the possible harms caused by commercialisation but we should also recognise that those harms provide justificatory grounds for legislative action on the part of the state. Such critics might also argue for the *pragmatic necessity* of state intervention. The idea would be that unless the state regulates the commercial development of sport, then some commercial initiatives would destroy or undermine the good-making features upon which commercial profits are based.[13] If fans become disenchanted with changes to their sport that are obviously driven by greed on the part of those commercially developing sport, this could, in the end, have counterproductive results and could ultimately undermine its financial viability. Alternatively, if the drive for profits is so relentless that the grassroots of the game are damaged then again this can undermine a sport itself in the long run.

Despite this disagreement, there is little controversy among the public at large that the state has a right to regulate sport for the public good. The real question is how extensive that right should be and, in our particular case, whether it can be extended to include concerns about the normative consequences of commercialisation.

Concluding remarks and future directions

Should we regard commercialisation with deep suspicion? In this chapter, I have explored a range of arguments that provide possible normative grounds for objecting to the commercialisation of sport. Unsurprisingly, such claims are highly contested and many thinkers reject objections to commercialisation based upon them. However, the arguments outlined herein do demonstrate that if we hold certain values dear to our hearts – such as equality of access or the idea of respect for persons – then commercialisation is of serious concern since it threatens to undermine them. The real question then becomes what ethical and political values we expect sport to realise and exemplify and, subsequently, if those are imperilled by commercialisation, how we should best respond to such threats.

Notes

1 There are a number of elite sports which are not highly commercialised. I have Olympic sports, such as judo, sailing and canoeing, in mind here.

2 There exists a vast social science literature on the commodification and globalisation of sport and, in particular, on the commodification of soccer. For a very useful survey of this literature see Giulianotti and Robertson (2009).

3 Here, critics of commercialisation would do well to remember that the market is not the only mechanism that has been employed historically for allocating scarce sporting goods.

4 See Walsh and Giulianotti (2007).

5 Notice here that it is not so much that the ideals are in conflict but that the motivational sets of agents cannot contain both monetary motives and these ideals of sport at the same time.

6 Michael Walzer (1983) famously talks of money being imperialistic and having a tendency towards domination in *Sphere of Justice*.

7 In Nozick's work, this falls under the category of 'justice in transfer', according to which the

fundamental rule is 'From each as they choose, to each as they are chosen'. See Robert Nozick, *Anarchy* (1974: 160).

8 Kant's work is illustrative since it captures on important way of understanding objectification. But it also highlights ways in which these critiques are prone to error in their tendency to see all human interaction that involves benefit on the part of at least one of the agents as objectifying.

9 For a comprehensive discussion of the sale of human organs and of prostitution, see Stephen Wilkinson (2003).

10 We might also usefully ask at this point what it means to treat someone as a mere commodity or as opposed to treating her as a commodity in some appropriate manner.

11 Although the EPL is soon to fall under UEFA's policy on these matters, which are more stringent.

12 In the New Testament of the Bible, riches and avarice are personified as the false god 'Mammon'.

13 For an extensive discussion of this idea, see Walsh and Giulianotti (2006): chapter 6 'Scoring an Own Goal: when markets undermine what they sell', pp. 107–19.

Bibliography

Allison, Lincoln. 2001. *Amateurism in Sport: An Analysis and Defence*. London: Frank Cass.

Anderson, Elizabeth. 1993. *Value in Ethics and Economics*. Cambridge, MA: Harvard University Press.

Andrews, David L. (ed.). 2001. *Michael Jordan Inc: Corporate sport, media culture, and late modern America*. New York: SUNY Press.

Bogusz, Barbara and Erika Szyszczak (eds) 2007. *The Regulation of Sport in the European Union*, Northampton: Edward Elgar.

Brohm, J. M. 1978. *Sport: A prison of measured time*, trans. I. Fraser. London: Ink Links.

Brown, A. and A. Walsh, *Not for Sale: Manchester United, Murdoch and the defeat of BskyB*. Edinburgh: Mainstream, 1999.

Cashmore, Ellis. 1996. *Making Sense of Sports*, 2nd ed. London: Routledge.

Coates, D. C. and B. R. Humphreys. 2000. 'The Stadium Gambit and Local Economic Development', *Regulation*, 23 (2): 15–20.

Downward, Paul M. and Alistair Dawson. 2000. *The Economics of Professional Team Sport*. London: Routledge.

Doyle, William. 1996. *Venality: The sale of offices in eighteenth-century France*. Oxford: Oxford University Press.

Dunning, Eric and Kenneth Sheard. 1979. *Barbarians, Gentlemen and Players: A sociological study of the development of rugby football*. Canberra: Australian National University Press.

Friedman, Milton. 1970. 'The Social Responsibility of Business is to Increase its Profits', *New York Times Magazine*, September 13: 122–6.

Giulianotti, Richard. 1999. *Football: A sociology of the global game*. Cambridge: Polity.

Giulianotti, R and R. Robertson. 2009. *Globalization and Football*. London: Sage.

Guevara, Arturo J. Marcano and David P. Fidler. 2002. *Stealing Lives: The globalization of baseball and the tragic story of Alexis Quiroz*. Bloomington, IN: Indiana University Press.

Guttmann, Allen. 1994. *Games and Empires, Modern Sports and Cultural Imperialism*. New York: Columbia University Press.

Hoch, P. 1973. *Rip Off the Big Game: The Exploitation of sport by the power elite*. New York: Anchor.

Hunter, Nick, 2012. *Money in Sport*. Ethics of Sport Series. London: Raintree.

Jennings, Andrew. 1996. *The New Lords of the Rings: Olympic corruption and how to buy gold medals*. London: Pocket Books.

Kant, Immanuel. 2012. *Groundwork of the Metaphysics of Morals*, translated and edited by Mary McGregor and Jens Timmerman. Cambridge: Cambridge University Press.

Kidd, B. 1984. 'The Myth of the Ancient Games' in A. Tomlinson and G. Whannel (eds), *Five Ring Circus: Money, power and politics at the Olympic Games*. London: Pluto.

Kretchmar, R. Scott. 1994. *Practical Philosophy of Sport*. Champaign, IL: Human Kinetics.

LaFeber, W. 2002. *Michael Jordan and the New Global Capitalism*. New York: W. W. Norton.

Loland, Sigmund. 2001. *Fair Play in Sport: A moral norm system*, London: Routledge.

Long, Judith Grant. 2005. 'Full Count: The Real Cost of Public Funding for Major League Sports Facilities', *Journal of Sports Economics*, 6 (2): 119–43.

MacIntyre, Alasdair. 1985. *After Virtue*. London: Duckworth.

McNamee, M. 1995. 'Sporting Practices, Institutions and Virtues: A critique and restatement', *Journal of the Philosophy of Sport*, 22: 61–82.

McNamee, M. J. 2008. *Morality Play: Sports, virtues and vices*. London: Routledge.

McNamee, M. J. and S. J. Parry (eds) 1998. *Ethics and Sport*. London: Spon.

Morgan, W. J. 1993. *Leftist Theories of Sport: A critique and reconstruction*. Urbana, IL: University of Illinois Press.

Morgan, William J., Klaus V. Meier and Angela J. Schnieder (eds) 2001. *Ethics in Sport*. Champaign, IL: Human Kinetics.

Novak, Michael. 1976. *The Joy of Sports*. New York: Basic Books.

Nozick, Robert. 1969. 'Coercion' in S. Morgenbesser *et al.* (eds) 1969. *Philosophy, Science and Method*. New York: St Martin's Press, 440–72.

Nozick, Robert. 1974. *Anarchy, State and Utopia*. Oxford: Blackwell.

Rowe, David. 2004. 'Watching Brief: Cultural citizenship and viewing rights', *Sport in Society*, 7 (3): 385–402.

Sandel, Michael. 2012. *What Money Can't Buy: The moral limits of markets*. New York: Macmillan.

Sandy, R., P. J. Sloane and M. S. Rosentraub. 2004. *The Economics of Sport: An international perspective*. Basingstoke: Palgrave.

Satz, Debra. 2010. *Why Some Things Should Not Be for Sale: The moral limits of markets*. Oxford: Oxford University Press.

Schmitz, K. 2001. 'Sport and Play: Suspension of the Ordinary' in W. Morgan and K. Meier (eds), *Philosophical Inquiry into Sport*. Champion IL: Human Kinetics, 29–38.

Scully, Gerald W. 1997. *The Market Structure of Sport*. Chicago, IL: University of Chicago Press.

Simon, Robert L. 1991. *Fair Play: Sports, values and society*. Boulder, CO: Westview.

Simon, Robert L. 2004. *Fair Play: The ethics of sport*, 2nd ed. Boulder, CO: Westview.

Simson, Vyv and Andrew Jennings. 1992. *The Lords of the Rings*. New York: Simon and Schuster.

Sloane, P. J. 1971. 'The Economics of Professional Football: the Football Club as a Utility Maximiser', *Scottish Journal of Political Economy*, 18(2): 121–46.

Steenbergen, Johan and Jan Tamboer. 1998. 'Ethics and the Double Character of Sport: An attempt to systematise discussions of the ethics of sport', in M. J. McNamee and S. J. Parry (eds), *Ethics and Sport*. London: Routledge, 35–54.

Tuxill, Cei and Sheila Wigmore. 1998. 'Merely Meat? Respect for persons and games', in Mike McNamee and Jim Parry (eds), *Ethics and Sport*. London: Routledge, 104–18.

Vamplew, Wray. 1988. *Pay up and Play the Game*, Cambridge: Cambridge University Press.

Walsh, Adrian and Richard Giulianotti. 2001. 'This Sporting Mammon: a normative critique of the commodification of sport, *Journal of the Philosophy of Sport*, 28(1): 53–77.

Walsh, Adrian and Richard Giulianotti, 2007. *Ethics, Money and Sport: This sporting Mammon*. Abingdon: Routledge.

Walzer, M. 1983. *Spheres of Justice*. Oxford: Blackwell.

Wilkinson, Stephen. 2003. *Bodies for Sale: Ethics and exploitation in the human body trade*. London: Routledge.

28

TECHNOLOGY AND SPORT

Rasmus Bysted Møller and Verner Møller

Introduction

The relationship between sport and technology is close and can be both fruitful and destructive. Technology has a constitutive function in sport, as it makes the activity possible. Moreover, it can enhance performance as well as the sporting experience. The use of football boots is clearly more comfortable and effective than playing football in bare feet. However, sport challenges its athletes by demanding the employment of less efficient means rather than more efficient means in pursuit of sport-specific goals (Suits, 2005). Technology can therefore potentially detract from the sporting experience. If, for instance, very efficient hail cartridges were allowed for use in double-trap shooting, it would reduce the skills required to excel at that discipline, reducing its value for participants and spectators alike. Similarly, the use of forbidden performance-enhancing substances has long been a much debated topic in sports philosophy and, with gene technology waiting around the corner, the relationship between sport and technology has become strained and is often viewed with concern and scepticism.

In this chapter, we analyse this trend and thereby expose what we consider a tendency towards an overly pessimistic outlook on technology in sport. The chapter opens with a brief survey of some major works that have been written about various aspects of the topic, followed by examples, from the 1960s onwards, of technophobia in relation to sport. After this, an alternative position with a more neutral view on technology based on a social constructivist epistemology is presented. Having exposed this position as self-defeating, the chapter moves on to the building of a coherent understanding of the relationship between sport and technology. This section begins with an examination of the concept of technology whereby it lays the foundation for a thorough analysis of normative assessments of the relationship between sport and technology. At the end of the analysis, we reach the conclusion that a sound normative assessment of technological development in sport must be based on theory of sport that respects sportive values in its own right irrespective of their moral worth.

Previous contributions to the understanding of sport and technology

Sport and technology is a vast topic that comprises a variety of disparate phenomena. It is manifest in basic things that make sport possible such as balls, boats, bikes, cars, clubs, rackets, skis, and the development of these things that enhance the experienced quality of athletes in these respective sports. It is displayed in the gear that improves the athletes comfort and safety, and it is present in stadia facilities that standardise as well as improve the conditions for sport competitions by ground heating, artificial turf, polyurethane or latex tracks. Jenkins and Subic's edited works (2003, 2007) offer a thorough analysis of those issues. Infrastructure and transport that makes it possible to organise tournaments nationally and internationally and facilities which accommodate large crowds and standardise the competitive environment around the world are also part of the sport and technology complex. Sport geographer John Bale has provided recommendable analyses of these issues in *Sport, Space and the City* (1993), *Landscapes of Modern Sport* (1996) and *Sport Geography* (2003). Technology's influence on sport is furthermore pervasive through the media development. The invention of satellites has made it possible, on the one hand, to bring live broadcast sports events to global audiences, which has made sport one of the worlds most valuable marketing tools, as described in Amis and Cornwell (2005), and, on the other hand, influenced public attitudes toward race, gender and nationalism, as Boyle and Haynes (2009) argue.

Media technology has impacted the public perception of fair play because the replay of close-up and slow-motion images expose and (over-)emphasise misbehaviour such as diving, (or – to use the Federation of International Football Association's nomenclature – 'simulation') reckless tackles and hand-ball in soccer, for example. It has also become an aid to referees in many sports, the 'Hawk-Eye' in tennis being perhaps the most successful from a spectator's point of view. At the same time, these technologies have been used as a means of controlling crowds. In fact, the wish to eradicate hooliganism by the means of surveillance paved the way for Britain's now general policy of camera surveillance of public spaces, according to McGrath (2004). Finally there are the performance-enhancing technologies. While the above-mentioned subjects mostly have drawn attention from sociology and cultural studies, performance-enhancement technologies, both legal and illegal, have been subject to intense discussion and analysis in the philosophy of sport.

The love of the past and the fear of future technologies

Discussions about the relationship between sport and technology often revolve around ethical issues and reflect different understandings and valorisations of both phenomena. An old but interesting example is Umminger's (1962) compelling introduction to the cultural history of sport. Umminger is fascinated by human creativity and scientific breakthroughs and he praises past achievements, but concerns arise when he envisions the future. The problems he foresees relate to the record mania captured in Pierre de Coubertin's Olympic motto: *citius, altius, fortius*. According to Umminger, the quest for records is a potent driving force. During modern sport's first hundred years, he claims, even world records were the product of a single person's unassisted effort. This is no longer the case. Today, world records are usually the outcome of teamwork. Scientists, physicians, trainers and the athlete's entourage also play a big part in the achievement of victory.

Umminger predicted that horrific times were not far away. An American scientist, he noted, had seriously recommended that genuinely elite sportsmen and women should marry to have children and thus create future world-record breakers. Moreover, *in vitro* fertilisation (IVF) – he claimed – was a public obsession. Dystopian novels like Aldous Huxley's *Brave New World* (1932) and the Danish physician Knud Lundberg's *The Olympic Hope – A story from the Olympic Games 1966* (1958) may foretell where sport is heading, Umminger maintains, stressing that he fears the future of the real world will be even more horrendous than that depicted by these writers.

IVF was, in fact, still 16 years away from becoming a reality when Umminger published his book. Today, it is commonplace. By the time that Robert G. Edwards, the father of this ground-breaking reproductive technology, won the Nobel Prize in 2010, four million children had been born using this technology (Russell 2010). In the USA alone, 58,000 babies resulted from IVF each year, to the joy of otherwise infertile couples. In light of this, Umminger's concern about a future where superhuman athletes would be created by IVF is striking and adds perspective to more recent concerns about scientific and technological progress. Apparently, the human capacity to reflect before new possibilities are put into practice is greater than he anticipated.

In 1992, following the Ben Johnson scandal at the 1988 Seoul Olympics and the fall of the Berlin wall in 1989, which symbolised the end of the Cold War and led to the exposition of the heinous regime behind East German sport's success, John Hoberman (1992) published a book with the telling title *Mortal Engines – The Science of Performance and the Dehumanization of Sport*. The book gives an eye-opening account of the historical development of the relationship between science and sport. Hoberman emphasises how sport was exploited during the Cold War, with detrimental effects on the health of the athletes involved. Hoberman meticulously documents the scientifically developed performance-enhancing drug regime and its political and financial underpinnings. However, in the final chapter of the book he, like Umminger, cannot resist the temptation to look into the crystal ball, and, like Umminger, he also foresees an emerging dystopia. Modern sports' inhuman demands on athletes' physiques pave the way for a new understanding of the concept 'necessity', according to which everything that can be done in the name of competitiveness must be done: 'Today the question is whether the sweat-stained athletes and the men in white coats will be able to persuade publics and parliaments that the future of sport requires a new medical realism' (Hoberman 1992: 286). Athletes may thus become pioneers in high-tech societies. If competition is constantly encouraged and increased competitiveness is made a prerequisite for success in all areas, leaders may 'want to apply genetic engineering to an entire range of performers' (ibid.). In such societies, athletes could serve:

> as the most promising experimental subjects because it will be easier to identify correlations between the actions of particular genes and performance-related traits if the test performances are physical and quantifiable in a way that [e.g.] musical and scientific talent are not.
>
> *(Hoberman 1992: 286)*

Hoberman makes a bold comparison between equine and human athletes and envisions a time where athletes will be genetically exploited as racehorses have been for centuries through breeding. Hoberman does not fear IVF. What he is concerned about is the Human Genome Project 'that will supposedly identify in sequence all three billions base pairs of DNA that constitutes the human genome by about year 2005' (Hoberman 1992: 287). This could lead to a situation where it would be possible to compare the genes of talented and less talented people of all kinds. If that happens it will:

> presumably lead to the identification of performance-linked genes and even, perhaps, their synthesis and *in utero* insertion into the genome of a gestating foetus. An even more futuristic scenario would be the 'cloning' of genetically identical individuals from the genome of a great athlete or some other kind of overachiever.
>
> *(Hoberman 1992: 287)*

Ten years later – one year before the Human Genome Project was in fact declared complete – similar concerns over future technologies' impact on sport and humanity appeared in the Research in Philosophy and Technology Handbook series volume 21, *Sport and Technology: History, Philosophy and Policy* (Miah and Eassom 2002). As usual in handbooks, we find contrasting views. Tamburrini's (2002) chapter 'After Doping What? The morality of the genetic engineering of athletes', for instance, offers an uncompromising defence of gene technology against the sensationalist fear-provoking portrayal of it. However, the undercurrent of the majority of articles is that we should be cautious about embracing human-enhancement technologies. Butryn's (2002) contribution 'Cyborg Horizons: Sport and the ethics of self-technologization' delves into the prospect of the dehumanization of sport of which Hoberman warns. As an echo of Umminger, Butryn warns that while 'genetic engineering for example, in elite sport may seem futuristic, scientists working on a muscle-building vaccine derived from engineered genes have already recognised the implications of their work for sport' (Butryn 2002: 113). According to Butryn, such future technologies threaten the integrity of sport.

History is full of examples of concerns over technological advances that have proven to be baseless or exaggerated long after the new technologies have been introduced. This does not prove, of course, that new technologies are harmless. Some old as well as new technologies are potentially harmful. The same can be said about an overly cautious approach to new technologies, which might prevent us from exploiting valuable opportunities. The point we want to make by drawing attention to the apparently ageless concern over emerging technology is that fear, worry and vigilance are features of human nature, which counterbalance human curiosity and innovation and make us act reasonably according to the circumstances in most cases. If there were no immediate concern about unknown effects of new and unfamiliar inventions, the risk they pose would be so much bigger. Unsurprisingly, therefore, we rarely find people who promote new technologies such as genetically modified organisms (GMO), radiation preservation of food, and so on, without implicitly or explicitly making cost-benefit analyses and risk assessments. Those who argue in favour of such technology usually do so on the basis of necessity (such as the need to feed a rapidly growing world population). The food industry's opposition to mandatory GMO labelling indicates that there is an understanding that visible labels which inform consumers that food products are modified by technology may harm sales (Strom 2013). Notwithstanding the fact that people enthusiastically yield to technologically advanced gadgets and so forth, the lay understanding is still that natural food is better than artificial food, and this further indicates that ordinary people recognise that the body is a natural biological organism which can be harmed by consuming artificial products. Tara Magdalinski's (2009) *Sport, Technology and the Body – The nature of performance* is interesting in this respect because it applies a constructivist perspective to the body. This view allows for a different more neutral perspective on sport and technology and therefore deserves separate treatment.

The social constructivist perspective

True to the constructivist epistemology, according to which knowledge is socially constructed and therefore without universal validity, Magdalinski opposes essentialism and dismisses the idea of a 'natural body'. The 'natural body' is nothing but a concept in the essentialist binary construction of 'natural' versus 'unnatural' – like 'nature' versus 'artifice' – she claims. In reality, there is no natural body. She admits, however, that: 'Although social theorists have written convincingly about the social constructedness of the body, the concept of the body as 'natural' retains primacy in the public consciousness' (Magdalinski 2009: 37).

It is an unsophisticated public's false consciousness that is responsible for the ambivalent and cautious approach to sports technology including the use of performance-enhancing drug. This public's consciousness is formed by popular media representations which evoke the illusion that it is natural bodies spurred by inner desire that exert themselves in sport competitions. And anti-doping programmes 'reinforce the authority of the natural body, utilising images that warn of the monstrous consequences of illicit enhancement' (Magdalinski 2009: 37). According to Magdalinski, '"natural" bodies are the stuff of sporting mythology, presented and represented to remind us of the horrors of technology and their potential to disrupt the otherwise uncontaminated' (Magdalinski 2009: 38). It goes without saying that Magdalinski understands this mythology as a narrative without foundation in any real nature, bodily or otherwise.

At the end of her introduction, she stresses that her book 'takes no particular stance in relation to performance enhancement, illicit or otherwise'. Instead, it 'interrogates those external and internal technologies that threaten to dismantle the carefully constructed athletic body' (Magdalinski 2009: 13).

Her reluctance to arrive at any normative conclusions concerning sport and technology is consistent with her view on health and the body as social constructs. This view leads her to the following statement on anti-doping strategies:

> Safeguarding the health of athletes may lie at the heart of anti-doping policies; however, it is clear that 'health' is an elusive concept, which is inextricably linked to broader moral and national discourses. In essence, these strategies are based on controlling and regulating athletes' bodies to conform to normative standards.
>
> *(Magdalinski 2009: 90)*

Magdalinski's understanding of health is common among social constructivist thinkers (Lupton 2003; Robertson 2001; Larson 1991; Crawford 1984). Although viewing the body as a social construct may seem baffling to common people, it is 'now accepted amongst cultural theorists', as Magdalinski (2009: 39) puts it. And it is truly in accordance with the thinking of Michael Foucault, one of the major inspirations for the social constructivist movement. One of Foucault's prominent protagonists, Chris Shilling, explains Foucault's position as follows:

> The biological, physical or material body can never be grasped by the Foucauldian approach as its existence is permanently deferred behind the grids of meaning imposed by discourse ... To put it bluntly, the bodies that appear in Foucault's work do not enjoy a prolonged visibility as corporeal entities. Bodies are produced, but their own powers of production, where they have any, are limited to those invested in them by discourse. As such, the body is dissolved as a causal phenomenon into the determining power of discourse, and it becomes extremely difficult to conceive of the body as a material component of social action.
>
> *(Shilling 2005: 70–1)*

While some may find Shilling's interpretation exaggerated, few philosophers and social scientists who have read the oeuvre of Foucault will disagree that he indeed presents the embodied subject as a social construct.

Taking a constructivist approach to sport and technology is attractive to those who might argue in favour of technological advances and enhancement in sports. First, the idea that a new technology poses a threat to sport as a meaningful activity implies that sport has essential characteristics that need protection whereas from a constructivist point of view essentialism is seen as an illusion. Second, from the constructivist perspective, both 'natural talent' and 'health' are concepts invented to discriminate between people and to achieve power. Those who accept that there is nothing essential about sport but oppose a new technology if it is thought to alter sport in a way that devalues the sporting test of athletes' natural capabilities or if they are thought to endanger athletes' health, are thus disarmed.

As attractive as the social constructivist perspective may be, it is ultimately an intellectual *cul-de-sac* or dead end. In philosophical terms, it goes nowhere. To realise why this is so, one just needs to consider the difficulty involved in explaining what a social construction actually is *without* making use of a world view that takes the existence of communicative human beings living in a shared physical world for granted. The existence of conscious human beings with cognitive skills that allow them to communicate about mental states and the physical world is a precondition for social constructions and therefore cannot be such constructions themselves. It seems that basic common-sense assumptions about the world and what is a human being are impossible to consistently contest. Consequently, if we want to say something consistent about human beings and the world we cannot avoid implicitly – if not explicitly – to build our argument on basic common-sense assumptions, and this immediately bring us back to the normative dimension involved in the relationship between sport and technology.

The concept of technology

As a precondition for dealing with philosophical questions pertaining to sports technology, we need an elaborated understanding of technology itself. We are familiar with technological devices such as bicycles, cars, cell phones, computers, and so on. But what is the essence of technology? In the sport literature, Sigmund Loland defines technology as '*human-made means* to reach *human interests and goals*' (Loland 2002: 158). This definition is consistent with common understandings of technology and is often implicitly at use when sport technological issues are being addressed. Nevertheless, this understanding had already been challenged by the German philosopher Martin Heidegger in his influential essay published in the middle of the twentieth century, *The Question Concerning Technology*. Thus, before we return to Loland's definition it will repay the effort to consider Heidegger's own view of the matter.

According to Heidegger, the claim that technology is a human contrivance designed to secure humanly chosen ends prevent us from really grasping the essence of technology. Heidegger is critical of the instrumental (means to an end) and anthropological (human-made) conceptions of technology, because they suggest that humans control technology and can thus freely choose its proper application (Heidegger 1993: 312).

Technology, Heidegger claims, is not primarily a set of tools we use to reach our ends more efficiently. Rather, it is a dangerous power that has changed the way we perceive and understand being as such. Technology has made us look on nature with an instrumental gaze. This instrumental outlook has become so all-encompassing in the modern age that it is easy to neglect and therefore hard to counteract. As counterintuitive as it may sound, technology is represented by the very perception of nature as a container of raw materials, as sources of energy that are available for our exploitation to met our needs and goals. Thus conceived, an apple or a pear is understood as an ingredient in a balanced diet or as a source of vitamins and minerals. Similarly, when a beautiful landscape in France is looked upon as a resource that could function well as a stage in the Tour de France, it shows we are in the grip of this technological world-picture.

Because of our technological stance towards our surroundings, the sun no longer fills our hearts with awe and wonder as it once did. Instead it is perceived as a source of energy that can be stored by solar cells. Farmers in preindustrial times also used their animals but they felt more connected to them and nature. Therefore they did not view farm animals as mere production units or nature as standing-reserve. Technology interprets or 'uncovers' nature as essentially a collection of material objects that can be combined in various useful ways. Technology also shows in our will to reveal the underlying mechanics of everything that seems unintelligible to us. For example, when a sublime feint in soccer is interpreted as a logical consequence of hours of repetitive training instead of an instance of 'divine' inspiration on behalf of the player.

This change in our worldly outlook has resulted in what Heidegger calls the *oblivion of Being*, because we have abandoned an understanding of the world as sacred and awe-inspiring. This oblivion is present even in our understanding of our selves. Human beings are looked upon as purely interchangeable material parts, as, for example, bodily organs that can be mended or transplanted to prolong our life. Accordingly, the body of an athlete is likewise viewed in a machine-like fashion, as a storage site of energy reserves, as an instrument that needs to be modelled to satisfy sporting demands.

In his article *Sport and the Technological Image of Man*, Hoberman (1988: 203) draws inspiration from Heidegger when he claims that high-performance sport 'contains, and in some ways conceals, an agenda for human development'. As a logical consequence of sports pursuit of records and victory, elite-level athletes are engineered in various ways by sport scientists to make them more proficient. According to Hoberman, this instrumental view of athletes' bodies is not condemned by the public. On the contrary, it is viewed as an ideal way of reaching their full potential as successful and efficient human beings. The widespread use of physical and cognitive enhancement drugs outside the realm of sport speaks in favour of Hoberman's analysis. To Hoberman 'the pursuit of the record performance … is a celebration of the logic of technological civilization (Hoberman 1988: 206). He quotes approvingly the French philosopher Jacques Ellul in this regard, who has this to say about sport and technology:

> In every conceivable way sport is an extension of the technical spirit. Its mechanisms reach into the individual's innermost life, working a transformation of his body and its motions as a function of technique and not as a function of some traditional end foreign to technique, as, for example, harmony, joy, or the realization of spiritual good.
>
> *(Ellul 1964: 384)*

If this description is accurate, then sport leads directly to the oblivion of being that Heidegger identifies as a hallmark of modernity and its technological outlook. For ways to transcend this technological world view, Heidegger looks to art since great art has the capacity to reveal the sacredness of being and once again to inspire awe. However, he might as well have looked to sport, since it is probably the most accessible way of transcending the technological outlook on being. At first glance, this claim may appear self-contradictory in light of the quotes of Hoberman and Ellul just noted. How can athletes possibly transcend technology when sport itself seems to model its logic of efficiency in total accordance with an instrumental rationality? If we look upon sport from the outside, the answer inevitably comes up negative: from such a perspective sport simply seems to instantiate technology by chasing effective procedures in every conceivable way. But if, instead, we turn to the athletes' perspective we find tales of 'runner's high', 'heightened awareness in defining moments', 'experiences of "deep flow"' (Jackson and Csikszentmihalyi 1999) and even quasi-mystical experiences of being one with the situation and ones surroundings (Breivik 2013). Such moments often leave a lasting impression on the sportspersons who experience them. These experiences are not just experiences of pleasure. They are life-defining moments with existential significance because they point to other modes of being and other ways of being in the world (Ogles *et al.* 1993–94).

Müller (2007) provides a compelling analysis of the existential dimension involved in high-risk sports' flirtatious relationship with death in his dissertation *Sterben, Tod und Unsterblichkeit im Sport – Eine existenzphilosophishe Deutung*. Müller's analysis focuses on high-risk sports but, according to the Norwegian philosopher Gunnar Breivik, the kind of heightened consciousness often associated with high-risk sports is also called for in elite sports in situations of great importance or difficulty (Breivik, 2013: 94).

Mindful of this decidedly non-technological side of sport, the relationship between sport and technology appears more complex than Hoberman, after Heidegger, would have us believe. Rather, sport offers an opportunity to turn technology, as it were, on its head; to transcend it. That is, even from a Heideggerian perspective there is no need to be excessively pessimistic about the role of technology in sport.

We now outline an approach to normative questions on sport and technology that differentiates between sportive and ethical norms. We do so based on Loland's straightforward, common-sense definition of technology, because it paves the way for a clearer understanding of the conflict between these two levels of normative enquiry and makes it possible to deal with them in a systematic manner.

Normative assessments of sport and technology

In his article *Sport Technologies – A moral view*, Loland (2002) puts forward his definition of technology in order to normatively evaluate various forms of sport technology and their desirability in relation to the purpose of sport. Loland differentiates between three ideal-typical interpretations of sport; what he calls the 'non-theory', the 'thin theory' and the 'thick theory'. Only the thin and thick theories are relevant to the present chapter, since they are the only ones that have normative implications and are built on a philosophical understanding of sport.[1] Loland defends the thick theory, which links 'sport to general moral ideals' (Loland 2002: 165).

Loland wants sport to accommodate disparate moral ideals. Ancient moral ideals are in play when he claims that sport 'ought to be an arena for human development and flourishing and one among many elements of the good life' (Loland 2002: 165). But modern moral ideals of beneficence and non-maleficence must also be incorporated in our theoretical understanding of sport. Accordingly, sport 'ought to take place within a framework of non-exposure to unnecessary harm' (Loland 2002: 167).

In an earlier article, *Fair Play: Historical anachronism or topical ideal?* Loland (1998) claimed that sportspersons should not try to win at sport for external reasons such as profit or prestige but rather for internal reasons, where winning means 'to end on top on the final ranking of competitors according to performance of the skills defined by the shared ethos of the game' (Loland 1998: 95). This claim is based on a utilitarian calculus that shows that if all players play to win for internal reasons, it will most likely contribute to positive experiences for all involved (Loland 1998). When sport is interpreted as an activity that ought to live up to these shared ideals, it provides normative reasons to dismiss certain technologies as relevant to genuine athletic excellence. For example, doping should be dismissed if it exposes athletes to unnecessary harm, by damaging their health.

At first glance this seems reasonable. One problem, however, is that neither does the 'thick' interpretation provide an accurate description of the relationship between sport and morality, nor does it provide a framework for systematic deliberations on sport technological issues. It fails to do so because, by insisting that sporting values must be in line with moral ideals, it masks existing differences between sporting and moral norms making it impossible to understand and deal with cases in which sportive and moral norms conflict. Such cases are arguably the most complicated and therefore those that need systematic sport philosophical consideration. Before considering examples of such cases, we need to understand what non-moral sportive norms could be. In other words, what we need is an understanding of sport as an autotelic activity with its own inner logic and values. We need in Loland's terms a 'thin' theory of sport.

The thin theory of sport, according to Loland, is a theory of the value of sport in which value is related to performance in competition and not to general moral values. Loland relates this theory to the logic of quantitative growth and objective measurements that fits athletics well but, if it is supposed to be a general theory of sport, we need to include a qualitative or an aesthetic dimension as well. Thus, the thin theory is a normative theory of sport that derives its norms and values directly from the internal logic of sport without an attempt to integrate general moral principles such as the principle of utility or the golden rule.[2]

In the present context, we are concerned only with what we find to be the key element in sporting contests. As Scott Kretchmar (1998) has pointed out, it is the goal of a sport competition to test the abilities of athletes through a contest. The result of a sports contest can only be a valid measure of superior sporting abilities if victory signifies athletic superiority in relation to the specific abilities that a given sport is designed to measure. If victory in a certain contest is not the result of athletically superior abilities, then that particular contest has failed as a test of such abilities and therefore has lost its *raison d'être*. Therefore, victory in a sporting competition *ought* to signify true athletic superiority. This, we suggest, is the key sportive norm to be observed. In order for a competition to be meaningful as a test of those abilities, everyone participating ought to behave in a manner that ensures that the result is indeed a valid measure of athletic superiority. In other words, they ought to play fairly. But fair play in the sense of abiding by the rules is not a moral duty. It is a purely sporting norm, as Bernard Suits seems to recognize when he writes: 'In morals obedience to rules makes the action right, but in games it makes the action' (Suits 2005: 46). Needless to say, this norm may be breached; for example, if one attempts to bribe the judge to secure victory.

Bearing this in mind, let us take another look at Loland's thick theory. According to Loland, the norm of non-maleficence should be incorporated into our theoretical understanding of sportive values and norms. If a boxer shows up in a ring with iron-packed gloves he is violating a sport-ethical norm of non-maleficence, according to the thick theory, since the intention of the boxer is to hurt his opponent beyond what a boxer can be thought to have agreed to. Similarly, it is unsporting according to the thick theory to trip an opponent in a running race since it is an act of maleficence that, if practised widely, would prevent these athletic competitions from being an arena for human flourishing. According to the thin theory of sport, such behaviour is most certainly also unacceptable. But it is unacceptable for a very different reason. It is unacceptable for sport internal reasons since cheating by tripping an opponent or entering the ring with iron-packed gloves prevents running races and boxing from functioning properly, as a reliable test of abilities. In other words, they are unsportsmanlike because they are at odds with the very idea of the particular sport competitions. It is also immoral, since it goes against moral principles, such as those of beneficence or non-maleficence, but such reasons are based on a moral rationality, not a sporting one. The aforementioned reasons make tripping opponents in running races or knocking down opponents in boxing with iron-packed gloves *immoral*, but these are not the reasons why they are unsporting. What makes these actions unsporting is the simple fact that they prevent the particular instances of running and boxing from functioning properly, as a reliable test of abilities. In other words, they are unsportsmanlike because they are at odds with the very idea of the particular sport competitions.

If an athlete deliberately hurts an opponent in pursuit of victory, the person in question ignores sporting as well as moral norms and is both immoral and unsporting. But the fact that ethical and sportive norms sometimes correlate does not mean that they *always* correlate or that sportive norms are instances of general moral norms. This becomes apparent in cases where there is conflict between the two. Such conflicts may be out of sight in sports like cricket and golf, but they appear as soon as we turn our attention to boxing and mixed martial arts (MMA). As with any other sport, there are standards of excellence and therefore norms and values attached to boxing and MMA. But are they moral? Not in a modern sense of the word 'moral', in which altruism plays a crucial part.[3] The goal in boxing and MMA is to conquer one's opponent by way of physically harm, either by blows to the head or body. Doing so by way of a knock out is to be preferred and applauded. To participate with success takes virtues such as courage, endurance, resilience and discipline but that does not render the activity or the attitudes it fosters moral in nature.

In his article 'Violence in Sports', Robert L. Simon argues in favour of morally reforming boxing and points to fencing as a positive historic example (Simon 2007: 386). Rule changes and the use of technology transformed duelling with a deadly outcome into modern bloodless fencing. Perhaps something similar could be achieved with regard to boxing, Simon speculates. Rules against blows to the head and various forms of equipment protecting the body could be a recommendable way forward – from a moral perspective, that is. However, such inventions would be disastrous from a boxing perspective, because they would in effect bring an end to the 'noble art of self defence'. Instead, they would result in the birth of an entirely new sport, with emphasis on different skills and standards of excellence. The thin theory of sport would be able to understand and respect the rationality behind those who wish to defend boxing and MMA from 'game-changing' moral intervention. Proponents of the thin theory might still opt in favour of moral arguments and support certain changes but, because they also respects the pure sporting side of the matter, they might be looking for some sort of compromise. According to the thick theory of sport, boxing and MMA are essentially flawed, since they are not in accordance with general moral principles. The proposed changes will eradicate those flaws, elevating them into a more true form of sport. In this view, there is no real conflict between moral and sportive interests and values and therefore no need to be particular sensitive towards sports that seems immoral but are valued nevertheless by those engaged within them. Boxing and MMA could be first in line for revision at the hands of the thick theory, but many more could follow. And now, let us take a closer look at elite sport in general.

One of the key moral principles on which Loland has based his thick theory is the Aristotelian principle of human flourishing. From the perspective of the thick theory: 'sport ought to be arena for human development and flourishing and one among many elements of the good life' (Loland 2002: 165). Surely sport in moderate doses can be one element in a good life. Elite sport today, however, demands an extreme, time-consuming, one-minded focus on very specific physical abilities on athletes. Such demands are not easy to harmonise with Aristotle's idea of human flourishing, to say the least. For sport to be in line with Aristotle's vision of a good life – an ideal that entailed the development of a variety of human abilities – elite sport would have to be given up in favour of the kind of amateur sports found in twentieth-century England. A good man in Aristotle's mind looked more like an aristocratic rationally enlightened and physically skilled gentleman than a modern elite athlete. Consistently thought through, Loland's thick theory ought to be far more critical towards sport technology associated with elite sport, including the employment of doctors, trainers, advanced fitness machines, and so on. Loland admits that the thick theory is historically related to the amateur ideologies found in the early twentieth-century England. As it turns out, his version of the thick theory is not as far removed from its historical roots as he would like to believe. A 2012 debate in the journal *Sport, Ethics and Philosophy* concerning sport and goal-line technology illustrates the clash between the thick and the thin theory of sport well.

In his article 'The Fallacies of the Assumptions Behind the Arguments for Goal-Line Technology in Soccer', Nlandu (2012) implicitly defends the thick theory by presenting an argument against goal-line technology that is based on a highly idealistic framework. The proponents of goal-line technology unintentionally reinforce the corruption of sport by putting too much importance on the final result and not enough on the play spirit, according to Nlandu. Instead of goal-line technology we should educate players to take personal responsibility in protecting the integrity of the game so that less involvement will be required from game officials (Nlandu 2012: 462). The proposed education should be ethical in nature and should 'construe sport as a *striving together* towards a common goal" (Nlandu 2012: 463). The goal of sport in Nlandu's understanding is not primarily personal or team victory but the common goal of achieving the best sport experience enjoyable by all. Again, the link to historical British amateur ideals is obvious.

In contrast to Nlandu's view, the British sport philosopher Ryall (2012: 448) implicitly uses a thin theory perspective to defends the use of goal-line technology in football by insisting that the essence of good sport is justice. Ryall does not define 'justice' but it is clear from her argument that she understands justice in sport to have been served when victory really does signify athletic superiority in relation to the rules of the game. Rule keeping and impartial officiating is crucial in attaining that end but if technology can also assist us in this regard it should be endorsed for that reason alone.

The thin theory is a theory about sport as realised in the present. It respects sport and morality as different normative realms and will listen to both in its attempt to deliberate on sport technological issues. The thick theory on the other hand builds its normative views on sport technology on an idealistic notion of sport that entails the same love of the past and fear of the future that we encountered at the beginning of this chapter.

Concluding remarks

Technology, whether medical, material or mechanical, does not pose any serious threat to sport as such unless it threatens the internal logic of sport. From a sporting perspective, it makes no difference whether the abilities being tested stem from nature's genetic lottery or gene technology. Still, there may be moral reasons to oppose the development of gene technology or other forms of technology for sporting purposes. We must acknowledge that there can be conflicts between sportive and moral norms and try to grasp the nature of those conflicts duly taking into account the importance of both sportive and moral values. Thus, the thin theory of sport – based only on autotelic sportive norms – provides a crucial contribution to an overall systematic approach to difficult sport technological issues in which morality must also play its proper role.

Notes

1   The non-theory of sport has no interest in sport *per se* but finds sport useful as a means to an external end. Such sport external goals could be everything from personal status over financial rewards to political and national prestige. If a certain technologies can increase the likelihood of attaining such ends via sport, they are accepted, otherwise not.
2   The competitive element found in sport and its constitutive relation to excellence is very closely linked to what was considered ethical in ancient Hellenic times. However, it is not upon this ancient

understanding of virtue that Loland's thick theory is based. His aim is to provide us with a theory of sport that is in accordance with a more modern understanding of ethics in which altruism plays a crucial part. It is the thick theory's attempt to interpret sportive norms in such a manner that we oppose.

3   In his book *The Ethics of Doping and Anti-Doping – Redeeming the Soul of Sport?* Møller (2010) argues that immoral characteristics can be found in many forms of sport. The goal of sport in general is victory, not a Christian form of altruism.

References

Amis, J. and Cornwell, T. B. eds (2005) *Global Sport Sponsorship*. Oxford: Berg.

Bale, J. (1993) *Sport, Space and the City*. London: Routledge.

Bale, J. (1996) *Landscapes of Modern Sport*. Leicester: Leicester University Press.

Bale, J. (2003) *Sport Geography*. London: Routledge.

Boyle, R. and Haynes, R. (2009) *Power Play – Sport the Media and the Popular Culture*. Edinburgh: Edinburgh University Press.

Breivik, G. (2013) 'Zombie-Like or Superconscious? A Phenomenological and Conceptual Analysis of Consciousness in Elite Sport', *Journal of the Philosophy of Sport* 40: 85–106.

Butryn, T. (2002) 'Cyborg Horizons: Sport and the Ethics of Self-Technologization' in: Miah, A. and Eassom, S. B., eds. *Sports Technology: History, Philosophy and Policy*. Oxford: Elsevier Science, 111–34.

Crawford, R. (1984) 'A Cultural Account of "Health"' in: J. B. McKinlay, ed. *Issues in the Political Economy of Health Care*. London: Tavistock, 61–103.

Ellul, J. (1964) *The Technological Society*. New York: Vintage.

Heidegger, M. (1993) 'The Question Concerning Technology', translated by W. Lovitt with revision by D. F. Krell, in D. F. Krell, ed. *Basic Writings*, 2nd ed. London: Routledge

Hoberman, J. (1992) *Mortal Engines: The science of performance and the dehumanization of sport*. New York: Free Press.

Hoberman, J. (1988) 'Sport and the Technological Image of Man' in: W. J. Morgan and K. V. Meier, eds. *Philosophic Inquiry in Sport*. Champaign, IL: Human Kinetics, 319–27.

Jackson, S. and Csikszentmihalyi, M., eds (1999) *Flow in Sports: The keys to optimal experiences and performances*. Champaign, IL: Human Kinetics.

Jenkins, M. and Subic, A. eds (2003) *Materials in Sport Equipment*, vol. 1. Cambridge: Woodhead.

Jenkins, M. and Subic, A. eds (2007) *Materials in Sport Equipment*, vol. 2. Cambridge: Woodhead.

Kretchmar, R. S. (1998) 'Soft metaphysics: a precursor to good sports ethics', in: M. J. McNamee and S. J. Parry, eds. *Ethics and Sport*. London: E. and F. N. Spon.

Larson, J. S. (1991) *The Measurement of Health: Concepts and indicators*. Westport, CT: Greenwood.

Loland, S. (1998) 'Fair Play: Historical anachronism or topical ideal?' in: M. J. McNamee and S. J. Parry, eds. *Ethics and Sport*. London: E. and F. N. Spon, 79–103.

Loland, S. (2002) 'Sport Technologies: A moral view' in: Miah, A. and Eassom, S. B., eds. *Sports Technology: History, philosophy and policy*. Oxford: Elsevier Science, 157–71.

Lupton, D. (2003) *Medicine as Culture: Illness, disease and the body in western societies*. 2nd ed. London: Sage.

McGrath, J. (2004) *Loving Big Brother: Performance, privacy and surveillance space*. Abingdon: Routledge.

Magdalinski, T. (2009) *Sport, Technology and the Body. The nature of performance*. Abingdon: Routledge.

Miah, A. and Eassom, S. B. eds. (2002) *Sports Technology: History, Philosophy and Policy*. Research in Philosophy and Technology Handbook series, vol. 21. Oxford: Elsevier Science.

Müller, A. (2007) *Sterben, Tod und Unsterblichkeit im Sport: Eine existenzphilosophishe Deutung* [*Dying, Death and Immortality in Sports: An existential philosophical interpretation*]. Doctoral dissertation, Institute for Education and Philosophy, German Sport University Cologne.

Møller, V. (2010) *The Ethics of Doping and Anti-doping: Redeeming the soul of sport?* Abingdon: Routledge.

Nlandu, T. (2012) 'The Fallacies of the Assumptions Behind the Arguments for Goal-Line Technology in Soccer', *Sport, Ethics and Philosophy* 6 (4): 451–66.

Ogles, B. M., Lynn, S. J., Masters, K. S., Hoefel, T. D. and Marsden, K. A. (1993–1994) 'Runners' Cognitive Strategies and Motivations: Absorption, fantasy style and dissociative experiences', *Imagination, Cognition and Personality* 13(2): 163–74.

Robertson, A. (2001) 'Biotechnology, political rationality and discourses on health risk', *Health* 5(3): 293–309.

Russell, C. (2010) 'Four Million Test-Tube Babies and Counting', *The Atlantic* 7 October. Available online at www.theatlantic.com/technology/archive/2010/10/four-million-test-tube-babies-and-counting/ 64198 (accessed 23 October 2014).

Ryall, E. (2012), 'Are there any Good Arguments Against Goal-Line Technology?' *Sport, Ethics and Philosophy* 6 (4): 439–50.

Shilling, C. (2005) The Body and Social Theory. London: Sage.

Simon, R. L. (2007) 'Violence in Sports' in: W. J. Morgan, ed. *Ethics in Sport*, 2nd ed. Champaign, IL: Human Kinetics, 379–88.

Strom, S. (2013) 'Genetic Changes to Food May Get Uniform Labeling' *New York Times* 31 January. Available online at www.nytimes.com/2013/02/01/business/food-companies-meet-to-weigh-federal-label-for-gene-engineered-ingredients.html?pagewanted=all&_r=0 (accessed 23 October 2014).

Suits, B. (2005) *The Grasshopper: Games, Life, and Utopia*, 2nd ed. Peterborough, Ontario: Broadview.

Tamburrini, C. (2002) 'After Doping What? The Morality of the Genetic Engineering of Athletes' in: Miah, A. and Eassom, S. B., eds. *Sports Technology: History, Philosophy and Policy*, Oxford: Elsevier Science, 253–68.

Umminger, W. (1962) *Supermen, Heroes and Gods – The Story of Sport Through the Ages*. New York: McGraw-Hill.

INDEX

Abe, Shinobu 106, 109
ability: connection to knowing-how 121
ableism 306
abnormality 304
Abrahams, Harold 30–1
absence: and causation 280
absurdity 150–1
acceptance: movement of 186
acknowledgement 291
acrobatism 156
Acromegaly 87
activity limitations 304–5, 306, 307
ACTN3 (alfa-actinin 3 polymorphism) 81, 82
Adams, Jeff 310
Addams, Jane: immigrant populations 214
additive drugs 321
adjudication 255; principles of 266, 267, 269
Adorno, Theodore W. 220
advantage: competitive 86, 87, 342–3, 371; and
    penalties 343; performance 87, 88; positional
    353, 358; property 87–8; unearned 328–9;
    unfair 86, 87, 311
aesthetics: art and sport 74–8; artistic vs.
    aesthetic 74; athletes' movement 70; beauty
    see beauty; conservatism 73; and
    disinterestedness 72; judgement 72, 73;
    narrow and conservative approach 71;
    pleasure 70, 71, 74; possibilities linked to
    hierarchy of games 70; qualities of sport 70;
    realm 152; rejection of 72; spectators 73;
    sport as life enhancing 71; sporting drama 71;
    and taste 71–2, 73; theodicy 154; and
    winning/professionalism 74
After Virtue (MacIntyre) 135
Agassi, Andre 149
agon 154–5, 333
agreements: and conventions 38; social 38, 44

alfa-actinin 3 (ACTN3) polymorphism 81, 82
alienation: of athletes 225; concept of 225;
    possibilities of disalienation 226; of sport 225;
    turning away from reality 225
Allen-Collinson, J.: woman's running body 202–3
Althusser, Louis 224
Alzheimer's disease 85
amateurism 40; anti-commercial ideals 416;
    conventional norms 40; correcting bad calls
    48; ethos of sport 40–1; hybrid construction
    45; intelligible conception of sport 46;
    opposed to playing for money 40, 51n7;
    opposite view to professionalism 41–2;
    purpose of sport 41–2; rational reconciliation
    with professionalism 45–6; selectively
    borrowing from professionalism 46;
    sportsmanship 30–1, 36; use of strategy 47–8
amputee athletes 303–4; amputation surgery
    312; competing at Olympic Games 90, 92;
    recategorization of Olympic events for 92; *see
    also* Pistorius, Oscar
anabolic steroids 320
analytical philosophy 55, 137
Anarchy, State and Utopia (Nozick) 412–13, 422
anatman 101
Ancient Greek Athletics (Miller) 239–40
Ancient Greeks 370; competitive advantage at
    Olympic Games 371; cultivating excellence
    through sport and philosophy 372; excellence
    of body and mind 372
Ancient Greek sport 239
ancient Olympic Games: educational function of
    athletes 373; equality of opportunity 333;
    exclusion of women 378, 380n17; influence
    on Olympism 368, 370, 372, 373; larger
    community 380n15; statues of winners 373;
    victory odes 373; *see also* Olympic Games

ancient world: and religion 242–3
Anderson, Douglas: growth through endurance
    sport 210
Anderson, Elizabeth 413, 417
androgens 86
androgen-suppressive therapy 86
androgyny 164
anitya 101–2
anomalous monism 194
anorexia 187
Anscombe, Elizabeth 55
antagonistic reciprocity 150
anti-doping: athlete biological passport 318;
    banning drugs 341; burden of proof 320;
    conceptual ambiguities 321–2; cost and
    effectiveness 318; expense and practical
    difficulties of programs 318; harm prevention
    as goal 320–1; injustices 319–20; line drawing
    321–2; preserving meaning 328–30; privacy
    319; promoting fairness 327, 341; protecting
    health 327–8; strategies 430; war on drugs
    363
anti-intellectualism 120
anxiety 148
apodictic truth 180
apolipoprotein epsilon 4 allele (ApoE4) 85
Apollonia: artistic power 154
appearances *see* phenomenology
appropriation 150
Aquinas, Thomas 241
arbitrary conventions 42, 42–3
archery: and Zen 249
Arendt, Hannah 142–3, 143
aretē 372, 373
argumentative discourse 47
Aristotle 3, 132, 135, 185, 210, 275; causation
    278; concept of beauty 375; definition of
    formal justice 336; human flourishing 435;
    human happiness 372; rational activities 357;
    rationality 356–7
Arjuna 100
Armstrong, David: on driving automatism
    124–5; mind-brain identity theory 196
Armstrong, Lance 315–16; lifetime sanction 320;
    medals achieved through cheating 374
Arnold, Thomas 235n8
arrivistes 407
art: definition 74–5; differences with sport 75–6;
    expression 75; imaginary quality 75;
    institutional theory of 53, 54, 55, 56–7, 57;
    and sport 74–8; worldmaking 76
artificial intelligence (AI) 196, 393–4
artistic theodicy 154
Asad, Talal: pre-modern religious writing 244
asceticism 155
áskēsis 155–6, 157
Asociación Latina de Filosofía del Deporte

(ALFiD; Latin Association for Philosophy of
    Sport) 5
Aspin, D. N.: aesthetic qualities of sport 70
athlete biological passport 318
athletes: alienated robots 225, 227; amputation
    surgery 312; amputee 92, 303–4; androgen
    thresholds 88; anorexia 187; bionic 354, 356;
    body movement and capitalism 223; brain
    injuries 391; and commercialisation 416; and
    communities 212–13; competing at Olympic
    Games 90, 92; consciousness of 199; creativity
    of 78; deaf 300; disabled 302–4, 306;
    discrimination against females 88; doping
    93–4, 174; educational function 373;
    eligibility criteria of female athletes 86;
    endurance 87; enhancement *see*
    enhancement; equity of access 91; facticity
    and transcendence 149; fulfilling the poetic
    task of life 151; genetic engineering 428, 429;
    guinea pigs 93; IAAF regulations for female
    athletes 86; importance of bodily differences
    162; instrumental view of athletes' bodies
    432; language of 416; market value 170;
    movement of 70, 182, 223; mutual
    manifestation 280–1; out-of-competition
    testing for drugs 319; preceding conscious
    processes 203; pressure to return to play 84;
    professionalization of 418; recategorization of
    Olympic Games for 92; relevant inequality in
    performance 339–41; role models 373–4;
    rules, challenge and acceptance 87, 187; strict
    liability condition 310; striving to improve
    358; technology and 432, 433; testosterone
    levels 86–7; training for women 214;
    transcending technology 432, 433; unfair
    advantage 86–7; use of potions 315;
    wheelchair 307; women outperforming men
    169–70; *see also* performance
athletic competition 27
athletic enterprise: amateur and professional
    approaches 41–2
Atlas Sports Genetics 81, 82
atman 99
Atry, Ashkan: on responsibility for doping 94
Augustine 241
Aurelius, Marcus 380n15
Austin, J. L. 59; verdictives 256
authenticity 148, 184
automatism 124–5
autonomic dysreflexia 310
autonomy 166–7
avidya 101
Awa, Kenzo 107
awareness: reflective 123, 126; in-zone 123–4;
    zoned-out 124–5

bad faith 148–9

Baker, William J. 240

Bale, John: technology and sport 427

banned substances 310

Bargh, John 395

Barron, Robert: on play 247

baseball 16; electronic aids 263; interference 26; perfect games 261; questions about formalism 26; strike zone 263

beauty: bringing disparate elements into a harmonious whole 71; concept of 375; and justice 375; and pleasure 71; as private ecstasy 71; sport as life enhancing 71

Beauvoir, Simon de 143

Beck, Simon: legal positivism 266–7

behaviorism 194, 391–2

Beijing Games (2008) 301, 375

Being and Nothingness (Sartre) 147

Beller, Jennifer 132

Bell, Melina Constantine Bell: emancipatory potential of women's bodybuilding 174

Belmont Report 362

benchwarmers 387–8

Berenson, Bernard 70; imaginary quality of art 75

Berger, Peter 242; play 246

Bergson, Henri 143

Berkeley, George: idealism 194, 195

Berlin Olympic Games (1936) 229, 231

Berlin Sports Club for the Deaf 300

Berman, Mitchell N.: defence and revision of formalism 267, 268; technological aids 261–2; temporal variance 264–5

Berra, Yogi 391

Best, David 5; aesthetic and purposive sports 73; aesthetic definition of art 75; difference between sport and art 75; Indian dance 76; sport and the subject 75–6

Best, Steven: megaspectacle 228

betting 401–2

Beyond a Boundary (James) 70

Bhagavad Gita 100

bio-Amazons 170, 171

bioethics: biotechnology and the categorization of sport 91–2; concussions and return to play issues 84–6; conflict of interest 83–6; conflict of interest dilemmas 92–4; direct-to-consumer genetics for talent identification 81–3; future directions 91–4; gender issues 86–9; Hastings Center 325; responsibility for doping 93–4; role of biotechnology in the Paralympics 89–91; top-down 325

biological absolutes 339

biological naturalism 196

biomedical enhancements 323, 329

bionic athletes 354, 356

biotechnology: performance-enhancing in sport 90–1; role in the Paralympics 89–91; running style of Oscar Pistorius 91–2

Birch, Jens 125

blades (prosthetic limbs) 89–90, 311

Bloch, Ernst 224–5

blocked exchanges 422

bodily differences 162

body: lived 183; and soul 241; and sport 230–1

body and mind: holistic approach 371, 372; separation 371, 372

bodybuilding 173–4, 325

body dysmorphic disorder 312

body modification 173–4

bog-snorkelling 60

Bok, Derek 379n11

Boorse, Christopher: definition of health 303

boosting 310

Bordner, Seth: unrestricted use of technological aids 262, 263

Borg, Bjorn 78

Bossuet, Jacques-Bénigne 218

Boulmerka, Hassiba 378

bounding 91, 92

'bounty' scandal 295

boxing 61, 435; dementia pugilistica 85

BPSA (British Philosophy of Sport Association) 5

Bradbury, Steven 374

Brahman 99, 100

BRAINBOUND 198

brain injuries 391

Brandes, Georg 143

breaking records 23, 47

breathing (Japanese philosophy) 107

Breivik, Gunnar: bodily existence related to sport 183; challenges Heidegger's concrete human body 201; consciousness of athletes 199; on Heidegger's equipmentality 200, 201; on reflective deliberations 125–6

Brett, George 37, 48–9, 389

A Brief Theology of Sport (Harvey) 245

British Philosophy of Sport Association (BPSA) 5

British Society of One-Armed Golfers 300

broad internalism 25–8, 30, 241, 266, 389

Brockport 3, 4

Brohm, Jean-Marie: alienation in sport 225; athletes as alienated robots 227; attacks sport ideology 223; background 221–2; on Baron Pierre de Coubertin 233; commercialisation of sport 412; false consciousness of sport 223; ideological mechanisms of capitalist society 224; massification of conscience 227; on spectacular sport 229; on sport and fascism 231; sport as embodiment of global capitalism 229; on sport as opium 231–2; sport slavery 227; on stupefied crowds 227

Brown, Albert 3

Brüggemann, Professor Gert-Peter 89, 90; on Oscar Pistorius's running style 91–2

brute reality 13
Bryant, Kobe 84
Buber, Martin 143
Buchanan, Allen 355, 362
Buckley, Anthony D.: sport as drama 78
Buddhism 243; accepts some Hindu views 101; *anatman* 101; *anitya* 101–2; *avidya* 101; *dharma* 101; *dukkha* 101; *magga* 101; metaphysical elements 101–2; *Middle Way* 101; *nirvana* 101; noble truths 101; origin 251–2n7; role of the body 105–6; *samudhaya* 101; Zen 106–9
Bugbee, Henry: nature of embodiment and meaning-making 211
bull run 156–7
Burghardt, Gordon M.: on play 118–19
Burke, Michael: segregation in sport 168
Burkett, B.: biotechnology and athletic performance 91; technology in sport 90
Butryn, T.: dehumanization of sport 429
Butt, Salman 402

Cagigal, José María 5
calls: in baseball 263; deception 257; genuine 256–7; made facts by umpires 256; make-up 263–4; open to review and revision 257; replays 257–8; technological aids 257–9, 260, 261–2; umpires' mistakes 261
Calvin and Hobbes 24
Calvinball 24
Campos, Daniel 212
Camus, Albert 143; existential experience of resistance and struggle 150; overcoming absurdity 150–1
capitalism: conflicts 219; false consciousness of sport 223–4; ideological mechanisms 224; pacifying the masses through sport 227; shambles post-First World War 221; sport as embodiment of 229
Carr, David 121
Carter, Robert 108
Cartesianism: clear and distinct ideas 193
The Case Against Perfection (Sandel) 353
Cassidy, Josh 307
Caulfield, T.: genetic tests 82
causation: by absence 280; doctrine of 193; empowered agency 278–80; mutual manifestation 280–1; powers 282–3; in sport 277–8
Cavanaugh, William 243; definition of religion 244
Center for Philosophic Exchange 4
Chalmers, David 394
Chamberlain, Wilt 15
Chan Buddhism 105
Chariots of Fire 30–1
Charlton, Bobby 281
cheating 12, 295, 343–4, 345

chess: versions 58–9
children: purpose and meaning of sport 83
China: Chan Buddhism 105; Confucianism 102–3; Daoism 103–5; patriarchal society 102
Chisholm, Roderick 117
Christianity: and ancient sport 239–40; and dualism 193; and embodiment 249–50
On Christian Teaching (Augustine) 241
chronic traumatic encephalopathy (CTE) 84–5
Chuang Tzu 103, 104
Ciomaga, Bogdan 44
Clark, K.: on cognition 197
clinical research 359–62; adults 359–60; benefits 363; children 360–1; equal distribution of benefits 363; germ line research 361–2; risks 360
Clough, Brian 281–2
coaching: behaviorism 391–2; benchwarmers 387–8; brain injuries suffered by athletes 391; coaching philosophy 383; enlightened generalists 386–7; epistemic virtues 386–7; ethical theory 387–90; ethical treatment of coaches 386; fast and slow thinking 396–7; functionalism 392–3; good coach 384–7; hidden brain 397; identity theory 392; Kantian approach 388; mental causation 391; panpsychism 394; philosophy of coaching 383; philosophy of the mind 390–4; situated 396; strong artificial intelligence 393–4; trustworthiness 386, 388; unconscious mind 395; and winning 384–5
cocaine 310
cognition: embodied 181; parity principle 197–8
cognitivism 123–4, 196, 203–4
Collected Papers (Peirce) 208
Collins, Harry: conceptualizing umpires' performance 258; justice 259–60
commercialisation: access to the goods of sport 413–16; and amateur ideals 416; availability of sport entertainment 413–14; blocked exchanges 422; contracts 418, 419; corporate boxes 413, 415; desperate exchanges 419; dignity 420; economic literature 413; exclusion of minorities 415–16; exploitation 418–19; improved facilities and resources 415; incentive structure 414; increased ticket prices 413; language of athletes 416; losing touch with local communities 414–15; loss of the class-mixing experience 415; market systems of distribution 414; meanings of sport 417–18; moral education 422; objectification 419–21; philosophical literature 412–13; principle of respect for persons 420; and pursuit of excellence 416–17; regulating the market 422; role of the state 421–3; salary caps 422
Common Rule 361

communication: natural 13–14
community: athletes and 212–13; larger 380n15;
losing touch with 414–15; and pragmatism
212–13; theory of world community 377–8;
under Confucianism 103
competition: athletic 27; categories and their
psychologies 293–4; distinction between tests
and contests 289–90; domestications of war
288; institutional varieties 287, 288; mutual
quest for excellence 297; nature of 289; non-
competitive activities of sport 289;
non-competitive and competitive
characteristics 290; opponents 290–1, 292;
paradox of 291, 291–2; as relationship 290–3;
self-competition approach 292–3; sport
paradigm 288; theory of the dialectic 291–2;
virtues and vices 294–7; zero-sum logic 294,
297, 298
competitive advantage 86, 87, 342–3, 371
competitiveness 225
concentrated spectacle 228
concept game 56
The Concept of Law (Hart) 25
The Concept of Mind (Ryle) 120, 131
concern for excellence 209–10
concrete appearances 179
concussion 84–6
confidentiality 83–4
conflict 150
conflict of interest 83–5
Confucianism 102–3, 105, 243; *ren* 102–3; and
sport 103; *yi* 103
Connor, Steven: changed meaning of sport 289;
competitive paradox 291–2
Conolly, Maureen: education-based embedded
curriculum 146
conquistadors 116
consciousness 395, 397; false 223; false
consciousness of sport 223–4; preceding
conscious processes 203; social and historical
195; in sport performance 199–200;
transcendental 197; whole person 195
consent, informed 360
consequentialism 134
conservatism: judging aesthetic qualities 73
constant conjunction 277, 278
constitutive rules: and conventional agreements
13; and games 11; importance of 24; integral
to knowledge of sport 119–20; levels of
violation 18–19; meaning of 308, 335;
normative support of deep conventions 39;
and play 119; tools used by gamerights 15;
total adherence to 18
contests 154–5; comparison with tests 118,
289–90
contextualism 269–70
contingent identity 194

contracts 418, 419
*A Contribution to the Critique of Hegel's Philosophy
of Right* (Marx) 231
conventionalism 25; and agreements 38;
arbitrary nature 42–3; compliance of
directives 41; coordination 37–8, 38;
criticisms of 35–7; deep 29, 30; features 40–2;
and internalism 29–32; multiform character
37; normative principles 35–6, 40, 41, 42, 44,
45; subject to moral scrutiny 29; surface 29;
ubiquitous nature 37
conventionalists 25
Convention (Lewis) 37
Cooper, Adam: on corporeality 250
coordinating conventions 38, 41
coordination problems 37, 38
co-participation 307, 346
Cordner, C. D.: creativity of athletes 78
corporate boxes 413, 415
corporeality 196, 250
corruption 376
cosmopolitanism 377
Coubertin, Baron Pierre de 6, 132, 301, 368;
critique by Simonovic 223; Olympism 152,
156, 184, 369; reactionary ideology 223, 233;
viewed as reactionary reformer 233
Council of Europe's Bioethics Convention
Article 12 82
Cranston, Toller 75
cricket: aesthetic pleasure 70; consciousness of
batsmen 199–200
criterion/criteria: and play 117–18, 118;
problem of 117; and sports 120
critical theory 219–20
critique: notion of 219–20
Crouch, Brent: Royce's conception of loyalty
212
Culbertson, Leon: bad faith 149
Curry, Wesley 26
cycling: doping scandals 93

DaCosta, Lamartine: Olympism 369
D'Agostino, F.: constitutive rules 18; on ethos 62
Daly, John 402
dangerous sports 156–7
danza de los voladores (dance of the flyers) 116
Daoism 103–5; self-cultivation 104; *shen* 104;
wuwei 104; *xing* 104
darshanas 98, 99
Dasein 197
Davidson, Donald 30; anomalous monism 194
Davis, P.: vices of partisan fans 408
Dawkins, Richard 251n1
Debord, D.: media spectacle 227
Debord, Guy: occult controlling centre 228;
spectacle critique 228
declarative knowledge 120

deep conventions 29, 30; arbitrary nature 42–3; evolving 39; normative responses 39; practice-dependent, internal purpose 41; of sport 38–9
defence: movement of 186
definitional deception 343
DeKosky, S. T.: screening for ApoE4 85
Delattre, Edwin J.: essence of sport 294, 298
dementia 84; pugilistica 85
Democritus 194
de novo review 262
depression 195
Descartes, Rene 193; clear and distinct ideas 193; method of radical doubt 193; separation of body and mind 371, 372, 390
descriptive ethics 139
desperate exchanges 419
dharma 99, 101; in Buddhism 101; in Hinduism 100
dialectical theory 291–2
Dickie, George 54
diffuse spectacle 228
dignity 420
Diogenes 380n15
Dionysian: artistic power 154
direct-to-consumer (DTC) companies 81–2
disability sport: amputation surgery 312; athletes' rejection of disability label 306; body parts and whole persons 302, 303; co-participation 307; deaf athletes 300; differences between the ICF and the ICIDH 306–8; disabled athletes 302–4; and disease 303, 304; doping and TUEs 310; environmental factors 305; ICF definition of disability 304–5; ICIDH definition of disability 302, 303, 304; intellectual disability 309; origins of Paralympic movement 300–1; permanence of impairment 307; taxonomy of disablement 302; vital goals 306; *see also* Paralympic Games; Paralympic sports
disabled sportspersons 198
disclosure 83–4
discourse approach 36
discourse perspective 48; normative theory 45
discovery approach 36–7
discretion 269
discrimination: equality and non-discrimination 162; against women in sport 168, 169–70
Discus Thrower (Myron) 372
disease: and disability 303, 304
disinterestedness 72
dismissive judgements 257
disqualifications 18
distributive norms 336–7
diversity: and Olympism 377–8
diving 25, 32n4, 344–5
Dixon, Nicholas 257; fans' loyalty 404–6;

patriotism in sport 408; winning and losing 295
do (Japanese philosophy) 107, 108; application to sport 108
doping 93–4, 134, 137; anti-doping *see* anti-doping; definitions 316; effect of ban on female athletes 174; and horseracing 315; libertarianism 322, 412–13; and Olympism 376; potions 315; pro-doping 317, 322–4; scholarship 325–6; therapeutic use exemption (TUE) certificates 310; transhumanism 322–3; WADA Code 316
Doris, John 396
double-aspect theory 195–6
double horizon 183
Dowey, John: concept of growth 210
Downcast Eyes (Jay) 230
Dreyfus, Hubert: expert performance 122–3; on language skills 203; skilful coping 123, 182; on tennis swings 123
driving: side of road chosen by drivers 37–8
drugs: additive 321; banning 341; EPO (erythropoietin) 316, 320, 322; and genetics 352–3; out-of-competition testing 319; performance enhancement in sport 341–2; restorative 321; safe 327–8; war on 363; *see also* anti-doping; doping; enhancement
dualism 2, 192–3, 211, 390
dukkha 101
Durant, Will: on habit formation 210
du Toit, Natalie 90
Dworkin, Ronald: characterization of law 26; conservatism of 17; legal precedent 16; precedent 19; predictability 17; principles of law 26; respect for games' rules 17

Eagleman, David 397
Eastern philosophy: Buddhism 101–2, 105–6; Chan Buddhism 105; Confucianism 102–3, 105; Daoism 103–5; *do* 107, 108; environmental studies 110; gender studies 109; genetic enhancement 110; Hinduism 101; Japanese sport philosophy 109–10; philosophies and sciences of the mind 109–10; Zen Buddhism 106–9
Edgar, A.: narrow and conservative approach of aesthetics 71
education: theory of 373–5
Edwards, Lisa: challenging masculine ideology of sport 171–2; relational approach to sport 172
Edwards, Robert G. 428
Edwards, Steven: on Oscar Pistorius's running style 91
effects: causation and 277–8
eidetic universals 180
Einstein, Albert 49
Either - Or (Kierkegaard) 152

Eitzen, D. Stanley 294
Elcombe, Tim L. 78, 212
elective amputation 312
Elias, N.: betting 402
Elliott, R. K.: aesthetic qualities of sport 70
Ellis, Robert 245
Ellul, Jacques 432
emancipation: human 219; mainstream 230;
    political 219; sexual 230
embedded cognition (HEMC) 198
embodied cognition 181
embodiment 183; and Christianity 249–50; in
    human nature 248–9; and pragmatism
    210–11; in sport 173; and Zen 249
Emerson, Ralph Waldo 209
emotion: in sport 198–9
emotional integrity 199
empowered agency 278–80
encumbered competitions 293
endurance athletes 87
endurance sport: growth through 210
Engels, Friedrich: on phantasmagorical and
    ideological rule 232–3
English, Jane 162; basic benefits 163; on equality
    of access to sports 163; on new sports for
    women's distinctive abilities 164; skill classes
    163–4
enhancement 323; benefits of clinical research
    363; biomedical research 354, 355; case for
    354–5; distinguishing between biomedical
    and medical treatments 355; and drugs
    352–3, 354; mastery 357–8; nature, human
    nature and the natural 356; nature of 355–6;
    positional advantages 353; psychological risks
    of 357–9; restriction on technologies 363–4;
    risks of clinical research 359–62; tactics to
    counter drugs and genetic engineering 364;
    war on drugs 363
enhancements 329
enlightened generalists 386–7
Enlightenment 106, 219; source of modern
    philosophical critique 233
Epic period 100
epistemic virtues 386–7
epistemology: cognitivism 123–4; expert
    performance 123–6; knowing sports 116–19;
    methodists 117; *particularists* 117, 119; problem
    of the criterion 117; ways of knowing in
    sports 119–22
EPO (erythropoietin) 316, 320, 322
equality: access to sport 161–3; bodily
    differences in sport 162; equal opportunity to
    perform 337–9; and non-discrimination 162;
    system inequalities 339; treatment of
    individuals 308
equipmentality 200
equity of access 91

erythropoietin (EPO) 316, 320
Escobar, Andrés 402
essences: phenomena 180
essentialism 276; gender 213–14
ethical realm 152
ethicists 135–7
ethics: authority and expertise 135–8; Baron
    Pierre de Coubertin 132; conceptual and
    normative analysis 132; consequentialism 134;
    corruption of external goods 135; in-depth
    collections focused on single sports 138;
    descriptive 139; empirical data 137; ethicist
    135–7; facts and data 139; future prospects
    138–9; history and philosophical influences
    131–3; and Paralympic sports 308–12; and
    phenomenology 186–7; policy critique
    138–9; scholarship 132–3; scope of 133–5;
    sport and law 138; system of duties 132;
    utilitarianism 134; Victorian Britain 132;
    virtue 135
Ethics and Sport (McNamee and Parry) 132–3
Ethics (Keating) 334
Ethics, Money and Sport: This Sporting Mammon
    (Walsh and Giulianotti) 412
The Ethics of Sports Coaching (Hardman and
    Jones) 387
ethos 62
etiquette: sporting 31
Eudemian Ethics (Aristotle) 375
Eurocentrism 377
European Association for the Philosophy of
    Sport (EAPS) 5
European Rationalism 379–80n12
European Society of Human Genetics (ESHG)
    82
events: double-aspect theory 195
excellence: and commercialisation 416–17;
    concern for 209–10; pursuit of 176n10; quest
    for 27–8, 30–1, 297; theory of 371–3
existence *see* existential philosophy
existential freedom 148
Existentialism is Humanism (Sartre) 147
existential phenomenology 197; on existential
    phenomenology 201
existential philosophy: absence and nothingness
    147; alternative to objectifying tendencies
    143; *becoming* 144; being for the subject 144;
    choice and anxiety 147–9; condemned
    freedom 147–8; condemned to meaning
    145–6; conflict and resistance 149–52;
    experience related to existence 143–4;
    heightening of human existence 153–7;
    history of 142–3; human existence 143–5;
    motor meaning 147; perceptual faith 146–7;
    primordial faith 146; primordial relation
    145–6; rebuttal of intellectualism and
    rationalism 144; stages towards transcendent

aspects of existence 152–3; struggle and resistance in relation to necessary obstacles 150–2; synthesis of possibility and necessity 144; *see also* Kierkegaard, Søren A.; Nietzsche, Friedrich; Sartre, Jean-Paul

Expert Medical Panel 86

expert performance: heightened reflective awareness 126; information processing 123; modes of 124–6; ongoing and nonreflective 123; tennis 123; in-zone awareness 123–4

exploitation 418–19

expression: in art 75

externalism: distinction from internalism 22–3

external purposes: sport 73–4

Eyser, George 90

facticity 144, 148, 149

failure: intrinsic ingredient of sport 78

Fairhall, Neroli 90, 309

fair play: anti-doping 327; background and interpretations 333–5; and cheating 343–4, 345; distributive norms 336–7; fairness in sport 335–6; formal 345; formal justice *see* formal justice; informal 345; justice in sport 336–45; moral obligation 335, 336; normative rationale of fairness 335–6; opportunity and 309–10; and play tradition 345–7; spirit of sport 341

Fair Play: Ethics in Sport and Education (McIntosh) 334

Fair Play: Historical anachronism or topical ideal? (Loland) 433

Fair Play in Sport: A Moral Norm System 334, 412

Fair Play. Journal of Sport: Philosophy, Ethics and Law 5, 133

Fair Play (Lumpkin, Stoll & Beller) 132

Fair Play: Sport, Values, and Society (Simon) 334

Fair Play: The Ethics of Sport (Simon) 334

false consciousness 223; of sport 223–4

false reality 223

family: under Confucianism 103

fans: blind to sports negative features 227; concern for victory of individual or team 403; loyalty 404–6; partisan 403–6; purist 406–7; purist and partisan 294

fascism: and sport 231

Federal Policy for the Protection of Human Subjects 362

femininity: concept of 164, 165; male and female bodybuilders 173–4; value of women-only sport 168

feminism: androgyny 164–5; autonomy 166–7; basic benefits 163; bio-Amazons 170, 171; bodies and practices 171–5; bodily differences in sport 162; comparison of men and women in sport 213–14; control of sport 169; definition of woman in sport context 167; difference and integration 163–6; equality of

access to sport 161–3; gynocentric 171–2; humanist 171–2; identifying and valuing traits 172; integration-segregation debate 169; male standards 170–1; masculinity of sports 162–3; new sports for women 164; paternalism 166; performance of women compared to men 169–70; pressure to exhibit male determined ideals of femininity 164; relational approach to sport 172; separation in sport 168; social facts mistaken as natural facts 166; withdrawing from masculine sports 165–6

fencing 435

Fever Pitch (Hornby) 58

fiduciary commitment 242

first philosophy 275

fishing 13

fit 27–8

Flanagan, Owen: dualistic view of the mind 390

football (UK) *see* soccer

formal fair play 335, 345

formalism: and aesthetics 76; approach to adjudication 269; bad name 11; content of sport 77; criticisms of 24–5; critique of 15–17; defence and revision of 17–19, 267; definition 11–12; foundations of 12–15; and internalism 24–5

formal justice 336; cheating 343–4, 345; competitive advantage 342–3; equality in external conditions 338; equality in personal characteristics 338–9; equality in system strength 339; equal opportunity to perform 337–9; penalties and reduction of advantage 343; performance-enhancing drugs 341–2; play-acting 344–5; professional fouls 344; relevant inequality in athletic performance 339–41; unequal treatment 342–5

forms, theory of 193

Fosbury flop 61

Foucault, Michel 143, 224, 230, 430

fouling 27; strategic 29

Foust, Mat: Royce's conception of loyalty 212

Fraleigh, Warren 3, 132; fair play 334; installs philosophy of sport in new curriculum 3; opponents 290–1; proposed Weiss–Schacht exchange 4

Frankfurt school 219–20

freedom: condemned 147–8

free will 278

Frege, G.: on concepts 61

French Royal Academy 218–19

Freud, Sigmund 224

Frisbee 55

Fromm, Erich 220

From Ritual to Record (Guttmann) 238

Fry, J.: cognitivist view of emotion 198; emotional integrity 199; emotions of self-assessment 199

functionalism 23, 196, 392–3
functionalist definition of religion 243

Galarraga, Armand 261
Gallagher, Shaun: embodied cognition 181
gamblers 334, 401–2
gamerighting 15, 20n8
games: penalties 14, 16; philosophical
    implications 56; rulebooks 15–16; rules *see*
    rules; synthesis between necessity and
    possibility 151; turning into sport 275–6; *see
    also* play
The Games People Play: Theology, religion, and sport
    (Ellis) 245
Gandy, S.: screening for ApoE4 85
Gasset, José Ortega y 143
Gautama, Siddhartha 101
The Gay Science (Nietzsche) 153
Geist 225
gender: essentialism 213–14; issues in sport
    86–9; sport as historically gendered activity
    213–14, 351
Geneffect 81
genetically modified organisms (GMO) 429
genetic engineering 428, 429
genetic modifications 170, 324
genetics: enhancement *see* enhancement; gene
    testing 318; legacy 351–4; performance
    enhancing drugs 352–3; research 82; sport
    segregated by sex 351; variations 352
genetic testing 81–2; consent for 82–3; false
    negatives 82; predictive ability of 82
gentleman-amateur concept 30–1, 36, 40; anti-
    commercial ideals 416; conventional norms
    40; correcting bad calls 48; ethos of sport
    40–1; hybrid construction 45; intelligible
    conception of sport 46; opposed to playing
    for money 40, 51n7; opposite view to
    professionalism 41–2; purpose of sport 41–2;
    rational reconciliation with professionalism
    45–6; selectively borrowing from
    professionalism 46; sportsmanship 30–1, 36;
    use of strategy 47–8
Gerber, Ellen 4, 145
The German Ideology (Marx and Engels) 232–3
German International Tennis Championship 296
germ line research 361–2
Ghose, Z.: beauty as private ecstasy 71
Gigerenzer, Gerd 396
Giordana, Simona 171
Gipp, George 199
Giulianotti, Richard 412
Gladwell, Malcolm 316
globalization: and Olympism 377
goal–line technology 260, 436
goals 281–2; lusory 24, 26
God in the Stadium (Higgs) 240

golf: British Society of One-Armed Golfers
    300; etiquette 31, 33n11, 268; meticulous
    application of rules 268–9; self-officiating
    268–9
Good Game (Hoffman) 240
Goodman, Nelson 76
Grassbaugh Forry, Joan: habits 214
The Grasshopper: Games, Life and Utopia (Suits)
    24, 151
gratuitous logic 23, 118
Green, Ronald 362
Greig, Tony 56
Grey-Thompson, Dame Tanni 306
Groundwork of the Metaphysics of Morals (Kant)
    420
growth: and pragmatism 209–10
Guardini, Romano: distinction between purpose
    and meaning 247; on play 246
Guernica (Picasso) 75
Gulyas, Istvan 296
Guttmann, Allen 240; modern sport 238, 244
Guttmann, Dr Ludwig: spearhead of the
    Paralympic movement 301
gymnastics 73
gynocentric feminism 171–2

Habermas, Jürgen 12
habit formation 182, 210–11
Hämäläinenm, M.: on competitive advantage 87
Hamilton, Mark: make-up calls 263–4
handicaps 302, 303
happiness 372
harm: prevention 320–1; and segregation 168; to
    women in sport 166, 167
Harman, Gilbert 396
Harris, Bucky 268
Harris, John 171
Hartel, Liz 309
Hart, H. L. A.: characterization of law 25;
    primary roads 24
Hartshorne, Charles 208
Harvey, Lincoln 245
Hastings Center 325
Hawk-Eye technology 258
health: definition 303; protection 320, 327–8;
    sport ideology 225, 225–6
Hegel, Georg Wilhelm Friedrich 40, 49;
    alienation 225; idealism 194–5; paradox of
    competition 291; recognition 291; theory of
    the dialectic 291
Hegelian left 219
hegemony 377
Heggie, Vanessa: on androgen thresholds for
    athletes 88
Heidegger, Martin 3, 122–3, 143; account of
    existence 143; and art 432; authenticity 184;
    conception of being in the world 200;

concrete human body 201; *Dasein* 197;
  equipmentality 200; inauthenticity 184;
  Oblivion of Being 432; skilful coping 182;
  technology 431, 432; thrownness 144;
  understanding of human existence 179–80
heightening 153–7
Heinilä, K.: totalization process of modern sport
  339
Hellenes 370
hemoglobin 352
hermeneutic phenomenology 197
Herr, Hugh 89
Herrigel, Eugen 107; Zen and archery 249
heteronormative gender 173, 174
heteronormativity 168
Higgs, Robert J. 240
high-jumping 61
high-velocity bounding 92
high-velocity branding 91
Hinduism: *atman* 99; *Bhagavad Gita* 100; *Brahman*
  99, 100; *darshanas* 98, 99; detachment from
  ego and results 100; *dharma* 99, 100; Epic
  period 100; fundamental reality 99; *Karma* 99;
  maya 99; *moksha* 99; *prajna* 99; *samadhi* 101;
  sruti 98; *Sutra* period 100; *Upanishads* 99;
  Vedic period 98; *Yoga* 100–1
historical epochs 194–5
history, sport 239–40
Hobbes, Thomas 194; natural state of
  humankind 290
Hoberman, John 428; Human Genome Project
  428; instrumental view of athletes' bodies 432
Hoch, Paul 412
Hochstetler, Douglas: Dowey's concept of
  growth 210; truth is in the making 209
Hoffman, Shirl 240
Hogeveen, B.: skilful coping 182
Hohler, V.: athletes' movement 70
holism 281
Holm, S. R.: conflicts of interest 84
Homer 154
homogenization 377
Homo Ludens (Huizinga) 99, 242
homophobia 230–1
Hopsicker, Peter Matthew: Dowey's concept of
  growth 210
Horkheimer, Max 220
Hornby, Nick 58
horseracing: and doping 315
Howard, Dwight 84
Howe, Leslie A. 214; risk in remote sports 157
Hsu, Leo 109
Hughson, J.: contrast of movement between
  males and females when heading footballs
  202; on soccer and socioeconomic power 202
Huizinga, Johan 99, 117, 242; on play 245–6
human emancipation 219

human existence 143–5
human experience: measuring truth against 180;
  understanding of 179; universal-personal 179;
  see also phenomenology
human flourishing 435
Human Genome Project 428
human happiness 372
humanist feminism 171–2
humanistic image 390
human nature 248–9
Hume, David 137; constant conjunction 277,
  278; doctrine of causation 193
Hunter, Nick 412
Husserl, Edmund 143; phenomenological
  conception of time 185; phenomenological
  method 178, 197
hydrodynamic swimsuits 375–6
Hyland, Drew A. 109, 148
Hyman, Flo 87
hyperandrogenism 86–9; advantages bestowed
  86, 87; androgen limits 86, 87; discrimination
  against female athletes 88
hypothesis of extended cognition (HEC) 198
hypoxic chambers 322, 326

IAAF (International Association of Athletics
  Federations): androgen limits 86, 87, 88; ban
  of stimulants 315; bars Oscar Pistorius from
  competing 89; eligibility criteria of female
  athletes 86; equity of access 91
ICF (International Classification of Functioning,
  Disability and Health): definition of disability
  304–5; differences with the ICIDH 306–8
ICIDH (The International Classification of
  Impairment, Disability and Handicap):
  definition of disability 302, 303, 304;
  differences with the ICF 306–8
idealisation 58
idealism 194–5
ideals: relativity of 28–9
identity theory 392
ideology: capitalist mechanisms 224;
  contemporary usage 223; contradictory field
  of false ideas 224–5; false consciousness
  223–4; origins of 223; reactionary ideology of
  Olympism 223; sport 224
Ilundáin-Agurruza, Jesus: dangerous sports
  156–7
immaterial soul 193
impairments 302, 303, 307
imperfect procedural justice 337, 338
inauthenticity 148, 184
Incognito: The secret lives of the brain (Eagleman)
  397
Indian dance 76
indisputable visual evidence (IVE) 262
informal fair play 335, 345

informed consent 360
Inglis, David 151; on soccer and socioeconomic power 202
inquiry: philosophical approach 208
institutional theory of art: authoritative body 55; characterization 55; definition 53, 54, 56–7; training 57
institutional theory of sport: completeness 58; constraints 60–1; context 59; defective instances 60; definitions not required 54–5, 57–8; different levels and statuses 57, 58; differing versions 60; normativity of institutions 62–4; real institutions 55–6; real sport 57–61; rule-related character 55, 56, 62–3
institutions: language 13; normativity of 62–4; stipulations and agreements 12
instrumental goodness 385–6, 398n3
integrated spectacle 228
integration: refusal of, positive potential 169
intellectual disability 309
intentionality 197; motor 201
intentional rule violations 343, 344–5
interference: baseball 26
internal goods 172–3
internalism: broad 25–8, 30; and conventionalism 29–32; criticisms 28–32; definition 23; formalist approaches 24–5; internalism-externalism distinction 22–3; relativity of ideals 28–9
International Association for the Philosophy of Sport (IAPS) 4, 208
International Association of Athletics Federations (IAAF) *see* IAAF
International Classification of Functioning, Disability and Health (ICF) *see* ICF
The International Classification of Impairment, Disability and Handicap (ICIDH) *see* ICIDH
International Fair Play Committee 334
International Journal of Religion and Sport 245
International Judo Federation 378
International Olympic Committee (IOC) 63
International Paralympic Committee (IPC): eligibility to compete in Paralympic sports 302
International Silent Games 300
international sports competitions 229
International Swimming Federation 375–6
interpretivism 267
intersubjectivity 187
invisible hand 227
in-zone awareness 123–4
IOC (International Olympic Committee): androgen limits 86, 87, 88; introduction of testing 315; Olympic Solidarity 371; sex verification tests 352
IPC (International Paralympic Committee) 306;

activity limitations 305, 307; fundamental principles 329
IVF (*in vitro* fertilisation) 427–8

Jacklin, Tony 31
Jackson, Phil 245, 398n2
Jaksche, Jörg: on responsibility for doping 93
James, C. L. R. 70; aesthetic pleasure 71; sport as life enhancing 71
James, Lebron 329
James, William 288; pragmatic maxim 207, 209; process of habituation 211
Japan: Buddhism 105–6; Confucianism 105; *do* 107, 108; *Kami* 105; popularity of Olympic Games in philosophy 109; sport philosophy 109–10; Zen Buddhism 106–9
Japan Society for the Study of Sport 4
Jaspers, Karl 143
Jay, Martin 230
Jirásek, Ivo: authenticity 184
John of Damascus 242
Johnson, Ben 376
Jones, Carwyn: challenging masculine ideology of sport 171–2; relational approach to sport 172
Jones, Marion 374
Jordan, Michael 226, 229, 416, 417
Journal of the Philosophy of Sport and Physical Education 4
Journal of the Philosophy of Sport (JPS) 4, 69, 145
Joyce, Jim 261
The Joy of Sports (Novak) 243
judgement 72, 73
justice 259–60; Ancient Greek philosophy 375; anti-doping 319–20; and beauty 375; definition of formal justice 336; distributive norms 336–7; formal *see* formal justice; norms and procedures 337; procedural 337; serving the common interests 376; theory of 375–7; transparency 376
justice (*yi*) 103
Juvenal 372

kabbadi 63
Kahneman, Daniel 396
kalarippayattu 100
Kami 105
Kant, Immanuel 49; approach to coaching 388; disinterestedness 72; notion of critique 219; pleasure and agreeableness 71; on price and dignity 420; treating people as ends not means 420
Karma 99
Karolyi, Bela 198–9, 199
Kass, Leon 353
Keating, Justin: sportsmanship as a moral category 334

Kellner, Douglas 222; alienation 226; ideology as contradictory field of false ideas 224–5; manipulation 227–8; media spectacle 227, 229–30; megaspectacle 228; on Michael Jordan and alienation 226; religious significance of sport 232

Kena Upanishad 99

Kiefer, Howard 4

Kierkegaard, Søren A. 143; aesthetic realm 152; *becoming* 144; ethical realm 152; internalising the infinite 152–3; leap of faith 153; opposed to Hegel 143; passionate interest 153; religious realm 152–3

Kihlstrom, John 395

Kipsang, Wilson 306–7

Klein, Gary 396

Klem, Bill 256

Knight, Bob 391

knowing-how 115; amounting to knowing-that 121; connection to skills 121; football 120; parallel with knowing-that 121; in-zone awareness 123–4; zoned-out awareness 124–5; *see also* expert performance

knowing-now: and performance 121–2

knowing-that 115; football 120; parallel with knowing-now 121

knowledge *see* epistemology

Koller, John 99

Kongzi (Confucius) 102–3

Körper 183

Kovich, M.: on aesthetic aspects of sport 72

Kram, Rodger 89

Kreft, Lev 5; whereabouts systems 319

Kretchmar, Scott 117, 412; distinction between tests and contests 118, 289; human nature 248; knowing how to win 31–2; moral dimension of coaching 388; sports ethics 132; transcending winning/losing 209

Kripke, S.: contingent identity 194

Krishna 100

Kuhn, Thomas 49

Kukai 106

Kukal, Jan 296

Kupfer, J. H.: hierarchy of games 70; lack of external purposes in sport 73–4, 77; sporting drama 71; winning and professionalism 74

Kyle, Don 240

Lally, Richard 109; sport and inquiry 208

language: and conventions 38; institutions 13; proto- 14

language game 56

Laozi 103, 104

Lavine, Thelma 207

law: characterization 25–6; principles 26

law of nature 274

Lazzeri, Tony 268

Lefort, Claude: empty places of power 228, 235n6

Leftist Theories of Sport: A critique and reconstruction (Morgan) 412

legal positivism 266–7

legal precedent 16

legal principles 26

legal system *see* sport as a legal system

Leib 183

leisure: philosophical views 242

Leisure, The Basis of Culture (Pieper) 242

Lenk, Hans 4; formal and informal fair play 334–5

Lenta, Patrick: legal positivism 266–7

level playing field 279

Leviathan (Hobbes) 290

Lewis, David 37–8

libertarianism 322

Liezi 103, 104–5

lifestyle sports 198

lived body 183

Lock, Rebecca Ann: effect of doping ban 174

logical behaviorism 391, 392

logic, gratuitous 23, 118

Loland, Sigmund 133, 412; coaches as enlightened generalists 386–7; definition of sports technology 89; definition of technology 433; fair play 334; Olympism 369; thick theory of sport 433, 434, 436; thin theory of sport 433, 434, 435, 436; winning for internal reasons 433

London Games (2012): disqualification of badminton players 376; pressure on Saudi Arabia to include female athletes 378

London Marathon 307

London Paralympics (2012) 308

Louis the Great 218–19

Löwenthal, Leo 220

loyalty: fans' 404–6; philosophy of 212

luck 279

Lumpkin, Angela 132

Lund Svindal, Aksel 125–6

lusory goals 24, 26

Luther, Martin: on God becoming man 250

MacArthur, Ellen 108–9

MacIntyre, Alasdair 135; practice 65n4

Mack, Reddy 26

Magdalinski, Tara 429–30; on anti-doping strategies 430

magga 101

Mahabharata 100

managerial ingenuity 49

manipulation: concept of 226–8; natural state of affairs 227; in sport 227

Man, Sport and Existence (Slusher) 2, 145, 181

Mäntyranta, Eero 87, 88

Maradona, Diego 58, 126, 343
Marcel, Gabriel 143
Marcuse, Herbert 220, 230
Marfan syndrome 87
market standards 171
market value 170
Marmor, A. 38
martial arts 107; comparison with western sports 108
Martin, Andy: existential consciousness in sport 149–50
Martin, Billy 49, 389
Martin, Casey 309–10
Marx, Karl: exploitation 418–19; false consciousness 223; human emancipation 219; opium of the people 231–3; on phantasmagorical and ideological rule 232–3; political emancipation 219
masculinisation: in sport 162–3, 164
masculinity: concept of 164, 165; male and female bodybuilders 173–4
master-slave relationship 150
mastery 357–8
match fixing 402
materialism 194
maya 99
McDermott, John J. 207
McFee, Graham: contextualist view 269–70; judging aesthetic sports 265
McGee, Glenn 131
McGowan, Bill 256
McIntosh, P.: fair play 334
McNamee, Mike 5, 55, 132–3, 412; on bog-snorkelling 60; epistemic searches 386; on Olympism 377; players' self-officiating 272n11; sportspersonship 198; strong evaluation 198; youth coaching 388
McPhail, Lee 389
Mead, George Herbert 212
measuring truth against experience: phenomenology 180
media spectacle 227
Media Spectacle (Kellner) 229
media technology 427
medical treatments 355
megaspectacle 228
Mehlman, Maxwell: reproductive freedom 362
Meier, Klaus: on existential phenomenology 201; on the philosophy of sport 200
Meier, Klaus V. 57; embodiment 183
meliorism 209–10
mental causation 391
mental events 195
mental phenomena 194
mental set: philosophy of the mind 192–3
mental state: and functionalism 196
Merleau-Ponty, Maurice 143; double horizon 183; 'the Flesh' 183; intentionality of the body 197; motor intentionality 201; motor meaning 147; primordial faith 146; primordial relation 145–6; understanding of existence 143
metaphysics: causal powers 282–3; causation in sport 277–8; definition 274; empowered agents 278–80; essence of sport 276; essentialism 276; games and sport 275–6; law of nature 274; meaning of sport 275; mutual manifestation 280–1, 281–2; parts, wholes and goals 281–2
Metaphysics (Aristotle) 275
Metheny, Eleanor 2
methodists 117
methodological behaviorism 391, 392
Miah, A.: transhumanism 322–3
Middle Way 101
Millar, David 326
Miller, Stephen 239–40; connection between equal opportunity and the birth of democracy 371
Mill, John Stuart 134; subjection of women 166
mind: philosophy of 390–4
mind-body dualism 2, 211, 390
mind-brain identity theory 194, 196
Mitchell, Stephen 248
mixed martial arts (MMA) 135
modernism 218–19
modernity 218–19; and radicalism 220–1
modern sport: secularity of 238
Moe, Vegard F.: classical cognitivism in sport 203; skill acquisition 182
moksha 99
Money in Sport (Hunter) 412
monism 194–5
Moore, G. E. 137
moral education 422
moral harm 166
moral ideals 433
Morality Play: Sports, Virtues and Vices (McNamee) 412
Morgan, William J. 19n2, 145, 412; on cheating 11–12; conventionalism 29–32; conventionalist approach to coaching 389; conventional theory of sport 44; gratuitous logic of sport 23; training and sport 185
Morris, S. T.: partisan fans 404
Mortal Engines – The Science of Performance and the Dehumanization of Sport (Hoberman) 428
motor intentionality 201
motor meaning 147
Moussambani, Eric "The Eel" 374
movement: of acceptance 186; of defence 186; everyday coping skills 182; and phenomenology 185–6; skills of athletes 182; of truth 186

Movement and Meaning (Metheny) 2
Müller, A.: heightened consciousness in high-risk sports 433
Mullins, Aimee 302–3
Mumford, Stephen 116; contrast between purist and partisan fans 294; purist fans 406, 407
Muscular Christianity 372
mushin 107–8
Muslims 242
mutualism 27–8
mutual manifestation 280–1; parts, wholes and goals 281–2
Myers, Gerald: truth is in the making 209
The Myth of Sisyphus (Camus) 150

Nagel, T.: on philosophy 192
Nallin, Dick 268
National Academy of Sciences 361, 362
National Commission for the Protection of Human Subjects of Biomedical and Behavioural Research 361
National Football League (NFL): bounty scandal 295; lawsuits against 85
National Institutes of Health 362
national Olympic committees 374, 379n9
National Socialism 223
natural bodies 429–30
natural facts 166
nature: concept of 356
Nesti, Mark: anxiety 148
Neuhaus, Richard John: Christian idea of *prolepsis* 246–7
neutral monism 195
New Left: origins 223
new media spectacle: international competitions 229; rise of television 228
New York Times 315
Nicklaus, Jack 31, 33n11
Nicomachean Ethics (Aristotle) 336, 375
Nietzsche, Friedrich 3, 143; aesthetic and artistic theodicy 154; *agon* 154–5; *asceticism* 155; *askesis* 155–6, 157; on contests 154–5; heightening of human existence 153–7; natural world 153; Olympian gods 154; *ostrakismos* 154; self-overcoming 156; understanding of existence 143
Nike 226, 229
nirvana 101
Nishida, Kitaro 106
Nlandu, Tamba 210; opposition to goal-line technology 436; opposition to technological aids 260
Nongbri, Brent: modern ideas about religion 242
Nordenfeldt, L.: theory of disability 306
normative principles and theory 35–6; and conventionalism 35–7, 40, 41, 42, 44, 45; discourse version 45

normativity 27–8; institutions 62–4
Novak, Michael 243
Nozick, Robert: free market 422; libertarianism 412–13

Oakland Athletics 397
objectification 419–21
objective spirit 40
objective time 185
objects: quality of 200
objects of comparison 56
observed voiding 319
obstacles: overcoming 150–2
occasionalism 391
officials *see* umpires
Oliveira, Alan 91, 311
Olympia 370
Olympian gods 154
Olympic Charter 369, 378
Olympic Games: amputees competing at 90, 92; Ancient Greeks 371; Beijing (2008) 301, 375; Berlin (1936) 229, 231; criteria for inclusion of sports 370; focus on results 374; Japanese philosophy 109; London (2012) 376, 378; motto 370, 373; national committees 374, 379n9; pacifying conflicts of capitalist society 233; Paralympic Games 300–1; religious aspect of sport 152; Tokyo (1964) 109; *see also* ancient Olympic Games
Olympic Solidarity 371
Olympism: body, will and mind 371; complexity of non-discrimination policies 378; Coubertin's failure to define 369; and diversity 377–8; ethical imperialism 375; exclusion of participants from expensive sports 370–1; foundational qualities 370; free from economic disparities 371; fundamental principles 369, 377; and globalization 377; good examples 373, 374; ideals of equal opportunity 370, 371; inclusion of women 378; invisible problems of doping and corruption 376; Olympic Charter 369; Olympic motto and creed 370, 373, 374, 379n10; philosophical tradition from ancient Olympic Games 368, 370, 371, 372; philosophy of 368–70; political vision 369; reactionary ideology 223; rules and regulations of sport 375; social and political philosophy of sport 370; sound mind in sound body 372; sport as a human right 377; theory of education through sport 373–5; theory of human excellence through sport 371–3; theory of justice through sport 375–6; theory of world community 377–8; transparency 376; universal philosophy 377; Western heritage 370–1
opium of the people: religious significance in

the sport spectacle 232; sport and the industry of death 231; sport as 231–2
opponents 290–1, 292
ORGANISMBOUND 198
Ortega y Gasset, J. 151
Orwell, George 288, 408
Ossur 89
Osterhoudt, Robert 4
ostracism 155
ostrakismos 154
outdoor sports 338
out-of-competition testing 319

Paglia, Camilla: competitiveness 225; natural power of sex 225, 235n4
Palmeiras 408
Palmer, Arnold 78
panpsychism 394
parallelism 391
Paralympic Games: origins of Paralympic movement 300–1; *see also* disability sport
Paralympics: role of biotechnology in 89–91; and technology 90
Paralympic sports: amputee athletes 303–4; contrast with Olympic sports 301; eligibility to compete in 302; equality, fair opportunity and fair play 308–10; ethics, fairness and technology 311–12; *see also* disability sport
parity principle 197–8
Parry, Jim 132–3; criteria for inclusion of sports in Olympic program 379n1; risk of globalization to Olympism 377
participation restriction 305
particularists 117, 118
partisan fans 294; allegiance 403–4; differing demonstrations of allegiance 403–4; good partisan fans 404–6; randomness of allegiance 403; vices 408
parts 281–2
passionate interest 153
paternalism 166–7, 167, 327
Patočka, Jan: movement 185–6; referents 186
patriotism 408
patriots 407–8
Pawlenka, Claudia 376
Peirce, C. S. 208; pragmatic maxim 207
Pelletier, David 257
penalties 14, 16; appropriateness 19; and reduction of advantage 343
People of Prowess (Struna) 240
perceptual faith 146–7
perfect procedural justice 337, 338
performance: consciousness in 199–200; drugs and genetics 352–3; genetic testing on predisposition 82; and knowing-how 122; physical-mathematical measurements 342; relevant inequality 339–41; sport-specific

measurements 342, 343; *see also* drugs; expert performance
performance advantage 87, 88
performance-enhancing polymorphisms (PEPs) 81–2
Personal Knowledge (Polayni) 242
personhood 196
Phelps, Michael 87, 376
Phenomenological Approaches to Sport 181–2
phenomenology: apodictic truth 180; authenticity 184; classical cognitivism in sport 203–4; contribution of 179, differences with empirical science 188; eidetic universals 180; embodiment 183; essences of phenomena 180, 197; ethics 186–7; examination of own being 179; existential 197, 201; explanation of phenomenon 179; hermeneutic 197; intentionality 197; meaning 178; measuring truth against experience 180; method 178; movement 185–6; in the philosophy of sport 200–2; research 179; skilful coping 182; sociologically inflected 202–3; and sport sciences 187–8; time 185; truth 180; understanding the being of entities 180; universal-personal experiences 179
Phenomenology of Spirit (Hegel) 291
phenomenon: explanation of 179
phenotypes: sports segregated by 351–2
Philosophic Inquiry in Sport 183
Philosophic Society for the Study of Sport (PSSS) 4
Philosophy and Human Movement (Best) 5
philosophy of physical education 2
philosophy of the mind: classical cognitivism in sport 203–4; cognitivism 123–4, 196; consciousness in sport performance 199–200; double-aspect theory 195–6; dualism 192–3, 211; emotion and strong evaluation in sport 198–9; functionalism 196; idealism 194–5; materialism 194; mental set 192–3; personhood 196; phenomenology 197; phenomenology in the philosophy of sport 200–2; physical set 192–3; sociologically inflected phenomenology 202–3; supersized mind 197–8
physical education: philosophy of 2
physical harm 166
physicalism 194
physical set: philosophy of the mind 192–3
physicians: differing roles in sports medicine 83
Picasso, Pablo 75
Pieper, Josef 242
Pindar 373
pine tar incident 37, 48–9, 268, 389
Pistorius, Oscar: appeal to Supreme Court of Arbitration for Sport (CAS) 89–90; barred from IAAF competition 89; biomechanical

studies of running style 91–2; challenges
Paralympic category T43 302; competing in
Paralympics and Olympic Games 90;
performing against able-bodied athletes 89;
refusal to use disabled parking spaces 306;
unfair advantage concern 311
Plato 3, 132, 193, 372, 375; recollection
argument 193; theory of forms 193
play: aim of continuation 118–19; children 117;
Christian idea of *prolepsis* 246–7, 248;
constitutive rules 119; criterion/criteria
117–18, 118, 119; crucial features for 118;
experience of 246; non-human animals 117;
philosophical views 242; preceding sport 117;
profundity of 245–6; sacral aspects 248; signal
of transcendence 246, 247; social 118–19;
social space 118; spirit of 246; and sport
245–8; turning into sport 119; uselessness of
245, 246; and worship 247; *see also* games
play-acting 344–5
Playing with God (Baker) 240
pleasure: aesthetic 70, 71, 74; principle 224;
reality differences for men and women 225;
sexual 230
pluralism 213
Polayni, Michael 242
political economy 219, 220
Politics (Aristotle) 375
positional advantage 353, 358
Postow, Betsy: on masculinity in sports 162–3;
segregationist stance 165–6
potions 315
power: causal 283
practical knowledge 120
Practical Philosophy of Sport (Kretchmar) 412
practical reason 12
practice: definition 65n4; social 172; sport 211;
value of 172
pragmatic contextualism 213
pragmatic meliorism 209
pragmatism: anti-essentialism 213–14; basic
tenets 207; feminism 213–14; habit formation
and embodiment 210–11; history of 207;
meliorism and growth 209–10; pluralism
213–14; self and community 212–13;
strenuous progress 210; as theoretical
intervention 214–16
Pragmatism and the Philosophy of Sport 208
Pragmatism (James) 209
prajna 99
precedent 16, 19
predictability 17
President's Council on Bioethics 353
price money: in sport 170
Priest, Stephen: philosophy of the mind 192
primary familial and congenital polycythaemia
87

primary rules 24, 25
primary skills 27
principle of redress 324
principles: of adjudication 266, 267, 269;
embedded in sport 266; of law 26; vs. rules
26
Principles of Psychology (James) 211
privacy 319
private language 195
procedural knowledge 120
professional fouls 344
professionalism: concept 30–1; contemporary
sport 39; conventional norms 40, 41; golf 31;
hybrid construction 45; intelligible
conception of sport 46; purpose of sport,
opposite view to amateurism 41–2; rational
reconciliation with amateurism 45–6;
selectively borrow from amateurism 46;
serious occupation 41; use of strategy 47–8;
winning and aesthetics 74; *see also* winning
professionalization 418
prolepsis 246–7, 248
property advantage 87–8
propositional knowledge 120
proprioception 283
prosthetic limbs 89–90, 311
Protestant Reformation 244
proto-language 14
psychē 372
psychoanalysis 224
psychological harm 166
pure procedural justice 337
purist fans 294, 406–7
Puritans 240
purposive sports 73
putative harms 166
Pythagoras 372

quest for excellence 27–8, 30–1, 297
The Question Concerning Technology (Heidegger)
431
Quine, W. V. 38
Quinton, Lord Anthony 2–3

radical critique of sport: alienation 225–6; body
and sport 230–1; critique and critical theory
219–20; ideology 223–5; manipulation
226–8; modernity and modernism 218–19;
new media spectacle 228–30; Olympic
Games 233; opium of the people 231–3;
origins 222–3; radicalism 220–2; weak points
234
radical doubt 193
radicalism 220–2
Rahner, Karl 394
Randall, Derek 56
Rasmussen, Michael 319

rational dialogue 45, 46
rational self-determination 167
Ratjen, Herman 365n1
Rawls, John 28; practice 65n4; principle of
  redress 324
realists: and causation 278
realist-subjectivist debate 215
reality 195; and alienation 225; false 223
real sport 57–61
reason: philosophical approach 233
The Rebel (Camus) 150
recognition 291
recollection argument 193
Recombinant DNA Advisory Committee 362
records: breaking 23, 427; quest for 427
redress, principle of 324
reductionism 281
referees *see* umpires
reflective awareness 123, 126
reflective equilibrium 28, 389
regularity theory 277, 278
regulative rules 13; meaning of 308, 335
relativity of ideals 28–9
religio 242
religion: criticism of 232; functionalist definition
  243; meaning in antiquity 242; pre-modern
  244; private/public 244; religious aspect of
  sport 152; and sport *see* sport and religion;
  substantive definition 243; transcendence 243;
  understanding 242–5; universals 244
religious harm 166
remote sports 157
ren 102–3
Renaissance 45
replays: literature on 258; use of 257–8
reproductive freedom 362
Republic of Art 55
Republic (Plato) 372, 375
Research in Philosophy and Technology
  Handbook 429
resistance 150–1
respect: games rules 17
restorative drugs 321
restorative skills 27
return to play 84–6
revolutions: post-war failures 220, 221
Ricoeur, Paul 143
Riggs v. Palmer 26
Right Actions in Sport: Ethics for Contestants
  (Fraleigh) 132, 334
righteousness (*yi*) 103
Ring, "Doc" 315
*Rip Off the Big Game: The Exploitation of Sport by
  the Power Elite* (Hoch) 412
robots: athletes alienated as 225, 227
Rockne, Knute 199
Romans: cultivating excellence through sport

and philosophy 372; excellence of body and
  mind 372
Roman Stoics 372
Rorty, Richard 207–8; criticisms of work 215
Roth, S. M. 82
Rousseau, Jean-Jacques 49
Royce, Josiah: philosophy of loyalty 212;
  pragmatism 212
RTDs (reconstructed track devices): technology
  of 258
Rudnik-Schoeneborn, S.: on consent for genetic
  testing 83
rules: application of 265–70; challenge for
  athletes 77; constitutive *see* constitutive rules;
  freely accepted by athletes 187; game
  rulebooks 15–16; and games 11, 14–15;
  honouring 17; interpretation of 15; lawyering
  268; primary 24, 25; vs. principles 26;
  regulative 13; respect for 17; secondary 24,
  25; violations 343–5
A Rumor of Angels (Berger) 242, 246
Rumsfeld, Donald 387
Runyan, Marla 90
Russell, Bertrand: events 195
Russell, John 26; adjudication in sport 255;
  challenges the notion of rules as sole source
  of decision-making for umpires 265–6;
  discovery approach 36–7; internal principle of
  sport 26, interpretivist approach to coaching
  389; principle of adjudication 266;
  responsibility of coaches to correct bad calls
  31; sporting allegiances 404; trivial
  infringencies 48–9; umpires' reviewing calls
  257
Ryall, E.: defends use of goal-line technology
  436
Ryan, Joan 198–9, 199
Ryder Cup 31
Ryle, Gilbert 120–1, 131; behaviorism 194

Sacred Hoops (Jackson) 245
Sailors, Pam R.: control of sport 169
salary caps 422
Salé, Jamie 257
Saltman, Ken 173, 174
samadhi 101
samudhaya 101
Sandel, Michael 353, 413; bionic athletes 354;
  loss of shared experience 415; rejection of
  enhancement 355–6
Sartre, Jean-Paul 3, 143; absence and nothingness
  147; anxiety 148; appropriation 150; bad faith
  148–9; choosing actions 148; choosing
  projects 147; condemned freedom 147–8;
  conflict 150; ethics 187; existence precedes
  essence 143; facticity of existence 144; human
  relation to the field 150; social roles 149

satellites 427
Satz, Debra 413
Schacht, Richard 4
Schmitz, K. L.: sport and play 245
Schneider, Angela: on definition of woman in
sport context 167
Schwartz, Meredith: on male standards 170–1;
market standards 171; winning in sport 170
scienceploitation 82
scientific image 390
scoring 14–15; external purposes of sport 73–4
Searle, J.: Chinese room experiment 196;
constitutive rules of language 18; regulative
rules 13
Searle, John: computer functionalism 393;
institutional concepts 55
secondary rules 24, 25
secularization theory: criticisms of 238–9
segregation: and harm 168; phenotypes 351–2;
positive potential of 169; sex 169, 351; in
sport 168
Sein und Zeit (Heidegger) 182
self: and pragmatism 212–13
self-assessment: emotions of 199
self-competition 292–3
self-consciousness 291
self-determination: rational 167
self-overcoming 156
Semenya, Caster 86, 365n2
separation: in sport 168
sex *see* gender
sex discrimination: in sport 168, 169–70
Sex Equality in Sports (English) 162
sexuality: sport's role in defining 174–5
sex verification 352
Shahrkhani, Wojdan 374
Sheehan, George 108–9
shen 104
Sherwin, Susan: on male standards 170–1;
market standards 171; winning in sport 170
Shestov, Lev 143
Shilling, Chris: the body as a social construct 430
signposts 62–3
Simonovic, Ljubodrag: athletes' body movement
and capitalism 223; background 221; on
Baron Pierre de Coubertin 233; homophobic
views 230–1; London Olympics (2012): The
Death Games 229; manipulation in sport 227;
spectacles 228–9; sport spectacles and Roman
spectacles 231
Simon, Robert: broad internalism 266, 389;
conceptual and normative analysis 132;
discourse approach 36; discourse version of
normative theory 45; fair play 334; historical
understanding of athletic endeavour 45–6;
intelligible conception of sport 46; moral
dimension of coaching 387; mutual quest for

excellence 297; practical wisdom and good
judgement of coaches 388–9; rational
dialogue 45, 46; responsibility of coaches to
correct bad calls 36, 48
Simpson, Robert L.: on measuring improvement
292–3
Sisyphus 150–1
skating 73
skilful coping 182; philosophy of 123
skills 120; classes 163–4; and knowing-how 121;
primary 27; restorative 27
Skultety, Steven: sports categories and
psychologies 293–4
skydiving 184
Sloterdijk, Peter: vertical tension 155–6
Slusher, Howard 2, 181
Smith, Adam: invisible hand 227
Smith, John 207
soccer: analogous to capitalist development 202;
goal-line technology 260; knowing and
identifying 119–20; versions 58
social agreements 38, 44
social constructivism 429
social conventions 25
social democracy 220
social facts 166
social harm 166
Social Philosophy of Athletics (Lenk) 4
social practice 172–3; understanding 22–3
social roles 149; of sport 23
Society of the Spectacle (Debord) 228
Socrates 372, 373–4
Sokolowski, Robert: on phenomenology 179
Solo, Hope 212
s ma 372
Sorrell, T.: innocent Cartesianism 193
soul: and body 241
spectacle: new media 228–30
Spectacles of Death in Ancient Rome (Kyle) 240
spectators: and aesthetics 73; blind to sport's
negative features 227; fans 403–7; gamblers
334, 401–2; partisan fans 403–6; patriots
407–8; purist fans 406–7
Spheres of Justice (Walzer) 413
Spiel als Weltsymbol (Fink) 187
Spinoza, Baruch: double-aspect theory 195
spirituality 240–1
sport: and art 74–8; conventions 39; definition 6;
essence of 275; etymology 289; gratuitous
logic 118; lack of external purposes 76–7;
metaphysical view 275–6; references to the
non-sporting world 76–7; risk of failure 78;
segregation by sex and phenotypes 351–2;
social role 23; *see also* games; play
sport and religion: Marx and the opium of the
people 231–2; philosophy 242; sport history
239–40; theology and spirituality 240–1

Sport and the Body (Gerber and Morgan) 145
Sport and Work 234–5n1
Sport: A Philosophic Inquiry (Weiss) 2, 208
Sport: A prison of measured time (Brohm) 412
sport as a legal system: adjudication 255;
    applying the rules 265–70; consequences of
    umpires' mistakes 261; corrupt umpires 257;
    deception of umpires 257; *de novo* review
    262; desert and entitlement 262; embedded
    principle 266; genuine calls 256–7; judging
    aesthetic sports 265; and justice 259–60; legal
    positivism 266–7; literature on replays 258;
    make-up calls 263–4; meticulous application
    of rules in golf 268–9; opposition to
    technological aids 260; players self-officiating
    264, 272n11; players sharing responsibility for
    officiating 260; principle of adjudication 266;
    RTDs (reconstructed track devices) 258; rules
    as sole source of decision-making 265–6;
    rules lawyering 268; technological aids
    257–9, 260, 261–2; temporal variance 264–5;
    umpires' calls make facts 256; umpires'
    reviewing and revising calls 257; unrestricted
    use of technological aids 262, 263; use of
    replays 257–8; *see also* umpires
*Sport, Culture and Advertising: Identities, Commodities
    and the Politics of Representation* 226
Sport, Ethics and Philosophy (SEP) 5, 133, 145
sport history 239–40
sport medicine: and biotechnology 91–2;
    conflict of interest dilemmas 92–4; disclosure
    and confidentiality 83–4; roles of different
    physicians 83
sport medicine professionals: preserving meaning
    328–30
sport psychology 203
*Sports and Christianity: Historical and contemporary
    perspectives* (Watson and Parker) 245
Sports and Social Values (Simon) 132
sports doctors 83–4
sports ethics *see* ethics
Sports, Ethics and Philosophy 69
Sports in the Western World (Baker) 240
sportsmanship 30–1, 295
sportspersons *see* athletes
sportspersonship 198
Sport Technologies – A Moral View (Loland) 433
*Sport, Technology and the Body –The Nature of
    Performance* (Magdalinski) 429
Sport: The First Five Millennia (Guttmann) 240
spot fixing 402
sruti 98
Staal, Frits 100
Standal, Øyvind F.: skill acquisition 182
standardized, encumbered competitions 293, 294
standardized, unencumbered competitions 293,
    294

Standish, Paul: authenticity 184
Stanley, Jason 121; knowing-how and
    performance 121–2
state, the: and commercialisation of sport
    421–3
stimulants 315
Stoke Mandeville Games 301
Stoll, Sharon 132
Strawson, Galen 394
Strawson, P.: depression 195; double-aspect
    theory 195
strict liability condition 310
strike zones 263
strong evaluation 198–9
Stroud, Scott 209
struggle 150–1
Struna, Nancy 240
The Subjection of Women (Mill) 166
subjective approaches 179
subjects: and sport 76
substantive definition of religion 243
suicides: college footballers 84–5
Suits, Bernard 20n4; definition of sport 57; game
    playing 151, 275–6; importance of
    constitutive rules 24; unnecessary obstacles
    29; worship and play 247
Sullivan, Claire: on genetic variations 86; on
    level playing fields in athletics 87
Supreme Court of Arbitration for Sport (CAS)
    89–90
surface conventions 29
Sutra period 100
Sutton, J.: consciousness in cricket batsmen
    199–200
Suzuki, Daisetz 107, 108

Takuan, Soho 107–8
Tamburrini, Claudio 134; genetic modifications
    170, 324; male standards 170–1; market value
    of athletes 170; meaning of sport 323; sex
    segregation 169; total integration of sport 169
Tännsjö, Torbjörn 134; genetic modification
    170; level playing field 323–4; male standards
    170–1; market value of athletes 170; sex
    segregation 169; total integration of sport 169
Tao Te Ching (Tzu) 248
taste 71–2, 73
Taylor, Charles 40; corporeal person 196
teams 281–2
technical goodness 385
technological aids 257–9, 260, 261–2
technology: concept of 431–3; fear of 428–9;
    genetic engineering 428, 429; goal-line 260,
    436; Human Genome Project 428; influence
    on sport 427; media 427; normative
    assessments 433–6; satellites 427; social
    constructivist perspective 429; transcended by

athletes 432, 433; *in vitro* fertilisation (IVF)
427–8
television: rise of 228
temporal variance 264–5
tennis: expert performance 123
testosterone 86–7
tests: comparison with contests 118, 289–90
theology 240–1; and sport 245
Theology, Ethics and Transcendence in Sports 245
theoretical knowledge 120
theory of forms 193
A Theory of Justice (Rawls) 28
therapeutic use exemption (TUE) certificates
310
thick theory of sport 433, 434, 436
thin theory of sport 433, 434, 435, 436
Thompson, John 287
Throwing Like a Girl (Young) 173, 214
Thus Spoke Zarathustra (Nietzsche) 153
ticket prices 413
time: and phenomenology 185
Title IX 161; support for pragmatist-feminist
commitments 214
token identity theory 392
Tokyo Olympic Games (1964) 109
Torres, Cesar 27, 374
totalitarianism 220
totalized social fact: sport 225
Tracey, Jill: progress 210
Tracy, Destutt de 223
training: and sport 185; women athletes 214
traits: valuing 172
transcendence 148, 149, 152, 243; signals of 246
transcendental consciousness 197
transcendentalism: growth through endurance
sport 210
transcendent perspective 44, 45, 48
transfer system 419–20
transhumanism 308, 322–3
Trebilcot, Joyce: statistical differences between
men and women performers 170
Trevino, Lee 342
truth: movement of 186; and phenomenology
180
Turing, Alan 196, 393
Turkle, Sherry 393–4
Tversky, Amost 396
type identity theory 392

Umminger, W.: cultural history of sport 427;
quest for records 427
umpires: calls make facts 256; conceptualizing
performance 258; consequences of mistakes
261; corrupt 257; deceived 257; discretion
269; formalist approach 267; Frisbee playing
55; genuine calls 256–7; indisputable visual
evidence (IVE) 262; and justice 259–60;

make-up calls 263–4; reviewing calls 257;
rules as sole source of decision-making
265–6; scapegoating 261; technological aids
257–9, 260; traditional roles 259–60; use of
principles 266; use of replays 257–8; witnesses
to events 256; zones of uncertainty 259
unconscious mind 395
understanding: characteristic of humanity
179–80
unearned advantage 328–9
unencumbered competitions 293
unfair advantage 86, 87, 311
unintentional rule violations 343, 343–4
United States Professional Golf Association
(USPGA) 309–10
universalism 30
universals: eidetic 180; and religion 244
University of Notre Dame 199
Unnatural Doubts (Williams) 215
unnecessary obstacles 29
Upanishads 99
USADA (United States Anti-Doping Agency)
318, 320
utilitarian goodness 386
utilitarianism 134, 415–16
Utopia 151

Value on Ethics and Economics (Anderson) 413,
417
The Varieties of Goodness (von Wright) 384
vaulting 73
Vedas 98
Vedic period 98
verdictives 256
vertical tension 155–6, 157
Vetterling-Braggin, Mary: on withdrawing from
masculine sports 166
A Vindication of the Rights of Woman
(Wollstonecraft) 166
violations: levels of 18–19
violence: sanctioned in sports 227
virtue 135
vis-à-vis, encumbered competitions 293, 293–4
vis-à-vis, unencumbered competitions 293,
293–4
vital goals 306
in vitro fertilisation (IVF) 427–8
Vivas, Eliseo: disinterestedness 72
Vodeb, Roman: background 222;
competitiveness 225; manipulation 227; on
sport ideology 224; theory of alienation 225
von Wright, Georg Henrik 384; instrumental
goodness 385–6; utilitarian goodness 386

WADA (World Anti-Doping Agency) 310;
appeal to the spirit of sport 364–5; Code
316, 341; equity of access 91

Walsh, Adrian 412
Walzer, Michael 413
Warrior Roots 81
Watsuji, Tetsuro 105
Weiss, Paul 2, 207; concern for excellence 209; contribution to pragmatism 208; habit formation 210–11; inquiry 208; on pragmatic contextualism 213; on sport practice 211; stature of 3; team play 212; women in sport 213–14
Welsch, W. 78
Wertz, Spencer 109
Weyand, P. G.: on running style of Oscar Pistorius 92
What Is Existential Philosophy? (Arendt) 142–3
What Money Can't Buy (Sandel) 413
wheelchair athletes 307
whereabouts programs 319
White, Cindy 153
Whitehead, Alfred North 208
wholes 281–2
Why Some Things Should Not Be for Sale: The Moral Limits of Markets (Satz) 413
Williams, Michael 215
Williamson, Timothy 121; knowing-how and performance 121–2
Wilson, Timothy: consciousness 395
winning: and aesthetics 73; attributes of 31–2; external purposes of sport 73–4; fleeting nature of 247–8; and good coaching 384–5; overemphasis on 295; purpose in sport 170, 247–8, 434; significance 27, 33n8; and technological aids 260–1; *see also* professionalism
Wittgenstein, Ludwig 3, 48; on completeness 64; concept game 56; language game 56; private language argument 195, 292; say what you choose 59; signposts 62–3

Wolbring, Gregor 91; ableism 306; recategorization of Olympic events for double amputees 92
Wollstonecraft, Mary 166; on women's autonomy 167
women: equal access in sport *see* feminism
World Anti-Doping Agency *see* WADA
world community: theory of 377–8
World Health Organization (WHO): differences between the ICF and the ICIDH 306–8; ICF definition of disability 304–5; ICIDH definition of disability 302, 303, 304
worldmaking 76
worship 247
wuwei 104

X Factor Sports Training 81
xing 104

yi 103
yoga 100–1
Young, Iris Marion 173; body movements and gendered power 202, 214
youth sport: purpose and meaning of 83

Zahavi, Dan: on the differences between phenomenology and empirical science 188
Zaner, Richard 4
Zanetti, Allessandro 309
Zen: and archery 249; and embodiment 249
Zen Buddhism 106–9; *mushin* 107–8
Zen in the Art of Archery (Herrigel) 249
zero-sum logic: competition 294, 297, 298
Ziff, P.: rejects aesthetics of sports 72
zoned-out awareness 124–5
zones of uncertainty 259
Zuelle, Alex: on doping 93

eBooks
from Taylor & Francis

Helping you to choose the right eBooks for your Library

Add to your library's digital collection today with Taylor & Francis eBooks. We have over 50,000 eBooks in the Humanities, Social Sciences, Behavioural Sciences, Built Environment and Law, from leading imprints, including Routledge, Focal Press and Psychology Press.

Choose from a range of subject packages or create your own!

Benefits for you
- Free MARC records
- COUNTER-compliant usage statistics
- Flexible purchase and pricing options
- 70% approx of our eBooks are now DRM-free.

Benefits for your user
- Off-site, anytime access via Athens or referring URL
- Print or copy pages or chapters
- Full content search
- Bookmark, highlight and annotate text
- Access to thousands of pages of quality research at the click of a button.

Free Trials Available

We offer free trials to qualifying academic, corporate and government customers.

eCollections

Choose from 20 different subject eCollections, including:

| Asian Studies |
| Economics |
| Health Studies |
| Law |
| Middle East Studies |

eFocus

We have 16 cutting-edge interdisciplinary collections, including:

| Development Studies |
| The Environment |
| Islam |
| Korea |
| Urban Studies |

For more information, pricing enquiries or to order a free trial, please contact your local sales team:

UK/Rest of World: **online.sales@tandf.co.uk**
USA/Canada/Latin America: **e-reference@taylorandfrancis.com**
East/Southeast Asia: **martin.jack@tandf.com.sg**
India: **journalsales@tandfindia.com**

www.tandfebooks.com